$28.00
direct
06-19-89

THE GERMAN HYMNODY
OF THE BRETHREN
1720-1903

by
Hedwig T. Durnbaugh

Published By The
BRETHREN ENCYCLOPEDIA, INC.
Philadelphia, Pennsylvania

1986

BRETHREN ENCYCLOPEDIA MONOGRAPH SERIES
William R. Eberly, editor

Number 1

THE GERMAN HYMNODY OF THE BRETHREN
1720-1903
Hedwig T. Durnbaugh

Copyright 1986 by The Brethren Encyclopedia, Inc.

Related materials are available from The Brethren Encyclopedia, Inc.: THE
BRETHREN ENCYCLOPEDIA, Volumes I, II, and III (1983-1984); and a paperback
book entitled MEET THE BRETHREN (1984). Requests for information or
orders may be sent to The Brethren Encyclopedia, Inc., 313 Fairview Ave.,
Ambler, PA 19002.

EXPLANATION OF LOGO
    The logo used on the title pages of the volumes of this series is
derived from a seal which has been attributed to Alexander Mack, Jr.
(1712-1803), son of the first Brethren minister and himself an active
elder in colonial America. The Brethren Encyclopedia article on this
"Mack seal" states, referring to the religious symbols: "Central to these
is the cross, on which is superimposed a heart, suggesting a strong emphasis on sacrifice and devotion. The importance of bearing spiritual fruit
is represented graphically by a vine, laden with grapes, whose branches
spring from the heart. All of these symbols express an understanding of
discipleship that was significant in the early history of the Brethren"
(p. 775). The "Mack seal" has often been used by Brethren congregations
on stationery, artwork, and publications.

Durnbaugh, Hedwig T.
    The German Hymnody of the Brethren, 1720-1903.
    v, 322 p., [7] leaves of plates : ill. ;
    (Brethren Encyclopedia Monograph Series ; no. 1)
    Bibliography: p. 298-315.
    Includes indexes.

    1. Brethren Church (Ashland Group)--Hymns--History and criticism. 2.
Church of the Brethren--Hymns--History and criticism. 3. Dunkard Brethren
--Hymns--History and criticism. 4. Fellowship of Grace Brethren Churches
--Hymns--History and criticism. 5. Old German Baptist Brethren--Hymns--
History and criticism. 6. Hymns, German--History and criticism. 7.
Hymns, German--Indexes. I. Title. II. Series.

BV403.G4D86 1986

ISBN   0-936693-21-5

Printed in the U.S.A. by Light and Life Press, Warsaw, IN.

CONTENTS

FOREWORD   ii
PREFACE   iii

INTRODUCTION   1

Chapters

    I.   GEISTREICHES GESANG-BUCH   12
   II.   DAS KLEINE DAVIDISCHE PSALTERSPIEL   41
  III.   DIE KLEINE HARFE   61
   IV.   DIE KLEINE LIEDER SAMMLUNG   68
    V.   DIE KLEINE PERLEN-SAMMLUNG   81
   VI.   NEUE SAMMLUNG VON PSALMEN, LOBGESÄNGEN UND GEISTLICHEN
         LIEDERN   92
 VII.   DAS CHRISTLICHE GESANG-BUCH   104
VIII.   EINE SAMMLUNG VON PSALMEN, LOBGESÄNGEN, UND GEISTLICHEN
         LIEDERN   114
   IX.   OCCASIONAL COLLECTIONS   124

CONCLUSION   130

Appendixes

     INTRODUCTION   137

    I.   GEISTREICHES GESANG-BUCH   138
   II.   DAS KLEINE DAVIDISCHE PSALTERSPIEL   146
  III.   DIE KLEINE HARFE   149
   IV.   DIE KLEINE LIEDER SAMMLUNG   150
    V.   DIE KLEINE PERLEN-SAMMLUNG   152
   VI.   NEUE SAMMLUNG VON PSALMEN, LOBGESÄNGEN UND GEISTLICHEN
         LIEDERN   154
 VII.   DAS CHRISTLICHE GESANG-BUCH   155
VIII.   EINE SAMMLUNG VON PSALMEN, LOBGESÄNGEN UND GEISTLICHEN
         LIEDERN   158
   IX.   FIRST-LINE INDEX OF HYMNS   160
    X.   PUBLISHING RECORD OF HYMNS   230
   XI.   INDEX OF MELODIES
         1. First-Line Index   257
         2. Metric Index   278
 XII.   INDEX OF HYMN-WRITERS   284

SELECTED BIBLIOGRAPHY   298

ADDENDUM   316

INDEX TO CHAPTERS I - IX   319

FOREWORD

During the editorial production of THE BRETHREN ENCYCLOPEDIA, historians from the five major Brethren bodies considered how they might continue to work together in the interest of the entire Brethren family of churches. Projects were desired which could be undertaken in the same fine spirit of cooperation which characterized the production of THE BRETHREN ENCYCLOPEDIA.

A growing interest across denominational lines in the heritage of the Brethren has become apparent in recent years. In order better to understand ourselves and our differences, we are driven to our sources. A spate of historical work at the turn of the last century by Brumbaugh, Holsinger, Falkenstein, and others laid a foundation for Brethren historical study. The work commencing in the 1950s by Mallott, Durnbaugh, Kimmel, and others has kindled renewed interest in our European and Colonial American sources. The four volumes of source material published in recent years by The Brethren Press at Elgin, Illinois, have proven indispensable to scholars who would encounter early Brethren thought first-hand and savor the fervor and spirit of their lives.

Some excellent dissertations and scholarly monographs have been produced which need to be put into print for scholars and interested laymen. These in-depth studies illuminate special parts of our history and draw together the work of many scholars. Some of these studies are little known and there is reason to believe that a carefully selected line of monographs would find a select audience.

The Board of Directors of Brethren Encyclopedia, Inc., chose the name BRETHREN ENCYCLOPEDIA MONOGRAPH SERIES and has selected William R. Eberly to edit the series. It is a pleasure to present Hedwig T. Durnbaugh's THE GERMAN HYMNODY OF THE BRETHREN as the first selection in this new series.

Fred W. Benedict
President, Board of Directors
Brethren Encyclopedia, Inc.

PREFACE

In the nineteen-fifties, my husband and I conducted extensive archival research into the European origins and common early history of five present-day denominations, namely, the Brethren Church, the Church of the Brethren, the Dunkard Brethren, the Fellowship of Grace Brethren Churches, and the Old German Baptist Brethren.

The members of these five denominations are the natural and/or spiritual descendants of the Schwarzenau Täufer (Baptizers from the village of Schwarzenau/Eder, Germany) or Neutäufer (New Rebaptizers). The early Brethren had come primarily from the German Palatinate and had been awakened around the turn of the eighteenth century by itinerant Pietist preachers, such as Ernst Christoph Hochmann von Hochenau (1670-1721), to lead a life consistent with the teachings of the New Testament. However, when they turned to preaching and practicing their faith in public, they ran afoul of the law. Private meetings for Bible study and prayer were not permitted by the established church, much less a public demonstration of faith.

Although religious dissent was prohibited, certain rulers practiced religious toleration in their lands. In the Germanies there were three areas where religious dissenters found refuge, namely the counties of Wittgenstein and Ysenburg-Büdingen in Hesse and the city of Krefeld on the Lower Rhine. When forced to leave the Palatinate, the Brethren found refuge in the small village of Schwarzenau in the county of Sayn-Wittgen-stein-Hohenstein. Here relative security and peace enabled them to formu-late their theology. Through studying the New Testament, the history of the early church, and the writings of the Anabaptists they came to the con-clusion that as Christians they had to live in a covenanted fellowship, the seal of which covenant was immersion baptism of believers. Thus, three women and five men were the first to be baptized in the river Eder in 1708. Among these early leaders were Alexander Mack (1679-1735) and his wife Anna Margaretha Mack (1680-1720).

As a result of the Schwarzenau Brethren's preaching missions, another group soon formed in the Büdingen area, but circumstances forced them to emigrate to Krefeld whence they migrated to Pennsylvania in 1719. The group at Schwarzenau continued there until 1720 when, for various reasons, they migrated to the Netherlands where they settled in the Mennonite colony of Surhuisterveen. In 1729 they joined the other Brethren in Penn-sylvania.

In the course of the historic research into Brethren beginnings, we discovered a small hymnal that appeared to have been compiled and published by the early Brethren in 1720. In the preface, mention is made of one hundred hymns written by Brethren then in prison for their beliefs. As no authors' names were given with any of the hymn-texts, I decided to try to identify those one hundred Brethren hymns. By determining hymns of known authorship, either through reliable secondary works or the published works of the poets themselves, it would be possible to locate those texts that might have been written by Brethren. This small project soon grew in scope to include the study of all German hymns in Brethren hymnals, smaller hymn-collections, and other printed formats.

The German Hymnody of the Brethren is the result of many years of searching, verifying, reading, compiling, and writing at intermittent times between tasks of greater claim upon my time. Although some additional research could be done, the project has reached a level at which it was ready for publication. Before describing the scope and use of this study, I wish to acknowledge the practical assistance, moral support, and scholarly nurture which I have received from many different people in the course of these years.

Numerous librarians in Europe and the United States and some private collectors of hymnals granted me access to their valuable materials, for which I have been very grateful. Equally important to me, the intellectual nurturing which I have received from teachers, friends, and colleagues needs to be acknowledged. This includes my husband Donald F. Durnbaugh, from whom I learned how to "do history" and undertake historical research, my friends in the Hymn Society of America who led me more deeply into the study of hymns, religious poetry, and church music, and my various teachers of early music performance who initiated me into the richness and subtleties of musical styles. At the very time when I was ready to turn the manuscript into presentable form, I was given permission to use one of the office word processors at Bethany Theological Seminary during after-hours. I am greatly indebted to the members of the Brethren Historical Committee who became interested in this study and its publication, especially chairman William R. Eberly. Dr. Wilfred Eckhardt, Director of the Hessian State Archives in Marburg, Germany, Donald R. Hinks, Brethren hymnal collector and bibliographer, and Dr. Paul Westermeyer, professor at Elmhurst College, Elmhurst, Illinois, and editor of The Hymn gave the manuscript careful and critical readings. Any shortcomings in the treatment of the subject matter, in style and language are entirely my own.

This study permits a glimpse into one aspect of the devotional life of the German-speaking Brethren from their beginning in 1708 until the early twentieth century. It was written primarily for the benefit of the descendants of the Schwarzenau Brethren and it is hoped that the material presented here will aid pastors, seminarians, and church members involved in music and worship in gaining a better understanding of hymnody in general and Brethren hymnody in particular. Nonetheless, it has been my goal throughout to present the results of this study in such a form that readers outside of the Brethren tradition might also find useful information among this material.

The subject matter of this study, then, is the body of German hymns which the Brethren used in print between the years 1720 and 1903. Although all publications containing Brethren hymns are here discussed, this study emphasizes hymnody, not bibliographical detail. Those interested in the latter should consult the recent monograph by Donald R. Hinks. Discussion of Brethren history is limited to providing the historical context for each of the hymn collections. Suggestions for further reading may be found in the bibliography. The introduction to German history and hymnology is presented as a brief, popular rather than scholarly, survey intended to provide some basic background necessary for this study.

Each chapter deals with one hymnal, describing and analyzing its contents. Each chapter concludes with two tables listing the hymn-writers under certain categories, which are explained in the first two chapters. A separate appendix provides supplementary material for each chapter, notably lists of unidentified hymns which are the material among which texts of Brethren authorship might be found. It is due to the nature and contents of the individual hymnals that the earlier chapters are considerably longer than the later ones. Hymn-texts published in smaller collections and on broadsides are discussed in the last chapter. Five appendixes provide detailed information on individual hymns, publication, melodies, meters, and authors. Specific instructions for the use of these are given at the beginning of each appendix. A select bibliography provides full bibliographical information about the works cited and others found especially useful in the course of this study. Primary source material, which came to hand just as the manuscript was prepared for publication and could therefore not be integrated into the main body of this study, is presented in an Addendum. Finally, an index provides access to the authors, hymns, and hymn-subjects in chapters one through nine.

Geistreiches Gesang-Buch/

Vor alle Liebhabende

Seelen der Warheit/

sonderlich

Vor die Gemeine

Des

HERRN

In sich fassend

Die Auserlesenste und nöthigste

Lieder/

Aus andern Gesang-Büchern ausgezogen/

Nebst 100. neue Lieder/ so zum ersten
mahl aufgesetzt worden/ zum Trost und
Erquickung allen wahren Nachfolgern des
HErrn JEsu/ und in gegenwärtiger Form
ans Licht gegeben/

Zum

Lobe GOTTES.

BERLENBURG/
Gedruckt bey Christoph Konert/ Anno 1720.

Geistreiches Gesang-Buch
(pp. 12-40)

INTRODUCTION

> We were bound two by two around our arms, John Carl, as the seventh, had one of his arms tied to the other with a rope behind his back. We were thus led away to Düsseldorf, which journey we passed mostly in singing.[1]

The event described above occurred on February 1, 1717, and the story is that of the Solingen Brethren. One of the songs which these men sang on their twenty-mile march was the hymn, O Jesu, mein Bräut'gam, wie ist mir so wohl (O Jesus, my bridegroom, how happy I feel). This event was recorded forty-six years later in a faithful account of their imprisonment written by one of the group, Wilhelm Grahe, representing one of the rare instances when a specific reference to the use of hymns by the early Brethren can be found in historical sources. As the first line of the quotation indicates, this was a hymn devoted to Jesus and written in the manner of what is called "mystical eros:"

> O Jesus, my bridegroom, how happy I feel; your love quite intoxicates and fills me: o heavenly hours! I have found what will give pleasure and satisfy in eternity. (:1)
> You have refreshed me most generously, o Jesus, and pressed me to the comfort-breasts of love; you have showered me with presents, quenched me with sensual pleasure, indeed, transported me into heavenly ecstasy. (:2)
> What is it, that tempts me still? It is the sight of my parents, my brothers, my children. Off with you, off with you, you relations, you friends, and acquaintances, cease your words, I do not know you! (:4)
> Come, rejoice, all you pious ones! Rejoice with me, I have the very fountain of joys right here: come, let us leap and sing and make noise, yes, even become inflamed with the desire for love. (:5)
> Fie, devil, world, hell, flesh, sin, and death! I fear no tribulation, neither suffering nor misery: as long as Jesus loves me, what can disquiet me? Whatever confronts me must become a mockery. (:7)
> Away, crowns, away, sceptre, away, majesty of the world! Away, riches and treasures, away, goods and money! Away, sensual pleasures and splendour! My only desire is Jesus the most beautiful in the heavenly spheres. (:8)

The text of this hymn is not quite what one would expect seven men to have sung on their way to prison. One wonders whether there were not any more suitable hymns available to them at that time. Before this question can be pursued, it will be helpful to outline briefly the events that influenced German hymnody up to the time of the early Brethren.

Church reformers of the sixteenth century, such as Luther and the leaders of the Anabaptists and the Czech Brethren, attached great importance to hymns; for them the function of hymns in worship was closely related to the preaching of the word, which had Christ, the incarnate Word, at its center. He was the only way leading to the knowledge of God and the only foundation of Christian community. This teaching was at the heart of German hymn-texts written during the first half of the sixteenth century.

The period following the emergence of Protestantism in Germany was marked by bitter religious strife and wars. Internal controversies arose among the Lutherans, who had separated into several factions of differing doctrinal persuasion. Persecution of all Protestants set in as the concerted action by the Roman Catholic Church to win the people back from Protestantism gained momentum, especially in South-German lands. This is known as the time of the Counter-Reformation. Both Protestants and Roman Catholics were united, however, in their view of the Anabaptists as a movement that must not be tolerated. Concern for and defense of the right doctrine, persecution and elimination of those who threatened a particular system of doctrines eventually culminated in the outbreak of the Thirty Years' War (1618-1648), which raged through most of the German-speaking lands. Hymns became vehicles for defending the true faith against the enemies of pure doctrine as well as a means for finding consolation in all manner of personal trials and great suffering.

The question of rightful religious persuasion, which had lain at the heart of the Thirty-Years' War, was finally settled at the Treaty of Westphalia in 1648. Henceforth, three Christian bodies were to be recognized as lawful churches: the Roman Catholic, the Lutheran, and the Reformed, although not simultaneously. It became the prerogative of the ruler of each of the countless German principalities to establish the church of his choice in his land, which then was binding for all subjects. A second consequence of this agreement was that the subjects in a given land had to change their church affiliation whenever a succeeding ruler embraced a different religious persuasion from the one before.

In the cultural context, the seventeenth and the first quarter of the eighteenth centuries are referred to as the Baroque era. The term, "baroque," was first applied to the visual arts, describing something that had grown beyond its normal proportions and design. Later, the term was used to include all aspects of the arts and society during that period. Baroque art was on the one hand the art of the courts, notably that of Louis XIV of France, the Sun King; on the other, it was the art of the Roman Catholic Church, which sought to solidify its gains among the war-battered populace through the magnificence of its church edifices, a foretaste of heaven for the poor. This juxtaposition already hints at the basic characteristic of the Baroque era: it was a time of extreme contrasts. Great splendour and flowering of the arts at the secular and ecclesiastical courts existed side by side with countrysides devastated by prolonged wars and inhabited by a decimated and demoralized populace.

In the areas of natural science and technology great advances had been made. Unlimited possibilities seemed to open themselves to human creativity and yet there was death and decay all around. Thus the people were filled on the one hand with a heightened sense of achievement and, on the other, with a general mood of deep pessimism. Flight into illusion provided release from these grim realities. At the courts, great festivities were staged that dazzled eyes and ears. For the common people, if they were Catholic, the pageantry and splendour of the church's feast and holy days provided similar aesthetic pleasures. Still, whether high-born or low, everyone was faced with the same problem: how to master life in a world that was in great tension between reality and illusion.

One way to resolve the dilemma was to embrace this world fully and equip oneself with a belief in fate. A stoic attitude toward life's vicissitudes and a bourgeois morality provided the means for coping and achieving some sense of security. The alternative was a complete turning away from the world and what it had to offer, both good and bad. For people who chose this way, the watchword was Andreas Gryphius' famous poem, Vanitas! Vanitatum vanitas! (Vanity! All is vanity!) Some form of asceticism or of mysticism determined their mode of living. Eventually, it became almost fashionable to embrace this all-pervasive pessimism as one's lifestyle. Quite genuinely, however, people had indeed been living in full awareness of their mortal state, an attitude prevailing from the Middle Ages well into the nineteenth century to which many so-called memento mori emblems, symbols, and writings testify. In the same way the turmoil of the period following the Thirty-Years' War found reflection in the secular as well as the religious poetry of the time.

It was during the era of the Baroque that numerous poetic and literary societies came into existence which had a twofold aim, namely, to purify and to enrich the German language and improve the quality of poetic writing. The members of these societies - chiefly court poets and scholars - held that the art of writing poetry could be learned by adhering to certain rules. Certain circles of poets were more influential in this endeavor than the rest.

The Gekrönte Pegnesische Blumenorden (Crowned Order of the Flowers on the Pegnitz River) of Nuremberg was known for its sentimental Arcadian poetry and somewhat moralizing spiritual shepherds' poetry. The Song of Solomon served as a model for imagery and style. The main themes were the battle with Satan, the world, and the flesh. All this was couched in a pervasive mood of deep remorse in which the sinful soul yearned for salvation. Another society, whose members found their spiritual roots in medieval mysticism, had its center in Silesia. This group provided the ground that nourished the Catholic Johann Scheffler (1624-1677), also known by his pen-name, Angelus Silesius, the "angel from Silesia." Scheffler's poetry, which was partly pan-theistic, partly purely lyrical, but always mystical, had a very great and lasting influence on later hymnwriters. One of the elements which he introduced into religious poetry was Psyche (Seele), the poet's ego, a female being enamored with Jesus. Königsberg in East Prussia was the seat of the third of the leading literary societies, the Fruchtbringende Gesellschaft (The Fruitbearing Society) or Palmenorden (Order of the Palms). In this city, intellectual and cultural activities of great significance were carried on safely removed from the horrors of the Great War, although many members of the society resided in different German principalities and cities.

The poets of the Baroque era sought to develop a style that was adequate for the times and capable of speaking to the human condition which was so subject both to highest exaltation as well as darkest dejection. The result was a type of poetry that centered on the human being with the whole spectrum of a person's emotions, and in a style that tended to use words for their own sake. Descriptive adjectives, imperatives, questions, exclamations, subjunctives, and mere filler words succeeded one another in long sequences. As in architecture and the visual arts, only that which broke through the norms, that which was unusual and far-fetched, found approval. Despite the efforts of the societies, poetic conventions became more and more artificial and elaborate until many poetic creations not only bordered on but actually were in bad taste.

Not all German poets and hymn-writers were associated with literary societies. The most notable among these was Paul Gerhardt (1607-1767), who in the course of time gathered a considerable informal following of his own. His poetry remained largely unaffected by poetic conventions and his Christian faith unshaken despite personal and national tragedy.

Church life, limited chiefly to attendance at Sunday services, was in many areas a matter of obligation to the authorities and frequently consisted of listening to the pastor's harangues against the other faiths. Whoever felt the need could observe private devotions at home, but only individually, never in groups. Such meetings were forbidden by law and subject to severe punishment, as was failure to attend the Sunday worship services. The bailiffs saw to it that the people adhered to these rules.

Hostility among the three established persuasions was not the only manifestation of the religious strife that marked the latter half of the seventeenth century. The Protestant churches themselves, especially the Lutherans, were torn between extremes in which they found themselves caught either between orthodoxy and Pietism or orthodoxy and emerging rationalism.

Partly out of reaction to the sterile and factious condition of the churches, there arose in the Germanies a popular movement around several preachers which sought to bring about a reformation of the Christian life. Its detractors gave it the then derogatory name of "Pietism", which was derived from the title of a slim work, Pia desideria (Pious desires)[2], published in 1675. The author of this book was Jakob Philipp Spener (1635-1705), then pastor in Frankfurt/Main where he had been conducting house meetings for prayer, Bible study, and singing, undisturbed by the authorities because of the great esteem in which he was held by the town. In his book, Spener outlined a "program" for a reformation of the Christian life, little expecting that it would have far-reaching influence. This was the movement that provided the spiritual nurture of the early Brethren in Europe.

During the centuries that followed the German Reformation, German hymnody underwent marked changes from the form in which it had begun. The earlier hymn-writers had been leaders as well as common members of the various movements, whose main purpose in writing had been the proclamation of the Word and the confession of their faith. In later centuries hymn-writers were, for the most part, highly educated people such as pastors, educators, lawyers, church musicians, and poets, who wrote secular as well as religious poetry. Many of them were members of literary societies. As poets, they endeavored to adhere to the rules of poetic diction. Consequently, hymns gradually lost their function of serving the word of God and of professing the faith. They became increasingly individualistic and subjective although that, also, represented a poetic convention. The poetic "I", for example, so prevalent in many hymn-texts, must be understood as a device to express universal experiences and feelings representative of the entire human race. Gerhard Tersteegen (1697-1769), the great Reformed separatist poet and writer of the eighteenth century, expressed his use of the poetic "I" in this way:

... whenever I speak of such matters as some profound truth or a state of the soul, and, in that context, use the little word "I", I am speaking only in the [place of the] person [possessing] such a soul and placed in such a state or experience. By no means do I claim to own all this out of my own experience, even though, out of grace, I may have been given to understand such truths with sufficient certainty in divine light. That, however, is far from having actually partaken and experienced the thing itself. I feel like a sickly person who enjoys hearing and talking about good health and yearns for it himself. Thus I occasionally speak in my poetry of very spiritual and innermost truths, not because I already possess them but because I, through the grace of God, recognize them as so precious and desirable that I embrace them with all my heart longing to experience them myself. Indeed, on occasion I cannot help but commend them to others.[3]

Apart from the multitude of political events on the political and ecclesiastical scene, three movements influenced German hymnody in particular. The first was mysticism, a legacy of Roman Catholicism which had found some followers in early Protestantism. Its chief characteristic was the belief, first, that there existed in every human being at least a small remnant of the divine substance and, secondly, that it was possible for a mortal being to return to God, but only by means of a re-enactment of Christ's incarnation within that human being who thus became a child of God and Christ himself. This union of a human being and God could take the form of ecstasy, which was then called the mystic union of the spirit and the divine, or it could take the form of a complete negation of the world, a flight into nonbeing or quietism.

Traces of mysticism are found in countless hymns. They can be recognized in such expressions as "drowning," "sinking into," "ocean," "melting away," "being enraptured," "divine ray," or "fire," "lightning," "spark," and by the strong renunciation of all self-will and self-expression of the individual. This self-will and ego-centricity was considered the one real temptation humans had to contend with, whereas a stoic passivity (Gelassenheit) afforded the greatest attainable joy.

Pietism was the second movement that had contributed to the fabric of German hymnody. Pietist poetry, like Baroque poetry, its secular counterpart, centered on the individual human being but went beyond the poetic convention of describing the typical by dwelling on very subjective emotionalism, which ranged from highest bliss to deepest dejection and feelings of lostness in sin. Most importantly, however, it was the true believer on whom these hymns centered. Adjectives like "true," "right," "Christian," and "spiritual" abounded, which served both as a tool to teach the meanings of the precepts found in the hymns as well as a polemical device used against those who were Christian in name only. Another characteristic was that of the Christian addressing his or her own person, soul, will, mind, or heart as something special.

One of the concepts which Pietism upheld especially was that of the high birth or nobility of the believers as creatures formed in the image of God. This attitude corresponded very closely to the heightened sense of the importance of self in the secular sphere. The Pietist counterpart of Baroque negativism on the other hand, was a renunciation of life and the world often coupled with a considerable degree of self-abasement.

A product of mysticism and Pietism was a certain type of Jesus-hymn which reflected both the secular erotic poetry and the Baroque reaching for the infinite. The result was religious poems about Jesus, which had themes of mystical eros and/or mystical union and language which borrowed heavily from the Song of Solomon. The hymn which the Solingen Brethren sang on their way to prison belongs into this category even though it is not as erotically explicit as many. This hymn displays all the characteristics of Baroque poetry: the wordiness, the enumerations, exclamations, questions, heaven-soaring ecstasy, denial of the world and of those outside the fold, exaltation of self and excessive self-contemplation culminating in the anticipated mystical marriage.

This particular hymn displays another trait so typical for that time. If it were not for the mention of the name of Jesus, there is nothing in this text to indicate to a twentieth-century reader that this was a hymn for Christian worship or a poem for private devotional reading. Gottfried Arnold (1666-1714), the great church historian, whose writings were so important to the early Brethren, wrote numerous hymns of this nature, addressing either Jesus or Sophia, the Divine Wisdom.

Although the movement of Pietism originated around Spener at Frankfurt/Main, the most influential center of Pietist activity was later found at Halle in Saxony, where August Hermann Francke (1663-1727) was the spiritual and practical leader. The poets of the Halle movement spanned two generations, from those who had been very close to Spener and Francke during the early years, to the circle gathered around the latter's son-in-law, Johann Anastasius Freylinghausen (1670-1739), best known for his publication of Pietist hymnals.

Another center of Pietism formed in the South-German state of Württemberg which had a more churchly and biblical orientation and whose hymnody remained freer of the current conventions of poetry than that of the Halle poets. The chief concern of the Württemberg Pietists was not so much the individual but the expectation of the glory of the coming kingdom of God.

A circle of Pietist hymn-writers also existed in Upper Lusatia, a part of the Germanies formerly known as Silesia. However, many of the poets who identified themselves with this circle did not actually reside in the area. Like the earlier Silesian poets, these Pietists turned to the inner life of the soul and the workings of the Holy Spirit as their chief concerns.

Although for a long time the leaders of the Reformed church in the German-speaking countries recognized only metric psalm translations as acceptable hymnody, Reformed Christians found a new way for expressing their faith in hymns under the influence of evangelistic preachers who, in their own understanding of the relationship between Christian doctrine, faith, annd life anticipated the Pietist movement. The greatest of these Reformed hymn-writers, who also occasionally composed his own tunes, was Joachim Neander (1650-1680), whose collection of hymns bore the title, Bundeslieder (Hymns of the Covenant).

The third movement that had left its stamp on German hymnody by the beginning of the eighteenth century was early rationalism. Movements seldom begin spontaneously. They usually have long roots which reach back

in time and nourish what later becomes known by a certain name. Similarly, new movements do not replace the old but exist side-byside with them
for a considerable time. Thus, "Pietist" concerns existed long before the
movement itself came into being. The same was true for rationalism. In
Germany, although the Enlightenment superseded the Baroque era, its beginnings reached much further into the past. In hymnody, this meant that
rationalist expressions existed alongside those of Pietism and mysticism
for a long time.

Rationalism imbued people with a much more positive outlook on life
than the Baroque era had done. This was now the age of the absolutist
ruler - prefigured earlier in the Sun-King Louis XIV of France - and of
the autonomous human being. The mood of pessimism and the cry of Vanitas!
had given way to an all-pervasive optimism; the new watchword became "God,
Virtue, and Conscience." Instead of mysticism, there was natural theology, instead of emotionalism, intellectualism. Moralism, the path of which
had been so well prepared by the Pietist emphasis on a virtuous life had
become even more important than before. It epitomized virtue as the means
to the supreme goal which constituted the happiness of the individual, and
moralism itself had become a means for salvation.

In hymnody, the influence of rationalism can be seen by the new term-
inology that was introduced which substituted "improved" words for the
old, thereby purging German hymnody of language objectionable to the new,
enlightened times. Thus, instead of "faith" (Glaube), the poets now used
"religion," instead of "joy in the Lord" (Gottseligkeit), "virtue"
(Tugend). "Improvement" (Besserung) replaced "penance" and "repentance"
(Busse, Bekehrung), and "immortality" (Unsterblichkeit) and "a better
world" (eine bessere Welt) were substituted for "eternal life" (ewiges
Leben). No longer did the hymn-writers speak of "God the Father" (Gott
Vater) but of the "godhead" (Gottheit) and "providence" (Vorsehung).
"Sanctification" (Heiligung) and "new birth" (Wiedergeburt) were reduced
to the endeavor to "lead a different life." Many more examples could be
given.

These, then, were the three main influences on German hymnody preceding and during the time of the early Brethren. Considering some of the
extremes to which hymn-writers had been led, questions will inevitably
arise about the role of church leaders and theologians in these develop-
ments. The fact is that after the time of the early Protestant reformers,
church leaders and theologians took little or no interest in hymnody; it
was thought a part of practical theology which was left entirely to the
parsons.

By the turn of the eighteenth century, true spiritual creativity as
well as the certain profit promised by a constant demand for devotional
literature of all kinds had caused an enormous output in hymns. Johannes
Westphal states that as early as the year 1700 there already existed two
thousand chorale melodies to accomodate a volume of approximately forty
thousand German hymn-texts produced by some five hundred writers. It is
easy to see that prolific output of such magnitude could not have produced
poetry of consistently good quality.

Martin Luther (1483-1546), who had given such great impetus to German
hymn-writing, came to recognize the risks inherent in encouraging the

people to express their faith through this medium. He found it necessary to preface the last hymnal he was to edit with this warning:

> Viel falscher Meister izt Lieder tichten
> Sihe dich für, und lern sie recht richten
> wo Gott hin bauet sein kirch und sein wort
> Da wil der Teuffel sein mit trug und mord.

(Many who falsely claim to be master poets are writing hymns these days. Take heed and learn to judge them properly. Wherever God establishes his church and his word, the devil is bound to be with falsehood and murder.)[4]

Luther took another precaution with the hymnal published by Klug in 1531.[5] In his preface he stated that, although heretofore, hymn-writers' names had not been printed along with their hymns, this had now become necessary because too often texts were submitted under his own or other reformers' names, thus deceitfully assuring the faithful of the hymns' purity of teaching and content.

On the whole, until the end of the sixteenth century, the Lutheran hymnals retained their intended character as instruments of proclamation of the faith, confession of sin, and preaching of the word. Usually these hymnals were published by laymen, which practice continued throughout the following century. Frequently it was an enterprising publisher who compiled a hymn-book, often by copying extensively from other hymnals. Occasionally it was an individual hymn-writer who brought his works before the public in this manner. Such lack of control again came to a head in the latter part of the seventeenth century when, during the dogmatic controversies of Lutheran orthodoxy in Prussia, all the hymnals published in Berlin listed the name of the writer with each hymn to assure the users of the doctrinal purity of the texts.

Around the turn of the eighteenth century, a new type of hymn-book emerged: the "official church-hymnal." These hymnals were published with the purpose of being adopted as the only authorized hymnal of the principality in which each was issued, sanctioned by the leaders of the respective state or established church, and endowed with the seal of the secular ruler. Such hymnals had titles like Neu vollständiges Marggräflich Brandenburgisches Gesang-Buch (New and complete hymn-book of the Duchy of Brandenburg), Churländisches vollständiges Gesangbuch (Complete hymnal for Kurland), or Eisenachisches Neu-vermehrtes und beständiges Gesang-Buch (Newly enlarged and permanent hymnal of the principality of Eisenach).

The fact that these hymnals were called official signified nothing in regard to their format and content, however. Appearances notwithstanding, theologians still considered hymnody too insignificant for their sphere of interest. They viewed hymn-texts as literature for the laity and produced by the laity. As such they followed other rules than those of dogmatic and systematic theology.

For Spener, the "Father of Pietism," hymnody was very important. In his view, singing constituted a large part of public worship and devotions in the home. Through it souls were prepared for other spiritual exercises. Printed hymns - in contrast to thanksgiving and prayer, which could much more easily be uttered without prescribed formulae - were a necessity for worship. This is what he wrote:

> I do not know that it would be easy to find anyone who is capable of singing spontaneously or extemporaneously an entire hymn from his heart. Since, then, such formulae are more necessary for hymns than for prayer, it is very important how [hymn-texts] are written. It is not enough that they should be in keeping with the pure doctrine and devoid of errors. They must also be phrased according to the spirit in order to express the concerns which are to be brought before God in such a way that our own hearts might be beneficially moved.[6]

The above sentiment notwithstanding, Spener opened the way for great freedom in the publishing of hymns in another statement, where he recommended two types of hymnals. The first was to be a church hymnal for use in public worship. It should be small so as to be convenient for carrying to services and should consist primarily of the time-tested hymns of the church which the people knew well enough to sing, German hymnals as a rule being printed without music. As space allowed, such newer hymns that were the richest in content and spirituality might also be included in this church hymnal.

The second hymnal was to be a book for private devotions. Here, great freedom should be allowed. This hymnal might contain all hymns that afforded any degree of edification. Only hymns that contained errors or other indecent matter were to be excluded. Spener liked those hymnals the best that contained the greatest number of hymns. He also favored adding to them frequently so that "everybody could choose to use those that moved and edified the most."[7]

Tersteegen, in his preface to the fifth edition of Joachim Neander's _Gott-geheiligtes Harfen-Spiel der Kinder Zion_ elaborated on the use of hymnals for private devotions. He conceived of a hymnal as an aid in the outward worship of God:

> ... among these external aids, the reading and singing of pious hymns is not the least ... . First of all, experience has clearly shown that the devout reading of godly hymns has at all times had its special blessing and good use with many a soul. Hymnals, more than other books, contain a variety of lively descriptions of special states of the soul. A God-seeking mind (whatever its need or status) can easily find something therein which harmonizes with its condition and may provide instruction, strength, awakening, and comfort. Besides, a graceful rendition conveys a charming power through which the Christian truths are depicted very agreeably to the mind and are imbued with pleasure. Furthermore, rhymed speech is retained in one's memory much more easily than unrhymed speech and can therefore serve a soul much better in all possible circumstances for instruction and strength through the intervention of God.[8]

The eighteenth-century theologian, scholar, and poet, Johann Gottfried Herder (1744-1803), made this statement about hymns and hymnals:

> The hymnal is the versified Bible for the common Christian: it is his consolation, his teacher, his refuge and delight at home; in public

meetings, hymn-texts and their accompanying melodies should be like wafting ether, like refreshing breezes from heaven that unite and edify those gathered. The nature of the music that contributes to this end, especially the nature of the highest kind - sacred music - cannot be described but only felt. It moves by its simplicity and exalts by its dignity ... .

It is regrettable that with the large number of inferior hymns in our old hymnals, the good ones are almost never found together in one volume, but scattered here and there in provincial [i.e., "official"] hymnals and hidden, again, among the chaff ... [one ought to] gather the best hymns - old and new - from all provinces [i.e., principalities] regardless of branch of Protestantism, along with their melodies. This would then be the foundation of a good hymnal for the Germans. The bad hymns - regardless of name and rank of the writers - would have to be removed, and even from the good hymns, bad verses would have to be deleted. Many of them are too long as it is and it is always preferable to remove what is poor than to alter poorly. ... All changes in the new hymns ought to be aimed only at removing what is objectionable. Never must the tone of the writer be lost, much less the hymn moulded into our own way of thinking. ... In short, a practicing theologian must needs know the best of the old and the best, or best-altered, new hymns. The comparison of the two is a vast area for studying language and sentiment in relation to spiritual matters and for providing the most memorable sermon materials.[9]

On the whole, however, the church paid little, if any, attention to the hymns that were sung by her people. The hymns used for the various Sundays and holy days of the ecclesiastical year as well as those for communion, baptismal, and funeral services were part of the liturgy and thus were generally prescribed by the order accompanying the lectionary. Hence, many people knew these hymns from memory. There was more flexibility in the choice of hymn following the sermon, although, in some cases, even those were established for the entire year. Nevertheless, it was generally after the sermon that new hymns could be introduced and taught to the congregation. Sometimes this was done by the pastor who might have written a hymn himself as a summary of his sermon, sometimes by the cantor or even by custodian. The writing of hymns as sermon summaries was a fairly common practice especially among the Pietists.

These, then, were the circumstances in which the early Brethren found themselves. They had grown up in the established churches of the principalities whose subjects they were. The influence of the Pietist movement had brought them to a biblical understanding of the Christian life. Their desire to practice this life within the twin institutions of church and state met with punishment, imprisonment, loss of property, and eventually, eviction. Counting the cost of their discipleship, the Brethren removed themselves to those few areas whose rulers, out of tradition or necessity, practiced tolerance in religious matters. There, their formation could take place, their first theological statements were composed, and their first hymnal was compiled and printed.

11

NOTES

1 Donald F. Durnbaugh, ed., <u>European Origins of the Brethren</u> (Elgin, Ill.: Brethren Press, 1958), p. 243.

2 Philipp Jacob Spener, <u>Pia desideria</u>. Herausgegeben von Kurt Aland. 2. Auflage (Berlin: Walter de Gruyter, 1955).

3 Gerhard Tersteegen, "Vorbericht," <u>Geistliches Blumengärtlein Inniger Seelen</u> ... . 5. und vermehrte Edition (Duisburg am Rhein: Johann Sebastian Straube, 1751), pp. [3-4].

4 <u>Geystliche Lieder. Mit einer neuen vorrhede D. Martin Luth.</u> (Leipzig, Valentin Babst, 1545).

5 <u>Das Klug'sche Gesangbuch 1533</u>, ed. Konrad Ameln (Kassel und Basel: Bärenreiter Verlag, 1954).

6 Philipp Spener, <u>Theologische Bedenken</u>, 4. Teil (Halle, Waysenhaus, 1715), p. 320-321, <u>passim</u>.

7 <u>Ibid.</u> 3. Teil, p. 562.

8 Gerhard Tersteegen, "Vorrede," <u>Gott-geheiligtes Harfen-Spiel der Kinder Zion; Bestehend in Joachimi Neandri sämtlichen Bundes-Liedern und Danck-Psalmen</u> ... 5. Aufl. (Solingen, Johann Schmitz, 1763), pp. [4-5] <u>passim</u>.

9 Johann Gottfried Herder, <u>Briefe, das Studium der Theologie betreffend</u>, 3. und 4. Teil. Nach der 2. verbesserten Ausgabe 1785 (Stuttgart und Tübingen, J. G. Cotta, 1829), pp. 230-237 <u>passim</u>.

Chapter I

GEISTREICHES GESANG-BUCH

The first hymnal attributable to the Brethren is the Geistreiches
Gesang-Buch printed at Berleburg, Germany in 1720. There is no mention of
it in early Brethren records. What little is known about it is derived
from internal evidence linking this hymnal to the Brethren.

Much can be learned about a hymnal from its title-page, its foreword,
and the subject index to its hymns. The Geistreiches Gesang-Buch contains
only the first two features. From its title-page the reader learns that
it is a

> Spirit-filled hymn-book for all souls who love the truth, especially
> for the church [Gemeine] of the Lord: comprising in it the choicest and
> most necessary hymns selected from other hymn-books, along with one
> hundred new hymns that have been set down for the first time for the
> comfort and consolation of all true followers of the Lord Jesus and
> brought to light in this present form for the praise of God.[1]

According to the imprint, the hymnal was printed at Berleburg, seat
of the counts of Sayn-Wittgenstein-Berleburg. This principality, together
with its neighbor, the county of Sayn-Wittgenstein-Hohenstein, made up the
territory of Wittgenstein, a haven for religious dissenters at the time of
the early Brethren. It is in the latter of the two counties that Schwarzenau is located. The hymnal's date of publication was given as 1720, the
year of the Schwarzenau Brethren's exodus from Wittgenstein. The name of
the publisher was Christoph Konert.

The foreword reads like a personal letter explaining how a group of
people decided to end the prevailing dissatisfaction with the current
hymnal situation among the "Baptist-minded" (Taufgesinnte) by printing a
hymn-book of their own. This, and the mention that most of the one
hundred new hymns were written "by brethren who have now been kept prison-
ers for almost three years for witnessing to Jesus," leads to the conclusion that this book was indeed published by and for the early members
in Europe of the Brethren movement.[2]

The description of the imprisoned brethren agrees perfectly with the
story of the Solingen brethren. Those seven men had been arrested and
brought before the authorities in 1717 for preaching and having been re-
baptized. While imprisoned in Düsseldorf during their trial, one of them,
Wilhelm Knepper, wrote approximately four hundred hymns.

THE ANTECEDENTS

Most of the early Brethren came from the Reformed church; some had been Lutherans. Both churches had their own hymnals with specific region-al hymnals in the various principalities. The Mennonites, with whom the Brethren were in contact, often used the hymnals prevalent in the region in which they lived or, when publishing their own hymnals, drew on Lutheran or Reformed hymnody to which they had become accustomed. The six-teenth-century Anabaptist hymnal, Ausbund, was not widely used by Menno-nites during the early eighteenth century.[3] As this hymnal had remained virtually unchanged since the late sixteenth century, neither its language nor its contents seemed relevant any longer.

Indeed, the Ausbund was no significant source of hymns for the Brethren. Of the five hymns by Anabaptist writers which the Brethren in-cluded, only two (158, 258) can be located in the Ausbund.[4] Two others (360, 744) were printed in the two hymnals which were the most important sources. These two hymnals will be discussed later in greater detail. A possible source for the fifth hymn (83) could not be ascertained. Ana-baptist tendencies are nevertheless noticeable in Brethren hymnody as will be shown later.

Two Pietist hymn-books probably served as the chief sources and models for the first Brethren hymnal. The richest source was very likely the Geistreiches Gesang-Buch (Spirit-filled hymn-book), published by Jo-hann Anastasius Freylinghausen in two parts in 1704 and 1714.[5] If not the first, it was nevertheless the largest and most significant Pietist hymn-book which soon became the model for later Pietist hymnals. (Henceforth, this hymnal will be referred to as "Freylinghausen's.") The other hymnal was the Davidisches Psalter-Spiel (Davidic psaltery).[6] It was published anonymously in 1718 by the Community of True Inspiration, Radical Pietists who were well-known to the early Brethren.[7]

The two above hymnals suggested themselves as the chief sources for the compilation of the Brethren's Geistreiches Gesang-Buch after several hymnals had been examined and compared. These were Freylinghausen's, the Davidisches Psalter-Spiel, an edition of Johann Arndts Paradiesgärtlein (1718),[8] and another Pietist hymnal printed in 1700 at Darmstadt, Hesse, close to the time and not far from the area of early Brethren activity.[9] Each hymn in the Brethren hymnal was checked in these hymn-books with the following results: 157 hymns appear both in Freylinghausen's and in the In-spirationist hymnal, with sixteen exclusively in the latter and two exclu-sively in the former. Eighteen hymns were located in other earlier hymnals. This left 101 hymns that could neither be documented in hymnals published before 1720, nor located in primary sources or reliable reference works to establish their authorship. Consequently, the assumption was made that these unidentified hymns are those that had been written by Solingen brethren.

The European hymnal of the Brethren is a small book, one page measuring 15.4 by 6.5 centimeters. Each page contains a single column of text. When closed, the hymnal is 2.8 centimeters thick including the covers. Title and format of the 1720 hymnal quite clearly follow Freyling-hausen's model, but here any resemblance ends. The Brethren hymnal not only lacks an index to subjects but the hymns themselves are arranged without a plan and are accessible only through an index of first lines. It is noteworthy that, although the arrangement of the body of hymns seems to follow no obvious order, the majority of the new, unidentified (Brethren) hymns are found in two large segments, namely, numbers ten through thirty-six and 161 through 217 in the hymnal.

THE RUBRICS

Since the compilers of the first Brethren hymnal did not provide any guide to its contents, a hypothetical list of subjects or rubrics, as they were then called, was constructed for this study. The rubrics thus supplied were based on those established by Freylinghausen and the Inspirationists. Before the rubrics for the Brethren hymnal can be discussed, a brief explanation about rubrics in general and Freylinghausen's in particular, is necessary.

In the early decades of German hymnal-printing during the sixteenth century, hymn-books were arranged in a very simple fashion. The hymnal which Luther edited before his death, the so-called Babstsches Gesangbuch served as a model for German hymn-books through the remainder of the century. It consisted of 130 hymns grouped in two parts. The first contained the core of the Reformation message: hymns for the festivals of the church; hymns explaining Luther's Small Catechisms (i.e., the ten commandments, the creed, the Lord's Prayer, baptism, and the Lord's Supper); psalms; and the liturgical hymns (i.e., the German litany, etc.). The second part consisted of other new hymns of the Reformation; hymns written by Christians of earlier times; hymns based on Scripture; and hymns for burial.

The hymnal which Freylinghausen compiled and edited almost 150 years later is a good example of the development of German hymn-books since the Reformation. His hymnal reached the proportions of fifteen hundred hymns in two volumes with the number of rubrics having grown from eight to sixty. The division into two parts was retained but instead of hymns about the heart of Protestant teaching, the first part consists of hymns for the ecclesiastical year following closely the chief Roman Catholic feast and holy days (rubrics 1-17). These, Freylinghausen explains in his preface, depict "Christ, the foundation of our salvation, with his attributes and endowments." The second part is almost twice as long and deals with "the order of our salvation." Lastly, the preface is now extended to a small treatise on Pietist theology.

This order of our salvation (Oeconomie unserer Seligkeit) originated neither with Freylinghausen nor with the Pietist movement. Its genesis is found much earlier in the medieval order of salvation in Roman Catholic mysticism. In Protestantism this idea was developed as a specially important doctrine of seventeenth-century orthodoxy. Here, the order progressed through the three stages of Illumination of Man, Conversion, and Rebirth.

For the Pietist Francke, it was important that each sermon encompass the entire order of salvation as he understood it. This Pietist emphasis was carried over into Freylinghausen's hymnal. Here, the three phases are extended over six sections. They are headed by the rubric, "Of the benevolence of God and Christ" (no. 18) and deal with the following: 1. the means by which God intends to restore mankind into communion with him (rubrics 19-23); 2. the order to which the Christian must submit to have part in Christ, and the salvation earned by Christ (rubrics 24-28); 3. the spiritual exercises and virtues required of the true Christian (rubrics 29-41); 4. the fruits of these virtues (rubrics 42-46); 5. God's promise (rubrics 47-48); and 6. the final and complete happiness awaiting the Christian (rubrics 51-53).

By means of this Pietist order, the Christian was led from the cradle of faith to the physical grave and life beyond. By following this path of progression, which began with teaching and instruction, the Christian was not only gradually guided on the right road toward salvation but was also given the means with which to attain it. This, however, was not sufficient. The order also pointed out quite clearly the possibilities and necessities for checking and testing one's faith experience - be it newly found or of long standing - and finally even the achieved state of one's own salvation.[10]

In the following, the rubrics of the Palter-Spiel and of Freylinghausen's hymnal will be discussed and compared.[11] These two hymnals seem closely related because the Inspirationists had apparently followed Freylinghausen's order; 664 hymns (or seventy-four percent of their entire hymnal) are also found in that collection.

The main difference between the arrangements of these two hymnals is that the Psalter-Spiel has no rubrics for Epiphany, the three Marian feast days, and for the feast day of John the Baptist. Likewise, there is no category for baptism, because the Inspirationists did not believe in that practice. "Of the holy supper" (Freylinghausen, rubric no. 23) was expanded here to "Of the holy supper and love-feast of believers" (Psalter-Spiel, rubric no. 30) and was moved from the means of grace to the place between "Of brotherly and universal love" and "Of following Jesus." This was a more logical sequence for Radical Pietists such as the Community of True Inspiration who, unlike the churchly Pietists at Halle, held a non-sacramental stance.

Similarly, Freylinghausen's rubric, "Of the divine word" (no. 21) was rephrased in the Psalter-Spiel as "Of the inner and outer word" (no. 16), an Anabaptist concept which Alexander Mack, Sr., also embraced in his writings. "Of Jesus, his name and offices" (Freylinghausen, no. 5) was expanded to "Of the transfiguration of Jesus in his manifold names, offices, and favors" (Psalter-Spiel, no. 5). "Of the ascension of Jesus Christ" (Freylinghausen, no. 12) became "Of the ascension of Jesus Christ and his sitting at the right hand of God" (Psalter-Spiel, no. 9).

An interesting contraction occurred in a Psalter-Spiel rubric which was perpetuated in later Brethren and other hymnals. Freylinghausen's "Of the nature of God and his attributes or, for the feast-day of the holy trinity" (no. 14) became "Of the nature and attributes of God, or the holy trinity" (Psalter-Spiel, no. 11). This marks perhaps one difference in hymnals serving churchly Pietists and Radical or Separatist Pietists. The former observed the feasts of the ecclesiastical year, whereas the latter were opposed to all outward rituals.

Checking the locations of those hymns in the 1720 hymnal which appeared both in Freylinghausen's as well as in the Inspirationist hymnal, it was found that only two hymns are listed under different rubrics in the two collections (108, 1219).

For the purpose of supplying a working order, or rubrics, for the first Brethren hymnal, it seemed preferable to follow the basic arrangement of the Inspirationists. Besides the fact that the Brethren were closer to the stance of the radical than that of the churchly Pietists, there is the compelling reason that the basic order of rubrics used in the Psalter-Spiel later served the Brethren as a model for their first hymnal produced in America. For the 1720 hymnal, some rubrics had to be added, such as "Baptism," "Footwashing," "Parting hymns," and "Hymns of supplication." The rubric, "Closing hymn" was omitted and "Travelling hymns" substituted. To demonstrate the arrangement of the rubrics, each section is headed by the description provided in Freylinghausen's preface. Numbers in parentheses denote the number of hymns in each rubric.

RUBRICS PROVIDED FOR
Geistreiches Gesang-Buch, 1720

[Feast Day Hymns in Which Christ, the Foundation of Our Salvation is Depicted with all His Graces and Attributes]
1. Of the coming of Christ to judgment (7)
2. Of the incarnation and birth of Christ (3)
3. Of the transfiguration of Jesus in his manifold names, offices, and favors (10)
4. Of the suffering and death of Jesus Christ (8)
5. Of the resurrection of Jesus Christ (3)
6. Of the ascension of Jesus Christ and his sitting at the right hand of God (1)
7. Of the holy ghost and his manifold gifts and workings (3)
8. Of the nature and attributes of God, or the holy trinity (2)

[The Source and Well-Spring from Which Flows Our Salvation and Blessed Estate]
9. Of the benevolence of God and Christ (9)

[The Means through Which God Will Restore Us into Communion with Him]
10. Of the works of creation and the divine love and glory reflected therein (2)
11. Of divine providence and lordship (7)

[The So-Called Means of Grace]
12. Of the inner and the outer word (2)

[The Order Which You Must Observe if You Will Have Part in Christ and the Salvation Earned by Him]
13. Of the true and the false Christendom (9)
14. Of human misery and damnation (4)
15. Of the true repentance and conversion (6)
16. Of the true faith (4)
17. Of Christian life and conduct (5)

[Exercises and Virtues Required for Christian Life and Conduct]
   18. Of the true spiritual prayer (1)
   19. Of spiritual watchfulness (12)
   20. Of spiritual battle and victory (13)
   21. Of the true chastity (3)
   22. Of denial of self and the world (16)
   23. Of the desire for God and Christ (16)
   24. Of the love for Jesus (12)
   25. Of brotherly and universal love (3)
   26. Of the holy supper and love-feast of believers (7)
   27. Of following Jesus (11)
   28. Of the mystery of the cross (which is laid upon you) (11)
   29. Of Christian resignation [Gelassenheit] (2)
   30. Of true steadfastness (6)
   31. Of the heart's complete surrender to God (3)

[Your Reward for Your Christian Life and Conduct]
   32. Of divine peace and rest of the soul (5)
   33. Of the joy in the holy ghost (7)
   34. Of the joyfulness of faith (10)
   35. Of the praise of God (16)
   36. Of the divine wisdom (1)

[The Blessed Estate of the Kingdom of Grace]
   37. Of the spiritual marriage [to Jesus] (2)
   38. Of the high birth of believers (1)

[Reminders that Despite of All This, You Have Not Yet Attained the Goal]
   39. Of the hidden life of the believers (2)
   40. Of the lament of Zion (4)

[The Hope with Which One Sustains Oneself amidst All the Lament in This Vale of Sorrows]
   41. Of the hope of Zion (12)
   42. Of death and resurrection (2)
   43. Of heaven and the heavenly Jerusalem (5)

[Hymns for Various Occasions]
   44. Morning hymns (4)
   45. Evening hymns (7)
   46. Table hymns (3)
   47. In times of distress (1)
   48. Baptism (7)
   49. Footwashing (1)
   50. Parting hymns (1)
   51. Hymns of supplication (9)
   52. Travelling hymns (2)

The list of subjects provided in Appendix I/4 shows which hymns fall into each rubric. All texts that appeared later in the first American hymnal, Das kleine Davidische Psalterspiel (1744), were assigned according to the rubrics used there, and the others were grouped where they seemed to fit best.

Any user of these rubrics will soon be frustrated by the seemingly arbitrary method with which individual hymns are grouped. It must be remembered that in most cases the relationship between a hymn's content, its title - if it has one - and the rubric(s) under which it is listed is very slight. Hymns were written to serve as meditations, to teach individuals how to become better followers of Jesus, to reinforce sermon content, to undergird people's faith, to give succor in all manner of adverse and trying circumstances, to encourage the Christian not to give up hope but to set the goal upon heavenly things - the list could go on and on. In all of these purposes a single hymn often covered a wide range of topics and attitudes as a rule. The order of rubrics must be understood as a system that was imposed on an existing and an emerging body of hymns in order to make a given hymnal's contents more easily accessible for use in private and public worship.

Although the relationship between a hymn's content and the rubric under which it is grouped is very slight, it is nevertheless interesting to examine the distribution of the hymns in this first Brethren hymnal. Some hymn studies place quantity in direct relationship to significance and popularity. If this were applied to the 1720 hymnal, then the most important rubric would have been "Of the praise of God" (no. 35) with fifteen hymns, followed by "Of denial of self and the world" (no. 22) and "Of the desire for God and Christ (no. 23) with fourteen hymns each. "Of spiritual battle and victory" (no. 20) had thirteen, "Of spiritual watchfulness" (no. 19) and "Of the love for Jesus (no. 24) had twelve hymns each.

No hymns at all could be found under the Psalter-Spiel rubrics of "New-Year's hymns," "Of the burial of Jesus Christ," and "Of the holy angels." Only one hymn each appears under the topics "Of the ascension of Jesus Christ and his sitting at the right hand of God" (no. 6), "Of the true spiritual prayer" (no. 18), "Of Christian resignation" (no. 29), "Of the divine wisdom" (no. 36), "Of the spiritual marriage" (no. 37), "Of the high birth of believers" (no. 38), "In times of distress" (no. 47), "Footwashing" (no. 49), and "Parting hymns" (no. 50). Six new and one old hymn make up the rubric "Of the holy supper and love-feast of believers" (no. 26) and five new and two old hymns that of "Baptism" (no. 48).

DOCUMENTED HYMNS

Among a total number of 295 hymns, 159 came from the stock of German hymnody representing eighty-two poets. Thirty-five texts can be documented but their authors remain as yet anonymous. Hymns in the manner of the Pietists predominate. There were probably two hymns by the Radical Pietist Wilhelm Petersen (1649-1727). He, along with the hymn-writer Johann Jakob Schütz (1640-1690), had been an influential member of a chiliastic circle of Pietists in Frankfurt/Main. These people had broken away from Spener and later helped finance the emigration of the Mennonites and Quakers from Krefeld, Germany, to Germantown, Pennsylvania, in 1683. Petersen's two hymns are expressions of both his chiliasm and his view of Jesus as the arriving bridegroom. His Liebster Jesu, liebstes Leben, der du bist (791) emphasizes the believer's readiness and is rather objective in tone. Wann erblick ich dich einmal (1190) is written in the style of the Song of Solomon.

Several hymns came from the pens of sixteenth-century Anabaptists. The hymn that expresses Anabaptist teachings on the gathered church and believers' baptism most distinctly is Hans Betz's (d. ca. 1537) Christus das Lamm auf Erden kam (158). Kommt her zu mir, spricht Gottes Sohn (744) by Georg Grünwald (ca. 1490-1530) deals with the suffering which following Jesus brings with it and with the joy and glory which the faithful can expect after death. Leupold Scharnschlager's Die Lieb' erkalt' jetzt in der Welt (258) deplores the human condition in this world which is without love. Two prayer hymns dealing with personal discipleship, the suffering here on earth and the glory of heaven were written by Michael Weisse (ca. 1448-1534), a leading elder of the Bohemian Brethren (83) and Adam Reissner (1496-1575), a Schwenkfelder scholar (635). Herr Jesu Christ, dich zu uns wend (484) by Wilhelm II of Sachsen-Weimar is known to have been sung at a Brethren baptism in Marienborn.[12]

Although it was probably not the result of intentional planning, one fifth of all the documented hymns were taken from the spiritual poetry of three well-known poets namely, the great hymn-writer of the Reformed tradition, Joachim Neander (twenty hymns), the Roman Catholic convert Johannes Scheffler (twelve), and the Lutheran Pietist Gottfried Arnold (ten). Sixty-three percent of all the hymn-writers were of the Pietist persuasion and account for approximately one third of all documented texts.

In their selection of hymns the Brethren differed very little from other hymnal publishers. Following the taste of the period, more than half of the hymns place great emphasis on sentiment and emotion. Jesus, mystical eros, denial of the world, and the Christian virtues as propounded by Pietism were the favorite themes. However, there are many hymns in this collection that have stood the test of time and are well-known and sung in Germany even in the latter part of the twentieth century. At the same time one wonders why some of the very good hymns in Freylinghausen's hymnal and the Psalter-Spiel were not included. Although Luther's hymns - of which the latter contained eleven - may have lost their appeal to the average church-goer during the seventeenth and early eighteenth centuries, their simplicity and plain speech should have appealed to the early Brethren more than the verbosity of the Baroque poets.

A list at the end of this chapter provides a summary of the hymn-writers according to historical periods and movements to which they belonged. It should be noted that there is a chronological overlap between the seventeenth century and the era of Pietism's forerunners. For the purpose of this study, it seemed helpful to create two categories and borrow the German term Vorläufer used in several works on hymnology. Thus, authors who elsewhere might be defined as members of Paul Gerhardt's circle or as Erbauungsliederdichter (writers of hymns of an edifying or devotional nature) are here grouped under "Forerunners." All others are found under "Late seventeenth century." A less noticeable and perhaps more debatable overlap occurs between the two categories of "Counter-Reformation" and "Thirty-Years' War." The distinction here depends in some cases entirely on the viewpoint of this writer. In later chapters, similar instances of overlap will occur. However, inasmuch as these categories are intended merely as an aid to gain some perspective and not as definitive statements, the possibility of divergence of opinion can be admitted without apology. The criterion for inclusion of hymn-writers in this and subsequent lists is reliable documentation as outlined in the introductory remarks to the cumulative index of first lines.

A second list notes all hymn-writers in alphabetical order with the number of hymns found in this hymnal in each case.

UNDOCUMENTED HYMNS

In this study, all hymn-texts for which neither authorship nor publication prior to the hymnal under discussion could be established are considered undocumented. In each chapter, special attention is given to such undocumented texts for it is these that are potentially Brethren-authored. In the present hymnal, one hundred new hymns were said to have been included which had been written by Brethren during their imprisonment. Exactly 101 texts cannot be identified as to their origins. One of these, as will be shown below, was in all probability written by Alexander Mack. It may therefore be assumed that the remaining one hundred were indeed authored by one or several of the Solingen Brethren. As it is known, however, that it was Wilhelm Knepper who wrote about four hundred hymns during that period, these texts will henceforth be attributed to him. A complete list of these new hymns is given in Appendix I/5.

Baptism

The most specific contemporary account of the use of a Brethren hymn by the Brethren is found in the Chronicon Ephratense (1786) where George Adam Martin (1715-1794) describes a Brethren baptism: "As soon as you came to the water, this hymn was usually sung: 'Count the cost, says Jesus Christ, when the foundation Thou wouldst lay,' etc. which A[lexander] M[ack] had composed [i.e., written] already in Germany."[13]

The inclusion of this baptismal hymn near the beginning of the European hymnal seemed substantial proof that the "Baptist-minded" mentioned in the preface were indeed the Schwarzenau Brethren. This is the only German or English hymnal in which this particular hymn was included. Four of its original thirteen stanzas were later on translated by Ora W. Garber (1903-1981) on the occasion of the 250th anniversary of the first baptism.[14]

Ueberschlag die Kost (1155) is a teaching hymn, in which one of the early Brethren leaders, Alexander Mack (1679-1735), explains the meaning of baptism, compares the church to the vine, gives a brief sketch of God's plan for the restoration of humankind, adds some sound Christian advice, and concludes with a call to action against the evils of the times. The language is very direct and somewhat reminiscent of sixteenth-century poetry, being not very polished but also free of unnecessary embellishments and exaggerations. The text is given here in a close prose translation:

"Count the cost," says Jesus Christ, when you will lay the foundation. Are you willing, in your own mind, to risk your wealth, body, possessions, and your honor, in following Christ's example, as you are about to promise? (:1)

Through baptism you are buried into Christ's death and will no longer be allowed to be your own, if you are minded to be co-inheritor with Christ's church [Gemeinde] and his bride, whom he has created through his word. (:2)

If you hate sin from the bottom of your heart, you will succeed; gird yourself with righteousness and you will be able to do battle with your enemy, the god of the world, who is obstructing your path. (:3)

The child is formed in the bosom of the church according to the Father's will. His spirit fills it and removes the [old] garments, the childish indecision disappears, and the child becomes an adult according to Christ's mind. (:4)

This adult is incorporated [into the church] to grow into a fruitful vine. To this end he will often be offered the bread of fellowship when the church gathers who are Christ's body and members. (:5)

They are truly in the house of God where God teaches them through his son, of whom it is said that one should listen to him in all that he teaches which is sealed through his own blood. (:6)

His testament is still as valid as it was a thousand years ago with the disciples to whom God had revealed it through signs, miracles, and through power, through which the old was abolished. (:7)

When later on it was destroyed, there was no evidence of any sign any more. When Joshua heard it read, he believed and no longer asked for a sign. (:8)

Whoever believes in the word of God will not demand a sign, for Christ reprimanded the evil band whose unbelief became manifest when they demanded a sign. When he did acceed, they did not believe it. (:9)

O dear soul [Mensch], remember the words which Abraham said to the rich man who, after he had died, asked Lazarus to tell his brothers about the agony and pain that they might believe it. (:10)

Abraham denied him this, he took it as unbelief. Their hearts had to be directed towards faith in God and his word, as the writings of Moses and the prophets directed towards Christ, the light. (:11)

Keep your heart from false teachings and do not be deceived by those who pretend that they, too, listen to Christ. If someone does not follow Christ's word in his own teaching, then what such a person says is not true. (:12)

Arise, dear soul [Menschen-Kind], the time is now to stem the evil, for Christ himself goes into battle against those who will not listen to him in his outer and inner word. But those who do, have the mind of Christ. (:13)

Allusion to believers' baptism is a rather certain indication of Brethren authorship. Several instances can be found among the new hymns:

Lord Jesus, you did profess in your holy baptism, to which you submitted yourself as an example, how you would fulfill all righteousness in all strife and thus prepare the way. (40:7)

This was done so that people would follow your example if they wanted to inherit your kingdom. Whoever was prepared to serve you was to be baptized into death and resurrection, no longer to be a servant of sin but of the true life. (:8)

Just as baptism represents a burial of sins and resurrection is true, and all the old is gone, and the new is beginning, in this way one is truly in the Lord's way. Blessed are they who follow it. (:9)

Through the chosen baptism one must shun and flee the old way.   (610:7)

Baptism is the resurrection with Christ from the dead, in which you had yourselves baptized.   (804:1)

The most direct reference to believers' baptism is found in the hymn, Wenn man allhier der Welt ihr Tun (1245):

Although they reprimand and call us re-baptizers [Wieder-Täufer], we shall live faithfully according to Christ's teachings.   (:4)

Occasionally, the writer waxed quite didactic as in the hymn, Ach Jesu, schau hernieder (34):

Another soul has been awakened from the sleep of sinfulness and is pre-pared to deny self and enter your covenant ... . She [i.e, the soul] desires to be baptized, Lord Christ, into your death, to leave the world of sin and follow your commandment. To this we shall be wit-nesses and listen to it carefully so that we may be taught anew our duty ... . We, too, have renounced in baptism sin and the world's ways, have laid our sinful bodies into their graves and submitted to you, in order to follow you in teaching and living in the way of the cross ... . One does not remain in the grave, ... one rises again, the sinful body is removed in baptism, the new creation emerges, lays the cross on his back ... .   (:1, 3, 4, 8 passim)

Baptism was understood not only as a symbol of the burying of sin and resurrection of that which was new, but also as a requirement of anyone who followed Jesus and desired to enter the kingdom of God. It signified death of the old being and resurrection to the new and true life.

Footwashing

Another mark of Brethren authorship may be the topic of footwashing. The best example is found in the hymn, Ach wie so lieblich und wie fein (68):

O how lovely and fine it is when brethren are united in faith and love, when they can truly wash one another's feet as faithful servants out of their hearts' humble desire.   (:1)
Let us then as faithful servants properly contemplate in this hour the meaning of footwashing, so that in humility we may observe this custom out of love and prepare ourselves for suffering.   (:5)
For whoever will have one's feet washed must remember how the Lord did this and what an important part of it is in the cleansing of the soul and the sanctification, washed by the Lord.   (:7)
For whoever refuses to be washed by the Lord and his congregation [Gemeine] has no part in her life and will remain in his or her own ways and the soul will remain a withered vine in all eternity.   (:8)
[All this in order] that we may continue to proclaim your death and your great anguish [Angst], and in so doing break your bread and learn what it means to have communion [Gemeinschaft] with your true life.
                                                                       (:10)

Thus, footwashing signified true unity, mutual love without envy, humility, proclamation of Christ's death, and the breaking of bread.

Love-Feast

A few references are found among the undocumented hymns pertaining to the ordinance of fellowship meal or love-feast of believers, which the Brethren had in common with the Inspirationists. An interesting detail is found in the new Brethren hymn, Ach Herr Jesu, sei uns freundlich (23):

Command your angels to serve and fill us now with good manners, let them be seated around us so that nothing may transpire that disgraces this table. (:8)

Another description reads as follows:

Since we who are on this course - those of us who are known - are willing to live faithfully, we break the bread of fellowship and thus submit to the death on the cross of our savior. (196:4)
The members who are founded in Christ and those who are united by love attain power and strength from this bread, from above, according to Christ's teaching, so that they can discern it in themselves. (:11)

It is not clear whether the following referred to the love-feast or a communion service. The time, however, was in the evening:

We have now come to this evening hour desiring to praise you, o Lord Jesus Christ, for your love, with singing and other melodies, for you are merciful. (752:10)
Therefore we now praise your death, Lord Jesus Christ, your mercy be highly exalted for you are risen. In so doing we break the bread in faith and love. (:11)

The Church

The view of the community of believers expressed in the new hymns conformed in part with that found in the traditional hymns of the church as, for example, when she was

hidden to the world but known to and cared for by God. (178:1)

Or, when she was juxtaposed to Babel, the false Christendom. In Brethren and Pietist terms, "Babel" referred to the established church:

The shepherd is Jesus Christ, Zion, the flock ... . Leave Babel's world and join Zion's band in spirit and life ... . By rational thinking alone Jesus' followers cannot be recognized because they appear blackened. The horde of blasphemers calls them heretics. (610: 2, 4, 8)

On the other hand,

If they see that children [of the faith] live in harmony in this world, and that all strive faithfully after love, people will be gladdened in their spirits to praise the Lord with love-inflamed hearts. They will encourage one another to risk their lives even unto death. (605:2)

How precious and noble is brotherly love ... .   (:3)

However, the world at large, whose way it was to repay good with evil, condemned the church altogether:

[If one] manifests in unity one spirit, one body, one faith, one baptism, and if one follows in everything Christ's way and does away with
all wrong as the gospel teaches us, one is easily despised.   (1245:2)

The World

Following Jesus' way rather than the world's was never easy for the
Christian. In the eyes of Pietist as well as Brethren hymn-writers, the
world and the apostate church were often identical. Here follow some
typical polemic passages:

It is true, in her delusion the world calls herself Christ's kingdom,
too, but resembles much more a Sodom ... . The Lord calls: "You, who
have truly come to know Christ, leave her behind, Babylon, the whore
and the beast!"   (604:6)

To call oneself Christian and yet be headed toward hell is the usual
way of things nowadays. ...   (806:4)
Too few, alas, too few are wearing white robes that are not soiled.
Too few are the souls that choose him who is on the cross, truly in
accordance with the teaching of his spirit ... .   (:6)
Drive them away from their high places where they are established,
gather your flock! ...   (:15)
Let thousands choose this way, let them be wedded to Jesus, to run
naked after Jesus together with his small band whose faces are still
and who shun neither cross nor shame.   (:16)

O Jesus, you called many [when you were] here on earth, to the goal [of
a new life]. They were to be adorned only as you desired.   (985:4)
But evil and false teaching led them away from you, so that every one
of them thought to be right, but was in reality beguiled.   (:5)
It is the same way still [today]; everybody finds a loophole in his or
her own will. Where does that leave the brotherhood which we must
faithfully fulfill?   (:6)
They do truly believe in a brotherhood, that is what they profess, yet
it is nothing but a mere pretense. This we deplore.   (:7)

There are many these days who are lame on both legs [i.e., they cannot
make up their minds]: they call themselves Christians, yet they avoid
suffering ... . Where have those brave heroes gone who used to profess
such staunch faith and love?   (278:4-5)

The early Brethren meant to remain faithful in the midst of all this
apostasy. This they expressed in one hymn as follows:

Truth has taught us to live in that spirit. Whoever repents, will
submit to God in faith, confess this in baptism, and turn away from
what is wrong, [turn] to God and strive for all truth.   (1245:3)

<u>Weltangst</u> (a feeling of being at the mercy of a blind faith)

Although the early Brethren lived as a fellowship of believers, they also lived in an age when sin, the devil, Satan, and hell were very real to the common people. They were expected to support through their labor and taxes the courts and their frivolous and lavish entertainments and the displays of wealth and splendor which, to a certain extent, set the tone for the ever upwardly-mobile middle class. Perhaps it was this situation which caused one of the Brethren hymn-writers to exclaim:

Lament this age, you children of Men on this earth, when everyone is busy about nothing else but how to become rich in possessions and how to give honor to this world, which is pleasing only to the flesh and up-lifts but the earthly heart and that for a short while only.   (129:1)

At the same time continuous wars with France repeatedly levelled towns and villages, changed the official religion of a principality over night, brought additional hardships on the lower classes, and gave every-body the feeling of being at the mercy of a blind and hostile fate. This, too, found expression in a Brethren hymn:

There seems to be no safe place left on earth, wherever I may be. Even if all goes well, I am still exposed to many dangers and wish I could sufficiently protect myself. When things go badly, nothing will avail ... .   (1301.0)

Even the churches had ceased to retain any vestiges of that place where a foretaste might be had of the kingdom of God. Politicking, polem-ics, and petty legalisms were the chief concerns voiced on many a pulpit. No wonder, then, that to the early Brethren, as to all early and radical Pietists, the established churches had indeed become apostate, a Babel.

The following is a long lament about this situation found in the hymn, <u>Wie lange willst du noch</u> (1291):

How long, you strong God, will you tarry before you stem this lament-able misery? It seems as if there were no God and helper, because faith, love, faithfulness, and right are perverted and all the world has turned from you.   (:1)
My soul is often in great sorrow and laments loudly the horror of the devastation, because the spirit of deceit has exalted itself so highly and has injured the poor people through deception. But, o my God! what am I to think of you, o that you would soon lead the souls in different paths!   (:2)
You act as if you were unaware of how all the people in the land are living these days. They are like sheep without shepherd, because they are not founded in Christ but cling to human beings and illusions. Indeed, they do not seem to wish for anything better.   (:3)
It is true, they mouth your counsels but they are nonetheless in league with the world who acknowledges neither you nor Jesus Christ. Even though [the people of] the world very liberally call themselves by his name, they are far from his ways whoring openly with alien lovers. (:4)
That is why the enemy nowadays deceives the people so much, because they do not gather at the well where the waters of life are gushing

forth abundantly. Instead, they run to empty wells whose water was stolen.   (:5)
Arise soon, you lion out of the tribe of Judah, to be victorious now, you true lamb of God, over the spirit that is of the abyss, which leads astray the whole world through its cunning. Pour out your clear rivers that the frogs may die; make us soon heirs of your kingdom   (:8)

The anguished cry for succor was sounded repeatedly in the hymns as, for example, in the following stanzas:

How long, how long, how long will you tarry, God's hero? You cannot help but know how fearful your chosen ones are. Go forth in us to victory. May you overcome the world, the devil, all the sins. Fight them with all your might.   (1027:6)
Come soon, hear the cry of the frightened dove ... .   (:7)

In another hymn, Jesus was urged to save his pious followers:

Do you not see how they moan with thirst for a drink, how they lament, wail, sigh, thirst ... .   (56:2)

Although it is impossible to state to what degree these effusions were merely imitations of the prevailing style of poetry or how much was the expression of genuine feelings, it is safe to say that these hymns spoke to situations in which many early Brethren found themselves.

Denial of the World

The individual human being living during the Baroque era had two alternatives for dealing with Weltangst and the stresses of life: either to renounce the world completely or to defy the dangers and calamities surrounding everyone and to embrace the more positive aspects of the world namely, the newly discovered possibilities and amazing achievements of the age. The Brethren writers tended to favor the first alternative, lavishing their euphoria not on human achievements but on the splendor of the new Zion, the bridal city on the hill where all things would be changed. However, there is among the new hymns one stanza that might be considered a Christian version of the world-conqueror idea:

Lions, bears, wolves, and dragons - a faithful Christian can laugh at them [and] whatever it is that may have to be faced. Whosoever turns to the Lord and walks in his ways will surely be victor over all the world.   (338:8)

The above stanza is, indeed, the exception rather than the rule, for the mood of Brethren as well as non-Brethren hymns of that era was much more like that expressed in the hymn, Ihr jungen Helden, aufgewacht! (602) This must have been a favorite with the Brethren because it appeared in all the editions of their German hymnals:

What is the world with all its activity? ...   (:2)
To cease loving the world and to embrace Jesus is the way to receive the power of the spirit so that one may soon punish [the world's] actions.   (:3)

Vanish, then, o vanity, time has grown too precious for me now to apply
it in a way that blasphemes the name of God.   (:4)
To the deceitful world and her guiles my soul says: it is enough - too
long have I loved pleasure and saddened my God.   (:6)

Another writer expressed the same idea without resorting to the flowery
conventions of Baroque style:

Teach me to know the futility of time, direct my thoughts only toward
eternity.   (238:3)

Government (Obrigkeit)

The hymn, Zion soll billig freudig sein (1352) deals in three of its
five stanzas with the relationship of the Christian to the state. As the
sole hymnic statement on this subject, it is remarkable only in the degree
in which it conforms with the established theology of instituted government:

This is the reason why God ordained the government that in this time it
may curb evil and work what is right, protect the pious and punish the
evil, so that good may grow ... .   (:3)
[This,] because people are wont to do what is wrong, they will not
remain within the boundaries which God's wise counsel has ordained in
all the world and which cannot waver: to honor princes and lords, as
faithful witnesses have taught, and to submit to them.   (:4)
This only in order that there remain freedom and no coercion of conscience arise against living according to God's word, because God in
his wisdom commanded through his son to strive after his righteousness
even in small things, to fulfill God's will here upon earth, and to
become completely subject to him.   (:5)

The Individual

One part of Baroque pessimism which was opposite to the idea of the
hero and world conqueror was a very bleak view of the individual human
being. The Brethren hymn-writers' view was not very different. At best,
the Christian was a pilgrim, stranger (863:7) or useless servant (1258:6),
but also - in true self-abasement of the time - a withered flower and
miserable worm (1002:5, 12), even a dead dog (1013:3) or, more poetically,
an arid desert, longing for rain, a withered tree barely alive, a child
naked and bare, a muddy spring (727, passim).

Jesus Christ

During the perplexing and frightening time out of which grew the
Pietist and, later, the Brethren movement, the Christian experienced Jesus
as the only way through and out of the confusion surrounding him. Mein
Herz, wach auf und singe (835) might be entitled, "A hymn about the divine
nature of Jesus Christ:"

He came from heaven, the true son of God; he assumed the body of a
servant and left his throne and all the glories he had in his father's
presence ... .   (:2)

He appeared to the world as a small child, born of Mary, laid in swaddling clothes. He was also raised like a child of Man [Menschen-Kind] and bore much suffering because of our sins.   (:3)
... He did not take on Mary's flesh and blood but the Word came from heaven ... the Word became flesh as it was recorded by John ... .   (:5)
That which was born in her was of the Holy Ghost and was chosen for this by the Father to be the savior of the world ... .   (:6)
The son of God did not come - as the world believes - to take on flesh and blood but he was made by his Father's spirit ... .   (:7)

A compilation of the attributes given to Jesus in the hymns of the early Brethren runs the gamut from the biblical to the mystical and the rationalistic:

Truth, Way Life;
Lord, Prince, King, King of Glory, King of Salem;
Priest, Prince of Priests, Great Prophet;
Mediator, Reconciler, Savior, Restorer of All Things;
Son of God, Son of Man, Righteous One;
Lamb of God, Good Shepherd, Staff;
Strong Hero, Shield, Refuge;
Light, Unadulterated Treasure, Precious Crown;
Bridegroom, Soul's Treasure, Beloved, Desire;
Creator of All Things, Fatherly Power;
Friend, Friend of Man, Friend of the Soul.

Only one of these attributes is found only in hymns of Brethren origin, namely, Restorer of All Things. Hardly ever used, this term did occur in one hymn by Gottfried Arnold which was not included in the 1720 hymnal. All the other attributes were very common in the religious poetry of the time. Jesus occupied a central place in the piety of Christians and far more hymns centered on Jesus than on God. Through his death he had earned for the Christian salvation, power, and life. It was he who bestowed grace. His coming was very often interpreted as his entering a person's soul, which religious experience then led to faith (788).

Discipleship (Nachfolge)

Just as Christ's coming was understood as an event taking place within an individual's soul, so discipleship or the following of Christ was understood in a very personal way and was limited to coping with the adversities of this life and to striving for steadfastness of faith and peace and rest of the soul. Brethren writers also dealt with discipleship in the context of the community of faith which was expressed in one prayer hymn in this way:

... work in us through the Spirit's moving that we might willingly bear your cross, with which we have already made a beginning.   (915:2/3)

One writer described discipleship in very concrete and down-to-earth examples:

Alas, what struggle it is to set one's mind on other things than sheep, oxen, horses, cows. Turning one's back on fields, pastures, lovely meadows brings greater reward.   (338:4)

To be sure, it is necessary to have faith to dig up this pearl which delights everlastingly, to attach less importance to father, mother, wife, and children. The power of faith conquers all.   (:5)

However, in these early Brethren hymns - just as was the case in most of the religious poetry of the time - discipleship was not so much the expression of obedience to him who had brought reconciliation with God and thereby salvation for the people, than a way of attaining that salvation. Discipleship was often understood only as the act of an individual:

Jesus' life is a light that has gone before us. Whoever does not follow it remains captured by sin ... .   (179:1)
Jesus' life is a garment. Whoever puts it on will be delivered from the wrath of God, will escape judgment and enter eternal joy where all strife has come to an end, where true rest is found.   (:2)
O life, you are everything, whoever finds you in faith attains the jubilee when all misery disappears ... .   (:7)

A virtuous life on earth was the only way in which one could be sure to be received into and rewarded in heaven after the great judgment:

Whoever is willing to suffer here, patiently and quietly, and will shun all sin to do only the will of God, will surely partake of that great joy of which one will not grow weary in all eternity.   (1188:6)
But whoever will not suffer here and refuses to be a seed, who wishes to enjoy pleasures here only, will have to suffer there, will have to be eternally banished from God's countenance and be subject to the divine judgment along with the godless.   (:7)
Eternal life is at stake, whoever wishes to enter it, must strive for virtue, must be holy and pure and must die here with Christ. Only then can rest be found. Otherwise a person will inherit nothing. O child of Man [Menschen-Kind], beware!   (:9)

Universal Restoration

Antithetical to the above views which demanded an active decision to follow Jesus if one hoped to inherit eternal life, was the idea of Jesus the restorer of all things:

Restorer of all things, restore my soul. Grant that I might succeed here completely in being wedded to you, that I might always conquer through you till I have been completely renewed. Give me the power of the spirit for warring, arm me with your mind.   (1304:1)
Restore in this life also many thousand souls to whom you are granting - like unto us - this time of grace for repentance. They are your creatures even though they are blind in sins and stillborn like us as Adam's race.   (:2)
With you, o Lord, there is no pleasure in the sinner's death. That is why you restore every one even though it is done after much sorrow and misery. But those who follow you in this time in pure love are made ready for you in love through the same reasons.   (:3)
You will restore everything under your government. Those who cannot be won through love in this time of grace shall - as a just punishment - bow down together with all the world. ...   (:4)

The fifth stanza of this hymn begins a long admonition to lead a repentant
life which culminates thus in stanza eleven:

> One does well to think here of the vast eternity, when the sinner sinks
> into such great pain and suffering being engulfed by the wrath until it
> has burned to the ground all the unclean evil things: lies, vices,
> sins, and shame. (:11)

Finally, in the concluding two stanzas, the writer returned to the idea of
universal restoration:

> Although our king will eventually restore everything in submission to
> his father for the final year of rest, it is nevertheless a great dis-
> grace for him who does not repent in time while he is still living in
> this land; before the great eternity. (:12)
> Teach us, Jesus, to lament what is subjected to the wrath, do not allow
> us to unite ourselves with anything that you are not. To you, Jesus,
> the restorer, the victor over hell and death, my soul gives thanks. Re-
> store for ever and ever. (:13)

Mysticism

In all of the preceding examples there were traces of one of the
strands that made up the German hymnody from which the Brethren drew in
their own writings, namely Pietism. This movement placed great emphasis
on the true believer, things spiritual, the faithful followers, and the
distinction between the true and the false, the Christian and the world.
Mysticism was another element that was quite well known to the Brethren
through the writings of Jakob Böhme (1575-1624), Antoinette Bourignon
(1616-1680), Gottfried Arnold, and others.

In Brethren hymns, mysticism is reflected through such expressions
as:

> O penetrating light, that explores the innermost recesses of the heart,
> o river that fills empty souls ... (1013:1)

> O life that gives life which fills many a soul, you are dealing with me
> as you see fit, therefore my heart sings [your praise]. My spirit
> revels in my God and my heart desires to be completely engulfed by
> Christ. (551:2)

> O life, I long for you, make yourself known. O take me away from my
> own self and give me to you. Purge in me all self-will and all self-
> being. ... (179:8)

> I do not live for myself, for Jesus has drowned me completely in the
> water bath [of baptism]. It is good that I am devoid of any will. I
> do not live for myself. I am immersed in God. (562:1)

Much of the mysticism in Brethren hymns expresses a desire to seek
spiritual union with Jesus rather than with God. The following is one
example of this sentiment:

Tie my soul close to you, Jesus, in love. Teach me how to live always
according to the prompting of your spirit. Open up, you well-spring of
life, flow into my soul.   (135:1)

Mystical Eros

From mysticism it is only a small step to mystical eros, the chief
distinction between the two being the object of the union. Whereas in expressions of mystical union the lines between God and Jesus are occasionally blurred and crossed, with mystical eros, Jesus is always quite clearly the object. As in other instances, the Brethren hymn-writers expressed
themselves in the conventional images but never went to the extremes of
many other Christian poets of the time in emulating the playfulness, almost frivolity and artificiality of secular erotic poetry. As might be expected, Brethren authors were never as erotically explicit as others. The
Moravian hymn-writers were among the most prominent exponents of mystical
eros. Nevertheless, very few hymns were completely without a trace of
this element. Here follow several examples:

What am I, o love [i.e., Jesus], that you should enter deep into [my
heart], therein to dwell in ardent love?   (1026:2)

Pure water, love of God [i.e., Jesus], flow into my tired soul. O let
me enter into you with ardent desire, fountain of life; let me, o let
me in this life cling to you more and more.   (56:4)

I live very well, indeed, for Jesus himself kisses me as often as I
wish it. ...   (562:2)

My beloved, look upon me with the hot gaze of your love.   (135:5)

The following is from a hymn on the passion of Christ:

He it is who conquers my heart, for he lies between my hot breasts like
a sprig of myrrh arousing in me holy lust.   (1232:2)
His faithfulness, his love plunge my heart into burning desire and
constant longing, hurting as unrequited love is wont to do.   (:3)
Draw me near to you with your love and teach me, my most dearly beloved
lamb, to return your embrace with love, and not to let you go, my
sweet, my bridegroom.   (:17)
Do not begrudge me the sweet kisses and delights, nor [refuse] my kiss
of love. I cannot live without you, give me the honey-flow of your
mouth.   (:18)

Christ's Passion

Most hymns on the passion of Christ - and there are only a few - are
written rather soberly, painting detailed word-pictures of the events of
Good Friday, such as Die Zeit ist hin, die Stund' ist da (274), Hindurch,
hindurch, mein träger Sinn (514), and especially, Wenn an Jesu ich gedenke
(1231) which has fourteen stanzas. However, in the hymn, Ach Jammer, es
ist um dich, Jesu, geschehen (32), which is a dramatic dialogue between
Jesus and the soul extending over eighteen stanzas, one is reminded of the
mystical cult of Jesus' wounds and especially the side-wound which, again,
the Moravians developed to such a high degree:

Beneath his side which they pierced with their spears and from which water and blood flowed so mightily, I shall place myself letting my heart be filled [with the water and the blood] and be truly refreshed.

(:1)

Come, Jesus, come, I shall engulf you in me. You shall stay in me to make me remember you always. It was for me that you died, for me you suffered, for me you rose and ascended into heaven. (:17)

Expectation of the End-Time

If looking beyond the vanity, finiteness, and misery of this world was one solution for secular people in coping with life's perplexing questions and terrors, how much more reason did the Christian have to choose that alternative. The Brethren writers felt the same way. They understood life as preparation for eternity:

All the way to the gate of heaven, continue to walk in pure love, devote yourself to living for eternity in this life. (276:3)

The Christians as the servants of the Lord would have to give an accouting of their lives before their savior:

How is it with the power of faith? How is it with the divine love? For Christ demands an accounting of how every one has performed [in respect to] these. Faith is good and of the right nature if love and action follow indeed. (613:3)
The Lord will not be satisfied with words about the faith only. Many display delusion and hypocrisy before the eyes of people. If faith does not work light and justice, you are but an idle servant. (:4)
For only those who do good will go forth into life, but those whose faith is delusion and who still continue to do evil must go to judgment. Their calling "Lord! Lord!" will be of no avail. (:5)

In some hymns, the imminence of the last judgment is described very vividly as in the following:

This is the last hour, o souls, awake, the world will soon perish. It has run its course ... . (357:1)
Since the hour is now come, the tribulation begins. In all lands the Antichrist seems to have gained the upper hand perverting Christ's teaching. Therefore the Lord will come soon to save his flock. (:4)
It cannot last much longer, midnight is now ... . (:5)
Since we know this, dear little children, let us take care and be of good cheer and anticipate with joy that hour when Jesus Christ will completely destroy the scheming of the evil spirits ... . (:7)

Much of the religious poetry of the early Brethren is permeated with eschatological hope just like the poetry of contemporary hymn-writers. Some hymns can be pointed out which deal very specifically with this belief such as, Es ist die letzte Stunde (357), Ihr Knecht' des Herren, kommt heran (613), Wacht auf, ihr Christen alle (1187), and Was machen doch und sinnen wir (1212). The very first hymn in the 1720 hymnal, which also seems to be of Brethren authorship, Die Zions Gesellen, die müssen stets wachen (278) strikes one like a rousing theme song, calling the Christian to be watchful and to prepare for the end-time. O Gott, was wird sich dort vor grosse Freud' erheben (961) paints a very vivid description of that event:

> O God, what great joy will there be among those who love you, who have passed through the narrow gate and who never ceased striving until they reached it - they will live there. (:1)
> Those who carried your cross and shame here in this time patiently and without complaining - all the misery, fear, and pain - those who are devoted to you here, shall live with you in all eternity after this time of grace. (:2)
> In that new world all pain will cease for those who honor you, who risked here their possessions and means, life and blood, renounced sin, and arose into heaven from this evil world. (:3)
> They will, time without end, praise you in pure power from above, out of true love, in all eternity. No more outcry will be heard, only praise and honor, which you have prepared in all eternity. (:4)
> When all war and strife everywhere will have ceased, how they will then honor you, indeed in all eternity sing with all the angels and bring praise and thanksgiving unto you. Glory, honor, and majesty be unto our God. (:7)
> Where all the apostles, the martyrs and prophets worship you unceasingly as the Lord, removed from all pain, that is where those will be who accepted Jesus, whom he has redeemed from suffering everywhere. (:8)
> Those who washed their garments in the blood of the lamb will no longer be touched by Satan and hell. They will forever be upright, and walk along the shining sea with pure body and soul, with the bright harps of God. (:9)
> There they will praise you, o God, with unheard-of hymns in complete love ... . (:10)

A feeling of urgency in the expectation of the end-time is expressed in Nun wollen wir jetzt alle schicken (931):

> Now, dearest Jesus, help us to be truly watchful in these last dark times. O save the embattled souls from the lion's teeth ... . (:5)
> [That we may always] be mindful of our end and the fact that we are all mortal ... . (:7)
> ... so that you may find us awake like the wise virgins. (:9)

The above is a prayer hymn for the sending out of the believers to witness to the world. It is written in very clear and concise language, much in the style of the early Reformation writers. Although it is a very good hymn, it was later on included only in the first American hymnal (and its later editions) but not in any other Brethren hymnals. However, the Reformed preacher, Daniel Hertz, incorporated it into his collection, Poetischer Himmelsweg, published in 1828. Here, the word schicken was changed to scheiden, which changed the opening mood from the active sending forth to the passive parting.

Closely related to the belief in a future life was the idea of future compensation for faithfulness on earth:

> In that new world all suffering will cease for those who honor you [i.e., God], who risked here their possessions and means, life and blood, renounced sin and arose into heaven from this evil world. (961:3)

Whoever confesses this teaching [i.e., Christ's] will there be crowned.
Here, he must bow his head in shame, contempt, and lies. But it brings
joys to the heart as long as one shuns evil.
(178:3)

Zion

Beyond the event of the Second Coming, the Brethren hymn-writers,
like many of their contemporaries, turned their imagination toward the
heavenly Zion, the desired city of God (597:7) which he had built in the
spirit according to his plan (646:1), and which was a city of peace
(1363:1) in the land called Beloved Lover (1363:2). However, Zion also
stood for Christ's church on earth, his small, despised (605:1) but chosen
(1349:11) flock. While awaiting Christ's coming, Zion must gird her loins
and draw her sword (1349:11).

Christ's heart has already been stirred, his love has been aroused
toward the beloved city, who shines like burnished gold, adorned with
sufferings here on earth.
(1353:2)

CONCLUSION

From the study of this first Brethren hymnal one gains the impression
of a fellowship of Christians who sought to create, on what turned out to
be the eve of their dispersion to distant countries, a means of unifying
their devotional life and worship. At the time of this writing, no
records had been found that would shed some light on the story of this
hymn-book. Many questions must as yet remain unanswered: Why was the work
undertaken so shortly before the Brethren left Schwarzenau for the Netherlands? Could it be that the compilation and printing of the hymnal was
begun in the assumption that the Brethren would continue to live in Wittgenstein? Did some unexpected circumstances lead to the emigration in the
same year during which their first hymnal was published?

It is possible to interpret some of the flaws of the 1720 hymnal as
indications of the fact that it was indeed published under pressure of
time. The most obvious is the lack of both a table of contents as well as
a list of rubrics. There are some typesetting errors in the numbering of
the hymns: 54 is printed as 53, 207 as 270, and 210, 211, and 213 bear the
numbering of 282, 283, and 285, respectively.

Whatever the circumstances were under which this hymnal was
published, it became a vehicle through which the early Brethren preserved
a large number of hymns that had originated in their own midst. Who the
writers were seemed to be of no significance. Perhaps the old hymns were
so well known to the Brethren that the new ones stood out recognizably.
It is more probable, however, that the compilers followed the prevailing
custom of not printing the authors' names and would have considered it an
evidence of vanity to do so.

Another feature which twentieth-century hymnal-users might expect to
find is the printed melodies to which the hymns are to be sung. These
were not usually provided in hymnals of earlier centuries. If the
Brethren had indeed been under pressure of time, printing the music would
have prolonged the process even more, not to mention the required additional cost and space. Thus, melodies are indicated in the customary manner

by reference at the beginning of each hymn to the first words of a well-known hymn that has the identical poetic meter. This reference is preceded by the abbreviation Mel. (i.e., Melodie).

In this first hymnal, all hymns were sung in the style of chorales. As one can see from the melodies printed in Freylinghausen's hymnal, the strong rhythms of the earlier melodies had by then been made less rhythmical and more florid in conformity with the taste of the Baroque era. Chorales were to remain the core of the melodies in the German hymnals of the Brethren, although gradually other genres were introduced as new types of hymns were incorporated into their hymnody. The first such instance will be seen in the next hymnal which the Brethren published.

If this hymnal is a true reflection of the early Brethren's devotional life and worship, one is led to assume that in this area they were most strongly influenced by the Pietist movement. As has become apparent in this chapter, Pietist sentiments are rather unlike the Anabaptist beliefs which the Brethren held. This discrepancy between the Brethren's theology and their hymnody is not a unique phenomenon, however. Ingeborg Röbbelen demonstrates a similar occurrence in her thorough study on piety and theology in the early hymnals of the German Lutheran church.[15]

In their selection of old hymns, the Brethren kept closely to the middle of the road. Although some of the great hymns contained in the hymnals, which the Brethren appear to have used, as sources had not been included, the worst excesses of taste and teaching had likewise been avoided. Together with the forerunners of the Pietist movement, there are altogether fifty poets of that persuasion represented by approximately one hundred hymns, with Neander by far the most popular of all. Nineteen of his hymns are found in this hymnal. These Pietist hymn-writers unquestionably were the models for the Brethren in their writing of hymns.

Although Pietist influence was almost all-pervasive, Anabaptist leanings can be discerned in a certain quietist attitude, the denial of worldly things, even of family, and the understanding and centrality of the church which is implicit in some of their hymns. Discipleship (Nachfolge), perhaps the most central Anabaptist teaching, is also mostly implicitly present in several Brethren hymns and not found in any specific place such as the hymns in the rubric "Of following Jesus" which are invariably expressions of the individualistic Pietist interpretation of this concept.

Peculiarly Brethren concerns can be found in only few of their hymns. Twentieth-century Brethren are probably struck by a complete lack, both in the rubrics as well as in the hymn contents, of social concern. The time was then far in the future when such would be proper subject matter for hymns. European Christians of the early eighteenth century still conceived of themselves as placed through their birth into the existing social order as into a divine plan. Thus they saw no reason to rebel against or feel any desire for changing their social condition. The following examples are taken from documented hymns. They are the closest, in the entire hymnal, to reflections on the social order:

Remain ever faithful to God in your estate wherein he has established you.
(1093:4)

Praise to the Lord who has visibly blessed your estate.   (795:4)

   Generally, quietism accepted the Christian's lot as sent by God to
purge the individual of the sins of the world and prepare the way to
heaven:

   If God takes away your money, property, honor, repute, flesh and blood,
   soul, mind, and senses - you are not worthy of it, for by this he
   desires to win you [unto himself].   (870:3)
   It is impossible to enter God's kingdom with such encumbrances, therefore he desires to take from you whatever hates, loves, gives pleasure
   and saddens, in order to prepare you for the journey.   (:4)

The same thought is expressed in almost identical words in the third
stanza of the hymn, Wenn dir das Kreuz dein Herz durchbricht (1234). Yet,
although God visited upon his faithful, he was also the one who would come
to their aid. European Christians had been taught for a long time to look
to Jesus rather than to fellow Christians for succor:

   Even if everyone has deserted you and everyone takes advantage of you,
   I [i.e., Jesus] shall stand by you. Even when you are without help and
   counsel night and day, do not despair, for I, I shall never forsake
   you.   (588:9)
   Indeed, I shall always be with you: in life and in death, at home and
   on the highway, in distress by fire and water, in good days and in evil
   days, in times of joy and in times of mourning, in pain of body and in
   pain of the soul, now and in eternity.   (:12)

   Even if my enemies are openly against me, Jesus will snatch me from all
   distress, he will destroy the devil, hell, and death.   (687:3)
   If I am ill and there is nobody to alleviate my weakness, Jesus will be
   my physician and aid in suffering.   (:4)
   If I am naked, poor, and destitute, and my stores are scant, Jesus will
   assist me in his time.   (:5)
   If I must go forth into poverty, to a strange place, Jesus takes care
   of me and protects me.   (:6)

   The idea of God's sending trials to prepare the Christian for the
kingdom is closely linked with the religious (Anabaptist and Pietist) and
secular (Baroque) concept of the evil and transitory nature of the world
which must be rejected in all its aspects. This, in turn, relates to the
Pietist understanding of discipleship as the practicing of all the
Christian virtues and the overcoming of the vices of the flesh.

   Indications of concern for the neighbor and active Christianity are
found in two documented hymns:

   Do not return evil with evil, see to it that you live without guilt
   here on earth ... leave vengeance and honor to God, walk the narrow
   road, God will punish the world.   (744:12)

   ... grant that we may begin the work ...   (345:4)
   You do show us what must be done on our path of faith ... .   (:5)

The only explicit statements of social concern are also expressed in documented hymns. The first is a revision of a hymn on the beatitudes by Justus Gesenius (1601-1673) and David Denicke (1603-1680), Kommt, und lasst euch Jesum lehren (757):

> Blessed are they who sincerely strive for justice and faithfulness, that in their deeds and life there be neither force [Gewalt] nor injustice [Unrecht] ... . (:5)
> Blessed are they who out of pity concern themselves with other people's distress, who take pity on the poor and faithfully intercede for them with God; who are ready to give counsel and, if possible, aid. (:6)

The second hymn is a paraphrase of psalm 133 by Michael Müller (1673-1704), Sieh, wie lieblich und wie fein (1106):

> Everyone lives unto himself in the world and does as he pleases, thinks of no one else - what then about the commandment of loving [one's neighbor]? (:6)

Inasmuch as the Brethren - true to the Anabaptist and Pietist traditions - sought to live in obedience to God's word and especially the commandment to love, it can be assumed that other texts dealing with these concerns only implicitly were read and understood explicity.

In their hymns, Brethren hymn-writers repeatedly refer to Christ's teachings and the mind of God. In several instances, scripture references are given at the end of stanzas. However, there is one sentence in a hymn which has been quoted several times, that leaves one with tantalizing speculations about the way the early Brethren interpreted scripture:

> Whatever God has not commanded must not be condoned. (1245:3)

At this point one must hasten to remind oneself that hymnals, by the very nature of their purpose, must not be read like doctrinal treatises. This applies perhaps in an even greater measure to the first Brethren hymnal. Nevertheless, given the dearth of early Brethren writings, one is tempted to look to these hymns for theological statements in order to fill a gap that is very acutely felt.

In summary it may be stated that the body of hymns in the Geist-reiches Gesang-Buch of 1720 probably derives from two different sources. Almost two thirds represent those hymns from the stock of German hymnody that were probably familiar and dear to the early Brethren and which they enjoyed singing. With the exception of one hymn, the remainder were in all likelihood written by Wilhelm Knepper, one of the Solingen Brethren during the first phase of their imprisonment. A poet without higher education, this brother "composed" a total of four hundred hymns following metric patterns he knew well. The 1720 hymnal contains only a fourth of the texts he wrote. There is no telling what hymns might have been lost or what texts the hymnal compilers discarded. In addition, the Geist-reiches Gesang-Buch of 1720 preserved for the spiritual descendants of the Schwarzenau Brethren the one significant hymn attributed to Alexander Mack, Ueberschlag die Kost, which would otherwise have remained lost. Yet this very hymn, along with forty-five other new texts, was never again included in another Brethren hymnal. Fifty-six new hymns did find their way into some later German hymnals of the Brethren, but only three became "core-hymns" [Kernlieder] that appeared in all of the subsequent German hymnals.

Without rubrics and an index to the melodies, the first Brethren hymnal appears sadly inadequate. The reader who hopes to find here a well laid out structure of early Brethren piety and, possibly, theology will undoubtedly be disappointed. If the first Brethren hymnal seems to have been compiled rather carelessly, it was probably not for reasons of ineptitude. That the early Brethren were very well able to apply theological thinking to the enterprise of compiling a collection of hymns and to produce a complete hymnal will become evident in the following chapter which deals with the first Brethren hymnal to be published in the American colonies.

HYMN-WRITERS REPRESENTED IN
GEISTREICHES GESANG-BUCH, 1720
ARRANGED ACCORDING TO HISTORICAL PERIODS
AND MOVEMENTS

	Writers	Hymns
REFORMATION:		
Orthodox: Decius, Gramann, Heyd, Kreuziger, Luther.	5	6
Anabaptists: Betz, Grünwald, Ringwald, Scharnschlager.	4	4
Schwenkfelder: A. Reissner.	1	1
Czech Brethren: Weisse.	1	1
COUNTER-REFORMATION: Helmbold, Leon, Nicolai.	3	4
THIRTY-YEARS' WAR: Dach, Heermann, Held, Rinkart, Rist, Rosenmüller, Sonnemann.	7	10
LATE 17TH CENTURY: Bucholtz, Denicke, Gesenius, Strattner; Lodenstein (Reformed).	5	6
PIETISM:		
Forerunners: Anton Ulrich, Clausnitzer, Finx, J. Franck, M. Franck, Fritsch, Gerhardt, Haack, Herzog, Keimann, Knorr, Kongehl, Liscow, Lochner, H. Müller, B. Prätorius, Quirsfeld, Scheffler, Schirmer, Senitz, Sieber; Neander (Reformed).	22	63
Early Pietists: Arnold, Astmann, Dessler, Drese, Freystein, Laurenti, Schade, Schütz, B. E. Zeller.	9	21
Halle and late Pietists: Baumgarten, Bernstein, Crasselius, Falkner, Francke, Gotter, Herrnschmidt, Koitsch, Lackmann, J. Lange, J. C. Lange, M. Müller, Nehring, Richter, J. E. Schmidt, J. H. Schröder, R. F. Schultt, Schwedler, Winkler.	19	36
Radical Pietists: Petersen?	1?	2?
Brethren: Knepper, Mack.	2	101
Württemberg Pietists: Hedinger.	1	1
Reformed: Buchfelder.	1	1
Orthodox: Menken, Weise, Zihn.	3	3

HYMN-WRITERS REPRESENTED IN
GEISTREICHES GESANG-BUCH
ARRANGED ALPHABETICALLY AND NUMBER OF THEIR HYMNS

Anton Ulrich: 1
Arnold: 10
Astmann: 1

Baumgarten: 1
Bernstein: 2
Betz: 1
Buchfelder: 1
Bucholtz: 1

Clausnitzer: 1
Crasselius: 1

Dach: 1
Decius: 1
Denicke: 1
Dessler: 1
Drese: 2

Falkner: 1
Finx: 2
Franck, J.: 3
Franck, M.: 2
Francke: 1
Freystein: 1
Fritsch: 2

Gerhardt: 4
Gesenius/Denicke: 2
Gotter: 4
Gramann: 1
Grünwald: 1

Haack: 1
Hedinger: 1
Heermann: 1
Held: 1
Helmbold: 1
Herrnschmidt: 2
Herzog: 1
Heyd: 1

Keimann: 1
Knepper: 100
Knorr: 4
Koitsch: 1
Kongehl: 1
Kreuziger: 1

Lackmann: 5
Lange, J.: 2
Lange, J.C.: 1
Laurenti: 3
Leon: 2
Liscow: 1
Lochner: 1
Lodenstein: 1
Luther: 2

Mack: 1
Menken: 1
Müller, H.: 1
Müller, M.: 1

Neander: 20
Nehring: 1
Nicolai: 1

Petersen?: 2?
Prätorius, B.: 1

Quirsfeld: 1

Reissner, A.: 1
Richter: 6
Ringwald: 1
Rinkart: 1
Rist: 4
Rosenmüller: 1

Schade: 1
Scharnschlager: 1
Scheffler: 12
Schirmer: 1
Schmidt, J.E.: 1
Schröder, J.H.: 3
Schultt, R.F.: 1
Schütz: 1
Schwedler: 1
Senitz: 1
Sieber: 1
Sonnemann: 1
Strattner: 1

Weise: 1
Weisse: 1
Winkler: 1

Zeller, B.E.: 1
Zihn: 1

NOTES

[1] Geistreiches Gesang-Buch, vor alle liebhabende Seelen der Wahrheit (Berleburg: Christoph Konert, 1720).

[2] For a complete translation of the preface, see Appendix I/1.

[3] Ausbund, Etlicher schöner Christlicher geseng wie die in der Gefängnuss zu Passaw im Schloss von den Schweitzern und auch von andern rechtgläubigen Christen hin und her gedicht worden ... (n. p.: 1583).

[4] Numbers in parentheses refer to the numbers assigned the hymns in the alphabetical index of first lines (Appendix IX). A number following a colon refers to the number of a stanza.

[5] Johann Anastasius Freylinghausen, Geistreiches Gesang-Buch, den Kern alter und neuer Lieder in sich haltend ... (Halle: Waysenhaus, 1741). The first edition of this hymnal to be published in one volume, a careful combination of the two volumes published earlier, was used for this study.

[6] The title of this and similarly named hymnals is usually translated as "Psalter." Apart from the fact that this term refers to the body of biblical psalms, be it a translation or paraphrase, in prose or metric poetry, and not to a collection of hymns generally, it is an incorrect translation of the German word Psalterspiel, which means "psaltery," the name for an ancient musical instrument of the harp family.

[7] Davidisches Psalter-Spiel Der Kinder Zions ... (n. p.: 1718).

[8] Johann Arndt, Paradiesgärtlein Voller Christlichen Tugenden ... Nebst einem Gesang-Büchlein Zu desto mehrerer frommer Seelen Vergnügung vermehret ... (Stuttgart: Bernhard Michael Müller, 1718).

[9] Geistreiches Gesangbuch, Vormahls in Halle gedruckt, Nun aber ... vermehret (Darmstadt: Sebastian Griebel, 1700).

[10] For a translation of Freylinghausen's treatise on the order of salvation and the use of Freylinghausen's hymnal, see Appendix I/2.

[11] For a comparative listing of the rubrics of the Inspirationist and Freylinghausen's hymnals, see Appendix I/3. For a listing of the hymns in the 1720 hymnal by rubrics, see Appendix I/4.

[12] Heinz Renkewitz, Hochmann von Hochenau (1670--1721). (Breslau: Maruschke und Berendt, 1935), p. 277, note 54.

[13] J. Max Hark, tr., Chronicon Ephratense, a History of the Community of Seventh Day Baptists at Ephrata, Lancaster County, Penn'a, by "Lamech and Agrippa" (Lancaster, Pa.: S. H. Zahm, 1889), p. 224.

[14] Anniversary Hymns (Elgin, Ill.: Church of the Brethren General Offices, 1958).

[15] Ingeborg Röbbelen, Theologie und Frömmigkeit im deutschen evangelisch-lutherischen Gesangbuch des 17. und frühen 18. Jahrhunderts (Göttingen: Vandenhoeck und Ruprecht, 1957).

Chapter II

DAS KLEINE DAVIDISCHE PSALTERSPIEL

THE FIRST EDITION

In a letter to Obed Snowberger written on November 1, 1880 the Brethren historian and antiquarian Abraham H. Cassel (1820-1908) stated that

> Alexander Mack or his friends never published a hymn-book in Germany ... the Brethren were obliged to use different kinds of books in their public worship, which caused a great deal of confusion in their congregational singing, until about 1740, the brethren abridged the old big Psalterspiel, besides adding a number of new hymns ... .
> A number of Brethren assisted in the work, but Saur, Mack and Baker [i.e., Becker] were the principals that made the selection ... (the most of this information I have from old brethren that lived cotemporary [sic] with Mack and Saur.)[1]

A rare copy of the Inspirationist hymnal, the Davidisches Psalter-Spiel published in Europe in 1718 is located in the Cassel Collection at Bethany Theological Seminary, Oak Brook, Illinois. It contains the following manuscript entry by Cassel:

> This is the original Psalterspiel which the Brethren used in Europe and in this Country till 1744 when Bro. Christopher Sauer published an abridgement of it under the Title of Das "Kleine Davidische Psalterspiel" which passed through at least 13 edditions [sic] and which is still used in the German churches ... .

The events described above took place some twenty years after the publication of the first Brethren hymnal in 1720 and the arrival of the first group of Brethren immigrants from Krefeld, Germany under the leadership of Peter Becker (1687-1758). Twenty-four years had elapsed since the group led by Alexander Mack left Schwarzenau for Surhuisterveen in Friesland and fifteen since their emigration from the Netherlands to Pennsylvania. The Brethren in the American Colonies had been reorganized and founding new congregations for about twenty years. The congregation at Conestoga had suffered its schism under Conrad Beissel (1690-1768). His followers had already established the community at Ephrata, Pennsylvania which by then was flourishing. Christopher Saur, the elder (1695-1758) had printed his first book which, significantly, was the Ephrata Community's first hymnal, Zionitischer Weyrauchshügel, in 1739.[2]

It is greatly to be regretted that the Brethren kept no journals that might have come down to posterity. The oral tradition on which Cassel drew was obviously not entirely reliable. Neither the title-page nor the preface of the first edition of Das Kleine Davidische Psalterspiel offer any clues as to the individuals who were involved in the compilation of this hymnal. Based on historical research done since the 1950s, Cassel's information must be corrected not only regarding the history of Brethren hymn-books but also the status of the first Christopher Sauer who had only been a friend but never a member of the brotherhood and was therefore incorrectly referred to by Cassel as "Brother."

THE ANTECEDENTS

This first Brethren hymnal printed in America was indeed quite clearly modelled upon the Inspirationist Psalter-Spiel. In the letter mentioned above, Cassel had this to say about it:

The book [i.e, the 1718 edition] soon became such a favorite among all classes of spiritual worshipers that by 1740 three editions of it were printed. I have the 1st and 3d in my possession and are perhaps the only copies of it in America.
It appears that the Brethren brought very few of these along when they came over, and as they multiplied and increased very fast after they were here awhile, there was soon a very great lack of hymn-books, and to import that big Psalterspiel from Germany would have been too expensive, as there were but poor facilities for importing anything at that time - especially books; for all the imports had to come by way of England, and as the king's printers there claimed a monopoly throughout the British dominions, all the boxes or packages containing books were weighed and as high as 6 pence sterling per pound was charged as duty, besides commission and consignment which sometimes amounted yet to from 50 to 100 per cent of their value ... .

Thus the price for the original "big" Psalter-Spiel, which weighed 14.5 ounces could have amounted to a sum ranging from eight to eleven pence sterling including the commission. Later editions, which were not only printed with wider margins but also included more hymns, were considerably larger books than any of the Kleine Psalterspiel editions.

In this study, the 1718 rather than any later edition of the "big" Psalter-Spiel will be used as primary source of reference. Likewise, the first edition of Das Kleine Davidische Psalter-Spiel will be used as the basis of discussion in this chapter.[3]

There is no difference in the title-pages of the two hymnals except for the added word Kleine to signify a smaller, less significant, or even derivative version of the former:

The small Davidic Psaltery of the children of Zion [consisting] of old and new hymns of the spirit: collected with great care for all the suckling infants in the truth yearning for their salvation [Heil], but especially for the congregations [Gemeinden] of the Lord for their service [worship?] and use, and brought to light in this present form and order including a twofold index which is practical for its use and necessary [for choosing] the subject matters.

The title-page was not the only feature in which the Brethren hymnal was modelled upon the Psalter-Spiel: the hymns were arranged alphabetically throughout, and two indexes provided access to the hymns by subject and by first lines, respectively. The latter was not as redundant as it may seem because the Brethren hymnal, like its prototype, had a substantial appendix, the hymns of which were incorporated into a cumulative index.

By contrast, the preface to the Brethren hymnal was very different from that of the original Psalter-Spiel. Whereas the Inspirationists had couched theirs in eschatological concepts and the language of the Revelation of John, the Brethren editors were very down-to-earth. After providing a brief background on the treatment of singing in the Bible, they proceeded to describe the hymnal situation among the "meetings of the membership." In some of those meetings, two or three different hymn-books were in use at that time and therefore a new one was to be printed. The situation of the years preceding 1720 seemed to have repeated itself. It must be remembered that hymn-books were not furnished in the churches or meeting-houses but had to be brought along by the members. Personal preference and availability were probably factors in the choice of a hymnal.

The compilers of this first American hymn-book for the Brethren went about their task in a very circumspect way:

There was also consensus about selecting the best-known hymns from the well-known larger Psalter-Spiel, the melodies of which are most widely familiar, and about issuing it in this format. A great effort was made to do this in the most impartial way so that hymns were selected from other authors' hymn-books in addition to several which had been found in manuscripts, so that it can in fact be said that this is quite an impartial hymn-book, indeed, a guileless flower-garden containing all manner of flowers or songs for all those who praise the Lord with hearts and lips.[4]

A survey of the possible sources for the hymns proves this to be true. Most texts are found in the chief Pietist hymnals of the time. Of the 536 hymns, as many as 398 appeared in the original Psalter-Spiel, 319 in Freylinghausen's hymnal, 300 in other collections, and 224 in the first Brethren hymnal of 1720. Forty-one hymns appeared exclusively in the Psalter-Spiel, four exclusively in Freylinghausen's, fifty-five exclusively in the European hymnal of the Brethren, and forty-two in other hymn-books. The first Ephrata hymnal, Zionitischer Weyrauchshügel (1739), on the other hand, was in all probability not a significant source for Das Kleine Davidische Psalterspiel. It is true that 147 of the latter's hymns appear also in the Ephrata hymnal, but only 111 of those agree as to the number of stanzas and the melody reference in each case. Conversely, 104 of these same hymns also agree with the Psalter-Spiel of 1718. If there was any relationship among these three hymnals, it seems more likely that the Inspirationist hymnal served as one of the sources for the two American ones.

The most striking dissimilarity between the first American-printed Brethren hymnal and that of the Ephrata Community is the latter's arrangement of the hymns within the hymnal. The 654 texts are grouped in non-alphabetical sequence into thirty-three sections. The headings for these sections are deeply mystical and quite unlike those in other contemporary or earlier hymnals. Recurring themes are the light of God, the Church, chastity, and brotherly love. The following examples are representative: "III. The gates of the deep open and the perfections of the new world are beheld in holy contemplation", "XI. Of the sojourn of the church in darkness for want of the light and the power of grace", or, "XXXIII. Of the great pomp and splendor and gathering of the whole church of God under heaven; indeed the revelation of Jesus Christ, and how all nations and kingdoms on the entire earth will come honoring her with presents and gifts and worshipping her."

The question of what happened to the European hymnal of the Brethren arises again here. All of the hymns common to it and Das Kleine Davidische Psalterspiel appear in the latter unabridged (they are, on an average, ten stanzas long) and in all but two instances (117 and 752) with the same melody references, which is remarkable because these references are sometimes quite haphazard. Fifty-five of these texts had been new Brethren hymns in 1720. All of these factors lead to the assumption that the Brethren must have brought at least one copy of the 1720 hymnal to America. Yet, the baptismal hymn attributed to Alexander Mack was not included and none of the new Brethren hymns of 1720 found their way into the first Ephrata hymnal.

A new feature of this first American hymnal is the presence of two appendixes of hymns. The first, Anhang einiger Psalmen Davids, consists of twelve by Ambrosius Lobwasser (1515-1585) of Genevan psalm hymns and one documented anonymous text. The second appendix, simply entitled Zweyter Anhang, contains an assortment of documented and undocumented hymns from various periods including an epic passion hymn poem by Alexander Mack, Jr. which is discussed in detail below.

THE RUBRICS

The rubrics of Das Kleine Davidische Psalterspiel are almost identical with those in the Inspirationist hymnal and follow its sequence more closely than that in Freylinghausen's. Although the Brethren adhered very closely to the pattern established by the Pietist "Economy of Salvation," they reflected their own interpretation of it through the way in which they applied it. It is quite obvious that thought was given to the Brethren's understanding of the order or sequence in which salvation (Heil), the reconciliation of the individual to God, was attained.

The first nine categories follow the seasons of the church year beginning with Advent and leading up to Pentecost, just as was the case in the Inspirationist hymnal. However, that traditional aspect of Advent which deals with the coming of Christ to judgment and the call to repentance and which both Freylinghausen and the Inspirationists included here, was moved in the Brethren order to the rubric about the last things.

The next section comprises what might be called "The Brethren Order of Salvation" (rubrics 10-18). The opening includes three of Freylinghausen's rubrics pertaining to the Pietist economy: "Of human misery and damnation," "Of the true repentance and conversion," and "Of the true faith." In the Pietist hymnal, these were followed by "Of the true and the false Christendom," and "Of Christian life and conduct." The Brethren went on instead to "Of holy baptism," "Of the love for Jesus," "Of brotherly and universal love" (these latter two were among Freylinghausen's required spiritual exercises or virtues listed later on), "Of foot-washing at the love-feast," "Of the holy supper and the proclamation of the death of Jesus Christ on the cross," and finally, "Of following Jesus."

This group of rubrics is followed by a new category, "Hymns of supplication" (Bitt-Lieder), which includes six hymns (306, 332, 496, 668, 788, 1347) that had formerly been in various other rubrics in the original Psalter-Spiel. The following two rubrics, "Of the mystery of the cross" and "Of the nature and attributes of God, or the holy trinity" are somewhat out of context here except that the latter might be related to the following rubrics which also refer to God.

After this digression into their own theology, the Brethren took up the remnants of the Pietist economy again. Rubrics 22-25 follow Freylinghausen except for using the Inspirationist wording "Of the inner and outer word" instead of "the divine word." These rubrics describe the means of grace by which God restores humankind to himself, to which Freylinghausen naturally counted the two sacraments of the Lutheran faith namely, baptism and the Lord's Supper. The Brethren placed these two ordinances within their own order of salvation as shown above.

The two categories that did not fit very well into the Brethren order of salvation - "Of the true and the false Christendom" (no. 26) and "Of Christian life and conduct" (no. 27) - are listed next. These, in turn, are followed by the spiritual exercises and virtues required of the Christian (nos. 28-36) with the exception of Freylinghausen's rubrics 35-38. Three of these - "Of the love for Christ," "Of brotherly and universal love," and "Of following Christ" - were incorporated into the Brethren order of salvation. From here on, Freylinghausen's order was adhered to exactly except for listing "Of the coming of Christ to judgment" (no. 48) with the rubrics pertaining to the last things.

An examination of the number of hymns in the various rubrics reveals some interesting facts. The areas of greatest emphasis in the 1744 hymnal are similar to those of the earlier one namely, "Of the desire for God and Christ" (no. 33, thirty-two hymns) and "Of denial of self and the world" (no. 32, twenty-six hymns). "Of the love for Jesus" (no. 14) and "Of the hope of Zion" (no. 46) contain twenty-three hymns each. The areas of least emphasis are "Of the burial of Jesus Christ" (no. 6) and "Of foot-washing" (no. 16), with one hymn each.

It is surprising, however, that not more hymns were added to categories of peculiarly Brethren concern. Only one hymn, for example, is designated for the service of foot-washing (68), which was taken over from the 1720 hymnal. The entire hymnal provides only four hymns for baptism, three of which (34, 40, 1245) were new in 1720. A rare contemporary account in the diary of Christoph Wiegner (1714-1777), a member of the Schwenkfelders, records the singing of Scheffler's Mir nach, spricht Christus, unser Held (876) at a Brethren baptism in 1734.[5] This hymn was already present in the 1720 hymn-book. Mack's Ueberschlag die Kost (1155) and Ihr Kinder, merket wohl (610), another Brethren hymn of 1720, were not included again.

In this hymnal, a new type of hymn was introduced into Brethren hymnody namely, "Psalms from Lobwasser" (Psalmen Davids aus dem Lobwasser). Unlike other psalm-hymns, which are usually paraphrases of portions of psalms, these are translations of the Genevan psalter into German. The Genevan psalter was composed of metric translations of the psalms which, as biblical texts, were acceptable to the reformer John Calvin (1509-1564) for use as hymns in public worship. It was Ambrosius Lobwasser, professor of jurisprudence at Königsberg in East Prussia, who made the Genevan psalm-hymns popular in German-speaking countries. The great appeal of the French psalter lay in its rhythmic Renaissance melodies, and therefore the German translations had to be made to fit the French meters exactly which did not always have a felicitous result. Nevertheless, these new hymns, originally intended for private use only, soon became widely known and accepted in the churches. Thirteen of them were included in the 1744 hymnal. The melody references are made either to the appropriate psalm tunes in Lobwasser's collection or to the first line of a well-known hymn.

In the following, the rubrics of this hymnal are listed with the numbers of hymns in each category. As in the previous chapter, each section is headed by the description provided in Freylinghausen's preface, with the exception of the headings entitled "The Brethren Order of Salvation" and "Digression," which were added editorially.

Das Kleine Davidische Psalterspiel, 1744

[Feast Day Hymns in Which Christ, the Foundation of Our Salvation is Depicted with all His Graces and Attributes]
1. Of the coming of Christ in the flesh (2)
2. Of the incarnation and birth of Christ (9)
3. New-Year's hymns (4)
4. Of the transfiguration of Jesus in his manifold names, offices, and favors (12)
5. Of the suffering and death of Jesus Christ (14)
6. Of the burial of Jesus Christ (1)
7. Of the resurrection of Jesus Christ (12)
8. Of the ascension of Jesus Christ and his sitting at the right hand of God (5)
9. Of the holy ghost and his manifold gifts and workings (5)

[The Brethren Order of Salvation]
10. Of human misery and damnation (8)
11. Of the true repentance and conversion (10)
12. Of the true faith (9)
13. Of holy baptism (4)
14. Of the love for Jesus (23)
15. Of brotherly and universal love (6)
16. Of foot-washing at the love-feast (1)
17. Of the holy supper and the proclamation of the death of Jesus Christ on the cross (7)
18. Of following Jesus (7)

[Digression]
19. Hymns of supplication (19)
20. Of the mystery of the cross of Christ (20)

[The Source and Well-Spring from Which Flows Our Salvation and Blessed Estate]
21. Of the nature and attributes of God, or the holy trinity (3)
22. Of the benevolence of God (10)

[The Means through Which God Will Restore Us into Communion with Him]
   23. Of the works of creation and the divine love and glory emanating
       therefrom (5)
   24. Of divine providence and lordship (5)

[The So-Called Means of Grace]
   25. Of the inner and the outer word (7)

[The Order Which You Must Observe if You Will Have Part in Christ and the
Salvation Earned by Him]
   26. Of the true and the false Christendom (7)
   27. Of Christian life and conduct (11)

[Exercises and Virtues Required for Christian Life and Conduct]
   28. Of the true spiritual prayer (4)
   29. Of spiritual watchfulness (18)
   30. Of spiritual battle and victory (21)
   31. Of the true chastity (5)
   32. Of denial of the world and self (26)
   33. Of the desire for God and Christ (32)
   34. Of Christian resignation (8)
   35. Of the true patience and steadfastness (6)
   36. Of the heart's complete surrender to God (7)

[Your Reward for Your Christian Life and Conduct]
   37. Of divine peace and rest of the soul (8)
   38. Of the joy in the holy ghost (15)
   39. Of the joyfulness of faith (15)
   40. Of the praise of God (20)
   41. Of the divine wisdom (7)

[The Blessed Estate of the Kingdom of Grace]
   42. Of the spiritual marriage [to Jesus] (9)
   43. Of the high birth of the believers (2)

[Reminders that Despite of All This, You Have Not Yet Attained the Goal]
   44. Of the hidden life of the believers (3)
   45. Of the lament of Zion (8)

[The Hope with Which One Sustains Oneself amidst All the Lament in This
Vale of Sorrows]
   46. Of the hope of Zion (23)
   47. Of death and resurrection (6)
   48. Of the coming of Christ to judgment (4)
   49. Of heaven and the heavenly Jerusalem (7)

[Hymns for Various Occasions]
   50. Morning hymns (16)
   51. Evening hymns (12)
   52. Table hymns (5)

[Psalm-Hymns]
   54. Psalms of David from Lobwasser (13)

DOCUMENTED HYMNS

Das Kleine Davidische Psalterspiel of 1744 contains 536 hymns, of which 291 are newly introduced to Brethren hymnody from the stock of German hymnody. Thus there is a larger number of hymn-writers represented in this hymnal than in its European predecessor. Altogether, hymns by 128 different hymn-writers are included here. Fifty-one authors are newly added and five were dropped (Duke Anton Ulrich, Betz, Heyd, Leon, Weise). There are notable increases in the number of hymns by some less well-known poets, but even more so in the number of hymns by the favorite writers. Neander's hymns number thirty-two, Arnold's thirty-one, Scheffler's twenty-eight, and Gerhardt's twelve. Again, it must be remembered that in most cases the compilers were probably unaware of the authorship of most of the hymns they chose. Fifty-six of the original Brethren hymns written probably by Wilhelm Knepper were carried over into this hymnal. Mack's baptismal hymn, however, was not printed again.

Several additional hymns by Radical Pietists are included in the 1744 hymnal. At least one hymn, but possibly four hymns by Eberhard Ludwig Gruber (1665-1728) are added. Gruber was one of the leaders of the Community of True Inspiration in Europe. Whereas his Jesu, wahres Lebensbrot (689) and Jesus ist Je-süss (699) are true Jesus-hymns with elements of mysticism and mystical eros, Pflichtmässig gelebt (1041) and Wohlauf, zum rechten Weinstock her (1338) are conventional hymns about the Christian life and Christ, the true vine, respectively. As three of these hymns (689, 1041, 1338) were documented on the basis of hand-written entries in two separate later editions of the Inspirationist Davidisches Psalter-Spiel (1753 and 1869), the accuracy of this source may be assumed only with certain reservations. Another Radical Pietist newly introduced here was Johann Conrad Ziegler (1692-1731), who had collaborated on the publication of the first edition of Davidisches Psalter-Spiel. His Sei unverzagt, o frommer Christ (1096) is a hymn about trust in God.

The Anabaptist Lenaert Clock is introduced in this hymnal. He was an elder in the German Mennonite congregation at Cologne who moved to the Netherlands before 1590 to serve there. In his hymn of parting, Lebt friedsam, sprach Christus der Herr (733), the person leaving impresses upon the Christian brothers and sisters remaining behind the necessity to live peacefully, according to Christ's teaching. There are two additional hymns by anonymous Anabaptists which are sometimes attributed to Michael Sattler, a German Anabaptist martyr (d. 1527). The first is a paraphrase of psalm 23 (839), the second, another hymn of parting (882).

UNDOCUMENTED HYMNS

As there is no direct reference anywhere in this hymnal to hymns written by Brethren, one cannot readily assume that all or even most of the unidentified newly added hymns were written by Brethren authors. There are only twenty such hymns, a much smaller percentage than was the case in the European hymnal. (For a complete list of the new hymns, see Appendix II/2.) It is possible that the four new hymns which are included in the second appendix (28, 356, 948, 1320) were of Brethren authorship. This assumption might be made on the basis of the mention in the preface of the inclusion of some hymns from manuscripts. However, only the hymn Ach Herzensgeliebte, wir scheiden jetzunder (28) has contemporary, possibly Brethren character. It will be discussed later on in this chapter.

In light of the singular lack of information about any possible Brethren hymns, a marginal entry by Abraham H. Cassel in the copy of the 1744 edition at Juniata College, Huntingdon, Pennsylvania is all the more intriguing. The entry is found above the hymn, <u>Wo bleiben meine Sinnen</u> (1320) and states: <u>Alexsander</u> [sic] <u>Mack hat dieses Lied gemacht</u> (Alexander Mack made this hymn). If this is correct, then the writer was probably Alexander Mack, Jr., who wrote numerous poems and hymns during his life and who was a skilled poet. Furthermore, the poem extols the ideals of virginity and chastity, reflecting the teachings of the Ephrata Community where the younger Mack spent many years of his life.

This hymn is a poem on the passion of Christ in seven parts comprising a total of 110 stanzas. It is found along with numerous other hymns in the second appendix of <u>Das Kleine Davidische Psalterspiel</u>, 1744. All subsequent editions and reprints from the Sauer and other presses included it in full. The first part opens with a contemplation of Jesus on the cross:

Where have my senses gone? How dim is my mind! What is my heart to do? Who will tell me about the wonderful bridegroom who is nailed to the cross, bleeding, as our Pascal lamb? (:1)

The next six stanzas trace the prefigurations of this Pascal lamb in the slaying of the firstborn sons in Egypt, through Isaac, finally to Joseph as he was sold by his brothers, and as he was thrown into prison by the pharaoh. After three stanzas of contemplation, the writer described the scene in the garden of Gethsemane and followed the passion story through the incident with Peter in the courtyard after the interrogation by the Sanhedrin.

In the second part, the beginning five stanzas describe Judas' remorse and futile attempts to reverse his evil deed. The remainder is a dramatic retelling of Jesus' interrogation by Pilate and the latter's verdict. The writer used various conventional devices such as questions and imperatives, to render his description even more vivid:

Come now, you children of Jacob! Come and see what is about to happen. Come all, you sinners, come, if you will see Jesus. Here in this valley of tears he is bound to the stake ready to be scourged out of love for his spouse. (:16)
Who has vanquished you, noble hero? Bound with ropes, displayed as a spectacle you are being scourged by the mercenary. The angels shy away and let sinners whip you quite pitifully. (:17)

This part concludes with a reflection on Pilate and Herod:

Pilate and Herod - ordinarily enemies of each other - consider themselves quite without guilt in this death and through this [mutual attitude] become friends: the fox mocks, the judge would like to acquit if only the poor Jews did not raise such as clamor. (:24)

Part three describes the reactions of the people, especially the
women, as they watch Jesus carry his cross to Golgotha. The writer added
his own interpretation:

> Salem's daughters are weeping because they watch the most beautiful one
> (as it appears to all the world) go to such an early grave, because the
> like of him is nowhere to be found and he has not left any progeny as
> did others.   (:7)
> But our bridegroom is now founding a better marriage, which is not
> poisoned by the bitter pain of sin. Out of his body God is now forming
> him a chaste wife who even in the act of procreation remains the purest
> of virgins.   (:8)
> Yet, because the bridegroom knows what tender love is like he does not
> withdraw. His head stained with blood, he painfully casts one last
> look upon Jerusalem's daughters and wishes them good fortune!   (:9)
> He says: "Daughters, if you wish to weep, do not weep over me. Weep
> over no one who lived as I did. When he passes away from here and is
> raised with me he shall have seed that will last in eternity.   (:10)
> Truly, truly I say to you who see me today, the days of the great tribu-
> lation are yet to come when one will call blessed the virgin spirit
> that passed the breasts of lust by."   (:12)
> The breasts that do not suckle the child of vanity, the bodies that
> bend under the cross unencumbered, in virginal discipline - it is they
> whom Jesus seeks and brings fruit to their love in eternity.   (:13)

The fourth part elaborates on the actual act of crucifixion, and the
fifth dramatizes remarks of the passers-by and the words of Christ. The
death of Jesus, who is repeatedly likened to the sacrificial lamb, is described in part six. The final part deals with the events surrounding
Jesus' death and burial. Several stanzas are noteworthy because of some
references to the belief of the early Brethren in universal restoration:

> ... The power of restoration which creates all things new makes way for
> suffering.   (:5)
> How the earth heaves! What can be in the graves? To open them, Jesus'
> death-anguish breaks latches, locks, and doors of hell and grave: thus
> even the dead will soon come forth.   (:6)
> Many holy bodies are coming forth now after the hero in battle has
> taken away death's power. They are his booty who will rise with him
> and go forth from their graves. Here and there they can be seen in
> the holy city.   (:7)

Next the people gathered around the cross are described, from the captain
and his servants to Jesus' "friends and relations," "dear ones and acquaintances:" Mary Magdalene, Mary, Salome, and John. A narration of the
events surrounding the burial leads up to the two concluding stanzas. All
this is interspersed with admonitions to the writer's own "dear heart:"

> What is put into the ground will thereby increase manifold and there-
> fore it is not so hard to bear. In the same manner our Lord died so
> that in his grave and death he might (pro)create a heavenly host. (:19)
> Still, his own are deeply saddened because they feel deserted. Mary,
> weeping, keeps looking for the Lord until she finds him. My heart,
> what are you doing? O weep also until Jesus lives within you after his
> rest in the grave.   (:20)

None of the other twenty new, unidentified hymns in this hymnal were in any way pointed out as Brethren-authored texts, and none bear any peculiarly Brethren traits. However, if there were indeed any new Brethren hymns present in this hymnal, they could only be found in this group. In the following, some noteworthy aspects of the new unidentified hymns will be discussed. The topics do not necessarily coincide with the rubrics under which the cited hymns are found.

Parting Hymns

Taking leave of one's brothers and sisters in the faith was frequently expected of people on the American frontier. Ach Herzens-Geliebte, wir scheiden jetzunder (28) is a hymn of parting consisting of four stanzas:

O most dearly beloved, we now part from one another. Let each keep a steadfast heart that joins me in calling out longingly for love: Lord Jesus, Lord Jesus, draw us after you!   (:1)
Yes, dear brothers and sisters, let us be watchful because our enemies are getting ready. They wish to steal from us our faith in God with which they hinder childlike trust.   (:2)
And since we are now parting from one another, let us sincerely intercede for one another so that none may stray from the path, that we may tread the right paths.   (:3)
O dearest members! it might come about that we shall never see one another again. Let each be diligent on the journey so that we may gain the crown as a prize.   (:4)

Teaching the Faith

Bewahre dich, o Seel' (133) is concerned with the right preparation for teaching the faith to others. It warns the soul against being enticed away from Jesus characterizing false preachers thus:

Whosoever does not have the spirit of Christ cannot hear his voice, much less teach others. Whosoever claims such is truly like the fools - his prattle is for nothing. For whosoever is without power does not have the spirit of Christ.   (:3)
It is only through the spirit that one gains insight into the great mysteries, the spirit's rivers of grace ... .   (:4)

A very good hymn of proclamation is Dir sei Lob, Herrlichkeit und Preis (286), a free paraphrase of Johann Jakob Schütz's Sei Lob und Ehr' dem höchsten Gut (1095). Similarly, Es ist der Not ein Ziel gesteckt (356) is a somewhat didactic but concise and sound statement on the Christian faith which is devoid of the literary mannerisms that are evident in so many of the texts even of Brethren hymns.

Prayer-Hymns

There are several prayer-hymns among the new texts of the 1744 hymnal dealing with a variety of concerns. Jesu, wahres Gotteslamm (688), in referring to the person praying uses expressions like "little lamb," and "little orphan," while deploring the state of the church and entreating for succor, because

Midnight is near, therefore all is bent on sleep and the power of the first love - o what can one say - has diminished greatly among serious-minded members. O that this were not so among fellow believers! (:5)

Ein König gross von Macht und Ehr' (321) combines the Old Testament language of describing Jesus as a king great in power and honor to whose banner the poet has sworn allegiance, with that of the New Testament. In stanza ten, the poet implores Jesus to teach him how to be lowly like a lamb, friendly, meek, and mild.

The attainment of perfection is the prayer-concern of Beweg mein Herz durch deine Kraft (134):

And whatever moves me to sin in my flesh, let it die so that my spirit may move in your spirit, increase and constantly plead [werben] until I, too, shall become a perfect human being in you, o Lord, which is what you desire. (:2)
... continue in me, then, your work until it is completed here on earth ... . (:3)
Let in me burn the fire of love that I may strongly feel it inside, which totally consumes the monster of sin and adorns me with virtue, so that I might become pure and chaste here [on earth] and some day be completely freed from the power of sin. (:4)

An evening and a morning hymn might be counted among this group also. These are Der Tag ist hin mit seinem Lichte (237) and Herzliebster Abba, deine Treue (501), which latter distinguishes itself through great clarity of thought and economy of words. Clearly the best of all new prayer-hymns is Dies ein, das not, lehr mich (279):

Teach me this one thing that is needed, that I may love you steadfastly, o Jesus. Grant that all my actions may be done to your glory whatever they may be. (:1)
Grant that whatever I think and speak may be generated by your love lest I offend your spirit who teaches me to love. (:2)
Make me ready to speak a word in its time in a wholesome way. Likewise, teach me, o my God, to keep silent when it is not necessary [to speak]. (:3)
Move my heart, purge it of all tort [Scherz], dwell in it, let me be your temple, and sanctify all my undertakings. (:4)
O creator, I, your clay, beseech you through Christ your son that you might prepare me to be a vessel that does you honor. (:5)
Among this wicked race let me shine as a light so that everyone might recognize by their fruits those who serve you. (:6)
Becalm my mind in you forever, to be steadfast without wavering, that my whole body might serve you to your praise and thanksgiving. (:7)

Jesus-Hymns

A hymn about Jesus and individual discipleship is Ein König gross von Macht und Ehr' (321). Here, Jesus is described as a king great of power and honor. The one praying has sworn fealty to his standard. For all the pain and struggle which this causes here, there will be great reward in heaven. Conversion and sanctification are two of the themes in Die Freundlichkeit meines Geliebten mich rühret (247):

... cease opposing God in your hearts lest your hearts become quite hardened in the end. O flee the evil and let yourselves be invited; the wedding of the lamb is all ready for everyone who does battle and fights diligently.   (:4)
It is not enough to set about this once, one must also complete it and achieve victory here, and then after the battles gain the crown promised to the victors by you, Jesus ... .   (:5)

Mysticism

Elements of mysticism found expression in Herr Jesu, deine Macht (488), a hymn of twenty-eight stanzas. It opens with the statement that Jesus' power has subjugated Satan and continues as follows:

A spark of your power has become flesh in our hut [Hütte, i.e., body]: that is what drives out the dragon. You are now the master of the house ruling in peace.   (:2)
The [very] angels cannot comprehend what you have prepared for us through this incarnation ... .   (:4)
The little child grows out of you and [yet] remains securely within you: we have nothing [i.e., no merit] in that; you alone are the one from whom it sprang.   (:5)
If you are quite emptied from inside, you are yourself the ocean, his very own [i.e., Christ's]. All that is yours must go if the vast house, the godhead, is to become visible.   (:21)
Then take a good look at it and you will have done enough; be content to have witnessed the power that is God's within your hut.   (:22)
But do not think that the spirit is safely yours: no, friend, you must be still: it blows where it will and where it is experienced.   (:23)
In the vast ocean there is neither way nor path except the one that is prepared by him who himself drives the winds, and yet the ocean endures and bears everything.   (:24)
I am only his spark and know not his way nor how he came: I am only waiting in patience until I am enfolded by his grace.   (:25)
He who has made me from nothing has entered me: if he is to place me into the nothingness whence he came when he was revealed, I shall be content.   (:26)

The stanzas not quoted deal chiefly with discipleship: to love shame and to take up the cross in patience; there is no other crown than in praising Christ despite ridicule and derision; a true son does not live in this world in honors, nor does he try to please everyone; only by leaving one's self behind and all that one owns can one become Christ's guest; there must be a death and a burial.

Death

Wann willst du, meiner Seele Trost (1191) describes the anguish of one who fears an early death before he has "seen his sun:"

My body is about to fade away, my strength has left me, I am growing old in the best years of my life, because I cannot grasp him who loved me but has now left me. That is why I am dying.   (:3)

The poet continues by imploring the daughters of Salem to intercede for him should they succeed in speaking with "Him," until he shall take his abode with the poet. At the same time, the writer addresses all those who, like him, had lost their lives:

> Now then, I say this unhesitatingly: let us nevertheless not despair, God's mercy is new despite of everything and he will hear our lament. Even in his judgment God's heart breaks and he will have mercy on us and embrace us as our father. (:7)

There are two points of similarity between this hymn and Wo bleiben meine Sinnen (1320), the poem attributed to Alexander Mack, Jr. Both address the "daughters of Salem" and both use the unusual term Marter-Pfahl (martyr's stake).

Expectation of the End-Time

Four of the new hymns (388, 621, 1022, 1239) deal with the end-time, the victory of the lamb, the coming of the heavenly Zion, all depicting the joyful events that await those who suffered here on earth for their faith.

Ihr Zions Bürger allzumal (621) describes the commencing of the millennium thus:

> Make sure your lamps are adorned, be yourselves alert and ready to see your bridegroom arrive, the most beautiful lamb of God, and to enter with him to his great wedding feast and to adorn his great hall which is full of joys. (:2)
> Then you will be offered for your suffering the garment of salvation made of beautiful white silk; the time of mourning will be over, no more crying will be heard, there will be only joyfulness. The song of the lamb will be heard and joy will increase continuously. (:3)
> Then love will triumph, she will adorn the citizens of peace who have done battle here for her and who spent their brief lifetime here in battle and strife and have kept the lust of the world in check. Their suffering will have come to an end, there will be nothing left to give them pain. (:4)
> When the kingdom of Zion is revealed, the millenium, promised for so long, commences. Then the earth will be freed of Babel's pride and whoring splendor, the Lord will destroy her; then the beast will be full of suffering when it is engulfed by the pool of flames. (:5)

Universal Restoration

In addition to the poem by Alexander Mack, Jr., the belief in universal restoration is expressed also in Ich will von deiner Güte singen (595), a beautiful morning-hymn of praise. This text is a good example for a characteritistic tendency of many hymn-writers of the time who, for want of clarity of thought or expression often interchange or confuse the persons of God and Christ.

> I want to sing of your mercy and praise your kindness [Freundlichkeit]. I want to make a sacrifice to you in this early morning hour of my heart, mind, and soul ... . (:1)

This sacrifice is quite insignificant, but you are the great God, the restorer of all things, whose name is Lord Sabaoth. Yet since I have nothing else to give you, receive it, o Lord, in mercy.   (:2)
Asperse it completely with your mild lamb's blood which was shed for me ... .   (:3)

From this point on the concept of the mighty Lord Sabaoth is fused with that of the sweet lamb, the treasure of the soul, the sweetest love, and ends with an attempt at clarifying the trinitarian stance albeit not very well:

My dearest Abba [God the Father?], bless, o bless and protect me! Lord Jesus Christ, graciously reveal yourself to me in your light! God, the holy ghost, bestow upon me your sweet kiss of peace.   (:8)

LATER EDITIONS

After 1744, Das Kleine Davidische Psalterspiel went through several further editions and reprints. The first four - 1744, 1760, 1764, 1777 - were printed and published by the Christopher Sauers of Germantown. After the American Revolution, the Philadelphia firm of Steiner and Cist printed the fifth edition in 1781 and, ten years later, Samuel Sauer of Chestnut-hill, Pennsylvania published the sixth edition in 1791. In 1795, Salomon Mayer at Ephrata, Pennsylvania published a reprint of the first edition with further appendixes. After this date, the numbering of the editions became irregular.

In the fourteen editions that followed the first, only thirteen new undocumented hymns were introduced. Five were added in 1760 (351, 382, 410, 1146, 1229) and five in 1764 (123, 251, 292, 299, 1208). Two of the latter (292, 299) were attributed to Benjamin Schmolck in a later, non-Brethren hymnal of 1832, not considered a reliable source. Three new hymns were added to Billmeyer's edition of 1797 (1042, 1132, 1252). In addition to these new hymns, a total of sixty-three were newly introduced which had been taken from the existing stock of German hymnody. It is interesting to note that as many as twenty such hymns were included in the appendix of Billmeyer's first edition of Das Kleine Davidische Psalter-spiel in 1797 but in no subsequent one.

One hymn-text introduced in 1760 mentions baptism albeit in a rather general manner. It is possible, however, that in its first line this text refers to the Brethren: "There are only few who live a godly life" (1229):

This bath [i.e., baptism], which we profess, is the old Adam's misery [Not]: and what we call baptism here, is his cross, his grave, and his death. Jesus' destiny must be universal and so must be that of his disciples.   (:3)

Zionitischer Weyrauchshügel (1739), the first hymnal of the Ephrata Community, seems to have been the source of two newly introduced hymns in the 1764 edition. Not all the texts in the first Ephrata hymnal were products of the community. However, Jauchzet, ihr Kinder, von Zion geboren (645), an eschatological hymn about the future glories, was indeed written by the community's leader, Conrad Beissel. The second hymn, Wenn ich mit geistlicher Habe versehen (1241) may well have been written by one of the brothers or sisters of the community. In twenty-five stanzas the hymn describes the futility and vanity of earthly things, wants, and desires, and points instead to all the spiritual values. There is a strong strain of asceticism present, albeit somewhat trite on occasions, but certainly offering good insights into the psyche of an Ephrata mystic.

CONCLUSION

Unlike the European hymn-book, the first American hymnal of the Brethren contains all the necessary features of such a work. Title-page, preface, an index to the subjects of the hymns (rubrics), an index to the first lines of the hymns, and an index to the melodies are all present. Also from its first edition, the hymnal contained two appendices: the first consisting of psalm-hymns by Lobwasser, the second, of additional hymns. Both in the main body of the hymnal and the appendixes, the hymns are arranged in alphabetical order, with the index of first lines providing access to all three parts.

This second Brethren hymnal was still very much a product and reflection of Pietism even though its span of publication reached far beyond the period referred to by that name. Hymn-writers from the movement of Pietism and its forerunners outnumber any other group by far. The three authors represented by the largest number of hymns are Neander, Arnold, and Scheffler. As was the case with the European hymnal of 1720, social concern was not one of the subjects expressed in any of the new undocumented hymn-texts, nor could this be found in any of the newly introduced documented hymns. The exception is one anonymous hymn, documented in the 1740 edition of Das Davidische Psalter-Spiel, which must be mentioned especially. This hymn, Wenn unsre Augen schon sich schliessen (1250), in its three stanzas, gives the best hymnic statement on the Anabaptist concept of mutual aid that can be found in Brethren hymnals thus far:

> If our eyes close while danger still lurks at our door ready to engulf us, then the best means [of help] is when friends gather together and thus render sleep powerless. (:1)
> The brotherhood of the children of God does not allow us to fall victims to sleep. The one renders aid faster than the other is able to promise it. A Christian conversation can result in our waking up from the deepest sleep. (:2)
> O if only the citizens of Zion would faithfully stand by one another, how one could then see the strangler of souls sink down towards hell. How the house of hell would shake in its foundations and Christ's kingdom live again. (:3)

Of the twenty-one new hymns that were introduced in Das Kleine Davidische Psalterspiel of 1744, twelve were printed only in the first edition. Four found their way into some later editions of this and/or other Brethren hymnals and five were included in all subsequent German hymnals of the Brethren. Although this was definitely a hymnal by and for the Brethren in Colonial America, it soon became the most widely used hymn-book among the German settlers in Pennsylvania. With its numerous editions and later reprints extending over more than one hundred years, it was the longest-lived of all Brethren hymnals. At the same time it was, together with its supplement, Die Kleine Harfe, which is the subject of the next chapter, a remnant of German seventeenth- and eighteenth-century piety. During the years of its existence it witnessed the increasing use of the English language in worship and hymnody among the settlers and, of course, the Brethren. Nevertheless it held its own for many more years and became the chief source from which the hymns compiled in Die Kleine Lieder Sammlung, the next main hymnal of the Brethren, were taken.

Das Kleine Davidische Psalterspiel will be remembered for three reasons: first, the authorship of the passion poem of 110 stanzas by Alexander Mack, Jr.; secondly, the introduction of Lobwasser's psalm-hymns. This latter fact further signifies that in addition to introducing a new type of hymn-text, the Brethren also introduced the new type of melody to which these texts were sung, namely, French Renaissance tunes. Although these tunes had lost most of their characteristic rhythms by the mid-eighteenth century, they nevertheless represent a different genre from the German chorales. Thirdly, and most significantly of all, this hymnal, despite its strong Pietist orientation, can nevertheless be considered peculiarly Brethren by virtue of its arrangement of rubrics which un-doubtedly reflects the theology of the Brethren in Colonial America during the first half of the eighteenth century.

The following table provides a summary of the hymn-writers according to historical periods and movements to which they belong. Although the basic list focuses on the first edition, information pertaining to the later ones is included. Asterisks denote those writers that entered Brethren hymnody for the first time here. Names in parentheses indicate writers that appeared in later editions. Numbers of hymns given in parentheses are inclusive of all editions.

HYMN-WRITERS REPRESENTED IN
DAS KLEINE DAVIDISCHE PSALTERSPIEL
ARRANGED ACCORDING TO HISTORICAL PERIODS AND MOVEMENTS

	Writers	Hymns
REFORMATION:		
Orthodox: Decius, Gramann, Herman*, Kreuziger, Luther, Renau*; Zwick* (Reformed)	7	12
Anabaptists: Clock*, Grünwald, Ringwald, Scharnschlager.	4	5
Schwenkfelder: A. Reissner.	1	1
Czech Brethren: Weisse.	1	2
COUNTER-REFORMATION: Behm*, Helmbold, Lobwasser*, Moller*, Nicolai, Weingärtner*.	6	19
THIRTY-YEARS'WAR: Albert*, Dach, Frankenberg*, Heermann, Held, Rinkart, Rist, Rosenmüller, Sonnemann, Wilhelm II*.	10	19
LATE 17TH CENTURY: Bucholtz, Denicke, Flitner*, Frentzel*, Gesenius, Strattner, Weydenheim*; Lodenstein (Reformed).	8	12
PIETISM:		
Forerunners: Aemilie Juliane*, Arnschwanger*, Birken*, Clausnitzer, Finx, J. Franck, M. Franck, Fritsch, Gerhardt, Haack, Herzog, Homburg*, Keimann, Knorr, Kongehl, Liscow, Lochner, Ludämilie Elisabeth*, H. Müller, Olearius*, B. Prätorius, Quirsfeld, Rodigast*, Sacer*, Scheffler, Schirmer, Scriver*, Senitz, Sieber, Stark*, Tietze*, Weber*; Neader (Reformed)	33	123 (128)
Early Pietists: Arnold, Astmann, Dessler, Drese, Freystein, Funke*, Heine*, Laurenti, Neuss*, Schade, Schütz, B. E. Zeller.	12	58 (59)
Halle and late Pietists: Baumgarten, Bernstein, Böhmer*, Bonin*, Breithaupt*, Crasselius, Falkner, Francke, Freylinghausen*, Gotter, Herrnschmidt, Kellner*, Koitsch, Lackmann, J. Lange, J. C. Lange, Lehr*, M. Müller, Nehring, Pfefferkorn*, Richter, Rothe*, Ruopp*, Schlicht*, J. E. Schmidt, J. H. Schröder, T. S. Schröder*, J. P. Schultt*, R. F. Schultt, Schwedler, Winkler, Wolff*.	29 (32)	71 (76)
Radical Pietists: (Annoni*), Gruber*, Petersen?, J. C. Ziegler*.	3 (4)	7 (8)
Brethren: Knepper.	1	56
(Moravians: N. L. Zinzendorf*.)	(1)	(1)
Württemberg Pietists: Erhard*, Gmelin*, Hedinger, (P. F. Hiller*)	3 (4)	3 (4)
Reformed: Buchfelder, Pauli*, Tersteegen*.	3	11 (26)
Orthodox: (Cramer*), Günther*, (Hübner*), Menken, Möckel*, Schmolck*, Sinold*, (Sporleder*), Zihn.	6 (9)	7 (16)
(Enlightenment: Diterich*, Gellert*, Schlegel*)	(3)	(10)
GERMAN-AMERICANS:		
Brethren: Mack, Jr.	1	1
(Ephrata: Beissel*)	(1)	(1)

HYMN-WRITERS REPRESENTED IN DAS KLEINE DAVIDISCHE PSALTERSPIEL
ARRANGED ALPHABETICALLY AND NUMBER OF THEIR HYMNS

Aemilie Juliane*: 1	Haack: 1	Reissner, A.: 1
Albert*: 1	Hedinger: 1	Renau*: 1
(Annoni*: 1)	Heermann: 4	Richter: 10
Arnold: 32	Heine*: 1	Ringwald: 2
Arnschwanger*: 1	Held: 2	Rinkart: 3
Astmann: 1	Helmbold: 1	Rist: 4
	Herman*: 2	Rodigast*: 1
Baumgarten: 1	Herrnschmidt: 3	Rosenmüller: 1
Behm*: 1	Herzog: 1	(Rothe*: 1)
(Beissel*: 1)	(Hiller, P.F.*: 1)	Ruopp*: 1
Bernstein: 3	Homburg*: 1	
Birken*: 3	(Hübner*: 1)	Sacer*: 1
Böhmer*: 1		Schade: 5
Bonin*: 1	Keimann: 1	Scharnschlager: 1
Breithaupt*: 1	Kellner*: 1	Scheffler: 28 (29)
Buchfelder: 1	Knepper: 56	Schirmer: 1
Bucholtz: 1	Knorr: 7	(Schlegel*: 2)
Clausnitzer: 1	Koitsch: 3	Schlicht*: 1
Clock*: 1	Kongehl: 1	Schmidt, J.E.: 1
(Cramer*: 2)	Kreuziger: 1	Schmolck*: 1 (6)
Crasselius: 4		Schröder, J.H.: 2
Dach: 1	Lackmann: 5	Schröder, T.S.*: 2
Decius: 2	Lange, J.: 2	Schultt, J.P.*: 1
Denicke: 1	Lange, J.C.: 4	Schultt, R.F.: 1
Dessler: 1	Laurenti: 8 (9)	Schütz: 1
(Diterich*: 3)	(Lehr*: 2)	Schwedler: 1
Drese: 3	Liscow: 2	Scriver*: 1
Erhard*: 1	Lobwasser*: 13	Senitz: 1
	Lochner: 1	Sieber: 1
Falkner: 1	Lodenstein: 2	Sinold*: 2
Finx: 4	Ludämilie Elis.*: 2	Sonnemann: 1
Flitner*: 1	Luther: 4	(Sporleder*: 1)
Franck, J.: 3		Stark*: 1
Franck, M.: 2	Mack, Jr.*: 1	Strattner: 1
Francke: 2	Menken: 1	
Frankenberg*: 1	Möckel*: 1	Tersteegen: 9 (24)
Frentzel*: 1	Moller*: 2	Tietze*: 1
Freylinghausen*: 3 (4)	Müller, H.: 2	
Freystein: 1	Müller, M.: 3	Weber*: 1
Fritsch: 5		Weingärtner: 1
Funke*: 1	Neander: 31	Weisse: 2
	Nehring: 1	Weydenheim*: 1
(Gellert*: 2)	Neuss*: 3	Wilhelm II.*: 1
Gerhardt: 12 (16)	Nicolai: 1	Winkler: 2
Gesenius/Denicke: 4		Wolff*: 2
Gmelin*: 1	Olearius*: 1	
Gotter: 8	Pauli*: 1	Zeller, B.E.: 1
Gramann: 1	Petersen?: 2	Ziegler, J.C.*: 1
Gruber*: 1	(Pfefferkorn*: 1)	Zihn: 1
Grünwald: 1	Prätorius, B.: 2	(Zinzendorf, N.L.*: 1)
Günther*: 1	Quirsfeld: 1	Zwick*: 1

NOTES

[1] "Das Davidische Psalterspiel - David's Psalm-Song," The Primitive Christian, 31 January, 1882, p. 67.

[2] Zionitischer WeyrauchsHügel Oder: Myrrhen Berg ... (Germantown: Christoph Sauer, 1739).

[3] Das Kleine Davidische Psalterspiel der Kinder Zions ... (Germantown: Christoph Sauer, 1744).

[4] For a complete translation of the preface, see Appendix II/1.

[5] Peter Erb, "The Brethren in the Early Eighteenth Century: an Unpublished Contemporary Account," Brethren Life and Thought, Spring 1977, pp. 105-112.

Chapter III

DIE KLEINE HARFE

THE FIRST EDITION

In the year 1792, a slim hymnal called Die Kleine Harfe (The Small Harp)[1] was published by Samuel Sauer. It contained fifty-eight hymns never before printed for the Brethren and was bound with Das Kleine Davidische Psalterspiel. Thus it was the first hymnal-supplement published by the Brethren. In the course of its subsequent six editions until 1830, it was occasionally published as a separate hymnal, but no new hymns were added to it.

In English translation, the title-page reads as follows:

The small harp, tuned [made to sound] by various beautiful hymns or songs of praise, which are heard from the ends of the earth to the glory of the righteous one. This small harp sounds beautifully, albeit only of earthly music [im niedrigen Ton], until that time when the great host of harp-players will elevate the singing. Unto God and the lamb be honor and praise in time and eternity! Amen.

Neither foreword nor rubrics were provided, only an index of first lines. The index to the melodies is incorporated into the list of melodies for Das Kleine Davidische Psalterspiel. The hymnal is divided into eight sections representing the eight strings of the Davidic harp, with two morning and two evening hymns added. Again, the headings of the eight sections are much more specific than the hymns printed under each. The number of hymns found in each section are given in parentheses.

The first string of this harp sounds happily and peacefully of the revelation of God in the flesh, particularly in the incarnation of Christ (4)
The second string sounds comfortingly and sweetly of the revelation of God in the cross (5)
The third string sounds beautifully and sweetly of the power of God in the order of salvation (11)
The fourth string sounds of following Christ in the new birth (13)
The fifth string sounds of the meekness and humility that can be learned from Christ (4)
The sixth string sounds lowly, yet kindly, of patience (4)
The seventh string sounds the most lowly yet sincerely and proclaims to all people repentance in the face of mortality (7)
The eighth string entices the power of the soul to the higher music [zum höhern Ton] through devout praise and thanksgiving for spiritual and physical blessings (7)

DOCUMENTED HYMNS

Only a few more than half of the texts in this collection are documented hymns. The poet most often represented is Gerhard Tersteegen (seven hymns). Three hymns were written by Nikolaus Ludwig von Zinzendorf, two by Freylinghausen, and one each by Gerhardt and Scheffler. The most significant of these is Gerhardt's O Haupt voll Blut und Wunden (965).

More hymns are included here from the Ephrata community than was the case with Das Kleine Davidische Psalterspiel. Two hymns are from the pen of Conrad Beissel. His Der bitt're Kelch und Myrrhen Weine (202) is found in the second string of the harp. The tenor of this hymn is the spiritual battle of the Christian, which is one's cross. This battle is likened to that of one who has sworn fealty, which demands that one first renounce one's own life before one can even enter into battle. It is necessary to leave behind wife and children in order to follow in the footsteps of Jacob and eventually inherit the new name of Israel. Such faithfulness is to be rewarded by God through the fulness of his grace. Beissel's second hymn, Nun ist die frohe Zeit erwacht (908) is the opening hymn of Die Kleine Harfe, a Christmas hymn. Stanza eight states that through the incarnation itself,

... because God himself awakens as a child - that which was lost is restored: the virgin consecrated unto God has fulfilled the wondrous counsel of God.   (:8)

The two other Ephrata hymns are Was ist das Leben dieser Zeit (1207) by Sister Naëmi (Naomi Eicher), and Wie freuet sich mein Geist (1285) by Sister Jaël (Barbara Meyer). The former is a hymn of renunciation of the world and the self, in which the author writes about the pain of this life and the early difficulties in seeking Jesus' way:

I have from my childhood been diligently seeking this way [of Jesus], but because of my childish ways I often stumbled.   (:5)
Because I was unable to see clearly that one can enter the kingdom of God only through sorrow, pain, cross, and distress, from youth until death.   (:6)

The latter hymn belongs to the fourth string of following Christ in the new birth. Jesus Christ is never mentioned here by name, however. Instead, the "pure lamb" is the object, who leads his followers through narrow, rough paths, even to the cross and the dark valley of death, even to the gates of hell. Eventually, one is to be led into paradise after having been wed to pure love and being directed by it.

The tenor of these hymns is still individual experience, love for Jesus, striving for a virtuous life, the battle with sin, the anticipation of the heavenly Jerusalem. Surprisingly, it is one of Scheffler's hymns, Wie süss ist dein Gebot (1299) that turns away from the self and makes some mention of the "sweet commandment" of loving one's neighbor:

You demand nothing of me but the holy zeal of love: I am to love my neighbor and practice love. You enable me to do this by kindling a fire in me yourself.   (:3)

Day and night I shall diligently seek to turn my heart to you and my neighbor. Only grant, sweet Lord, what your commandment demands.   (:7)

UNDOCUMENTED HYMNS

Although the contents of this slim hymnal did not change in the later editions, in the second edition, 1797, the publisher, Samuel Sauer, added at the end of four hymns the names of their Brethren authors, namely, Peter Becker, Jakob Danner, and Johann Naas. Furthermore, internal evidence of one hymn-text points to Christopher Sauer II as its author and three are documented as texts by Alexander Mack, Jr. The text by Sauer (154) and one by Mack (695) had been printed with the authors' names in 1788 in a small collection of hymn-texts. All of these hymns were still very much in the Pietist style and manner. The following is a discussion of their content. (For a list of the new hymns, see Appendix III.)

Peter Becker (1687-1758)

Du armer Pilger wandelst hier (291). This is a poem rather than a hymn. Because of the two-syllabic word, Geduld (patience) at the end of each stanza, the text could not have lent itself very well to singing. It is therefore not surprising that no existing melody could be found to fit it. In fourteen stanzas the writer addresses the Christian, a poor pilgrim, who is making his way through this vale of tears which is his life. He is being admonished to stay on the straight and narrow path, no matter what might befall, and to look to his savior's sufferings as a comfort. None of these earthly tribulations and trials are significant in comparison with the heavenly glory awaiting the pilgrim.

Jakob Danner (1727-ca.1800)

Gute Nacht, ihr meine Lieben (462) is a hymn for the dying.

Alexander Mack, Jr. (1712-1802)

Du forschest mich (294). This is a poem of twenty stanzas and fairly intricate meter and rhyme which now and then results in textual ambiguity. The first eight stanzas deal with the fact that nothing is hidden from God who sees and knows all. Then, through stanza fourteen, the poet expresses praise and adoration for the wonders of God's ways with Man and the works of his creation. There may also be a remnant of Calvinistic theology in these stanzas:

My bones could not be hid from you, my Lord, o no, when I was formed from clay. That which I was to look and be like was already revealed before you.   (:10)
You knew me already in your son and I knew nothing of it, was unprepared, my days written in the book, how many of them there were to be ... .   (:11)

Later on, the poet expresses his hope for a betterment of the world:

May the godless power of the many sinners soon die so that I may no longer be troubled by bloodthirstiness and mercilessness along with all cruelty [which is] of Satan's realm.   (:16)

The following two stanzas are even more personal although these formulas were also rather typically Pietist:

> When people blaspheme you [i.e., God] in my presence, I am appalled: for your enemies are rising up against you without cause, and that disquiets me as well as your friends! (:17)
> I hate those who are so anxiously envious here of your kingdom of grace. And they take this very much amiss of me and can hardly abide me any longer. (:18)

Nun bricht der Hütten Haus entzwei (898) was written on the death of Christopher Sauer II, July 26, 1784. Mack had the soul of the deceased speak about his life on earth as a pilgrimage from the hut of the body to a better house which Jesus had built for him in heaven. The tenor of the text is praise of Jesus for his work of salvation.

Jesus Christus, Gottes Sohn (695) is the last hymn of the last string. It was given a very fine translation by Ora Garber as "Bless, o Lord, this church of thine."[2] In the English version, the original four stanzas were reduced to three and rearranged in such a manner that the English stanzas 1, 2, and 3 correspond to the German stanzas 2, 4, and 1.

Johann Naas (1669-1742)

Eins betrübt mich sehr auf Erden (331). This hymn is an eloquent description of the condition of humankind. After eleven stanzas of timely commentary, Naas admonishes his fellow man to turn to Christ, his teachings, and his way. He advises him to pay attention to those who please God, namely those who humble themselves before others because "humility is their foundation" (:13). Stanzas fourteen through sixteen continue to elaborate on this order for one's salvation. Stanza seventeen offers the advice to cast one's lot with the small band of believers.

Heiland meiner Seel' (470) is known as "Savior of my soul." The English translation by Lillian Grisso (1889-1974)[3] is a very free paraphrase utilizing only stanzas 1, 3, and 8 of the original seventeen stanzas. This poem is even more subjective than the previous one but much more like a typical Pietist hymn. It deals with the individual's troubles in this world and life and with the state of one's soul. Mankind is on the wrong path and yet seems to feel safe because God is silent. Many God-fearing people are carrying a foreign yoke which leads to this plea in the last stanza:

> Lord, it is up to you! Salvage your honor, dearest king Jesus Christ! You have, after all, paid with your blood. O therefore salvage your honor, Lord, it is up to you! (:17)

Christoph Sauer II (1721-1784)

Christen müssen sich hier schicken (154). This is one of Sauer's numerous birth-day poems, his sixtieth, in which the intitials of the thirteen stanzas, when read downwards, spell his name. It is found in the second string of the harp because it is a hymn about the cross. Sauer wrote it several years after his loss of his business and all of his property during the American Revolution:

... Those who wept many tears here shall there be united with God ... .
Calling, shouting, sighing, praying, paves the way to God. To implore
him in every distress comforts us in all distress. No one ever lacked
comfort who set his hopes in him. Whosoever fixes his eyes in faith
only on him has truly built upon a rock ... .   (:1/2)
O, I cannot be but deeply ashamed and I deplore it that so many a worldly worry has often filled by breast and so beguiled my heart that it
interfered with love and the task which I should have been about was
often left undone. ... withouth [God] I should have perished in the ex-
tremity that engulfed me.   (:11)

Later Brethren hymnals included all of the identified Brethren hymns
with the exception of Mack's Du forschest mich. Naas's Heiland meiner
Seel' found its way only into Neue Sammlung (1870).

Other Undocumented Hymns

In addition to the eight hymns of known Brethren authorship there are
twenty-three new hymns of unknown authorship. These neither distinguish
themselves from other religious poetry of their time nor do they propound
any peculiarly Brethren tenets.

A few observations can be made, however. The opening hymn of the
second string, which deals with the cross, is Der bitt're Kelch und
Myrrhen Weine (202), in which the Christian is depicted as a valiant
warrior or knight. Its first stanza reads:

The bitter chalice and wine of myrrh tastes good to a Christian who is
fighting to the blood [death]: this testing sweetens the pain of the
cross because one can find in it many things that make for peace.   (:1)

An allusion to universal restoration is found in the first line of
Wiederbringer des Verlornen (1305): "Restorer of that which is lost." The
concept of Gemeinde (church, congregation) is evoked in the hymn, Jesus,
wahrer Mensch in Gnaden (708) which begins with these words:

Jesus, truly human [Mensch], full of [in] grace, come into our midst
today. We ask you in humility to be with us this day for we are aware
of your faithfulness.   (:1)

The rather unusual designation Goel for Christ occurs in the hymn,
Kaufet, kauft die Zeit (718). The word means "one who ransoms."[4] Alexander Mack, Jr. used it in his Wo bleiben meine Sinnen (1320, I:10). It is
also found in Tersteegen's poetry and, before that, in the writings of the
French mystic Jeanne Marie Guyon (1648-1717) with which the early Brethren
were quite familiar.

John Jacob Stoudt attributes the Christmas hymn, Mein Gemüt bedenket
heut' (813) to a Brethren author.[5] It is a very straightforward text with
a well developed line of thought - the contemplation of the Christ-child -
and mastery of a simple poetic meter. The hymn ends with an idea that is
found in no other hymn text:

O could I yet this day on earth become my savior's mother!   (:14)

LATER EDITIONS

Seven years after the publication of the first edition of this hymnal, Samuel Saur printed a "second improved" edition in Baltimore in 1797. The third and fourth editions were published by Michael Billmeyer in Philadelphia, in the years 1813 and 1817, respectively. A "first" edition was issued by Schäffer and Maund in Baltimore 1816, which was bound with their "first improved" edition of Das Kleine Davidische Psalterspiel. Germania was the location of a fifth edition in 1829; no publisher's name was given in the imprint. Lastly, there followed another Philadelphia edition in 1830 by Mentz and Rovoudt. In most instances, Die Kleine Harfe was bound with corresponding editions of Das Kleine Davidische Psalterspiel. The contents remained the same throughout.

CONCLUSION

Die Kleine Harfe was the first hymnal-supplement published by the Brethren. Its arrangement is quite unlike that of any other hymnal in that it is divided into eight parts symbolizing the eight strings of the Davidic harp. No new type of hymns was introduced here and the character of the hymnal is still clearly Pietist. Of the twenty-one new hymns, twelve appeared only in Die Kleine Harfe. All others were printed in several later German hymnals of the Brethren, but only Danner's Gute Nacht, ihr meine Lieben (462) found its way into all of them.

The special significance of this hymnal lies in the fact that beginning with its second edition of the Saur press (1797), the names of three Brethren authors were affixed to their hymns. This is not only significant in itself but also a marked departure from the common practice of keeping hymns anonymous.

HYMN-WRITERS REPRESENTED IN
DIE KLEINE HARFE
ARRANGED ACCORDING TO HISTORICAL PERIODS AND MOVEMENTS

	Writers	Hymns
LATE 17TH CENTURY: C. Prätorius*.	1	1
PIETISM:		
Forerunners: Fritsch, Gerhardt, Scheffler.	3	3
Early Pietists: Arnold, Canitz*.	2	2
Halle and late Pietists: Edeling*, Freylinghausen, Herrnschmidt, Wolff.	4	6
Moravians: N. L. Zinzendorf.	1	3
Reformed: Tersteegen.	1	7
Orthodox: Hübner.	1	2
GERMAN-AMERICANS:		
Brethren: Becker*, J. Danner*, Mack, Jr., Naas*, Saur II*.	5	8
Ephrata: Beissel, Jaël*, Naëmi*.	3	4

HYMN-WRITERS REPRESENTED IN
DIE KLEINE HARFE
ARRANGED ALPHABETICALLY AND NUMBER OF THEIR HYMNS

Arnold: 1

Becker*: 1

Beissel: 2

Canitz*: 1

Danner, J.*: 1

Edeling*: 1

Freylinghausen: 2

Fritsch: 1

Gerhardt: 1

Herrnschmidt: 2

Hübner: 2

Jael*: 1

Mack, Jr.: 3

Naas*: 2

Naemi*: 1

Prätorius, C.: 1

Saur II: 1

Scheffler: 1

Tersteegen: 7

Wolff: 1

Zinzendorf, N.L.: 3

NOTES

[1] Die Kleine Harfe, Gestimmet von unterschiedlichen Lieblichen Liedern oder Lob-Gesängen ... (Chestnuthill: Samuel Saur, 1792).

[2] The Brethren Hymnal (Elgin, Ill.: House of the Church of the Brethren, 1951), no. 493.

[3] Ibid., no. 361.

[4] Johannes Kulp, Die Lieder unserer Kirche. Eine Handreichung zum Evangelischen Kirchengesangbuch. Bearbeitet und herausgegeben von Arno Büchner und Siegfried Fornacon (Göttingen: Vandenhoeck und Ruprecht, 1958), p. 68.

[5] John Joseph Stoudt, Pennsylvania German Poetry 1695-1830 (Pennsylvania German Folklore Society, 1956), p. 23.

Chapter IV

DIE KLEINE LIEDER SAMMLUNG

THE FIRST EDITION

In 1826 the first of several editions and reprints of a Brethren hymnal was published which displayed a rather different appearance from the earlier ones. It was Die Kleine Lieder Sammlung, published by Gruber and May of Hagerstown, Maryland.[1] The small format of this hymnal - 12 x 7.5 x 2 cm - was designed "for the convenience of travellers." Indeed, it could easily fit into one's coat pocket. Furthermore, it was intended for those young people who still desired to use their German mother-tongue. Again, the lack of hymn-books in public worship was mentioned in the preface. The present collection of 197 hymns had been compiled to remedy that situation.[2]

The translation of the title-page reads as follows:

The small collection of hymns or extract from the Psalterspiel of the children of Zion, for the use [i.e., service] of sincere souls seeking salvation, but especially for the brotherhood of baptizers [Täufer] and compiled for [their] use and service in this present small format and supplied with a two-fold index ... .[2]

The two-fold index mentioned provides an alphabetical list of first lines and a grouping of hymns and psalm-hymns according to the melodies to which they can be sung. Within the hymnal, the hymns are arranged alphabetically. There is neither a register of categories nor a table of contents in the first edition of this hymnal. In the later editions the former was provided, the order and distribution of the hymns on the whole remaining the same throughout.

THE CATEGORIES

Since no rubrics of topics were provided in the first edition, those of the third (1829) are applied here. This arrangement of rubrics differs quite markedly from any that were discussed earlier, even from those in Das Kleine Davidische Psalterspiel from which most of the hymns are said to have been taken. The headings are simply arranged alphabetically. The table of contents or arrangement of rubrics no longer conveys any meaningful order.

Several hymns appear in more than one rubric, which means either that the publishers took pains to provide various access points to the contents or that those hymns were found under different categories in the hymnals which had been used as models.

In comparing the rubrics of this hymnal with those of Freylinghausen's and of the two Psalterspiel hymnals, Die Kleine Lieder Sammlung strikes one as rather colorless and functional. For example, the "manifold attributes of God," which the earlier hymnals had named, are grouped together into "God's omnipresence," which category contains all of one hymn. Similarly, "Resurrection" and "Ascension" are condensed into one rubric. Of "Christendom," only the "true" one is left. Lobwasser's psalm-hymns are not listed as a separate category, nor are the hymns on "Following Jesus," Easter, Christ's resurrection and second coming. Only two hymns are found under "Baptism."

Two new categories are introduced, namely, "Hymns of invitation" and "[Spiritual] awakening," which latter contains eighteen hymns, the largest number in any category. This is not surprising, because by 1826, several collections of hymns had been published by and for the evangelical Christian groups related to the camp-meeting and revivalist movement of the early nineteenth century. The movement had also produced several prolific hymn-writers who are grouped in this study under the category of German-American Evangelicals. All of these influences may well be reflected in the importance given to the new rubrics in Die Kleine Lieder Sammlung. Inasmuch as the camp-meeting movement had appropriated many texts and some melodies of older English and German hymns for their own use, many hymns had dual identities as camp-meeting songs on the one hand and as "churchly" hymns on the other. It was in the melodies, the manner of singing, and the way in which the text was rearranged, often including refrain and chorus, that such camp-meeting songs differed from conventionally sung hymns. It is impossible to tell by the melody references how the "double-duty" hymns in this hymnal were sung by the Brethren.

Among the "Hymns of invitation," there are three (433, 1131, 1280) that appeared in the earliest hymnal published by German camp-meeting groups, Das Aller Neueste Harfenspiel (1795).[3] Two of these are hymns by Tersteegen, the third, Steh, armes Kind (1131), is anonymous. Ihr jungen Helden, aufgewacht (602), which is one of the two hymns under "Hymns of invitation especially for youth" is mentioned by Yoder in his list of the eighteen "most popular High-German hymns among [the] Bush-Meeting Dutch."[4] Yoder does not identify the authors of these texts; however, all but this latter one can be readily documented. Ihr jungen Helden is, in fact, one of the new Brethren hymns, probably by Wilhelm Knepper, in Geistreiches Gesang-Buch, 1720. It reappeared in all subsequent German hymnals of the Brethren.

"Hymns of awakening" includes only one hymn that comes close to its definition. This is Geh, Seele, frisch im Glauben fort (400). It appears in this hymnal for the first time in Brethren hymnody as an undocumented new hymn:

Go, o soul, go on undaunted in faith and do not lose heart and pass here through the narrow gate, follow Jesus. (:1)
Your savior himself leads the way through cross and tribulation, therefore you, too, must follow through the Red Sea: it will bring you much gain. (:2)
O Jesus, savior of my soul, I come to you without fear; wash off my sin, Emmanuel, o do come to me yourself! (:3)
Forgive my transgressions and that which eats away at my heart, and grant me, o Jesus, your grace that I might be undaunted. (:4)

The remaining hymns in this category deal mostly with the end-time, calling for watchfulness in awaiting the bridegroom. Only three hymns which are newly introduced here (348, 1050, 1089) had been adopted by the German camp-meeting movement. All three are from the stock of older German hymnody. Ermuntert euch, ihr Frommen (348) is also one of the eighteen most popular German camp-meeting songs listed by Yoder.

Below is a list of the hymns in Die Kleine Lieder Sammlung, with documentation, which are known to have been used as German bush-meeting songs. Their first appearance in Brethren hymnody is indicated by the abbreviations used in the appendixes.

"HIDDEN" CAMP-MEETING SONGS IN
Die Kleine Lieder Sammlung, 1826

Alle Christen hören gerne (75) / Documented (ANH 1795)
Denket doch, ihr Menschenkinder (198) / Hübner / KDP 1797-G.
Ermuntert euch, ihr Frommen (348) / Laurenti / GGB.
Ewig, ewig heisst das Wort (374) / Schmolck.
Gott rufet noch (433) / Tersteegen.
Ihr jungen Helden, aufgewacht (602) / Knepper / GGB.
Jauchzet, ihr Himmel (644) / Tersteegen / KH 1792.
Jesu, Jesu, Brunn' des Lebens (670) / Annoni / KDP 1760.
Mein Gott, das Herz ich bringe dir (816) / Schade / KDP 1744.
Ringe recht, wenn Gottes Gnade (1050) / Winkler / GGB.
Sei getreu bis in den Tod (1089) / Schmolck / ELEL 1812.
Steh, armes Kind (1131) / Documented (ANH 1795).

In the absence of a subject index to the hymns in the first edition of Die Kleine Lieder Sammlung, a table of rubrics is provided below which is based on that found in the 1829 edition. As was mentioned above, the arrangement of the headings in the original was alphabetical, which is, of course, not reflected in the translation. Numbers in parentheses refer to the number of hymns in each category.

RUBRICS PROVIDED FOR
Die Kleine Lieder Sammlung, 1826

1. Evening hymns (10)
2. Hymns for the Lord's Supper (4)
3. Parting hymns (4)
4. Hymns of supplication and profession (18)
5. Hymns of repentance and faith (8)
6. Hymns about Christ in general (7)
7. Hymns about Christ's
   a) birth (3)
   b) teaching and life (4)
   c) suffering and death (6)
8. Hymns of invitation (5)
9. Hymns of invitation especially for youth (2)
10. Hymns of awakening (18)
11. Hymns of love (2)
12. Hymns of humility (2)
13. Hymns of the true Christendom (2)

14. Hymns of God's omnipresence (1)
15. Hymns at the tolling of the bell (1)
16. Hymns of praise and thanksgiving (11)
17. Morning hymns (8)
18. Hymns about Pentecost and the Holy Spirit (4)
19. Hymns of death and for burial (12)
20. Baptismal hymns (2)
21. Table hymns (4)
22. Hymns of consolation (5)
23. Hymns for the meeting (11)
24. Miscellaneous hymns (2)

DOCUMENTED HYMNS

A survey of the documented hymns shows that in 1826 the same poets seem to have been favorites with the Brethren as had been the case earlier. Of the 140 hymns in the first edition of Die Kleine Lieder Sammlung, fourteen are by Tersteegen, nine by Neander, and eight by Scheffler. On the other hand, for the first time in Brethren hymnody, a non-Brethren German-American writer can be documented here. Christopher Dock (ca. 1710-1771) was probably a Mennonite schoolteacher and educator. Six of the original twenty-four stanzas of his Ach Kinder, wollt ihr lieben (35) were printed in this hymn-book in 1826, in the rubric of "Hymns of invitation especially for youth:"

O children, if you will love, then love something worthy of being loved. If you will be joyful, then love what is worthy of rejoicing. Love God, the highest good with spirit, heart, soul, and mind and such love will refresh your heart and mind. (:1)
If you love vain things, if you love the desires of the flesh, then you suckle brief joys from the wrong breast of love. Upon this will follow misery, pain, and suffering in eternity, unless in this time of grace the soul is freed through repentance. (:2)
We find it written quite clearly about a rich man who practiced such love as Luke records. He lived during his short time on earth in the desires and joys of the flesh and fed his heart on vain things. (:3)
He clothed himself in this life in purple cloth yet he had to part with it. His joy lasted only a short while. Upon his death he found himself in great need, no one was willing to save him from such pain and misery. (:4)
Then he cried out for mercy: o Father Abraham, come and help me from these great flames! I beg you to send Lazarus with a drop of water to cool my tongue. (:5)
No comfort was granted him but this: Remember, son, that in your life you chose that good which was your reward. Therefore, dear little children, let this be a warning to you. Forsake the life of vanity that you might escape the pain. (:6)

As indicated in the preface, the compilers had drawn substantially on the contents of Das Kleine Davidische Psalterspiel. As many as 107 hymns in the 1826 edition of the Lieder Sammlung are also present in the various editions of the Psalterspiel. Eight hymns, including Jakob Danner's Gute Nacht, ihr meine Lieben (462), originally appeared in Die Kleine Harfe. The European hymnal does not appear to have served as a source. It is possible that by this time it was completely forgotten, which might explain why Abraham H. Cassel had no knowledge of it.

UNDOCUMENTED HYMNS

In the 1826 edition, only twelve newly added hymns cannot be identified as to their authors and/or earlier publication. These are listed in Appendix IV/2. Three of these deal with the theme of death. Gottlob, das Leiden dieser Zeit (441) is kept in very general terms. In Gottlob, mein Leben ist vollbracht (450), the poet assumes the voice of a dying husband and father. Theologically more interesting is So gehe nun in deine Gruft (1114), a hymn for burial. It begins with these words:

Enter your tomb until Jesus Christ calls from on high with a loud voice, "Arise, all you dead!"
(:1)

The hymn continues by describing how those who lived good lives on earth will join the choir of angels, but woe to them who had not chosen to prepare themselves through God's free grace.

Nun scheiden wir, ihr Herzens-Freund' (925) is a hymn of parting, perhaps the parting through death. The first stanza reads as follows:

We depart now, dear friends, from this place. Though you are saddened now, we shall meet again there.
(:1)

After admonitions to the brothers and sisters the hymn concludes:

Now let us all be cheerful on our pilgrimage until we enter into rest, the heavenly paradise.
(:4)

The eschatological theme is further elaborated in Ihr Freunde Jesu allzumal (599), a hymn calling to watchfulness in expectation of the "midnight." Jesus' friends and disciples are to be the ones that will fill the hall of heaven. The call goes out to all sisters and brothers to fill their lamps with oil. There is still time to hear God's word which he has entrusted to Jesus' friends. It pains him that so many are still going astray. The hymn concludes thus:

You beloved all, compose yourselves, stand by God always, that we may meet again in his kingdom of joy. Though the parting here causes much grief, one day of eternal joy will erase it all: when God gathers us into his blessed state.
(:6)

Wer Ohren hat zu hören (1267) states the poet's conception of the narrow and low gate which leads into heaven: it is humility, which is also the great treasure offered to anyone in return for his own will. Two very good, relatively short, prayer-hymns are, Mein Herzens-Jesu, meine Freud' (837) and Wir danken dir, du grosser Gott (1311). The former especially is reminiscent in style and content of Reformation-era hymns. Both succeed in conveying with great economy of words a clear statement of Christian faith and doctrine albeit with neglect of the significance of God the Father in the case of the former hymn, and of the Holy Spirit in the case of the latter.

One of these new hymns was written for the celebration of the Lord's Supper. It is the very didactic Nun kommt, ihr Christen alle (912):

Come now, all you Christians, listen in love at this supper to what Jesus has done ... . (:1)

The poet goes on to give a detailed depiction of Jesus washing the feet of the disciples, including the verbal exchange between Jesus and Peter. The hymn concludes with Jesus' admonition to the disciples to do as he had done and wash one another's feet,

that everyone may recognize you for certain as my disciples. I have given you an example to do as I have done for you: let each be as a servant and consider it right because I have commanded it myself. Now do it as faithful servants. (:7)

A rather interesting case is that of O meine Seele, sinke (1008), a hymn "for the Lord's Supper." Ada Kadelbach in her thorough study of Mennonite hymnody in America[5] found it in Gemeinschaftliche Liedersammlung (1836), a Mennonite hymnal, and commented that according to content and style the hymn might have been written by the Mennonite poet Christian Herr. However, from the perspective of the present study this hymn might as justifiably be attributed to Alexander Mack, Jr. Style and content are strongly reminiscent of Wo bleiben meine Sinnen (1320), which appeared for the first time in Das Kleine Davidische Psalterspiel. Furthermore, the melody reference in the present hymnal is to the above-named hymn which in turn was sung to its "own melody." An additional link might be the use of the unusual term "Goel" in both hymns.

Another hymn for the Lord's Supper is the very didactic Nun kommt, ihr Christen alle (912). In seven stanzas the first footwashing as instituted by Jesus is described in great detail. This, and the fact that the hymn is grouped with those for the Lord's Supper might indicate Brethren authorship.

THE LATER EDITIONS

Between 1827 and 1853 twenty further editions and reprints were published by eight different publishers. While some were issued individually, others were bound together with the English-language Brethren hymnal, A Choice Collection.[6] Following an edition printed in 1829 by Salomon Sala at Canton, Ohio, Henry Kurtz (1796-1874) began publishing editions of Die Kleine Lieder Sammlung in 1833 at Osnaburgh, Ohio. (A supposed first edition of his, Osnaburgh, 1826, seems to be non-existent.) This German-born Lutheran educator, pastor, and publisher had been attracted to the Brethren and become one of their ministers. Three further editions followed from the same house (1835, 1837, 1841). Afterwards, Kurtz's editions were published at Poland, Ohio in 1844, 1848, 1850, and 1853, the latter three as stereotyped editions.

The publishing history of this hymnal illustrates the westward movement of the Brethren, for by the time Kurtz began publishing hymnals, there existed many Brethren settlements in Ohio which were separated from the East by much wilderness country. Thus a tradition of publishing for the "Western Brethren" was begun with this hymnal while in the East publishing continued as before: 1827 by Baumann of Ephrata, 1832 by Miller of Neu-Berlin, 1834, 1836, 1841, and 1848 by Neinstedt of Gettysburg, 1838, 1843, 1847, and 1849 by Peters of Harrisburg, and 1850 by Lutz and Scheffer of Harrisburg.

Although the individual editions are almost identical with one another, significant variances are to be noted. During the years 1827 to 1853, fifty-nine hymns were added to the original stock of 1826. Others, of course, were omitted. All told, 197 different hymns appeared in the course of time in the various editions of Die Kleine Lieder Sammlung. Among the newly added hymns, eleven are unidentified.

In 1827, a new Brethren hymn-writer was introduced. This was Henrich (Heinrich, Henry) Danner of whom very little was known beyond the facts that he was a Dunker and the brother of Jacob Danner.[7] In the spring of 1982, this writer discovered numerous old papers in an eighteenth-century Bible which proved to have been written by this very Henrich Danner. From these papers it was possible to establish that he was born on 12 February, 1742 and died before February, 1814. The hymn which was included in the 1827 edition is, Was hat uns doch bewogen (1202). It consists of eight stanzas and was translated by Ora Garber.[8] Yoder found it to have been a Pennsylvania-German camp-meeting song and it indeed deals with the typical theme of the sadness of parting and the yearning for the life hereafter. The first stanza, however, seems more down-to-earth and raises interesting conjectures about its significance in relationship to Danner's life and, in turn, his relationship to the Brethren when he writes about leaving the home (homeland?) and setting out to join the church that God had established in a foreign country.

A new baptismal hymn appeared in the 1829 edition. Diesen Täufling bringen wir (283) is remarkable for several reasons. First, it is the congregation who are speaking here saying, "We are bringing this person who wishes to be baptized." They are asking Jesus to be merciful on this soul so that the one to be baptized may become holy here on earth and blessed when in heaven. Secondly, the middle three stanzas embody the baptismal formula of the Brethren. Each of the next three stanzas, which address the Täufling, begins with the word eingetaucht (immersed) and ends in a refrain (as does the first) thus emphasizing the role of the congregation. As a whole, the hymn, with its introductory stanza and its refrains could be called a Brethren litany for baptism:

In accordance with the word of God you are being immersed in the name of the Father, that you might believe in him as a true refuge, in childlike faith! Amen! Amen! Father, may you be well pleased with this our faith! (:2)
In accordance with the word of God you are being immersed in the name of the Son, that you might forever love him from your heart. Amen! Amen! Jesus, may you be well pleased by this our love! (:3)
In accordance with the word of God, you are being immersed in the name of the Holy Spirit, that you might remain in joyful hope until you reach the safe haven. Amen! Amen! Holy Spirit, may you be well pleased with this our hope! (:4)

The last stanza again addresses Jesus:

> Jesus, accept this little lamb, make it into one of the members [of your body]. Show it the right way, faith, love, hope, humility, peace. Let it be consecrated even unto death if that were to your honor. (:5)

The description of trine immersion in this baptismal hymn is the most specific of all in German Brethren hymnody thus far. Brethren authorship is probable. Apart from the poetic conventions of Pietism, especially in the last stanza, it is a well-composed poem.

Another new hymn in the 1829 edition was written for the love-feast and is very likely also of Brethren authorship. _Kommet, ihr lieben Geschwister, zum festlichen Mahle_ (737) is divided into three parts: the first two stanzas were to be sung before, the last two after the love-feast. Thus, presumably, the middle two were sung during the love-feast.

> Come, dear brothers and sisters, to the feast which has been prepared for us in this simple room. Come, eat and drink in peace that which God has given for our sustenance. (:1)
> Let us give high praise to God's infinite love which desires to refresh and feed us in body and soul ... . (:2)
> May this love-feast kindle love in all and proclaim them as true disciples of the Lord. May the church [_Gemeinde_] be one heart and one soul and be truly founded in Christ. (:3)
> Bless, o Jesus, all these your gifts of love that they may strengthen heart, soul, and body to your praise. Be our guest, who has himself given [us] this meal. (:4)
> Thank the Lord, his name be eternally praised, who has fed us plentifully at the table of his love. Grant now, o Lord, that we shall always find the way which only love shows. (:5)
> And further we pray, in a child-like spirit, o king of honor, that you keep and increase in us the gifts of the spirit so that after death and misery are overcome we may be fed by heavenly food. (:6)

This hymn was written by a rather skillful poet. Meter and melody are those of _Lobet den Herren_ ("Praise to the Lord, the almighty").

Die Kirche Jesu ("The Church of Jesus") is the heading for another new hymn in the 1829 edition (1324). This hymn is interesting for its description of the life of the church. Could it have referred to the Brethren as they were in the early nineteenth century?

> Where is the church of Jesus? Where is Christ's yoke taken up gladly? Where is his word still being taught pure? Where is evil still being resisted? Where does the word of God still count more than the host of doctrinal writings? (:1)
> (Answer by the congregation:) We are grieved to confess that we cannot deny that there is still evil among us, but we may also freely profess that all is not lost. For when Elias thought that he was alone, the Lord knew that there were seven thousand. (:2)
> He himself is still in his city, although it has a thousand holes. He whose merciful presence has saved our reputation of being the church of the Father and the Son in spite of all prevailing misery. (:3)

Halleluiah! Halleluiah! The word of the Lord is still there: we baptize as the Lord has taught, the Lord's Supper is not being perverted; also, [church] discipline is still practiced according to the Word wherever necessary, although we do not like to offend [any of our brothers and sisters].   (:4)

The hymn, Dankbar lasst uns Christum preisen (164), which first appeared in 1829, bears the title, Das Amt der Schlüssel ("The office of the keys"). It consists of four long stanzas and sounds more like a versified sermon than anything one would sing. The poet must not have had any known melody for his poem in mind because the reference is to sing it to its "own melody." The office of the keys is given by Christ to his people on earth, it is his way of bestowing grace upon them. With these keys, they can open the door to the poor sinners that they might enjoy his blessing (Heil), but it is also meant to keep out those who are still in sin. "To this end he anoints his servants, for the administering of these rights, that they loose and that they bind, and that they attain heaven's help." After two stanzas dealing with conversion and salvation and instruction as to how these servants of Christ are to go about their tasks, the fourth stanza concludes thus:

Do not mock these rights of the house [of God], o you Christians; the one before whom you speak untruth is God. If you desire to eat the bread of life and yet be unmindful of the testing, if you ignore [your] sins, alas, you eat to [your] judgment. Therefore let everyone be watchful and pray lest he or she stray from the path, and [let everyone] reach out his hand to the brother or sister lest they, too, go astray.   (:4)

There have been other didactic, sermon-like poems among those that might be attributed to Brethren authors. This, however, is the only one thus far that alludes to the "rights of the house" of God, a phrase which is rather reminiscent of the elder Alexander Mack's treatise on Brethren beliefs, The Rights and Ordinances of the House of God.[9]

Five new hymns were printed in Kurtz's editions only. However, they do not distinguish themselves in any way from other texts. They are: Der Herr schickt seine Diener aus (221), Der Herr sei selbst in unsrer Mitt' (222), Ew'ges Evangelium (373), Herr Jesu, sei an diesem Tage (493), and O du Heiliger, Allbarmherziger (946). The first two consist of one stanza each, which may well be stanzas taken out of their original context. A rather unusual plea is found in one of them (221):

The Lord sends out his servants. We find ourselves very weak. O, our common head! Grant that our witness be believed; let [our] shouting penetrate ears and hearts and when we direct [them] to you, appear!

The fourth of these new hymns is appended to a text by Tersteegen, Herr Jesu Christe, mein Prophet (486) and numbered as stanzas eleven through fourteen, even though there is no internal connection between the two hymns. The appended text is a hymn for congregational meetings and contains this significant prayer:

Keep everything that is deliberated this day in your hand and let it be done according to your will so that it may serve to your glory. (493:2)

CONCLUSION

Die Kleine Lieder Sammlung was published at a time when the English language was increasingly being used in Brethren congregations. The new, small format was intended to appeal to those Brethren who had to travel much, either as preachers or in attending meetings, and to those who desired to cultivate their mother tongue, especially young people. The change in format seems to have met with approval, because the last four German and most of the nineteenth-century English hymnals of the Brethren followed this model.

The smaller format of the hymnal resulted in a reduction of the number of hymns and of the number of stanzas. In the first edition, fifty-three hymn-writers are represented with ninety hymns. The character of the hymnal still bears the stamp of Pietism as can be seen from the tables at the end of this chapter. Christoph Dock, eighteenth-century German-American hymn-writer, who may have been a Mennonite, is newly introduced here and three earlier Brethren authors are included. In the edition of 1827, the contemporary German-American Mennonite Christian Herr and the Brethren poet Henrich Danner were introduced. Jakob Danner's Gute Nacht, ihr meine Lieben (462) is found in full in all editions, but Becker's Du armer Pilger wandelst hier (291) did not appear in this hymnal until 1829. The strange fate of Mack's Wo bleiben meine Sinnen (1320) will be described below.

The largest number of significant hymns was added in the 1829 edition. Disappointingly, the editorship of Henry Kurtz made no impact on the content or the quality of this hymnal. As a matter of fact, Kurtz availed himself of the deplorable custom of hymnal publishers of filling half-page spaces with single stanzas taken out of the context of their hymns. The best example for this is provided by Mack, Jr.'s epic passion poem. After having been printed in full in all editions and reprints of Das Kleine Davidische Psalterspiel, a truncated version consisting of the original stanzas I:1, VII:15, VII:8, and VII:2 appears in the four eastern editions (1834, 1836, 1841, 1848) and in two of Kurtz's western editions. Furthermore, stanzas two and three of the truncated hymn are printed as two separate single-stanza "hymns" in the 1829 edition as Nun kommt die Abendstunde (911) and Was soll ich weiter sagen? (1216). As single stanzas, these "hymns" make no sense, especially the latter. Nevertheless, they were subsequently included in several other later editions. Similarly, Liebe, hast du es geboten (779) is not a hymn in its own right but two stanzas lifted from Zinzendorf's well-known Herz und Herz vereint zusammen (500), which latter hymn was not included in Brethren hymnals until 1870.

The most significant of all new unidentified hymns is undoubtedly the baptismal hymn, Diesen Täufling bringen wir (283) which was added to the 1829 edition. At this time in the history of Brethren hymnal publishing, it would not have been surprising to discover songs of the German camp-meeting movement in this hymnal. Fourteen texts that have been identified by various scholars as German camp-meeting songs were indeed published in editions of Die Kleine Lieder Sammlung. Three of these are listed under "Hymns of awakening." They are older German hymns and are newly introduced to Brethren hymnody here. Three other such hymns are found under "Hymns of invitation."

Die Kleine Lieder Sammlung will be remembered for several reasons. First, this was the hymnal that began the long tradition of pocket-sized hymn-books among the Brethren. Although successful from a practical viewpoint it does display the drawbacks of its format. Secondly, it contains four significant hymns. Three were introduced in 1729. The first, a hymn for baptism (283) contains a "litany for trine immersion;" the second is a love-feast hymn (737); the third describes the church around the turn of the nineteenth century (1324). The fourth hymn-text was first introduced in the 1720 hymnal as a hymn probably authored by a Brethren writer. During the years that this hymnal was in use, this hymn, Ihr jungen Helden, aufgewacht (175), became one of the most popular songs of the German camp-meeting movement in America. Although there is no evidence in this hymnal that the Brethren actually sang the new songs of the camp-meeting movement, at least some Brethren must have been familiar with it because, as will be seen in the next chapter, one concerned brother set about to provide such songs for them.

HYMN-WRITERS REPRESENTED IN
DIE KLEINE LIEDER SAMMLUNG
ARRANGED ACCORDING TO HISTORICAL PERIODS AND MOVEMENTS

	Writers	Hymns
REFORMATION:		
Orthodox: Kreuziger.	1	1
COUNTER-REFORMATION: Behm, Lobwasser, Moller, (Nicolai),		
Weingärtner.	4 (5)	4 (5)
THIRTY-YEARS' WAR: Albert, (Bachmeister*), Heermann,		
Held, Rinkart, Rist, Rosenmüller, Wilhelm II.	7 (8)	7 (9)
LATE 17TH CENTURY: Denicke, Gesenius.	2	1
PIETISM:		
Forerunners: Aemilie Juliane, (Birken), Clausnitzer,		
J. Franck, (M. Franck), Gerhardt, Herzog, Homburg,		
Knorr, Sacer, Scheffler, H. Schenk*, Schirmer,		
Weber; Neander (Reformed).	13 (15)	31 (36)
Early Pietists: Drese, Freystein, Laurenti, Schade,		
Schütz.	5	7
Halle and late Pietists: Baumgarten, Bonin, (Francke),		
Freylinghausen, Gotter, Lackmann, Lehr, M. Müller,		
Richter, Winkler, (Woltersdorf*).	9 (11)	12 (20)
Radical Pietists: Annoni.	1	1
Brethren: Knepper.	1	10
Moravians: N. L. Zinzendorf, (R. Zinzendorf*,		
Steinhofer*)	1 (3)	1 (5)
Württemberg Pietists: Gmelin, (F. K. Hiller*),		
P. F. Hiller.	2 (3)	2 (5)
Reformed: Tersteegen.	1	14 (16)
Orthodox: Günther, (Hübner, Menken), Möckel,		
Neumann*, Schmolck.	4 (6)	6 (8)
ENLIGHTENMENT: Klopstock*, (Liebich*).	1 (2)	1 (2)
GERMAN-AMERICANS:		
Brethren: (Becker, H. Danner*), J. Danner,		
(Mack, Jr.)	1 (4)	1 (7)
Mennonites: Dock*, (Herr*).	1 (2)	1 (2)
(Moravians: Loskiel*)	(1)	(1)

HYMN-WRITERS REPRESENTED IN
DIE KLEINE LIEDER SAMMLUNG
ARRANGED ALPHABETICALLY AND NUMBER OF THEIR HYMNS

Aemilie Juliane: 1
Albert: 1
Annoni: 1

(Bachmeister*: 1)
Baumgarten: 1
(Becker: 1)
Behm: 1
(Birken: 1)
Bonin: 1

Clausnitzer: 1

(Danner, H.*: 1)
Danner, J.: 1
Dock*: 1
Drese: 2

Franck, J.: 1 (2)
(Franck, M.: 1)
(Francke: 1)
Freylinghausen: 1 (2)
Freystein: 1

Gerhardt: 3
Gesenius/Denicke: 1
Gmelin: 1
Gotter: 3
Günther: 1

Heermann: 1 (2)
Held: 1
(Herr*: 1)
Herzog: 1
(Hiller, F.K.*: 1)
Hiller, P.F.: 1 (2)
Homburg: 1
(Hübner: 1)

Klopstock*: 1
Knepper: 10
Knorr: 1 (2)
Kreuziger: 1

Lackmann: 1 (2)
Laurenti: 1
Lehr: 1
Lobwasser: 1
(Loskiel*: 1)

(Mack, Jr.: 4)
(Menken: 1)
Möckel: 1
Moller: 1
Müller, M.: 1 (2)

Neander: 9 (11)
Neumann*: 1
(Nicolai: 1)

Richter: 2
Rinkart: 1
Rist: 1
Rosenmüller: 1

Sacer: 1
Schade: 2
Scheffler: 8 (9)
Schenk, H.*: 1
Schirmer: 2
Schmolck: 3
Schütz: 1
(Steinhofer*: 1)

Tersteegen: 14 (16)

Weber: 1
Weingärtner: 1
Wilhelm II.: 1
Winkler: 1
(Woltersdorf*: 4)

Zinzendorf, N.L.: 1 (4)
(Zinzendorf, R.*: 1)

NOTES

[1] Die Kleine Lieder Sammlung, oder Auszug aus dem Psalterspiel der Kinder Zions ... . (Hägerstadt: Gruber und May, 1826).

[2] For a complete translation of the preface, see Appendix IV/1.

[3] Das Aller Neueste Harfenspiel, oder Zugabe einiger Lieder, auf Begehren von J. Engel, P. Eby, C. Grosch und anderen Mitglieder der Vereinigten Brüderschaft in Pennsylvanien (n. p.: 1795).

[4] Don Yoder, Pennsylvania Spirituals (Lancaster: Pennsylvania Folklore Society, 1961), p. 349.

[5] Ada Kadelbach, Die Hymnodie der Mennoniten in Nordamerika (1742-1860) (Mainz: 1971).

[6] A Choice Selection of Hymns, from Various Authors, Recommended for the Worship of God.

[7] John Joseph Stoudt, Pennsylvania German Poetry 1695-1830 (Lancaster: Pennsylvania Folklore Society, 1956), pp. 18-20.

[8] Donald F. Durnbaugh, ed., The Brethren in Colonial America (Elgin, Ill.: The Brethren Press, 1967), pp. 558-560.

[9] Alexander Mack, Kurtze und einfältige Vorstellung, Der äussern aber doch heiligen Rechten und Ordnungen des Hauses Gottes ... ([Berleburg: Christoph Konert?], 1715).

Chapter V

DIE KLEINE PERLEN-SAMMLUNG

The next hymnal to be published for the Brethren was again in the nature of a supplement. J. E. Pfautz compiled a collection of eighty-three hymns which he called Die kleine Perlen-Sammlung ("The Small Collection of Pearls"). It was published at Ephrata, Pennsylvania in 1858. A translation of the title-page reads as follows:

The small collection of pearls or selection of spiritual songs, mostly taken from manuscripts, for the service, use, and edification of all god-loving brothers and sisters in Christ. Compiled in the present small format by J. E. Pfautz.

Praise, ye sisters and brothers / praise with spiritual songs / praise with heart and mouth / praise and make known God's praise.[1]

The verso of the title-page contains a small poem of dedication:

The pearls are now here, collected onto paper. May God lay his blessing upon them that the labor applied here may not have been in vain, but that it be truly turned in every heart, even in this time on earth to truth, power, and life with all who read them.

The reasons for publishing this collection are explained in the preface:

... the small collection appears ... not because of the opinion that there is a dearth in hymn-books. Rather, it is hoped that some who love hymns might be edified by it inasmuch as most of the added hymns were written by pious teachers of the gospel such as Jacob Stoll, William Preis, and others, under whose preaching many brothers and sisters still living used to refresh, delight, and edify themselves. Many of the hymns never appeared in print before ... .[2]

Indeed, all but one of the eighty-three hymns in this collection had never before been printed in any earlier Brethren hymnal. The body of hymns in this small hymnal comprises only 109 pages. The contents are found on page 110. The alphabetical register of first lines takes up pages 111 through 115. In the copy at hand, the verso of page 115 is the title-page for the English A Small Collection of Pearls ..., compiled also by J. E. Pfautz which, however, is not a translation of the former but a separate collection comprising only thirty-seven pages of hymns. The English first-line index is followed by a list of the authors of the German hymn-texts giving the number of the hymn in the German hymnal and the source from which the text was taken.

THE RUBRICS

As might be expected, the rubrics in this small collection are not comprehensive. However, an attempt had been made at arranging them in some order. This order leads from spiritual awakening through exhortation to the fruits and rewards of faith which results in prayer. There is a remnant of two rubrics from the life of Christ and one from the church-year. The order is completed by three rubrics with hymns for various occasions including one general category "On various subjects." Apart from this last rubric, which contains twenty-two hymns, the largest number is found under "Hymns for dying and for funerals" (thirteen), followed by "On the blessed state" (eleven) which deals variously with eternity, the coming glory of life after death, and love for Jesus, and, thirdly, "Hymns of awakening" (ten).

Die kleine Perlen-Sammlung, 1858.

Hymns of awakening (10)
Hymns of exhortation (5)
On the blessed state (11)
Of the desire for Jesus (1)
Of the heavenly homeland (4)
Of the love for Jesus (2)
Prayer-hymns (2)
Praise and thanksgiving (3)
Of the incarnation of Jesus (4)
Of the crucifixion (3)
New Year's hymn (1)
Parting hymn (1)
Hymns about death and for burial (13)
On various subjects (22)

A new element was introduced here into German Brethren hymnody probably due to the influence of the camp-meeting movement earlier in the century. Certain texts reveal the influence of that movement through increased emphasis on the need for conversion and for mending one's ways while there is yet time, on the sorrows in this life and the comfort of looking beyond it to the life to come. Although these themes were certainly not new, the form of the hymns was altered through the addition of refrains and choruses which were perhaps the most characteristic traits of the camp-meeting songs.

DOCUMENTED HYMNS

Only nine of the hymn-writers encountered in earlier hymnals are represented here. Typical entries in the authors' list are: "Written by S. D. Miller," "Composed by a youth on his death-bed," "From B. H. Sasse's Spiritual Songs," "From the Lutheran hymnal," "Poet's name withheld," "From the English, by W. Preiss," "From Ter Stegen's Blumen-Gärtlein," and "Unknown." In twenty cases, the authors' names could be documented in reliable sources. Two hymns which were attributed to W. Preiss had actually been written by P. F. Hiller (653) and H. Danner (846).

In this hymnal, the documented hymns from earlier periods are in the minority. Among the newly introduced hymn-writers are two that were contemporary with Pfautz. The first, Albert Knapp (1798-1864), noted hymnologist and hymn-writer, consistently endeavored to stem the corruption of hymnody by rationalist writers. Nurtured by Württemberg and Moravian Pietism, he was a proponent of the movement in nineteenth-century Germany to renew and revitalize the church. The two hymns contributed by

Knapp (968) and the other nineteenth-century poet, Karl Plank (1801-1825) (289) were probably taken from Hermann's very popular Der Sänger am Grabe (The bard at the graveside),[3] a collection of hymns for the dying and for use at funerals.

For the first time identifiable translations of English hymns were incorporated. Three English-language poets are represented here. The Irishman Thomas Kelly (1769-1854) was a learned evangelical preacher and fine hymn-writer. His "Hark, ten thousand harps and voices" was somewhat freely translated in the original meter by Wilhelm Preiss as Hör viel tausend Harfen (525). Joseph Swain (1761-1796), an engraver from Birmingham, England, was converted by John Rippon (1751-1836), one of the most influential Baptist preachers of his time; Swain became a preacher himself later on. One of his best-known hymns, "O thou in whose presence," was ably translated in the original meter into O Heiland, in dem meine Seele sich freut (966). William Williams (1717-1791), the "sweet singer of Wales," was both a deacon in the established church and a well-known revivalist preacher who wrote hymns both in Welsh and English. His "Guide me, o thou great Jehova" is very beautifully rendered in the original meter as Leite mich, o mein Jehova (776). There is no indication as to the identity of the translators of the last two hymns.

Among the German-American hymns there emerged, also for the first time in Brethren hymnody, revival hymnody in recognizable form. One of the newly introduced hymn-writers is Johannes Walter (1781-1818) whose Wer will mit uns nach Zion gehen (1278) was one of the most popular camp-meeting songs.[4] Pfautz provided an additional chorus for this hymn which is printed at the end of the hymnal. The chorus, O dort wird sein Freude which is printed with the hymn proper, is a translation of the English chorus "O that will be joyful."[5] Two revival songs were taken from Bernhard Heinrich Sasse's collection of spiritual songs and may have been written by him. One is a conversion hymn (725) the other, a prayer-hymn for Christian life and virtues (1063).

NEW AND UNDOCUMENTED HYMNS

In the authors' list several of the new hymns are marked Unbewusst (unknown). One of these can be traced to Philip Friedrich Hiller (632), but five could not be identified (215, 241, 423, 513, 1140). Yoder lists the second and third of these among the Pennsylvania German camp-meeting songs.[6] Five others were marked D. N. v, i.e., "A[uthor's] n[ame] w[ithheld]" (70, 508, 648, 781, 1143). (For a list of the new hymns, see Appendix V/2.) Most of these texts, like the one written "by a young man on his death-bed" (197), are eternity oriented, intended to call people back from their ways to turn to Jesus where they can find comfort in the midst of death and life. The hymn, Mein Leben ist mühsam allhier auf der Erd' (848), written "by a sister in her suffering" is in the same vein:

My life is hard here on this earth, full of heartache and misery and hardship, nothing but sorrow and suffering comes my way, but I trust in Jesus, my only repose.   (:1)
Here I must suffer in manifold ways, outwardly and inwardly I am often full of anxiety, but from all of this my God will deliver me when the time has come, he will lead me out of all misery.   (:2)

Yet often our sufferings are good for us even though according to our nature and flesh we hurt greatly. It prostrates us and makes our spirits humble and causes us to give up our own will. (:3)

But at last all misery will come to an end and blessed will be the one who knows Jesus the savior, who will lead us into peace and joy where there will be love and joy and blessed time. (:4)

One text seems to be using contemporary imagery when describing the way to heaven which had been prepared by Christ:

Faith and repentance worked by love lead pilgrims ... free of charge across into that glorious land ... The Bible functions as engineer in leading the throng ... (241: passim)

This was obviously written during the time of the expansion of the railroad and the migration of many to newly opened territories.

It is assumed that the authors' names which Pfautz listed refer to Brethren, although some of these cannot be so documented. He did not identify the authors of hymns from the stock of German or English hymnody, but only the hymnals from which the hymns were taken. The following is a discussion of the hymn-texts by Brethren authors in this collection.

C. Bamberger

Two hymns are attributed to C. Bamberger. This may have been Christian Bomberger (1801-1880), an elder in the Conestoga congregation.[7] Bleibe bei mir, liebster Seelenfreund (142) is a Jesus hymn on prayer and conversion. The "dearest soul-friend" stands both for Jehova and Jesus. Der Vater, der hat mich gezeugt (240) is about the death of a young child.

Heinrich Danner (1742-before 1814)

Although Pfautz attributes Mein Leben auf Erden ist mühsam allhier (846) to W. Preiss, according to Yoder it was actually written by Heinrich Danner.[8] This is a long hymn of twelve stanzas. The first seven describe the writer's own condition and pilgrimage, the eighth, the joys of heaven. The remaining stanzas admonish the sinner to come to Jesus:

Therefore, o you children, do be pious! O comfortless sinner, welcome! Do come and receive freely mercy upon mercy, because God, who is now inviting you, is very merciful. (:9)

O come from afar and hasten here because God wants so very much to give you peace. Why do you stay away? O do enter! For God wants to be your God, too. (:10)

O do come! Purchase, and that without money; o hasten and hurry from the ends of the world! Let nothing delay you, o do come, all of you! Love is inviting you to the wedding-feast. (:11)

In heaven yonder we shall be truly joyous, when we shall declare: "My A[lpha] and O[mega]! My Lord and my God!" Whoever [would have] believed here what one beholds yonder with [one's] eyes? (:12)

David Gerlach (ca. 1811-1879)

Gerlach was a minister and elder in the Eastern Pennsylvania district and was known as an outstanding preacher. His Schon lang hört' ich ein' Stimm' in mir (1066) reveals good mastery of language and meter. This hymn is about personal conversion which means repentance here and now,

> ... to mourn over one's sins in order to unite onself with God and his son in eternity, to follow God and his word and to renounce oneself in deed, as Jesus himself teaches us.   (:3)

Samuel Grebil (1809-1881)

A minister at White Oak, Pennsylvania, Grebil wrote Ach Gott, wie plagt man sich (19), a hymn of personal confession and conversion. It is written in the style of a revival hymn and describes in the course of fifteen stanzas a personal spiritual pilgrimage.

Jakob Haller (ca. 1777-1865)

A very eloquent preacher, Jakob Haller applied the same gift when writing the text of the hymn printed in this present hymnal (673). It is a doctrinally sound but rather dry teaching hymn about the love of Jesus, which is given the following attributes: it is a light and incomprehensibly great, it frees from sin, it is a beautiful silken garment, it is beautiful, it is one's goal for ever, it is a treasure, it supports, it makes us rich and like the angels, it has shed its [i.e., Jesus'] blood, it gives courage and joy. In three of its seventeen stanzas this hymn deals with Brethren teachings:

> Jesus' love also commands to keep the covenant in baptism. It [i.e., Jesus' love? the covenant?] will prevail in eternity.   (:5)
> Jesus' love is so sweet that it washes the disciples' feet so that one would follow him even though it is quite humiliating to do so.   (:6)
> Jesus' love takes bread and wine. Whoever wishes to be his disciple must follow his examples in all things and obey all his teachings.   (:7)

J. Hoffer

There are no sources to document that J. Hoffer was a Brethren preacher or even a member of the church. As is the case with C. Bamberger and, below, S. D. Miller, the only indication that these writers might be Brethren is the fact that their names were listed along with the others. Hoffer's is a New-Year's hymn that alludes to some of the secular and religious customs of the time.

> Another beautiful New Year has arrived. The good and the pious observe it in the proper way.   (365:1)
> The sinners hail the beginning of the year with drinking and firing of rifles, in great danger [to their souls].   (:2)
> They think no further than just of the world and, alas, are hardly aware of what sustains them still.   (:3)
> The Christians welcome the New Year with praying and beautiful speeches of happiness and danger.   (:4)

They prepare themselves to go out from here, from sadness and suffering, from daily toil.   (:5)
Then they can depart and leave the world behind and go with great joy
to Christ, the hero.   (:6)

Jakob W. Meyer, Sr. (1832-1906)

A hymn of praise comes from the pen of the young Jakob W. Meyer,
later to be elder in the Eastern Pennsylvania district:

God, you are worthy of praise, because you give us at all times, from
heaven and earth, food for the body and the soul.   (421:1)
We exalt your name for all of this now, o God. Laud, praise, and
honor be unto you in time and eternity.   (:2)

A second contribution by the same author, Ihr Kinder, habt Mut (609) is a
hymn of admonition which encourages the believers to hold fast and not
lose sight of the goal and also reminds them of their mortality. It
concludes thus:

Let us then, therefore, turn to the Lord in true repentance, honor him
with all our hearts, both young and old.   (:6)

J. W. Meyer's third hymn in this hymnal (1317) strikes a similar tone
but with more orientation toward eternal life:

O God, help all of us here and remain with us always. Bring us home at
last where there will be no more sorrow.   (:4)
Thus your praise is sung even here by us poor ones, how much more in
your kingdom where we shall be like the angels.   (:5)
Where the beautiful host of angels joyfully walk two by two -- o, how
glorious that will be when we shall at last enter there.   (:6)

Abraham Miller (died 1843)

Abraham Miller was a minister in Mifflin County, Pennsylvania. His
Ehr' sei Gott in der Höh (313) is a Christmas hymn of fourteen stanzas.
The first ten tell the story of the birth of Christ at Bethlehem. The
last four address the people:

Come, then, dear people, call on the name of Jesus and work your
salvation; whoever will follow, come.   (:11)
In heaven, we are to be in a blissful state with Jesus if we were obedi-
ent to his word here.   (:12)
Lord Christ, our hero, is the one who caused these verses to be formed
and made known.   (:13)
O savior of all the world, create in us the new world and close the
ark.   (:14)

S. D. Miller

Thus far, S. D. Miller has remained an unknown hymn-writer who cannot
be documented as Brethren. However, the fact that five of his hymns were
included in this hymnal, taken together with the strong allusion to adult

baptism in one of them, support the assumption that he may have indeed been a member, perhaps even a preacher.

Auf, auf, du junger Mensch (93) is a well-written hymn of admonition consisting of five stanzas. Mention of adult baptism is made in Ihr jungen Helden, auf (601), which has four stanzas:

> You young heroes, arise, leave the whole world behind, follow Jesus through this covenant in your baptism. (:1)
> Whoever believes and is baptized shall be blessed. Such a one has been purchased with Jesus' blood, if he or she honors only him. (:3)

The third of Miller's hymns, Kurz war mein Leben hier auf Erden (760), is about the death of a young child and consists of three stanzas. The last texts are prayer hymns addressing Jesus (988, 993).

Wilhelm Preiss (1789-1849)

The most prolific Brethren hymn-writer was Wilhelm Preiss, or William Price, as his name is known in English. This hymnal includes eleven original texts and five translations of English hymns by this author. Two of the originals and one translation are in the style of Pennsylvania-German camp-meeting songs. However, the mood of longing for the heavenly home which is so characteristic for this type of hymn, pervades most of his other texts also.

Original hymns

Ach kommt, ihr lieben Brüder (37): a hymn of following Jesus. (Three stanzas.)

Einst fiel vom ewigen Erbarmen (333): a hymn about the longing for heaven, the true homeland. (Three stanzas.)

Heimweh fühl' ich, Sohn vom Hause (472): a hymn about heaven, the true home, and about the longing for it. This hymn was written in the style of and sung to a traditional German chorale melody. However, either Preiss himself or Pfautz, the editor, added the chorus, Hallelujah, wir sind auf der Reise heim! This is a direct translation of the English camp-meeting chorus, "Halleluiah, we are on our journey home!"[8] (Three stanzas.)

Ich walle stündlich hin (577): a hymn about the battle, sadness, and trials of life here on earth. The Christian is on the way to eternity where there will be freedom. It is necessary to be watchful and ready. (Three stanzas.)

Ihr Lieben, weinet nicht (616): although grouped with "Hymns of admonition," this hymn is about the sorrow of parting, the anticipation of the joys and peace of eternity after the world, the devil , and sins have been overcome. (Six stanzas.)

Im Grabe ist Ruh' (626): a hymn of comfort for funerals. (Three stanzas.)

Jesus, mein Trost und Heil (704): a hymn of comfort for the pilgrim through this vale of tears. (Seven stanzas.)

Jetzt ist die schöne Gnadenzeit (712): a hymn of awakening and call to conversion. (One stanza.)

Mein Jesu kaufte mich mit Blut (843): a typical camp-meeting song with chorus. (Four stanzas.)

> My Jesus purchased me with blood, he dearly paid for me. All the wrath of hell engulfed him. (:1)
> Thus he overcame hell and death for me and for my benefit. May he reign in my soul and give me much courage. (:2)
> My savior, I recognize you, because you are white and red. Yes, your love urges me, which is as strong as death. (:3)
> Yes, your love urges me to long for you that I, o dear savior, may love you there [in eternity] for ever. (:4)

The chorus following each stanza is a translation of the English camp-meeting chorus "O the lamb, the loving lamb, the lamb on Calvary, the lamb that was slain, yet lives again, to intercede for me."[9]

Was ich euch nun sage hier (1205): a hymn of parting with a strong admonition to use this time of grace well, to be prayerful and watchful. (Six stanzas.)
Wenn mein Gemüt erfüllet ist (1246): a heaven-directed hymn. (Two stanzas.)

Translations

Hör viel tausend Harfen (525): Thomas Kelly's "Hark, ten thousand harps and voices." The first two stanzas are a very good and close, the last two a very free, translation of the original.
Sorgloser Sünder du (1129): the original of this hymn has not been located. It is a typical revival hymn, urging the sinner to come to Jesus before it is too late and the world comes to an end. (Nine stanzas.)
Tochter von Zion, steh auf von Betrübnis (1139): "Daughter of Zion, awake from thy sadness." This is a very close but somewhat clumsy translation. (Three stanzas.) A chorus was added which was not part of the original hymn:

> Daughter of Zion, awake from thy sadness, awake, for thy foes shall oppress thee no more, no more, no more.

Wach auf, mein Herz, und singe nun (1184): the original of this hymn has not been located. If the authors' list did not state that it was a translation, one would assume it to be an original poem. Content and language of this hymn of praise are equally good. (Seven stanzas.)
Wenn nach dem Friedensland wir geh'n (1247): the same comments apply here as to the text above. This hymn is about the heavenly homeland. (Three stanzas.)

Jakob Stoll (1731-1827)

Three hymns included in this hymnal were taken from Jakob Stoll's Geistliches Gewürz-Gärtlein, published at Ephrata, Pennsylvania, in 1806.[10] It may be assumed that these hymns were written by Stoll himself.
Ach, mein Jesu, mein Verlangen (42) is a Jesus-hymn of six stanzas, rather in the style of Baroque poetry with numerous exclamations, sighings, questions, and similar devices.

In der frühen Morgenstund' (630): a morning hymn of praise.

Liebe Seele, lass dir raten (782): this hymn is much more realistic and moralizing than the first although still encumbered with many Baroque conventions such as enumerations and questions:

Dear soul, let me warn you that you are headed for eternity: and your deeds that you have scattered here [like seeds] will follow you. (:1)
Do you love Jesus, the life and the source of peace? Or do you love what is secondary, and have you attained it by kissing it? (:2)
For what we choose here in this dear time of grace is what will give us life throughout eternity. (:3)
There are indeed many things in this wide world that dazzle your eyes and lure you in many ways. (:4)
Pride, temporal vanity, greed and desire are the things that distract the heart from the true goal. (:5)
Therefore it is necessary to wrestle seriously on this narrow pilgrim's path and abstain from everything. Bowed, one ascends to heaven. (:6)
Watching, entreating, sighing, fighting, wrestling, in prayer with God, subduing all evil inclinations -- then everything will be alright with us. (:7)
Then I shall here in this time and there in eternity spread the glory of your name. Prepare me for that only. (:8)
Thus everything will be well with me on my pilgrimage, even all my actions; let them be done to your glory and praise. (:9)

CONCLUSION

Die kleine Perlen-Sammlung was the second German Brethren hymnal that served as a supplement. Its format matches that of Die Kleine Lieder Sammlung, the German hymnal then in use, but since by that time that hymnal was no longer printed, the two were never bound together in one volume. This supplement came closer to including near-contemporary hymnody than did Die Kleine Harfe before it. Numerous hymns came from the pens of well-known Brethren preachers and one by Albert Knapp, a continental German poet still living at the time.

This slim hymn-book is significant for two other reasons. The first is the inclusion, for the first time, of identifiable translations of English hymns, the second, the introduction of camp-meeting songs in their characteristic form. The implications of this for the choice of melodies to be sung are obvious. Although the majority of the hymns were still printed with the conventional German melody references, new texts were to be sung to their own melodies. Such information often included the syllabic structure of the stanza, for example, "6.5.6.5." Camp-meeting songs and choruses, especially those translated from the English, were undoubtedly sung to their original or other suitable new melodies. The same applies to conventional hymns translated from the English.

Thus, although small and modest, Die kleine Perlen-Sammlung can claim some significance in German Brethren hymnody. Seventeen of its thirty-nine new hymn-texts, many of which were written by Brethren, found their way into later German Brethren hymnals. It is noteworthy that only one of these texts appeared in all subsequent hymnals and ten in all but Neue Sammlung, the next German hymnal and the first such authorized by Annual Meeting. Twelve Brethren-authored texts were reprinted in later hymnals

(142, 846, 1066, 673, 365, 760, 472, 577, 712, 1205, 1129, and 782), which
constitutes a high percentage of the new Brethren hymns and, indeed, of
the entire hymnal.

Die kleine Perlen-Sammlung was the last collection of hymns to be
published for the Brethren through private initiative. During the ensuing
years, the annual meetings began to deal with queries related to the use
of hymnals in the church. At last the first hymnal to be compiled by an
officially appointed committee was published in 1867. However, since by
that time the English language was widely used among the Brethren, that
hymnal was in English. Three years later, the first authorized hymnal in
the German language appeared in print, which will be the subject of the
next chapter in this study.

HYMN-WRITERS REPRESENTED IN
DIE KLEINE PERLEN-SAMMLUNG
ARRANGED ACCORDING TO HISTORICAL PERIODS AND MOVEMENTS

	Writers	Hymns
COUNTER-REFORMATION: Helmbold.	1	1
LATE 17TH CENTURY: Bucholtz.	1	1
PIETISM:		
Forerunners: Connow*.	1	1
Halle and late Pietists: Rambach, Rothe, H. T. Schenk*, Woltersdorf.	4	4
Württemberg Pietists: P. F. Hiller.	1	2
Reformed: Tersteegen.	1	1
ENLIGHTENMENT: Diterich, Gellert.	2	3
GERMAN-AMERICANS:		
Brethren: Bamberger?*, H. Danner, Gerlach*, Grebil*, Haller*, Hoffer?*, Meyer*, A. Miller*, S. D. Miller?*, W. Preiss*, Stoll*.	11	31
Evangelicals: Sasse*, Walter.*	2	4
ENGLISH AUTHORS: Kelly*, Swain*, Williams*.	3	3
19TH CENTURY GERMAN AUTHORS:		
Church renewal movement: Hoffmann*, Knapp*.	2	2
Others: Plank*.	1	1

HYMN-WRITERS REPRESENTED IN
DIE KLEINE PERLEN-SAMMLUNG
ARRANGED ALPHABETICALLY AND NUMBER OF THEIR HYMNS

Bamberger*: 2
Bucholtz: 1

Connow*: 1

Danner, H.: 1
Diterich: 1

Gellert: 2
Gerlach*: 1
Grebil*: 1

Haller*: 1
Helmbold: 1

Hiller, P.F.: 2
Hoffer*: 1
Hoffmann*: 1

Kelly*: 1
Knapp*: 1

Meyer*: 3
Miller, A.*: 1
Miller, S.D.*: 5

Plank*: 1
Preiss, W.*: 11

Rambach: 1
Rothe: 1

Sasse*: 1
Schenk, H.T.*: 1
Stoll*: 3
Swain*: 1

Tersteegen: 1

Walter*: 1
Williams*: 1
Woltersdorf: 1

NOTES

1 *Die kleine Perlen-Sammlung, oder Auswahl Geistreicher Lieder* ... (Ephrata: J. E. Pfautz, 1858).

2 For a complete translation of the preface, see Appendix V/1.

3 [Charles G. Hermann], *Der Sänger am Grabe. Eine Auswahl Lieder zum Gebrauch bei Leichenbegängnissen, wie auch Trost-Lieder für solche, die um geliebte Tote trauern* (Philadelphia, Pa.: J. Rohr, 1851).

4 Don Yoder, *Pennsylvania Spirituals* (Lancaster: Pennsylvania Folklore Society, 1961), p. 349.

5 Ellen Jane Lorenz, *Glory, Hallelujah! The Story of the Campmeeting Spiritual* (Nashville: Abingdon, 1978), p. 88.

6 Yoder, p. 372, 399.

7 *History of the Church of the Brethren of the Eastern District of Pennsylvania* (Lancaster, Pa.: New Era Printing Co., 1915), p. 366-367.
   Information on the other Brethren hymn-writers in this chapter may also be found in this source.

8 Yoder, p. 406.

9 Lorenz, p. 92.

10 Lorenz, p. 106.

11 J[akob] St[o]ll, *Geistliches Gewürz-Gärtlein Heilsuchender Seelen; Oder kurz-gefassten Betrachtungen ... Nebst einem Anhang, Bestehend aus Geistlichen Lieder und Andachten* (Ephrata: Johannes Baumann, 1806).

CHAPTER VI

NEUE SAMMLUNG

About the middle of the nineteenth century the Brethren began taking
a critical look at their hymnals. A query was brought before the Annual
Meeting of 1849 asking whether the hymn-books then in use might not be
improved by a better selection of hymns. These hymnals were, for the
German-speaking Brethren, Die Kleine Lieder Sammlung and Das Kleine
Davidische Psalterspiel and, for the English-speaking members, A Choice
Selection of Hymns[1] and the earlier The Christian's Duty[2] with its
supplement, A Selection of Hymns[3]. The response of Annual Meeting was,
however, that the currently used hymnals served the Brethren's purpose
very well.[4] Nine years later, the question was raised again and referred
to the next Annual Meeting.[5]

At long last, in 1860, Annual Meeting appointed a committee of five
consisting of James Quinter, Samuel Garber, John Metzger, John H. Umstad,
and John Kline, who were to compile a new (English) hymn-book.[6] However,
the following year, Annual Meeting postponed the revision of the hymn-
books.[7] When a new hymnal was at last published, it was A Collection of
Psalm, Hymns, and Spiritual Songs, which came to be known as "The
Brethren's Hymnal."[8] Considerable resistance to the use of this hymnal
arose in congregations where the German language was still spoken and the
need was expressed for a hymnal that contained both English and German
hymns. Binding a small collection of the choicest German hymns with the
new English hymnal would avoid the necessity of carrying more than one
hymn-book to church. Thus, Annual Meeting appointed a committee
consisting of Paul Wetzel, Henry Kurtz, F. P. Loehr, and D. M. Holsinger
"to select a number of German hymns, not exceeding two hundred, to be
added to as many of the English books as it is necessary to supply the
want of the German Brethren."[9]

Two hundred hymn-texts are not very many. Consequently, on behalf of
the committee, Henry Kurtz asked the 1869 Annual Meeting for permission to
select a larger number. This request was denied despite the fact that the
German members were very anxious to see the hymn-book completed.[10] Finally, in 1870, James Quinter published a slim, pocket-sized German hymnal
containing 303 hymns entitled: Neue Sammlung von Psalmen, Lobgesängen und
Geistlichen Liedern.[11] This "New collection of psalms, hymns of praise
and spiritual songs" was published for die Alten Brüder or "old Brethren."
It contained only the text of the hymns; music was not yet printed in
Brethren hymnals. Henry Kurtz as one of the compilers and editors wrote a
long preface which is given here in full.

Beloved friends and fellow-pilgrims, brothers and sisters in the Lord,
peace! For more than a century the Davidische Psalterspiel has been in
general use and much appreciated by our brotherhood. It was probably
printed first by our dear, long departed Brother Christopher Sauer in
Germantown, Pennsylvania, and by his descendants after that. In its
last editions it contained 634 hymns among which were several of twenty, thirty, even one of over one hundred stanzas which, however, made

it very heavy and cumbersome when traveling. This caused several Brethren near Hagerstown, Maryland, about forty years ago, to publish Die Kleine Lieder Sammlung, which we have been using up to now. Originally it contained only 140 hymns but was later enlarged to 175. Nevertheless, it was not quite satisfactory.

Since the English hymnals had also become too large, the Kleine Lieder Sammlung was followed by a small English book of the same size and format [A Choice Selection of Hymns]. Both were frequently bound together into one volume and generally met with great approval, except where English was used exclusively. There the demands for a better and more complete hymnal were voiced the loudest. Consequently, a few years ago, "A Collection of Psalms, Hymns, and Spiritual Songs, &c. Covington, Miami County, Ohio, Published by James Quinter" appeared in print. It sold well and was accepted in almost all congregations, East and West, North and South, which it deserved, being a complete and excellent work that contains 818 hymns.

Now this writer was asked as early as 1867 to prepare a German work of similar character and format so that it could be bound with the former and be equal to its stature. However, as this writer, due to his advanced age and then poor health did not wish to undertake this by himself, the Brethren Paul Wetzel, F. P. Löhr, and Daniel M. Holsinger were appointed at the annual meeting of 1868 to serve as a committee. They were to select two hundred hymns for this purpose.

This was done at a meeting in August of last year. But instead of selecting only two hundred, they came up with 325 and felt justified to use the larger number and shorten some hymns, since in all the world two halves or three thirds count only for one whole and the committee was convinced that only in this way could the needs of the congregations be met.

The manuscript was prepared accordingly, exactly as the book was to appear in print, page by page. Already in the English book there were several instances where smaller print was used with individual hymns, such as nos. 30, 121, 123, 139, etc. We hoped to do the same when and where it became necessary in order to retain the same arrangement of the pages.

If this simple rule had been observed from the beginning, this book would have taken on a different form. It is the fault of the editor [i.e., Kurtz], that it was not communicated to the type-setter, because he thought that it had been done orally. Forgive him this omission, dear Brethren, and do not let this cause you to despise the good which is contained in this little book. If we had had more space it would have been better looking in layout and type. God's blessing be with all of you.

In the name of the Committee,
Henry Kurtz.
Columbiana, O., February 1870.

THE RUBRICS

The arrangement of the rubrics in this hymnal does not resemble any of the earlier ones, nor does it follow any consistent general plan as can be seen below. Numbers in parentheses refer to numbers of hymns in each category.

Neue Sammlung, 1870.

Several psalm hymns (9)
General hymns of supplication, praise, and thanksgiving, as well as for
   the beginning and the closing of the meeting (15)
For family and private devotions:
   Morning hymns (11)
   Evening hymns (10)
   Seasons of the year and times of the day (3)
   Table-songs (7)
Christian beliefs [Glaubenslehren des Christentums]:
   God's being, nature, and perfection (5)
   Man's sin and salvation (6)
   Christ's incarnation and birth (6)
   Christ's name and offices (5)
   Christ's life and conduct (3)
   Christ's suffering and death (8)
   Christ's resurrection and ascension (7)
   Christ's coming again (4)
More Jesus hymns (6)
Of the Holy Spirit and his workings (6)
Of the Word of God and the gospel (6)
The church [Gemeinde] of Jesus (6)
The teaching office (4)
True and false Christendom (3)
Of prayer (3)
Of holy baptism (6)
Of holy foot-washing (3)
Love-feast and communion (11)
Penitence, faith, and new birth (13)
The new life in love and sanctification (7)
Spiritual battle and victory (10)
Denial of self and the world (5)
Hope and trust in God and Christ (6)
Hymns of awakening and invitation (17)
Hymns of encouragement and consolation (12)
Self-examination and preparation for death and eternity (7)
Death and burial (12)
Resurrection, judgment and eternal life (12)
Appendix of miscellaneous hymns (42)
Some more Brethren hymns (7)

In this hymnal there is again a rubric of "Hymns of awakening and invitation," which is the largest of the categories. Only five of these hymn-texts, however, are written in the style of German camp-meeting songs (602, 729, 740, 878, 1131). Scattered throughout the hymnal in various categories are another twenty-seven hymns the texts of which were used by the German camp-meeting movement. One hymn by Heinrich Danner, which had become a popular camp-meeting song, was grouped more appropriately in this hymnal with "Some more Brethren hymns." In the body of the hymnal, this rubric is introduced as follows:

Although there is reason to believe that some of the preceding hymns [in the rubric, "Appendix of miscellaneous hymns"] were written by Brethren, their names are not known. Those that follow here are inserted in memory of their long deceased authors, abbreviated but with the names given.

This rubric contains six hymns by Brethren authors that were documented earlier (291, 331, 470, 665, 1202, 1205). The hymn, Ich bin ein Herr, der Sünd' vergibt (540), which introduces this group of Brethren hymns, is ascribed to "Alexander Mack sen.", but was actually written by Joachim Neander. Jesu, auferstand'ner Held (655), an Easter hymn, is attributed to Alexander Mack, Jr. Although the authorship cannot be documented, this hymn, which is discussed below, may well have been written by Mack, Jr.

Among the miscellaneous hymns, there are only three new undocumented texts (21, 640, 1099); three had appeared as new undocumented texts in earlier Brethren hymnals (26, 225, 599).

DOCUMENTED HYMNS

At first glance it appears that the composition of this hymnal regarding documented hymns closely follows the earlier pattern. The favorite hymn-writers are still Tersteegen (eleven hymns), Scheffler (ten hymns), and Neander (eight hymns). Luther is represented only by his Erhalt uns, Herr, bei deinem Wort (343). All but one of the Brethren hymns had appeared in earlier Brethren hymnals.

The number of newly-introduced hymn-writers had levelled off to about one fourth of the total number of authors represented in this hymnal. On the other hand, more English hymns in translations were incorporated here than at any time before. The history of the most famous hymn by the English Baptist minister, David Denham (1791-1848) ilustrates what often happened to texts in evangelical hymnody. "'Mid scenes of confusion and creature complaints" became, by way of translation, the German hymn, Bei aller Verwirrung und Klage allhier (127). This version, in turn, seems to have been used both as a churchly hymn and as a German camp-meeting spiritual with an additional chorus. The chorus, in its turn, is a direct translation of an independent English camp-meeting chorus, "Home, home, sweet, sweet home! Prepare me, dear savior, for glory, my home." The German rendition of this, Heim! heim! ach, nur heim! copied the English meter exactly and was probably sung to the same melody but had different endings for the separate stanzas.

UNDOCUMENTED HYMNS

Among a total of 303 hymns, there are twenty-five in this hymnal that cannot be documented elsewhere. It is possible that some of these were written by Brethren, although there is no external evidence to support this assumption. (For a list of the undocumented hymns, see Appendix VI.)

Baptism

One hymn among those "On holy baptism," alludes rather clearly to adult baptism:

> Come, Father, Son, and Holy Ghost, honor now your means of grace. Prove that that which has been called apostolic was instituted by you yourself. (736:1)
> Reveal, o Father, your Son to those who are now standing before you. Open to them the mystery of the purifying grace. (:3)
> O that the souls who have now been baptized into the name of Jesus might feel the grace which you, o Lord, have purchased for them through your blood. (:5)

The Lord's Supper

Only one text among those for "Love-feast and communion" remains undocumented. It barely fits into this category. This hymn (31) opens with the words, Ach, ich Sündenwurm der Erden, with which the poet is referring to himself as a sinful worm on this earth. The first three stanzas contemplate the atoning work of Christ. The fourth is probably the one which qualified this particular hymn for this rubric:

> Give me, a poor creature, drink of your blood, [for] it breaks the power of sin. It can warm my heart and create new life. O fill and sweeten me with this sap of life! (:4)

Foot-Washing

One new hymn was added to two earlier (Brethren-authored?) texts in the rubric "Of holy foot-washing." Herr Jesu, der du in der Nacht (489) is a very long and didactic hymn of thirteen stanzas. It was written to the complicated meter of Wie schön leuchtet der Morgenstern. Consequently, there are many very awkward passages due to the incompatibility of meter and text. Furthermore, the jubilant melody does not suit the contemplative text at all. The heading for this hymn reads: "John 13, a rhymed paraphrase." Within the hymn, however, there are also scripture references to Luke 22:24 (:2), Luke 22:31, John 17:12, and John 12:4-6 (:8). At the end of the hymn a source reference states that it was "written from a manuscript, August 1829." The hymn concludes with some strong polemics and a firm resolution:

> You despisers, tell us what it is that moves you to heap shame and despicable mockery [Spott] upon us because we obey this word. If we overdo it, know then that we do it unto God. Therefore, whoever acts so boldly and does not walk in the way of Christ, beware of [God's] displeasure. (:12)
> Therefore, o Lord Jesus Christ, we are minded to serve you according to your word at all times among your members and gladly follow your example, and return our brothers' love without pride and haughtiness, so that you, o Jesus, might recognize us and call us by name as those who are yours, who are a bright light unto the world. (:13)

The Church

Although they are not all found in this category, three new hymns address themselves to the topic of the church. The first is a teaching hymn (161) but is relatively free of the tedium that usually accompanies this style:

Christ is the head of the church who believes in his name. She holds him to be her husband and clings to him in love. (:1)
He recognizes her as his wife and loves her as his own body, nourishes and cares for her, is her Lord and never deserts her. (:2)
To make her holy, he washed her in the blood. Her magnificent wedding gown is the righteousness of the Lord. (:3)
You foes, do not touch her, for he who is able [to do so] will punish you. You, o church, remain faithful to him only; your savior sets you free. (:4)
Jesus, I too am a member that draws life from you. Adorn me most beautifully with your blood so that I might go along on that wedding day. (:5)

Noch ist der Herr in seiner Stadt (896) uses the metaphor of the city in speaking of the church:

The Lord is still within his city, although she has a thousand holes [Lücken]. It is he who delighted his Zion and is today renewing his church. (:1)
You are helping us freely to confess on earth as in heaven that nothing else saves the sinner but that you died on the cross. (:2)
We still baptize as you taught it and your supper remains inviolate. O help us, Lord, that the power of both may work true fruits in us. (:3)

This text borrows several lines from the undocumented hymn, new in 1829, Wo ist die Kirche Jesu doch (1324).

The last hymn, O dass ob dieser Gnadenstätt' (941) is found among the "Hymns of praise and thanksgiving." It is an invocation of the power of the word of God through the holy spirit concluding as follows:

You brothers, surrender to the Lord, let us follow Jesus only. You sisters, live quietly unto the savior who will adorn you royally. (:4)
O let us all walk in unity through this beautiful time of grace, and never live divided. (:5)

The Trinity

Generally speaking, there have not been many undocumented hymns specifically on the trinity, but occassionally the triune God is addressed in a last stanza as in a doxology. Neig, o mein Gott, dein Ohr zur mir (889), a doctrinally sound hymn, is one of the few that address the trinity:

Incline, o my God, your ear to me! I, mere earth and ashes, am entreating you -- I, a sinner, am entreating you! O do not turn your merciful countenance from me! (:1)

You, o Father, in your good work did create even me in your image.
When I lost it, you renewed me in your Son.   (:2)
Now you, who did not cast me off, are giving me each day what I need.
Many times you have saved me in the hour when I least expected it. (:3)
God the Son, you have purchased me through your blood from the eternal
fire. It is you who mightily intercedes for me. In pain, my comfort,
in night, my light.   (:4)
God the Holy Spirit, only your power can work good in sinners. If
there is any good to be found in me it is truly your work.   (:5)
Through you it is that I came to know God and Christ whom he has sent
on my behalf, and that I rejoice in the true teaching in the word of
the cross.   (:6)
Absolve me of all my guilt and continue to bear with me in patience.
If I should err, do not cast me off but lead me back to my duty yourself.   (:7)

Christ's Incarnation and Birth

Among the seven hymns on Christ's incarnation and birth, one is
undocumented. Like several of those described above, it is rather concise, sparse, yet lively and singable:

You sinners all, rejoice in God who became human like you, in the word
which came to earth and assumed your flesh and blood.   (617:1)
The word was itself the true God who had created all things. Through
him, all that is in the whole circle of the wide world has its being.
                                                                     (:2)
He created the human being pure and beautiful, reflecting his own
image. But through Satan's cunning and envy this blessed state was
lost.   (:3)
Yes, hear and ponder this aright, God is doing a work that nobody would
have expected: in the fullness of time he has clothed himself with our
humanity.   (:4)
Why is it that he becomes a child? So that he might shed his blood.
Thanks be to him, he has finished it, for his death has brought us
life.   (:5)
Therefore let us all be glad and dedicate our hearts to the child who
has brought peace to earth and is called Jesus because he saves.   (:6)

Christ's Resurrection

The Easter hymn, Jesu, auferstand'ner Held (655) is attributed in
this hymnal to Alexander Mack, Jr. It was first published by Christoph
Sauer II in the second edition of the elder Alexander Mack's treatise
popularly known as Grundforschende Fragen, 1774.[12] On the last pages of
this book, Sauer printed as an addendum (Beylage) "A Letter Concerning
Foot-Washing" (Ein Brief wegen dem Fusswaschen) by Mack, Jr. and the hymn
under discussion, entitled Oster-Lied. Whereas the name of Alexander Mack
appears at the end of the letter, the hymn is not attributed to any
author. Sauer, a close friend of the younger Mack, had printed many of
the latter's religious poems and hymns in his periodical publication Ein
Geistliches Magazien.[13] If this hymn was indeed written by Mack, Jr., it
is somewhat puzzling why Sauer did not attach Mack's pen-name, Theophilus,
to it as he had done in the Magazien. Another anonymous hymn, Ich bin ein
Herr, der Sünd' vergibt (540), mentioned above, was added by the same

publisher to the elder Mack's <u>Rechte</u> <u>und</u> <u>Ordnungen</u>, 1774.[14] The authorship of this hymn, however, although in the present hymnal ascribed to
Alexander Mack, Sr., can be disproven. In both instances, authorship may
have been attributed by association with the authors of the publications
to which they were appended. Although the hymnal publishers were wrong in
one instance, they may have been right in the case of the Easter hymn. It
is, however, surprising that Heckman did not include this text in his book
on the religious poetry of Alexander Mack.

Given the fact that thus far it has not been possible to document
this hymn in any available source, it is not unreasonable to look for
internal evidence pointing to the authorship of Mack, Jr. The hymn is a
rhymed, very detailed narrative of the resurrection story involving numerous biblical characters and events extending over forty-one stanzas.
These features are very much in keeping with Mack's style of religious
poetry. One need only read some of the texts printed in Heckman's book to
sense the same author behind them. The authorship of Alexander Mack, Jr.
of this hymn will be accepted on the same basis and with the same reser-
vation as with <u>Wo</u> <u>bleiben</u> <u>meine</u> <u>Sinnen</u> (1320). It is felt that in these
two cases it is safe to overrule the basic guideline applied in this study
of not accepting authors' names printed in hymnals as authoritative until
such a time when authorship can be documented definitively.

In Brethren hymnals, only the first four stanzas of the hymn under
discussion were ever printed. Although they do not represent a completely
developed idea, they are the only stanzas capable of being made into a
shorter hymn:

> Jesus, risen hero, king without equals [<u>sonderbarer</u> <u>König</u>], at last all
> the world will be subject to you, for you have mightily defeated
> Satan's power and joyfully displayed the glory of your victory. (:1)
> Royal spirit of David, you have overcome; you have found life even in
> death: therefore I shall all my life long joyfully go wherever your
> people exalts you with hymns of praise. (:2)
> Our Joseph is still alive, he will feed us, o you unenlightened ones,
> listen! God will present us with a rich Easter bounty in the kingdom
> of grace. That is why he is having us invited yet today to the
> wedding. (:3)
> Whoever has truly mourned his or her sinful being can be healed in God
> through Jesus' heroic deed. The power of Christ's resurrection
> strengthens our faith; wherever thorns have been removed, sweet grapes
> can grow. (:4)

The next six stanzas deal with the story of the women ("Christ's
sisters") at the empty tomb and later, when they encounter the risen
Christ. This is followed by ten stanzas describing Christ's appearances
among the asesmbled disciples and on the way to Emmaus. Stanzas twenty-
one through twenty-four are devoted to the story of Thomas. The remainder
summarizes the resurrection passages in the gospels of Matthew, Mark,
Luke, and John.

A practice of nineteenth-century hymnal publishers encountered
earlier in this study was that of lifting one or more stanzas (not necessarily in their original sequence) from other hymns and printing them as
hymn-texts in their own right. In many cases an obvious loss of meaning

occurred as was the case, for example, with Mack Jr.'s hymn, Wo bleiben meine Sinnen (1320). Such "hymns" can be identified only through chance recognition. In this hymn-book there is at least one such "new" hymn name-ly, Halte deine Krone feste (469), which consists of four stanzas that are actually stanzas nine through twelve of Ringe recht, wenn Gottes Gnade (1050) by Johann Joseph Winkler (1670-1722). The hymn proper entered Brethren hymnody in 1720. Yoder shows that it was one of the eighteen most popular German camp-meeting songs of the early nineteenth century.[15] It is possible that this "hymn" had its origin in the custom of creating new songs by shortening longer ones or as composites of stanzas from several different hymns. It will be seen later that even the shortened Easter hymn discussed above became the source for two such truncated "hymns" lifted from others.

Another undocumented hymn of one stanza may have had a similar history although its original has not yet been found. This is the hymn, So lass dein Bild aufgehen (1119) under "The new life in love and sancti-fication:"

So let then your likeness arise from which we have turned away and let our will remain under your strict rule and in your hand, so that we might live in divine purity and strive for that nature in which you yourself live in us.

CONCLUSION

After 150 years of hymnal-publishing through private initiative, Neue Sammlung was the first German hymnal of the Brethren to be authorized by the Annual Meeting and compiled by an appointed committee. It appeared in 1870, three years after its English counterpart and was published both separately as well as bound with A Collection of Psalms, Hymns, and Spiritual Songs. In either case, the format was small and compact enough to fit easily into a coat pocket. As before, only the words were printed. Although still strongly oriented towards Pietism, this hymnal's compilers seemed to have made an effort at including more recent hymns. There is some representation of European and American nineteenth-century hymnody both in the conventional as well as the evangelical idiom. Several hymns were borrowed from English hymnody through translations. Occasionally in the main body of the hymnal and in all cases in the appendix of Brethren hymns, the texts are attributed to certain authors, although not always correctly. The two tables below provide an overview of the hymn-writers and their hymns contained in this hymnal. Asterisks denote authors appearing here for the first time in Brethren hymnody.

Despite the many years of preparation and the great efforts of the appointed committee, the membership was not completely satisfied. The trials and errors of one particular district's leaders who attempted to remedy the situation for themselves will be described in the following chapter.

HYMN-WRITERS REPRESENTED IN
NEUE SAMMLUNG
ARRANGED ACCORDING TO HISTORICAL PERIODS AND MOVEMENTS

	Writers	Hymns
REFORMATION:		
Czech Brethren: Herbert*.	1	1
COUNTER-REFORMATION: Behm, Höfel*, Lobwasser,		
Nicolai, Ringwald.	5	5
THIRTY-YEARS' WAR: Albert, Heermann, Held, Rist,		
Rosenmüller, Sonnemann, Wilhelm II.	7	7
LATE 17TH CENTURY: Denicke, Gesenius.	2	2
PIETISM:		
Forerunners: Aemilie Juliane, Birken, M. Franck,		
Gerhardt, Herzog, Homburg, Liscow, Ludämilie		
Elisabeth, Neumark*, B. Prätorius, Sacer,		
Scheffler, Schirmer, Scriver, Weber; Neander		
(Reformed).	16	37
Early Pietists: Drese, Freystein, Laurenti,		
Mentzer*, Schade, Schütz.	6	10
Halle and late Pietists: Bogatzky*, Freylinghausen,		
Gotter, Kunth*, Lackmann, M. Müller, Rambach,		
Ruopp, H. T. Schenk, Schwedler, Winkler,		
Woltersdorf.	12	22
Radical Pietists: Annoni.	1	1
Brethren: Knepper.	1	5
Moravians: N. L. Zinzendorf.	1	5
Württemberg Pietists: P. F. Hiller, Pfeil*.	2	18
Reformed: Tersteegen.	1	13
Orthodox: Adolph*, Günther, Hübner, Löscher,		
Möckel, Neumann, Schmolck, Schrader*, Stübner,		
Sturm*.	10	16
ENLIGHTENMENT: Claudius*, Diterich, Gellert, Klopstock,		
Lavater*, Liebich, Schlegel.	7	13
GERMAN-AMERICANS:		
Brethren: Becker, H. Danner, J. Danner, Mack, Jr.,		
Naas, W. Preiss.	6	9
Moravians: Loskiel.	1	1
Evangelicals: Bertolet*, Dreisbach*, Orwig*, Sasse,		
Walter.	5	11
Others: Jörgens.	1	1
ENGLISH AUTHORS: Addison*, Denham*, Newton*, Watts*,		
C. Wesley*.	5	9
19TH-CENTURY GERMAN AUTHORS:		
Church renewal movement: Bahnmeier*, Conz*, Hoffmann,		
Knapp, Schlatter*, C. H. Zeller*.	6	6

HYMN-WRITERS REPRESENTED IN
NEUE SAMMLUNG
ARRANGED ALPHABETICALLY AND NUMBER OF THEIR HYMNS

Addison*: 1
Adolph*: 1
Aemilie Juliane: 1
Albert: 1
Annoni: 1

Bahnmeier*: 1
Becker: 1
Behm: 1
Bertolet*: 2
Birken: 1
Bogatzky*: 1

Claudius*: 1
Conz*: 1

Danner, H.: 1
Danner, J.: 1
Denham*: 1
Diterich: 1
Dreisbach*: 3
Drese: 3

Franck, M.: 1
Freylinghausen: 1
Freystein: 1

Gellert: 4
Gerhardt: 4
Gesenius/Denicke: 2
Gotter: 3
Günther: 1

Heermann: 1
Held: 1
Herbert*: 1
Herzog: 1

Hiller, P.F.: 17
Höfel*: 1
Hoffmann: 1
Homburg: 1
Hübner: 1

Jörgens*: 1

Klopstock: 2
Knapp: 1
Knepper: 5
Kunth*: 1

Lackmann: 2
Laurenti: 2
Lavater*: 1
Liebich: 2
Liscow: 1
Lobwasser: 1
Löscher*: 2
Loskiel: 1
Ludämilie Elis.: 2

Mack, Jr.: 3
Mentzer*: 1
Möckel: 1
Müller, M.: 3

Naas: 2
Neander: 8
Neumann: 1
Neumark*: 1
Newton*: 1
Nicolai: 1

Orwig*: 3

Pfeil*: 1
Prätorius, B.: 1
Preiss, W.: 1

Rambach: 2
Ringwald: 1
Rist: 1
Rosenmüller: 1
Ruopp: 1

Sacer: 1
Sasse: 2
Schade: 2
Scheffler: 10
Schenk, H.T.: 1
Schirmer: 2
Schlatter*: 1
Schlegel: 2
Schmolck: 6
Schrader*: 1
Schütz: 1
Schwedler: 1
Scriver: 1
Sonnemann: 1
Stübner*: 1
Sturm*: 1

Tersteegen: 13

Walter: 1
Watts*: 3
Weber: 1
Wesley, C.*: 3
Wilhelm II: 1
Winkler: 2
Woltersdorf: 4

Zeller, C.H.*: 1
Zinzendorf, N.L.: 5

NOTES

[1] *A Choice Selection of Hymns from Various Authors Recommended to all Denominations for the Worship of God* (Gettysburg, Pa.: H. C. Neinstedt, 1834).

[2] *The Christian's Duty, Exhibited in a Series of Hymns* ... (Germantown: Peter Leibert, 1791).

[3] *A Selection of Hymns from Various Authors, Supplementary for the Use of Christians* (Germantown: John Leibert and G. and D. Billmeyer, 1816).

[4] *Minutes of the Annual Meetings of the Church of the Brethren. Containing All Available Minutes from 1778 to 1909.* Published by The General Mission Board Under Authority of Annual Conference, June 1-3, 1909. (Elgin, Ill.: Brethren Publishing House, 1909), p. 112. (*Minutes*, 1849, art. 38.)

[5] *Ibid.*, p. 172. (*Minutes*, 1858, art. 23.)

[6] *Ibid.*, p. 197. (*Minutes*, 1860, art. 9.)

[7] *Ibid.*, p. 203. (*Minutes*, 1861, art. 14.)

[8] *A Collection of Psalms, Hymns, and Spiritual Songs; Suited to Various Kinds of Christian Worship; and Especially Designed for and Adapted to the Fraternity of the Brethren* ... (Covington, Miami Co., Ohio: James Quinter, 1867).

[9] *Minutes of the Annual Meetings*, p. 272. (*Minutes*, 1868, art. 18.)

[10] *Ibid.*, p. 283. (*Minutes*, 1869, art. 25.)

[11] *Neue Sammlung von Psalmen, Lobgesängen und Geistlichen Liedern* ... (Covington, Miami Co., Ohio: James Quinter, 1870).

[12] Alexander Mack, *Eberhard Ludwig Gruber's Grundforschende Fragen* ... (Baltimore: Christoph Sauer, 1774), p. 37-41.

[13] *Ein Geistliches Magazien* ... (Germantown: Christoph Sauer, 1764 and 1770).

[14] Alexander Mack, *Kurtze und einfältige Vorstellung, Der ässern aber doch heiligen Rechten und Ordnungen* ... (Germantown: Christoph Sauer, 1774), p. [100].

[15] Don Yoder, *Pennsylvania Spirituals* (Lancaster, Pennsylvania: Pennsylvania Folk Life Society, 1961), p. 349.

CHAPTER VII

DAS CHRISTLICHE GESANG-BUCH

As was shown in the preceding chapter, the great efforts of the
hymnal committee appointed by Annual Meeting had finally resulted in the
publication by James Quinter of one English and one German hymnal, namely,
A Collection of Psalms, Hymns, and Spiritual Songs, better known as The
Brethren's Hymnal (1867) and Neue Sammlung von Psalmen, Lobgesängen und
Geistlichen Liedern (1870). These two hymnals were to have provided all
the congregations with uniform hymn-books. Still, a considerable number
of congregations preferred the earlier ones, so that, in some areas, a
variety of hymnals continued to be used in the meetings. Consequently, a
query was brought before the Annual Meeting of 1872 requesting that action
be taken to recommend that only one hymnal, which was to consist of the
two new Quinter publications, be used in Brethren congregations. In
response the congregations were reminded that these new hymnals had after
all met on the whole with satisfaction, that official sanction had been
given, and their use by all members been recommended.[1]

Thus the two publications were declared the official hymnals of the
church and the excuse offered by some congregations for not using the new
hymnals was eliminated. However, dissatisfaction in this matter continued
in the Eastern District of Pennsylvania until in 1874 a separate hymnal,
Das Christliche Gesang-Buch, was published under the district's auspices.[2]
It contained 399 hymns.

The various hymnals in use among the Brethren at that time are enumer-
ated in the preface. These were: Das kleine Davidische Psalterspiel; the
very popular Die kleine Perlen-Sammlung; the "Hymn-Book of the New
Brethren" (probably Eine Sammlung von Geistlichen Liedern, the River
Brethren hymnal which was published in the same year and place as Das
Christliche Gesang-Buch;[3] "Das Viole" (i.e., Die Geistliche Viole, an
important hymnal of the evangelical camp-meeting movement);[4] the hymnals
of the Winebrennerians and of the United Brethren; Jacob Erb's Eine Sammlung von Geistlichen, Lieblichen Liedern;[5] and "Der Sänger" (probably Der
Christliche Sänger).[6] Neue Sammlung is not mentioned.

The preface, which is written in the simplest verse form, concludes
with the statement that the compilers had asked and received permission
for this undertaking and, since many of the church members sang in
English, they had added some English hymns at the end, "so that no one
would be cheated."[7] However, even this hymnal did not meet with the full
and general approval among those Brethren who had felt the need for its
publication as is evident from the preface to the second edition five
years later:

It is a widespread custom for every book to contain a preface and this
was indeed the case with the first edition of this hymn-book. However,
the said preface was not found to be appropriate for a second edition
which had become necessary due on the one hand to the many errors in

the old book and, on the other, because there was demand for it but no more copies left.[8]

The revision affected most the appendix of hymns which in the first edition consisted virtually in its entirety of the poems by the Württemberg Pietist Philipp Friedrich Hiller (1699-1769).

THE RUBRICS

The rubrics are listed as the table of contents. With very few exceptions, the headings and the numbers of hymns in each category (given in parentheses below), though not necessarily the hymns themselves, are the same in both editions.

Das Christliche Gesang-Buch

Of the word of God (9)
Of the fall (1)
Christmas-hymns (5)
Of the cross of Christ and the disciples (19)
Of the resurrection of Christ (4)
Of the merciful call of God (19)
Of the repentance before God (7)
Of faith and steadfastness (8)
Of conversion (8)
Of baptism (4)
Of spiritual life (7)
Of spiritual battle (7)
Of Christian duties (6)
Of the love of God (7)
Of the praise of God (11)
Of footwashing and the Lord's Supper (5)
Of the breaking of bread and the [holy] kiss (4)
Hymns about resurrection and temptation (4)
Of praying and watching (6)
At the beginning and conclusion of the meeting (13)
Of grace and the blessed estate (2)
Of brotherly love (2)
New-Year's hymns (6)
Hymns about sowing and harvesting (3)
Morning and evening hymns (19)
Table-songs (5)
Hymns for the sick and for burial (49)
Of the judgment (2)
Of heaven (12)
Parting-hymns (7)
For general use (23)
Of humility and denial [of self and the world] (1) [This rubric was
   eliminated in the second edition, where this hymn was incorporated
   into the preceding rubric.]
Of the kingdom of God (2)
Of the house of God (28)
Of the teaching office (5)
Of marriage (1)
Appendix (82) [This number was reduced to 40 in the second edition.])

Although some vestiges of earlier orders can be discerned, the arrangement of the rubrics is not systematic. In the first edition, several hymns were printed twice in the body of the hymnal, such as Denket doch, ihr Menschenkinder (198) which appears in the index of first lines as number 201 and 214, both times in the category of "Hymns for the sick and the dead." Herr Jesu, Gnadensonne (491) is found twice in the 1874 edition, once under "Of the merciful call of God" and also under "At the beginning and conclusion of the meeting." Under the latter rubric it was replaced in 1879 by a new hymn, Ach Herr, erleuchte deine Knecht' (20). Likewise, Kommt, ihr überzeugten Herzen (750) was originally listed under "Of the merciful call of God" and "Hymns about resurrection and tempt- ation," but was replaced later on by a new hymn under the latter rubric, Diese Welt gering zu schätzen (282). On the other hand, the conversion hymn, Will ich mich denn nicht bekehren (1308), which is found both under "Of conversion" and "For general use" in 1874, is listed only under the latter in 1879. Finally, another hymn dealing with illness and death, Ich mag mich, wo ich will, hinkehren (566) was originally quite unsuitably grouped with "Hymns for sowing and harvesting."

Several hymns in the main body of the 1874 edition were not reprinted in 1879, such as the table-song, Abermal uns deine Güte (2); Ach, wann werd' ich schauen dich (55), a praise hymn by Ahasverus Fritsch; Scriver's evening hymn, Der lieben Sonne Licht und Pracht (226); Ein von Gott gebor'ner Christ (327); the funeral hymn, O wie so selig schläfest du (1037); and the German camp-meeting song by Dreisbach, Wie prächtig ist der Nam' (1294).

DOCUMENTED HYMNS

In this hymnal, the body of documented texts is remarkable for several reasons. A noticeable shift in the "popularity" of hymn-writers has taken place. Among newly introduced poets are some from rather early periods and movements as well as very recent times. The most striking feature, however, is found in the appendix of the first edition. This consisted almost in its entirety (seventy-seven of eighty-two) of hymns by Philipp Friedrich Hiller, the foremost hymn-writer of Württemberg Pietism. The members of this branch of Pietism remained within the established church and did not separate themselves like many of the more radical groups. Hiller had been a disciple of Johann Albrecht Bengel (1687-1752), the "Father of Württemberg Pietism." While serving as a pastor, Hiller lost the use of his voice for eighteen years and turned from preaching to writing hymns and devotional literature. Like many other prolific hymn-writers especially of the late period of Pietism he produced many hymns of lesser quality. Nevertheless he was the best and most beloved poet of his time and country. Next to the Bible, his own collection, Geistliches Liederkästlein[9] (Little Treasure Trove of Hymns) and his editions of Johann Arndts Paradies-Gärtlein[10] (Johann Arndt's Little Garden of Paradise) were the most widely read books in Württemberg during his lifetime.

Philipp Friedrich Hiller had become quite popular among the German Americans in the nineteenth century; his texts can be found in increasing numbers in the hymn-collections of that time. In Brethren hymnody, Hiller's hymns were given a prominent place for the first time in Neue Sammlung. The editors of the 1874 Brethren hymnal, however, favored his poetry to a degree never before or after accorded any other hymn-writer in Brethren hymnology. Although the editors may not have been aware of the authorship of the three texts by Hiller which they included among the other hymns, the same assumption cannot be made in the case of the appendix. Even after the drastic cutting in the second edition it still included twenty-four of Hiller's texts.

Tersteegen, who had been gaining in popularity with the Brethren since publication of Die Kleine Lieder Sammlung, is here represented by thirteen hymns. The third place is taken by the German-American Evangelical Dreisbach (eleven texts and translations). The number of early Brethren hymns by Knepper was raised to ten. Seven hymns each are included by Gerhardt and Neander, six each by Heermann and Wilhelm Preiss, and five each by Bertolet and Schmolck. The great majority of sixty-four poets are represented by one hymn only.

Of special interest among the documented hymns is a Winebrennerian text on footwashing (169). The first stanza states that this rite is a duty which the Christian is obligated to fulfill. The next polemicizes against people who deny the validity of this commandment of God. The third praises those who gladly obey God's commandment in the face of mockery and disdain. Finally, the fourth stanza testifies that

They practice humility and love which makes them like Christ here on earth. That is why they practice footwashing and why they greet one another with the kiss of love.

By the time the 1874 edition was compiled, the influence of the re-awakening which occurred in the German churches of the early nineteenth century had made itself felt through that movement's hymnody. Philipp Spitta (1801-1859), preacher and tutor in North Germany, was one of the leaders of the movement in his area. This hymnal contains his Ein lieblich Los ist mir gefallen (323), a hymn about eternal life. It is the most contemporary documented text in this collection.

UNDOCUMENTED HYMNS

There are altogether twenty-nine newly added hymns in the 1874 edition that cannot be documented elsewhere and whose authors are unknown. The largest number - seven - are in the category "Hymns for the sick and for burial." The others are found in smaller numbers in almost all of the other rubrics. Several of these merit some detailed description, especially those dealing with peculiarly Brethren tenets. (For a list of the new hymns, see Appendix VII/3.)

Baptism

Two of the new hymns are found under the heading, "Of baptism." Der Herr hat uns befohlen (216) is a teaching poem rather than a hymn:

The Lord commanded us that we, his servants, go out into all the world to teach.   (:1)
Go and teach and baptize [everyone] whom I have purchased dearly, so that here on earth they may be consecrated to me.   (:2)

Indeed, this must be done; whosoever desires to see God's kingdom must be born anew or else perish. (:3)
You must be baptized and grasp the promise if you would have the gifts of the spirit sealed on you. (:4)
Come then, and put baptism into practice, postpone it no longer and the Lord will strengthen you in all good works. (:5)

By contrast, Herr, hier sind nun deine Kinder (482) is a prayer hymn for the occasion of baptism:

Lord, here are your children. Come and bless them when they descend into this water and be baptized here. (:1)
Bless also, o God, their example in the hearts of these people. Yea, awaken, convert the sinners and establish your kingdom yet today. (:2)

One additional hymn seems to address Anabaptist teachings. Hört hier den alten Täufergrund (530) is a long teaching poem which is found with the hymns "Of the word of God." However, the emphasis is placed chiefly on the individual's path to salvation rather than the concept of the church:

Hear, then, the old Anabaptist foundation which I confess with heart and lips, the foundation that will endure for ever while heaven and earth perish. (:1)
"Whence is this teaching?" you ask. "Is there scripture foundation to it?" "It is founded in God's word and is firmly grounded in it." (:2)
"Is there then no other teaching than that of the despised Jesus?" "No, this is the only pathway upon which I can be saved." (:3)
"How do I enter this pathway?" "You must begin to pray, you must truly awake from sleep so that you can in truth realize the course of your sins. (:4)
For you are so blind by nature that you are in death and sin; you must be converted from your heart as the word of God clearly teaches. (:5)
You must, in true repentance, from your heart fall at the feet of God; through repentance and faith one comes with a penitent heart to the son of God. (:6)
Repentance and faith, it is said, must be followed by baptism for the forgiveness of your sins as it is found in the word of God. (:7)
You must obey God's word as Jesus commanded; therefore do not ignore even the least of the commandments because Jesus brought them all from heaven. (:8)
This is the true path of life and there is neither comfort nor counsel without it; whoever does not follow Jesus' commandment will lose his soul. (:9)
Many a one will follow Jesus who does not awaken from his sleep of sin; such a one has not yet passed through the narrow gate according to God's word. (:10)
Such a person is a member of the church [Gemeinde], that is almost his only God [?]; he has not been made free from from sin, his heart is still full of hatred and envy. (:11)
Many a one who is converted does not obey the teaching of the word of God; he does not wish to be so despised as Jesus was. (:12)
Another, who is still full of pride, believes he is a Christian, and yet he is as far from being minded like the son of God as heaven [is from earth]. (:13)

There will be many who will find themselves disappointed when they expect to enter, who will find the gate locked because they were not truly children of God." (:14)

Heaven

The yearning for heaven pervades many hymns in various categories. Ich mag mich, wo ich will, hinwenden (566) is one of these:

Wherever I turn, I see nothing but misery. Everyone has a cross to bear and eats his humble bread with tears. And this is ever on the increase. O if I but were in heaven! (:1)
It is in heaven that we find the best gifts, there all of us are rich; in heaven everything is to be had and we are like the angels. In heaven there is no more misfortune: O if I but were in heaven! (:2)

Judgment

The hymn, Dem Lämmlein nachgehen (190) describes how one can prevail before the judgment seat:

By following the little lamb in virginity and purity one will pass before the judgment seat. Virginal souls are the reflection of Jesus because they have chosen him from their hearts and that wholly. (:1)
The lamb can be seen transfigured on Zion: whoever desires to stand there with Jesus must leave this sinful world behind and cling to that only which pleases Jesus. (:2)
Whoever properly comprehends here what is to be expected there will then joyfully leave this world: such a one will strive, by grace only, to be a citizen of the lamb, of heaven. (:3)
Up there, in heaven, we will be well off. Whoever believes it and lives accordingly will have increasing courage. There, the savior will say to us: inherit the kingdom, the father gave it to me, I give it to you. (:4)
Up there one enjoys eternal rest, up there, everything is done gloriously and royally. The savior is priest, king, and lord. No thirst, hunger, or heat will affect us there. (:5)
There we shall see what no eye has ever seen; there we shall feel what no heart has ever felt; there we shall hear what no ear has ever heard: that which Jesus prepares for those who worship him. (:6)

One hymn is found under "Of the judgment" which is written in the idiom of a ballad memorializing the untimely death of a young man:

He was like the roses in spring; his lips were beautiful like lilies, his heart full of well-being [Wohllust] as it is with you, and on the surface, everything seemed to be joyful. (340:1)

Life was good for this young man who did not give much thought to the possibility of his own death. Death, however, did overcome him prematurely. In none of the stanzas is there any allusion to God's judgment or any indication of the spiritual state of the young man as he faced death. Instead, the text seeks to convey comfort and reassurance to those left behind. In the words of the last two stanzas,

He has now completed his journey on earth and has gone the way of all flesh. He left us with the hope that in his misery he has found the love that endures in death. (:5)
Although his passing saddens our hearts because in life we loved him so dearly, hope does not allow us to mourn so much and lessens the sorrow for the friend who is no more. (:6)

THE 1879 EDITION

Apart from being provided with a conventional preface, the second edition of Das Christliche Gesang-Buch differs from the first chiefly in the contents of its appendix of hymns. In the first edition, the appendix consisted of seventy-seven hymns by P. F. Hiller, two new anonymous and three anonymous documented hymns. None of these are retained in the appendix of the second edition, but twenty-three of Hiller's texts are distributed among certain categories where they replace other hymns.

Seven new undocumented hymns are introduced in the second edition, of which one is remarkable for its biographical content. Höret, wie im fernen Lande (529) is entitled: "At the death of J. H. Balsbaugh." A translation of this text follows:

Listen [to the story of] how our friend and brother died in a far-away land. Strangers (for no one knew him there) laid him into his coffin. They sent him in great haste many hundred miles to his neighbors and his family who deeply mourn his parting. (:1)
Adieu, then, I must leave my children and my wife. I commend my affairs to God in my last days. My children, who are still small and who will then be orphans, may God grant them in their time a blessed death and make them heirs of heaven. (:2)
What great sorrow has come over me because my husband has been taken from me. O how it has saddened me because we loved each other. Many tears have been shed because of the misery that has befallen me. (:3)
I hope to see my relatives there again, my friends and acquaintances who are standing before the throne of God. Also my husband and my child who are with that throng there I hope to see in joy [in that place] where we shall never part in eternity. (:4)
There, all sorrow will be made sweet, there will be no more dying. In the kingdom where love flows, there will be no pain in eternity. There will be great glory as Paul writes, which no ear has yet heard and which will last in eternity. (:5)

CONCLUSION

Several aspects set this hymnal apart from other German-language hymn-books of the Brethren. First and most obviously, it was compiled out of dissatisfaction with the officially authorized and recommended denominational hymnal. Secondly, when published, it did not meet with the whole-hearted approval of the district that had authorized its compilation. A properly revised second edition was likewise never republished.

This hymnal bears the stamp of Pietism much more than any other before it. Almost three fourths of its authors are from that tradition. Even without the hymns of the predominant author, Philipp Friedrich Hiller, the balance would still be heavily on the Pietist side. The increase in hymns from nineteenth-century German-American evangelicalism is striking, which may be due to the fact that the Brethren of Eastern Pennsylvania were closer to that movement both geographically and theologically than the rest of the denomination.

Das Christliche Gesang-Buch was to be followed by only one further hymnal before German hymnal printing came to an end for the Brethren.

HYMN-WRITERS REPRESENTED IN
DAS CHRISTLICHE GESANG-BUCH, 1874
ARRANGED ACCORDING TO HISTORICAL PERIODS AND MOVEMENTS

	Writers	Hymns
COUNTER-REFORMATION: Behm, Helmbold, Moller, Nicolai, Ringwald, Schechs*, Schneegass*, Selneccer*.	8	8
THIRTY-YEARS' WAR: Albert, Bachmeister, Heermann, Held, Rist, Rosenmüller, Sonnemann, Wilhelm II.	8	17
LATE 17TH CENTURY: Denicke, Gesenius, Strattner.	3	2
PIETISM:		
Forerunners: Aemilie Juliane, Albinus, Bornmeister*, Clausnitzer, Connow, M. Franck, Fritsch, Gerhardt, Herzog, Keimann, Knorr, Liscow, Ludämilie Elisabeth, Neumark, B. Prätorius, Rodigast, Scheffler, H. Schenk, Schirmer, Schwämlein*, Scriver, Weber; Neander (Reformed)	23	40
Early Pietists: Freystein, Laurenti, Sacer, Schade, Schütz.	5	7
Halle and late Pietists: Breithaupt, Francke, Gotter, Herrnschmidt, Lackmann, M. Müller, Rambach, Richter, Rothe, H. T. Schenk, Schwedler, Starck, Winkler, Wolff, Woltersdorf.	15	21
Radical Pietists: Annoni, Gruber, Ziegler.	3	3
Brethren: Knepper.	1	10
Moravians: Steinhofer, N. L. Zinzendorf.	2	4
Württemberg Pietists: F. K. Hiller, P. F. Hiller.	2	81
Reformed: Lampe*, Tersteegen.	2	14
Orthodox: Günther, Hübner, Möckel, Neumeister*, Schmolck, Stübner, Sturm.	7	11
ENLIGHTENMENT: Diterich, Gellert, Klopstock, Liebich.	4	7
GERMAN-AMERICANS:		
Brethren: Becker, H. Danner, J. Danner, Haller, Hoffer?, Mack Jr., Meyer, S. D. Miller?, Naas, W. Preiss, Stoll.	11	18
Ephrata: Naëmi.	1	1
Mennonites: Herr.	1	1
Evangelicals: Bertolet, Dreisbach, Orwig, Sasse, Walter.	5	20
ENGLISH AUTHORS: Adams*, Denham, Hart*, Newton, Watts, C. Wesley, Williams.	7	9
19TH-CENTURY GERMAN AUTHORS:		
Church renewal movement: Spitta.	1	1
Others: Plank.	1	1

HYMN-WRITERS REPRESENTED IN
DAS CHRISTLICHE GESANG-BUCH, 1874
ARRANGED ALPHABETICALLY AND NUMBER OF THEIR HYMNS

Adams*: 1
Aemilie Juliane: 1
Albert: 2
Albinus: 1
Annoni: 1

Bachmeister: 1
Becker: 1
Behm: 1
Bertolet: 5
Bornmeister*: 1
Breithaupt: 1

Clausnitzer: 1
Connow: 1

Danner, H.: 1
Danner, J.: 1
Denham: 1
Diterich: 2
Dreisbach: 8

Franck, M.: 1
Freystein: 1
Fritsch: 1

Gellert: 3
Gerhardt: 7
Gesenius/Denicke: 1
Gotter: 3
Günther: 1

Haller: 1
Hart*: 1
Heermann: 6
Held: 2
Helmbold: 1
Herr: 1
Herrnschmidt: 1
Herzog: 1

Hiller, F.K.: 1
Hiller, P.F.: 80
Hoffer: 1
Hübner: 1

Keimann: 1
Klopstock: 1
Knepper: 10
Knorr: 1

Lackmannn: 1
Lampe*: 1
Laurenti: 3
Liebich: 1
Liscow: 1
Ludämilie Elis.: 1

Mack, Jr.: 3
Meyer: 1
Miller, S.D.: 1
Möckel: 1
Moller: 1
Müller, M.: 1

Naas: 1
Naemi: 1
Neander: 7
Neumark: 1
Neumeister*: 1
Newton: 1
Nicolai: 1

Orwig: 1

Plank: 1
Prätorius, B.: 1
Preiss, W.: 4

Rambach: 1
Richter: 1
Ringwald: 1
Rist: 3
Rodigast: 1
Rosenmüller: 1
Rothe: 2

Sacer: 1
Sasse: 4
Schade: 1
Schechs*: 1
Scheffler: 5
Schenk, H.: 1
Schenk, H.T.: 1
Schirmer: 2
Schmolck: 5
Schneegass*: 1
Schütz: 1
Schwämlein*: 1
Schwedler: 1
Scriver: 1
Selneccer*: 1
Sonnemann: 1
Spitta: 1
Starck: 1
Steinhofer: 1
Stoll: 3
Strattner: 1
Stübner: 1
Sturm: 1

Tersteegen: 13

Walter: 2
Watts: 1
Weber: 1
Wesley, C.: 3
Wilhelm II: 1
Williams: 1
Winkler: 1
Wolff: 1
Woltersdorf: 4

Ziegler: 1
Zinzendorf, N.L.: 3

NOTES

[1] <u>Minutes of the Annual Meetings of the Church of the Brethren. Containing All Available Minutes from 1778 to 1909.</u> Published by The General Mission Board Under Authority of Annual Conference, June 1-3, 1909. (Elgin, Ill.: Brethren Publishing House, 1909), p. 304-305. (<u>Minutes</u>, 1872, art. 18.)

[2] <u>Das Christliche Gesang-Buch. Eine Zusammenstellung der Besten Lieder der alten und neuen Dichter, zum Gottesdienstlichen Gebrauch aller Gott suchenden und heilsbegierigen Seelen</u> ... (Lancaster, Pa.: Druck und Verlag von Johann Bär's Söhnen, 1874).

[3] <u>Eine Sammlung von Geistlichen Liedern, angepasst den verschiedenen Arten des Christlichen Gottesdienstes, und besonders bestimmt für den Gebrauch der Brüder in Christo, bekannt als die "River-Brüder."</u> Zusammengestellt nach den Bestimmungen der General-Conferenz (Lancaster, Pa.: 1874).

[4] <u>Die Geistliche Viole oder Eine kleine Sammlung alter und neuer Geistreicher Lieder, zum Gebrauch in den Gemeinden der Evangelischen Gemeinschaft</u> ... 8. Auflage (Neu-Berlin, Pa.: T. Buck, für die Evangelische Gemeinschaft, 1842).

[5] Jacob Erb, <u>Sammlung von Geistlichen, Lieblichen Liedern, Aus verschiedenen Gesangbücher gesammlet zum Gebrauch des Oeffentlichen und privat Gottesdienst</u> (Harrisburg, Pa.: 1830).

[6] <u>Der Christliche Sänger, Eine Sammlung der vornehmnsten und gebräuchlichsten Lieder, zum Gebrauch des öffentlichen und privat Gottesdienstes für alle heilsuchende Seelen Jeder Christlichen Benennung</u> (Skippachsville, Pa.: Samuel K. Cassel, 1855)

[7] For a complete translation of the preface to the first edition, see Appendix VII/1.

[8] For a translation of the preface to the second edition, see Appendix VII/2.

[9] Philipp Friedrich Hiller, <u>Geistliches Liederkästlein zum Lobe Gottes, bestehend aus 366 kleinen Oden über ebenso viele Bibelsprüche. Kindern Gottes zum Dienst aufgesetzt</u> (Stuttgart: 1762-1767).

[10] Johann Arndt, <u>Paradies-Gärtlein Geistreicher Gebeter in Liedern</u>, Dritter Druck, ed. Philipp Friedrich Hiller ... (Tübingen: Johann Christoph Löffler, 1751).

CHAPTER VIII

EINE SAMMLUNG VON PSALMEN,
LOBGESÄNGEN, UND GEISTLICHEN LIEDERN

In the year 1891, the District Meeting of eastern Pennsylvania passed
on to the Annual Meeting several queries in reference to German hymn-
books. The district petitioned that a hymnal committee of three be appointed, with two members from the German churches of Pennsylvania.
Selection of hymns was to be made from the Brethren's (i.e., Neue Sammlung) and the Lancaster (i.e., Das Christliche Gesang-Buch) hymn-books.
The petition was granted and S. R. Zug, J. H. Longenecker, and Jacob
Aldinger were appointed to serve on the committee.[1] Two years later, the
annual meeting received a report from the committee stating that 380 hymns
had been selected from the suggested sources.[2] The title of the new
German hymnal was Eine Sammlung von Psalmen, Lobgesängen, und Geistlichen
Liedern (A Collection of Psalms, Hymns, and Spiritual Songs).[3]

This slim, pocket-sized hymnal went through three editions. The
first two were published at Mount Morris, Illinois (1893 and 1895), the
last, at Elgin, Illinois (1903), Only few and insignificant changes were
made in the latter two editions. An index of melodies and meters and an
alphabetical index of first lines are provided at the end of the volume.

According to the preface, as directed by the Annual Meeting, the
hymns were taken chiefly from two sources, namely, Neue Sammlung, or, as
it had come to be known by then, the General Brüder Buch ("The General
Brethren Book") and Das Christliche Gesang-Buch or the Lancaster Buch.[4]
This is indeed the case. Of the 367 hymns in the first edition, 334 are
in both these hymnals, eighty only in the former, and 141 only in the
latter. This leaves thirty-three hymns that were newly added in 1893.
Where applicable, reference is made to the hymns contained in those two
hymnals by using the letter "A" for the former and "B" for the latter,
followed by the appropriate number in the respective hymnal. Melodies are
indicated both by reference to the first line of the hymn to the melody of
which the text in question is to be sung and to the number in the index of
melodies and meters. In many instances the meter is indicated at the top
of the hymn.

THE RUBRICS

Although this hymnal provides no separate list of rubrics, the hymn-
texts themselves are arranged within the body of the hymnal according to
subjects and following a certain discernible order. The table of contents
lists the headings for these groups of texts in alphabetical sequence. Inasmuch as the arrangement of subjects or rubrics may well represent a
theological exposition, it is reconstructed below with the number of hymns
in each category indicated. The first prominent group is devoted to God's
plan of salvation for human kind, with "The Fall" placed as a link between
"Creation" and "Christ" (rubrics 1-4). This is followed by what might be
called "An evangelical (or revivalistic) order of salvation" (rubrics

5-12) in which the first four elements lead up to the conviction of the sinner, then the invitation is given, which leads to penitence and conversion. This sequence of rubrics is concluded and sealed by prayer.

Three rubrics illustrating the Reformation teaching of justification through faith, namely, "Faith," "Of justification," and "Of the new birth," link this order of salvation to the Brethren ordinances (rubrics 16-22). Of these, the love-feast is represented in most detail including self-examination, footwashing, communion, the meal, and hymns to be sung at the table. This sequence is followed by "Of marriage," which is placed in the somewhat ambivalent location between the Brethren ordinances and the Pietist virtues which begin with "Of love" (rubrics 24-27).

Five requirements for and aspects of leading a Christian life (rubrics 28-32) are linked to the fruits of such a life (rubrics 34-37) by the category of "Battle and victory." After "Praise and thanksgiving have been rendered, the Christian turns to contemplate "Christian duties" (rubric 38), after which attention is given to the church in its various aspects as people of God, building, and meeting (rubrics 39-44). Seven categories of hymns for various occasions and seasons lead up to the final group of rubrics about the last things (rubrics 52-55). The very last group of hymns are four praise hymns (rubric 56).

Thus, in their last German-language hymnal, the Brethren once again arranged their hymns within a theological framework. The table of the rubrics given below is supplied with the headings as interpreted above. Numbers in parentheses indicate the number of hymns.

Eine Sammlung von Psalmen,
Lobgesängen, und Geistlichen Liedern, 1893.

[God's plan of salvation for human kind]
   [1] God, his being, essence and perfection (2)
         his omniscience (1)
         his love and mercy (6)
         of creation (3)
   [2] The Fall (2)
   [3] Christ. His incarnation (8)
           Name and offices (8)
           Life and conduct (2)
           Suffering and death (6)
           Resurrection and ascension (8)
           His second coming (6)
   [4] Of the Holy Spirit (5)

[An evangelical order of salvation]
   [5] The word of God and gospel (6)
   [6] The teaching office (6)
   [7] Mission hymns (5)
   [8] The merciful calling of God (6)
   [9] Conviction (3)
   [10] Invitation (19)
   [11] Penitence and conversion (9)
   [12] Prayer (2)
   [13] Faith (5)

[Reformation teachings]
    [14] Of justification (2)
    [15] Of the new birth (3)

[Brethren ordinances and practices]
    [16] Of baptism (3)
    [17] Of self-examination (3)
    [18] Of footwashing (2)
    [19] Of the Lord's Supper (3)
    [20] Of breaking the bread (4)
    [21] Table songs (5)
    [22] Of anointing (3)
    [23] Of marriage (1)

[The Pietist virtues]
    [24] Of love (7)
    [25] Of humility (3)
    [26] Of patience (1)
    [27] Of hope (3)

[Requirements for leading a Christian life]
    [28] Of watchfulness (5)
    [29] Of denial of self (3)
    [30] Encouragement (12)
    [31] Steadfastness (3)
    [32] Trust in God (4)

[33] Battle and victory (12)

[The fruits of a Christian life]
    [34] Sanctification (3)
    [35] Of perfection (1)
    [36] Peace and joy in God (11)

[37] Hymns of praise and thanksgiving (12)

[38] Christian duties (5)

[The church]
    [39] Of the true and the false Christendom (3)
    [40] The church [Gemeinde] of Jesus (3)
    [41] The house of God (5)
    [42] Dedication [of buildings] (2)
    [43] Prayer-hymns (7)
    [44] Meeting. Beginning (6)
                 Closing (5)

[Hymns for various occasions, times of day and year]
    [45] Parting hymns (6)
    [46] Morning hymns (9)
    [47] Evening hymns (9)
    [48] Sabbath (1)
    [49] Seasons of the year (5)
    [50] Sowing and harvesting (3)
    [51] Passage of time (6)

[52] Hymns for sickness and death, and burial.
          For children (11)
          For unmarried young men and women (4)
          For families, fathers and mothers (6)
          For old persons (4)
          For general and special cases (30)

[Last things]
     [53] Resurrection and judgment (4)
     [54] Eternity (2)
     [55] Heaven and eternal salvation [Seligkeit] (13)

[56] Praise hymns [Lob-Sprüche] (4) (Hymns 374-377 only; the table of
     contents incorrectly lists 374-380.)

     Although the hymns were almost in their entirety taken over from the
two preceding German hymnals, the arrangement of the rubrics follows
neither. Two categories are newly introduced here namely, "Mission hymns"
and "Dedication." Two of the mission hymns were taken from the two
earlier Brethren hymnals (137, 1189), two are newly introduced documented
hymns (1104, 1180), and one is a new, undocumented hymn (1053). The
rubric, "Dedication" of church buildings contains one documented (436) and
one new undocumented hymn (437).

     It is interesting to note the great emphasis on "Hymns for sickness,
death, and funerals" which amount to fifty-five hymns altogether and are
by far the largest category. Thirty-eight are devoted to "Christ," con-
stituting the second-largest group, the third being hymns of "Invitation"
with nineteen. Although accorded places of importance in the structure of
the hymnal, the rubrics of "God" and the Brethren ordinances did not receive much attention when hymn-texts were assigned.

     Of the three baptismal hymns, Rambach's Ich bin getauft in deinen
Namen (542) would be much more suitable as a Lutheran confirmation hymn.
Rambach's original title for this hymn was, "For the daily renewal of the
baptismal covenant."[5] Herr, deine Rechte und Gebot' (478) by Denicke
which is here introduced into Brethren hymnody is not specifically a
baptismal hymn but does mention the baptismal covenant in the second
stanza:

     Help me ... to contemplate every day and every hour how firmly my
     baptismal covenant commits me to your service.   (:2)

To be sure, both these writers had infant baptism in mind. The third hymn
in this category, Geh, Seele, frisch im Glauben fort (400) is an undocumented hymn that entered Brethren hymnody in 1826. It is a hymn of personal, individual commitment rather than one for baptism. The only reference
to that ordinance is found in the supplication in stanza 3, "Wash away my
sin, Immanuel." In the sixth and last stanza mention is made of the
fellowship of believers:

     Let all the members of the congregation be one soul and let them be com-
     mended to your faithfulness, o guardian of Israel.   (:6)

In the love-feast sequence, two of the hymns of self-examination are by P. F. Hiller. Although very subjective in tone, they are useful. The third, O Christenmensch, erbarme dich (938) is a documented hymn that does evoke the spirit of examining oneself as a member of the church. Its opening and closing stanzas read as follows:

O Christian, have mercy, for your God also has mercy. The attitude that you hold towards your brother will be that of God towards you. (:1) O Lord and father, endow us with your spirit of truth that it may rule our hearts and lips to be faithful in our covenant with you.   (:5)

Only one of the two hymns under "Of footwashing," Nun kommt, ihr Christen alle (912) deals with that ordinance. It is an undocumented hymn that entered Brethren hymnody in 1826. The first two hymns under "Anointing" are not related to the Brethren ordinance in any way. The third, O Herr, dein heilig Wort uns lehrt (969), a new undocumented hymn in the 1893 edition, deals specifically with anointing for healing. Similarly, only one of the three hymns under "The church" is somewhat related to Brethren tenets. This is Christus ist der Kirche Haupt (161), which was a new undocumented hymn in 1870. Jesu, baue deinen Leib (656) is a documented anonymous hymn dated before 1718, which was incorporated into Brethren hymn-books in 1744 and continued to be included in every successive hymnal since. The third hymn, Dein Garten, Herr, mit Sehnsucht wart't (187) came into Brethren hymnody from German collections of camp-meeting songs in 1870.

DOCUMENTED HYMNS

The 1893 edition of Eine Sammlung contains 367 hymns. P. F. Hiller is again the most popular writer (seventeen hymns), followed by Tersteegen (fourteen). Eight of Neander's hymns are included and seven each by Gellert, Scheffler, and Schmolck. Dreisbach, the American evangelical and W. Preiss are represented by six hymns each. Most of the rest are represented by only one hymn each. Hymns in the style and tradition of Pietism still dominate by far, as can be seen from the two tables at the end of the chapter. The differences between the three editions of this hymnal are so insignificant that they are not accounted for as was done for earlier hymnals.

UNDOCUMENTED HYMNS

In all three editions, a total of twelve undocumented hymns were introduced. However, one of these (1160) is in actuality stanzas three and four of Jesu, auferstand'ner Held (655). It was first printed in the second edition of Mack's Grundforschende Fragen and appeared in Brethren hymnody for the first time in Neue Sammlung where it is attributed to Mack (Jr.?). Three of the new texts are hymns of praise and thanksgiving (404, 921, 1111). The second of these, Nun lobet und ehret, seems to be one of those curious instances where a new hymn was created from an existing one. Its second (and last) stanza appeared earlier in the 1879 edition of Das Christliche Gesang-Buch as a hymn of one stanza (167). Similarly, Segne deiner Knechte Lehren (1083), to be sung at meeting, consists of two totally unconnected stanzas and might well have been lifted from another hymn. (For a list of the new undocumented hymns, see Appendix VIII/2.)

119

Ruft laute, ihr Wächter (1053) is a new hymn in the rubric of "Missions," which is a new category in German Brethren hymnals:

Shout loudly, you watchmen, by day and by night, until all tribes have been brought to Jesus. Let the nations be astonished and perplexed, you keep on playing the trumpets with a happy sound.   (:1)
O wonder of wonders, the proudest people are lowering themselves and are bending their knees before Jesus in humility. They have but one desire: to serve Christ only here on earth.   (:2)

One undocumented hymn each is found in the rubrics for the Lord's Supper (194) and the ordinance of anointing (969). The latter category contains also two documented hymns which, however, are quite unrelated to the ordinance, whereas the new text deals specifically with anointing for healing:

O Lord, your holy word teaches us to anoint with oil, and this brother (sister) desires to keep your commandment.   (:1)
Let the prayer of faith now be answered here and let this anointing which we perform be blessed by you.   (:2)
Anoint him yourself with your hand, saturate him with holy oil; release him from this bond, refresh body and soul.   (:3)
If his conscience is burdened by many a care, absolve him from everything that preys on him.   (:4)
If it be that this illness is not unto death, let him soon rise again, break the fetters apart.   (:5)
But if his journey is completed, the suffering here soon to be over, grant him that he will be crowned by you in your father's house.   (:6)

Gott Vater, dir, dir weihen wir (437) is the new hymn written for a church dedication, applying a very liturgical concept of the building:

Father God, we now dedicate to you this temple, that it be your dwelling place for ever and ever.   (:1)
Come, Jesus, come, prepare for yourself in this temple a place and dwell yourself therein.   (:2)
You spirit of power, let your light, let your presence dwell in this temple - o sanctify this place!   (:3)
Come, Father, Son, and Holy Ghost, enter to your glory that your name be praised in your property.   (:4)

Death and the life hereafter are addressed in two of the new undocumented hymns (172, 527) where the traditional stances of Christian resignation or stoicism and the yearning for the life after death are expressed in familiar terms. Höre auf, lass Trauern fahren (527) consists of five stanzas, the last two of which are identical with the last two stanzas of the hymn written on the death of J. H. Balsbaugh, which was introduced in the 1879 edition of Das Christliche Gesang-Buch (529). In the present instance they are totally out of context. The original hymn to which they were attached, perhaps erroneously, must have been a shorter one, because its third stanza concludes with these words:

... Glory be to God and his lamb who helped us on the cross; praise and glory be to his name for ever and ever, Amen, Amen.   (:3)

THE LATER EDITIONS

The second and third editions of Eine Sammlung which were published in 1895 and 1903, are practically identical with the first, even regarding the number of stanzas in each hymn. Four hymn-texts occur exclusively in 1895: one anonymous documented hym (263) appears here for the first time again since 1744, albeit substantially shortened; two are new undocumented hymns of praise (404, 1111); and the fourth (1160) is actually stanzas three and four of Jesu, auferstand'ner Held (655). Three texts appear only in 1893 and 1903 (194, 198, 1052) of which Der Tag vor Christi Leiden (194) is a new undocumented hym.

CONCLUSION

Eine Sammlung was published during the years which followed the rise and widespread popularity of English gospel hymnody and which witnessed the greatest spurt of creativity in Brethren hymnody in English. Whereas this was not true for the German hymnody, the significant factor about this last German hymnal is the rather successful attempt at reintroducing into the arrangement of the contents a theological structure. Although Eine Sammlung went through three editions within ten years, it is not difficult to see that German hymnody was coming to an end among the Brethren. Drawing very heavily on the two preceding hymnals, both of which had met with much criticism, this last collection offered very little that was new in Brethren hymnody in German besides five hymns on the mission theme and one on anointing. The relatively large number of hymns in this collection (381 in the first edition) was possible only because most of the texts were shortened considerably, often to the detriment of the context. Yet it is remarkable that such a large body of German texts was still in use even after English hymns had been sung in Brethren congregations for more than one hundred years.

HYMN-WRITERS REPRESENTED IN
EINE SAMMLUNG VON PSALMEN, LOBGESÄNGEN, UND GEISTLICHEN LIEDERN
ARRANGED ACCORDING TO HISTORICAL PERIODS AND MOVEMENTS

	Writers	Hymns
COUNTER-REFORMATION: Behm, Helmbold, Moller, Nicolai, Ringwald, Schneegass.	6	6
THIRTY-YEARS' WAR: Albert, Heermann, Held, Rinkart, Rist, Rosenmüller, Sonnemann, Wilhelm II.	8	11
LATE 17TH CENTURY: Denicke, Gesenius.	2	2
PIETISM:		
Forerunners: Aemilie Juliane, M. Franck, Gerhardt, Herzog, Homburg, Keimann, Knorr, Liscow, Ludämilie Elisabeth, Neumark, Rodigast, Sacer, Scheffler, H. Schenk, Schirmer, Schwämlein, Scriver, Sieber, Weber; Neander (Reformed).	20	38
Early Pietists: Drese, Freystein, Laurenti, Schade, Schütz.	5	8
Halle and late Pietists: Bogatzky, Gotter, Herrnschmidt, Kunth, Lackmann, M. Müller, Rambach, Richter, Rothe, Ruopp, H. T. Schenk, Starck, Winkler, Wolff, Woltersdorf.	15	23
Radical Pietists: Annoni, Gruber.	2	2
Brethren: Knepper.	1	9
Moravians: Garve*, N. L. Zinzendorf.	2	4
Württemberg Pietists: F. K. Hiller, P. F. Hiller, Pfeil, Steinhofer.	4	20
Reformed: Lampe, Tersteegen.	2	15
Orthodox: S. Franck*, Günther, Hübner, Krause*, Liebich, Löscher, Möckel, Neumann, Neumeister, Schmolck, Schrader, Stübner, Sturm.	13	21
ENLIGHTENMENT: Cramer, Diterich, Gellert, Klopstock, Schlegel.	5	15
GERMAN-AMERICANS:		
Brethren: Becker, H. Danner, J. Danner, Gerlach, Haller, Mack Jr., Meyer, S. D. Miller?, Naas, W. Preiss, Sauer II, Stoll.	12	18
Ephrata: Naëmi.	1	1
Mennonites: Herr.	1	1
Evangelicals: Bertolet, Dreisbach, Orwig, Sasse, Walter.	5	17
Others: Jörgens.	1	1
ENGLISH AUTHORS: Adams, Denham, Hart, Heber*, Hunter*, Newton, Swain, Watts, C. Wesley, Williams.	10	16
19TH-CENTURY GERMAN AUTHORS:		
Church renewal movement: Bahnmeier, Conz, Hoffmann, Knapp, C. H. Zeller.	5	6
Others: Hölty*, Plank, Sachse.	3	3

HYMN-WRITERS REPRESENTED IN
<u>EINE</u> <u>SAMMLUNG</u> <u>VON</u> <u>PSALMEN,</u> <u>LOBGESÄNGEN,</u> <u>UND</u> <u>GEISTLICHEN</u> <u>LIEDERN</u>
ARRANGED ALPHABETICALLY AND NUMBER OF THEIR HYMNS

Adams: 1	Hölty*: 1	Rambach: 3
Aemilie Juliane: 1	Homburg: 1	Richter: 1
Albert: 2	Hübner: 1	Ringwald: 1
Annoni: 1	Hunter*: 1	Rinkart: 1
		Rist: 1
	Jörgens: 1	Rodigast: 1
Bahnmeier: 1		Rosenmüller: 1
Becker: 1	Keimann: 1	Rothe: 2
Behm: 1	Klopstock: 2	Ruopp: 1
Bertolet: 5	Knapp: 1	
Bogatzky: 1	Knepper: 9	Sacer: 1
	Knorr: 1	Sachse: 1
Conz: 1	Krause*: 1	Sasse: 2
Cramer: 1	Kunth: 1	Sauer II: 1
		Schade: 1
Danner, H.: 1		Scheffler: 7
Danner, J.: 1	Lackmann: 1	Schenk, H.: 1
Denham: 1	Lampe: 1	Schenk, H.T.: 1
Denicke: 1	Laurenti: 3	Schirmer: 2
Diterich: 4	Liebich: 2	Schlegel: 1
Dreisbach: 5	Liscow: 1	Schmolck: 7
Drese: 2	Löscher: 2	Schneegass: 1
	Ludämilie Elis.: 2	Schrader: 1
Franck, M.: 1		Schütz: 1
Franck, S.*: 1		Schwämlein: 1
Freystein: 1	Mack, Jr.: 3	Scriver: 1
	Meyer: 1	Sieber: 1
	Miller, S.D.: 2	Sonnemann: 1
Garve*: 1	Möckel: 1	Starck: 1
Gellert: 7	Moller: 1	Steinhofer: 1
Gerhardt: 4	Müller, M.: 2	Stoll: 1
Gerlach: 1		Stübner: 1
Gesenius/Denicke: 1		Sturm: 1
Gotter: 2	Naas: 1	Swain: 1
Gruber: 1	Naëmi: 1	
Günther: 1	Neander: 8	Tersteegen: 14
	Neumann: 1	
Haller: 1	Neumark: 1	Walter: 2
Hart: 1	Neumeister: 1	Watts: 3
Heber*: 1	Newton: 1	Weber: 1
Heermann: 2	Nicolai: 1	Wesley, C.: 5
Held: 2		Wilhelm II: 1
Helmbold: 1	Orwig: 3	Williams: 1
Herr: 1		Winkler: 2
Herrnschmidt: 1	Pfeil: 1	Wolff: 1
Herzog: 1	Plank: 1	Woltersdorf: 3
Hiller, F.K.: 1	Preiss, W.: 4	
Hiller, P.F.: 17		Zeller, C.H.: 2
Hoffmann: 1		Zinzendorf, N.L.: 3

NOTES

[1] *Minutes of the Annual Meetings of the Church of the Brethren. Containing All Available Minutes from 1778 to 1909.* Published by The General Mission Board Under Authority of Annual Conference, June 1-3, 1909. (Elgin, Ill.: Brethren Publishing House, 1909), p. 538. (*Minutes,* 1891, art. 11.)

[2] *Ibid.,* p. 579. (*Minutes,* 1893, report 3.)

[3] *Eine Sammlung von Psalmen, Lobgesängen, und Geistlichen Liedern* (Mount Morris, Ill.: The Brethren's Publishing Company, 1893).

[4] For a translation of the entire preface, see Appendix VIII/1.

[5] Johannes Kulp, *Die Lieder unserer Kirche. Eine Handreichung zum Evangelischen Kirchengesangbuch.* Bearbeitet und herausgegeben von Arno Büchner und Siegfried Fornacon (Göttingen: Vandenhoeck und Ruprecht, 1958), p. 68.

CHAPTER IX

OCCASIONAL COLLECTIONS

Hymn-texts authored or used by Brethren are found not only in hymnals but also in various other publications, such as occasional collections of hymns, magazines, or even on a broadside. The following is a discussion of those sources and the hymns which they contain.

GEISTLICHE UND ANDÄCHTIGE LIEDER[1]

This is a collection of thirteen "Spiritual and Pious Songs" which were written by Johannes Preiss (1702-1724), who was, in the words of the title-page, "one who had much experience in the bearing of the cross." The collection was published in Germantown, Pennsylvania, probably in 1753, twenty-nine years after the author's untimely death by drowning. The hymn-texts deal with a variety of subjects.

Alles, was lebt in der Welt (81): This hymn is "A Christian ABC," in which the initial letters of each stanza form the alphabet from A to Z. The letter "I" is omitted because at the time of its writing "I" and "J" were interchangeable. It is amusing to note how the letter "X" was used to form the word G'sellen (i.e., Gesellen - fellows, fellow-...). In the colloquial form, the prefix Ge- drops the vowel, which places the initial consonant into a different context and causes the sound to change from "g" as in "grate" to "k" as in "crate." The combination with the following "s" results in the sound represented by the letter "X." The word in its correct spelling was used quite frequently in German writings at that time so that there is every reason to assume that the present form was used on purpose to supply a stanza for the difficult letter "X".

Christus hat uns erwählt (160): on following Christ.

Der Mensch ist wie ein' schöne Blum' (228): on the finiteness of life.

Ich ruf zu dir, Herr Jesu Christ (567): supplication to Jesus; a paraphrase of Psalm 100.

Ich weiss ein ewig' Himmelreich (583): on the heavenly kingdom.

Ihr lieben Freunde, hört nur zu (614): on watchfulness and preparation for the end-time. Two unique attributes for Jesus are used here: "Lord and President" (:14) and "Examiner" (Examinant) (:24).

In dieser Morgenstunde (636): a morning hymn.

Jesu, hilf mir, so will ich danken dir (666): a Jesus-hymn.

Lasset uns Gott herzlich lieben (766): a praise and prayer hymn.

Sei getreu in deinem Leiden (1090): on steadfastness in suffering.

Selig sind, die geistlich arm sind (1097): "A Hymn on the 9 Beatitudes."

Was vor viel Lob und Lieb's-Getöne (1217): on expectation of the end-time.

Wie eine Blum', o Mensch, du bist (1283): a memento mori hymn. In light of the general lack of concrete expressions of social concern in Brethren hymnody, two stanzas in this collection are noteworthy in this context:

> Do good to the poor here in your life and then you will receive mercy from God in all your need.   (81:19)

> Blessed is who is always merciful to the poor. Such a one is a true Christian upon whom God will have mercy and who will find mercy yet in this time.   (1097:5)

ETLICHE LIEBLICHE UND ERBAULICHE LIEDER[2]

Six hymns in this collection of "Several lovely and edifying songs" are attributed to several Brethren and non-Brethren authors; the seventh, mentioned especially on the title-page, is an anonymous hymn in the manner of a Christian ballad about the maiden Angnes [Agnes?] who died a martyr's death.

Angnes keusch und voll von Tugend (90): A young Christian girl who early in her life had dedicated herself to Jesus as her bridegroom, rejected the attentions of the heathen son of a mighty judge. For this she was punished and publicly humiliated. When the young man arrived at the scene, "about to play his Venus-game with Angnes, an evil spirit appeared who choked him to death." Angnes' prayer for the life of the young man was heard, he was restored to life, declared his belief in God, and witnessed as a Christian. The priests pronounced this to be witchcraft and condemned Angnes to be burned at the stake, but she remained unharmed by the flames, so that the executioner had to run his sword through her. The body was buried in an honest grave and Angnes' soul, beautifully adorned, triumphed in heaven.

Fromm sein ist ein Schatz der Jugend (391): "Piety, a treasure of youth" is a hymn for the young people and attributed to the German-American U. Grumbacher, probably a Mennonite (d. ca. 1745). His advice is that one should

> ... honor all people, serve everyone, teach and edify everyone to the best of one's ability, have mercy with the sick, aid everyone who is in need, share one's bread with the poor ...   (:5)
> ... sadden no child, love not only one's dear friends but also one's enemies, even if they do not deserve it ...   (:6)

Three hymns are attributed to the German-American mystic Johann Kelpius (1673-1706). All deal with denial of the world and directing one's mind to the life hereafter.

Ach wie so gar verblend' muss sein das Aug' den Zeiten (67)

In dieser Welt, wem sie gefällt, ist keine Ruh' zu finden (637)

Wenn ich in Angst und Not mein Augen heb empor (1240)

The very first hymn in this collection, Jesus Christus, Gottes Sohn (695) is attributed to "Theophilus," which was the pen-name of Alexander Mack, Jr. This text was discussed in Chapter III.

The last hymn, Christen müssen sich hier schicken (154) is by Christoph Sauer II and was discussed in Chapter III.

EIN LIED VON DER TAUFE[3]

The text of this "Hymn about Baptism," In der Schrift des neuen Bundes (631), was published on a broadside. It is attributed to Henry Kurtz. As no melody reference is given, one cannot be certain that the text was ever used as a hymn. It was nevertheless included in this study because of its apology of adult or believers' baptism. A prose translation of all nine stanzas is given below.

In the scriptures of the new covenant you will find this ordinance: the way in which the sinner is to enter the kingdom of grace and rest is written in the third chapter of Matthew where Jesus, the Savior of the world, submits himself to it.   (:1)
He is baptized in the Jordan, not alongside of, no, in the river; therefore everyone can from now on draw this conclusion: if Jesus, the Son of God, lowered himself into, and then rose from the water, no doubt quite soaked through,   (:2)
Human beings ought not try to know better. All of us are sinners and wholly unclean. Therefore it is obvious, not just the face, no, but also the body and soul must be cleansed again.   (:3)
Jesus gave us an example in his baptism that we should follow him in all his ways. The forerunner points to the Lamb, the Christian follows the Lamb -- that is where the baptizers (Anabaptists? [Täufer]) have their roots; so remember who you are!   (:4)
Many say that our baptism is in the place of circumcision, but the word of God informs us that Jesus had been first circumcised and then baptized, and so he proved the futility of this error.   (:5)
They brought the little children to be blessed by the Lord; therefore no one is to despise them, for the Lord will bless them. Do come, dear parents, and bring your children along, but not in order to have them baptized, because Jesus does not baptize them.   (:6)
Many will say that this is wrong, but do not let it distress you. The word teaches that none were baptized except those who believed. Woe to those who teach otherwise and who rob God of his glory.   (:7)
You have read the scriptures, come, read them again. If you will become truly whole and numbered among the disciples who follow their Lord in all things, then believe and repent and be baptized.   (:8)
This is the true door to the kingdom of Jesus Christ. May his Holy Spirit guide me lest I stray. For this will prevail against the gate of hell. When everything fails, Jesus will remain my refuge.   (:9)

GEISTLICHES GEWÜRZ-GÄRTLEIN[4]

The author of this slim book, "A Small Spiritual Herb-Garden," (published in 1806), was the Brethren writer and poet, Jakob Stoll (1731-1827). The first part consists of 114 rhymed meditations on brief selections from the Bible, the second contains twenty-five hymn-texts and twenty-five religious poems. All hymns are fairly subjective and introspective. The main themes are love for Jesus (thirteen) and the pilgrim life (four); two are hymns of praise. One text merits a separate discussion.

O wie ist die Zeit so wichtig, die uns Gott vergönnet noch (1033)

The second stanza of this hymn on the finiteness of life, which begins with the words O wie ist die Zeit so wichtig, die uns Gott nur einmal gibt (1032), appeared for the first time as an independent anonymous "hymn" in the first edition of Das Christliche Gesang-Buch. It was subsequently included in the second edition and all three editions of Eine Sammlung. Finally it was incorporated into The Brethren Hymnal (1951) together with an English translation by Ora Garber as "O How Is the Time So Urgent," and attributed to Alexander Mack, Sr. There are no records to document this assumption and no evidence has been found to support Mack's authorship. Indeed, there is no reason to assume that any of the hymn-texts in Geistliches Gewürz-Gärtlein were written by anyone but Jakob Stoll. None of them could be documented anywhere else or prior to 1806. The list of Stoll's hymns follows below.

Ach es fleucht der Menschen Leben wie ein Pfeil zur Ewigkeit (9)
Ach ich hör ein Stimme klingen, die durchschallet Berg und Tal (30)
Ach mein Jesu, mein Verlangen, wo bist du, mein Seelen-Freund (42)
Ach wie ist der Weg so schmal, der zum Leben gehet (66)
Bald kommt der Abend, liebe Seel', dann ist der Tag vergangen (118)
Der Tag hat sich nun geendet und die Nacht herfür getan (235)
Die Glock' hat ja nun geschlagen und mir wieder angedeut' (250)
Ich will meinen Jesum lieben meine ganze Lebens Zeit (592)
Jesu, Brunn' des Lebens, lass mich nicht vergebens (657)
Jesu, Hirte meiner Seelen, dir bin ich so wohl bekannt (669)
Jesu, teurer Schatz der Seelen, komm, ach komm, kehr bei mir ein (687)
Jesus ist mein höchstes Gut, aller Weisheit ew'ger Güte (701)
Jesus, lieber Meister, Prüfer aller Geister (703)
Liebe Seele, lass dir raten, du gehst nach der Ewigkeit (782)
Liebster Jesu, liebstes Leben, Brunnquell aller Seligkeit (790)
Lobet unsern Gott und Herrn, preiset ihn von Herzen gern (799)
Meine Seele lobe Gott, der ein mächtig', heilig' Wesen (860)
O dass ich nur Jesum wählen konnte in der Gnaden-Zeit (939)
O mein starker Bundes König, Jesu, treuer Seelen Hirt (1006)
O milder Heiland Jesus Christ, der du die Quell' des Lebens bist (1011)
O wie ist die Zeit so wichtig, die uns Gott vergönnet noch (1033)
Ringe recht, weil Gottes Gnade dir dein armes Herze regt (1049)
Sanfte Lebensquelle, lauter, klar und helle (1056)
Sieh doch, holder Ehren-König, mit Erbarmen ja auf mich (1103)
Wo kommst du dann her, Pilger, so beschwert mit der Last (1329)

THE RELIGIOUS POETRY OF ALEXANDER MACK, JR.

The religious poetry of Alexander Mack, Jr. was printed at different times in Geistliches Magazien (referred to as GM in the list below), a journal published by the Sauer press, and in other German-American publications. Samuel B. Heckman, in his The Religious Poetry of Alexander Mack Jr.[5] has reprinted that body of Brethren poetry with his own prose translations into English.

The hymn Wo bleiben meine Sinnen (1320), which appeared in Das Kleine Davidische Psalterspiel, was not included in Heckman's book. It was attributed in this study to Alexander Mack, Jr. A comparison of this text with others in the book by Heckman supports the argument in favor of Mack's authorship. A very similar case is that of Ich walle stündlich näher hin (578), although the internal evidence of this text is not as strong. Jesu, auferstand'ner Held (655) was attributed to Alexander Mack, Jr. in Neue Sammlung, but no valid outside documentation could be found. However, internal and circumstancial evidence, however, is rather strongly in favor of Mack's authorship. This hymn-text is discussed in Chapter VI.

The following is a list of the hymn-texts published by Heckman with references to his sources and to the hymnals and occasional collections, in which these texts were printed. For a list of the abbreviations used see Appendix XI.

Auf, lasst uns nun mit Ernst erwägen (107). In GM, no. 10.
Das macht Satanas so rasen (181). In Der kleine Kempis, Leibert, 1795.
Du forschest mich, o Herr (294). Sauer, 1760. KH.
Ehre, dem die Ehr' gebühret (312). In GM?
Eine Seele, die Gott liebet (328). In Der kleine Kempis, Leibert, 1795.
Endlich wird es doch gelingen, jeder Seele (337). From a manuscript.
Es sind gewiss die letzten Zeiten (370). In GM, no. 9.
Gott allein ist gut (413). In Über die Rechtmässigkeit der Kriege, Leibert, 1796.
Gross und mächtig muss man nennen (453). In GM, no. 12?
Herrlichkeiten, gross und kleine (497). In GM, no. 12?
Heute wollen wir begraben (504). From a manuscript.
Hohe Häupter Kronen tragen (521). In GM, no. 12?
Jesu Adel ist alleine (654). In GM, no. 12.
Jesus Christus, Gottes Sohn (695). ELEL 1788, KH, KLS 1834.
Nun bricht der Hütten Haus entzwei (898). KH, KLS 1829, NS, CG, ES.
Nur Gott allein woll' uns genädig sein (934). In Über die Rechtmässigkeit der Kriege, Leibert, 1796.
Über alle Menschenkinder (1154). In GM, no. 12?
Unter lieben Menschenkindern (1165). In GM, no. 12?
Unter reichen Menschenkindern (1166). In GM, no. 12?
Unter schönen Menschenkindern (1167). In GM, no. 12.
Weit für allen Menschenkindern (1223). In GM, no. 12?
Wohl, ja ewig wohl ist denen (1336). From a manuscript.

Only three of the above hymn-texts found their way into Brethren hymnals (294, 695, 898). Twelve appeared in Geistliches Magazien, of which ten were addressed to "the dear young people" (312, 453, 497, 521, 654, 1154, 1165, 1166, 1167, 1223).

NOTES

[1] Johann Preisz, _Geistliche und andächtige Lieder._ (Germantown: Christoph Sauer, 1753).

[2] _Etliche liebliche und erbauliche Lieder._ (Germantown: Peter Leibert, 1788).

[3] _Ein Lied von der Taufe._ (Lancaster: H. W. Ville, [n.d.]).

[4] Jakob Stoll, _Geistliches Gewürz-Gärtlein Heilsuchender Seelen._ (Ephrata: Johann Baumann, 1806).

[5] Samuel B. Heckman, _The Religious Poetry of Alexander Mack, Jr._ (Elgin, Illinois: Brethren Publishing House, 1912).

CONCLUSION

The German hymnals of the Brethren underwent various changes in size, number of hymns, contents, and number and type of hymn-writers in the course of the almost two hundred years during which they were published. In outward form, the hymnals dwindled to about half their original size during the second century of their history while the number of hymns and hymn-writers increased and the length of the individual hymns was greatly reduced. (The average length of a hymn-text published in the eighteenth century was seven stanzas, in the nineteenth, three stanzas.) These factors had a direct bearing on the contents of the hymnals. In the following, some of these trends will be summarized and other features not mentioned in the previous chapters discussed.

A comparison of the hymnals according to the number of hymns contained in each is made in the following table. The standard abbreviations for the hymnals as listed in the appendixes are used here; the total number of hymns in the respective first editions are given in parentheses.

GGB (295)

KDP (536)

KH(58)

KLS (140)

KPS (83)

NS (303)

CG   (398)

ES (367)

In order to complete the picture of which the above diagram can convey only one dimension, one would have to add the actual size of each hymnal. This would show, for example, that GGB is a much larger book than CG, and that there is not much difference in size between NS and CG. As indicated, the large number of texts in the later hymnals was possible only at the cost of omitting most of the stanzas of originally much longer texts.

The entire German hymnody of the Brethren as compiled in this study encompasses 1364 hymns. However, not all of them are discrete hymn-texts. It was not an unusual practice in nineteenth-century hymnal publishing to lift individual stanzas from existing texts and print them as hymn-texts in their own right. There are numerous examples of this in the Brethren hymnals, all of which are noted in the First Line Index (31, 272, 275,

281, 290, 469, 716, 746, 761, 779, 807, 819, 911, 1032, 1160, 1216, 1266a, 1275). There may also be the case of a double or reciprocal lift (167 and 921).

Lifted stanzas can often be discovered because, having been taken out of context, such "hymns" make very little sense. Another method for creating new hymns from old ones is that of paraphrasing, which has been practiced by hymn-writers ever since hymns were written. In Brethren hymnody, seven pairs of originals and paraphrases have been discovered (219/220; 286/1095; 653/654; 916/917; 920/923; 955/956; 1029/1222). Two texts are paraphrases of which the originals do not occur in Brethren hymnody (343, 394).

Related to paraphrases are variant translations of hymns from a different language. Two such texts occur in Brethren hymnody as German versions of Charles Wesley's hymn "A charge to keep I have" (318, 324).

One of the features looked for in any study of poetry is whether there are any acrostics present. These are poems in which the first letter or word of each stanza, when read downward, result in a name or a sentence. Below is a list of the first lines and the acrostics which the stanzas form of the nine hymns which display this feature.

Allein zu dir, o Vater, ist meine Zuversicht (79) / Knepper
   A-N-D-R-E-A-S (the German name for Andrew)

Alles, was lebt in der Welt (81) / J. Preiss
   A-B-C-...-Z (the alphabet)

Befiehl du deine Wege (122) / Gerhardt
   Befiehl-dem Herren-dein'-Weg'-und-hoff-auf-ihn-er-wird's-wohl-mach End
   [i.e., machen] (Trust all things to the Lord and hope in him; he will
   bring everything to a good end.)

Christen müssen sich hier schicken (154) / Sauer
   C-H-R-I-S-T-O-P-H-S-A-U-E-R

Jesus ist Je-süss (699) / Gruber
   J-E-S-U-S-Jesus

Jesus, Jesus, nichts als Jesus (702) / Ludämilie Elisabeth
   J-E-S-U-S

Meines Lebens beste Freude (868) / Liscov
   M-A-R-G-A-R-E-T-E (the name of the author's wife)

Schaffet, schaffet, meine Kinder (1058) / Gotter
   Schaffet-dass-ihr-selig-werdet-mit-Furcht-und-Zittern-Amen (Work your
   salvation with fear and trembling. Amen.)

The hymns which a hymnal contains are like the individual bricks and stones used in the construction of an edifice, the appearance of which is greatly influenced by the shape, color, and texture of these elements. By analogy, the character of a hymnal is determined by the type of hymns found in it which, in turn, is determined to a certain degree by the historical background against which the texts were written. The following table is a summary of the lists of hymn-writers found at the end of each chapter. The categories are the same except for some instances where several smaller ones were grouped together, such as the non-orthodox movements of the Reformation era and the German-American religious bodies that are neither Brethren nor Evangelical (all of which are listed under "Other"), and all periods and branches of Pietism (other than Brethren), which are referred to as "General." The number of documented anonymous hymns are listed at the end. The hymnals are referred to by the standard abbreviations. Numbers signify the numbers of hymns in each category in the first editions of the hymnals.

	GGB	KDP	KH	KLS	KPS	NS	CG	ES
REFORMATION								
Orthodox:	6	12		1				
Other:	6	8				1		
COUNTER-REFORMATION:	4	19		4	1	5	8	6
THIRTY-YEARS' WAR:	10	19		7		7	17	11
LATE 17TH CENTURY:	6	12	1	1	1	2	2	2
PIETISM								
General:	124	273	21	68	8	106	170	110
Brethren:	101	56		10		5	10	9
ORTHODOX:	3	7	2	6		16	11	21
ENLIGHTENMENT:				1	3	13	7	15
GERMAN-AMERICANS								
Brethren:		1	8	1	31	8	17	17
Evangelicals:					4	11	10	17
Other:			4	1		2	2	3
ENGLISH AUTHORS:					3	9	9	16
19TH-CENTURY GERMAN								
Church renewal:					2	6	1	6
Other:					1		1	3
DOCUMENTED ANONYMOUS:	34	109	6	16	5	66	65	114

The predominance of Pietist hymns throughout Brethren hymnody becomes quite clear in the above table and would be even more pronounced if one were to add the hymns of the German-American Brethren to that number, which were, for the most part, still strongly influenced by Pietism. Although the documented anonymous texts have not been identified as to their first appearance in the history of German hymnody, many date from the periods listed under the category of Pietism.

Throughout the German hymnody of the Brethren, certain writers were favorites, probably more by accident than design, with the exception of P. F. Hiller in Das Christliche Gesang-Buch, whose texts could only have been included intentionally in such large numbers. The table below lists the three hymn-writers for the first edition of each of the six major hymnals which are represented by the largest number of texts. The figures represent the hymns by each writer both in absolute numbers and in percentages.

	GGB	KDP	KLS	NS	CG	ES
Arnold	10 3.4%	21 3.9%				
Dreisbach					10 2.5%	
P.F.Hiller				16 5.3%	79 19.8%	16 4.4%
Neander	20 6.8%	32 6%	9 6.4%			8 2.2%
Scheffler	12 4.1%	28 5.2%	8 5.7%	10 3.3%		
Tersteegen			14 10%	11 3.6%	13 3.3%	13 3.5%

Several women authors were positively documented in the total body of German Brethren hymnody. They are Sarah Adams, Aemilie Juliane, Maria Magdalena Böhmer, two members of the Ephrata Community, namely Sister Jaël and Sister Naëmi, Elisabeth Kreuziger, Ludämilie Elisabeth, Anna Schlatter, Tranquilla Sophia Schröder, Juliane Patientia Schultt, and Elisabeth von Senitz. Together they contributed sixteen hymns to Brethren hymnody (38, 44, 474, 543, 628, 643, 702, 887, 937, 947, 1144, 1207, 1277, 1285, 1325, 1326).

As the eighteenth century drew to its close, the Brethren began using English hymns in their meetings and published their own English-language hymnal, The Christian's Duty, which was printed by Peter Leibert at Germantown, Pa. in 1791. Translations of English hymns entered the German hymnody in 1858 via Die kleine Perlen-Sammlung. In the course of time, twelve English hymn-writers were represented in Brethren German-language hymnody, namely, Sarah Adams, Joseph Addison, David Denham, Joseph Hart, Reginald Heber, William Hunter, Thomas Kelly, John Newton, Joseph Swain, Isaac Watts, Charles Wesley, and William Williams. They are represented by twenty translations of their hymns (127, 132, 137, 318, 324, 341, 353, 384, 525, 532, 733, 748, 776, 887, 966, 1035, 1057, 1180, 1233, 1290).

The order of the rubrics can reveal a great deal not only about the care with which a hymnal was compiled but also whether or not such an order is a reflection of a church's theology. The first American hymnal of the Brethren, which was published privately and without naming the persons responsible for it, reflected a very good theological statement in its arrangement of rubrics. As the names of the compilers of Brethren hymnals were made public and church leaders became increasingly involved in the process of hymnal publication, the arrangement of the rubrics seemed to lose significance. (The same can be observed with the prefaces, which began as small treatises and exhortations in the early hymnals and became less so as time progressed.) It was not until the last German hymnal of the Brethren that a systematic arrangement of rubrics was once more achieved.

The subject or rubric under which a given text is grouped is not necessarily a true reflection of the hymn's content. Nevertheless, the significance attached to a category may be reflected by the number of hymns assigned to it. In the table below, the three rubrics with the largest number of hymns are given for each of the six major hymnals, showing the percentages of the total number of texts in each case. The headings for the rubrics are given in condensed form. There is a certain amount of overlapping of headings in some hymnals due to the wording in each case. Headings which cover several subjects are not considered here.

	GGB	KDP	KLS	NS	CG	ES
Awakening (and invitation)			12.8	5.6		
Battle and victory						3.3
Cross of Christ					4.8	
Death and burial			8.6			
Denial of self and world	5.4	4.9				
Desire for God and Christ	5.4	6.0				
Encouragement and consolation				4.0		
Heaven and eternal salvation						3.5
Hope of Zion		4.3				
House of God					7.0	
Invitation						5.2
Love for Jesus		4.3				
Meeting				7.9		
Merciful call of God					4.8	
Penitence, faith, new birth				4.3		
Praise and thanksgiving			7.9			3.3
Praise of God	5.4					
Resurrection, judgment, eternal life				4.0		
Sickness and burial					12.3	
Supplication and confession			12.8			

It is interesting to note a shift after the turn of the nineteenth century from strongly Pietist to Anabaptist ("Meeting") and revival ("Awakening," "Invitation," "Supplication and confession," "Merciful call of God") emphases. Another shift occurred in the texts dealing with death and dying. In earlier Pietist hymnody the awareness of human mortality and the finiteness of one's existence, and the longing for the life in God's kingdom were implicit in most hymns. After the middle of the nineteenth century numerous hymns appeared that dealt quite explicitly with sickness, death, and burial. In none of the hymnals, however, did the rubrics on the Brethren ordinances ever contain a significant number of hymns.

In any study of hymnody covering more than one hymnal it is interesting to discover whether or not there exists a core of hymn-texts that occurs consistently in all editions of all the hymnals under study, and what the nature of this core is. In the case of the German hymnody of the Brethren, which spans 183 years and includes six major hymnals and a total of 1364 hymns, there is a core of fourteen texts which occurs in all the editions of all the major hymnals. These hymns are listed below in alphabetical order, each with its number in the index of first lines, the name of the author and a brief description of its content.

Alle Menschen müssen sterben (76) / Rosenmüller / On the finiteness of life; anticipation of the heavenly Jerusalem.

Auf, Christen-Mensch, auf, auf (98) / Scheffler / The Christian's battle against sin and the world.

Binde meine Seele wohl (135) / Knepper / Mystical eros.

Das Leben Jesu ist ein Licht (179) / Knepper / Of following Jesus which leads to sanctification.

Ermuntert euch, ihr Frommen (348) / Laurenti / Expectation of the end-time.

Guter Hirte, willst du nicht (463) / Scheffler / Christ, the shepherd; the Christian, the helpless lamb.

Ihr jungen Helden, aufgewacht (602) / Knepper / Denial and rejection of the world, turning to God.

Komm, o komm, du Geist des Lebens (732) / Held / Supplication to God.

Kommt, und lasst euch Jesum lehren (757) / Gesenius/Denicke / Paraphrase of the beatitudes.

Mache dich, mein Geist, bereit (803) / Freystein / Watchfulness.

Mir nach, spricht Christus, unser Held (876) / Scheffler / Following Jesus.

O heil'ger Geist, kehr bei mir (uns) ein (967) / Schirmer / One of the few hymn-texts that address the holy spirit.

Ringe recht, wenn Gottes Gnade (1050) / Winkler / Christian battle, life and conduct.

Sei Lob und Ehr' dem höchsten Gut (1095) / Schütz / Praise of God.

All but three of these core hymns are written in the spirit of Pietism. Of the three exceptions, two date from the time of the Thirty-Years' War (76, 732) and one from the late seventeenth century (757). This latter text is a biblical paraphrase written in language which still speaks to modern Christians. Similarly, the hymns by Held (732) and Schütz (1095) are sound both from the theological as well as the literary point of view and of enduring value.

The starting point and entire reason for this study has been a quest for the German hymnody of the Brethren generally and the hymns written by Brethren in particular. The total hymnody has been examined under various aspects both in some detail and through broad summaries. Twenty Brethren hymn-writers have been discovered along the way and approximately 150 new undocumented texts have been made accessible, which constitute a possible source for additional Brethren-authored hymns.

At the present state of research into Brethren hymnody, the following are the names of the Brethren who wrote religious poetry and hymns in the German language:

Bamberger, C[hristian] (1801-1880) - 2 hymns.
Becker, Peter (1687-1758) - 1 hymn.
Danner, Heinrich (1742-before 1814) - 2 hymns.
Danner, Jakob (fl. 1800) - 1 hymn.
Gerlach, David (ca.1811-1879) - 1 hymn.
Grebil, Samuel (1809-1881) 1 hymn.
Haller, Jakob (ca.1777-1865) - 1 hymn.
Hoffer, J. (19th cent.) - 1 hymn.
Knepper, Wilhelm (1691-ca.1743) - 100 hymns.
Kurtz, Heinrich (1796-1874) - 1 hymn.

Mack, Alexander (1679-1735) - 1 hymn.
Mack, Alexander, Jr. (1712-1802) - 24 hymns.
Meyer, Jakob (1832-1906) - 3 hymns.
Miller, Abraham (d. 1843) - 1 hymn.
Miller, S. D. (19th cent.) - 5 hymns.
Naas, Johann (1669-1742) - 2 hymns.
Preiss, Johannes (1702-1724) - 13 hymns.
Preiss, Wilhelm (1789-1849) - 14 original texts and translations.
Sauer, Christoph, II (1721-1784) - 1 hymn.
Stoll, Jakob (1731-1822) - 24 hymns.

Not all of the hymns referred to above appeared in Brethren hymnals. Most of the hymns of Mack, Jr. and all of Johannes Preiss's were printed elsewhere. Although the majority of these hymns had a rather short life in Brethren hymnody, three of Knepper's texts became core hymns. Three texts were later incorporated in English translation into The Brethren Hymnal (1951). They are Mack, Jr.'s "Bless, o Lord, this Church of Thine" (695), Naas's "Savior of My Soul" (331), and one stanza of a hymn by Stoll, "O How is the Time So Urgent" (1032), although incorrectly attributed to Alexander Mack. Mack's baptismal hymn, never reprinted in any American hymnal, was translated and published in 1958 on the occasion of the 250th anniversary of the first Brethren baptism at Schwarzenau.

Although this study is ready for publication, it is by no means considered closed. Further Brethren hymns in print might be discovered yet. References to German hymn-writers among the Brethren are found here and there in secondary literature. Thus there is mention of one John Berkley, Sr. of the Elk Lick congregation in Pennsylvania, of whom it is said that "He was quite a poet, and composed a number of German hymns, which, however, were never published, owing to his having sent them to Editor Kurtz, founder of the Gospel Visitor, who, at a time of removing his printing office, either lost or mislaid the manuscript."[1]

The German hymnody of the Brethren both in its entirety as well as its Brethren component is distinctly marked by the movement of Pietism rather than by Anabaptism. This is neither surprising nor unique. Hymns in the Pietist manner had been around for a very long time, even before the movement called by that name had actually come into existence. The old hymns of the Anabaptists had become irrelevant even to the German Mennonites. In their hymnal publishing the early Brethren followed the pattern of Pietist hymnals.

Thus, in one way, one cannot speak of a peculiarly and distinctly "Brethren" hymnody as such. On the other hand, if one considers that almost one seventh of all the hymns published in Brethren hymnals were written by Brethren (even though half of these came from one source) there exists a fairly large body of religious poetry which does indeed constitute the German hymnody of the Brethren.

NOTES

[1] Jerome E. Blough, History of the Church of the Brethren of the Western District of Pennsylvania (Elgin, Ill.: Brethren Publishing House, 1916), p. 86.

Das Kleine Davidische Psalterspiel
(pp. 41-60)

Die Kleine

Harfe,

Gestimmet von unterschiedlichen Lieblichen

Liedern oder Lob-Gesängen,

Welche gehöret werden

Von den Enden der Erden,

zu Ehren dem Gerechten.

--◇--◇--◇--◇--◇--◇--◇--◇--

Diese Kleine Harfe klinget zwar lieblich,
aber doch noch im niedrigen Thon;

Bis das grosse

Harfen = Spieler Heer

den Gesang erhöhen wird.

• • •

Gott und dem Lamm sey die Ehre und
das Lob in Zeit und Ewigkeit! Amen.

———————————————————

Zum ersten mal ans Licht gegeben.

———————————————————

Chesnuthill. gedruckt bey Samuel Saur, 1792.

Die Kleine Harfe
(pp. 61-67)

Geistliches

Gewürz-Gärtlein

Heilsuchender Seelen;

Oder kurz-gefaßten

Betrachtungen,

Ueber einige auserlesene Sprüche der heilig-
en Schrift, in gebundenen

Schluß-Reimen
und
Geistliche Brosamen,

Zur Erweckung, Stärkung und Erquickung, auf
das Innere Leben gerichtet, von einem
Kinde in der Schule JEsu Christi.

Nebst einem

Anhang,

Bestehend aus Geistlichen Lieder und
Andachten, ans Licht gegeben, von

J. St—ll.

Ephrata:
Gedruckt und zu haben, bey Johannes Baumann,
Im Jahr 1806.

Geistliches Gewürz-Gärtlein
(p. 127)

Die kleine
Perlen-Samlung.
oder Auswahl Geistreicher
Lieder,

Mehrstentheils von Manuscripten genommen, zum Dienst, Gebrauch und Auferbauung aller Gottliebenden Brüder und Schwestern in Christo.

Zusamen getragen in gegenwärtiger kleiner Form,
von J. C. Pfautz.

Lobsinget ihr Schwestern und Brüder,
Lobsinget mit Geistlichen Lieder,
Lobsinget mit Herzen und Mund,
Lobsinget, mach't Gottes Lob kund.

Erste Auflage.

Ephrata:

Gedruckt bey J. C. Pfautz. 1858

Die kleine Perlen-Sammlung
(pp. 81-91)

Die kleine
Lieder Sammlung,
oder Auszug aus dem
Psalterspiel
der
Kinder Zions,

zum Dienst inniger heilsuchender Seelen, insonderheit aber der Brüderschaft der Täufer zum Dienst und Gebrauch zusammengetragen in gegenwärtig kleiner Form, und mit einem zweyfachen Register versehen.

"Ich will den Herrn loben, so lange
ich lebe, und meinem Gott lobsingen,
weil ich hie bin." Ps. 146, 2.

Erste Auflage.

Hägerstadt:
Gedruckt bey Gruber und May.
1826.

Die Kleine Lieder Sammlung
(pp. 68-80)

Das Christliche Gesang-Buch.

Eine Zusammenstellung

der

Besten Lieder der alten und neuen Dichter,

zum

Gottesdienstlichen Gebrauch

aller

Gott suchenden und heilsbegierigen Seelen.

Singet und spielt dem Herrn in Euren Herzen.
Eph. 5, 19.

Lancaster, Pa.:

Druck und Verlag von Johann Bär's Söhnen.
1874.

Das Christliche Gesang-Buch
(pp. 104-113)

Neue Sammlung

von

Psalmen, Lobgesängen

und

Geistlichen Liedern,

zum Gebrauch für den Privat-, Familien- und
öffentlichen Gottesdienst der

Alten Brüder,

und

aller innigen, heilsuchenden Seelen,

Zusammengetragen auf Anordnung der jährlichen Versammlung
aus unsern ältern, sowie aus neuern Gesangbüchern
von einem Committee.

"Ich will den Herrn loben, so lange ich lebe, und meinem Gott
lobsingen, weil ich hier bin." Psalm 146, 2.

Covington, Miami Co., O.

Herausgegeben von James Quinter.
1870.

Neue Sammlung
von Psalmen, Lobgesängen
und Geistlichen Liedern
(92-103)

Eine Sammlung

—von—

Psalmen, Lobgesängen,

—und—

Geistlichen Liedern,

Zum Gebrauch für den Privat-, Familien- und
Öffentlichen Gottesdienst der Brüder
(German Baptist Brethren.)

—und—

aller innigen, heilsuchenden Seelen,

zusammengetragen auf Anordnung der Jährlichen Versammlung, von einer Committee.

„Singet dem Herrn ein neues Lied.“ Jes. XLII. 10.
„Ich will dem Herrn singen mein Lebenlang, und meinen
Gott loben, so lange ich bin.“ Pf. CIV., 33.

Mount Morris, Ill.:
THE BRETHREN'S PUBLISHING COMPANY,
1893.

Eine Sammlung
von Psalmen, Lobgesängen
und Geistlichen Liedern
(pp. 114-123)

THE APPENDIXES

The reference material for this study consists of twelve appendixes.
The first eight provide supplementary material to each of the first eight
chapters. The last four are of larger scope and allow access to the body
of hymns from various aspects. Two objectives are common to all: first,
to provide the fullest possible useful information; secondly, to do this
with the greatest economy of space. The first was achieved by designing
the several indexes in such a way that the information provided by each
can be related to and supplemented by the others. The latter objective
was achieved by avoiding redundancies and unnecessary data, such as page
references in sources where the user can locate an item through that
work's own index.

The most significant part of the chapter appendixes are the lists of
new hymns for each hymnal. Those texts are the material among which as
yet unidentified hymns of Brethren authorship might be found through
further study and research.

The most comprehensive of the general appendixes is the First-Line
Index (Appendix IX). Here, all the hymn-texts, which are known to date to
have been published by the Brethren, are listed in alphabetical order.
The fullest possible description is given for each hymn at its first publication in Brethren hymnody: first line of text, often including the second
line for further identification; melody reference(s); name(s) of all
author(s) associated with a given hymn-text supported by documentation;
reference to publication in earlier non-Brethren hymnals; chorus, if
present; in the case of translations from English, the original author and
first line with documentation where possible; reference(s) to trans-
lation(s) into English; earliest publication in Brethren hymnody.

The remaining appendixes are auxiliary to the First-Line Index. Occurrence of a given hymn-text in later Brethren hymnals can be located
through the Publishing Record of Hymns (Appendix X). The Index of Hymn-
Writers (Appendix XII) provides minimal biographical information about
each person mentioned in the First-Line Index, again directing the user to
the literature through the references given with each name. This index
also lists all the hymn-texts associated with a person by their numbers in
the First-Line Index.

The Index of Melodies (Appendix XI) consists of two parts. The first
is similar to the First-Line Index of hymn-texts. Each melody is described according to the number of lines per stanza; the poetic meter; the
number of syllables per line; source references; first mention in Brethren
hymnody; and the numbers of the texts with which the melody was associated
in Brethren hymnody. The metric index provides access to these melodies
by stanza length and meter.

APPENDIX I

Geistreiches Gesang-Buch

1. PREFACE

May God grant much blessing and mercy.
Dear Friends and Brethren:

Several years ago, dissatisfaction was felt, in the meetings of the Baptist-minded, about the many different hymnals. For this reason, we have been led to select the most edifying hymns from all of them and compile them in one volume. One hundred new hymns were added, most of which were written by brethren who have been imprisoned now for almost three years for the sake of their witness to Jesus, in which imprisonment God's goodness has not been lacking. Rather, it has refreshed and strengthened the inward man, so that they have written these spiritual hymns for the comforting and strengthening of all those who are resolved to follow Jesus, the crucified Savior, in His saving words and commandments, and because of this must take upon themselves cross, shame, and various temptations.

Yes, I say it again, these hymns will be able to serve them to the awakening and joy of their hearts to look even more steadfastly to Jesus, the Author and Completer of the faith, to bear always more willingly the shame of Jesus with the people of God, and to rejoice in the imminent great happiness when we will hear the hymns of praise resound from all corners of the earth to the honor of the righteous (Isaiah 24:16). Yes, eventually, all creatures in heaven, on earth, and under the earth -- yes, on the sea and all that is in it -- will bring praise and gratitude to God and the Lamb. To this end may the almighty God also bless this little book for all who have turned their faces toward the heavenly Jerusalem (which is the mother of all true believers). May he grant all blessing and grace here in this world-wilderness to serve God in spite of this in spirit and in truth, and also to sing hymns to the Lord in spirit, to whom alone belongs honor from all creatures. To Him, the only true and living God and to Jesus, His most beloved Son, the crucified Savior, and also to the Holy Spirit, be praise, honor, glory, gratitude, fame, might, ... from eternity to eternity. Amen. Hallelujah.

(Donald F. Durnbaugh, European Origins of the Brethren, Elgin, Ill.: The Brethren Press, 1958, pp. 407-408)

2. EXTRACT FROM THE PREFACE TO FREYLINGHAUSEN'S HYMNAL

As regards the order of the rubrics, it is arranged in accordance with and as a consequence of the economy of our salvation.

For, placed at the beginning are those rubrics that pertain to the feast days, in which CHRIST, THE FOUNDATION OF OUR SALVATION [Heil], with his attributes and endowments, is brought before our eyes in the most lovely manner. The first 17 rubrics belong here. Next follows the rubric ON THE BENEVOLENCE [Leutseligkeit] OF GOD AND CHRIST as the SOURCE AND WELL-SPRING, whence flows all our salvation and blessed estate [Heil und Seligkeit].

Next follow those [rubrics] which represent the MEANS, through which God desires to restore us into union [Gemeinschaft] with him. To this belongs the instruction, which can be derived both from the WORKS OF CREATION as well as from the DIVINE PROVIDENCE AND GOVERNMENT [Regierung], but especially the appropriately named means of grace of the WORD and the SACRAMENTS, that is, BAPTISM and LORD'S SUPPER. After this follow those [rubrics] which tell you the ORDER, which you must follow if you desire to partake of Christ and the salvation which he has earned. According to this order you, dear soul [lieber Mensch], are being both warned against THE FALSE CHRISTENDOM as well as instructed in the TRUE AND UPRIGHT CHRISTENDOM. In particular, THE HUMAN MISERY AND DAMNATION is put before your eyes, to which you must submit in order to attain TRUE REPENTANCE AND CONVERSION and the TRUE FAITH in Jesus, the savior of the world: this faith, provided it is a true faith, not only accepts the JUSTIFICATION in the blood of Christ, but also results in a CHRISTIAN LIFE AND WALK IN GOD as an inevitable fruit.

If you now desire to know more particularly what exercises and virtues are implied by a Christian life and a walk in God, you need only contemplate devoutly what, in Christian hymns, you are being told here about PRAYER, about the SPIRITUAL WATCHFULNESS, about SPIRITUAL BATTLE AND VICTORY, about CHASTITY and the DENIAL OF SELF AND THE WORLD, about THE DESIRE FOR GOD AND CHRIST, THE LOVE TO JESUS, about BROTHERLY AND UNI-VERSAL LOVE, about FOLLOWING CHRIST, THE MYSTERY OF THE CROSS which is or-dained for you, about CHRISTIAN RESIGNATION [Gelassenheit], PATIENCE, AND STEADFASTNESS which you must prove under it [i.e., the cross], and about THE HEART'S SURRENDER TO GOD.

If you are found faithful in all of these, you will already in this life receive the reward of DIVINE PEACE, THE JOY IN THE HOLY GHOST and a TRUE JOYFULNESS OF FAITH. Indeed, your heart and mouth will daily over-flow with the PRAISE OF GOD, and the WISDOM of those not yet of age will protect you. But there is more! Your bridegroom will UNITE WITH YOU IN MARRIAGE so that you may thus share THE HIGH BIRTH OF THE BELIEVERS, which infinitely surpasses all majesty and glory of this world. All of this is what constitutes the BLESSEDNESS [Seligkeit] OF THE KINGDOM OF GRACE and the savory foretaste of the eternal life to come.

However, since despite all of this you will not yet have reached the goal or attained the treasure, you are being further reminded that the LIFE OF THE BELIEVERS here is still HIDDEN with Christ in God, and that the spiritual ZION cannot yet cease her LAMENTATIONS. Yet, in all of this, that HOPE is not being denied through which one must fortify and strengthen oneself despite all lament in this vale of tears, lest one's courage flag and cease. This hope leads THROUGH DEATH and THE BLESSED RESURRECTION INTO HEAVEN AND INTO THE HEAVENLY JERUSALEM, where the FINAL AND PERFECT BLESSEDNESS [Seligkeit] and glory shall be revealed, and where the fullness of God's riches will pour into his church [Gemeine] from one eternity into the next.

At the end, there are the MORNING-, EVENING-, and TABLE-HYMNS and those which one needs in times of COMMON DISTRESS and WHILE TRAVELLING.

3. A COMPARISON OF THE RUBRICS:

Freylinghausen's _Geistreiches Gesang-Buch_	Davidisches _Psalter-Spiel_
CONTENTS ... OF THE MATTERS CONTAINED IN THE HYMNS:	THE CHIEF SUBJECTS OF THE TRUE THEOLOGY AND ORDER OF SALVATION:
1. Of the coming of Christ in the flesh, or, Advent hymns.	1. Of the coming of Christ in the flesh.
2. Of the coming of Christ to judgment.	2. Of the coming of Christ to judgment.
3. Of the incarnation and birth Christ.	3. Of the incarnation and birth of Christ.
4. New-Year's hymns.	4. New-Year's hymns.
5. Of Jesus, his name and offices.	5. Of the transfiguration of Jesus in his manifold names, offices, and favors.
6. For the feast-day of Epiphany.	
7. For the feast-day of the purification of Mary.	
8. For the feast-day of the annunciation to Mary.	
9. Of the suffering and death of Jesus Christ.	6. Of the suffering and death of Jesus Christ.
10. Of the burial of Jesus Christ.	7. Of the burial of Jesus Christ.
11. Of the resurrection of Jesus Christ.	8. Of the resurrection of Christ.
12. Of the ascension of Jesus Christ.	9. Of the ascension of Christ and his sitting at the right hand of God.
13. Of the holy ghost and his manifold gifts and workings, or, Pentecost hymns.	10. Of the holy ghost and his manifold gifts and workings.
14. Of the nature of God and his attributes, or, for the feast-day of the holy trinity.	11. Of the nature and attributes of God, or the holy trinity.
15. For the feast-day of John the Baptist.	
16. For the feast-day of the visitation of Mary.	
17. Of the holy angels, or, for the feast-day of Michaelmas.	12. Of the holy angels.
18. Of the benevolence [_Leutseligkeit_] of God and Christ.	13. Of the benevolence [_Leutseligkeit_] of God and Christ.
19. Of the works of creation, etc.	14. Of the works of creation and the divine love and glory reflected therein.
20. Of divine providence and government.	15. Of divine providence and government.
21. Of the divine word.	16. Of the inner and the outer word.
22. Of holy baptism.	
23. Of the holy supper.	

24. Of the true and the false
    Christendom.
25. Of human misery and damnation.
26. Of the true repentance and
    conversion.
27. Of the true faith.
28. Of Christian life and conduct.
29. Of prayer.
30. Of spiritual watchfulness.
31. Of spiritual battle and victory.
32. Of chastity.
33. Of denial of self and the world.
34. Of the desire for God and Christ.
35. Of the love to Christ.
36. Of brotherly and universal love.

37. Of following Christ.
38. Of the mystery of the cross
    [which is laid upon you].
39. Of Christian resignation
    [Gelassenheit].
40. Of patience and steadfastness.
41. Of the heart's complete surrender
    to God.
42. Of divine peace.

43. Of the joy in the holy ghost.
44. Of the joyfulness of faith.
45. Of the praise of God.
46. Of the true wisdom.
47. Of the spiritual marriage
    [to Jesus].
48. Of the high birth of believers.
49. Of the hidden life of the
    believers.
50. Of the lament of Zion.
51. Of the hope of Zion.
52. Of death and resurrection.
53. Of heaven and the heavenly
    Jerusalem.
54. Morning hymns.
55. Evening hymns.
56. Table hymns.
57. In times of common distress.
58. Travel hymns.

17. Of the true and the false
    Christendom.
18. Of human misery and damnation.
19. Of the true repentance and
    conversion.
20. Of the true faith.
21. Of Christian life and conduct.
22. Of the true spiritual prayer.
23. Of spiritual watchfulness.
24. Of spiritual battle and victory.
25. Of the true chastity.
26. Of denial of self and the world.
27. Of the desire for God and Christ.
28. Of the love for Jesus.
29. Of brotherly and universal love.
30. Of the holy supper and
    love-feast of believers.
31. Of following Jesus.
32. Of the mystery of the cross
    [which is laid upon you].
33. Of Christian resignation
    [Gelassenheit].
34. Of the true steadfastness.
35. Of the heart's complete surrender
    to God.
36. Of divine peace and rest of the
    soul.
37. Of the joy in the holy ghost.
38. Of the joyfulness of faith.
39. Of the praise of God.
40. Of the divine wisdom.
41. Of the spiritual marriage
    [to Jesus].
42. Of the high birth of believers.
43. Of the hidden life of the
    believers.
44. Of the lament of Zion.
45. Of the hope of Zion.
46. Of death and resurrection.
47. Of heaven and the heavenly
    Jerusalem.
48. Morning hymns.
49. Evening hymns.
50. Table hymns.
51. In [times of] common distress.

52. Closing hymn.

4. RUBRICS SUPPLIED FOR <u>Geistreiches</u> <u>Gesang-Buch</u>, 1720.

The numbers refer to the numbers in the First-Line Index of this study. Asterisks denote new hymns.

1. Of the coming of Christ to judgment — 357*, 360, 371, 613*, 1186, 1188*
2. Of the incarnation and birth of Christ — 403, 474, 835*
3. Of the transfiguration of Jesus in his manifold names, offices, and favors — 24*, 293*, 458, 677, 678, 696*, 698, 838, 869, 930
4. Of the suffering and death of Jesus Christ — 32, 514*, 857, 947, 997, 1030, 1231*, 1232*.
5. Of the resurrection of Jesus Christ — 95, 907, 1023
6. Of the ascension of Christ and his sitting at the right hand of God — 976
7. Of the holy ghost and his manifold gifts and workings — 732, 897, 967
8. Of the nature and attributes of God, or the holy trinity — 647, 1211
9. Of the benevolence of God and Christ — 39, 536, 539, 778, 977, 1013*, 1081, 1174
10. Of the works of creation and the divine love and glory reflected therein — 622*, 623*
11. Of divine providence and lordship — 122, 431, 572, 588, 855, 1148, 1195, 1352*
12. Of the inner and the outer word — 672, 792
13. Of the true and the false Christendom — 83, 129*, 284*, 347, 611*, 753*, 757, 985*, 1291*
14. Of human misery and damnation — 56*, 61, 206, 812*
15. Of the true repentance and conversion — 13, 200, 538*, 597*, 661, 1031
16. Of the true faith — 338*, 366*, 607*, 963
17. Of Christian life and conduct — 491, 586*, 615*, 841*, 951 1360*
18. Of the true spiritual prayer — 1105
19. Of spiritual watchfulness — 54, 178*, 278*, 608*, 791, 803, 804*, 1187*, 1212*, 1224, 1349*, 1352*
20. Of spiritual battle and victory — 98, 104, 185, 269, 506, 635, 700, 852*, 862*, 863*, 1017, 1027*, 1050
21. Of the true chastity — 724, 1175, 1181
22. Of denial of self and the world — 259, 339, 502, 568, 570, 602* 675, 836, 943, 1045*, 1162, 1204*, 1214, 1219
23. Of the desire for God and Christ — 300*, 302, 444, 463, 561, 571, 589, 854, 858, 983, 1016, 1190, 1323, 1345
24. Of the love for Jesus — 258, 310, 515, 552, 565, 587, 659, 811*, 864, 868, 1068, 1269
25. Of brotherly and universal love — 605*, 606, 1106
26. Of the holy supper and love-feast of believers — 23*, 36, 196*, 274*, 752*, 794*, 998*

27. Of following Jesus	4*, 179*, 180*, 379, 471, 604*, 876, 995*, 1220*, 1258*, 1310
28. Of the mystery of the cross [which is laid upon you]	108, 192*, 297, 412, 744, 865, 870, 932, 1120, 1234
29. Of Christian resignation	439
30. Of the true steadfastness	361*, 375, 867, 1082, 1091, 1093
31. Of the heart's complete surrender to God	517, 562*, 1199
32. Of divine peace and rest of the soul	386, 555, 1256, 1303*
33. Of the joy in the holy ghost	60, 261, 467*, 544, 987, 1002*, 1026*
34. Of the joyfulness of faith	3, 201, 276*, 316, 582*, 1179, 1213*, 1227, 1361*, 1362*
35. Of the praise of God	79, 314, 352*, 465, 516, 522, 551*, 795, 798*, 805, 918, 1044, 1095, 1316*, 1341
36. Of the divine wisdom	829*
37. Of the spiritual marriage [to Jesus]	559
38. Of the high birth of believers	1036
39. Of the hidden life of the believers	355, 806*
40. Of the lament of Zion	135*, 456, 769*, 1159
41. Of the hope of Zion	377*, 498, 646*, 650, 667, 1084, 1209, 1236, 1304*, 1353*, 1363*
42. Of death and resurrection	359, 553
43. Of heaven and the heavenly Jerusalem	76, 348, 961*, 964, 1295
44. Morning hymns	345, 535, 936, 992
45. Evening hymns	234, 236, 238*, 239*, 445, 927, 1327
46. Table hymns	369*, 464*, 797
47. In [times of] common distress	1259
48. Baptism	34*, 40*, 158, 610*, 905, 1155*, 1245*
49. Footwashing	68*
50. Parting hymns	931*
51. Hymns of supplication	117*, 306, 332, 487, 496, 668, 727*, 788, 1007*, 1347
52. Travelling hymns	639

5. NEW HYMNS

Single asterisks denote hymns that appear only in this hymnal; double asterisks denote hymns that appear in all subsequent German Brethren hymnals.

(4)	Ach armer Christ, wo willst du hin auf diesen schmalen Wegen.*
(23)	Ach Herr Jesu, sei uns freundlich jetzt in dieser Abend Stund'.
(24)	Ach Herr Jesu, sieh, wir Armen sind vor deinem Angesicht.*
(34)	Ach Jesu, schau hernieder auf uns, dein' arme Schaf'.
(40)	Ach liebster Jesu, sieh auf mich, weil ich jetzt zu dir schreie.
(56)	Ach wann willst du, Jesu, kommen einst mit deiner vollen Kraft.
(68)	Ach wie so lieblich und wie fein ist es, wenn Brüder einig sein.
(129)	Beklagt doch diese Zeit, ihr Menschen-Kind' auf Erden.*
(135)	Binde meine Seele wohl an dich, Jesu, in der Liebe.**
(178)	Das Leben dieser Zeit ist voller Kampf und Streit.*
(179)	Das Leben Jesu ist ein Licht, das mir ist vorgegangen.**
(180)	Das Leben Jesu war zur Zeit der ersten Zukunft in dem Streit.
(192)	Den am Kreuz ich nur erwähle, meine ganze Lebenszeit.
(196)	Den Wunder-Gott, den Wunder-Gott, der uns im Geist vereinigt hat.
(238)	Der Tag ist nun vergangen, die dunkle Nacht bricht an.*
(239)	Der Tag verschwind't, der Abend kommt, sei munter, meine Seele.*
(274)	Die Zeit ist hin, die Stund' ist da.*
(276)	Die Zeit ist nah, Hallelujah, der Tag beginnt zu blicken.*
(278)	Die Zions-Gesellen, die müssen stets wachen.
(284)	Dieses ist der Weg, der eine, wo man auch sich selbst nicht traut.*
(293)	Du Brot, das von dem Himmel kommt, du Speis' der frommen Seelen.*
(300)	Du Licht, das ohne Wechsel ist, ich tu nach dir verlangen.
(338)	Endlich wird es uns gelingen, dass wir alle Welt bezwingen.
(352)	Es gehet wohl, Hallelujah. Der liebe Gott ist denen nah.
(357)	Es ist die letzte Stunde, ach Seelen, wachet auf.
(361)	Es ist mir die beste Sach', dass mein Jesus ist mein Leben.*
(366)	Es koste, was es will, ich will Gott halten still.
(369)	Es sei dem Schöpfer Dank gesagt, denn er ist gut.
(377)	Fliehet aus Babel, ihr Kinder aus Zion geboren.
(464)	Hab Dank, hab Dank, du guter Gott, hab Dank für deine grosse Liebe.
(467)	Halleluja wird man mit Freuden endlich singen.
(514)	Hindurch, hindurch, mein träger Sinn, richt dein Gesicht auf Jesu hin.
(538)	Ich bin ein Christ und Gottes Kind, weil Christus ist gestorben.*
(551)	Ich hab' die Hoffnung noch zu dir, zu dir, der Lebensquelle.*
(562)	Ich leb' mir nicht, denn Jesus hat durchs Wasser-Bad mich ganz und gar ertränket.*
(582)	Ich weiss, das mein Jesus lebet, der einmal für mich gestorben.*
(586)	Ich weiss nun, was ich suche, weil ich dasselb' verfluche.*
(597)	Ich wollte gerne Christum rein bekennen, wie es sollte sein.*
(602)	Ihr jungen Helden, aufgewacht, die ganze Welt muss sein veracht'.**
(604)	Ihr Kinder auf der Glaubens-Bahn, lasst euch dies nicht verdriessen.*
(605)	Ihr Kinder der Liebe, was wird es einst werden.
(607)	Ihr Kinder, fasset neuen Mut in eurem Stand.
(608)	Ihr Kinder Gottes allzugleich, seid munter und tut wachen.
(610)	Ihr Kinder, merket wohl, wie es noch werden soll.*
(611)	Ihr Kinder Zion, schauet, in was Gefahr ihr seid.*
(613)	Ihr Knecht' des Herren, kommt heran, eu'r Zentner darzulegen.*

(615)   Ihr lieben Menschen-Kinder und ja auch arme Sünder.*
(622)   Im Anfang aller Dinge schuf Gott Himmel und Erd'.*
(623)   Im Anfang als Gott schuf den Himmel und die Erden.*
(646)   Jauchzet im Vorspiele freudig alle Frommen.*
(696)   Jesus ist der gute Hirt, der in diese Welt ist kommen.*
(727)   Komm doch, mein Jesu Christ, du weisst wohl, wie mir ist.
(752)   Kommt, lasset uns bedenken des Herren Wunderwerk.
(753)   Kommt, lasst uns aus Babel fliehen, wer sich noch drin finden mag.
(769)   Lasst uns innigst, seufzend klagen, Gott zu fragen.
(794)   Lob sei dir, du erwürgtes Lamm, Lob sei dir an des Kreuzes Stamm.
(798)   Lobet Gott zu jeder Stunde und auch jetzt mit Herz und Munde.
(804)   Macht euch bereit zur Ewigkeit, die ihr seid aufgestanden.*
(806)   Man mag wohl ins Klaghaus gehen und den Lauf der Welt besehen.
(811)   Mein erwünschter Lebensbrunn gibt nicht Wasser süss und bitter.*
(812)   Mein ganzes Herz beweget sich, mein Gott, wann ich gedenk' an dich.
(829)   Mein Herz, dich schwing zum höchsten Gut.
(835)   Mein Herz, wach auf und singe, betracht das grosse Werk.*
(841)   Mein Jesu, Gottes Sohn, der du zuvor und nun.*
(852)   Mein schwacher Geist von Innen wirf du doch deine Sinnen.
(862)   Meine Seele sei getrost, Jesus hat ja überwunden.*
(863)   Meine Seele, tu dich schwingen hin durch alle Berg' und Tal'.*
(915)   Nun, liebster Jesu, sieh, wir wallen allhier in dieser Wüstenei.*
(931)   Nun wollen wir jetzt alle schicken ein jegliches an seinen Ort.
(961)   O Gott, was wird sich dort vor grosse Freud' erheben.*
(985)   O Jesu, lehre doch dein Volk, das allhier noch auf dieser Erden.*
(995)   O Kreatur, lass ab, mit deinem Gott zu streiten.*
(998)   O Lammes Blut, wie trefflich gut bist du in meiner Seelen.
(1002) O liebste Liebe, wie ist mir so wohl. Wenn man dir nur lebet.
(1007) O mein starker Bundeskönig, wunderbare Lebenskraft.
(1013) O scharfes Licht, das Herz und Nieren prüft.*
(1026) O Vater der Liebe, lass mir es sein wohl.
(1027) O Vater, Himmels-König, du Schöpfer aller Welt.*
(1045) Preise den Herren, der wunderlich uns allhier führet.
(1155) Ueberschlag die Kost, spricht Jesus Christ.* (A. Mack, Sr.)
(1187) Wacht auf, ihr Christen alle, es ist nun hohe Zeit.
(1188) Wacht auf, ruft uns die Stimme in dieser letzten Zeit.*
(1204) Was hier dem Fleisch oft bitter schmeckt und sehr zuwider ist.*
(1212) Was machen doch und sinnen wir? Ach, dass wir munter wachten.
(1213) Was mag uns von Jesu scheiden? Weder Leiden, falsche Freuden.
(1220) Weil Christus uns erschienen ist mit seinem Wort und Leben.*
(1231) Wenn an Jesu ich gedenke und auch lenke meine Sinnen da hinan.
(1232) Wenn an meinen Freund ich denke und versenke in sein Leiden.
(1245) Wenn man allhier der Welt ihr Tun beschämt in keuschem Leben.
(1258) Wer hier will finden Gottes Reich, der werde einem Kinde gleich.
(1291) Wie lange willst du noch, du starker Gott, verziehen.*
(1303) Wie wohl ist mir, wie wohl ist mir! Wenn unser Gott im Geiste.
(1304) Wiederbringer aller Dinge, Wiederbringer meiner Seel'.
(1316) Wir loben dich, o Herre Gott, du väterlich Gemüte.
(1349) Zion, brich herfür jetzt durch Tor und Tür.
(1352) Zion soll billig freudig sein, weil Gottes Wahrheit bricht herein.*
(1353) Zion, Zion, du geliebte und von Herzen oft betrübte.
(1360) Zu wachen lehrt uns Gottes Sohn, gerecht zu leben für sei'm Thron.*
(1361) Zuletzt, wenn wir einst zum Ziele gelangen.
(1362) Zum Nach-Denk will den Meinen hier, den Rat nun geben.*
(1363) Zur Friedensstadt, nach Gottes Wort und Rat.

APPENDIX II

Das Kleine Davidische Psalterspiel

1. PREFACE.

In Jesus, the crucified head of his church [Gemeinde], whom he has won and bought with his blood and death as his own in time and eternity; through this true son of God may the Father of all spirits give his blessing [Heil] and grace in this sincere work of love.

Most dearly beloved friends and brethren, indeed, all lovers of the divine truth who are receiving this small Psaltery with favor: the spirit of truth and true praise and thanksgiving desires that in the same measure as externally the mouth permits the voice to sound, so should the heart become harmonious before the Lord, because to God, the sacrifice of one's lips alone is not sufficient. That is why the Lord lamented over his Israel of old saying: "This people draweth nigh unto me with their mouth, and honoureth me with their lips: but their heart is far from me. But in vain they do worship me, teaching for doctrines the commandments of men" (Matt. 15:8[-9]). To such a nation the Lord speaks thus: "Take thou away from me the noise of thy songs, for I will not hear the melody of thy viols" (Amos 5:23).

If God demanded in his old covenant that he should be served with heart and mouth, how much more so in the new covenant, when God desires to be served and worshipped in spirit and in truth. And since this world is full of such lip-servants, with singing and beautiful resounding of songs and prayers and speeches, let those souls who are concerned about their salvation [Heil] conduct their worship - be it now through song, prayer, or speech - in such a manner that it flows from the bottom of their hearts and that it be done to the honor and glorification of God. Let their loins be girded so that their fleeting senses be kept in rein and that everything be done in the name of Jesus Christ to the honor of the Father, etc.

Das Kleine Davidische Psalterspiel was published because there has often been a great lack of hymn-books in the meetings of the membership, and in some meetings two or even three different hymnals were being used. Therefore it was decided to have a hymn-book printed. There was also unanimity in selecting the majority and the best-known hymns from the well-known larger Psalter-Spiel, namely those with the most widely familiar melodies, and to issue it in this format.

Great pains have been taken to go about this in the most impartial way so that hymns have been selected from other authors' hymn-books in addition to several hymns which had been found in manuscripts. Thus it can in fact be said that this is quite an impartial hymnal, indeed, an artless flower-garden containing all manner of flowers or songs for all those who praise the Lord with heart and lips.

Since there is no desire to boast of this hymn-book in this foreword (as many other authors are wont to do), this work will be allowed to sing its own praises, for one knows full well that everything is still in a state of imperfection on earth. Thus all hymn-books must be reckoned among these imperfections which is the reason why there has never yet been a perfect hymn-book published. Each still has its shortcomings and needs to be put right. Therefore this hymn-book is likewise left open to judgment and is simply called The Small Psaltery, just as the most precious teachings of Jesus are very simply called by the unassuming title, The New Testament.

Inasmuch as all good things which the spirit of God works, be they in speaking, praying, or singing, derive from the perfect ocean of the divine, everything in like manner hastens to return to this, its origin, where, in a state of perfection everything again attains to the perfect praise before the throne of God. Therefore, let all believers on earth edify one another according to the admonition of the holy apostle Paul when he says: "Speaking to your selves in psalms and hymns, and spiritual songs, singing and making melody in your heart to the Lord" (Eph. 5:6 [i. e., 19]).

Therefore the praise of the believers on earth will last until the perfect praise is revealed. Let us now therefore offer through Him the sacrifice of praise unto God always, which is the fruit of the lips of those who confess his name (Heb. 13:15). The time will come when that will be fulfilled of which the prophet Isaiah says: "We hear hymns of praise from the end of the earth to the glory of the righteous one." But now this is often true: "O how lean [wanting?] I am."

Now may the Lord soon fulfill his promise to the comfort of all souls that wait upon him in the faith of Zion, and that the spirit and the bride may say: Come, and he who hears it, let him say: Come, and he who so wishes let him take the water of life free.

Halleluiah, praise, honor, and power to God our Lord in eternity, Amen!

2. NEW HYMNS

Single asterisks denote hymns that appear only in the edition under which they are listed. Double asterisks denote hymns that appear also in all subsequent German hymnals of the Brethren.

1744

(28)   Ach Herzens-Geliebte, wir scheiden jetzunder.
(133) Bewahre dich, o Seel', dass du nicht abgeführet.
(134) Beweg mein Herz durch deine Kraft und es zu deiner Liebe richte.
(140) Bleibe bei mir, liebster Freund, Jesu, mein Verlangen, weil die Sonne nicht mehr scheint.
(237) Der Tag ist hin mit seinem Lichte, die Nacht ist da mit Dunkelheit.**
(247) Die Freundlichkeit meines Geliebten mich rühret.
(279) Dies ein', das not, lehr mich, dass ich beständiglich dich, Jesum, liebe.
(286) Dir sei Lob, Herrlichkeit und Preis, Immanuel, gegeben.
(321) Ein König gross von Macht und Ehr ist, dem ich mich vertraue.

(356)   Es ist der Not ein Ziel gesteckt. Geduld, Gott hat den Held erweckt.
(388)   Fröhlich soll mein Herze springen, weil die Zeit voller Freud'.
(501)   Herzliebster Abba, deine Treue und herzliche Barmherzigkeit.
(595)   Ich will von deiner Güte singen und rühmen deine Freundlichkeit.**
(621)   Ihr Zions Bürger allzumal, die ihr nun hört den Ruf und Schall.
(688)   Jesu, wahres Gotteslamm, meiner Seele Leben.**
(948)   O du Menschen-Kind, eile doch geschwind.
(1022) O teure Seelen, lasst euch wachend finden.
(1191) Wann willst du, meiner Seelen Trost, ein wenig mich erquicken.
(1239) Wenn ich es recht betracht' und sehe Tag und Nacht.
(1320) Wo bleiben meine Sinnen, wie trüb ist mein Verstand.
        (A. Mack, Jr.)

1760

(351)   Es eilt heran und bricht schon wirklich an.
(382)   Fort, ihr Glieder und Gespielen und wer sonst den Bräut'gam liebt.
(410)   Glaube, Liebe, Hoffnung sind das Geschmeide wahrer Christen.
(1146) Treuer Gott, wie bin ich dir jetzt und ewiglich verpflichtet.
(1229) Wenig sind, die göttlich leben und für Gottes Angesicht.

1764

(123)   Befiehl, mein Herze, deine Wege alleine dem, der alles ist.
(251)   Die Glocke schlägt und zeigt damit, die Zeit hat abgenommen.
(292)   Du Aufgang aus der Höh', du Glanz der Herrlichkeit.
(299)   Du Herr des Himmels und der Erden, woher kommt diese Knechts-Gestalt.
(1208) Was ist die Gebühr der Christen anders als ein ernster Streit.

1797 (Billmeyer)

(1042) Prächtig kommt der Herr, mein König.
(1132) Stimmt unserm Gott ein Loblied an mit freudigem Gemüte.
(1252) Wenngleich aus tiefer Mitternacht Gewitter um mich blitzen.

APPENDIX III

Die Kleine Harfe

NEW HYMNS

Single asterisks denote hymns that appear only in this hymnal. Double asterisks denote hymns that appear also in all subsequent German hymnals of the Brethren.

(26)   Ach Herr, wie billig schäm ich mich, wenn ich gedenk an dich.
(69)   Ach wie war ich in meinem Schlummer versunken zum Abgrund hin.*
(154)   Christen müssen sich hier schicken in des Kreuzes schmale Bahn.
        (Saur, II)
(219)   Der Herr ist mein getreuer Hirt, der mich behüt' mit Fleisse.*
(225)   Der Herr uns segne und behüt' und lass sein Antlitz leuchten.
(291)   Du armer Pilger wandelst hier in diesem Jammertal. (Becker)
(294)   Du forschest mich, o Herr, wie wunderlich.* (Mack, Jr.)
(331)   Eins betrübt mich sehr auf Erden, dass so wenig selig werden.
        (Naas)
(462)   Gute Nacht, ihr meine Lieben, gute Nacht, ihr Herzens-Freund'.**
        (J. Danner)
(470)   Heiland meiner Seel', schaff, dass ich erwähl. (Naas)
(520)   Hoffnung lässt nicht zu Schanden werden, die auf den Herren ist
        gegründet.*
(549)   Ich folge dir bis an dein Kreuze hin, weil ich in dich, mein Lieb',
        verliebet bin.*
(629)   In dem Anfang war das Wort, wie uns Sanct Johannes schreibet.*
(695)   Jesus Christus, Gottes Sohn, dir sei Lob und Ehr' gegeben.
        (Mack, Jr.)
(708)   Jesus, wahrer Mensch in Gnaden, kehre heute bei uns ein.*
(813)   Mein Gemüt bedenket heut', wie in der bestimmten Zeit.*
(898)   Nun bricht der Hütten Haus entzwei, nun kann der Leib verwesen.
        (Mack, Jr.)
(1000) O Liebe, labe doch das sehnende Verlangen, das sich befindet noch.*
(1004) O mein armes Herze, glaub, Gott wird alles doch gut machen.*
(1289) Wie hochvergnügt bin ich, wenn mich die Welt entblösset.*
(1305) Wiederbringer des Verlor'nen, höre doch, was von dir heischt.*

APPENDIX IV

Die Kleine Lieder Sammlung

1. PREFACE

Speaking to your selves in psalms, and hymns, and spiritual songs, singing
and making melody in your heart to the Lord. (Eph. 5:19)

Most dearly beloved friends, brethren, and fellow-pilgrims to the blessed
eternity!

The small collection of songs [Lieder Sammlung] is herewith coming to
light for the first time. However, it has by no means been the intention
to detract from the so well-arranged Psalterspiel. Rather, it [i.e., the
Psalterspiel] is being warmly commended to all god-loving fathers of house-
holds and all mothers for diligent use in their families. This [present]
small book also shows that the Psalterspiel is being held in high esteem
because most of its hymns [i.e., the Lieder Sammlung's] were taken from
it. For the rest, various hymns were added from other hymnals and several
from manuscripts, so that it may indeed be called a very impartial little
hymn-book, for the convenience of travellers and especially for those
among our dear youth, who still desire to honor their mother-tongue. And
inasmuch as there has been evidence of a general lack of hymnals in public
worship-services, it is hoped that this may be remedied with the help of
this small collection of hymns.

Now then, beloved young hearts and god-loving souls! Here you have a
small book with beautiful hymns - a most fragrant flower-garden - use it
diligently in the meetings. Allow the meaning of the verses to penetrate
deep into your hearts. Thus it will benefit you toward your eternal state
of bliss [Glückseligkeit].

A special effort was made to keep this book small and therefore, for
the most part, only the best-known hymns and, in some cases, only their
most touching stanzas have been included. Some of the most beautiful
hymns, especially from the Psalterspiel could not be shortened because of
their dignity and context and were too lengthy to be included in full in
this format.

May the Lord bless this humble work to his praise and the fulfillment
of his word when he says in Isaiah 12:5: Sing unto the Lord; for he hath
done excellent things: this is known in all the earth. And in Psalm
149:1: Praise ye the Lord. Sing unto the Lord a new song, and his praise
in the congregation of saints.

Let every thing that hath breath, praise the Lord. Praise ye the Lord.
Ps. 150:6.

2. NEW HYMNS

Single asterisks denote hymns that appear only in the edition under which they are listed. Double asterisks denote hymns that appear also in all subsequent German hymnals of the Brethren.

1826

(400)   Geh, Seele, frisch im Glauben fort, und sei nur unverzagt.**
(441)   Gottlob, das Leiden dieser Zeit ist ein(st)mals überwunden.
(450)   Gottlob, mein Leben ist vollbracht, das Kreuz ist überwunden.**
(492)   Herr Jesu, möchten's alle wissen, wie gut man's bei dir haben kann.*
(599)   Ihr Freunde Jesu allzumal, die ihr tut seinen Willen.**
(837)   Mein Herzens-Jesu, meine Freud', wie innig liebst du doch die
         Leut'.*
(912)   Nun kommt, ihr Christen alle, aus Liebe höret an.**
(925)   Nun scheiden wir, ihr Herzens-Freund', von diesem Orte fort.**
(1008) O meine Seele sinke vor deinen Goel hin.
(1114) So gehe nun in deine Gruft, bis Jesus Christus aus der Luft.**
(1267) Wer Ohren hat zu hören, der merk', was ich ihm sag'.
(1311) Wir danken dir, du grosser Gott, dass du von deinem Throne.

1827

(1202) Was hat uns doch bewogen, zu gehen aus von heim.   (H. Danner?)

1829

(164)   Dankbar lasst uns Christum preisen, der sein Volk auf Erden liebt.
(283)   Diesen Täufling bringen wir, Jesu, deinen Liebes-Armen.
(737)   Kommet, ihr lieben Geschwister, zum festlichen Mahle.
(826)   Mein Heiland, mein Erlöser, blick unsre Sehnsucht an.
(1324) Wo ist die Kirche Jesu doch? Wo trägt man freudig Christi Joch.

1841

(221)   Der Herr schickt seine Diener aus, wir finden schwach uns überaus.
(222)   Der Herr sei selbst in unsrer Mitt' und segne uns mit Frieden.
(373)   Ew'ges Evangelium, das wie Milch und Honig schmecket.
(493)   Herr Jesu, sei an diesem Tage so mit uns, dass man's fühlen mag.
(946)   O du Heiliger, Allbarmherziger, Herr und Schöpfer der Welten.

APPENDIX V

Die kleine Perlen-Sammlung

1. PREAFCE

Die kleine Perlen-Sammlung appears herewith for the first time in print, but not because there is a dearth of hymn-books. Rather, because it is hoped that some especially interested people might edify themselves with it, for most of the hymns here included were written by pious teachers of the gospel. These are Jacob Stoll, William Preis, and others by whose sermons many a brother and sister still living has often been refreshed, delighted, and edified.

Many of the hymns have never before been published in print.

It is hoped that the Lord will bless this small book to his glory and to the edification of all souls that are seeking their salvation, Amen.

The author.

2. NEW HYMNS (not including translations from the English)

Single asterisks denote hymns that appear only in this hymnal. Double asterisks denote hymns that appear also in all subsequent German hymnals of the Brethren.

(37)   Ach kommt, ihr liebe Brüder, seht euren Jesum an.* (W. Preiss)
(70)   Ach wie wichtig ist die Zeit, worin wir nun leben.* (Author's name withheld)
(93)   Auf, auf, du junger Mut, auf, auf zu deinem Gott.* (S. D. Miller)
(142)   Bleibe bei mir, liebster Seelen-Freund, Jehova, dem ich mich vereint.* (Bamberger)
(197)   Denket doch, ihr Adams-Kinder, denket an die Ewigkeit. (By a young man on his death-bed)
(215)   Der Herr hat euch jetzt sehr betrübt, indem dass er. (Unknown)
(240)   Der Vater, der hat mich gezeugt, die liebe Mutter mich gesäugt.* (Bamberger)
(241)   Der Weg zu dem Himmel von Christus gemacht.* (Unknown)
(313)   Ehre sei Gott in der Höh', dem Heiland aller Welt.* (A. Miller)
(333)   Einst fiel vom ewigen Erbarmen ein Strahl in meine Nacht herein.* (W. Preiss)
(365)   Es ist wieder kommen ein schönes Neu-Jahr. (Hoffer)
(421)   Gott, du bist lobenswert, weil du uns gibst allzeit.* (Meyer)
(472)   Heimweh fühl' ich, Sohn vom Hause, draussen ist es kalt und kahl. (W. Preiss)
(508)   Hier sind wir in der Trauer-Zeit und müssen streiten viel.* (Author's name withheld)
(513)   Himmel, Erde, Luft und Meere, grosser Gott, ist all dein Werk.* (Unknown)
(577)   Ich walle stündlich hin zur frohen Ewigkeit. (W. Preiss)
(601)   Ihr jungen Helden, auf, verlasst die ganze Welt.* (S. D. Miller)
(609)   Ihr Kinder, habt Mut, wir kommen bald all' dort zusammen.* (Meyer)

(616)   Ihr Lieben, weint nicht, wir seh'n uns in Ewigkeit wieder.*
(W. Preiss)

(626)   Im Grabe ist Ruh', drum wanken dem tröstenden Ziele.* (W. Preiss)

(630)   In der frühen Morgenstund', da noch alles stille. (Stoll)

(648)   Jehova, o du schönster Nam', wie reizend ist ja deine Lieb.'*
(Author's name withheld)

(673)   Jesu Liebe ist ein Licht, das ich will verlassen nicht. (Haller)

(704)   Jesu, mein Trost und Heil auf meiner Pilger-Reis'.* (W. Preiss)

(712)   Jetzt ist die schöne Gnadenzeit und auch das angenehme Heut'.
(W. Preiss)

(760)   Kurz war mein Leben hier auf Erden, kurz, ja nur eine kleine Zeit.
(S. D. Miller)

(781)   Liebe Seele, denk daran, suche doch die Lebensbahn. (Author's name
withheld)

(782)   Liebe Seele, lass dir raten, du gehst nach der Ewigkeit. (Stoll)

(843)   Mein Jesus kaufte mich mit Blut, er hat mich teu'r bezahlt.* (W.
Preiss)

(846)   Mein Leben auf Erden ist mühsam allhier. (H. Danner)

(848)   Mein Leben ist mühsam allhier auf der Erd'.* (Written by a sister
in her suffering)

(988)   O Jesu, meine Freud', mein Trost, mein Heil und Licht. (S. D.
Miller)

(993)   O Jesu, wahrer Lebens-Brunn', du Ausfluss aller Güt'.* (S. D.
Miller)

(1066)   Schon lang hört' ich eine Stimm' in mir so dauernd zu mir sagen.
(Gerlach)

(1140)   Tod, wie bist du durchgedrungen durch des Adams Glieder all'.*
(Unknown)

(1143)   Traurig muss man oftmals sein, tut man überlegen. (Author's name
withheld)

(1205)   Was ich euch nun sage hier, nehmt es an aus Lieb' zu mir.** (W.
Preiss)

(1246)   Wenn mein Gemüt erfüllet ist mit Kummer mancherlei.* (W. Preiss)

(1317)   Wir sind herzlich schön vermahnt, wie uns ist der Weg gebahnt.
(Meyer)

154

APPENDIX VI

Neue Sammlung

NEW HYMNS

Single asterisks denote hymns that appear only in this hymnal. Double asterisks denote hymns that also appear in all subsequent German hymnals of the Brethren.

(21)   Ach Herr Jesu, mein Erretter, rette mich verlor'nes Kind.
(72)   Ach wohin soll ich geh'n, beladen, krank und matt.*
(125)   Begrabet mich nun immerhin, wo ich so lang verwahret bin.
(150)   Busse ist der Weg zum Leben, bitte, fahr im Bitten fort.
(161)   Christus ist der Kirche Haupt, die an seinen Namen glaubt.
(223)   Der Herr steigt aus des Jordans Flut, der Geist der Salbung auf ihm ruht.*
(325)   Ein Streiter bei der Kreuzesfahn' bin ich für Jesus Christ.
(489)   Herr Jesu, der du in der Nacht vor deinem Sterben hast bedacht.*
(574)   Ich trau' dem Herrn, mein Schatz ist er.
(617)   Ihr Sünder alle, freuet euch des Gottes, der euch Menschen gleicht.*
(640)   Israels Wächter rufet laut auf Zions hohen Mauern.
(736)   Komm, Vater, Sohn und heil'ger Geist, ehr deine Gnadenmittel jetzt.*
(889)   Neig, o mein Gott, dein Ohr zu mir. Ich Erd' und Asche fleh' zu dir.*
(892)   Nicht um Reichtum, nicht um Ehre bitt' ich, bester Vater, dich.
(896)   Noch ist der Herr in seiner Stadt, wiewohl sie tausend Lücken hat.*
(941)   O dass ob dieser Gnadenstätt' der Himmel sich eröffnen tät'.*
(1099)   Selig sind die geistlich Armen, denn das Himmelreich ist ihr.
(1119)   So lass dein Bild aufgehen, wovon wir abgewandt.*
(1128)   Sorgen, Furcht und manche Plagen setzen uns im Leben zu.
(1135)   Sünder, lernt das Blut erkennen, das das Lamm vergossen hat.*
(1136)   Sünder, lernt die Ordnung fassen, die zum Seligwerden führt.
(1185)   Wach auf zum Dank, o mein Gemüt, und preise Gottes Tun.**
(1313)   Wir danken dir, o treuer Gott, in dieser Morgenstund'.
(1337)   Wohlauf, mein' Seel', wohlauf, wirf alle Furcht beiseit'.*
(1343)   Zeuch durch deines Todes Kräfte mich in deinen Tod hinein.*

APPENDIX VII

Das Christliche Gesang-Buch

1. PREFACE TO THE FIRST EDITION

A Rhymed Preface
for the
New Christian Hymn-Book

Is any among you afflicted? let him pray. Is any merry? let him sing psalms. James 5. 13.

People will have their prefaces. It can do no harm to write a poem which says why the Brethren have again collected many hymns for the praise and glory of God. These now appear in this small volume which handily fits into a pocket while travelling. Thus one has available the abundance of beautiful flowers from above which smell delightfully and lovely, not deceptively. The fragrance is always present. Foreign parts [das Ausland, i.e., Europe] and America are two different countries which results in very expensive [import] duties. [The next two verses are unintelligible.] Well, that is the way it is [?] and many are sighing "Ach" and "Oh." There is no end to book publishing, yet not of certain ones, if one knows of the scarcity. It would be good to be united in song, but how can that be if there is no harmony in the use of books among Christ's disciples. One of them has the Psalterspiel; the Perlen-Sammlung is used by many as is the "Book of the New Brethren." Then there is "The Viol," the "Wine-brennerian Hymns," and "United Brethren." After that, there appears "Erb's [hymns]." Many a one struggles with the "Bard." There seems to be no end to this situation and confusion is caused when everyone pulls out of his sack what he has. The singing will not work, like [the one] above, one cannot praise it. Some have no books at all. To remedy this and turn this situation around we asked for advice. We were given permission to collect the essence (marrow) into a small book, not to bother with the shell, because one eats only the nut (core). We collected [this core], let the diversity be. But as there are a goodly number of those who like English, we are adding also English [hymns] lest somebody feel cheated.

2. PREFACE TO THE SECOND EDITION

It is customary for every book to have a preface, as was the case with the first edition of this hymn-book. However, that particular preface was not considered quite appropriate for a second edition. The latter had become necessary, partly because many errors had crept into the old book, partly because there has been a demand for more copies and none are available any more. For these reasons the brotherhood of the Eastern District of Pennsylvania appointed a committee to prepare and publish a second improved edition of the book. However, as far as possible, the number of hymns was to be the same as that in the old book. In the course of certain necessary changes individual hymns were placed differently. A small numeral in parentheses after the main number indicates the number which the hymn had in the old edition. Also, several entirely new hymns were included which are marked with the letter N following the main number.

Most of the hymns contained in the appendix of the old book have been omitted. They were replaced in the new edition by more substantial and spiritual hymns.

No changes were made in the English portion of this book; merely a number of edifying, beautiful hymns were added.

The Committee.

3. NEW HYMNS

1874

Single asterisks denote hymns that appear only in the edition under which they are listed. Double asterisks denote hymns that also appear in Eine Sammlung.

(10)   Ach es ist betrübt zu lesen, was man von dem Joseph hört.
(74)   Adje, mein vielgeliebter Mann (Weib) und liebe Kinder alle.**
(88)   An meiner Gruft stärkt euren Glauben, ihr Eltern, die ihr mich geliebt.
(171) Das Grab ist aller Totenhaus, heut' trägt man mich, bald dich hinaus.**
(190) Dem Lämmlein nachgehen, jungfräulich und rein, so wird man bestehen.
(216) Der Herr hat uns befohlen, wir seine Diener sollen in alle Welt hingehen.
(224) Der Herr uns segne und behüt' und lass sein Antlitz leuchten.
(273) Die Zeit gehet zum End', nicht aber Gottes Tun.**
(334) Einst riefen Gottes Boten den Heiden trostvoll zu.
(340) Er gleichte den Rosen im Frühling gar schön.**
(427) Gott ist es, der alle Dinge, die herrlichen und die geringe.*
(442) Gottlob, dass ich den Tag vollbracht durch Gottes Gnad und Güte.**
(482) Herr, hier sind nun deine Kinder, komm, o komm und segne sie.
(530) Hört hier den alten Täufergrund, den ich bekenn' mit Herz und Mund.
(566) Ich mag mich, wo ich will, hinwenden, da seh' ich nichts denn tausend Not.**
(714) Johannes war ein Gottesmann, ja, voller Geist und Gnade.
(754) Kommt, lasst uns Jesum suchen bald, wir werden sonsten träg und kalt.
(913) Nun kommt, ihr frommen Seelen, all', die ihr Jesum liebt.**
(974) O ihr jung und alten Leut', ihr müsst trag'n das Sterbekleid.**
(994) O Jesu, wär' ich armes Kind in allem so wie du gesinnt.
(1014) O selig ist der Stand allhier in dieser Welt.**
(1019) O süsser Gott, du selig's Gut, wie liebest du die Leute.**
(1037) O wie so selig schläfest du nach manchem schweren Stand.**
(1070) Schreib alles fest in meinen Sinn, dass ich nicht nur ein Sieger bin.
(1071) Schreib alles, was man heut' gelehrt.**
(1163) Unsre Zeit ist kurz und bündig, die wir noch auf Erden sein.**
(1230) Wenig waren meine Tage, da ich lebte in der Zeit.**
(1251) Wenn wir des Herren Wort als heilsbegierig lieben.
(1339) Womit gleicht sich das Himmelreich? Ist es nicht dem Hausvater gleich.

157

1879

(167)   Dankt Jesu, dem Retter, dankt Jesu, dem Hort.*
(175)   Das Jerusalem, das droben, wo die Schar das Lämmlein loben.*
(262)   Die lieblichen Lehrer, die Christus gesandt.**
(311)   Durch Kreuz und Trübsal können schon die Menschen sich bekehren.**
(524)   Hör, ach erhör mein seufzend Schreien, du allerliebstes Vaterherz.*
(529)   Höret, wie im fernen Lande unser Freund und Bruder starb.*
(942)   O denke stets an deinen Tod! Du bist noch wohl, gesund und rot.**

APPENDIX VIII

Eine Sammlung von Psalmen, Lobgesängen, und Geistlichen Liedern

1. PREFACE

At the annual meeting of the "German Baptist-Brethren" held at Hagerstown, Md., June 2-4, 18991, a committee was nominated to compile a German hymnal.

The present work is the result of their difficult task. The committee was concerned, as far as possible to meet the wishes of their German brethren. For this reason, preference was given in their selections especially to the "General Brethren Book" as well as that known by the name of "Lancaster Book."

With few exceptions the hymns are printed in the way in which they were found in the above-named hymnals. However, the committee found it necessary to shorten several texts and to drop others entirely lest the size of the book became too unwieldy.

As the committee was not completely limited in their selection, several hymns from other works were added as well as some that are published for the first time.

To those members who lent their kind aid in this undertaking, we extend our heartfelt thanks.

Finally, the committee, which was appointed by annual meeting, wishes to state that they have been mindful of the significance of the task entrusted to them. By night and day they have worked with prayerful hearts to make a selection that would be appropriate both for the private and the public worship of their dearly beloved brethren and the next generation, as well as for all souls seeking salvation [Heil].

Being well aware that on earth everything is surrounded by imperfection, we expect that this work, too, will reveal its flaws.

We now send this work on its mission and pray that it might become a means for honoring the Lord. May it bring consolation, succor and inspiration to many thousands who read it and sing from it, that they may be faithful unto death -- to attain the crown and to appear by the shiny sea -- where "Each will bring his harp and sing his special song of praise."

S. R. Zug, J. H. Longenecker, Jacob Aldinger, Committee.

2. NEW HYMNS

Single asterisks denote hymns that appear only in the edition under which
they are listed. Double asterisks denote hymns that appear in all subsequent editions.

1893

(172)   Das Grab ist da, so heisst es immer, wir gehen ein, wir gehen aus.**
(194)   Den Tag vor Christi Leiden, beim letzten Abendmahl.
(437)   Gott Vater, dir, dir weihen wir jetzt diesen Tempel ein.**
(527)   Höre auf, lass Trauern fahren, ich fahr' auf zu Gottes Stuhl.**
(921)   Nun lobet und ehret Gott Vater und Sohn.**
(969)   O Herr, dein heilig' Wort uns lehrt, die Salbung mit dem Öl.**
(1053) Ruft laute, ihr Wächter, bei Tag und bei Nacht.**
(1083) Segne deiner Knechte Lehren, öffne selber ihren Mund.**

1895

(404)   Gelobet seist du, Schöpfersmacht, denn gross ist dein Erbarmen.*
(1034) O wie rein ist doch dein Blut, Jesu, meine Wonne.*
(1111) Singt unserm Gott ein neues Lied, ihm, der nur Wunder schafft.*

APPENDIX IX

First-Line Index of Hymns

   This index lists the German hymns published for and by the Brethren in
hymnals, small collections of hymns, individually on broadsides, or in
early magazines. The entries are listed alphabetically in word-by-word
arrangement. Every entry consists of several elements in a certain
sequence. Irrespective of sequence, four principles are observed: 1. elements are set off from one another by slashes; 2. separate items within
each element are set off from one another by semicolons; 3. sources of
documentation are enclosed in parentheses; 4. information supplied by the
author is enclosed in brackets. In the following, each element is described in detail.

1. The first line of the hymn, printed in capital letters, in many cases
actually includes the second line as well for the sake of more exact identification. As the spelling in the various hymnals is not uniform, it has
been moderately modernized except where such editing would interfere with
rhyme or meter. Variant text is given in parentheses. Elisions are indicated by an apostrophe except in the verb forms of the first person
singular, present tense, indicative, subjunctive and the second person
singular, imperative. The exclamations "Oh" and "O" are always spelled
"O". Although commas have been supplied where required, they have been
omitted after the exclamations "Ach" and "O". In most instances, excla-
mation marks have been replaced by commas. Vowels displaying an Umlaut
are alphabetized in their pure form. Hyphenated words are considered
single words. Occsasionally, the first line is followed by a reference
which is given in parentheses.

2. The melody reference for each hymn at its first publication in
Brethren hymnody follows the abbreviation "Mel." and consists of the initial words of the first line(s) of the hymn(s) to which the text in
question was to be sung. Certain abbreviations used in the hymnals are to
be interpreted as follows:
          e. M.: eigene Melodie (the text has its own melody)
          C. M.: Common Meter
          L. M.: Long Meter
          P. M.: Peculiar or Particular Meter
          S. M.: Short Meter
          "Psalm ... Lobwasser:" this refers to the French or Genevan
melody of the psalm indicated.

   Where references are unspecific, such as "melody type no. 55", they
were omitted. Instead, a bracketed reference directs the reader to that
number in the metric index (Appoendix XI), which represents the
appropriate meter for the hymn in question. Since the melody references
apply only to the first appearance of a given hymn in Brethren hymnody,
they may vary from those in the original sources and/or later Brethren and
non-Brethren hymnals.

3. The number of stanzas for each hymn at its first publication in
Brethren hymnody is followed by the abbreviation "st." These numbers may
vary from those in the original sources and/or those in later Brethren and
non-Brethren hymnals.

4. The first line of the chorus, where present, follows the abbreviation "Ch." Occasionally, a source reference is given in parentheses either for the documentation of the original or a translation.

5. Documentation. The author's name follows the descriptive elements. If the "author" is a translator, this is indicated by "tr." Only the last names are given unless this causes ambiguity. For brief biographies, see Appendix XII. Unknown authorship is indicated by the abbreviation "Anon." In the case of the first Brethren hymnal, Geistreiches Gesang-Buch, the reference to the anonymous author may be interpreted as Wilhelm Knepper.

Although not all entries display all sub-elements, documentation is arranged in the following sequence: the author's work (indicated by a group of capital letters); German secondary works; English secondary works; a hymnal predating first publication of the hymn in a Brethren hymnal (usually an alpha-numeric symbol).

For the sake of brevity, no page references are provided for works in which hymns can be located by their first lines through the index. Hymnal citations are not comprehensive but limited, as far as possible, to certain key sources. For a key to the abbreviations, the list following this introduction may be consulted.

Where more than one author is cited, the name considered to have the most reliable documentation precedes the other(s) with source reference(s) following immediately. As a rule, authors' references in hymnals have not been considered sufficiently reliable documentation. The following hymnals are an exception:

Davidisches Psalter-Spiel, 1753: a copy of this Inspirationist hymnal in the archives of the Amana Community, Amana, Iowa contains hand-written entries of authors' names. Careful examination proved these to be eighty percent correct. It was therefore assumed that the references to Inspirationist and Radical Pietist authors may be recognized as valid sources.

Die Kleine Harfe, 1797: names of eighteenth-century Brethren hymn-writers were supplied by the publisher, Christoph Sauer II, himself a Brethren.

Die kleine Perlen-Sammlung: names of contemporary and near-contemporary Brethren authors were supplied by the publisher, J. E. Pfautz, himself a Brethren.

6. English versions are referred to by "Tr." (translations), followed by a source where either references to translators and translations or complete translations can be found. In the case of a German translation from the English, the original is referred to by "Or." Where possible, both author and original first line of the text are given. Page references are provided only where a hymn cannot be located by its German first line.

7. First publication in Brethren hymnals is indicated by an alpha-numeric symbol referring to the appropriate Brethren hymnal and the year of publication. A letter following the year refers to the place of publication in cases where further identification is necessary. If first publication in a hymnal was preceded by publication in a small occasional hymn-collection, both are listed.

8. The number of the hymn by which it is referred to when mentioned in the text is given on the right-hand margin.

List of Abbreviations

For full bibliographical records, see the Selected Bibliography. Asterisks indicate Brethren hymnals and hymn-collections.

A	Arndt, Paradiesgärtlein.
AHS	Schmolck, Eines andächtigen Herzens Schmuck und Asche.
ALS	Die allgemeine Lieder-Sammlung.
ANH	Das Aller Neueste Harfenspiel.
ASGL	Eine auserlesene Sammlung Geistlicher Lieder.
AU	Ausbund.
Bachmann	Zur Geschichte der Berliner Gesangbücher.
BGB1545	Geystliche Lieder.
BGB1725	Sammlung geistlicher und lieblicher Lieder.
BLT	Brethren Life and Thought.
Brumbaugh	History of the Brethren.
CG*	Das Christliche Gesang-Buch.
CGB	Churländisches vollständiges Gesangbuch.
CGW	Christliche Glaubens-Bekentnus Der Waffenlosen.
CH	Gerhart, Choral Harmonie.
Christ-Janer	American Hymns Old and New.
Colonial	Durnbaugh, The Brethren in Colonial America.
Cunz	Geschichte des Kirchenliedes.
DG	Schaff, Deutsches Gesangbuch.
DGM	Deutsches Gesangbuch der Bischöflichen Methodisten-Kirche.
DP	Davidisches Psalter-Spiel.
EE	Eyn Enchiridion.
EG	Eisenachisches Neu-vermehrtes und beständiges Gesang-Buch.
EGB	Erfurter Gesang Buch.
EGS	Evangelisches Gesangbuch oder, eine Sammlung.
Ehmann	Philipp Friedrich Hiller's sämmtliche Geistliche Lieder.
ELEL*	Etliche liebliche und erbauliche Lieder.
ELS	Orwig, Evangelisches Liederbüchlein für Sonntagsschulen.
ENGL*	Etliche Neue Geistliche Lieder.
ENL	Woltersdorff, Einige neue Lieder.
ES*	Eine Sammlung.
ESL*	Eyn schön Lied.
EUL	Arnold, Das Eheliche und Unverehelichte Leben.
F	Freylinghausen, Geistreiches Gesang-Buch.
Farlee	"A History of the Church Music of the Amana Society."
Fischer	Das deutsche evangelische Kirchenlied.
Flory	Literary Activity of the Brethren.
Funk	A Biographical Sketch of Bishop Christian Herr.
G	Hölty, Gedichte.
GAL*	Geistliche u. andächtige Lieder.
GBG	Tersteegen, Geistliches Blumengärtlein.
GG	Geistreiches Gesang-Buch.
GGB*	Geistreiches Gesang-Buch, 1720.
GGG*	Stoll, Geistliches Gewürz-Gärtlein.
GGLR	Das Gemeinschaftliche Gesangbuch.
GGS	Arnold, Das Geheimnis der göttlichen Sophia.
GKW	Gesangbuch für die evangelische Kirche in Württemberg.
GL	Gerhardt, Geistliche Lieder.
GL1811	Sasse, Geistliche Lieder.
GLK	Hiller, Geistliches Liederkästlein.

GLL	Beissel, Göttliche Liebes und Lobesgethöne.
GLL1612	Geistliche Lieder D. Martin Lutheri.
GLO	Klopstock, Geistliche Lieder und Oden.
GLS	Geistlicher Liederschatz.
GLU	Neander, Glaub- und Liebesübung.
Goedeke	Deutsche Dichter des 18. Jahrhunderts.
GOL	Gellert, Geistliche Oden und Lieder.
GS	Das Geistliche Saitenspiel.
GV	Dreisbach, Die Geistliche Viole.
GVB	Gesangbuch der Vereinigten Brüder in Christo.
Heckman	The Poetry of Alexander Mack, Jr.
HGB	Sammlung Geist- und lieblicher Lieder.
HS	Scheffler, Heilige Seelenlust.
Hymnal 1951	The Brethren Hymnal, 1951.
JK	Beissel, Jacobs Kampff.
JL	Gruber, Jesus-Lieder.
Julian	Dictionary of Hymnology.
Kadelbach	Die Hymnodie der Mennoniten.
KDP*	Das Kleine Davidische Psalterspiel.
KGL	Kern Geistlicher Lieblicher Lieder.
KH*	Die Kleine Harfe.
KK	Der kleine Kempis.
KLS*	Die kleine Lieder Sammlung.
Knapp	Evangelischer Liederschatz, 4th ed., 1891.
Knapp 1837	Evangelischer Liederschatz, 1837.
Knapp/Z	Knapp, Geistliche Gedichte des Grafen von Zinzendorf.
Koch	Geschichte des Kirchenlieds.
KP	Evangelisches Gesangbuch. Die kleine Palme.
KPS*	Die kleine Perlen-Sammlung.
Kulp	Die Lieder unserer Kirche.
LF	Arnold, Göttliche Liebes-Funken.
LHB	Die Lieder der Hutterischen Brüder.
Lorenz	Glory, Hallelujah!
LS	Schmolck, Der Lustige Sabbath.
MG	Vollständiges Marburger Gesang-Buch.
Mützell	Geistliche Lieder der evangelischen Kirche.
NE	Neu-Eingerichtetes Gesang-Buch.
Nelle	Geschichte des deutschen evangelischen Kirchenliedes.
NG	Weisse, Ein New Geseng buchlen.
NGW	Des Neu-verbesserten Gesang-Buchs Anderer Theil.
NS*	Neue Sammlung.
NVG	Das neue und verbesserte Gesangbuch.
Origins	Durnbaugh, European Origins of the Brethren.
PD	Lobwasser, Die Psalmen Davids.
Pfeiffer	Dichtkunst und Kirchenlied.
PH	Spitta, Psalter und Harfe.
PI	Einige Psalmen Israels.
PPM	Praxis Pietatis Melica.
PUL	Psalmen und Lieder.
Röbbelen	Theologie und Frömmigkeit.
SAG	Hermann, Der Sänger am Grabe.
SAZ	Stimmen aus Zion.
Seipt	Schwenkfelder Hymnology.
SEL	Eine Sammlung Evangelischer Lieder.
SGL	Sammlung von Geistlichen Liedern.

SGR	Sonntagsschul-Gesangbuch der Reformirten Kirche.
Stoudt	Pennsylvania-German Poetry.
TH	Starck, Tägliches Hand-Buch.
UCH	Die Union Choral-Harmonie.
UG	Bogatzky, Die Übung der Gottseligkeit.
UG[date]	Ein Unpartheyisches Gesang-Buch.
UL	Unparteiische Liedersammlung.
VGLU	Neander, Vermehrte Glaub- und Liebes-Übung.
Viehmeyer	"An Index to Ephrata Hymnological Materials."
Wackernagel	Das deutsche Kirchenlied.
Westphal	Das evangelische Kirchenlied.
Willard	Johannes Kelpius.
Wolkan	Die Lieder der Wiedertäufer.
Yoder	Pennsylvania Spirituals.
ZP	Lorenz, Zions Pilgerschatz.
ZSGL	Zwey schöne geistliche Lieder.
ZW	Zionitischer WeyrauchsHügel.

ABERMAL EIN TAG (NACHT, JAHR) VERFLOSSEN   1
    Mel.: Freu dich sehr, o meine / 7 st. / Neander (GLU, Koch; DP1718)
    / KPD1744.

ABERMAL UNS DEINE GÜTE AUF GANZ WUNDERBARE WEIS'   2
    Mel.: Es ist gewisslich / 1 st. / Anon. / (UG1804) / CG1874.

ACH ALLES, WAS HIMMEL UND ERDE UMSCHLIESSET   3
    Mel.: Ich liebe dich herzlich / 8 st. / Anon. / (Koch; Julian;
    DP1718, F) / Tr.: Julian / GGB1720.

ACH ARMER CHRIST, WO WILLST DU HIN AUF DIESEN SCHMALEN WEGEN   4
    Mel.: So wünsch ich nun ein' gute Nacht; Wo Gott der Herr nicht /
    10 st. / Anon. / GGB1720.

ACH BEDENK ES WOHL, WIE MAN FLEISSIG SOLL DIESE GNADENZEIT AUSKAUFEN   5
    Mel.: Seelen-Bräutigam / 4 st. / Anon. / KPS1858.

ACH BLEIB BEI UNS, HERR JESU CHRIST, WEIL ES NUN ABEND WORDEN IST   6
    Mel.: Du unbegreiflich höchstes Gut / 3 st. / Selneccer (Fischer,
    Koch, Kulp, Mützell, Westphal; Julian); (F) / Tr.: Julian /
    ELEL1812, CG1874.

ACH BRÜDER, LASST ZUM KAMPF UND STREIT EUCH NIEMALS TRÄGE FINDEN   7
    Mel.: Es ist gewisslich / 4 st. / Anon. (EGS1821) / KPS1858.

ACH DASS EIN JEDER NÄHM' IN ACHT, WAS DORT MARIA WOHL BEDACHT   8
    Mel.: Kommt her zu mir / 12 st. / Anon. (DP1718, F) / KDP1744.

ACH ES FLEUCHT DER MENSCHEN LEBEN WIE EIN PFEIL ZUR EWIGKEIT   9
    Mel.: O der alles hätt' verloren / 12 st. / Stoll (GGG) / GGG1806.

ACH ES IST BETRÜBT ZU LESEN, WAS MAN VON DEM JOSEPH HÖRT   10
    Mel.: Alle Menschen müssen sterben / 3 st. / Anon. / CG1874.

ACH GOTT, ERHÖR MEIN SEUFZEN UND WEHKLAGEN   11
    Mel.: e. M. / 1 st. / Schechs (Fischer; A1718) / CG1874.

ACH GOTT, IN WAS FÜR FREUDIGKEIT SCHWINGT SICH MEIN HERZ ZU JEDER ZEIT   12
    Mel.: Herr Jesu Christ, mein's Lebens / 23 st. / Schade (Knapp,
    Koch; DP1718) / KDP1744.

ACH GOTT, IN WAS FÜR SCHMERZEN BRINGT MICH DIE MISSETAT   13
    Mel.: Helft mir Gottes Güte / 10 st. / Anon. (GG1700) / GGB1720.

ACH GOTT, MAN KENNET DICH NICHT RECHT   14
    Mel.: Kommt her zu mir / 14 st. / Tersteegen (GBG) / KPS1858.

ACH GOTT, MICH DRÜCKT EIN SCHWERER STEIN   15
    Mel.: Christ lag / 9 st. / Laurenti (Koch; DP1718, F) / KDP1744.

ACH GOTT, WIE IST DAS CHRISTENTUM ZU DIESER ZEIT VERFALLEN   16
    Mel.: Es ist gewisslich / 2 st. / Anon. (GGBLR1828) / NS1870.

ACH GOTT, WIE MANCHER KUMMER MACHT, DASS ICH MICH HERZLICH KRÄNKE   17
    Mel.: Es ist gewisslich / 4 st. / Anon. (MG1759) / ES1893.

ACH GOTT, WIE MANCHES HERZELEID BEGEGNET MIR ZU DIESER ZEIT   18
    Mel.: Herr Jesu Christ, mein's Lebens / 18 st. / Moller (Knapp,
    Koch, Kulp, Mützell, Westphal; Julian); Hojer (Cunz,
    Mützell, Wackernagel); (DP1718, F) / Tr.: Julian / KDP1744.

ACH GOTT, WIE PLAGT MAN SICH MIT SELBSTGEWIRKTEN WERKEN   19
    Mel.: Die Nacht ist vor der / 15 st. / Grebil (KPS) / KPS1858.

ACH HERR, ERLEUCHTE DEINE KNECHT', DIE VOR DICH SOLLEN TRETEN   20
    Mel.: Mir nach, spricht / 2 st. / Anon. (ALS1871) / CG1879.

ACH HERR JESU, MEIN ERRETTER, RETTE MICH VERLOR'NES KIND   21
    [Mel.: 19] / 5 st. / Anon. / NS1870.

ACH HERR JESU, SCHAU IN GNADEN UNSERE VERSAMMLUNG AN   22
    Mel.: Mir nach, spricht / 3 st. / Herr (Funk, Kadelbach) / KLS1827.

ACH HERR JESU, SEI UNS FREUNDLICH JETZT IN DIESER ABEND-STUND'   23
    Mel.: Zeuch mich / 9 st. / Anon. / GGB1720.

166

ACH HERR JESU, SIEH, WIR ARMEN SIND VOR DEINEM ANGESICHT   24
   Mel.: Jesu, der du meine Seele; Jesu, meines Lebens Leben / 9 st. /
   Anon. / GGB1720.

ACH HERR, LEHRE MICH BEDENKEN, DASS ICH EINMAL STERBEN MUSS   25
   Mel.: Abermal ein Tag / 3 st. / Schmolck (AHS; Knapp, Koch;
   EGS1850) / CG1874.

ACH HERR, WIE BILLIG SCHÄM ICH MICH, WENN ICH GEDENK AN MICH UND DICH   26
   Mel.: O starker Gott / 10 st. / Anon. / KH1792.

ACH HERR, WIE DÜRSTET MEINE SEELE   27
   Mel.: Ich suche dich in dieser Ferne / 6 st. / Neander (GLU;
   DP1718, F) / KDP1744.

ACH HERZENS-GELIEBTE, WIR SCHEIDEN JETZUNDER   28
   Mel.: Ach Jesu, mein Schönster / 4 st. / Anon. / KDP1744.

ACH HÖR DAS SÜSSE LALLEN, DEN ALLERSCHÖNSTEN TON   29
   Mel.: Befiehl du deine Wege / 8 st. / Anon. (DP1740) / KDP1764.

ACH ICH HÖR EIN' STIMME KLINGEN, DIE DURCHSCHALLET BERG UND TAL   30
   Mel.: Ringe recht / 11 st. / Stoll (GGG) / GGG1806.

ACH ICH SÜNDENWURM DER ERDEN, JESU, STIRBST DU MIR ZU GUT   31
   (= st. 6-9 of 1100)
   [Mel.: 127] / 4 st. / Tersteegen / NS1870.

ACH JAMMER, ES IST UM DICH, JESU, GESCHEHEN   32
   Mel.: e. M. / 18 st. / Anon. (F) / GGB1720.

ACH JESU, MEIN SCHÖNSTER, ERQUICKE MICH ARMEN   33
   Mel.: Ich liebe dich herzlich / 7 st. / Anon. (DP1718, F, ZW) /
   KDP1744.

ACH JESU, SCHAU HERNIEDER AUF UNS, DEIN' ARME SCHAF'   34
   Mel.: Von Gott will ich nicht lassen / 16 st. / Anon. / GGB1720.

ACH KINDER, WOLLT IHR LIEBEN, SO LIEBT, WAS LIEBENSWERT   35
   Mel.: Ihr Sünder, kommt / 6 st. / Dock (Stoudt; UG1804) / KLS1826.

ACH KOMM, DU SÜSSER HERZENSGAST, DU LABSAL MEINER SEELEN   36
   Mel.: Ich dank dir schon / 17 st. / Menken (Knapp; Julian; DP1718,
   F) / Tr.: Julian / GGB1720.

ACH KOMMT, IHR LIEBE BRÜDER, SEHT EUREN JESUM AN   37
   Mel.: Wo bleiben meine Sinnen / 3 st. / W. Preiss (KPS) / KPS1858.

ACH LASS DICH JETZT FINDEN, KOMM, JESU, KOMM FORT   38
   Mel.: e. M. / 7 st. / Ludämilie Elisabeth of Schwarzburg-Rudolstadt? (Koch; A1718) / KDP1744.

ACH LIEBSTER JESU, RUFE MICH, DASS ICH DIE STIMM' ERKENNE   39
   Mel.: Wo Gott der Herr nicht / 7 st. / Weise (Koch; F) / GGB1720.

ACH LIEBSTER JESU, SIEH AUF MICH, WEIL ICH JETZT ZU DIR SCHREIE   40
   Mel.: Wo Gott der Herr nicht / 12 st. / Anon. / GGB1720.

ACH MEIN GOTT, WIE LIEBLICH IST DEINE WOHNUNG, DA DU BIST   41
   Mel.: Schwinge dich, mein schwacher Geist / 12 st. / Anon. (DP1718,
   F, ZW) / KDP1744.

ACH MEIN JESU, MEIN VERLANGEN, WO BIST DU, MEIN SEELENFREUND   42
   Mel.: Ringe recht / 6 st. / Stoll (GGG) / GGG1806, KPS1858.

ACH MEIN JESU, SIEH, ICH TRETE, DA DER TAG NUNMEHR SICH NEIGT   43
   Mel.: Ach was soll ich Sünder machen / 7 st. / Schlicht (Knapp,
   Koch; DP1718, F, ZW) / KDP1744.

ACH MÖCHT ICH MEINEN JESUM SEHEN, DER MEINE SEEL' SO HERZLICH LIEBT   44
   Mel.: Wo ist der Schönste/ 5 st. / Böhmer (Koch; DP1718, F, ZW) /
   KDP1744.

ACH MÖCHT ICH NOCH AUF DIESER ERDEN MIT ENGELS-SITTEN UND GEBÄRDEN   45
   Mel.: Psalm 80 Lobwasser / 13 st. / Anon. (DP1718, ZW) / KDP1744.

ACH MUSS DANN DER SOHN SELBST LEIDEN UND ERDULDEN HOHN UND SPOTT   46
   Mel.: Gott des Himmels und der Erden / 3 st. / Anon. (F) / CG1874.

ACH SAGT MIR NICHTS VON GOLD UND SCHÄTZEN   47
   Mel.: Wer nur den lieben Gott / 9 st. / Scheffler (HS; Knapp, Koch,
   Nelle; Julian; DP1718, F) / Tr.: Julian / KDP1744.

ACH SCHONE DOCH, O GROSSER MENSCHEN-HÜTER   48
   Mel.: Der Tag ist hin, mein Jesu, bei mir bleibe / 6 st. / Neander
   (GLU; Knapp; DP1718, F) / KDP1744.

ACH SEI GEWARNT, O SEEL', FÜR SCHADEN   49
   Mel.: Wo ist mein Schäflein / 3 st. / Arnold (GGS; Koch; DP1718,
   ZW) / KDP1744.

ACH SIEHET (SEHET) DOCH DAS LAMME GOTTES, AN DEM KREUZ   50
   Mel.: e. M. / 6 st. / Anon. tr. (Lorenz, p. 49; KPS) / KPS1858.

ACH TREIB AUS MEINER SEEL', O MEIN IMMANUEL   51
   Mel.: Mein Jesu, der du mich / 21 st. / Gmelin (Koch, Kulp, Julian;
   DP1718, ZW) / Tr.: Julian / KDP1744.

ACH TREUER GOTT, BARMHERZIG'S HERZ, DES GÜTE SICH NICHT ENDET   52
   Mel.: Ach Gott, vom Himmel / 16 st. / Gerhardt (GL; Knapp, Koch;
   Julian; DP1718, F, ZW) / Tr.: Julian / KDP1744.

ACH TREUER GOTT, WIE NÖTIG IST, DASS WIR JETZUND RECHT BETEN   53
   Mel.: Ach Gott, vom Himmel / 14 st. / Anon. (DP1718, F, ZW) /
   KDP1744.

ACH WACHET, WACHET AUF, ES SIND DIE LETZTEN ZEITEN   54
   Mel.: e. M. / 8 st. / Neander (GLU; Koch; DP1718, F) / GGB1720.

ACH WANN WERD ICH SCHAUEN DICH, LIEBSTER JESU   55
   Mel.: Jesu, meines Herzens Freund / 6 st. / Fritsch (Koch; DP1718,
   F) / KDP1744.

ACH WANN WILLST DU, JESU, KOMMEN EINST MIT DEINER VOLLEN KRAFT   56
   Mel.: Zeuch mich / 5 st. / Anon. / GGB1720.

ACII WÄR ICH DOCH SCHON DROBEN, MEIN HEILAND, WÄR ICH DA   57
   Mel.: Bedenke, Mensch, das Ende / 2 st. / Woltersdorf (Koch; Yoder;
   GV1855) / CG1874.

ACH WÄR ICH GANZ IN GOTT VERSENKT, IN GOTT, DER LIEBREICH MEIN GEDENKT   58
   Mel.: L. M. / 2 st. / Anon. (DGM1865) / NS1870.

ACH WAS BIN ICH, MEIN ERRETTER UND VERTRETER   59
   Mel.: Hüter, wird die Nacht der Sünden; Ps. 38 / 6 st. / Neander
   (Knapp, Koch; DP1718, F, ZW) / KDP1744.

ACH WAS MACH ICH IN DEN STÄDTEN, DA NUR LIST UND UNRAT IST   60
   Mel.: Komm, o komm, du Geist / 15 st. / H. Müller (Fischer; DP1718,
   F) / GGB1720.

ACH WAS SIND WIR OHNE JESU, DÜRFTIG, JÄMMERLICH UND ARM   61
   Mel.: Unser Herrscher, unser König / 10 st. / Lackmann (Knapp,
   Koch; DP1718, F) / GGB1720.

ACH WENN DOCH ALLE SEELEN WÜSSTEN, WIE GUT MAN ES BEI JESU HAT   62
   Mel.: Wer nur den lieben / 2 st. / Sasse (GL1811; Yoder) / CG1874.

ACH WENN ICH JA GEDENK DARAN, WIE VIELE SÜND' ICH HAB GETAN   63
   Mel.: Herr Jesu Christ, dich zu uns wend / 3 st. / Herr (Kadelbach;
   UL1860) / CG1874.

ACH WIE BETRÜBT SIND FROMME SEELEN ALLHIE IN DIESER JAMMER WELT   64
   Mel.: Wer nur den lieben Gott / 8 st. / Pfefferkorn? (Koch; A1718)
   / ELEL1812, KLS1827.

ACH WIE HERRLICH IST DAS LEBEN, WELCHES GOTT NACH DIESER ZEIT   65
   Mel.: Schaffet, schaffet, meine / 5 st. / Anon. (NVG1806) / KLS1827.

ACH WIE IST DER WEG SO SCHMAL, DER ZUM LEBEN GEHET   66
    Mel.: O wie ist der Weg so schmal / 9 st. / Stoll (GGG) / GGG1806,
    CG1874.

ACH WIE SO GAR VERBLEND' MUSS SEIN DAS AUG' DEN ZEITEN   67
    [Mel.: 155] / Mel.: e. M. / 7 st. / Kelpius (ELEL1788) / ELEL1788.

ACH WIE SO LIEBLICH UND WIE FEIN IST ES, WENN BRÜDER EINIG SEIN 68
    Mel.: Kommt her zu mir, spricht / 11 st. / Anon. / Tr.: Origins,
    p. 415 / GGB1720.

ACH WIE WAR ICH IN MEINEM SCHLUMMER VERSUNKEN ZUM ABGRUND HIN   69
    Mel.: Wer nur den lieben Gott / 6 st. / Anon. / KH1792.

ACH WIE WICHTIG IST DIE ZEIT, WORIN WIR NUN LEBEN   70
    Mel.: Jesu, wahres Gotteslamm / 7 st. / Anon.: "Author's name
    withheld" (KPS) / KPS1858.

ACH WO STRÖMT DER BORN DES LEBENS, DER INS EW'GE LEBEN QUILLT   71
    Mel.: Ringe recht / 5 st. / Conz (Knapp; DGM1865) / NS1870.

ACH WOHIN SOLL ICH GEH'N, BELADEN, KRANK UND MATT   72
    Mel.: S. M. / 6 st. / Anon. / NS1870.

ADE, DU SÜSSE WELT, ICH SCHWING' INS HIMMELSZELT   73
    Mel.: Wo soll ich fliehen hin / 12 st. / H. Müller (Koch; DP1718,
    F, ZW) / KDP1744.

ADJE, MEIN VIELGELIEBTER MANN (WEIB) UND LIEBE KINDER ALLE   74
    Mel.: Es ist gewisslich an der Zeit / 1 st. / Anon. / CG1874.

ALLE CHRISTEN HÖREN GERNE VON DEM REICH DER HERRLICHKEIT   75
    Mel.: Alle Menschen müssen sterben / 1 st. / Anon. (Julian;
    ANH1795) / Tr.: Julian / KLS1826.

ALLE MENSCHEN MÜSSEN STERBEN, ALLES FLEISCH VERGEHT WIE HEU   76
    Mel.: e. M.; Jesu, der du meine Seele / 7 st. / Rosenmüller (Knapp,
    Kulp); Albinus (Knapp, Koch, Westphal; Julian) (DP1718, F) / Tr.:
    Julian / GGB1720.

ALLEIN GOTT IN DER HÖH' SEI EHR' UND DANK FÜR SEINE GNADE   77
    Mel.: e. M. / 4 st. / Decius (Knapp, Koch, Kulp, Mützell, Nelle,
    Wackernagel; Julian; DP1718, F, ZW) / Tr.: Julian / KDP1744.

ALLEIN UND DOCH NICHT GANZ ALLEINE BIN ICH IN MEINER EINSAMKEIT 78
    Mel.: Wer nur den lieben / 9 st. / Schmolck (Koch; DP1718, ZW) /
    KDP1744.

ALLEIN ZU DIR, O VATER, IST MEINE ZUVERSICHT, DU BIST EIN TREUER RATER 79
    Mel.: Herzlich tut mich verlangen / 7 st. / Anon.; signed: "J. F."
    / GBB1720.

ALLER GLÄUB'GEN SAMMELPLATZ IST DA, WO IHR HERZ UND SCHATZ   80
    [Mel.: 33] / 4 st. / N. L. von Zinzendorf (Knapp, Nelle; Julian;
    GKW1841) / NS1870.

ALLES, WAS LEBT IN DER WELT, GOTT GESCHAFFEN UND ERHÄLT   81
    Mel.: Höchster Priester / 25 st. / J. Preiss (GAL) / GAL1753.

ALLGENUGSAM WESEN, DAS ICH MIR ERLESEN EWIG HAB ZUM SCHATZ   82
    Mel.: Jesu, meine Freude / 8 st. / Tersteegen (GBG; Knapp, Koch,
    Kulp; Julian; ZW) / Tr.: Julian / KDP1744.

ALS CHRISTUS MIT SEIN'R WAHREN LEHR' VERSAMMELT HAT EIN KLEINES HEER 83
    Mel.: Dies sind die heiligen zehn Gebot' / 13 st. / Weisse and
    Sattler (Knapp, Wackernagel, Wolkan; BGB1545) / GGB1720.

ALS JESUS CHRISTUS IN DER NACHT, DARIN ER WARD VERRATEN   84
    Mel.: O Jesu, meines Lebens / 6 st. / Heermann (Mützell; F) /
    CG1874.

ALSO HAT GOTT DIE WELT GELIEBT, DASS ER AUS FREIEM TRIEB   85
    Mel.: C. M. / 6 st. / Anon. (GS1836) / NS1870.

AN JESUM DENKEN OFT UND VIEL   86
    Mel.: Vom Himmel hoch / 7 st. / Rinkart (Fischer; Julian; DP1718,
    F) / Tr.: Julian / KDP1744.
AN JESUM ZU GLAUBEN, IST HERZLICHE LUST   87
    Mel.: Die lieblichen Blicke / 3 st. / P. F. Hiller (GLK) / CG1874.
AN MEINER GRUFT STÄRKT EUREN GLAUBEN, IHR ELTERN, DIE IHR MICH GELIEBT   88
    Mel.: Wer weiss, wie nahe mir / 1 st. / Anon. / CG1874.
ANBETUNGSWÜRD'GER GOTT, MIT MAJESTÄT GESCHMÜCKET   89
    Mel.: O Gott, du frommer Gott / 10 st. / Diterich (Knapp 1837) /
    Tr.: Julian / KDP1797-G.
ANGNES KEUSCH UND VOLL VON TUGEND, WIE IHR NAME ZEIGET AN   90
    Mel.: Freu dich sehr / 18 st. / Anon. / ELEL1788.
ARME WITWE, WEINE NICHT, JESUS WILL DICH TRÖSTEN   91
    Mel: Liebster Vater, ich, dein Kind / 2 st. / Anon. (Knapp; UG1804)
    / CG1874.
AUCH DIE KINDER SAMMELST DU, TREUER HIRT, ZUR EW'GEN RUH'   92
    Mel.: Jesu, komm doch selbst zu mir / 4 st / Hoffmann (Koch;
    SAG1851) / KPS1858.
AUF, AUF, DU JUNGER MUT, AUF, AUF ZU DEINEM GOTT   93
    Mel.: Der Tag ist fort / 5 st. / S. D. Miller (KPS) / KPS1858.
AUF, AUF, MEIN GEIST UND DU, O MEIN GEMÜTE   94
    Mel.: Zerfliess, mein Geist / 6 st. / Scheffler (HS; DP1718, ZW) /
    KDP1744.
AUF, AUF, MEIN HERZ, MIT FREUDEN, NIMM WAHR, WAS HEUT' GESCHIEHT   95
    Mel.: e. M. / 9 st. / Gerhardt (CL, Knapp, Koch, Kulp; Julian;
    DP1718, F) / Tr.: Julian / GGB1720.
AUF, CHRISTEN, FREUET EUCH, DAS NEUE JAHR BRICHT EIN   96
    Mel.: Blast die Trompete / 4 st. / Ch.: Bald kommt das Jubeljahr
    herbei / Anon. tr. (Yoder; EGS1821) / CG1874.
AUF, CHRISTEN, PREIST MIT MIR DEN HERRN   97
    Mel.: L. M. / 4 st. / Schlegel (SGG; EGS1821) / NS1870.
AUF, CHRISTEN-MENSCH, AUF, AUF ZUM STREIT   98
    Mel.: Mein Geist frohlocket / 12 st. / Scheffler (Knapp, Koch Kulp;
    Julian; DP1718, F) / Tr.: Julian / GGB1720.
AUF DEN TAG DES HERRN SICH RÜSTEN   99
    Mel.: Alles ist an Gottes / 5 st. / P. F. Hiller (GLK) / CG1874.
AUF DICH, JESU, SCHAUEN WIR, LASS VEREINT UNS SEIN IN DIR   100
    Mel.: P. M. / 5 st. / Anon. (DGM1865) / NS1870.
AUF DIESEN TAG BEDENKEN WIR, DASS CHRISTUS GEN HIMMEL GEFAHREN   101
    Mel.: Allein Gott in der Höh' / 5 st. / Zwick (Koch, Kulp, Mützell,
    Nelle, Westphal; Julian; DP1718, F) / KDP1744.
AUF, DU PRIESTERLICH GESCHLECHTE, DAS DEN BUND DES HERRN BEWAHRT   102
    Mel.: Alle Menschen müssen sterben / 39 st. / Steinhofer (Koch;
    SGL) / ESL1832, KLS1834.
AUF, HINAUF ZU DEINER FREUDE, MEINE SEELE, HERZ UND SINN   103
    Mel.: e. M. / 5 st. / Schade (Knapp, Koch, Nelle; Julian; DP1718,
    F, ZW) / Tr.: Julian / KDP1744.
AUF, IHR CHRISTEN, CHRISTI GLIEDER, DIE IHR NOCH HÄNGT AN DEM HAUPT   104
    Mel.: Meine Hoffnung stehet; Christi Tod ist Adams Leben / 11 st. /
    Falckner (Knapp, Koch; Julian; DP1718, F) / Tr.: Julian / GGB1720.
AUF, IHR CHRISTEN, LASST UNS SINGEN, DEM HEILAND LOB UND EHRE BRINGEN   105
    Mel.: Wachet auf, ruft uns die Stimme / 12 st. / Arnschwanger
    (Fischer; Julian); Falckner (Stoudt); (DP1718, F) / Tr.: Julian /
    KDP1744.

AUF, JESU JÜNGER, FREUET EUCH, DER HERR FÄHRT AUF ZU SEINEM REICH   106
   Mel.: Herr Jesu Christ, dich zu uns wend / 3 st. / Diterich
   (Koch; Julian; NVG1799) / Tr.: Julian / CG1874.

AUF, LASST UNS NUN MIT ERNST ERWÄGEN DEN WICHTIG GROSSEN UNTERSCHEID   107
   Mel.: Nichts hilft uns doch mit hohen Gaben; Wer nur den lieben
   Gott lässt walten / 79 st. / Mack, Jr. (Heckman) / Tr.: Colonial,
   p. 577; Heckman.

AUF LEIDEN FOLGT DIE HERRLICHKEIT, TRIUMPH, TRIUMPH, NACH KURZEM STREIT 108
   Mel.: Kommt her zu mir, spricht; Geh aus, mein Herz / 8 st. /
   Lackmann (Koch; DP1718, F) / GGB1720.

AUF, MEIN HERZ, VERLASS DIE WELT, RICHTE DICH GEN HIMMEL   109
   Mel.: Mache dich, mein Geist bereit / 3 st. / Sasse (GL1811, Yoder)
   / CG1874.

AUF MEINEN LIEBEN GOTT TRAU ICH IN ANGST UND NOT   110
   Mel.: Wo soll ich fliehen hin / 5 st. / Weingärtner (Knapp, Koch,
   Kulp, Mützell); anon. (Nelle); (DP1718, F) / KDP1744.

AUF, SEELE, AUF UND SÄUME NICHT, ES BRICHT DAS LICHT HERFÜR   111
   Mel.: Lobt Gott, ihr Christen / 28 st. / M. Müller (Knapp, Koch,
   Kulp; Julian; DP1718, F, ZW) / Tr.: Julian / KDP1744.

AUF, SEELE, SEI GERÜST', DEIN HEILAND, JESUS CHRIST   112
   Mel.: Mein Jesu, der du mich / 18 st. / Heine (Knapp, Koch;
   Julian; DP1718, F, ZW) / Tr.: Julian / KDP1744.

AUF, TRIUMPH, ES KOMMT DIE STUNDE DA SICH ZION, DIE GELIEBTE   113
   Mel.: e. M. / 16 st. / J. C. Lange (Koch; DP1718, F, ZW) / KDP1744.

AUS DER TIEFE RUFE ICH ZU DIR, HERR, ERHÖRE MICH   114
   Mel.: Jesu, komm doch selbst / 4 st. / Schwämlein (Fischer; A1718)
   / CG1874.

AUS DER TIEFEN GRUFT MEIN GEIST ZU DIR RUFT   115
   Mel.: Seelen-Bräutigam / 7 st. / Anon. (Koch; DP1718, F, ZW) /
   KDP1744.

AUS GNADEN WIRD DER MENSCH GERECHT, AUS GNADEN NUR ALLEIN   116
   Mel.: C. M. / 6 st. / Liebich (Knapp 1837; EGS 1850) / NS1870.

AUS LIEB' VERWUND'TER JESU MEIN, WIE KANN ICH DIR G'NUG DANKBAR SEIN 117
   Mel.: e. M. / 9 st. / Anon. (Julian) / Tr.: Julian / GGB1720.

BALD KOMMT DER ABEND, LIEBE SEEL', DANN IST DER TAG VERGANGEN   118
   Mel.: Es ist gewisslich an / 10 st. / Stoll (GGG; ANH1795) /
   GGG1806.

BEDENK ICH SATANS STRICKE, DEN LAUF DER ARGEN WELT   119
   Mel.: Von Gott will ich nicht / 3 st. / P. F. Hiller (GLK) /
   CG1874.

BEDENKE, MENSCH, DAS ENDE, BEDENKE DEINEN TOD   120
   Mel.: P. M. / 3 st. / Liscow (Koch); anon. (Knapp); (DP1854, F) /
   NS1870.

BEFIEHL DU DEINE WEGE DEM HÖCHSTEN NUR ALLEIN   121
   Mel.: Ermuntert euch, ihr Frommen / 10 st. / Hübner (Koch) /
   KH1792.

BEFIEHL DU DEINE WEGE UND WAS DEIN HERZE KRÄNKT   122
   Mel.: Herzlich tut mich verlangen; Valet will ich dir geben /
   12 st. / Gerhardt (GL; Knapp, Koch, Kulp; Julian; DP1718, F) /
   Tr.: Julian / GGB1720.

BEFIEHL, MEIN HERZE, DEINE WEGE ALLEINE DEM, DER ALLES IST   123
   Mel.: Wer nur den lieben Gott / 7 st. / Anon. / KDP1764.

BEGLÜCKTER STAND GETREUER SEELEN, DIE GOTT ALLEIN ZU IHREM TEIL   124
    Mel.: Entfernet euch, ihr matten Kräfte / 8 st. / Bonin
    (Bachmann; DP1718, F, ZW) / KDP1744.

BEGRABET MICH NUN IMMERHIN, WO ICH SO LANG VERWAHRET BIN   125
    Mel.: L. M. / 3 st. / Anon. / NS1870.

BEGRABT DEN LEIB IN SEINE GRUFT BIS IHM DES RICHTERS STIMME RUFT   126
    Mel.: Nun lasst uns den Leib begraben / 7 st. / Klopstock (GLO;
    SAG 1851) / KLS1826.

BEI ALLER VERWIRRUNG UND KLAGE ALLHIER   127
    Mel.: Home / 4 st. / Ch.: Heim, heim, ach nur heim / Anon. tr.
    (DGM1865) / Or.: Denham: 'Mid scenes of confusion and creature
    complaints (Julian) / NS1870.

BEI DIR, JESU, WILL ICH BLEIBEN, HALTE SELBST DEIN SCHWACHES KIND   128
    Mel.: Alle Menschen müssen sterben / 2 st. / Loskiel (Koch,
    Kulp); anon. (Knapp 1837); Spitta (Nelle, Westphal; Julian) /
    KLS1841.

BEKLAGT DOCH DIESE ZEIT, IHR MENSCHEN-KIND' AUF ERDEN   129
    Mel.: O Gott, du frommer Gott / 7 st. / Anon. / GGB1720.

BERUF'NE SEELEN, SCHLAFET NICHT, ZUR EWIGKEIT STEHT AUFGERICHT'   130
    Mel.: Ich hab mein' Sach' / 6 st. / Tersteegen (GBG; Julian) /
    Tr.: Julian / KDP1760.

BEUG DICH TIEF, SEELE, BEUG DICH TIEF FÜR GOTT   131
    Mel.: Fahre fort / 5 st. / Anon. / ENGL1807.

BEUGT VOR JEHOVAS HEHREM THRON, BEUGT EUCH, IHR VÖLKER NAH UND FERN   132
    Mel.: Old Hundred / 5 st. / Anon. tr. (DGM1865) / Or.: Watts
    (ZP) / NS1870.

BEWAHRE DICH, O SEEL', DASS DU NICHT ABGEFÜHRET   133
    Mel.: Holdselig's Gotteslamm / 8 st. / Anon. / KDP1744.

BEWEG MEIN HERZ DURCH DEINE KRAFT UND ES ZU DEINER LIEBE RICHTE   134
    Mel.: Preis, Lob, Ehr', Ruhm / 6 st. / Anon. / KDP1744.

BINDE MEINE SEELE WOHL AN DICH, JESU, IN DER LIEBE   135
    Mel.: Jesus ist der schönste Nam' / 7 st. / Anon. / GGB1720.

BIST DU DENN, JESU, MIT DEINER HILF' GÄNZLICH ENTGANGEN   136
    Mel.: Hast du denn, Jesu, dein / 6 st. / Anon. (DP1718) /
    KDP1744.

BLAST DIE TROMPETE, BLAST DEN FROHEN FRIEDENS-TON   137
    Mel.: Jubilee / 6 st. / Ch.: Das frohe Jubeljahr bricht ein /
    Dreisbach, tr. (Yoder; GV1855) / Or.: C. Wesley: Blow ye the
    trumpet, blow (Julian) / CG1874.

BLEIB, JESU, BLEIB BEI MIR, ES WILL NUN ABEND WERDEN   138
    Mel.: O Gott, du frommer Gott / 4 st. / Neumeister (Knapp,
    Koch; Julian) / Tr.: Julian / ES1893.

BLEIB, LIEBSTER JESU, WEIL DIE NACHT DAS TAGESLICHT VERJAGT   139
    Mel.: C. M. / 5 st. / Scriver (Knapp; DGM1865) / NS1870.

BLEIBE BEI MIR, LIEBSTER FREUND, JESU, MEIN VERLANGEN, WEIL DIE SONNE
NICHT MEHR SCHEINT   140
    (Paraphrase of/Companion hymn to 141?)
    Mel.: Schwing dich auf zu deinem Gott / 13 st. / Anon. / KDP1744.

BLEIBE BEI MIR, LIEBSTER FREUND, JESU, MEIN VERLANGEN, WEIL DIE SONNE
WIEDER SCHEINT   141
    Mel.: Schwing dich auf / 14 st. / Anon. (Knapp 1837) / KDP1744.

BLEIBE BEI MIR, LIEBSTER SEELEN-FREUND, JEHOVA, DEM ICH MICH VEREINT   142
    Mel.: Wenn nach dem Friedens-Land wir geh'n / 9 st. / Bamberger
    (KPS) / KPS1858.

BLICKE MEINE SEELE AN, DIE SO FEST GEBUNDEN   143
    Mel.: Straf mich nicht / 13 st. / Anon. (DP1718, ZW) / KDP1744.

BLÜHENDE JUGEND, DU HOFFNUNG DER KÜNFTIGEN ZEITEN   144
    Mel.: Lobe den Herren / 9 st. / Woltersdorf (Knapp, Koch;
    NVG1806) / KLS1841.

BRICH AN, MEIN LICHT, ENTZIEH DICH NIMMER NICHT   145
    Mel.: Mein Bräutigam, du zartes / 7 st. / Arnold (EUL; DP1718,
    ZW) / KDP1744.

BRICH ENDLICH HERFÜR, DU GEHEMMETE FLUT   146
    Mel.: Mach endlich des vielen Zerstreuens ein End' / 10 st. /
    Arnold (GGS; DP1718, ZW) / KDP1744.

BRÜDER WACHT, IM GLAUBEN STEHT, NUR ALLEIN AUF JESUM SEHT   147
    Mel.: Mein Gemüt / 4 st. / Bertolet (Yoder; NVG1828) / CG1874.

BRUNN ALLES HEILS, DICH EHREN WIR UND ÖFFNEN UNSERN MUND VOR DIR   148
    Mel.: O starker Gott / 5 st. / Tersteegen (GBG; Knapp, Koch,
    Kulp; Julian) / Tr.: Julian / KDP1764.

BRUNNQUELL ALLER GÜTER, HERRSCHER DER GEMÜTER   149
    Mel.: Jesu, meine Freude / 8 st. / J. Franck (Koch; Julian;
    DP1718, F) / KDP1744.

BUSSE IST DER WEG ZUM LEBEN; BITTE, FAHR IM BITTEN FORT   150
    [Mel.: 35] / 5 st. / Anon. / NS1870.

CHRISTE, MEIN LEBEN, MEIN HOFFEN, MEIN GLAUBEN   151
    Mel.: Bist du denn, Jesu / 7 st. / Kellner von Zinnendorf (Koch;
    F, ZW) / KDP1744.

CHRISTE, WAHRES SEELENLICHT, DEINER CHRISTEN SONNE   152
    Mel.: Schwing dich auf / 6 st. / C. Prätorius (Koch; DP1718, F,
    ZW) / KH1792.

CHRISTEN ERWARTEN IN ALLERLEI FÄLLEN JESUM MIT SEINER ALLMÄCHTIGEN   153
    Mel.: Jesu, hilf siegen / 9 st. / Edeling (Knapp, Koch; Julian;
    F) / Tr.: Julian / KH1792.

CHRISTEN MÜSSEN SICH HIER SCHICKEN IN DES KREUZES SCHMALE BAHN   154
    Mel.: Meine Sorgen, Angst und Plagen / 13 st. / C. Sauer II
    (Stoudt) / Tr.: Colonial, p. 569; Flory, p. 278 / ELEL1788, KH1792.

CHRISTI BLUT UND GERECHTIGKEIT, DAS IST MEIN SCHMUCK UND EHRENKLEID   155
    Mel.: Herr Jesu Christ, dich zu uns wend / 3 st. / N. L. von
    Zinzendorf (Knapp, Nelle; Julian) / CG1874.

CHRISTI TOD IST ADAMS LEBEN, CHRISTI LEBEN ADAMS TOD   156
    Mel.: Meine Hoffnung stehet feste / 13 st. / Frankenberg (Fischer,
    Koch, Mützell; DP1718, F, ZW) / KDP1744.

CHRISTUM WIR SOLLEN LOBEN SCHON   157
    Mel.: e. M. / 8 st. / Luther (Koch; Julian; DP1718, F, ZW) /
    KDP1744.

CHRISTUS, DAS LAMM, AUF ERDEN KAM NACH'S VATERS RAT UND WILLEN   158
    Mel.: Ich dank dir schon / 23 st. / Betz (Wolkan); Büchel
    (Wackernagel); AU1767) / GGB1720.

CHRISTUS, DER IST MEIN LEBEN, STERBEN IST MEIN GEWINN   159
    Mel.: Bedenke, Mensch, das Ende / 2 st. / Anon. (Knapp, Kulp,
    Mützell, Westphal; Julian); Sömeren (Wackernagel); (F) / Tr.:
    Julian / CG1874.

CHRISTUS HAT UNS ERWÄHLT, ZU SOLCHER ZAHL GEZÄHLT   160
    Mel.: O Herr der Herrlichkeit / 8 st. / J. Preiss (GAL) / GAL1753.

CHRISTUS IST DER KIRCHE HAUPT, DIE AN SEINEN NAMEN GLAUBT   161
    Mel.: P. M. / 5 st. / P. F. Hiller (GL1840) / NS1870.

CHRISTUS LAG IN TODESBANDEN FÜR UNSRE SÜND' GEGEBEN 162
    Mel.: e. M. / 6 st. / Luther (GLL1612; DP1718) / KDP1744.

DANK SEI GOTT, DASS CHRISTI GEIST SEINER JÜNGER TRÖSTER HEISST 163
    [Mel.: 33] / 5 st. / P. F. Hiller (GLK) / NS1870.
DANKBAR LASST UNS CHRISTUM PREISEN, DER SEIN VOLK AUF ERDEN LIEBT 164
    Mel.: e. M. / 4 st. / Anon. / KLS1829.
DANKE DEM HERREN, O SEELE, DEM URSPRUNG 165
    Mel.: Lobe den Herren / 6 st. / Tersteegen (GBG; Koch) KDP1744.
DANKT DEM HERRN, IHR GOTTES-KNECHTE, KOMMT, ERHEBET SEINEN RUHM 166
    Mel.: e. M. / 7 st. / Neuss (Koch; DP1718, F, ZW) / KDP1744.
DANKT JESU, DEM RETTER, DANKT JESU, DEM HORT 167
    Mel.: Mein Leben auf Erden / 1 st. / Anon. / CG1879.
DAS AMT DER LEHRER, HERR, IST DEIN, DEIN SOLL AUCH DANK UND EHRE SEIN 168
    Mel.: L. M. / 5 st. / Anon. (NVG1799) / NS1870.
DAS FUSSWASCHEN IST EINE PFLICHT, WOZU DER CHRIST VERBUNDEN IST 169
    Mel.: Herr Jesu Christ, dich zu uns wend / 4 st. / Anon.
    (Yoder) / CG1874.
DAS GESETZ ZEUGT WIDER UNS WEGEN UNSRES ÜBELTUNS 170
    [Mel.: 33] / 6 st. / P. F. Hiller (GLK) / NS1870.
DAS GRAB IST ALLER TOTENHAUS; HEUT' TRÄGT MAN MICH, BALD DICH HINAUS 171
    Mel.: Herr Jesu Christ, dich zu uns wend / 3 st. / Anon. / CG1874.
DAS GRAB IST DA, SO HEISST ES IMMER, WIR GEHEN EIN, WIR GEHEN AUS 172
    Mel.: Wer nur den lieben Gott / 4 st. / Anon. / ES1893.
DAS GRAB IST LEER, DAS GRAB IST LEER, ERSTANDEN IST DER HELD 173
    Mel.: C. M. / 5 st. / Claudius (Pfeiffer; Julian) / NS1870.
DAS IST EINE WUNDERSACHE, SCHWACH SEIN, ABER DOCH IN KRAFT 174
    Mel.: Jesu, der du meine Seele / 3 st. / P. F. Hiller (GLK) /
    CG1874.
DAS JERUSALEM, DAS DROBEN, WO DIE SCHAR' DAS LÄMMLEIN LOBEN 175
    Mel.: Lobet Gott, zu jeder Stunde / 1 st. / Anon. / CG1879.
DAS KREUZ IST DENNOCH GUT, OBGLEICH ES WEHE TUT 176
    Mel.: Mein g'nug beschwerter Sinn / 10 st. / Tersteegen (GBG;
    Julian) / Tr.: Julian / KH1792.
DAS KURZGESTECKTE ZIEL DER TAGE IST SIEBENZIG, IST ACHTZIG JAHRE 177
    Mel.: Wer weiss, wie nahe mir / 2 st. / Anon. (SAG1851) / KPS1858.
DAS LEBEN DIESER ZEIT IST VOLLER KAMPF UND STREIT 178
    Mel.: Auf meinen lieben Gott / 9 st. / Anon. / GGB1720.
DAS LEBEN JESU IST EIN LICHT, DAS MIR IST VORGEGANGEN 179
    Mel.: Sei Lob und Ehr'; Es ist das Heil / 8 st. / Anon. / GGB1720.
DAS LEBEN JESU WAR ZUR ZEIT DER ERSTEN ZUKUNFT IN DEM STREIT 180
    Mel.: Wie fleucht dahin; Ich hab mein Sach' Gott heimgestellt /
    14 st. / Anon. / GGB1720.
DAS MACHT SATANAS SO RASEN, WENN MAN SCHÖNE WASSERBLASEN 181
    Mel.: Endlich wird es uns gelingen, dass wir alle / 5 st. /
    Mack, Jr. (Heckman; KK1795: signed: "Theophilus") / Tr.: Heckman.
DAS NEUGEBOR'NE KINDELEIN, DAS HERZELIEBE JESULEIN 182
    Mel.: Herr Jesu Christ, dich zu uns wend / 4 st. / Schneegass
    (Koch, Mützell; Julian; F) / Tr.: Julian / CG1874.
DASS JESUS UNS GERECHT GEMACHT, WEIL ER FÜR UNS GELITTEN 183
    Mel.: Allein Gott in der Höh' / 2 st. / Anon. / KDP1797-G.
DEIN BLUT, HERR, IST MEIN ELEMENT, DARIN ICH NUR KANN LEBEN 184
    Mel.: Mein Herzens-Jesu, meine / 7 st. / Arnold (EUL; Koch;
    DP1718, F) / KDP1744.

DEIN ERBE, HERR, LIEGT VOR DIR UND WILL IM BLUT DES LAMMES WERDEN   185
    Mel.: Preis, Lob, Ehr, Ruhm / 12 st. / Arnold (GGS; Koch;
    DP1718, F) / GGB1720.

DEIN' ERKENNTNIS, JESU CHRISTE HAT DEN ÜBERSCHWANG BEI MIR   186
    Mel.: O Durchbrecher / 4 st. / P. F. Hiller (GLK) / CG1874.

DEIN GARTEN, HERR, MIT SEHNSUCHT WART'T AUF DEINER GNADE GEGENWART   187
    Mel.: P. M. / 10 st. / Anon. (EGS1821) / NS1870.

DEIN WORT, O HÖCHSTER, IST VOLLKOMMEN, ES LEHRT UNS UNSRE GANZE PFLICHT   188
    Mel.: Wer nur den lieben / 4 st. / Cramer (Koch; NVG1806) / ES1893.

DEM HERREN DER ERDKREIS ZUSTEHT   189
    Mel.: Ps. 24 Lobwasser / 5 st. / Lobwasser (PD1710) / KDP1744.

DEM LÄMMLEIN NACHGEH'N, JUNGFRÄULICH UND REIN   190
    Mel.: The rock that is higher than I / 6 st. / Ch.: Eilt vorwärts,
    das Kleinod ist nah / Anon. / CG1874.

DEMUT IST DIE SCHÖNSTE TUGEND, ALLER CHRISTEN RUHM UND EHR'   191
    Mel.: Alle Menschen müssen sterben / 8 st. / P. F. Hiller
    (Kadelbach, Knapp; TH1776) / KDP1797-G.

DEN AM KREUZ ICH NUR ERWÄHLE, MEINE GANZE LEBENSZEIT   192
    Mel.: Der am Kreuz ist meine Liebe / 8 st. / Anon. / GGB1720.

DEN MEINE SEELE LIEBT, HAT GAR NICHT SEINES GLEICHEN   193
    Mel.: Nun danket alle / 13 st. / Anon. (Knapp; DP1718, F) /
    KDP1744.

DEN TAG VOR CHRISTI LEIDEN, BEIM LETZTEN ABENDMAHL   194
    Mel.: Ermuntert euch, ihr Frommen / 2 st. / Anon. / ES1893.

DEN WEISEN SCHIEN EIN NEUER STERN; VON OSTEN HER SIE KAMEN FERN   195
    Mel.: Herr Jesu Christ, dich zu uns wend / 7 st. / Dreisbach
    (Yoder; EGS1821) / CG1874.

DEN WUNDER-GOTT, DEN WUNDER-GOTT, DER UNS IM GEIST VEREINIGT HAT   196
    Mel.: Ich leb mir nicht / 12 st. / Anon. / GGB1720.

DENKET DOCH, IHR ADAMS-KINDER, DENKET AN DIE EWIGKEIT   197
    Mel.: Schaffet, schaffet, meine Kinder / 1 st. / Anon.: "By a
    youth on his death-bed" (KPS) / KPS1858.

DENKET DOCH, IHR MENSCHENKINDER, AN DEN LETZTEN TODESTAG   198
    Mel.: Werde munter / 29 st. / Hübner (Knapp, Koch; DP1740) /
    KDP1797-G.

DER ABEND KOMMT, DIE SONNE SICH VERDECKET   199
    Mel.: Der Tag ist hin, mein Jesu / 10 st. / Tersteegen (GBG;
    Knapp, Koch, Kulp; ZW) / KDP1764.

DER ALLES FÜLLT, VOR DEM DIE TIEFEN ZITTERN   200
    Mel.: Zerfliess, mein Geist / 15 st. / Herrnschmidt (Koch;
    DP1718, F) / GGB1720.

DER AM KREUZ IST MEINE LIEBE, MEINE LIEB' IST JESUS CHRIST   201
    Mel.: Werde munter / 6 st. / Fritsch (Fischer, Nelle; Julian;
    DP1718) / GGB1720.

DER BITT'RE KELCH UND MYRRHEN WEIN SCHMECKT EINEM CHRISTEN GUT   202
    Mel.: Kein Christ soll ihm / 16 st. / Beissel (JK; ZW) / KH1792.

DER BRÄUT'GAM KOMMT, DER BRÄUT'GAM KOMMT   203
    Mel.: Auf, Christenmensch, auf, auf zum Streit / 4 st. / Scheffler
    (HS; DP1718, ZW) / KDP1744.

DER ERSTEN UNSCHULD REINES GLÜCK, WOHIN BIST DU GESCHIEDEN   204
    Mel.: Es ist gewisslich an der Zeit / 3 st. / Garve (Knapp, Koch;
    Julian; GKW 1841) / ES1893.

DER GLAUB' IST EINE ZUVERSICHT ZU GOTTES GNAD' UND GÜTE   205
    [Mel.: 129] / 4 st. / Schrader (Koch; DP1854, F) / NS1870.

DER GNADEN-BRUNN' FLIESST NOCH, DEN JEDERMANN KANN TRINKEN   206
     Mel.: O Gott, du frommer / 6 st. / Knorr von Rosenroth (Koch;
     DP1718, F) / GGB1720.

DER GRUND, AUF DEM ICH FEST WILL STEHEN, IST JESUS CHRISTUS   207
     [Mel.: 96] / 5 st. / P. F. Hiller (GLK; EGS1850) / NS1870.

DER HEILAND RUFET MIR UND DIR: "WEN DÜRSTET, DER KOMM HER ZU MIR!"   208
     Mel.: L. M. / 6 st. / Bertolet (Yoder; EGS1821) / NS1870.

DER HEILAND WILL DER WEINSTOCK SEIN, DIE JÜNGER SIND DIE REBEN   209
     Mel.: Mir nach, spricht / 2 st. / P. F. Hiller (GLK) / CG1874.

DER HEILAND, ZUR RECHTEN DES VATERS ERHOBEN   210
     Mel.: O Jesu, wann soll ich / 3 st. / P. F. Hiller (GLK) / CG1874.

DER HERR BEFIEHLT DIE WACHSAMKEIT UND DAS GEBET DEN SEINEN   211
     Mel.: Gottlob, ein Schritt / 2 st. / P. F. Hiller (GLK) / CG1874.

DER HERR BRICHT EIN UM MITTERNACHT, JETZT IST NOCH ALLES STILL   212
     Mel.: C. M. / 5 st. / Anon. (Knapp); Rube (Knapp 1837; Julian);
     (HGB 1731) / NS1870.

DER HERR ERHÖR' DICH IN DER NOT; GOTT JAKOBS SCHÜTZE DICH   213
     Mel.: C. M. / 6 st. / Anon. (DP1854) / NS1870.

DER HERR ERMAHNT UNS ZUM GEBET, SEIN WILLE BLEIBET FEST UND STET   214
     Mel.: L. M. / 4 st. / Anon. (Knapp 1837; F) / NS1870.

DER HERR HAT EUCH JETZT SEHR BETRÜBT INDEM DASS ER, WAS IHR GELIEBT   215
     Mel.: Ach Gott, man kennet dich / 7 st. / Anon. / KPS1858.

DER HERR HAT UNS BEFOHLEN, WIR, SEINE DIENER, SOLLEN IN ALLE WELT   216
     Mel.: Wach auf, mein Herz, und singe / 5 st. / Anon. / CG1874.

DER HERR IST GOTT UND KEINER MEHR, FROHLOCKT IHM, ALLE FROMMEN   217
     Mel.: Es ist das Heil / 8 st. / Cramer (Koch; PUL1785) /
     KDP1797-G.

DER HERR IST KÖNIG, WEIT UND BREIT NICHT SEINES SZEPTERS HERRLICHKEIT   218
     Mel.: L. M. / 5 st. / Anon. (DGM1865) / NS1870.

DER HERR IST MEIN GETREUER HIRT, DER MICH BEHÜT' MIT FLEISSE   219
     (Paraphrase of 220?)
     Mel.: Sei Lob und Ehr' / 5 st. / Anon. / KH1792.

DER HERR IST MEIN GETREUER HIRT, HÄLT MICH IN SEINER HUTE   220
     Mel.: Allein Gott in / 5 st. / Anon. (Kulp); Meuslin (Kadelbach,
     Koch, Mützell; Julian); (DP1718, F, ZW) / Tr.: Julian / KDP1744.

DER HERR SCHICKT SEINE DIENER AUS, WIR FINDEN SCHWACH UNS ÜBERAUS   221
     Mel.: Ich hab ihn dennoch / 1 st. / Anon. / KLS1841.

DER HERR SEI SELBST IN UNSRER MITT' UND SEGNE UNS MIT FRIEDEN   222
     [Mel.: 19] / 1 st. / Anon. / KLS1841.

DER HERR STEIGT AUS DES JORDANS FLUT, DER GEIST DER SALBUNG AUF IHM   223
     Mel.: L. M. [i.e., C. M.] / 4 st. / Anon. / NS1870.

DER HERR UNS SEGNE UND BEHÜT' UND LASS SEIN ANTLITZ LEUCHTEN;
   ER WOLLE UNS   224
     Mel.: Sei Lob und Ehr' / 1 st. / Anon. / CG1874.

DER HERR UNS SEGNE UND BEHÜT' UND LASS SEIN ANTLITZ LEUCHTEN ÜBER UNS   225
     Mel.: Sei Lob und Ehr' / 1 st. / Anon. / KH1792.

DER HIMMEL UND ... see: DIE HIMMEL UND ...

DER LIEBEN SONNE LICHT UND PRACHT HAT NUN DEN LAUF VOLLFÜHRET   226
     Mel.: e. M. / 9 st. / Scriver (Knapp, Koch, Kulp; Julian; DP1718,
     F) / Tr.: Julian / KDP1744.

DER LIEBEN SONNE LICHT UND PRACHT SCHEINT UNSRER ERDE WIEDER   227
     (Paraphrase of/Companion hymn to 226)
     Mel.: Frisch, frisch hinach / 9 st. / Anon. (A1718) / KDP1744.

DER MENSCH IST WIE EIN' SCHÖNE BLUM', DIE OFTMALS HAT SEHR SCHÖNEN   228
    Mel.: e. M. / 3 st. / J. Preiss (GAL) / Tr.: Colonial,
    p. 552-553 / GAL1753.

DER NEID UND EHRGEIZ QUÄLEN DIE WELTGESINNTEN SEELEN   229
    Mel.: Nun ruhen alle Wälder / 4 st. / P. F. Hiller (GLK) / CG1874.

DER SATAN SUCHT, WIE ER GEWINN', WAS SICH VON IHM GESCHIEDEN   230
    Mel.: Es ist gewisslich / 3 st. / P. F. Hiller (GLK) / CG 1874.

DER SCHMALE WEG FÜHRT DOCH GERAD' INS LEBEN   231
    Mel.: Der schmale Weg ist breit genug / 13 st. / Lehr (Cunz,
    Koch) / KDP1764.

DER SCHMALE WEG IST BREIT GENUG ZUM LEBEN   232
    Mel.: e. M. / 11 st. / Richter (Knapp, Koch; DP1718, F, ZW) /
    KDP1744.

DER SPÖTTER STROM REISST VIELE FORT, ERHALT UNS, HERR, BEI DEINEM WORT   233
    Mel.: L. M. / 4 st. / Klopstock (GLO; EGB1848) / NS1870.

DER TAG HAT SICH GENEIGET, DIE NACHT HERVORGETAN   234
    Mel.: Ich dank dir, lieber Herre / 7 st. / Anon. 16th cent.
    (Kulp); Oderborn (Mützell) / GGB1720.

DER TAG HAT SICH NUN GEENDET UND DIE NACHT HERFÜR GETAN   235
    Mel.: Sieh, hier bin ich, Ehrenkönig / 9 st. / Stoll (GGG) /
    GGG1806.

DER TAG IST HIN, MEIN JESU, BEI MIR BLEIBE   236
    Mel.: e. M. / 6 st. / Neander (GLU; Knapp, Koch, Kulp; Julian;
    DP1718, F) / Tr.: Julian / GGB1720.

DER TAG IST HIN MIT SEINEM LICHTE, DIE NACHT IST DA MIT DUNKELHEIT   237
    Mel.: Wer nur den lieben Gott / 5 st. / Anon. / KDP1744.

DER TAG IST NUN VERGANGEN, DIE DUNKLE NACHT BRICHT AN   238
    Mel.: Herzlich tut mich verlangen / 6 st. / Anon. / GGB1720.

DER TAG VERSCHWIND'T, DER ABEND KOMMT, SEI MUNTER, MEINE SEELE   239
    Mel.: So wünsch ich ihr eine / 8 st. / Anon. / GGB1720.

DER VATER, DER HAT MICH GEZEUGT, DIE LIEBE MUTTER MICH GESÄUGT   240
    Mel.: Ihr jungen Helden, aufgewacht, die ganze / 3 st. /
    Bamberger (KPS) / KPS1858.

DER WEG ZU DEM HIMMEL VON CHRISTUS GEMACHT MIT KÖSTLICHEN RIEGEL   241
    Mel.: Ach lass dich jetzt finden / 7 st. / Anon. (Yoder) /
    KPS1858.

DER WEISHEIT LICHT GLÄNZT IMMERZU UND TREIBT DEN MÜDEN SINN ZUR RUH'   242
    Mel.: Herr Jesu Christ, meins Lebens / 12 st. / Arnold (EUL;
    Knapp 1859; DP1718, ZW) / KDP1744.

DER WELTGEIST IST DOCH CHRISTO FEIND, WILL ER ES GLEICH VERHEHLEN   243
    Mel.: Allein Gott in der Höh' / 4 st. / P. F. Hiller (GLK) /
    CG1874.

DER WELTMENSCH SORGT SICH BALD ZU TOD   244
    Mel.: Mir nach, spricht / 4 st. / P. F. Hiller (GLK) / CG1874.

DES HERREN WORT BLEIBT IN EWIGKEIT UND SCHALLET IN DER GNADENZEIT   245
    Mel.: L. M. / 6 st. / Herbert (Wackernagel, Wolkan; Julian);
    Czech Brethren (Knapp); (HGB1731) / Tr.: Julian / NS1870.

DIE BIBEL IST EIN KÖSTLICH BUCH, WO GOTTES BLUMEN BLÜH'N   246
    Mel.: Mein Gott, das Herz / 6 st. / Orwig (ELS1843) / CG1874.

DIE FREUNDLICHKEIT MEINES GELIEBTEN MICH RÜHRET   247
    Mel.: Es glänzet der Christen / 7 st. / Anon. / KDP1744.

DIE FREUNDLICHKEIT VON OBEN HER HAT MICH IM GEIST GETRIEBEN   248
    Mel.: Wer wird in jener neuen Welt / 6 st. / Anon.: "Sung at
    Sister Elisabeth Knepper's love feast." (Broadside, dated:
    Pentecost, 1796, Antietam)

DIE GANZE WELT GEWINNEN SCHEINT GROSS VOR MENSCHENSINNEN   249
    Mel.: Nun ruhen alle Wälder / 5 st. / P. F. Hiller (GLK) /
    CG1874.

DIE GLOCK' HAT JA NUN GESCHLAGEN UND MIR WIEDER ANGEDEUT'   250
    Mel.: Alle Menschen müssen sterben / 5 st. / Stoll (GGG) /
    GGG1806.

DIE GLOCKE SCHLÄGT UND ZEIGT DAMIT, DIE ZEIT HAT ABGENOMMEN   251
    Mel.: Es ist gewisslich an der Zeit / 2 st. / Anon. / KDP1764.

DIE GNADE SEI MIT ALLEN, DIE GNADE UNSRES HERRN   252
    Mel.: e. M. / 5 st. / P. F. Hiller (GLK; Knapp, Koch) / KLS1844.

DIE GNADE UNSRES HERRN JESU CHRISTI UND DIE LIEBE GOTTES   253
    Mel.: e. M. / 1 st. / Anon. (Koch; CGB1832) / KLS1844.

DIE GNADE WIRD DOCH EWIG SEIN, DIE WAHRHEIT DOCH GEWISS   254
    Mel.: C. M. / 5 st. / P. F. Hiller (GLK; Knapp, Koch) / NS1870.

DIE GÖTTLICHE LIEBE BRINGT LAUTER VERGNÜGEN   255
    Mel.: Es glänzet der Christen / 6 st. / Anon. (Knapp 1837) /
    KDP1744.

DIE HIMMEL UND DER HIMMEL HEER' ERZÄHLEN GOTTES MACHT UND EHR'   256
    Mel.: Wie schön leucht' / 8 st. / Anon. (DP1854, F, ZW) / NS1870.

DIE IHR DIE STILLEN HARFEN NOCH AN BABELS WEIDEN HÄNGET   257
    Mel.: Mein Herzens-Jesu / 4 st. / P. F. Hiller (GLK) / CG1874.

DIE LIEB ERKALT' (IST KALT) JETZT IN DER WELT   258
    Mel.: e. M. / 8 st. / Scharnschlager (Wackernagel; AU1767);
    Hetzer (LHB); anon. Anabaptist (Wolkan) / GGB1720.

DIE LIEBE LEIDET NICHT GESELLEN, IM FALL SIE TREU UND REDLICH BRENNT   259
    Mel.: Wer nur den lieben Gott / 8 st. / Finx (Fischer, Knapp,
    Koch; DP1718, F) / GGB1720.

DIE LIEBE, SO NIEDRIGEN DINGEN ENTGEHET UND EINIG IN JESU   260
    Mel.: Durch blosses Gedächtnis / 13 st. / Arnold (GGS; DP1718,
    ZW) / KDP1744.

DIE LIEBLICHEN BLICKE, DIE JESU MIR GIBT, DIE MACHEN MIR SCHMERZEN   261
    Mel.: e. M. / 6 st. / Quirsfeld (Fischer, Koch; DP1718, F) /
    GGB1720.

DIE LIEBLICHEN LEHRER, DIE CHRISTUS GESANDT, DIE MENSCHENBEKEHRER   262
    Mel.: Mein Leben auf Erden / 5 st. / Anon. / CG1879.

DIE MACHT DER WAHRHEIT BRICHT HERFÜR UND KLOPFT AN VIELER HERZEN TÜR   263
    Mel.: O Ewigkeit, du / 17 st. / Anon. (DP1718, ZW) / KDP1744.

DIE MORGENSTERNE LOBEN GOTT, WO BIST DU, MEINE SEELE   264
    Mel.: O Herre Gott, dein göttlich Wort / 6 st. / Anon. (Knapp;
    F) / KDP1744.

DIE NACHT DES GRABES WIRD VERGEHN, WENN EINST DER TAG GEKOMMEN IST   265
    Mel.: Der Tag ist hin, mein Geist und Sinn / 2 st. / Anon.
    (Knapp) / KLS1841-O.

DIE NACHT IST HIN, MEIN GEIST UND SINN SEHNT SICH NACH JENEM TAGE   266
    Mel.: Der Tag ist hin, mein Geist und Sinn / 14 st. /
    Freylinghausen (Knapp, Koch; DP1718, F) / KH1792.

DIE NACHT IST VOR DER TÜR, SIE LIEGT SCHON AUF DER ERDEN   267
    Mel.: e. M. / 7 st. / Weber (Fischer, Koch); C. Ziegler
    (Koch); (DP1718, F) / KDP1744.

DIE SEELE CHRISTI HEIL'GE MICH, SEIN GEIST VERSETZE MICH IN SICH   268
    Mel.: Du unbegreiflichs höchstes Gut / 5 st. / Scheffler
    (HS; Koch; Julian; DP1718, F) / Tr.: Julian / KDP1744.

DIE TUGEND WIRD DURCHS KREUZ GEÜBET   269
    Mel.: e. M. / 10 st. / Nehring (Knapp, Koch; DP1718, F) / GGB1720.

DIE WASSERBÄCHE RAUSCHEN DAR, DIE STERN' AM HIMMEL LEUCHTEN   270
    [Mel.: 84] / 4 st. / Bertolet (Yoder; EGS1821) / CG1874.
DIE WEISHEIT DIESER ERDEN IST DOCH DIE WAHRE NICHT   271
    Mel.: Herr Jesu, Gnadensonne / 5 st. / P. F. Hiller (GLK) /
    CG1874.
DIE WIR UNS ALLHIER BEISAMMEN FINDEN, SCHLAGEN UNSRE HÄNDE EIN   272
    (= last stanza of: Marter Gottes, wer kann dein vergessen)
    [Mel.: 198] / 1 st. / C. R. von Zinzendorf (Koch; Julian;
    HGB1778) / KLS1844.
DIE ZEIT GEHET ZUM END', NICHT ABER GOTTES TUN   273
    Mel.: Blast die Trompete / 1 st. / Anon. / CG1874.
DIE ZEIT IST HIN, DIE STUND' IST DA, DASS ICH VON EUCH SOLL SCHEIDEN   274
    Mel.: So wünsch ich nun ein' gute / 11 st. / Anon. / GGB1720.
DIE ZEIT IST KURZ, DER ABEND KOMMT, DA MAN SICH AUF DEN SABBATH FREUT   275
    (= st. 12 and 11 of 1181)
    Mel.: Entfernet euch, ihr / 2 st. / Francke (Koch; GL1801) /
    KLS1829.
DIE ZEIT IST NAH, HALLELUJA, DER TAG BEGINNT ZU BLICKEN   276
    Mel.: Ach Gott und Herr / 12 st. / Anon. / GGB1720.
DIE ZEIT IST NOCH NICHT DA, DA ZION TRIUMPHIERET   277
    Mel.: e. M. / 10 st. / Anon. (DP1718, F, ZW) / KDP1744.
DIE ZIONS-GESELLEN, DIE MÜSSEN STETS WACHEN   278
    Mel. : Ihr Kinder des Höchsten / 13 st. / Anon. / GGB1720.
DIES EIN', DAS NOT, LEHR MICH, DASS ICH BESTÄNDIGLICH   279
    Mel.: Mein Jesu, der du mich / 7 st. / Anon. / KDP1744.
DIES IST DER TAG, DEN GOTT GEMACHT, SEIN WERD' IN ALLER WELT GEDACHT   280
    Mel.: Du unbegreiflichs höchstes Gut / 11 st. / Gellert (GOL;
    Knapp, Koch, Kulp; Julian) / Tr.: Julian / KDP1797-G.
DIES IST MEIN SCHMERZ, DIES KRÄNKET MICH   281
    (st. 1 = st. 2 of 982)
    [Mel.: 226] / 2 st. / Heermann (Knapp, Koch, Mützell;
    DP1718) / KLS1841.
DIESE WELT GERING ZU SCHÄTZEN, IST DER CHRISTEN TEURE PFLICHT   282
    [Mel.: 35] / 4 st. / Anon. (GV1848) / NS1870.
DIESEN TÄUFLING (DIESE SEELE) BRINGEN WIR, JESU, DEINEN LIEBES-ARMEN   283
    Mel.: e. M. / 5 st. / Anon. / KLS1829.
DIESES IST DER WEG, DER EINE, WO MAN AUCH SICH SELBST NICHT TRAUT   284
    Mel.: Komm, o komm du Geist / 14 st. / Anon. / GGB1720.
DIR, DIR, JEHOVA, WILL ICH SINGEN   285
    Mel.: e. M. / 8 st. / Crasselius (Knapp, Koch, Kulp; Julian;
    DP1718, F, ZW) / Tr.: Julian / KDP1744.
DIR SEI LOB, HERRLICHKEIT UND PREIS, IMMANUEL, GEGEBEN   286
    (Paraphrase of 1095)
    Mel.: Sei Lob und Ehr' / 10 st. / Anon. / KDP1744.
DORNIG IST DIE FINSTRE WÜSTE WODURCH PILGER REISEN HIN   287
    [Mel.: 35] / 4 st. / Dreisbach (Yoder; GV1855) / NS1870.
DORT AUF JENEM TOTEN-HÜGEL HÄNGT AM KREUZ MEIN BRÄUTIGAM   288
    Mel.: e. M. / 4 st. / Anon. (SEL1842) / KPS1858.
DORT ÜBER JENEN STERNEN, DORT IST EIN SCHÖNES LAND   289
    Mel.: Bedenke, Mensch / 3 st. / Plank (Knapp; SAG1851) / KPS1858.
DROBEN, WENN WIR ÜBERWINDEN, WIRD IM PARADIESE SCHON   290
    (= st. 4 and 5 of 102; st. 8 and 37 of original)
    Mel.: Jesu, Jesu, Brunn' des Lebens / 2 st. / Steinhofer /
    (Koch; GL1811) / CG1874.

DU ARMER PILGER WANDELST HIER IN DIESEM JAMMERTAL   291
    Mel.: e. M. / 14 st. / Becker (Flory, Stoudt; KH1797) / Tr.:
    Brumbaugh, p. 209; Flory, p. 204 / KH1792.

DU AUFGANG AUS DER HÖHE, DU GLANZ DER HERRLICHKEIT   292
    Mel.: Von Gott will ich nicht / 4 st. / Anon. / KDP1764.

DU BROT, DAS VON DEM HIMMEL KOMMT, DU SPEIS' DER FROMMEN SEELEN   293
    Mel.: Allein zu dir, Herr Jesu / 7 st. / Anon. / GGB1720.

DU FORSCHEST MICH, O HERR, WIE WUNDERLICH PRÜFST DU MICH INNERLICH   294
    Mel.: Brich an, mein Licht / 20 st. / Mack, Jr. (Heckman) / Tr.:
    Heckman / KH1792.

DU GEIST, DER ALLE FROMMEN FÜHRT UND IN DIE WAHRHEIT LEITET   295
    Mel.: Der Herr ist mein getreuer / 7 st. / Anon. (DP1718) /
    KDP1744.

DU, GOTT, DU BIST DER HERR DER ZEIT UND AUCH DER EWIGKEITEN   296
    Mel.: Es ist das Heil uns kommen her / 8 st. / Anon. (Knapp1837;
    PUL1785) / KDP1797-G.

DU, GOTT, MEIN HEILAND BIST, LIEBSTER HERR JESU CHRIST   297
    Mel.: Mein Jesu, der du mich / 24 st. / Anon. (Bachmann; GG1700)
    / GGB1720.

DU GRÜNER ZWEIG, DU EDLES REIS, DU HONIGREICHE BLÜTE   298
    Mel.: Mir nach / 6 st. / Scheffler (HS; DP1718, F, ZW) / KDP1744.

DU HERR DES HIMMELS UND DER ERDEN, WOHER KOMMT DIESE KNECHTSGESTALT   299
    Mel.: Wer nur den lieben Gott / 7 st. / Anon. / KDP1764.

DU LICHT, DAS OHNE WECHSEL IST, ICH TU NACH DIR VERLANGEN   300
    Mel.: Es ist gewisslich / 6 st. / Anon. / GGB1720.

DU MEINE SEELE, SINGE, WOHLAUF UND SINGE SCHÖN   301
    Mel.: Ermuntert euch; Herzlich tut mich erfreuen / 10 st. /
    Gerhardt (GL; Knapp, Koch, Kulp; Julian); anon. Pennsylvania-
    German (Stoudt); (DP1718, F, ZW) / Tr.: Julian / KDP1744.

DU, O SCHÖNES WELTGEBÄUDE, MAGST GEFALLEN, WEM DU WILLST   302
    Mel.: Jesu, der du meine Seele / 8 st. / J. Franck (Knapp, Koch;
    Julian; DP1718, F) / Tr.: Julian / GGB1720.

DU SCHENKEST MIR DICH SELBST, O JESU CHRIST, MEIN LEBEN   303
    Mel.: O Gott, du frommer Gott / 13 st. / Anon. (DP1718) / KDP1744.

DU TAUSEND-LIEBSTER GOTT, MEIN INNIGSTES VERLANGEN   304
    Mel.: O Gott, du frommer / 5 st. / Scheffler (HS; DP1718) /
    KDP1744.

DU TOCHTER DES KÖNIGS, WIE SCHÖN IST DEIN GEHEN   305
    Mel.: Ach alles, was Himmel / 5 st. / Arnold (GGS; DP1718) /
    KDP1744.

DU UNBEGREIFLICH HÖCHSTES GUT, AN WELCHEM KLEBT MEIN HERZ UND MUT   306
    Mel.: Nun lasst uns den Leib begraben / 6 st. / Neander (GLU;
    DP1718, F) / GGB1720.

DU VATER ALLER GEISTER, DU STRAHL DER EWIGKEIT   307
    Mel.: Ach Herr, mich armen Sünder / 6 st. / N. L. von
    Zinzendorf (Julian; HGB1731) / Tr.: Julian / KH1792.

DU WESENTLICHES WORT VOM ANFANG HER GEWESEN   308
    Mel.: Ich hab ich dennoch lieb / 8 st. / Laurenti (Knapp, Koch;
    Julian; DP1718, F, ZW) / Tr.: Julian / KDP1744.

DURCH ADAMS FALL UND MISSETAT, DIE ER EHMALS VERÜBET HAT   309
    Mel.: L. M. / 5 st. / Anon. (Knapp; CH1822) / NS1870.

DURCH BLOSSES GEDÄCHTNIS DEIN, JESU, GENIESSEN   310
    Mel.: Ich liebe dich herzlich / 15 st. / Knorr von Rosenroth
    (Fischer; DP1718, F) / GGB1720.

DURCH KREUZ UND TRÜBSAL KÖNNEN SCHON DIE MENSCHEN SICH BEKEHREN   311
   Mel.: Die Morgensterne loben Gott / 4 st. / Anon. / CG1879.

EHRE, DEM DIE EHR' GEBÜHRET, DOCH DIE EHRE JESU CHRIST   312
   Mel.: Glück zu, Kreuz / 10 st. / Mack, Jr. (Heckman) / Tr.:
   Colonial, p. 568; Heckman.
EHRE SEI GOTT IN DER HÖH', DEM HEILAND ALLER WELT   313
   Mel.: Der Tag ist fort / 14 st. / A. Miller (KPS) / KPS1858.
EHRE SEI JETZO MIT FREUDEN GESUNGEN   314
   Mel.: e. M. / 6 st. / Neander (GLU; DP1718) / GGB1720.
EI, LOBET DOCH ALLE GESCHÖPFE DEN KÖNIG, DIES LOBEN IST DENNOCH   315
   Mel.: Ach alles, was Himmel / 5 st. / Anon. (DP1718, ZW) / KDP1744.
EI, WAS FRAG ICH NACH DER ERDEN, WENN JEHOVA BEI MIR IST   316
   Mel.: Meine Hoffnung / 6 st. / Neander (GLU; DP1718) / GGB1720.
EIL DOCH HERAN UND MACH DEM GUTEN BAHN   317
   Mel.: Brich an, mein Licht / 24 st. / Anon. (DP1718, ZW) / KDP1744.
EIN AMT IST MIR VERTRAUT, DAS TREU ICH SOLL VERSEH'N   318
   (Paraphrase of 324)
   [Mel.: 15] / 4 st. / Anon. tr. (GV1855) / Or.: C. Wesley: A charge
   to keep I have (Julian, Yoder) / NS1870.
EIN CHRIST SCHEINT EIN VERÄCHTLICH' LICHT UND IST DER STOLZEN SPOTT   319
   Mel.: C. M. / 5 st. / P. F. Hiller (GLK) / NS1870.
EIN KIND IST UNS GEBOREN HEUT', DER LIEBSTE SOHN IST UNS GESCHENKET   320
   Mel.: Preis, Lob, Ehr', Ruhm / 10 st. / Freylinghausen (Knapp,
   Koch / DP1718, F) / KDP1744.
EIN KÖNIG GROSS VON MACHT UND EHR' IST, DEM ICH MICH VERTRAUE   321
   Mel.: Allein Gott in der Höh' / 10 st. / Anon. / KDP1744.
EIN LÄMMLEIN GEHT UND TRÄGT DIE SCHULD DER WELT UND IHRER KINDER   322
   Mel.: e. M. / 9 st. / Gerhardt (GL; Knapp, Koch, Kulp; Julian;
   DP1718, F) / Tr.: Julian / KDP1797-G.
EIN LIEBLICH' LOS IST MIR GEFALLEN, EIN SCHÖNES ERBTEIL MIR BESCHERT   323
   Mel.: Wer nur den lieben / 2 st. / Spitta (PH; Knapp; Julian) /
   Tr.: Julian / CG1874.
EIN' PFLICHT ZU TUN ICH HAB, EIN' GOTT ZU EHREN FEIN   324
   Mel.: Ich traue meinem Gott / 4 st. / Anon. tr. / Or.: C. Wesley:
   A charge to keep I have (Julian, Yoder) / CG1874.
EIN STREITER BEI DER KREUZESFAHN' BIN ICH FÜR JESU CHRIST   325
   Mel.: C. M. / 9 st. / Anon. / NS1870.
EIN TRÖPFLEIN VON DEN REBEN DER SÜSSEN EWIGKEIT   326
   Mel.: Herzlich tut mich erfreuen / 10 st. / Finx (Knapp, Koch;
   DP1718, F) / KDP1744.
EIN VON GOTT GEBOR'NER CHRIST WIRD AUCH HERZLICH LIEBEN   327
   Mel.: Bleibe bei mir, liebster / 2 st. / Anon. (NVG1806) / CG1874.
EINE SEELE, DIE GOTT LIEBET, FINDET ANGST IN DIESER WELT   328
   Mel.: Gott des Himmels und der Erden / 10 st. / Mack, Jr.
   (Heckmann; KK1795: signed: "Theophilus") / Tr.: Flory, p. 255;
   Heckman.
EINEN GUTEN KAMPF HAB ICH AUF DER WELT GEKÄMPFET   329
   Mel.: Liebste Witwe, weine nicht / 2 st. / Albert (Knapp, Kulp,
   Westphal; F) / CG1874.
EINMAL IST'S GESETZT ZU STERBEN, NACH DEM STERBEN, DAS GERICHT   330
   Mel.: Werde munter / 4 st. / P. F. Hiller (GLK) / CG1874.

EINS BETRÜBT MICH SEHR AUF ERDEN, DASS SO WENIG SELIG WERDEN   331
    Mel.: Treuer Vater, deine / 18 st. / Naas (Stoudt; KH1797) / Tr.:
    Brumbaugh, p. 126-128 / KH1792.

EINS IST NOT, ACH HERR, DIES EINE LEHRE MICH ERKENNEN DOCH   332
    Mel.: e. M. / 10 st. / J. H. Schröder (Knapp, Koch, Kulp, Nelle,
    Westphal; Julian; DP1718, F) / GGB1720.

EINST FIEL VOM EWIGEN ERBARMEN EIN STRAHL IN MEINE NACHT HEREIN   333
    Mel.: Wer nur den lieben / 3 st. / W. Preiss (KPS) / KPS1858.

EINST RIEFEN GOTTES BOTEN DEN HEIDEN TROSTVOLL ZU   334
    Mel.: Bedenke, Mensch, das Ende / 1 st. / Anon. / CG1874.

ENDLICH, ENDLICH MUSS ES DOCH MIT DER NOT EIN ENDE HABEN   335
    Mel.: Guter Hirte / 4 st. / Schmolck (Koch; Julian; KGL1731) /
    Tr.: Julian / KDP1764.

ENDLICH SOLL DAS FROHE JAHR DER ERWÜNSCHTEN FREIHEIT KOMMEN   336
    Mel.: e. M. / 6 st. / Arnold (GL; Knapp); anon. Pennsylvania-
    German (Stoudt); (DP1718, F, ZW) / KDP1744.

ENDLICH WIRD ES DOCH GELINGEN, JEDER SEELE, DIE GOTT LIEBT   337
    Mel.: Meine Hoffnung stehet feste / 4 st. / Mack, Jr. (Heckman) /
    Tr.: Heckman.

ENDLICH WIRD ES UNS GELINGEN, DASS WIR ALLE WELT BEZWINGEN   338
    Mel.: O wie selig sind / 11 st. / Anon. / GGB1720.

ENTFERNET EUCH, IHR MATTEN KRÄFTE VON ALLEM, WAS NOCH IRDISCH HEISST   339
    Mel.: e. M. / 10 st. / Arnold (GL; Koch; DP1718, F) / GGB1720.

ER GLEICHTE DEN ROSEN IM FRÜHLING GAR SCHÖN   340
    Mel.: Heim, heim, wir gehen jetzt heim / 6 st. / Anon. / CG1874.

ER STIRBT, ER STIRBT, DER SÜNDERFREUND, SCHAU, SALEMS TÖCHTER WEINEN   341
    Mel.: L. M. / 6 st. / Anon. tr. (EGS1821) / Or.: Watts: He dies,
    the friend of sinners, dies (Julian, Yoder) / NS1870.

ER WIRD ES TUN, DER FROMME TREUE GOTT   342
    Mel.: Es kostet viel, ein Christ / 9 st. / Herrnschmidt (Knapp,
    Koch; Julian; DP1718, F) / Tr.: Julian / KH1792.

ERHALT UNS, HERR, BEI DEINEM WORT, WEHR ALLEN FEINDEN, STARKER HORT   343
    (st. 1 and 2 are a paraphrase of Luther's: Erhalt uns, Herr, bei
    deinem Wort)
    Mel.: Herr Jesu Christ, dich zu / 3 st. / Anon. (A1718) / KLS1829.

ERHEBE DICH, MEIN FROHER MUND, DIES IST DIE RECHTE ZEIT   344
    Mel.: L. M. / 6 st. / Löscher (Koch) / NS1870.

ERHEBE DICH, O MEINE SEEL', DIE FINSTERNIS VERGEHET   345
    Mel.: Mein Herzens-Jesu / 8 st. / Lackmann (Knapp, Koch; DP1718,
    F) / GGB1720.

ERINN'RE DICH, MEIN GEIST, ERFREUT DES HOHEN TAGS DER HERRLICHKEIT   346
    Mel.: L. M. / 6 st. / Gellert (GOL; Knapp, Koch; Julian) / Tr.:
    Julian / NS1870.

ERLEUCHT MICH, HERR, MEIN LICHT, ICH BIN MIR SELBST VERBORGEN   347
    Mel.: e. M. / 16 st. / Buchfelder (Knapp, Koch, Nelle; Julian;
    DP1718, F) / Tr.: Julian / GGB1720.

ERMUNTERT EUCH, IHR FROMMEN, ZEIGT EURER LAMPEN SCHEIN   348
    Mel.: Valet; Wacht auf, ihr Christen alle / 10 st. / Laurenti
    (Knapp, Koch, Kulp, Westphal; Julian; DP1718, F) / GGB1720.

ERNEURE MICH, O EWIG'S LICHT UND LASS VON DEINEM ANGESICHT   349
    Mel.: Erhalt uns Herr / 16 st. / Ruopp (Knapp, Koch, Kulp; DP1718,
    F) / KDP1744.

ERSTAUNET ALL, IHR HÖH' UND TIEFEN, SEHT EINST DIE HOHE WÜRDE AN   350
    Mel.: Wach auf, du Geist / 11 st. / Anon. (DP1718, ZW) / KDP1744.

ES EILT HERAN UND BRICHT SCHON WIRKLICH AN, MEHR, ALS MAN GLAUBEN KANN   351
    Mel.: Eil doch heran und mach / 22 st. / Anon. / KDP1760.

ES GEHET WOHL, HALLELUJAH, DER LIEBE GOTT IST DENEN NAH'   352
    Mel.: Kommt her zu mir, spricht / 9 st. / Anon. / GGB1720.

ES GIBT EIN WUNDERSCHÖNES LAND, WO REINE FREUDE WOHNT   353
    Mel.: C. M. / 6 st. / Anon. tr. (Knapp; DGM1865) / Or.: Watts:
    There is a land of pure delight (Julian) / NS1870.

ES GING EIN SÄMANN AUS ZU SÄEN, SPRACH JESUS DORT VON SEINEM WORT   354
    Mel.: Wer nur den lieben Gott / 7 st. / Anon. (HGB1731) / KDP1744.

ES GLÄNZET DER CHRISTEN INWENDIGES LEBEN   355
    Mel.: e. M. / 8 st. / Richter (Knapp, Koch, Kulp, Nelle; Julian;
    DP1718, F) / Tr.: Julian / GGB1720.

ES IST DER NOT EIN ZIEL GESTECKT, GEDULD, GOTT HAT DEN HELD ERWECKT   356
    Mel.: Kommt her zu mir, spricht / 4 st. / Anon. / KDP1744.

ES IST DIE LETZTE STUNDE, ACH SEELEN, WACHET AUF   357
    Mel.: Herzlich tut mich verlangen / 9 st. / Anon. / GGB1720.

ES IST EIN GOTT, O FÜHL ES, HERZ! ERHEBT EUCH, IHR GEDANKEN   358
    Mel.: Es ist gewisslich an der / 4 st. / Anon. (GGLR1828) / NS1870.

ES IST GENUG, MEIN MATTER SINN SEHNT SICH DAHIN, WO MEINE VÄTER   359
    Mel.: e. M. / 6 st. / Anton Ulrich of Braunschweig-Wolfenbüttel
    (Fischer; GG1700) / GGB1720.

ES IST GEWISSLICH AN DER ZEIT, DASS GOTTES SOHN WIRD KOMMEN   360
    Mel.: e. M. / 7 st. / Ringwald (Knapp, Koch, Kulp, Mützell;
    Julian); anon. Anabaptist (Wolkan); (DP1718, F) / Tr.: Julian /
    GGB1720.

ES IST MIR DIE BESTE SACH', DASS MEIN JESUS IST MEIN LEBEN   361
    Mel.: Guter Hirte, willst du nicht / 8 st. / Anon. / GGB1720.

ES IST NICHT SCHWER, EIN CHRIST ZU SEIN   362
    Mel.: Es kostet viel, ein Christ / 8 st. / Richter (Knapp, Koch,
    Kulp, Nelle, Westphal; Julian; DP1718, F) / Tr.: Julian / KDP1744.

ES IST NOCH EINE RUH' VORHANDEN FÜR JEDEN GOTT ERGEB'NEN GEIST   363
    Mel.: Wer nur den lieben / 3 st. / Kunth (Nelle; GGLR1828) / NS1870.

ES IST VOLLBRACHT, ER IST VERSCHIEDEN, MEIN JESUS SCHLOSS DIE AUGEN ZU   364
    Mel.: Wer nur den lieben Gott lässt / 2 st. / S. Franck (Cunz,
    Knapp, Koch) / ES1893.

ES IST WIEDER KOMMEN EIN SCHÖNES NEU-JAHR   365
    Mel.: e. M. / 6 st. / Hoffer (KPS) / KPS1858.

ES KOSTE, WAS ES WILL, ICH WILL GOTT HALTEN STILL   366
    Mel.: Auf meinen lieben Gott / 9 st. / Anon. / GGB1720.

ES KOSTET VIEL, EIN CHRIST ZU SEIN   367
    Mel.: Es ist nicht schwer, ein Christ / 8 st. / Richter (Knapp,
    Koch, Kulp, Nelle, Westphal; Julian; DP1718, F, ZW) / KDP1744.

ES LEBE GOTT ALLEIN IN MIR IN ZEIT UND EWIGKEIT   368
    Mel.: C. M. / 10 st. / Tersteegen (GBG) / NS1870.

ES SEI DEM SCHÖPFER DANK GESAGT, DENN ER IST GUT, DAS MACHT MIR MUT   369
    Mel.: Hab ich nur Gott / 10 st. / Anon. / GGB1720.

ES SIND GEWISS DIE LETZTEN ZEITEN, DENN WIE'S ZU NOAHS ZEITEN WAR   370
    Mel.: Die Liebe leidet nicht Gesellen / 78 st. / Mack Jr.
    (Heckman) / Tr.: Heckman.

ES SIND SCHON DIE LETZTEN ZEITEN, D'RUM, MEIN HERZ, BEREITE DICH   371
    Mel.: Freu dich sehr / 8 st. / Laurenti (Koch; DP1718, F) / GGB1720.

EW'GE WEISHEIT, JESU CHRIST   372
    Mel.: Jesu, meiner Seelen Ruh' / 18 st. / Arnold (GGS; Knapp, Koch;
    Julian; DP1718, F) / Tr.: Julian / KDP1744.

EW'GES EVANGELIUM, DAS WIE MILCH UND HONIG SCHMECKET   373
    Mel.: Meinen Jesum lass ich nicht / 5 st. / Anon. / KLS 1841.

EWIG, EWIG HEISST DAS WORT, SO WIR WOHL BEDENKEN MÜSSEN   374
    Mel.: Meinen Jesum lass / 3 st. / Schmolck (Koch; ANH 1795) /
    KLS 1826.

EY ... see: EI ...

FAHRE FORT, FAHRE FORT, ZION, IM LICHTE   375
    Mel.: e. M. / 7 st. / J. E. Schmidt (Knapp, Koch, Westphal; Julian;
    DP 1718, F) / Tr.: Julian / GGB 1720.

FASS, MEIN HERZ, WAS JESUS SPRICHT, EUER HERZ ERSCHRECKE NICHT   376
    Mel.: Gott sei Dank / 9 st. / P. F. Hiller (GLK; Knapp 1837) /
    CG 1874.

FLIEHET AUS BABEL, IHR KINDER AUS ZION GEBOREN   377
    Mel.: Lobe den Herren, den mächtigen / 6 st. / Anon. / GGB 1720.

FLIESST, IHR AUGEN, FLIESST VON TRÄNEN UND BEWEINET MEINE SCHULD   378
    Mel.: Zion klagt mit Angst / 5 st. / Laurenti (Knapp, Koch; Julian;
    DP 1718, F) / Tr.: Julian / KDP 1797-G.

FOLGET MIR, RUFT UNS DAS LEBEN, WAS IHR BITTET, WILL ICH GEBEN   379
    Mel.: e. M. / 14 st. / Rist (Knapp, Koch; Julian; DP 1718, F) / Tr.:
    Julian / GGB 1720.

FORT, FORT, MEIN HERZ, ZUM HIMMEL! FORT, FORT, ZUM LAMME ZU   380
    Mel.: e. M. / 10 st. / Anon. / ELEL 1812.

FORT, IHR GLIEDER, LASST UNS GEHEN AUS DEM WINTERQUARTIER AUS   381
    Mel.: Wo ist wohl ein süsser / 15 st. / Anon. (DP 1718) / KDP 1744.

FORT, IHR GLIEDER UND GESPIELEN, UND WER SONST DEN BRÄUT'GAM LIEBT   382
    Mel.: Werde munter, mein Gemüte / 14 st. / Anon. / KDP 1760.

FRAG DEINEN GOTT, HÖR, WAS ER ZEUGET IN SEINEM WORT   383
    Mel.: Wer nur den lieben Gott lässt / 4 st. / Arnold (GL; Knapp,
    Koch; DP 1718, ZW) / KDP 1744.

FREUDENVOLL, FREUDENVOLL WALLE ICH FORT, HIN ZU DEM LANDE   384
    Mel.: e. M. / 3 st. / Lyon, tr. (Yoder; ELS 1863) / Or.: Hunter:
    Joyfully, joyfully onward I move (Yoder) / ES 1893.

FREUND, ICH BIN ZUFRIEDEN, GEH' ES WIE ES WILL   385
    Mel.: Ach lass dich jetzt finden / 2 st. / Anon. (UCH) / CG 1874.

FRIEDE, ACH FRIEDE, ACH GÖTTLICHER FRIEDE   386
    Mel.: e. M. / 9 st. / Crasselius (Knapp, Koch, Westphal; DP 1718, F)
    / GGB 1720.

FRISCH, FRISCH HINACH, MEIN GEIST UND HERZ   387
    Mel.: Der lieben Sonne Licht und Pracht / 7 st. / Dessler (Fischer,
    Knapp, Koch; DP 1718, F) / KDP 1744.

FRÖHLICH SOLL MEIN HERZE SPRINGEN, WEIL DIE ZEIT VOLLER FREUD'   388
    Mel.: Der lieben Sonne Licht und Pracht / 20 st. / Anon. / KDP 1744.

FROHLOCKET, DER HEILAND IST MÄCHTIG ERSTANDEN   389
    Mel.: O Jesu, wann soll ich / 3 st. / P. F. Hiller (GLK) / CG 1874.

FROHLOCKET, IHR VÖLKER, FROHLOCKET MIT HÄNDEN   390
    Mel.: e. M. / 6 st. / Anon. (DP 1718, F, ZW) / KDP 1744.

FROMM SEIN IST EIN SCHATZ DER JUGEND, IHRE ZIER UND BESTE KRON'   391
    Mel.: O Durchbrecher / 10 st. / Grumbacher (ELEL 1788); Mennonite
    schoolmaster (Stoudt) / ELEL 1788.

FRÜHMORGENS, DA DIE SONN' AUFGEHT, MEIN HEILAND, CHRISTUS, AUFERSTEHT   392
    Mel.: Heut' triumphieret Gottes Sohn / 4 st. / Heermann (Knapp,
    Koch, Kulp, Mützell, Westphal; Julian; DP 1718, F) / Tr.: Julian /
    CG 1874.

FÜR SOLCHE WOHLTAT WOLLEN WIR, WIE LIEBE KINDER MÜSSEN 393
    Mel.: Sei Lob und Ehr' / 2 st. / Anon. (PI1725) / KLS1826.
FÜR UNSRE BRÜDER BETEN WIR, O VATER, WIE FÜR UNS, ZU DIR 394
    (Paraphrase of Cramer's: Für unsren Nächsten bitten wir)
    Mel.: L. M. / 5 st. / Anon. (DGM1865) / NS1870.
FÜRST DER FÜRSTEN, JESU CHRIST, DER DU ERDENRICHTER BIST 395
    [Mel.: 33] / 5 st. / Scheffler (HS) / NS1870.

GEDULDIG'S LÄMMLEIN, JESU CHRIST, DER DU ALL' ANGST UND PLAGEN 396
    Mel.: Mir nach, spricht Christus / 5 st. / Scheffler (HS; Knapp,
    Koch; DP1718, F) / KDP1744.
GEH AUF, MEIN'S HERZENS MORGENSTERN UND WERD' AUCH MIR ZUR SONNE 397
    Mel.: Was mein Gott will / 5 st. / Scheffler (HS; Koch; DP1718, F,
    ZW) / KDP1744.
GEH AUS, MEIN HERZ, UND SUCHE FREUD' IN DIESER LIEBEN SOMMER-ZEIT 398
    Mel.: Kommt her zu mir, spricht / 15 st. / Gerhardt (GL; Knapp,
    Koch, Kulp; Julian; DP1718, F) / Tr.: Julian / KDP1744.
GEH, MÜDER LEIB, ZU DEINER RUH', DEIN JESUS RUHT IN DIR 399
    Mel.: Nun sich der Tag geendet / 5 st. / Schmolck (Knapp, Koch;
    Julian) / Tr.: Julian / KDP1760.
GEH, SEELE, FRISCH IM GLAUBEN FORT UND SEI NUR UNVERZAGT 400
    Mel.: Mein Gott das Herz / 4 st. / Anon. / KLS1826.
GEHET DURCH DIE ENGE PFORTE AUF DEN SCHMALEN LEBENSWEG 401
    [Mel.: 196] / 3 st. / Anon. (EGS1850) / NS1870.
GELOBET SEIST DU, JESU CHRIST, DASS DU DER SÜNDER HEILAND BIST 402
    Mel.: L. M. / 12 st. / Woltersdorf (Knapp; GGLR1828) / NS1870.
GELOBET SEIST DU, JESUS CHRIST, DASS DU MENSCH GEBOREN BIST 403
    Mel.: e. M. / 7 st. / Luther (Knapp, Koch, Kulp; Julian; DP1718, F)
    / Tr.: Julian / GGB1720.
GELOBET SEIST DU, SCHÖPFERSMACHT, DENN GROSS IST DEIN ERBARMEN 404
    Mel.: Sei Lob und Ehr' / 1 st. / Anon. / ES1895.
GENUG, GENUG, ES IST GENUG, IHR KINDER EINER MUTTER 405
    Mel.: Ach Gott vom Himmel; Mein Herzens-Jesu, meine Lust / 24 st. /
    Anon. (DP1718) / KDP1744.
GIB DICH ZUFRIEDEN UND SEI STILLE IN DEM GOTTE DEINES LEBENS 406
    Mel.: e. M. / 15 st. / Gerhardt (GL; Knapp, Koch, Kulp; Julian;
    DP1718, F) / Tr.: Julian / KDP1744.
GIB, JESU, DASS ICH DICH GENIESS IN ALLEN DEINEN GABEN 407
    Mel.: Gottlob, ein Schritt zur Ewigkeit / 2 st. / Tersteegen (GBG;
    Knapp) / KDP 1764.
GLANZ VOLLER KRAFT, MACH DEINER EIGENSCHAFT UND LICHTES DOCH TEILHAFT 408
    Mel.: Eil doch heran und mach / 5 st. / Anon. (DP1740) / KDP1760.
GLAUB AN GOTT, ZION, GLAUB AN GOTT, DER EIN HEILIG, FREUNDLICH WESEN 409
    Mel.: Fahre fort, Zion / 11 st. / Anon. (DP1740) / KDP1760.
GLAUBE, LIEBE, HOFFNUNG SIND DAS GESCHMEIDE WAHRER CHRISTEN 410
    Mel.: Liebster Jesu, wir sind / 8 st. / Anon. / KDP1760.
GLAUBEN HEISST, DIE GNAD' ERKENNEN, DIE DEN SÜNDER SELIG MACHT 411
    [Mel.: 35] / 6 st. / Woltersdorf (Knapp; EGS1850) / NS1870.
GLÜCK ZU, KREUZ, VON GANZEM HERZEN, KOMM, DU ANGENEHMER GAST 412
    Mel.: e. M. / 21 st. / Gotter (Knapp, Koch; Julian; DP1718, F) /
    Tr.: Julian / GGB1720.
GOTT ALLEIN IST GUT, DIESES MACHT UNS MUT 413
    Mel.: Seelenbräutigam / 7 st. / Mack, Jr. (Heckman) / Tr.: Heckman.

GOTT, DER GROSSE HIMMELS-KÖNIG, WELCHER HEISST HERR ZEBAOTH   414
    Mel.: Unser Herrscher / 8 st. / Anon. (DP1718, F, ZW) / KDP1744.
GOTT DER WAHRHEIT UND DER LIEBE, DIR SEI LOB UND RUHM GEBRACHT   415
    Mel.: Abermal ein Tag / 1 st. / P. F. Hiller (Ehmann, Knapp, Koch)
    / KLS1841-O.
GOTT DES FRIEDENS, HEIL'GE MICH, DENN ICH SEHN MICH INNIGLICH   416
    [Mel.: 33] / 6 st. / Anon. (DGM1865) / NS1870.
GOTT DES HIMMELS UND DER ERDEN, VATER, SOHN, HEILIGER GEIST   417
    Mel.: Komm, o komm, du Geist / 8 st. / Albert (Knapp, Koch, Kulp;
    Julian; DP1718, F) / Tr.: Julian / KDP1744.
GOTT, DES SZEPTER, STUHL UND KRONE HERRSCHET ÜBER ALLE WELT   418
    Mel.: Freu dich sehr, o meine Seele / 12 st. / Neuss (Koch, Nelle;
    DP1718, F, ZW) / KDP1744.
GOTT, DESSEN LIEBEVOLLER RAT DEN EHESTAND GESTIFTET HAT   419
    [Mel.: 20] / 5 st. / Anon. (NVG1799) / NS1870.
GOTT, DIR SEI LOB VON ALLEN FÜR DIES, DEIN WOHLGEFALLEN   420
    Mel.: Wach auf, mein Herz / 6 st. / P. F. Hiller (GLK) / CG1874.
GOTT, DU BIST LOBENSWERT, WEIL DU UNS GIBST ALLZEIT   421
    Mel.: Der Tag ist fort und hin / 2 st. / Meyer (KPS) / KPS1858.
GOTT, GIB MIR DEINEN GEIST ZUM BETEN, ZUM BETEN OHNE UNTERLASS   422
    Mel.: Wer nur den lieben / 5 st. / P. F. Hiller (GLK; Knapp) /
    NS1870.
GOTT HAT DIE WELT GELIEBET, DASS ER SEIN KINDLEIN GIBET   423
    Mel.: e. M. / 4 st. / Anon. Winebrennerian hymn (Yoder) / KPS1858.
GOTT HAT SICH ZU UNS GENEIGET UND IN SEINEM SOHN GEZEIGET   424
    Mel.: Lobet Gott zu jeder Stunde / 4 st. / Anon. / CG1874.
GOTT, ICH PREISE DEINE GÜTE FÜR DEN SCHUTZ IN DIESER NACHT   425
    Mel.: Gott des Himmels und der / 3 st. / Anon. (DGM1865) / CG1879.
GOTT, ICH WILL VOR DIR MICH BEUGEN   426
    Mel.: Meine Armut macht / 4 st. / P. F. Hiller (GLK; Knapp) /
    CG1874.
GOTT IST ES, DER ALLE DINGE, DIE HERRLICHEN UND DIE GERINGE   427
    Mel.: Wachet auf, ruft uns die Stimme / 2 st. / Anon. / CG1874.
GOTT IST GEGENWÄRTIG, LASSET UNS ANBETEN   428
    Mel.: Wunderbarer König / 8 st. / Tersteegen (GBG; Knapp, Koch,
    Kulp; Julian; DP1740, ZW) / Tr.: Julian / KDP1744.
GOTT IST GUT, WAS WILL ICH KLAGEN, WENN DIE WELT ES BÖSE MEINT   429
    Mel.: Komm, o komm, du Geist / 6 st. / Anon. (KGL1731) / KDP1764.
GOTT IST MEIN HEIL, MEIN' HILF, MEIN TROST, MEIN' HOFFNUNG   430
    Mel.: e. M. / 4 st. / Renau (Koch); Sophia, Queen of Denmark
    (Knapp); (A1718) / KDP1744.
GOTT LEBET NOCH, SEELE, WAS VERZAGST DU DOCH   431
    Mel.: e. M. / 8 st. / Zihn (Koch; Julian; DP1718, F) / Tr.: Julian
    / GGB1720.
GOTT LOB ... see: GOTTLOB ...
GOTT, MEIN TROST, WER FRAGT DANACH, OB MICH GLEICH DIE WELT BETRÜBET   432
    Mel.: Meinen Jesum lass / 6 st. / Schmolck (Koch; KGL1731) / KDP1760.
GOTT RUFET NOCH, SOLLT ICH NICHT ENDLICH HÖREN   433
    Mel.: Der Tag ist hin, mein Jesu / 8 st. / Tersteegen (GBG; Knapp,
    Koch, Kulp; Julian; ANH1795) / Tr.: Julian / KLS1826.
GOTT SEI DANK DURCH ALLE (IN ALLER) WELT   434
    Mel.: Nun komm, der Heiden Heiland / 9 st. / Held (Knapp, Koch,
    Kulp, Mützell, Nelle; Julian; F) / Tr.: Julian / KDP1744.
GOTT UND WELT UND BEIDER GLIEDER SIND EINANDER STETS ZUWIDER   435
    Mel.: Liebster Jesu, du / 13 st. / Anon. (DP1718, ZW) / KDP1744.

GOTT VATER, ALLER DINGE GRUND, GIB DEINEN VATERNAMEN KUND   436
   Mel.: O heil'ger Geist, kehr / 4 st. / Knapp (Knapp, Koch; EGS1850)
   / ES1893.
GOTT VATER, DIR, DIR WEIHEN WIR JETZT DIESEN TEMPEL EIN   437
   Mel.: Mein Gott, das Herz ich bringe / 4 st. / Anon. / ES1893.
GOTT VATER, DIR SEI LOB UND DANK DURCH CHRISTUM FÜR DIE SPEIS'   438
   Mel.: Wie schön leucht' uns / 1 st. / Anon. (NE1762) / KH1792.
GOTT WILL'S MACHEN, DASS DIE SACHEN GEHEN, WIE ES HEILSAM IST   439
   Mel.: Seelenweide, meine Freude / 17 st. / Herrnschmidt (Knapp,
   Koch; Julian; DP1718, F) / Tr.: Julian / GGB1720.
GOTTES KIND SEIN UND DOCH WEINEN, WILL OFT UNBEGREIFLICH SCHEINEN   440
   Mel.: Alles ist an Gottes / 5 st. / P. F. Hiller (GLK) / CG1874.
GOTTLOB, DAS LEIDEN DIESER ZEIT IST EIN(ST)MALS ÜBERWUNDEN   441
   Mel.: Mir nach, spricht Christus / 6 st. / Anon. / KLS1826.
GOTTLOB, DASS ICH DEN TAG VOLLBRACHT DURCH GOTTES GNAD' UND GÜTE   442
   Mel.: Es ist gewisslich an der Zeit / 2 st. / Anon. / CG1874.
GOTTLOB, DIE STUND' IST KOMMEN, DA WERD ICH AUFGENOMMEN   443
   Mel.: O Welt / 5 st. / Heermann (Koch, Kulp, Mützell; F) / KLS1834.
GOTTLOB, EIN SCHRITT ZUR EWIGKEIT IST ABERMALS VOLLENDET   444
   Mel.: Mein Herzens-Jesu / 12 st. / Francke (Knapp, Koch, Nelle;
   Julian; DP1718, F) / GGB1720.
GOTTLOB, ES IST NUNMEHR DER TAG VOLLENDET   445
   Mel.: Der Tag ist hin, mein Jesu / 9 st. / Lackmann (Koch; DP1718,
   F) / GGB1720.
GOTTLOB, ICH BIN IM GLAUBEN, WER WILL MIR SCHADEN TUN   446
   Mel.: Bedenke, Mensch, das Ende / 2 st. / Anon. (NVG1799) / CG1879.
GOTTLOB, ICH HABE GNADE, AN GNADE IST'S GENUG   447
   Mel.: Valet will ich dir / 2 st. / P. F. Hiller (Ehmann) / CG1874.
GOTTLOB, ICH HABE WIEDER DEN SÜNDEN ABGESAGT   448
   Mel.: Befiehl du deine Wege / 5 st. / Anon. (KGL1731) / KDP1764.
GOTTLOB, ICH KANN MICH TRÖSTEN, AUCH WENN DIE NOT AM GRÖSSTEN   449
   Mel.: Nun ruhen alle / 4 st. / P. F. Hiller (Ehmann, Koch) / CG1874.
GOTTLOB, MEIN LEBEN IST VOLLBRACHT, DAS KREUZ IST ÜBERWUNDEN   450
   Mel.: Komm, Sterblicher, betrachte mich / 4 st. / Anon. / KLS1826.
GROSS IST UNSRES GOTTES GÜTE, SEINE TREU, TÄGLICH NEU   451
   Mel.: Warum willst du / 18 st. / Tersteegen (GBG; Koch) / KDP1764.
GROSS UND HERRLICH IST DER KÖNIG IN DER FÜLLE SEINER PRACHT   452
   Mel.: Jauchzet all mit / 14 st. / Anon. (DP1718, F, ZW) / KDP1744.
GROSS UND MÄCHTIG MUSS MAN NENNEN DIE GEWALTIGEN DER WELT   453
   Mel.: Ringe recht / 10 st. / Mack, Jr. (Heckman) / Tr.: Colonial,
   p. 592; Heckman.
GROSSER GOTT, IN DEM ICH SCHWEBE, MENSCHENFREUND, VOR DEM ICH LEBE   454
   Mel.: Liebster Jesu, du wirst kommen / 16 st. / Tersteegen (GBG;
   Knapp; Julian) / Tr.: Julian / KDP1760.
GROSSER GOTT, LEHR MICH DOCH SCHWEIGEN, MACH MEIN HERZ GANZ IN DIR   455
   Mel.: Komm, o komm / 13 st. / Anon. (DP1718, ZW) / KDP1744.
GROSSER IMMANUEL, SCHAUE VON OBEN AUF DEIN ERLÖSTES, ERKAUFTES   456
   Mel.: Grosser Prophete / 8 st. / Bernstein (Knapp, Koch; DP1718, F)
   / GGB1720.
GROSSER MITTLER, DER ZUR RECHTEN SEINES GROSSEN VATERS SITZT   457
   Mel.: Ringe recht / 6 st. / Rambach (Knapp, Koch, Nelle, Westphal;
   Julian; EGS1850) / NS1870.
GROSSER PROPHETE, MEIN HERZE BEGEHRET   458
   Mel.: e. M. / 4 st. / Neander (GLU; Koch; Julian; DP1718, F) /
   Tr.: Julian / GGB1720.

GUT' NACHT, IHR LIEBEN KINDER, GUT' NACHT, IHR HERZENSFREUND', SEHT   459
   Mel.: Kommt, Kinder / 4 st. / Anon. / CG1874.
GUTE LIEBE, DENKE DOCH, DENK IN GNADEN DEINER JÜNGER   460
   Mel.: Wann erblick ich dich einmal / 3 st. / Anon. (ZW) / KDP1744.
GUTE NACHT, IHR EITLEN FREUDEN, ICH GEH FREUDIG VON EUCH AUS   461
   Mel.: Alle Menschen müssen / 8 st. / Anon. (DP1718, F) / KDP1744.
GUTE NACHT, IHR MEINE LIEBEN, GUTE NACHT, IHR HERZENSFREUND', GUTE   462
   Mel.: Psalm 42 Lobwasser / 11 st. / J. Danner (Stoudt; KH1797) /
   Tr.: Colonial, p. 555 / KH1792.
GUTER HIRTE, WILLST DU NICHT DEINES SCHÄFLEINS DICH ERBARMEN   463
   Mel.: Jesus, meine Zuversicht und / 5 st. / Scheffler (HS; Julian;
   DP1718, F) / Tr.: Julian / GGB1720.

HAB DANK, HAB DANK, DU GUTER GOTT, HAB DANK FÜR DEINE GROSSE LIEBE   464
   Mel.: Preis, Lob, Ehr' / 4 st. / Anon. / GGB1720.
HALLELUJA, LOB, PREIS UND EHR' SEI UNSERM GOTT JE MEHR UND MEHR   465
   Mel.: Wie schön leucht' / 4 st. / Rinkart (Fischer); anon. (Koch;
   Julian); Crasselius? (Knapp); (DP1718, F) / Tr.: Julian / GGB1720.
HALLELUJA, SCHÖNER MORGEN, SCHÖNER, ALS MAN DENKEN MAG   466
   Mel.: Komm, o komm / 4 st. / Krause (Knapp, Koch; Julian; GEKW1841)
   / Tr.: Julian / ES1893.
HALLELUJA WIRD MAN MIT FREUDEN ENDLICH SINGEN DEM HERREN, UNSERM GOTT   467
   Mel.: Nun danket alle Gott / 5 st. / Anon. (Knapp) / GGB1720.
HALT IM GEDÄCHTNIS JESUM CHRIST, O MENSCH, DER AUF DIE ERDEN   468
   Mel.: Mein Herzens-Jesu, meine Lust / 6 st. / Günther (Knapp, Kulp,
   Westphal; Julian; DP1718, F) / Tr.: Julian / KDP1744.
HALTE DEINE KRONE FESTE, HALTE MÄNNLICH, WAS DU HAST   469
   (st. 1 = st. 8 of 1050; = st. 8-12 of original)
   Mel.: Ringe recht / 5 st. / Winkler (Yoder) / NS1870.
HEILAND MEINER SEEL', SCHAFF, DASS ICH ERWÄHL   470
   Mel.: Seelenbräutigam / 17 st. / Naas (KH1797) / Tr.: Hymnal 1951,
   no. 361; Brumbaugh, p. 129; Flory, p. 217 / KH1792.
HEILIGSTER JESU, HEILIGUNGSQUELLE, MEHR ALS KRISTALL REIN, KLAR UND   471
   Mel.: Wachet auf, ruft / 9 st. / Lodenstein; tr. from Dutch into
   German by Crasselius (Koch; Julian), Arnold (Knapp); (DP1718, F) /
   Tr.: Julian / GGB1720.
HEIMWEH FÜHL ICH, SOHN VOM HAUSE, DRAUSSEN IST ES KALT UND KAHL   472
   Mel.: Komm, o komm / 3 st. / Ch.: Halleluja, halleluja, wir sind
   auf der Reise heim / W. Preiss (KPS) / Or. Ch.: Halleluiah,
   halleluiah, we are on our journey home (Lorenz, Yoder) / KPS1858.
HERR, BEI JEDEM WORT UND WERKE MAHNE MICH DEIN GEIST DARAN   473
   [Mel.: 35] / 5 st. / Pfeil (Koch; SEL1842) / NS1870.
HERR CHRIST, DER EIN'GE GOTT'S SOHN   474
   Mel.: e. M. / 5 st. / Kreutziger (Knapp, Koch, Kulp, Nelle,
   Röbbelen; Julian; DP1718, F) / Tr.: Julian / GGB1720.
HERR, DA DU EINST GEKOMMEN UND UNSRE MENSCHHEIT ANGENOMMEN   475
   Mel.: Wachet auf, ruft uns die / 2 st. / P. F. Hiller (GLK) /
   CG1874.
HERR, DEIN' OHREN ZU MIR NEIGE UND DICH GNÄDIG MIR ERZEIGE   476
   Mel.: Psalm 77 Lobwasser / 9 st. / Lobwasser (PD1710) / KDP1744.
HERR, DEIN WORT, DIE EDLE GABE, DIESEN SCHATZ ERHALTE MIR   477
   Mel.: Alle Menschen müssen sterben / 2 st. / N. L. von Zinzendorf
   (Knapp, Koch, Westphal) / KLS1841l-O.

HERR, DEINE RECHTE UND GEBOT', DANACH WIR SOLLEN LEBEN 478
  Mel.: Es ist gewisslich / 4 st. / Denicke (Koch; F) / ES1893.
HERR, DEINE TREUE IST SO GROSS, DASS WIR UNS WUNDERN MÜSSEN 479
  Mel.: Ach Gott, vom Himmel; Wo Gott der Herr nicht / 10 st. /
  Weydenheim (Knapp, Koch; DP1718, F) / KDP1744.
HERR, DU ERFORSCHT UND KENNEST MICH, DU SIEHST MICH SITZEN, STEHEN 480
  Mel.: Es ist das Heil / 8 st. / Anon. (A1751) / KLS1826.
HERR, ES IST VON MEINEM LEBEN ABERMAL EIN TAG DAHIN 481
  [Mel.: 192] / 2 st. / Neumann (Knapp; A1718, DP1842) / NS1870.
HERR, HIER SIND NUN DEINE KINDER, KOMM, O KOMM UND SEGNE SIE 482
  Mel.: Ringe recht / 2 st. / Anon. / CG1874.
HERR, ICH PREISE DEIN ERBARMEN, DEINE TREU' UND GÜTIGKEIT 483
  [Mel.: 116] / 4 st. / Anon. (NVG1799) / NS1870.
HERR JESU CHRIST, DICH ZU UNS WEND, DEIN' HEIL'GEN GEIST DU ZU UNS SEND 484
  Mel.: Du unbegreiflichs höchstes Gut / 4 st. / Wilhelm II. of
  Sachsen-Weimar (Knapp, Koch, Kulp, Westphal; Julian; DP1718, F) /
  Tr.: Julian / KDP1744.
HERR JESU CHRIST, DU HÖCHSTES GUT, DU BRUNNQUELL ALLER GNADEN 485
  Mel.: Ach Gott, vom Himmel sieh darein / 8 st. / Ringwald (Knapp,
  Koch, Kulp, Nelle, Wackernagel, Westphal; Julian; DP1718, F) / Tr.:
  Julian / KDP1744.
HERR JESU CHRISTE, MEIN PROPHET, DER AUS DES VATERS SCHOSSE GEHT 486
  Mel.: O starker Gott / 10 st. / Tersteegen (GBG; Koch) / KDP1744.
HERR JESU, DEINE HINDIN SCHREIT, ACH IST DES LEBENS QUELL NOCH WEIT 487
  Mel.: In dich hab ich gehoffet / 11 st. / Anon. (DP1718) / GGB1720.
HERR JESU, DEINE MACHT HAT SATAN UNTERBRACHT 488
  Mel.: Mein Jesu, der du mich / 28 st. / Anon. (DP1718, ZW) /
  KDP1744.
HERR JESU, DER DU IN DER NACHT VOR DEINEM STERBEN HAST BEDACHT 489
  [Mel.: 226] / 13 st. / Anon.: "From a manuscript written in August,
  1829" (NS) / NS1870.
HERR JESU, EW'GES LICHT, DAS UNS VON GOTT ANBRICHT 490
  Mel.: e. M. / 7 st. / Crasselius (Knapp, Koch; DP1718, F, ZW) /
  KDP1744.
HERR JESU, GNADENSONNE, WAHRHAFTES LEBENSLICHT 491
  Mel.: Herr Christ, der ein'ge Gott's Sohn / 8 st. / Gotter (Knapp,
  Koch, Kulp, Westphal; Julian; DP1718, F) / Tr.: Julian / GGB1720.
HERR JESU, MÖCHTEN'S ALLE WISSEN, WIE GUT MAN'S BEI DIR HABEN KANN 492
  Mel.: Wer nur den lieben Gott / 4 st. / Anon. / KSL1826.
HERR JESU, SEI AN DIESEM TAG SO MIT UNS, DASS MAN'S FÜHLEN MAG 493
  [Mel.: 20] / 4 st. / Anon. / KLS1841-O.
HERR JESU, ZIEH UNS FÜR UND FÜR, DASS WIR MIT DEN GEMÜTERN NUR 494
  Mel.: Nun sieh, wie fein und / 4 st. / Anon. (DP1718) / KDP1744.
HERR, MEINER SEELE GROSSEN WERT, DEN MIR DEIN TEURES WORT ERKLÄRT 495
  Mel.: Wohlauf, mein Herz / 9 st. / Anon. (GGLR1828) / KDP1797-G.
HERR, WANN WIRST DU ZION BAUEN, ZION, DIE GELIEBTE STADT 496
  Mel.: Freuet euch, ihr Christen alle / 8 st. / J. Lange (Knapp,
  Koch; DP1718, F) / GGB1720.
HERRLICHKEITEN, GROSS UND KLEINE TRIFFT MAN ZWAR AUF ERDEN AN 497
  Mel.: O der alles hätt' verloren / 10 st. / Mack, Jr. (Heckman) /
  Tr.: Colonial, p. 593; Heckman.
HERRLICHSTE MAJESTÄT, HIMMLISCHES WESEN 498
  Mel.: Grosser Prophete / 10 st. / Arnold (GL; Koch; DP1718, F) /
  GGB1720.

HERZ, ACHT ES EITLE FREUDE, WENN DU VERSUCHET BIST   499
    Mel.: Von Gott will ich nicht / 5 st. / P. F. Hiller (GLK) /
    CG1874.

HERZ UND HERZ VEREINT ZUSAMMEN SUCHT IN GOTTES HERZEN RUH'   500
    [Mel.: 194] / 5 st. / N. L. von Zinzendorf (Knapp, Koch, Kulp;
    Julian; HGB1731) / NS1870.

HERZLIEBSTER ABBA, DEINE TREUE UND HERZLICHE BARMHERZIGKEIT   501
    Mel.: Wer nur den lieben Gott / 5 st. / Anon. / KDP1744.

HERZOG UNSRER SELIGKEITEN, ZEUCH UNS IN DEIN HEILIGTUM   502
    Mel.: Eins ist not, ach Herr / 8 st. / Arnold (GGS; Knapp, Koch;
    Julian; DP1718, F) / GGB1720.

HEUT' FÄNGET AN DAS NEUE JAHR MIT NEUEM GNADENSCHEIN   503
    Mel.: Lobt Gott, ihr Christen; Mein Gott, das Herz / 20 st. / Anon.
    (DP1718, F) / KDP1744.

HEUTE WOLLEN WIR BEGRABEN DEN UNREINEN SÜNDENLEIB   504
    Mel.: Werde munter / 5 st. / Mack, Jr. (Heckman) / Tr.: Heckman.

HIER BIN ICH, HERR, DU RUFEST MIR, DU ZIEHEST MICH, ICH FOLGE DIR   505
    Mel.: Herr Jesu Christ, dich zu uns wend / 3 st. / Rambach (Koch;
    Julian; NVG1828) / Tr.: Julian / CG1874.

HIER LEGT MEIN SINN SICH VOR DIR NIEDER   506
    Mel.: Zeuch meinen Geist / 12 st. / Richter (Knapp, Koch; Julian;
    DP1718, F) / Tr.: Julian / GGB1720.

HIER LIEGT EIN MENSCH, HIER FIEL ER NIEDER, ER FIEL DURCH EIG'NE HAND   507
    Mel.: Wer weiss, wie nahe / 2 st. / Anon. (SAG1851) / CG1874.

HIER SIND WIR IN DER TRAUERZEIT UND MÜSSEN STREITEN VIEL   508
    Mel.: Mein Gott, das Herz / 8 st. / Anon.: "Author's name withheld"
    (KPS) / KPS1858.

HILF GOTT, DASS WIR MIT DIESEM JAHR IN EINEM NEUEN LEBEN   509
    Mel.: O Jesu, meines Lebens Licht / 5 st. / Bertolet (Yoder;
    EGS1821) / CG1874.

HILF, HERR JESU, LASS GELINGEN, HILF, DAS NEUE JAHR GEHT AN   510
    Mel.: Schaffet, schaffet, meine Kinder / 2 st. / Rist (Knapp, Kulp;
    Julian; F) / CG1874.

HILF, JESU, HILF SIEGEN UND LASS MICH NICHT LIEGEN   511
    Mel.: e. M. / 18 st. / Anon. (DP1718, F, ZW) / KDP1744.

HIMMEL, ERDE, LUFT UND MEER ZEUGEN VON DES SCHÖPFERS EHR'   512
    Mel.: Nun komm, der Heiden / 6 st. / Neander (GLU; Knapp, Koch;
    Julian; DP1718, F) / Tr.: Julian / KDP1744.

HIMMEL, ERDE, LUFT UND MEERE, GROSSER GOTT, IST ALL DEIN WERK   513
    Mel.: Gott des Himmels und der Erden / 4 st. / Anon. / KPS1858.

HINDURCH, HINDURCH, MEIN TRÄGER SINN, RICHT DEIN GESICHT AUF JESU HIN   514
    Mel.: Ich hab mein' Sach' Gott / 16 st. / Anon. / GGB1720.

HÖCHSTE LUST UND HERZVERGNÜGEN AUSERKOR'NER UND ERWÄHLTER   515
    Mel.: Auf, Triumph, es kommt die / 8 st. / Lackmann (Koch; DP1718,
    F) / GGB1720.

HÖCHSTER FORMIERER DER LÖBLICHSTEN DINGE   516
    Mel.: Schönster Immanuel, Herzog der / 11 st. / Knorr von Rosenroth
    (Koch; DP1718, F) / GGB1720.

HÖCHSTER PRIESTER, DER DU DICH SELBST GEOPFERT HAST FÜR MICH   517
    Mel.: e. M. / 5 st. / Scheffler (HS; Knapp, Koch; DP1718, F) /
    GGB1720.

HÖCHSTER PRIESTER, DER DU DICH SO ERNIEDRIGT HAST FÜR MICH   518
    Mel.: Höchster Priester / 8 st. / Scheffler (HS; Knapp; Julian) /
    Tr.: Julian / KDP1760.

HOCHTEURER HEILAND, MILDES HERZ, IN DEINER LEIDENSPEIN 519
    Mel.: C. M. / 5 st. / Löscher (Knapp 1837; EGS1821) / NS1870.
HOFFNUNG LÄSST NICHT ZU SCHANDEN WERDEN, DIE AUF DEN HERREN IST 520
    Mel.: Wer nur den lieben Gott / 3 st. / Anon. / KH1792.
HOHE HÄUPTER KRONEN TRAGEN IN DER VORBEDEUTUNGSWELT 521
    Mel.: Wo ist Jesus, mein / 10 st. / Mack, Jr. (Heckman) / Tr.:
    Colonial, p. 595; Heckman.
HOLDSELIG'S GOTTESLAMM, SEI HOCHGEBENEDEIET 522
    Mel.: e. M. / 11 st. / Arnold (GL; Julian; DP1718, F) / Tr.: Julian
    / GGB1720.
HOLZ DES LEBENS, KOST DER SEELEN, DIE NACH GNADE HUNGRIG SIND 523
    Mel.: Jesu, deine tiefen Wunden / 12 st. / Anon. (DP1718) / KDP1744.
HÖR, ACH ERHÖR MEIN SEUFZEND SCHREIEN, DU ALLERLIEBSTES VATERHERZ 524
    Mel.: Wer nur den lieben Gott / 3 st. / Anon. / CG1879.
HÖR VIEL TAUSEND HARFEN STIMMEN DORT DAS LOB-GETÖNE AN 525
    Mel.: Komm, o komm / 4 st. / W. Preiss, tr. (KPS) / Or.: Kelly:
    Hark, ten thousand harps and voices (Julian) / KPS1858.
HÖR, WIE DER TOR IM HERZEN SPRICHT: ES IST, ES IST KEIN GOTT 526
    Mel.: C. M. / 7 st. / Anon. (SEL1842) / NS1870.
HÖRE AUF, LASS TRAUERN FAHREN, ICH FAHR AUF ZU GOTTES STUHL 527
    Mel.: Abermal ein Tag verflossen / 5 st. / Anon. / ES1893.
HÖRE MICH, ICH MUSS DICH FRAGEN, LIEBE SEELE, FASSE MICH 528
    Mel.: Ach, was mach ich in den Städten / 13 st. / Anon. / ELEL1812.
HÖRET, WIE IM FERNEN LANDE UNSER FREUND UND BRUDER STARB 529
    Mel.: Abermal ein Tag verflossen / 5 st. / Anon.: "At the death of
    J. H. Balsbaugh" (CG1879) / CG1879.
HÖRT HIER DEN ALTEN TÄUFERGRUND, DEN ICH BEKENN MIT HERZ UND MUND 530
    Mel.: Ihr jungen Helden, aufgewacht / 14 st. / Anon. / CG1874.
HÖRT, WIE DER ENGEL SCHAR AUF JUDAS FELDERN SINGT 531
    Mel.: S. M. / 6 st. / Anon. tr. (DGM1865) / NS1870.
HÖRT, WIE DIE WÄCHTER SCHREI'N. ES IST UM MITTERNACHT 532
    Mel.: S. M. / 5 st. / Dreisbrach, tr. (Yoder; EGS1821) / Or.:
    C. Wesley: Hark, how the watchmen cry (Julian) / NS1870.
HOSIANNA, DAVIDS SOHN KOMMT IN ZION EINGEZOGEN 533
    Mel.: Guter Hirte / 8 st. / Schmolck (LS; Koch) / KDP1764.
HOSIANNA, UNSER HORT, GOTTES EWIGLICHES WORT 534
    Mel.: Jesu, komm doch selbst / 6 st. / Bucholtz (Koch; F) /
    KPS1858.
HÜTER, WIRD DIE NACHT DER SÜNDEN NICHT VERSCHWINDEN 535
    Mel.: e. M. / 9 st. / Richter (Koch, Kulp; Julian; DP1718, F) /
    Tr.: Julian / GGB1720.

ICH BIN DEIN GOTT, DEIN HÖCHSTES GUT, ICH BIN MIT DIR VERSÖHNET 536
    Mel.: Nun freut euch; Aus tiefer Not / 5 st. / Neander (GLU;
    DP1718) / GGB1720.
ICH BIN EIN ARMER PILGER UND REISE DURCH DIE ZEIT 537
    Mel.: Kommt, Kinder / 3 st. / Dreisbach (Yoder; EGS1821) / CG1874.
ICH BIN EIN CHRIST UND GOTTES KIND, WEIL CHRISTUS IST GESTORBEN 538
    Mel.: Aus tiefer Not / 6 st. / Anon. / GGB1720.
ICH BIN EIN HERR, DER EWIG LIEBT UND NUR EIN'N AUGENBLICK BETRÜBT 539
    Mel.: Kommt her zu mir / 6 st. / Neander (GLU; DP1718, F) /
    GGB1720.

ICH BIN EIN HERR, DER SÜND' VERGIBT, ICH BIN, DER UNVERÄNDERT LIEBT   540
    Mel.: P. M. / 3 st. / Neander (GLU); Mack (Stoudt); (NGW1749) / Tr.:
    Christ-Janer, p. 264-265 / NS1870.

ICH BIN FROH, DASS ICH GEHÖRET, WEIL MICH CHRISTI GEIST GELEHRET   541
    Mel.: O wie selig sind die / 11 st. / Anon. (DP1718, F) / KDP1744.

ICH BIN GETAUFT AUF (IN) DEINEN NAMEN, GOTT VATER, SOHN UND HEIL'GER   542
    [Mel.: 96] / 4 st. / Rambach (Knapp, Koch, Kulp, Westphal; Julian;
    NVG1806) / Tr.: Julian / NS1870.

ICH BIN IN ALLEM WOHL ZUFRIEDEN, BEFIND MICH RUHIG UND VERGNÜGT   543
    Mel.: Wer nur den lieben Gott / 5 st. / Aemilie Juliane of Schwarz-
    burg-Rudolstadt (Koch; DP1718, ZW) / KDP1744.

ICH BIN VOLLER TROST UND FREUDEN UND VERGEH FÜR FRÖHLICHKEIT   544
    Mel.: e. M. / 12 st. / Scheffler (HS; DP1718) / GGB1720.

ICH DANKE DIR, MEIN GOTT, DASS DU MIR HAST GEGEBEN   545
    Mel.: Nun danket alle Gott / 6 st. / Olearius (Fischer, Koch;
    DP1718, F) / KDP1744.

ICH DENK AN DEINE GERICHTE, DU RICHTER ALLER WELT   546
    [Mel.: 161] / 4 st. / Schmolck (LS; Knapp, Koch; ANH1795) / NS1870.

ICH EILE MEINEM GRABE ZU, EIN SCHRITT, SO BIN ICH ERDE   547
    Mel.: Es ist gewisslich an / 2 st. / Anon. (GS1836) / CG1879.

ICH FINDE STETIG DIESE ZWEI IN MEINEM WANDEL UND GEMÜTE   548
    Mel.: On ne vit / 7 st. / Tersteegen (GBG) / KH1792.

ICH FOLGE DIR BIS AN DEIN KREUZE HIN, WEIL ICH IN DICH, MEIN LIEB'   549
    Mel.: Du Geist des Herrn / 6 st. / Anon. / KH1792.

ICH FÜHLE EINEN DURST IN MIR, FÜR SOLCHEN TAUGT KEIN WASSER HIER   550
    Mel.: Die Seele Christi heil'ge mich / 4 st. / P. F. Hiller (GLK;
    Knapp) / CG1874.

ICH HAB DIE HOFFNUNG NOCH ZU DIR, ZU DIR, DER LEBENSQUELLE   551
    Mel.: Sei Lob und Ehr' / 7 st. / Anon. / GGB1720.

ICH HAB IHN DENNOCH LIEB UND BLEIBE AN IHM HANGEN   552
    Mel.: Was frag ich nach der Welt; O Gott, du frommer / 5 st. /
    Anon. (DP1718, F) / GGB1720.

ICH HAB MEIN' SACH' GOTT HEIMGESTELLT, ER MACH'S MIT MIR, WIE'S IHM   553
    Mel.: e. M. / 18 st. / Leon (Knapp, Kulp, Wackernagel, Westphal;
    Julian); Pappus (Koch, Mützell); (DP1718, F) / Tr.: Julian /
    GGB1720.

ICH HABE 'FUNDEN, DEN ICH LIEBE, DEN LIEBSTEN FREUND UND BRÄUTIGAM   554
    (Answer to 1323)
    Mel.: Wo ist mein Schäflein / 6 st. / Anon. (DP1718, F) / KDP1744.

ICH HABE G'NUG IM HIMMEL UND AUF ERDEN, DER BESTE SCHATZ   555
    Mel.: e. M. / 4 st. / Anon. (Bachmann; GG1700) / GGB1720.

ICH HABE IMMERDAR ZU BAUEN, BALD KRIEGT DIE LIEBE EINEN RISS   556
    Mel.: Wer nur den lieben / 2 st. / P. F. Hiller (Ehmann) / CG1874.

ICH HABE NUN DEN GRUND GEFUNDEN, DER MEINEN ANKER EWIG HÄLT   557
    Mel.: Wer nur den lieben Gott / 6 st. / Rothe (Knapp, Koch, Kulp,
    Nelle, Westphal; Julian; ANH1795) / Tr.: Julian / KDP1797-G.

ICH HANGE DOCH AN DIR, MEIN GOTT UND WILL NICHT VON DIR LASSEN   558
    Mel.: Mein Herzens-Jesu / 12 st. / Anon. (DP1718, F, ZW) / KDP1744.

ICH HEILAND, SAGE DIR, SEI MUNTER, WENN ICH KOMME   559
    Mel.: O Gott, du frommer Gott / 6 st. / Anon. / GGB1720.

ICH KOMM JETZT ALS EIN ARMER GAST, O HERR, ZU DEINEM TISCHE   560
    Mel.: Es ist gewisslich / 3 st. / Sieber (Knapp, Koch; F) / ES1893.

ICH KOMME SELBST ZU DIR, DU MEINE SCHÖNE   561
    Mel.: e. M. / 9 st. / Anon. (DP1718, F) / GGB1720.

ICH LEB MIR NICHT, DENN JESUS HAT DURCHS WASSER-BAD MICH GANZ UND GAR   562
    Mel.: Es ist genug / 5 st. / Anon. / GGB1720.
ICH LEBE VON BARMHERZIGKEIT, VON NICHTS KANN ICH SONST LEBEN   563
    Mel.: Mir nach, spricht / 2 st. / P. F. Hiller (GLK) / CG1874.
ICH LIEB DEN HERREN UND IHM DRUM DANKSAG   564
    Mel.: Psalm 74 Lobwasser / 11 st. / Lobwasser (PD1710) / KDP1744.
ICH LIEBE DICH HERZLICH, O JESU, FÜR ALLEN, DU BIST ES, AN DEM ICH   565
    Mel.: Ach alles, was Himmel / 19 st. / Anon. (DP1718, F) / GGB1720.
ICH MAG MICH, WO ICH WILL, HINWENDEN, DA SEH ICH NICHTS DENN TAUSEND   566
    Mel.: Wer weiss, wie nahe mir mein Ende / 2 st. / Anon. / CG1874.
ICH RUF ZU DIR, HERR JESU CHRIST, DER DU MEIN GOTT UND HEILAND BIST   567
    Mel.: Psalm 100 Lobwasser / 8 st. / J. Preiss (GAL) / GAL1753.
ICH SAGE GUT' NACHT DEM IRDISCHEN PRACHT, VERLASSE DIE WELT   568
    Mel.: e. M. / 9 st. / Strattner (in Neander VGLU) / GGB1720.
ICH SEHE DICH, O GOTTES MACHT ALLHIER, VERWUNDRE MICH, O HERR   569
    Mel.: Psalm 116 Lobwasser / 6 st. / Anon. (DP1718, F) / KDP1744.
ICH STERBE DAHIN, MEIN BESTER GEWINN IST, STERBEN IN DIR   570
    Mel.: Ich sage gut' Nacht / 6 st. / Anon. (GG1700) / GGB1720.
ICH SUCHE DICH IN DIESER FERNE, MEIN AUFENTHALT, MEIN LICHT UND STERNE   571
    Mel.: e. M. / 12 st. / Anon. (Koch; DP1718, F) / GGB1720.
ICH TRAU AUF GOTT IN ALLEN SACHEN, DENN WER WOLLT' SONST MEIN HELFER   572
    Mel.: Wer nur den lieben Gott / 5 st. / Anon. (GG1700) / GGB1720.
ICH TRAU AUF GOTT IN ALLEN SACHEN, ER MAG ES MIT MIR, WIE ER WILL   573
    Mel.: Wer nur den lieben Gott / 12 st. / Anon. (DP1718) / KDP1744.
ICH TRAU DEM HERRN, MEIN SCHUTZ IST ER, WAS SPRECHT IHR MIR DENN ZU   574
    Mel.: C. M. / 5 st. / Anon. / NS1870.
ICH TU MICH OFT VERGLEICHEN MIT EINEM SCHIFF IM MEER   575
    Mel.: Kommt, Kinder / 6 st. / Dreisbach (Yoder) / CG1874.
ICH VERLASS'NES WAISENKIND MUSS IN TRÄNEN EINSAM GEHEN   576
    Mel.: Endlich, endlich muss es doch / 3 st. / Anon. / KPS1858.
ICH WALLE STÜNDLICH HIN ZUR FROHEN EWIGKEIT   577
    Mel.: Da Joseph sein' Brüder / 3 st. / W. Preiss (KPS) / KPS1858.
ICH WALLE STÜNDLICH NÄHER HIN ZUM STILLEN, KÜHLEN GRABE   578
    Mel.: Was Gott tut, das ist wohlgetan / 4 st. / Anon. (KPS); Mack?
    (A. H. Cassel manuscript note in ESL1832) / ESL1832, KPS1858.
ICH WAR EIN KLEINES KINDLEIN, GEBOR'N AUF DIESE WELT   579
    Mel.: Bedenke, Mensch / 2 st. / Anon. (Fischer; GS1836) / CG1874.
ICH WEISS, AN WEN MEIN GLAUB' SICH HÄLT, KEIN FEIND SOLL MIR IHN RAUBEN 580
    [Mel.: 129] / 4 st. / Sturm (Koch; NVG1806) / NS1870.
ICH WEISS, DASS MEIN ERLÖSER LEBT, AUF FELSEN STEHT MEIN GLAUBE   581
    Mel.: Es ist gewisslich an der Zeit / 4 st. / Gerhardt (GL; Koch;
    Julian; PPM1690) / CG1874.
ICH WEISS, DASS MEIN JESUS LEBET, DER EINMAL FÜR MICH GESTORBEN   582
    Mel.: Jesus ist der schönste Nam' / 10 st. / Anon. / GGB1720.
ICH WEISS EIN EWIG' HIMMELREICH, DAS GOTT SEHR SCHÖN WIRD BAUEN   583
    Mel.: Mein' Wallfahrt ich vollendet hab / 14 st. / J. Preiss (GAL)
    / GAL1753.
ICH WEISS EIN LAND VOLL LAUTER FREUD', WO HEILIGE ZU HAUS'   584
    Mel.: Mein Gott, das Herz / 4 st. / Dreisbach, tr. (Yoder; EGS1821)
    / Or.: Watts: There is a land of pure delight (Julian) / CG1874.
ICH WEISS NICHT, WANN MEIN ENDE KOMMT, WIE SOLLT ICH MICH DANN SCHICKEN 585
    Mel.: Der lieben Sonne Licht und Pracht / 4 st. / Anon. / ENGL1807.
ICH WEISS NUN, WAS ICH SUCHE, WEIL ICH DASSELB' VERFLUCHE   586
    Mel.: Wach auf, mein Herze / 16 st. / Anon. / GGB1720.

ICH WILL DICH LIEBEN, MEINE STÄRKE, ICH WILL DICH LIEBEN, MEINE ZIER   587
    Mel.: e. M. / 8 st. / Scheffler (HS; Knapp, Koch, Kulp; Julian;
    DP1718, F) / Tr.: Julian / GGB1720.
ICH WILL DICH NICHT VERLASSEN, NOCH SCHLAGEN IN DEN WIND   588
    Mel.: e. M. / 13 st. / Haack (Fischer; DP1718) / GGB1720.
ICH WILL EINSAM UND GEMEINSAM MIT DEM EIN'GEN GOTT UMGEH'N   589
    Mel.: Sieh, hier bin ich, Ehrenkönig / 5 st. / Lodenstein;
    Bernstein, tr. (Koch; DP1718, F) / GGB1720.
ICH WILL GANZ UND GAR NICHT ZWEIFELN IN DER GUTEN ZUVERSICHT   590
    Mel.: Psalm 50 Lobwasser / 6 st. / Neander (GLU; Koch; DP1718, ZW)
    / KDP1744.
ICH WILL LIEBEN UND MICH ÜBEN, DASS ICH MEINEN BRÄUTIGAM   591
    Mel.: Sieh, hier bin ich / 4 st. / Anon. (Knapp) / KDP1744.
ICH WILL MEINEN JESUM LIEBEN, MEINE GANZE LEBENSZEIT   592
    Mel.: Sieh, hier bin ich / 10 st. / Stoll (GGG) / GGG1806.
ICH WILL NICHT LASSEN AB, DES HERREN LOB IN MEINEM MUND ZU FÜHREN   593
    Mel.: Psalm 34 Lobwasser / 11 st. / Lobwasser (PD1710) / KDP1744.
ICH WILL STREBEN NACH DEM LEBEN, WO ICH SELIG BIN   594
    Mel.: e. M. / 4 st. / P. F. Hiller (Ehmann, Knapp, Koch) / CG1874.
ICH WILL VON DEINER GÜTE SINGEN UND RÜHMEN DEINE FREUNDLICHKEIT   595
    Mel.: Wer nur den lieben Gott / 8 st. / Anon. / KDP1744.
ICH WILL VON MEINER MISSETAT ZUM HERREN MICH BEKEHREN   596
    Mel.: Es ist gewisslich / 5 st. / Anon. (Kulp); Luise Henrietta of
    Brandenburg (Knapp; Julian); (F) / Tr: Julian / CG1874.
ICH WOLLTE GERNE CHRISTUM REIN BEKENNEN, WIE ES SOLLTE SEIN   597
    Mel.: Erschienen ist der; Gelobet seist / 17 st. / Anon. / GGB1720.
IHR CHRISTEN SEHT, DASS IHR AUSFEGT, WAS SICH IN EUCH VON SÜNDEN   598
    Mel.: Es ist das Heil / 6 st. / Denicke-Gesenius (Fischer; DP1718,
    F) / KDP1744.
IHR FREUNDE JESU ALLZUMAL, DIE IHR TUT MEINEN WILLEN   599
    Mel.: Es ist gewisslich an der Zeit / 6 st. / Anon. / KLS1826.
IHR GESPIELEN, LASST UNS WACHEN, DER KÖNIG WIRD SICH BALD AUFMACHEN   600
    Mel.: Wachet auf, ruft uns / 10 st. / Anon. (DP1718, ZW) / KDP1744.
IHR JUNGEN HELDEN, AUF, VERLASST DIE GANZE WELT   601
    Mel.: Der Tag ist fort / 4 st. / S. D. Miller (KPS) / KPS1858.
IHR JUNGEN HELDEN, AUFGEWACHT, DIE GANZE WELT MUSS SEIN VERACHT'   602
    Mel.: O starker Gott / 9 st. / Anon. / GGB1720.
IHR JUNGEN LEUTE, MERKET AUF, HÖRT, WAS ICH SAGEN WILL   603
    Mel.: Mein Gott, das Herz ich / 4 st. / Dreisbach (Yoder; EGS1821)
    / CG1874.
IHR KINDER AUF DER GLAUBENS-BAHN, LASST EUCH DIES NICHT VERDRIESSEN   604
    Mel.: Nun freut euch, lieben / 8 st. / Anon. / GGB1720.
IHR KINDER DER LIEBE, WAS WIRD ES EINST WERDEN MIT DEN JETZT IN CHRISTO 605
    Mel.: Ihr Kinder des Höchsten / 5 st. / Anon. / GGB1720.
IHR KINDER DES HÖCHSTEN, WIE STEHT'S UM DIE LIEBE   606
    Mel.: e. M. / 9 st. / Bernstein (Knapp, Koch; Julian; DP1718, F) /
    Tr.: Julian / GGB1720.
IHR KINDER, FASSET NEUEN MUT IN EUREM STAND, ZU GOTT GEWANDT   607
    Mel.: Hab ich nur Gott zum / 15 st. / Anon. / GGB1720.
IHR KINDER GOTTES ALLZUGLEICH, SEID MUNTER UND TUT WACHEN   608
    Mel.: Sei Lob und Ehr' / 8 st. / Anon. / GGB1720.
IHR KINDER, HABT MUT, WIR KOMMEN BALD ALLE ZUSAMMEN   609
    Mel.: Ihr Lieben, weint nicht / 6 st. / Meyer (KPS) / KPS1858.
IHR KINDER, MERKET WOHL, WIE ES NOCH WERDEN SOLL   610
    Mel.: Mein Jesu, der du mich / 10 st. / Anon. / GGB1720.

IHR KINDER ZION, SCHAUET, IN WAS GEFAHR IHR SEID   611
   Mel.: Schatz über alle Schätze / 8 st. / Anon. / GGB1720.

IHR KNECHT' DES HERREN ALLZUGLEICH, DEN HERREN LOBT IM HIMMELREICH   612
   Mel.: e. M. / 3 st. / Lobwasser (PD1710; Julian; DP1718) / Tr.:
   Julian / KDP1744.

IHR KNECHT' DES HERREN, KOMMT HERAN, EU'R ZENTNER DARZULEGEN   613
   Mel.: Jesus ist der schönste Nam' / 12 st. / Anon. / GGB1720.

IHR LIEBEN FREUNDE, HÖRT MIR ZU, WAS ICH EUCH JETZUND SAGEN TU   614
   Mel.: O starker Gott / 28 st. / J. Preiss (GAL) / GAL1753.

IHR LIEBEN MENSCHEN-KINDER UND JA AUCH ARME SÜNDER   615
   Mel.: Wach auf, mein Herze / 17 st. / Anon. / GGB1720.

IHR LIEBEN, WEINT NICHT, WIR SEH'N UNS IN EWIGKEIT WIEDER   616
   Mel.: Ihr Kinder, habt Mut / 6 st. / W. Preiss (KPS) / KPS1858.

IHR SÜNDER ALLE, FREUET EUCH DES GOTTES, DER EUCH MENSCHEN GLEICH   617
   Mel.: L. M. / 6 st. / Anon. / NS1870.

IHR SÜNDER, KOMMT GEGANGEN, SEHT EUREN JESUM AN   618
   Mel.: Wo bleiben meine Sinne / 6 st. / Anon. / ELEL1812, CG1874.

IHR VÖLKER AUF DER ERDEN ALL', DEM HERREN JAUCHZT UND SINGT MIT SCHALL   619
   Mel.: e. M. / 4 st. / Lobwasser (PD1710; ZW) / KDP1744.

IHR WAISEN, WEINET NICHT, WIE KÖNNT IHR EUCH NICHT FASSEN   620
   Mel.: O Gott, du frommer Gott / 2 st. / Starck? (TH1776) / CG1874.

IHR ZIONS BÜRGER ALLZUMAL, DIE IHR NUN HÖRT DEN RUF UND SCHALL   621
   Mel.: Die Macht der Wahrheit / 10 st. / Anon. / KDP1744.

IM ANFANG ALLER DINGE SCHUF GOTT HIMMEL UND ERD'   622
   Mel.: Ach Gott, in was für Schmerzen / 17 st. / Anon. / GGB1720.

IM ANFANG ALS GOTT SCHUF DEN HIMMEL UND DIE ERDEN   623
   Mel.: O Jesu, süsses Licht / 14 st. / Anon. / GGB1720.

IM BEWAHREN VOR GEFAHREN ZEIGST DU, GOTT, DICH WUNDERBAR   624
   Mel.: Ringe recht / 5 st. / P. F. Hiller (GLK) / CG1874.

IM FEUER WIRD DAS GOLD BEWÄHRT, DER GLAUBE IN DEM LEIDEN   625
   Mel.: Mein Herzens-Jesu, meine Lust / 3 st / P. F. Hiller (GLK) /
   CG1874.

IM GRABE IST RUH', DRUM WANKEN DEM TRÖSTENDEN ZIELE   626
   Mel.: Ihr Lieben, weint nicht / 3 st. / W. Preiss (KPS) / KPS1858.

IN CHRISTO SIND WIR REBEN, WEIL ER DER WEINSTOCK IST   627
   Mel.: Valet will ich dir geben / 4 st. / P. F. Hiller (GLK) /
   CG1874.

IN DEINEM NAMEN, JESU CHRIST, STEH ICH VOM LAGER AUF   628
   Mel.: C. M. / 5 st. / Schlatter (Knapp; DGM1865) / NS1870.

IN DEM ANFANG WAR DAS WORT, WIE UNS SANCT JOHANNES SCHREIBET   629
   Mel.: Jesus ist der schönste Nam' / 5 st. / Anon. / KH1792.

IN DER FRÜHEN MORGENSTUND', DA NOCH ALLES STILLE   630
   Mel.: Jesu, wahres Gotteslamm / 2 st. / Stoll (GGG) / GGG1806,
   KPS1858.

IN DER SCHRIFT DES NEUEN BUNDES DIE VERORDNUNG FINDEST DU   631
   [Mel.: 194] / 9 st. / Anon.: "Said to be composed by Elder Kurtz"
   (manuscript note by A. H. Cassel, broadside, no date)

IN DER SEL'GEN EWIGKEIT SIND VERSCHIED'NE STUFEN   632
   Mel.: Jesu, wahres Gotteslamm / 4 st. / P. F. Hiller (GLK) /
   ESL1832, KPS1858.

IN DER STILLE AUS DER FÜLLE MEINES HERZENS SING ICH DIR   633
   Mel.: Sieh, hier bin ich / 4 st. / P. F. Hiller (GLK) / CG1874.

IN DER STILLEN EINSAMKEIT FINDEST DU MEIN LOB BEREIT   634
   Mel.: Psalm 136 Lobwasser / 8 st. / Neander (GLU; Knapp, Koch;
   DP1718, ZW) / KDP1744.

IN DICH HAB ICH GEHOFFET, HERR, HILF, DASS ICH NICHT ZU SCHANDEN WERD   635
    Mel.: e. M. / 7 st. / A. Reissner (Koch, Kulp, Mützell, Nelle,
    Westphal; Julian; DP1718, F) / Tr.: Julian / GGB1720.

IN DIESER MORGENSTUNDE DICH LOBET JETZT MEIN MUNDE   636
    Mel.: Wach auf, mein Herz, und / 13 st. / J. Preiss (GAL) /
    GAL1753.

IN DIESER WELT, WEM SIE GEFÄLLT, IST KEINE RUH' ZU FINDEN   637
    Mel.: So wünsch ich nun ein' / 7 st. / Kelpius (Willard) /
    ELEL1788.

IN GOTTES REICH GEHT NIEMAND EIN, ER SEI DENN NEUGEBOREN   638
    [Mel.: 129] / 4 st. / Stübner (Knapp, Koch; SAZ1744) / NS1870.

IN JESU NAMEN REIS ICH AUS, DER SELBST AUS SEINES VATERS HAUS   639
    Mel.: Wenn wir in höchsten Nöten sein; Ich bin heilig, spricht der
    Herr / 11 st. / Heermann (Knapp; CGB1695) / GGB1720.

ISRAELS WÄCHTER RUFET LAUT AUF ZIONS HOHEN MAUERN   640
    [Mel.: 129] / 3 st. / Anon. / NS1870.

IST'S, ODER IST MEIN GEIST ENTZÜCKT, MEIN AUGE HAT JETZT WAS ERBLICKT   641
    Mel.: Wie schön leucht' uns / 8 st. / Fritsch (Knapp, Koch; DP1718,
    F) / KH1792.

JAHRE KOMMEN, JAHRE GEHEN, ACH WIE SCHNELL VERFLIESST DIE ZEIT   642
    Mel.: Ringe recht / 6 st. / Anon. (EGS1821) / NS1870.

JAUCHZET ALL' MIT MACHT, IHR FROMMEN   643
    Mel.: Lasset uns den Herren preisen / 9 st. / T. S. Schröder (Koch,
    Kulp; DP1718, F, ZW) / KDP1744.

JAUCHZET, IHR HIMMEL, FROHLOCKET, IHR ENGLISCHEN CHÖRE   644
    Mel.: Lobe den Herren / 8 st. / Tersteegen (GBG; Knapp, Koch, Kulp;
    Julian; ZW) / Tr.: Julian / KH1792.

JAUCHZET, IHR KINDER VON ZION GEBOREN, DANKET UND RÜHMET DEN KÖNIG   645
    Mel.: Herrlichste Majestät / 5 st. / Beissel (GLL; ZW) / KDP1764.

JAUCHZET IM VORSPIELE, FREUDIG ALLE FROMMEN   646
    Mel.: Wunderbarer König / 4 st. / Anon. / GGB1720.

JEHOVA IST MEIN LICHT UND GNADEN-SONNE   647
    Mel.: e. M. / 4 st. / Neander (GLU; Knapp, Koch; Julian; DP1718, F)
    / Tr.: Julian / GGB1720.

JEHOVA, O DU SCHÖNSTER NAM', WIE REIZEND IST JA DEINE LIEB'   648
    Mel.: Ihr jungen Helden, aufgewacht / 13 st. / Anon.: "Author's
    name withheld" (KPS) / KPS1858.

JEHOVA, VATER, SOHN UND GEIST, DER DREI UND DOCH NUR EINES HEISST   649
    Mel.: Herr Jesu Christ, dich / 1 st. / Orwig (ELS1853) / ES1893.

JERUSALEM, DU GOTTES-STADT, GEDENKE JENER PLAGEN   650
    Mel.: Mein Herzens-Jesu / 11 st. / Gotter (Fischer; DP1718, F) /
    GGB1720.

JERUSALEM, DU GOTTES-STADT, WIE SCHÖN BIST DU GEBAUET   651
    Mel.: Mir nach, spricht Christus / 12 st. / Anon. / KH1792.

JERUSALEM IST EINE STADT, DIE NICHT GEMEINE BÜRGER HAT   652
    Mel.: L. M. / 5 st. / P. F. Hiller (Ehmann) / NS1870.

JERUSALEM IST EINE STADT, DIE NICHT ZERTEILTE G'MEINDEN HAT   653
    (= 652, with the exception of st. 1, verse 2)
    Mel.: Ihr jungen Helden / 4 st. / P. F. Hiller (Ehmann) / KPS1858.

JESU ADEL IST ALLEINE EWIG ALLER EHREN WERT   654
    Mel.: Ringe recht / 10 st. / Mack, Jr. (Heckman) / Tr.: Colonial,
    p. 589; Heckman.

JESU, AUFERSTAND'NER HELD, SONDERBARER KÖNIG   655
   [Mel.: 186] / 4 st. / Mack, Jr.? / NS1870.
JESU, BAUE DEINEN LEIB, DEINEN TEMPEL BAUE WIEDER   656
   Mel.: Meinen Jesum lass ich nicht / 8 st. / Anon. (A1718) /
   KDP1744.
JESU, BRUNN' DES LEBENS, LASS MICH NICHT VERGEBENS ALLHIER SCHREIEN   657
   Mel.: Jesu, meine Freude / 8 st. / Stoll (GGG) / GGG1806.
JESU, DEINE HEIL'GEN WUNDEN, DEINE QUAL UND BITTERN TOD   658
   Mel.: Zion klagt mit Angst und Schmerzen / 6 st. / Heermann
   (Fischer, Mützell; Julian; DP1718, F); rewritten by Gesenius-
   Denicke (Fischer) / Tr.: Julian / KDP1744.
JESU, DEINE LIEBES-FLAMME MACHT, DASS ICH DIE WELT VERDAMME   659
   Mel.: e. M. / 5 st. / Anon. (DP1718, F) / GGB1720.
JESU, DEN ICH MEINE, LASS MICH NICHT ALLEINE   660
   Mel.: Name voller Güte / 11 st. / Tersteegen (GBG; Julian; ZW) /
   Tr.: Julian / KDP1744.
JESU, DER DU MEINE SEELE HAST DURCH DEINEN BITTERN TOD   661
   Mel.: e. M. / 12 st. / Rist (Goedeke, Knapp, Koch; DP1718, F) /
   GGB1720.
JESU, DU MEIN LIEBSTES LEBEN, MEINER SEELEN BRÄUTIGAM   662
   Mel.: Lasset uns den Herren preisen / 13 st. / Rist (Koch, Kulp; F)
   / KDP1744.
JESU(S), FROMMER MENSCHEN HERDEN GUTER UND GETREUER HIRT   663
   Mel.: Jesu, meines Lebens / 6 st. / Birken (Knapp, Koch; DP1718, F,
   ZW) / KDP1744.
JESU(S) GEH(T) VORAN AUF DER LEBENSBAHN   664
   [Mel.: 106] / 2 st. / N. L. von Zinzendorf (Knapp, Koch; Julian) /
   Tr.: Julian / KLS1844.
JESU, HILF MEIN KREUZ MIR TRAGEN, WENN IN BÖSEN JAMMERTAGEN   665
   Mel.: Liebster Jesu, du wirst / 11 st. / Anon. (DP1718) / KDP1744.
JESU, HILF MIR, SO WILL ICH DANKEN DIR UND ALLZEIT, FÜR UND FÜR   666
   Mel.: Eil doch heran und mach / 7 st. / J. Preiss (GAL) / GAL1753.
JESU, HILF, SCHAU DOCH IN GNADEN EINST DEIN ZION WIEDER AN   667
   Mel.: Freuet euch, ihr Christen alle / 10 st. / J. H. Schröder
   (Koch; DP1718, F) / GGB1720.
JESU, HILF SIEGEN, DU FÜRSTE DES LEBENS   668
   Mel.: Grosser Prophete / 14 st. / J. H. Schröder (Knapp, Koch,
   Kulp, Westphal; Julian; DP1718, F) / Tr.: Julian / GGB1720.
JESU, HIRTE MEINER SEELEN, DIR BIN ICH SO WOHL BEKANNT   669
   Mel.: Zeuch mich / 10 st. / Stoll (GGG) / GGG1806.
JESU, JESU, BRUNN' DES LEBENS, STELL, ACH STELL DICH BEI UNS EIN   670
   Mel.: Seelen-Weide / 10 st. / Annoni (Koch) / KDP1760.
JESU, KOMM DOCH SELBST ZU MIR UND VERBLEIBE FÜR UND FÜR   671
   Mel.: Nun komm, der Heiden Heiland; Liebster Jesu, du wirst kommen
   / 9 st. / Scheffler (HS; Koch; Julian; DP1718, F, ZW) / Tr.: Julian
   / KDP1744.
JESU, KOMM MIT DEINEM VATER, KOMM ZU MIR, ICH LIEBE DICH   672
   Mel.: Christi Tod ist Adams Leben / 12 st. / R. F. von Schult
   (Koch; DP1718, F) / GGB1720.
JESU LIEBE IST EIN LICHT, DAS ICH WILL VERLASSEN NICHT   673
   Mel.: Jesu, komm doch selbst / 17 st. / Haller (KPS) / KPS1858.
JESU, MEIN TREUER, LASS DOCH DEIN FEUER STETS IN MIR BRENNEN   674
   Mel.: e. M. / 8 st. / Knorr von Rosenroth (Knapp; DP1718, F, ZW) /
   KDP1744.

JESU, MEINE FREUDE, MEINES HERZENS WEIDE, JESU, MEINE ZIER   675
    Mel.: e. M. / 6 st. / J. Franck (Knapp, Koch, Kulp, Westphal;
    Julian; DP1718, F) / Tr.: Julian / GGB1720.

JESU, MEINER JUGEND LUST, MEINES FRÜHEN LEBENS SONNE   676
    Mel.: Endlich, endlich muss es / 6 st. / Anon. (TH1812) / KPS1858.

JESU, MEINER SEELEN LEBEN, DEM ICH MICH ZUM DIENST ERGEBEN   677
    Mel.: Liebster Jesu, du wirst / 21 st. / Anon. (Julian; DP1718, F)
    / GGB1720.

JESU, MEINER SEELEN RUH' UND MEIN BESTER SCHATZ DAZU   678
    Mel.: Jesu, komm doch selbst; Gott sei Dank durch / 12 st. / Sonne-
    mann, attr. (Fischer); Bachmeister (Koch); (DP1718, F) / GGB1720.

JESU, MEINES HERZENS FREUD', SEI GEGRÜSSET, MEINER SEELEN SELIGKEIT   679
    Mel.: Wann erblick ich dich einmal / 5 st. / Flitner (Nelle); anon.
    (Koch); (DP1718, F, ZW) / KDP1744.

JESU, MEINES HERZENS FREUDE, MEINE SONNE, LICHT UND HEIL   680
    Mel.: O du Liebe meiner Liebe / 11 st. / Anon. (DP1718, F) /
    KDP1744.

JESU, MEINES LEBENS LEBEN, JESU, MEINES TODES TOD   681
    Mel.: Jesu, der du meine Seele / 8 st. / Homburg (Knapp, Koch,
    Kulp, Westphal; Julian; DP1718, F) / Tr.: Julian / KDP1744.

JESU, NIMM DEN SINN, NIMM MEIN ALLES HIN   682
    Mel.: Seelenbräutigam / 9 st. / N. L. von Zinzendorf (Knapp/Z) /
    KH1792.

JESU, RUFE MICH VON DER WELT, DASS ICH ZU DIR EILE   683
    Mel.: e. M. / 9 st. / Drese (Koch; DP1718, F, ZW) / KDP1744.

JESU, SCHÄRFE DEINE WORTE MIR DOCH ALLE TAGE EIN   684
    [Mel.: 35] / 6 st. / Anon. (EGS1821) / NS1870.

JESU, SCHENK MIR BRUDERLIEBE, DIE NICHT BLOSS IN WORTEN STEHT   685
    [Mel.: 35] / 6 st. / Anon. (EGS1821) / NS1870.

JESU, SONN' IM HERZEN, JESU, FREUD' IN SCHMERZEN   686
    Mel.: Jesu, meine Freude / 6 st. / Fritsch (Fischer; DP1718) /
    KDP1744.

JESU, TEURER SCHATZ DER SEELEN, KOMM, ACH KOMM, KEHR BEI MIR EIN   687
    Mel.: O der alles hätt' verloren / 8 st. / Stoll (GGG) / GGG1806.

JESU, WAHRES GOTTESLAMM, MEINER SEELE LEBEN   688
    Mel.: Jesu, meiner Seelen / 10 st. / Anon. / KDP1744.

JESU, WAHRES LEBENS-BROT, LABSAL IN DER GRÖSSTEN NOT   689
    Mel.: Meine Seele, willst du ruh'n / 7 st. / E. L. Gruber (Farlee,
    DP1753; DP1718, ZW) / KDP1744.

JESU, WIE SÜSS IST DEINE LIEBE, WIE HONIGFLIESSEND IST DEIN KUSS   690
    Mel.: Ach wie glückselig ist ein Herze; Psalm 58 Lobwasser / 5 st.
    / Scheffler (HS; Koch; DP1718) / KDP1744.

JESU ... see also: JESUS ...

JESUM NUR ALLEINE LIEBEN, DER FÜR UNS GESTORBEN IST   691
    [Mel.: 35] / 4 st. / Anon. (Yoder; EGS1821) / NS1870.

JESUM ÜBER ALLES LIEBEN, ÜBERTRIFFT DIE WISSENSCHAFT   692
    Mel.: Meine Sorgen, Angst und Plagen / 6 st. / Anon. / CG1879.

JESUM WILL ICH LIEBEN, WEIL ER SICH VERSCHRIEBEN   693
    Mel.: Jesu, meine Freude / 7 st. / Anon. (DP1718) / KDP1744.

JESUS CHRISTUS GAB SICH UNS SELBST ZUM VORBILD ALLES TUNS   694
    Mel.: Gott sei Dank / 4 st. / P. F. Hiller (Ehmann, Knapp) /
    CG1874.

JESUS CHRISTUS, GOTTES SOHN, DIR SEI LOB UND EHR' GEGEBEN   695
    Mel.: Jesus ist der schönste Nam' / 4 st. / Mack, Jr. (Heckman;
    ELEL1788) / Tr.: Hymnal 1951, no. 493; Flory, p. 254; Heckman /
    ELEL1788, KH1792.
JESUS IST DER GUTE HIRT, DER IN DIESE WELT IST KOMMEN   696
    Mel.: Mensch, was suchst du / 12 st. / Anon. / GGB1720.
JESUS IST DER KERN DER SCHRIFT, WEIL AUF IHN ZUSAMMEN TRIFFT   697
    Mel.: Gott sei Dank durch alle / 6 st. / P. F. Hiller (GLK) /
    CG1874.
JESUS IST DER SCHÖNSTE NAM' ALLER, DIE VOM HIMMEL KAMEN   698
    Mel.: e. M. / 9 st. / Scheffler (HS; Koch; Julian; DP1718, F) /
    Tr.: Julian / GGB1720.
JESUS IST JE-SÜSS UND SCHÖN, ÜBER ALLES ZU BESINGEN   699
    Mel.: Meinen Jesum lass ich nicht / 6 st. / E. L. Gruber (JL;
    Farlee; DP1718) / KDP1744.
JESUS IST MEIN FREUDEN-LICHT, WENN ER HELL IN MIR ANBRICHT   700
    Mel.: Jesu, komm doch selbst / 9 st. / Anon. (DP1718) / GGB1720.
JESUS IST MEIN HÖCHSTES GUT, ALLER WEISHEIT EW'GE GÜTE   701
    Mel.: e. M. / 11 st. / Stoll (GGG) / GGG1806.
JESUS, JESUS, NICHTS ALS JESUS SOLL MEIN WUNSCH SEIN UND MEIN ZIEL   702
    Mel.: Komm, o komm / 5 st. / Ludämilie Elisabeth of Schwarzburg-
    Rudolstadt (Koch; Julian; DP1718, F) / Tr.: Julian / KDP1744.
JESUS, LIEBER MEISTER, PRÜFER ALLER GEISTER, DIR IST WOHLBEKANNT   703
    Mel.: Jesu, meine Freude / 8 st. / Stoll (GGG) / GGG1806.
JESUS, MEIN TROST UND HEIL AUF MEINER PILGER-REIS'   704
    Mel.: e. M. / 7 st. / W. Preiss (KPS) / KPS1858.
JESUS NIMMT DIE SÜNDER AN, DRUM SO WILL ICH NICHT VERZAGEN   705
    Mel.: Ach was soll ich Sünder / 8 st. / Anon. (DP1718) / KDP1744.
JESUS NIMMT DIE SÜNDER AN, SAGT DOCH DIESES TROSTWORT ALLEN   706
    Mel.: Binde meine Seele wohl / 3 st. / Neumeister (Knapp, Kulp,
    Westphal; Julian; KGL1731) / Tr.: Julian / CG1874.
JESUS SOLL DIE LOSUNG SEIN, DA EIN NEUES JAHR ERSCHIENEN   707
    [Mel.: 111] / 5 st. / Schmolck (Knapp, Kulp, Westphal; Julian ;
    KGL1744) / Tr.: Julian / NS1870.
JESUS, WAHRER MENSCH IN GNADEN, KEHRE HEUTE BEI UNS EIN   708
    Mel.: Jesu, du mein / 3 st. / Anon. / KH1792.
JESUS WIRD SEIN VOLK ERLÖSEN VON DEM BÖSEN   709
    Mel.: Meine Armut macht mich / 5 st. / P. F. Hiller (GLK) / CG1874.
JESUS-NAM', DU HÖCHSTER NAME, DEM SICH ERD' UND HIMMEL BEUGT   710
    Mel.: Werde munter, mein / 8 st. / Tersteegen (GBG; Julian; ZW) /
    Tr.: Julian / KDP1764.
JESUS ... see also: JESU ...
JETZT IST DIE ANGENEHME ZEIT, JETZT IST DER TAG DES HEILS   711
    Mel.: C. M. / 5 st. / P. F. Hiller (GLK; Knapp) / NS1870.
JETZT IST DIE SCHÖNE GNADENZEIT UND AUCH DAS ANGENEHME HEUT'   712
    Mel.: O heil'ger Geist, kehr / 1 st. / W. Preiss (KPS) / KPS1858.
JETZT SCHEIDEN WIR DEM LEIBE NACH, DOCH FEST VEREINT IM GEIST   713
    Mel.: Mein Gott, das / 6 st. / Dreisbach (Yoder; EGS1821) / CG1874.
JOHANNES WAR EIN GOTTESMANN, JA, VOLLER GEIST UND GNADE   714
    Mel.: Es ist gewisslich an der Zeit / 1 st. / Anon. / CG1874.
JUNGFRAUEN, HÖRT, WOMIT DIE KEUSCHHEIT LOHNT   715
    Mel.: Du Geist des Herrn / 5 st. / Anon. (DP1718) / KDP1744.

KANN DIE LIEBE DES GELIEBTEN UNSER HERZ ERWEICHEN NICHT   716
     (= st. 9 and 8 of 382)
     Mel.: Schaffet, schaffet, meine Kinder / 2 st. / Anon. / CG1874.

KANN MAN GOTT IN TRÜBSAL LOBEN? JA, O JA, ER IST NAH   717
     Mel.: Warum soll ich mich denn / 5 st. / P. F. Hiller (GLK) /
     CG1874.

KAUFET, KAUFT DIE ZEIT, WEIL ES HEISST NOCH HEUT'   718
     Mel.: Mein Seelen-Bräutigam / 9 st. / Anon. (BGB1725) / KH1792.

KAUM STARB NOCH DER HEILAND, SO HAT ER GELEBET   719
     Mel.: Ach alles, was Himmel / 4 st. / P. F. Hiller (GLK) / CG1874.

KAUM STEIGT ZU IHREM FROHEN LAUF DIE SONN' IN VOLLER KRAFT HERAUF   720
     Mel.: L. M. / 4 st. / Heermann (Schlegel; NVG1806) / NS1870.

KEIN CHRIST SOLL IHM DIE RECHNUNG MACHEN   721
     Mel.: e. M. / 7 st. / Dach (Knapp, Koch; Julian; DP1718, F, ZW) /
     Tr.: Julian / KDP1744.

KEINE SCHÖNHEIT HAT DIE WELT, DIE MIR NICHT FÜR AUGEN   722
     Mel.: Jesu, komm doch selbst zu mir / 17 st. / Scheffler (HS;
     Knapp, Koch; Julian; DP1718, F) / Tr.: Julian / KDP1744.

KEINE WEISHEIT MACHT MICH FROH, KEINE KUNST ERHEB ICH HOCH   723
     Mel.: Gott sei Dank durch alle / 6 st. / P. F. Hiller (GLK) /
     CG1874.

KEUSCHER JESU, HOCH VON ADEL, UNBEFLECKTES GOTTESLAMM   724
     Mel.: Jesu, der du meine Seele; Du, o schönes Weltgebäude / 21 st.
     / Baumgarten (Knapp, Koch; DP1718, F) / GGB1720.

KINDER, EILT EUCH ZU BEKEHREN, JESUS STEHET VOR DER TÜR   725
     Mel.: Ringe recht / 22 st. / Anon. (GL1811) / KPS1858.

KINDER, LERNT DIE ORDNUNG FASSEN, DIE ZUM SELIGWERDEN FÜHRT   726
     Mel.: Ringe recht / 9 st. / Woltersdorf (Koch; ELS1843) / KPS1858.

KOMM DOCH, MEIN JESU CHRIST, DU WEISST WOHL, WIE MIR IST   727
     Mel.: Auf, Seele, sei gerüst' / 10 st. / Anon. / GGB1720.

KOMM, GEIST, VOM THRON HERAB, HAUCH GOTTES, WEH UNS AN   728
     Mel.: S. M. / 4 st. / Orwig (Yoder; EGS1821) / NS1870.

KOMM JUNG, KOMM ALT ZUM GNADENBRUNN, DER HEUTE AUFSTEHT NOCH   729
     Mel.: C. M. / 6 st. / Dreisbach (Yoder; EGS1821) / NS1870.

KOMM, LIEBSTER, KOMM IN DEINEN GARTEN   730
     Mel.: e. M. / 7 st. / Scheffler (HS; Koch; DP1718, F, ZW) /
     KDP1744.

KOMM, MEIN HERZ, ZU DEINER TAUFE, TAUCHE DICH IM GEIST HINEIN   731
     [Mel.: 192] / 2 st. / Anon. (GVB1853) / NS1870.

KOMM, O KOMM, DU GEIST DES LEBENS, WAHRER GOTT VON EWIGKEIT   732
     Mel.: Gott des Himmels und der Erden / 9 st. / Held (Fischer,
     Knapp, Koch, Kulp, Mützell; Julian; DP1718, F) / Tr.: Julian /
     GGB1720.

KOMM, SEELE, BETEND ZU DEM HERRN, DEIN HEILAND HÖRT DIE BITTEN GERN   733
     Mel.: L. M. / 5 st. / Knapp, tr. (Knapp) / Or.: Newton / NS1870.

KOMM, STERBLICHER, BETRACHTE MICH, DU LEBST, ICH LEBT' AUF ERDEN   734
     Mel.: Es ist gewisslich / 13 st. / Sacer (Koch; DP1718, F) /
     KDP1744.

KOMM, TAUBEN GATTE, REINSTE LUST, KOMM, UNSER BETTE BLÜHET   735
     Mel.: Mein Herzens-Jesu / 7 st. / Arnold (GGS; DP1718, ZW) /
     KDP1744.

KOMM, VATER, SOHN UND HEIL'GER GEIST, EHR DEINE GNADENMITTEL JETZT   736
     Mel.: L. M. / 5 st. / Anon. / NS1870.

KOMMET, IHR LIEBEN GESCHWISTER ZUM FESTLICHEN MAHLE   737
     Mel.: e. M. / 6 st. / Anon. / KLS1829.

KOMMT, BETET DOCH DIE LIEBE AN, DIE KEIN VERSTAND BEGREIFEN KANN   738
    Mel.: L. M. / 6 st. / P. F. Hiller (GLK; EGS1850) / NS1870.
KOMMT, BRINGET EHRE, DANK UND RUHM DEM HERRN IM HÖCHSTEN HEILIGTUM   739
    Mel.: L. M. / 4 st. / Anon. (NVG1806) / NS1870.
KOMMT, BRÜDER, KOMMT, WIR EILEN FORT NACH NEU JERUSALEM   740
    [Mel.: 18] / 5 st. / Walter (KP; Yoder; EGS1821) / NS1870.
KOMMT, DANKET DEM HELDEN MIT FREUDIGEN ZUNGEN   741
    Mel.: Ach alles, was Himmel / 10 st. / Herrnschmidt (Julian); anon.
    (DP1718, F, ZW) / Tr.: Julian / KDP1744.
KOMMT DOCH, O IHR MENSCHENKINDER, KOMMT UND ZAUDERT LÄNGER NICHT   742
    [Mel.: 35] / 4 st. / Anon. (SEL1842) / NS1870.
KOMMT HER, IHR MENSCHENKINDER, KOMMT HER, IHR FRECHE SÜNDER   743
    Mel.: Nun ruhen alle Wälder / 18 st. / Rist (Fischer; CGB1695) /
    ELEL1812.
KOMMT HER ZU MIR, SPRICHT GOTTES SOHN, ALL', DIE IHR SEID BESCHWERET   744
    Mel.: e. M. / 16 st. / Grünwald (Kadelbach, Knapp, Kulp, Wolkan;
    Julian); anon. (Mützell); (DP1718, F) / Tr.: Julian / GGB1720.
KOMMT, IHR ARMEN, BLÖDEN SEELEN, DIE IHR MATT UND MÜDE SEID   745
    [Mel.: 35] / 4 st. / Bogatzky (UG; Knapp) / NS1870.
KOMMT, IHR ARMEN UND ELENDEN, DIE IHR AN DEN GASSEN LIEGT   746
    (= st. 22 and 10 of 1064)
    Mel.: Gott des Himmels und der / 2 st. / Anon. (EGS1850) / CG1874.
KOMMT, IHR KINDER UNSRER LIEBE, LASSET UNS MIT JESU ZIEH'N   747
    Mel.: Wo ist wohl ein süsser Leben / 13 st. / Anon. (DP1718, F, ZW)
    / KDP1744.
KOMMT, IHR SÜNDER, ARM UND DÜRFTIG, SCHWACH UND SCHRECKLICH   748
    Mel.: Setze dich, mein Geist, ein wenig / 3 st. / J. C. Reissner,
    tr. (Yoder; GV1855) / Or.: Hart: Come, ye sinners, poor and
    wretched (Julian) / CG1874.
KOMMT, IHR SÜNDER, LASST EUCH RATEN, NEHMT DIE ZEIT DER GEISTER AN   749
    [Mel.: 35] / 5 st. / Anon. (GV1855) / NS1870.
KOMMT, IHR ÜBERZEUGTEN HERZEN, KOMMT ZU JESU, KOMMT GEEILT   750
    Mel.: P. M. / 5 st. / Anon. (EGS1821) / NS1870.
KOMMT, KINDER, LASST UNS GEHEN, DER ABEND KOMMT HERBEI   751
    Mel.: Von Gott will ich nicht lassen / 19 st. / Tersteegen (GBG;
    Knapp, Koch, Kulp; Julian; DP1753) / Tr.: Julian / KDP1764.
KOMMT, LASSET UNS BEDENKEN DES HERREN WUNDERWERK   752
    Mel.: Von Gott will ich nicht lassen / 18 st. / Anon. / Tr.:
    Origins, p. 413 / GGB1720.
KOMMT, LASST UNS AUS BABEL FLIEHEN, WER SICH NOCH DRIN FINDEN MAG   753
    Mel.: Zeuch mich / 9 st. / Anon. / GGB1720.
KOMMT, LASST UNS JESUM SUCHEN BALD, WIR WERDEN SONSTEN TRÄG UND KALT   754
    Mel.: Herr Jesu Christ, dich zu uns wend / 4 st. / Anon. / CG1874.
KOMMT, MENSCHENKINDER, RÜHMT UND PREIST GOTT VATER, SOHN UND HEIL'GEN   755
    Mel.: L. M. / 5 st. / Orwig (ELS1843) / NS1870.
KOMMT UND BETET UNTERTÄNIG GOTT FÜR SEIN ERBARMEN AN   756
    Mel.: O Durchbrecher / 3 st. / P. F. Hiller (GLK) / CG1874.
KOMMT UND LASST EUCH JESUM LEHREN, KOMMT, UND LERNET ALLZUMAL   757
    Mel.: Zion klagt mit Angst und Schmerzen / 11 st. / Gesenius-
    Denicke (Fischer; Julian; DP1718, F) / Tr.: Julian / GGB1720.
KÖNIG, DEM WIR ALLE DIENEN, OB IM GEISTE, DAS WEISST DU   758
    Mel.: Seelen-Weide / 11 st. / N. L. von Zinzendorf (Knapp, Koch;
    HGB1731) / KDP1797-G.
KRONE SEL'GER LUST, HEIL GETREUER BRUST   759
    Mel.: Mein Seelenbräutigam / 4 st. / Anon. / BGB1725 / KH1792.

KURZ WAR MEIN LEBEN HIER AUF ERDEN, KURZ, JA, NUR EINE KLEINE ZEIT   760
    Mel.: Wer nur den lieben Gott lässt / 3 st. / S. D. Miller (KPS) /
    KPS1858.
KURZ WAR NUR MEIN IRDISCH LEBEN HIER IN DIESER PILGRIM ZEIT   761
    (= st. 4-6 of 1140)
    Mel.: Schaffet, schaffet, meine Kinder / 3 st. / Anon. / CG1874.

LASS, SEELE, DICH NICHT MEISTERN VON AUFGEBLAS'NEN GEISTERN   762
    Mel.: O Welt, sieh hier dein / 6 st. / P. F. Hiller (GLK) / CG1874.
LASSET AB, IHR MEINE LIEBEN, LASSET AB VON TRAURIGKEIT   763
    Mel.: Schaffet, schaffet / 3 st. / Heermann (Knapp, Mützell;
    PPM1690) / CG1874.
LASSET EURE LICHTER BRENNEN, SCMÜCKET EURER LAMPEN SCHEIN   764
    Mel.: Ringe recht / 5 st. / Anon. (DGM1865) / NS1870.
LASSET UNS DEN HERREN PREISEN UND VERMEHREN SEINEN RUHM   765
    Mel.: Jauchzet all mit Macht / 7 st. / Koitsch (Knapp, Koch;
    Julian; DP1718, F, ZW) / Tr.: Julian / KDP1744.
LASSET UNS GOTT HERZLICH LIEBEN UND UNS STETS DARINNEN ÜBEN   766
    Mel.: O wie selig sind die / 11 st. / J. Preiss (GAL) / GAL1753.
LASSET UNS MIT JESU ZIEHEN, SEINEM VORBILD FOLGEN NACH   767
    Mel.: Jesu, du mein liebstes Leben / 4 st. / Birken (Knapp, Koch,
    Kulp, Westphal; Julian; DP1718, F) / Tr.: Julian / KDP1744.
LASST NUR DIE LEUTE AUF UNS SCHMÄHEN, WENN UNS DER HERR DOCH SELIG   768
    Mel.: Wer nur den lieben / 5 st. / P. F. Hiller (Ehmann) / CG1874.
LASST UNS INNIGST SEUFZEND KLAGEN, GOTT ZU FRAGEN   769
    Mel.: Hüter, wird die Nacht / 16 st. / Anon. / GGB1720.
LEB WOHL, DIE ERDE WARTET DEIN, GEH IN DER MUTTER KAMMER EIN   770
    Mel.: Ach bleib bei uns / 5 st. / Sachse (Julian; SAG1851) /
    ES1893.
LEB WOHL, O VATERHERZ, LEB WOHL, O MUTTERLIEBE   771
    Mel.: Der Gnadenbrunn fliesst / 1 st. / Anon. (SAG1851) / CG1874.
LEBEN IST DIE ERSTE GABE UND DIE LETZTE, DIE MAN HAT   772
    Mel.: Ach was sind wir ohne / 4 st. / P. F. Hiller (GLK) / CG1874.
LEBT FRIEDSAM, SPRACH CHRISTUS DER HERR ZU SEINEN AUSERKOR'NEN   773
    Mel.: e. M. / 9 st. / Clock (Kadelbach; GGB1691) / KDP1744.
LEHR MICH DIE WORTE WÄGEN, EH' SIE NOCH DIE ZUNGE SPRICHT   774
    Mel: O Durchbrecher / 4 st. / P. F. Hiller (GLK; Knapp) / CG1874.
LEIDEN IST DIE BESTE LIEBE, DIE UNS JESUS HAT GELEHRT   775
    Mel.: Ei, was frag ich nach / 6 st. / Anon. (DP1718, ZW) / KDP1744.
LEITE MICH, O MEIN JEHOVA, PILGRIM DURCH DIES ÖDE LAND   776
    Mel.: Setze dich, mein Geist / 3 st. / Anon. tr. / Or.: Williams:
    Guide me, o Thou great Jehova (Julian) / KPS1858.
LIEBE BRÜDER AUF DER REISE, ZIONS KINDER, SEID DOCH WACH   777
    [Mel.: 35] / 5 st. / Dreisbach (Yoder; EGS1821) / NS1870.
LIEBE, DIE DU MICH ZUM BILDE DEINER GOTTHEIT HAST GEMACHT   778
    Mel.: Komm, o komm, du Geist / 7 st. / Scheffler (HS; Knapp, Koch,
    Kulp; Julian; DP1718, F) / GGB1720.
LIEBE, HAST DU ES GEBOTEN, DASS MAN LIEBE ÜBEN SOLL   779
    (= st. 4 and 5 of 500)
    Mel.: Sieh, hier bin ich / 2 st. / N. L. von Zinzendorf / KLS1841-O.
LIEBE IST DIE GRÖSSTE GABE, DIE DER GEIST DEN CHRISTEN GIBT   780
    Mel.: O Durchbrecher / 4 st. / P. F. Hiller (GLK; Knapp) / CG1874.

LIEBE SEELE, DENK DARAN, SUCHE DOCH DIE LEBENSBAHN 781
    Mel.: Jesu, komm doch selbst zu mir / 10 st. / Anon.: "Author's
    name withheld" (KPS) / KPS1858.

LIEBE SEELE, LASS DIR RATEN, DU GEHST NACH DER EWIGKEIT 782
    Mel.: Ringe recht, wenn Gottes Gnade / 9 st. / Stoll (GGG) / Tr.:
    BLT 19:4, p. 229 / GGG1806, KPS1858.

LIEBER VATER, UNS ERHÖRE, GIB, DASS DEINE LIEBES-GLUT 783
    Mel.: Werde munter, mein Gemüte / 11 st. / Anon. (DP1718) /
    KDP1744.

LIEBSTER ALLER LIEBEN, MEINER SEELEN RUHM 784
    Mel.: Schönster aller / 13 st. / Herrnschmidt (Bachmann; DP1718, F,
    ZW) / KH1792.

LIEBSTER BRÄUT'GAM, DENKST DU NICHT AN DIE TEURE LIEBESPFLICHT 785
    Mel.: Höchster Priester / 8 st. / Scheffler (HS; DP1718) / KDP1744.

LIEBSTER GOTT, WANN WERD ICH STERBEN, MEINE ZEIT LÄUFT 786
    Mel.: Unerschaff'ne Lebenssonne / 7 st. / Neumann (Knapp, Koch) /
    KLS1826.

LIEBSTER HEILAND, NAHE DICH, MEINEN GRUND BERÜHRE 787
    Mel.: Unerschaff'ne Gotteslieb' / 7 st. / Tersteegen (GBG; Knapp,
    Koch; ZW) / KDP1744.

LIEBSTER JESU, DU WIRST KOMMEN, ZU ERFREUEN DEINE FROMMEN 788
    Mel.: e. M. / 10 st. / Anon. (Knapp, Koch; Julian; DP1718, F, ZW) /
    Tr.: Julian / GGB1720.

LIEBSTER JESU, IN DEN TAGEN DEINER NIEDRIGKEIT ALLHIER 789
    Mel.: Jesu, der du meine Seele / 6 st. / Anon. (Julian; DP1718, F,
    ZW) / KDP1744.

LIEBSTER JESU, LIEBSTES LEBEN, BRUNNQUELL ALLER SELIGKEIT 790
    Mel.: Zeuch mich / 10 st. / Stoll (GGG) / GGG1806.

LIEBSTER JESU, LIEBSTES LEBEN, DER DU BIST DAS GOTTES-LAMM 791
    Mel.: e. M. / 5 st. / Petersen (Julian, Farlee; DP1718, F) / Tr.:
    Julian / GGB1720.

LIEBSTER JESU, WIR SIND HIER, DICH UND DEIN WORT ANZUHÖREN 792
    Mel.: e. M. / 3 st. / Clausnitzer (Fischer, Knapp, Kulp, Westphal;
    Julian; DP1718, F) / Tr.: Julian / GGB1720.

LOB SEI DEM ALLERHÖCHSTEN GOTT, DER UNSER SICH ERBARMET HAT 793
    Mel.: Von Himmel hoch / 14 st. / Weisse (NG1531; Knapp; DP1718, F)
    / KDP1744.

LOB SEI DIR, DU ERWÜRGTES LAMM, LOB SEI DIR AN DEM KREUZES STAMM 794
    Mel.: Gelobet seist du, Jesus Christ / 14 st. / Anon. / GGB1720.

LOBE(T) DEN HERREN, DEN MÄCHTIGEN KÖNIG DER EHREN 795
    Mel.: Hast du dann, Jesu / 5 st. / Neander (GLU; Knapp, Koch, Kulp;
    Julian; DP1718, F) / Tr.: Julian / GGB1720.

LOBE, LOBE, MEINE SEELE, DEN, DER HEISST GOTT ZEBAOTH 796
    Mel.: Liebster Jesu, liebstes Leben / 8 st. / Pauli (Koch; DP1718,
    F) / KDP1744.

LOBET DEN HERREN, DENN ER IST SEHR FREUNDLICH 797
    [Mel.: 12] / 7 st. / Anon. (Koch, Kulp, Mützell; Julian; DP1718, F)
    / GGB1720.

LOBET GOTT ZU JEDER STUNDE UND AUCH JETZT MIT HERZ UND MUNDE 798
    Mel.: Treuer Vater, deine Liebe / 11 st. / Anon. / GGB1720.

LOBET UNSERN GOTT UND HERRN, PREISET IHN VON HERZEN 799
    Mel.: Mein Gemüt erfreuet sich / 14 st. / Stoll (GGG) / Tr.:
    BLT 19:4, p. 230 / GGB1806.

LOBSINGET GOTT, WEIL JESUS CHRIST VON TOTEN AUFERSTANDEN IST 800
    Mel.: Triumph, Triumph / 11 st. / Anon. (DP1718, F) / KDP1744.

LOBT GOTT, IHR CHRISTEN ALLZUGLEICH, IN SEINEM HÖCHSTEN THRON 801
    Mel.: Auf, Seele, auf und säume nicht / 8 st. / Herman (Knapp,
    Koch, Kulp, Mützell; Julian; DP1718, F) / Tr.: Julian / KDP1744.

MACH ENDLICH DES VIELEN ZERSTREUENS EIN END', O SEELE 802
    Mel.: Brich endlich hervor / 18 st. / Anon. (DP1718, ZW) / KDP1744.

MACHE DICH, MEIN GEIST, BEREIT, WACHE, FLEH UND BETE 803
    Mel.: Straf mich nicht / 10 st. / Freystein (Knapp, Koch, Kulp,
    Westphal; Julian; DP1718, F) / Tr.: Julian / GGB1720.

MACHT EUCH BEREIT ZUR EWIGKEIT, DIE IHR SEID AUFGESTANDEN 804
    Mel.: O Traurigkeit, o Herzeleid / 12 st. / Anon. / GGB1720.

MAN LOBT DICH IN DER STILLE, DU HOCHERHAB'NER ZIONS-GOTT 805
    Mel.: Nun lob, mein Seel' / 3 st. / Rist (Koch, Kulp, Westphal;
    Julian; DP1718, F) / Tr.: Julian / GGB1720.

MAN MAG WOHL INS KLAGHAUS GEHEN UND DEN LAUF DER WELT BESEHEN 806
    Mel.: Treuer Vater, deine Liebe / 22 st. / Anon. / GGB1720.

MANCHER IST IN NACHT GERATEN, IN UNGLÜCK UND GROSSE NOT 807
    (= st. 2 and 6 of 1282)
    Mel.: Gute Nacht, ihr meine Lieben / 2 st. / Anon. (Knapp; Julian)
    / Tr.: Julian / CG1874.

MEIN BRÄUT'GAM, FÜHRE MICH SPAZIEREN IN DEIN VERSPROCH'NES PARADIES 808
    Mel.: Wo ist der Schönste, den ich / 8 st. / Arnold (LF; DP1718, F,
    ZW) / KDP1744.

MEIN BRÄUTIGAM, DU ZARTES GOTTES-LAMM, HERR ZEBAOTH 809
    Mel.: Eil doch heran / 7 st. / Arnold (EUL) / KDP1744.

MEIN ERLÖSER, GOTTES SOHN, DER DU FÜR MICH LITTEST 810
    Mel.: Bleibe bei mir / 9 st. / Diterich (Koch; PUL1785) /
    KDP1797-G.

MEIN ERWÜNSCHTER LEBENSBRUNN GIBT NICHT WASSER SÜSS UND BITTER 811
    Mel.: O du toll und töricht Volk / 5 st. / Anon. / GGB1720.

MEIN GANZES HERZ BEWEGET SICH, MEIN GOTT, WENN ICH GEDENK AN DICH 812
    Mel.: Wo Gott zum Haus / 7 st. / Anon. / GGB1720.

MEIN GEMÜT BEDENKET HEUT', WIE IN DER BESTIMMTEN ZEIT 813
    Mel.: Höchster Priester / 14 st. / anon. Brethren (Stoudt) / KH1792.

MEIN GEMÜT ERFREUET SICH, JESU, WENN ICH DENK AN DICH 814
    Mel.: Jesu, komm doch selbst / 6 st. / Anon. (Yoder; EGS1821) /
    CGB1695.

MEIN G'NUG-BESCHWERTER SINN, WIRF DIE GEDANKEN HIN 815
    Mel.: O Jesu, du bist mein / 14 st. / Anon. (DP1718, F, W) /
    KDP1744.

MEIN GOTT, DAS HERZ ICH BRINGE DIR ZUR GABE UND GESCHENK 816
    Mel.: Nun sich der Tag geendet hat / 24 st. / Schade (Knapp, Koch;
    Julian, Yoder; DP1718, F) / KDP1744.

MEIN GOTT, DU BRUNNEN ALLER FREUD', DER LEBEN FREUDIG MACHT 817
    Mel.: Mein Gottes Herz / 4 st. / Walter, tr. (Yoder; EGS1821) /
    Or.: C. Wesley / ES1893.

MEIN GOTT, DU WILLST, DASS ICH SOLL REIN UND IN DER LIEBE VÖLLIG SEIN 818
    Mel.: L. M. / 5 st. / Anon. (DGM1865) / NS1870.

MEIN GOTT, ICH WEISS NICHT, WANN ICH STERBE 819
    (= st. 2-5 of: Mein Gott, ich weiss wohl, dass ich sterbe)
    Mel.: Wer nur den lieben Gott / 4 st. / Schmolck (Knapp; Julian) /
    Tr.: Julian / ES1893.

MEIN HEILAND, DU HAST UNS GELEHRT, WER NICHT VON HERZEN UMGEKEHRT   820
    Mel.: Herr Jesu Christe, mein / 2 st. / Woltersdorf (Knapp;
NVG1806) / CG1874.

MEIN HEILAND, ES IST DEINE SACHE, DASS DU DIE DEINIGEN BEWAHRST   821
    Mel.: Wer weiss, wie nahe mir / 2 st. / P. F. Hiller (GLK) /
CG1874.

MEIN HEILAND, GIB MICH MIR ZU KENNEN, WEIL ICH MIR SONST VERBORGEN BIN 822
    Mel.: Entfernet euch, ihr / 10 st. / Anon. (DP1718, F, ZW) /
KDP1744.

MEIN HEILAND, HABE AUF MICH ACHT IN DIESER WÜSTENEI   823
    Mel.: Mein Gott, das Herz ich bringe / 1 st. / Anon. (ASGL) /
ES1893.

MEIN HEILAND HAT SICH MÜD' GEREIST   824
    Mel.: Mein Gott, das Herz ich bringe / 6 st. / P. F. Hiller (GLK;
Knapp) / CG1874.

MEIN HEILAND LEBT; ER HAT DIE MACHT DES TODES GANZ BEZWUNGEN   825
    Mel.: Es ist gewisslich an der / 3 st. / Diterich (Julian; NVG1806)
/ Tr.: Julian / ES1893.

MEIN HEILAND, MEIN ERLÖSER, BLICK UNSRE SEHNSUCHT AN   826
    Mel.: e. M. / 8 st. / Anon. / KLS1829.

MEIN HEILAND NIMMT DIE SÜNDER AN, DIE UNTER IHRER LAST DER SÜNDEN   827
    Mel.: e. M. / 11 st. / Lehr (Knapp, Koch; Julian; A1761) / Tr.:
Julian / KDP1777.

MEIN HERZ, ACH DENK AN DEINE BUSSE, DA NOCH DES HERREN STIMME LOCKT   828
    [Mel.: 96] / 4 st. / Adolph (Knapp; NVG1806) / NS1870.

MEIN HERZ, DICH SCHWING ZUM HÖCHSTEN GUT, DAS IST DIR WAHRLICH BESSER   829
    Mel.: Mein' Wallfahrt ich / 7 st. / Anon. / GGB1720.

MEIN HERZ, EIN EISEN GROB UND ALT   830
    Mel.: Psalm 24 Lobwasser / 8 st. / Tersteegen (GBG; Julian, Yoder;
GV1824) / Tr.: Julian / KH1792.

MEIN HERZ, GIB DICH ZUFRIEDEN UND BLEIBE GANZ BESCHIEDEN   831
    Mel.: Nun ruhen alle Wälder / 11 st. / Freylinghausen (Knapp, Koch,
Westphal; Julian; DP1718, F) / Tr.: Julian / KH1792.

MEIN HERZ, GIB DICH ZUR RUH', WAS SOLL DAS ZAGEN?   832
    Mel.: Wer Jesum bei sich hat / 4 st. / P. F. Hiller (GLK) / CG1874.

MEIN HERZ IST SCHON GEWÖHNET AN JESU SÜSSES WORT   833
    Mel.: Valet will ich / 4 st. / P. F. Hiller (GLK; Knapp) / CG1874.

MEIN HERZ, SEI ZUFRIEDEN, BETRÜBE DICH NICHT, GEDENK, DASS ZUM BESTEN   834
    Mel.: O Ursprung des Lebens / 6 st. / Anon. (DP1718, F) / KDP1744.

MEIN HERZ, WACH AUF UND SINGE, BETRACHT DAS GROSSE WERK   835
    Mel.: Herzlich tut mich verlangen / 15 st. / Anon. / GGB1720.

MEIN HERZE, WIE WANKEST UND FLATTERST DU NOCH   836
    Mel.: Die lieblichen Blicke / 8 st. / Koitsch (Julian; DP1718, F) /
Tr.: Julian / GGB1720.

MEIN HERZENS-JESU, MEINE FREUD', WIE INNIG LIEBST DU DOCH DIE LEUT'   837
    Mel.: Aus Lieb' verwund'ter Jesu mein / 5 st. / Anon. / KLS1826.

MEIN HERZENS-JESU, MEINE LUST, AN DEM ICH MICH VERGNÜGE   838
    Mel.: e. M. / 18 st. / J. C. Lange (Kulp; Julian; DP1718, F) / Tr.:
Julian / GGB1720.

MEIN HÜTER UND MEIN HIRT IST GOTT, DER HERRE   839
    Mel.: e. M. / 3 st. / Lobwasser (PD1710; anon. Anabaptist (Wolkan)
/ KDP1744.

MEIN JESU, DER DU MICH ZUM LUST-SPIEL EWIGLICH DIR HAST ERWÄHLET   840
    Mel.: e. M. / 14 st. / J. C. Lange (Koch; DP1718, F, ZW) / KDP1744.

MEIN JESU, GOTTES SOHN, DER DU ZUVOR UND NUN DIES TUST GEBIETEN 841
    Mel.: Mein Jesu, der du mich / 12 st. / Anon. / GGB1720.

MEIN JESU, HIER SIND DEINE BRÜDER, DIE LIEBE ANEINANDER HÄLT 842
    Mel.: Wer nur den lieben Gott lässt / 9 st. / Anon. (Koch; Julian);
    (DP1718) / Tr.: Julian / KDP1744.

MEIN JESU KAUFTE MICH MIT BLUT, ER HAT MICH TEU'R BEZAHLT 843
    Mel.: e. M.; Mein Gott, das Herz ich / 4 st. / Ch.: O das Lamm, das
    liebe Lamm / W. Preiss (KPS) / Or. Ch.: O the lamb, the loving lamb
    (Lorenz) / KPS1858.

MEIN JESU, SÜSSE SEELENLUST, MIR IST NICHTS AUSSER DIR BEWUSST 844
    Mel.: Wie schön leucht' / 10 st. / J. C. Lange (Koch; DP1718, F,
    ZW) / KDP1744.

MEIN KÖNIG, SCHREIB MIR DEIN GESETZ INS HERZ 845
    Mel.: e. M. / 16 st. / Arnold (GLU; Koch; Julian; DP1718, F, ZW) /
    Tr.: Julian / KDP1744.

MEIN LEBEN AUF ERDEN IST MÜHSAM ALLHIER UND VOLLER BESCHWERDEN 846
    Mel.: Ach lass dich jetzt finden / 12 st. / H. Danner (Yoder); W.
    Preiss (KPS) / KPS1858.

MEIN LEBEN IST EIN PILGERSTAND, DER HIMMEL IST MEIN VATERLAND 847
    Mel.: Herr Jesu Christ, dich zu uns wend / 5 st. / Lampe (Koch,
    Kulp; Julian; ANH1795) / Tr.: Julian / CG1874.

MEIN LEBEN IST MÜHSAM ALLHIER AUF DER ERD', VOLL KUMMER UND ELEND 848
    Mel.: Ach lass dich jetzt finden, komm / 4 st. / Anon.: "Written by
    a sister in her suffering" (KPS) / KPS1858.

MEIN LIEBSTER, MEIN SCHÖNSTER, MEIN TRÖSTER IN LEIDEN 849
    Mel.: Ich liebe dich herzlich / 18 st. / Fritsch (Fischer; DP1718,
    F, ZW) / KDP1744.

MEIN SALOMO, DEIN FREUNDLICHES REGIEREN STILLT ALLES WEH 850
    Mel.: So ist denn nun die Hütte / 11 st. / Richter (Koch; Julian;
    DP1718, F, ZW) / Tr.: Julian / KDP1744.

MEIN' SCHÖNSTE ZEIT IST SCHON VORBEI UND BIN VOM ELEND NOCH NICHT FREI 851
    Mel.: Wie schön bewohnt / 1 st. / Anon. / CG1874.

MEIN SCHWACHER GEIST VON INNEN WIRF DU DOCH DEINE SINNEN 852
    Mel.: Nun ruhen alle Wälder / 12 st. / Anon. / GGB1720.

MEIN' SEEL' GEDULDIG, SANFT UND STILL AUF GOTT IHR' HOFFNUNG SETZEN 853
    Mel.: Psalm 24 Lobwasser / 8 st. / Lobwasser (PD1710) / KDP1744.

MEINE ARMUT MACHT MICH SCHREIEN ZU DEM TREUEN 854
    Mel.: Hüter, wird die Nacht / 7 st. / Richter (Koch; Julian;
    DP1718, F) Tr.: Julian / GGB1720.

MEINE HOFFNUNG STEHET FESTE AUF DEN LEBENDIGEN GOTT 855
    Mel.: Jesu, komm mit deinem Vater / 5 st. / Neander (GLU; Knapp,
    Koch; Julian; DP1718, F) / Tr.: Julian / GGB1720.

MEINE LEBENSZEIT VERSTREICHT, STÜNDLICH EIL ICH ZU DEM GRABE 856
    [Mel.: 111] / 3 st. / Gellert (Koch; GKW1841) / NS1870.

MEINE SEEL', ERMUNT'RE DICH, DEINES JESU LIEB' GEDENKE 857
    Mel.: Liebster Jesu, wir sind hier / 15 st. / Schade (Koch; Julian;
    DP1718, F) / Tr.: Julian / GGB1720.

MEINE SEEL', KOMM IN DIE WUNDEN CHRISTI EIN ZUR SÜSSEN RUH' 858
    Mel.: O du Liebe meiner Liebe; O Durchbrecher aller Bande / 5 st. /
    Anon. (DP1718, F) / GGB1720.

MEINE SEEL' MIT ALLEM FLEISSE MEINES HERREN LOB ERHEB' 859
    Mel.: e. M. / 8 st. / Lobwasser (PD1710) / KDP1744.

MEINE SEELE LOBE GOTT, DER EIN MÄCHTIG', HEILIG' WESEN 860
    Mel.: e. M. / 12 st. / Stoll (GGG) / GGG1806.

MEINE SEELE SEHNET SICH NACH DER STILLE, DASS SIE, JESU, GANZ IN DICH   861
    Mel.: e. M. / 8 st. / Anon. (GL1801) / KPS1858.

MEINE SEELE, SEI GETROST, JESUS HAT JA ÜBERWUNDEN   862
    Mel.: Meinen Jesum lass ich nicht / 12 st. / Anon. / GGB1720.

MEINE SEELE, TU DICH SCHWINGEN HIN DURCH ALLE BERG' UND TAL'   863
    Mel.: Psalm 146 Lobwasser; Meine Hoffnung stehet / 7 st. / Anon. /
    GGB1720.

MEINE SEELE, WILLST DU RUH'N UND DIR IMMER GÜTLICH TUN   864
    Mel.: e. M. / 12 st. / Scheffler (HS; Koch; Julian; DP1718, F) /
    Tr.: Julian / GGB1720.

MEINE SORGEN, ANGST UND PLAGEN LAUFEN MIT DER ZEIT ZU END'   865
    Mel.: Freu dich sehr / 7 st. / Anon. (Fischer, Knapp; DP1718, F) /
    GGB1720.

MEINE ZUFRIEDENHEIT STEHT IN VERGNÜGLICHKEIT   866
    Mel.: Jesu, mein Treuer / 12 st. / Erhard (Koch; A1718) / KDP1744.

MEINEN JESUM LASS ICH NICHT, WEIL ER SICH FÜR MICH GEGEBEN   867
    Mel.: Jesus ist der schönste Nam' / 6 st. / Keimann (Fischer,
    Knapp, Koch, Kulp; Julian; DP1718, F) / Tr.: Julian / GGB1720.

MEINEN JESUM WILL ICH LIEBEN, WEIL ICH NOCH IM LEBEN BIN   868
    Mel.: Ach was soll ich Sünder machen / 5 st. / J. Franck (Fischer;
    GG1700) / GGB1720.

MEINES LEBENS BESTE FREUDE IST DER HIMMEL, GOTTES THRON   869
    Mel.: Komm, o komm; Gott des Himmels und der / 9 st. / Liscow
    (Knapp, Koch, Kulp; DP1718, F) / GGB1720.

MENSCH, DRÜCKT DEIN KREUZ DICH OHNE ZIEL, IST AUCH DES LEIDENS NOCH SO   870
    Mel.: In dich hab ich / 16 st. / Anon. (Knapp; DP1718, F) / GGB1720.

MENSCH, SAG AN, WAS IST DEIN LEBEN, EINE BLUM' UND DÜRRES LAUB   871
    Mel.: Gott des Himmels / 5 st. / Anon. (CGB1695); anon. Penn-
    sylvania Dutch (Stoudt) / KLS1826.

MENSCH, WAS SUCHST DU IN DER NACHT DIESER WELT, WAS WIRST DU FINDEN   872
    Mel.: Meinen Jesum lass ich / 11 st. / Finx (Fischer; F) / KDP1744.

MENSCHEN EILT, EUCH ZU BEKEHREN, JESUS STEHET VOR DER TÜR   873
    [Mel.: 35] / 7 st. / Anon. (DGM1865) / NS1870.

MERK, SEELE, WOHL DIES GNADENWORT, WENN JESUS WINKT, SO GEH   874
    Mel.: Mein Gott, das Herz ich / 4 st. / N. L. von Zinzendorf
    (Knapp; GL1801) / KLS1826.

MIR IST ERBARMUNG WIDERFAHREN   875
    [Mel.: 96] / 5 st. / P. F. Hiller (GLK; Knapp, Koch, Kulp; Julian)
    / NS1870.

MIR NACH, SPRICHT CHRISTUS, UNSER HELD, MIR NACH, IHR CHRISTEN ALLE   876
    Mel.: Mach's mit mir / 7 st. / Scheffler (Knapp, Koch, Kulp;
    Julian; DP1718, F) / Tr.: Julian / GGB1720.

MÖCHTEN'S CHRISTEN RECHT ERWÄGEN, WAS IM KREUZ FÜR NUTZEN LIEGT   877
    [Mel.: 35] / 5 st. / Anon. (EGS1821) / NS1870.

MÖCHTEN'S DOCH DIE MENSCHEN SEHEN, WIE SIE GOTT SO HERZLICH LIEBT   878
    [Mel.: 35] / 5 st. / Bertolet (Yoder; EGS1821) / NS1870.

MONARCHE ALLER DING', DEM ALLE SERAPHINEN MIT EHRERBIETIGKEIT   879
    Mel.: e. M. / 8 st. / Freylinghausen (Koch; Julian; DP1718, F, ZW)
    / Tr.: Julian / KDP1797-G.

MORGEN SOLL ES BESSER WERDEN, DIES VERHEISSET GOTTES WORT   880
    [Mel.: 35] / 5 st. / Anon. (Knapp) / NS1870.

MORGEN-GLANZ DER EWIGKEIT, LICHT VOM UNERSCHÖPFTEN LICHTE   881
    Mel.: e. M. / 7 st. / Knorr von Rosenroth (Knapp, Koch, Kulp,
    Westphal; Julian; DP1718, F, ZW) / Tr.: Julian / KDP1744.

MUSS ES NUN SEIN GESCHEIDEN, SO WOLL' UNS GOTT BEGLEITEN   882
    Mel.: Psalm 6 / 6 st. / anon. Anabaptist (Wolkan); Sattler
    (Kadelbach) / KDP1744.

NACH EINER RPÜFUNG KURZER TAGE ERWARTET UNS DIE EWIGKEIT   883
    Mel.: Wer nur den lieben Gott / 3 st. / Gellert (Knapp, Koch;
    Julian; GKW1841) / Tr.: Julian / ES1893.

NACH MEINER SEELEN SELIGKEIT LASS, HERR, MICH EIFRIG RINGEN   884
    Mel.: Es ist gewisslich / 2 st. / Diterich (Koch; NVG1806) /
    CG1874.

NACHDEM DAS ALTE JAHR VERFLOSSEN, UND WIR, DIE GOTT NUN MEHR VERNEUT   885
    Mel.: Wer nur den lieben Gott / 5 st. / Knorr von Rosenroth
    (Fischer; DP1718, F) / KDP1744.

NÄGELMAL UND SEITENSTICH TRÄGT DER HEILAND NOCH AN SICH   886
    Mel.: Höchster Priester / 6 st. / P. F. Hiller (GLK) / CG1874.

NÄHER, MEIN GOTT, ZU DIR, NÄHER ZU DIR! WENN AUCH DES KREUZES LAST   887
    Mel.: Nearer, my God / 4 st. / Anon. tr. (SGR1876) / Or.: Adams:
    Nearer, my God to Thee (Julian) / CG1879.

NAME VOLLER GÜTE, KOMM IN MEIN GEMÜTE   888
    Mel.: e. M. / 7 st. / Scheffler (Fischer; DP1718, F, ZW) / KDP1744.

NEIG, O MEIN GOTT, DEIN OHR ZU MIR, ICH ERD' UND ASCHE FLEH ZU DIR   889
    Mel.: L. M. / 7 st. / Anon. / NS1870.

NEIN, ICH MAG AUF SAND NICHT BAUEN, WER WILL FALLEN, SEI SO DUMM   890
    Mel.: Gott des Himmels und der / 5 st. / P. F. Hiller (GLK) /
    CG1874.

NETZE KEIN AUG', WENN DEIN FREUND IST ERBLASST   891
    Mel.: Shed not a tear / 4 st. / Anon. tr. (Yoder; EGS1821) / Or.:
    Shed not a tear (Yoder) / CG1874.

NICHT UM REICHTUM, NICHT UM EHRE BITT ICH, BESTER VATER, DICH   892
    [Mel.: 35] / 5 st. / Anon. / NS1870.

NICHTS HILFT UNS DORT MIT HOHEN GABEN UND WISSENSCHAFT GEZIERT   893
    Mel.: Wer nur den lieben Gott / 8 st. / Anon. (DP1718, ZW) /
    KDP1744.

NIE WILL ICH DEM ZU SCHADEN SUCHEN, DER MIR ZU SCHADEN SUCHT   894
    Mel.: e. M. / 10 st. / Gellert (GOL; PUL1785) / KDP1797-G.

NIMM HIN DEN DANK FÜR DEINE LIEBE, DU, MEIN ERLÖSER, JESU CHRIST   895
    [Mel.: 96] / 4 st. / Anon. (GKW1841) / NS1870.

NOCH IST DER HERR IN SEINER STADT, WIEWOHL SIE TAUSEND LÜCKEN HAT   896
    Mel.: L. M. / 6 st. / Anon. / NS1870.

NUN BITTEN WIR DEN HEILIGEN GEIST UM DEN RECHTEN GLAUBEN ALLERMEIST   897
    Mel.: e. M. / 4 st. / Luther (BGB1545; Knapp, Koch, Kulp, Mützell;
    Julian; DP1718, F) / GGB1720.

NUN BRICHT DER HÜTTEN HAUS ENTZWEI, NUN KANN DER LEIB VERWESEN   898
    Mel.: Allein Gott in der Höh' / 5 st. / Mack, Jr. (Heckman) / Tr.:
    (Brumbaugh, p. 257; Heckman) / KH1792.

NUN BRINGEN WIR DEN LEIB ZUR RUH' UND DECKEN IHN MIT ERDE ZU   899
    Mel.: Brunn alles Heils, dich / 5 st. / Liebich (Knapp, Koch, Kulp,
    Westphal; Julian; NVG1806) / Tr.: Julian / KLS1827.

NUN DANKET ALLE GOTT, MIT HERZEN, MUND UND HÄNDEN   900
    Mel. e. M. / 5 st. / Rinkart (Knapp, Koch, Kulp; Julian; DP1718, F)
    / Tr.: Julian / KDP1744.

NUN DAS ALTE JAHR IST HIN UND VORBEI GEGANGEN   901
    Mel.: e. M. / 16 st. / M. Müller (Koch; DP1718, F) / KDP1744.

NUN ERFAHR ICH AUCH BEI DER LIEBE BRAUCH, DIE ICH, JESU ZU DIR FINDE   902
    Mel.: O du süsse Lust / 15 st. / Anon. (DP1718, ZW) / KH1792.

NUN GIBT MEIN JESU GUTE NACHT, NUN IST SEIN LEIDEN GANZ VOLLBRACHT   903
    Mel.: Herr Jesu Christ, dich zu uns / 4 st. / Rist (Fischer;
    GS1836) / CG1874.

NUN GOTTLOB, ES IST VOLLBRACHT, SINGEN, BETEN, LEHREN   904
    Mel.: Liebster Jesu, wir sind hier / 2 st. / H. Schenk (Knapp,
    Koch, Kulp, Westphal; F) / KLS1826.

NUN GUTE NACHT, DU EITLES WELT-GETÜMMEL, MEIN HERZE SEHNT SICH FORT   905
    Mel.: Der Tag ist hin, mein Jesu bei mir bleibe / 7 st. / Anon.
    (DP1718, F) / GGB1720.

NUN GUTE NACHT, IHR LIEBSTEN MEIN, ICH MUSS NUN VON EUCH SCHEIDEN   906
    Mel.: Es ist gewisslich / 5 st. / Herr (Kadelbach) / ES1893.

NUN HAT DAS HEIL'GE GOTTESLAMM, DEM MAN AM KREUZ DAS LEBEN NAHM   907
    Mel.: Triumph, Triumph es / 13 st. / Bucholtz (Fischer, Koch; F) /
    GGB1720.

NUN IST DIE FROHE ZEIT ERWACHT, ALLWO DER VÄTER HOFFNUNG LACHT   908
    Mel.: O starker Gott / 9 st. / Beissel (Viehmeyer) / KH1792.

NUN IST (ES) ALLES WOHL GEMACHT, WEIL JESUS RUFT, ES IST VOLLBRACHT   909
    Mel.: Ich hab mein' Sach' Gott / 13 st. / Laurenti (Knapp, Koch;
    DP1718, F) / KDP1744.

NUN IST ES ZEIT ZU SINGEN HELL, GEBOREN IST IMMANUEL   910
    Mel.: Ihr jungen Helden / 5 st. / Helmbold (Koch; PPM1690) /
    KPS1858.

NUN KOMMT DIE ABENDSTUNDE, WER HAT EIN NEUES GRAB?   911
    (= st. 15, part VII of 1320)
    Mel. e. M. / 1 st. / Mack, Jr. / KLS1829.

NUN KOMMT, IHR CHRISTEN ALLE, AUS LIEBE HÖRET AN BEI DIESEM ABENDMAHLE   912
    Mel.: Ihr Sünder kommt / 7 st. / Anon. / KLS1826.

NUN KOMMT, IHR FROMMEN SEELEN, ALL, DIE IHR JESUM LIEBT   913
    Mel.: Kommt, Kinder, lasst uns gehen / 2 st. / Anon. / CG1874.

NUN, LIEBE BRÜDER, SCHEIDEN WIR, IHR SCHWESTERN, ES GEHT FORT VON HIER   914
    Mel.: Herr Jesu Christ, dich zu uns wend / 7 st. / Dreisbach
    (Yoder; EGS1821) / CG1874.

NUN, LIEBSTER JESU, SIEH, WIR WALLEN ALLHIER IN DIESER WÜSTENEI   915
    Mel.: Erheb dein Herz, tu auf den / 16 st. / Anon. / GGB1720.

NUN LIEG ICH ARMES WÜRMELEIN UND RUH IN MEIN'M   916
    Mel.: O Jesu Christ, mein's / 5 st. / Schirmer (Koch; PPM1690) /
    KLS1826.

NUN LIEG ICH SEL'GES KINDELEIN UND RUH IN MEINEM KÄMMERLEIN   917
    (= 916)
    Mel.: O Jesu Christ, mein's Lebens / 5 st. / Schirmer (Koch;
    PPM1690) / KLS1826.

NUN LOB, MEIN SEEL', DEN HERREN, WAS IN MIR IST, DEN NAMEN SEIN   918
    Mel.: e. M. / 5 st. / Gramann (Knapp, Koch, Kulp; Julian; DP1718,
    F) / Tr.: Julian / GGB1720.

NUN LOBET ALLE GOTTES SOHN, DER DIE ERLÖSUNG 'FUNDEN   919
    Mel.: Auf, Christenmensch / 8 st. / Tersteegen (GBG; Knapp, Koch;
    Julian) / Tr.: Julian / KDP1760.

NUN LOBET ALLE WÄLDER, VIEH, MENSCHEN, STÄDT' UND FELDER, ES LOBT   920
    (Paraphrase of 923)
    Mel.: e. M. / 9 st. / Gerhardt (Kadelbach) / KDP1744.

NUN LOBET UND EHRET GOTT VATER UND SOHN, DEN GEIST, DER UNS FÜHRET   921
    (st. 2 = 167)
    Mel.: Ach lass dich jetzt finden / 2 st. / Anon. / ES1893.

NUN MUSS ICH EUCH VERLASSEN, BETRÜBT IST MIR DIES WORT   922
   Mel.: Kommt, Kinder, lasst uns gehen / 3 st. / Anon. (Yoder;
   EGS 1821) / CG 1874.

NUN RUHEN ALLE WÄLDER, VIEH, MENSCHEN, STÄDT' UND FELDER   923
   Mel.: e. M. / 9 st. / Gerhardt (GLO; Knapp, Koch, Kulp; DP1718, F)
   / KDP1791.

NUN RUHT DOCH ALLE WELT UND IST FEIN STILLE   924
   Mel.: e. M. / 4 st. / Crasselius (Koch; DP1718, F, ZW) / KDP1744.

NUN SCHEIDEN WIR, IHR HERZENS-FREUND', VON DIESEM ORTE FORT   925
   Mel.: Mein Gott, das Herz / 4 st. / Anon. / KLS1826.

NUN SCHLÄFET MAN, UND WER NICHT SCHLAFEN KANN, DER BETE MIT MIR AN   926
   Mel.: Sie schläfet / 3 st. / Tersteegen (GBG; Koch) / KDP1777.

NUN SICH DER TAG GEENDET HAT UND KEINE SONN' MEHR SCHEINT   927
   Mel.: e. M. / 10 st. / Herzog (Fischer, Knapp, Koch, Kulp; Julian;
   DP1718, F) / GGB1720.

NUN SICH DIE NACHT GEENDET (GEWENDET) HAT, DIE FINSTERNIS ZERTEILT   928
   Mel.: Nun sich der Tag / 11 st. / Möckel (Knapp, Kulp; Julian; F) /
   Tr.: Julian / KDP1744.

NUN, SO BLEIBT ES FEST DABEI, DAS ICH JESU EIGEN SEI   929
   Mel.: e. M. / 6 st. / Woltersdorf (ENL) / KLS1841.

NUN WILL ICH MICH SCHEIDEN VON ALLEN DINGEN   930
   Mel.: e. M. / 13 st. / Scheffler (HS; DP1718, F) / GGB1720.

NUN WOLLEN WIR JETZT ALLE SCHICKEN EIN JEGLICHES AN SEINEN ORT   931
   Mel.: Zu deinem Fels / 12 st. / Anon. / GGB1720.

NUR FRISCH HINEIN, ES WIRD SO TIEF NICHT SEIN   932
   Mel.: e. M. / 13 st. / Kongehl (Knapp, Koch, Westphal; DP1718, F,
   ZW) / Anon. / GGB1720.

NUR GOTT ALLEIN, O GÜLD'NES WORT, SUCH'S, WO DU WILLST   933
   Mel.: e. M. / 7 st. / Tersteegen (GBG) / KD1792.

NUR GOTT ALLEIN WOLL' UNS GENÄDIG SEIN   934
   Mel.: Eil doch heran / 7 st. / Mack, Jr. (Heckman) / Tr.: Heckman.

O ABGRUND, TU DICH AUF, O TIEFE GOTTESLIEBE   935
   Mel.: Mein Vater, zeuge / 17 st. / Arnold (LF; DP1718, ZW) /
   KDP1744.

O ALLERHÖCHSTER MENSCHENHÜTER, DU UNBEGREIFLICH HÖCHSTES GUT   936
   Mel.: e. M. / 6 st. / Neander (GLU; Knapp, Koch; Julian; DP1718, F)
   / Tr.: Julian / GGB1720.

O AUFERSTAND'NER SIEGESFÜRST, DU LEBEN ALLER LEBEN   937
   Mel.: Was Gott tut, das ist wohlgetan / 2 st. / J. H. Böhmer
   (Knapp, Koch; Julian; F) / Tr.: Julian / KDP1797-G.

O CHRISTENMENSCH, ERBARME DICH, DENN AUCH DEIN GOTT ERBARMET SICH   938
   Mel.: L. M. / 5 st. / Anon. (Knapp; DGM1865) / NS1870.

O CREATUR ... see: O KREATUR ...

O CREUTZES ... see: O KREUZES ...

O DASS ICH NUR JESUM WÄHLEN KONNTE IN DER GNADENZEIT   939
   Mel.: O der alles hätt' verloren / 12 st. / Stoll (GGG) / GGG1806.

O DASS ICH TAUSEND ZUNGEN HÄTTE   940
   Mel.: Wer nur den lieben Gott lässt / 5 st. / Mentzer (Kulp,
   Westphal; Julian; F) / Tr.: Julian / NS1870.

O DASS OB DIESER GNADENSTÄTT' DER HIMMEL SICH ERÖFFNEN TÄT   941
   Mel.: L. M. / 5 st. / Anon. / NS1870.

O DENKE STETS AN DEINEN TOD, DU BIST NOCH WOHL, GESUND UND ROT   942
   Mel.: Herr Jesu Christ, dich zu uns wend / 3 st. / Anon. / CG1879.

O DER ALLES HÄTT' VERLOREN 943
    Mel.: e. M. / 8 st. / Arnold (Koch; Julian; DP1718, F) / Tr.:
    Julian / GGB1720.

O DU, DES HIMMELS ZIER UND KRON', DER SÜNDER HOFFNUNG, TROST UND LEBEN 944
    Mel.: L. M. / 5 st. / Knapp, tr. from Latin (Knapp) / NS1870.

O DU GEIST DER HERRLICHKEIT, GEIST DER KRAFT UND LIEBE 945
    Mel.: P. M. / 5 st. / Woltersdorf (Knapp, Koch) / NS1870.

O DU HEILIGER, ALLBARMHERZIGER, HERR UND SCHÖPFER DER WELTEN 946
    Mel.: Sicilian hymn / 5 st. / Anon. / KLS1841-O.

O DU LIEBE MEINER LIEBE, DU ERWÜNSCHTE (QUELL ALLER) SELIGKEIT 947
    Mel.: O Durchbrecher / 7 st. / Senitz (Knapp, Westphal); Drese?
    (Koch); (DP1718, F) / GGB1720.

O DU MENSCHEN-KIND, EILE DOCH GESCHWIND 948
    Mel.: Seelen-Bräutigam / 19 st. / Anon. / KDP1744.

O DU SÜSSE LUST AUS DER LIEBES-BRUST 949
    Mel.: Seelenbräutigam / 9 st. / Arnold? (GGS, LF; Julian; DP1718,
    F) / Tr.: Julian / KDP1744.

O DU TOLL UND TÖRICHT VOLK, DANKEST DU ALSO DEM HERREN 950
    Mel.: e. M. / 5 st. / Neander (GLU; ANH1795) / ELEL1812.

O DURCHBRECHER ALLER BANDE 951
    Mel.: O du Liebe meiner Liebe / 11 st. / Arnold (LF; Knapp, Koch,
    Kulp; Julian; DP 1718, F) / Tr.: Julian / GGB1720.

O ERDENPILGER, SEI BEREIT ZU DEINEM TODE JEDERZEIT 952
    Mel.: Ihr jungen Helden / 5 st. / Anon. (SAG1851) / KPS1858.

O EWIGKEIT, DU DONNERWORT, O SCHWERT, DAS DURCH DIE SEELE BOHRT 953
    Mel.: e. M. / 3 st. / Rist (Knapp, Koch, Kulp; Julian; A1718) /
    Tr.: Julian / ES1893.

O FINSTRE NACHT, WANN WIRST DU DOCH VERGEHEN 954
    Mel.: Zerfliess, mein Geist, in Jesu / 10 st. / Anon. (DP1718, F,
    ZW) / KDP1744.

O FRIEDENSFÜRST AUS DAVIDS STAMM, O MEINER SEELEN BRÄUTIGAM 955
    (st. 1 = 956; st. 2-3 identical with non-Brethren sources)
    Mel.: O heil'ger Geist / 3 st. / Anon. (NVG1806) / ES1893.

O FÜRSTEN-KIND AUS DAVIDS STAMM, O MEINER SEELE BRÄUTIGAM 956
    Mel.: Wie schön leuchtet / 1 st. / Anon. (A1718) / CG1874.

O GOTT, DER DU EIN HEERFÜRST BIST, WIE LUSTIG UND WIE LIEBLICH IST 957
    Mel.: e. M. / 6 st. / Lobwasser (PD1710); Schwerin (Koch) /
    KDP1744.

O GOTT DES HIMMELS UND DER ERDEN, DER DU ALLGEGENWÄRTIG BIST 958
    Mel.: Wer nur den lieben Gott / 4 st. / Anon. (PUL1785) / ES1893.

O GOTT, DU FROMMER GOTT, DU BRUNNQUELL ALLER GABEN 959
    Mel.: Die Nacht ist vor der Tür / 3 st. / Heermann (Knapp, Kulp,
    Mützell, Röbbelen, Westphal; Julian; DP1718, F) / Tr.: Julian /
    CG1874.

O GOTT, VON DEM WIR ALLES HABEN, DIE WELT IST EIN SEHR GROSSES HAUS 960
    Mel.: Wer weiss, wie nahe / 3 st. / Neumann (Knapp, Koch) / CG1879.

O GOTT, WAS WIRD SICH DORT VOR GROSSE FREUD' ERHEBEN 961
    Mel.: Holdselig's Gottes-Lamm / 11 st. / Anon. / GGB1720.

O GOTTES LAMM, MEIN ELEMENT IST EINZIG DEIN ERBARMEN 962
    Mel.: Mir nach, spricht Christus / 5 st. / Woltersdorf (Knapp,
    Koch; ANH1795) / KLS1835.

O GOTTES SOHN, HERR JESU CHRIST, DASS MAN RECHT KÖNNE GLAUBEN 963
    Mel.: Ach Gott, vom Himmel sieh darein / 10 st. / Denicke (Knapp,
    Koch; DP1718, F) / GGB1720.

O GOTTES STADT, O GÜLD'NES LICHT, O GROSSE FREUD' OHN' ENDE   964
   Mel.: e. M. / 16 st. / Rist (Fischer; DP1718, F) / GGB1720.

O HAUPT VOLL BLUT UND WUNDEN   965
   Mel.: Herzlich tut mich erfreuen / 10 st. / Gerhardt (GL; Knapp,
   Koch, Kulp; Julian; DP1718, F) / Tr.: Julian / KDP1797-G.

O HEILAND, IN DEM MEINE SEELE SICH FREUT, BEI DEM ICH IM LEIDEN SUCH   966
   Mel.: e. M. / 5 st. / Anon. tr. / Or.: Swain: O Thou, in whose
   presence my soul takes delight (Julian) / KPS1858.

O HEIL'GER GEIST, KEHR BEI MIR (UNS) EIN   967
   Mel.: Wie schön leuchtet / 7 st. / Schirmer (Knapp, Koch, Kulp,
   Westphal; Julian; DP1718, F) / Tr.: Julian / GGB1720.

O HERR, DAS HIMMLISCHE PANIER, AUF STUMMEN TOTENGRÜFTEN HIER   968
   Mel.: O heil'ger Geist, kehr bei / 3 st. / Knapp (Knapp; SAG1851)
   KPS1858.

O HERR, DEIN HEILIG' WORT UNS LEHRT DIE SALBUNG MIT DEM ÖL   969
   Mel.: Mein Gott, das Herz ich bringe / 6 st. / Anon. / ES1893.

O HERR DER HERRLICHKEIT, O GLANZ DER SELIGKEIT, DU LICHT VOM LICHTE   970
   Mel.: Mein Jesu, der du / 34 st. / Anon. (DP1718, F, ZW) / KDP1744.

O HERR, VERSAMMELT SIND WIR HIER WIE KINDER UM EIN LICHT   971
   Mel.: C. M. / 4 st. / C. H. Zeller (Knapp, Koch) / NS1870.

O HIMMLISCHE LIEBE, DU HAST MICH BESESSEN, MEIN HERZ IST MIT JESU   972
   Mel.: e. M. / 9 st. / Anon. (Julian) / Tr.: Julian / KDP1744.

O IHR AUSERWÄHLTEN KINDER, IHR JUNGFRAUEN ALLZUMAL   973
   Mel.: e. M. / 6 st. / Sporleder (Koch; BGB1725) / KDP1797-G.

O IHR JUNG' UND ALTEN LEUT', IHR MÜSST TRAG'N DAS STERBEKLEID   974
   Mel.: Jesu, komm doch / 3 st. / Ch.: Dann wünscht ihr zu sein
   bereit / Anon. / CG1874.

O JERUSALEM, DU SCHÖNE, DA MAN GOTT BESTÄNDIG EHRT   975
   Mel.: Gott des Himmels und der Erden / 7 st. / F. K. Hiller (Knapp,
   Koch; Julian; EGS1821) / KLS1827.

O JESU CHRIST, DER DU MIR BIST DER LIEBST' AUF DIESER ERDEN   976
   Mel.: Ach Gott und Herr / 6 st. / Scheffler (Julian; DP1718, F) /
   GGB1720.

O JESU CHRIST, MEIN SCHÖNSTES LICHT, DER DU IN DEINER SEELEN   977
   Mel.: Ich ruf zu dir / 16 st. / Gerhardt (GL; Knapp, Koch; Julian;
   DP1718, F) / Tr.: Julian / GGB1720.

O JESUS CHRIST, MEIN'S LEBENS LICHT, MEIN HÖCHSTER TROST   978
   Mel.: Die Seele Christi heil'ge mich / 15 st. / Behm (Knapp, Koch,
   Kulp, Mützell, Westphal; Julian; DP1718) / Tr.: Julian / KDP1744.

O JESU CHRISTE, WAHRES LICHT, ERLEUCHTE, DIE DICH KENNEN NICHT   979
   Mel.: Herr Jesu Christ, dich zu uns wend / 6 st. / Heermann
   (Fischer, Kulp, Mützell; Julian; F) / Tr.: Julian / CG1874.

O JESU, DU BIST MEIN UND ICH WILL AUCH DEIN SEIN   980
   Mel.: Mein g'nug beschwerter Sinn / 16 st. / Neuss (Koch; DP1718,
   F, ZW) / KDP1744.

O JESU, HOFFNUNG WAHRER REU', WIE GÜTIG BIST DU, WIE GETREU   981
   Mel.: O Jesu Christ, mein's / 14 st. / Finx (Fischer; DP1718, F) /
   KDP1744.

O JESU, JESU, GOTTES SOHN, MEIN MITTLER UND MEIN GNADEN-THRON   982
   Mel.: Wie schön leucht' uns / 7 st. / Heermann (Knapp, Koch,
   Mützell; Julian; DP1718, F, ZW) / Tr.: Julian / KDP1744.

O JESU, KOMM ZU MIR, MEIN RECHTES LEBEN, UND MACHE MICH AN DIR ZUM   983
   Mel.: e. M. / 6 st. / Anon. (DP1718, F) / GGB1720.

O JESU, KÖNIG HOCH ZU EHREN, DU HÖCHST-VERKLÄRTER GOTTES-SOHN   984
     Mel.: Zu deinem Fels / 12 st. / Tersteegen (GBG; Koch; Julian; ZW)
     / Tr.: Julian / KDP1744.

O JESU, LEHRE DOCH DEIN VOLK, DAS ALLHIER NOCH AUF DIESER ERDEN   985
     Mel: Mein Jesu, der du mich / 20 st. / Anon. / GGB1720.

O JESU, LEHRE MICH, WIE ICH DICH FINDE UND MICH DURCH DICH, MEIN HEIL   986
     Mel.: O Jesu, komm zu mir / 15 st. / Anon. (DP1718, F, ZW) /
     KDP1744.

O JESU MEIN BRÄUT'GAM, WIE IST MIR SO WOHL   987
     Mel.: e. M. / 9 st. / Fritsch (Fischer, Koch; DP1718, F) / GGB1720.

O JESU, MEINE FREUD', MEIN TROST, MEIN HEIL UND LICHT   988
     Mel.: Der Tag ist fort und / 6 st. / S. D. Miller (KPS) / KPS1858.

O JESU, MEINES LEBENS LICHT, NUN IST DIE NACHT VERGANGEN   989
     Mel.: Ich dank dir schon durch / 15 st. / Tersteegen (GBG; Koch;
     ZW) / KDP1744.

O JESU, SCHAU, EIN SÜNDER GANZ BELADEN SICH BEUGEN WILL   990
     Mel.: Der Tag ist hin, mein Jesu, bei mir bleibe / 8 st. /
     Tersteegen (GBG; ANH1795) / KH1792.

O JESU SÜSS, WER DEIN GEDENKT   991
     Mel.: Vom Himmel hoch / 19 st. / Moller (Knapp, Koch, Mützell;
     Julian); Arndt (Mützell); anon. (Wackernagel); (DP1718, F) /
     KDP1744.

O JESU, SÜSSES LICHT, NUN IST DIE NACHT VERGANGEN   992
     Mel.: O Gott, du frommer Gott / 8 st. / J. Lange (Knapp, Koch,
     Kulp; Julian; DP1718, F) / GGB1720.

O JESU, WAHRER LEBENS-BRUNN', DU AUSFLUSS ALLER GÜT'   993
     Mel.: Mein Gott, das Herz / 3 st. / S. D. Miller (KPS) / KPS1858.

O JESU, WÄR ICH ARMES KIND IN ALLEM SO WIE DU GESINNT   994
     Mel.: Herr Jesu Christ, dich zu uns wend / 5 st. / Anon. / CG1874.

O KREATUR, LASS AB, MIT DEINEM GOTT ZU STREITEN   995
     Mel.: O Gott, du frommer Gott / 12 st. / Anon. / GGB1720.

O KREUZES-STAND, O EDLES PFAND, DAS ALTE STREITER BINDET   996
     Mel.: O Traurigkeit / 11 st. / Anon. (DP1718) / KDP1744.

O LAMM GOTTES, UNSCHULDIG AM STAMM DES KREUZES GESCHLACHTET   997
     Mel.: e. M. / 3 st. / Decius (Knapp, Koch, Kulp, Mützell, Nelle;
     Julian; DP1718, F) / Tr.: Julian / GGB1720.

O LAMMES BLUT, WIE TREFFLICH GUT BIST DU IN MEINER SEELEN   998
     Mel.: Ich dank dir schon durch / 9 st. / Anon. / GGB1720.

O LAND DER RUH', NACH DIR ICH SEUFZ, WANN KOMM ICH DOCH HINEIN   999
     Mel.: Mein Gott, das Herz ich / 3 st. / Anon. tr. (KPS) / KSP1858.

O LIEBE, LABE DOCH DAS SEHNENDE VERLANGEN, DAS SICH BEFINDET NOCH   1000
     Mel.: Ich hab ihn / 7 st. / Anon. / KH1792.

O LIEBE SEELE, KÖNNT'ST DU WERDEN EIN KLEINES KINDCHEN NOCH   1001
     Mel.: Zeuch meinen Geist; Psalm 7 Lobwasser / 18 st. / Tersteegen
     (GBG; Julian) / Tr.: Julian / KDP1744.

O LIEBSTE LIEBE, WIE IST MIR SO WOHL, WENN MAN DIR NUR LEBET   1002
     Mel.: O Jesu, mein Bräut'gam, wie / 16 st. / Anon. / GGB1720.

O LIEBSTER HERR, ICH ARMES KIND, DAS NIRGENDS TROST NOCH RUHE FIND'T   1003
     Mel.: Herr Jesu Christ, dich / 4 st. / Tersteegen (Knapp; ANH1795)
     / CG1874.

O MEIN ARMES HERZE, GLAUB, GOTT WIRD ALLES DOCH GUT MACHEN   1004
     Mel.: Morgenglanz der Ewigkeit / 3 st. / Anon. / KH1792.

O MEIN HERZ, ZIEH (ZEUCH) DEIN BEGEHREN TIEF IN DIE VERBORGENHEIT   1005
     Mel.: Unerschaff'ne Lebenssonne / 9 st. / Arnold (EUL; DP1718, ZW)
     / KDP1744.

O MEIN STARKER BUNDESKÖNIG, JESU, TREUER SEELEN HIRT   1006
   Mel.: Zeuch mich / 10 st. / Stoll (GGG) / Tr.: BLT 19:4, p. 231 /
   GGG1806.

O MEIN STARKER BUNDESKÖNIG, WUNDERBARE LEBENSKRAFT   1007
   Mel.: Freu dich sehr, o meine Seele / 7 st. / Anon. / GGB1720.

O MEINE SEELE, SINKE VOR DEINEN GOEL HIN, IM GEISTE TIEF BEDENKE   1008
   Mel.: Wo bleiben meine Sinnen / 12 st. / Anon.; Herr? (Kadelbach) /
   KLS1826.

O MENSCH, BEKEHRE DICH, DIEWEIL DU LEBST AUF ERDEN   1009
   Mel.: Der Gnadenbrunn' fleusst / 2 st. / Anon. (NVG1799) / CG1974.

O MENSCH, WIE IST DEIN HERZ BESTELLT, HAB ACHTUNG AUF DEIN LEBEN   1010
   Mel.: Es ist gewisslich / 2 st. / Laurenti (Knapp, Koch; DP1718, F,
   ZW) / CG1874.

O MILDER HEILAND, JESUS CHRIST, DER DU DIE QUELL' DES LEBENS BIST,
   DURCHFLIESS MEIN GANZES HERZ UND SINN   1011
   Mel.: Du unbegreiflichs höchstes / 16 st. / Stoll (GGG) / Tr.:
   BLT19:4, p. 235 / GGG1806.

O MILDER HEILAND, JESUS CHRIST, DER DU DIE QUELL' DES LEBENS BIST,
   KOMM, WOHN UNS BEI MIT DEINER GNAD'   1012
   Mel: Du unbegreiflichs höchstes / 2 st. / Anon. (NE1762) / KLS1826.

O SCHARFES LICHT, DAS HERZ UND NIEREN PRÜFT, DU STROM, DER KLAR   1013
   Mel.: Psalm 50 Lobwasser / 7 st. / Anon. / GGB1720.

O SELIG IST DER STAND ALLHIER IN DIESER WELT, WER RECHT MIT DIR   1014
   Mel: Blast die Trompete / 1 st. / Anon. / CG1874.

O SELIG IST, WER EINWÄRTS KEHRET GANZ SANFT INS REINE LEBENSLICHT   1015
   Mel.: Verliebtes Lustspiel / 14 st. / Anon. (DP1718, ZW) / KDP1744.

O STARKER GOTT, O SEELENKRAFT, O LIEBSTER HERR   1016
   Mel.: Nun lasst uns den Leib / 6 st. / Neander (GLU; Koch; DP1718)
   / GB1720.

O STARKER ZEBAOTH, DU LEBEN MEINER SEEL' UND MEINES GEISTES KRAFT   1017
   Mel.: e. M. / 4 st. / Neander (GLU; Koch; DP1718) / GGB1720.

O SÜNDER, DENKE WOHL, DU LÄUFST ZUR EWIGKEIT   1018
   Mel.: e. M. / 6 st. / Neander (GLU; Koch; DP1718, F) / KDP1744.

O SÜSSER GOTT, DU SELIG'S GUT, WIE LIEBEST DU DIE LEUT'   1019
   Mel.: O Jesu, meines Lebens Licht / 3 st. / Anon. / CG1874.

O SÜSSER STAND, O SELIG LEBEN, DAS AUS DER WAHREN EINFALT QUILLT   1020
   Mel.: Die Tugend wird durchs Kreuz geübet / 8 st. / Winkler (Koch;
   Julian; DP1718, F, ZW) / Tr.: Julian / KDP1744.

O SÜSSES WORT, DAS JESUS SPRICHT ZUR ARMEN WITWE: "WEINE NICHT"   1021
   Mel.: L. M. / 9 st. / Höfel (Knapp; Julian; NVG1806) / Tr.: Julian
   / NS1870.

O TEURE SEELEN, LASST EUCH WACHEND FINDEN, ACH EILET ALL   1022
   Mel.: Psalm 8 Lobwasser / 6 st. / Anon. / KDP1744.

O TOD, WO IST DEIN STACHEL NUN? WO IST DEIN SIEG, O HÖLLE   1023
   Mel.: Mein Herzens-Jesu, meine Lust; Allein Gott in der Höh' /
   10 st. / Gesenius-Denicke (Fischer, Knapp, Koch, Kulp, Nelle;
   Julian); Bachmeister (Koch); Weissel (Nelle; Julian); (DP1718, F)
   / Tr.: Julian / GGB1720.

O UNBETRÜBTE QUELL', UNSCHULDIG'S EINFALTSWESEN   1024
   Mel.: Mein Vater, zeuge / 5 st. / Arnold (LF; DP1718, ZW) / KDP1744.

O URSPRUNG DES LEBENS, O EWIGES LICHT, DA NIEMAND VERGEBENS SUCHT   1025
   Mel.: Mein Herz, sei zufrieden / 7 st. / Koitsch (Knapp, Koch;
   Julian; DP1718, F, ZW) / Tr.: Julian / KDP1744.

O VATER DER LIEBE, LASS MIR ES SEIN WOHL, WENN LIEBEN IM LEIDEN   1026
   Mel.: O Jesu, mein Bräutigam / 7 st. / Anon. GGB1720.

O VATER, HIMMELS-KÖNIG, DU SCHÖPFER ALLER WELT, WIE LEBT MAN HIER SO   1027
    Mel.: Aus meines Herzens Grunde / 7 st. / Anon. / GGB1720.
O WAS FÜR EIN HERRLICH WESEN HAT EIN CHRIST, DER DA IST RECHT IN GOTT   1028
    Mel.: Warum sollt ich mich denn grämen / 11 st. / Wolff (Knapp,
    Koch; DP1718, F, ZW) / KDP1744.
O WEISHEIT, ALLER HIMMEL ZIER, KOMM VON DEINEM GLORIA-SITZ   1029
    Mel.: Mein Gott, das Herz / 3 st. / Tersteegen (GBG) / KDP1791.
O WELT, SIEH HIER DEIN LEBEN AM STAMM DES KREUZES SCHWEBEN   1030
    Mel.: Nun ruhen alle Wälder / 16 st. / Gerhardt (Knapp, Koch, Kulp;
    Julian; DP1718, F) / Tr.: Julian / GGB1720.
O WIE IST DER WEG SO SCHMAL, DER UNS EINIG FÜHRT   1031
    Mel.: Christus, der uns selig macht / 8 st. / Finx (Julian; GG1700)
    / Tr.: Julian / GGB1720.
O WIE IST DIE ZEIT SO WICHTIG, DIE UNS GOTT NUR EINMAL GIBT   1032
    (= st. 2 of 1033)
    Mel.: Alle Menschen müssen sterben / 1 st. / Stoll (GGG) / Tr.:
    Hymnal 1951, no. 428 / GGG1806, CG1874.
O WIE IST DIE ZEIT SO WICHTIG, DIE UNS GOTT VERGÖNNET NOCH   1033
    Mel.: Alle Menschen müssen sterben / 7 st. / Stoll (GGG) / GGG1806.
O WIE REIN IST DOCH DEIN BLUT, JESU, MEINE WONNE   1034
    Mel.: Mache dich, mein Geist, bereit / 2 st. / Anon. / ES1895.
O WIE SELIG SIND DIE, DIE MIT ARBEIT UND MÜH' IHREN SCHATZ IN DEN   1035
    Mel.: O how happy are they / 4 st. / Anon. tr. (Yoder; EGS1821) /
    Or.: C. Wesley / CG1874.
O WIE SELIG SIND DIE SEELEN, DIE MIT JESU SICH VERMÄHLEN   1036
    Mel.: Fröhlich, fröhlich, immer fröhlich / 10 st. / Richter (Knapp,
    Koch; Julian; DP1718, F) / Tr.: Julian / GGB1720.
O WIE SO SELIG SCHLÄFEST DU NACH MANCHEM SCHWEREN STAND   1037
    Mel.: Mein Gott, das Herz / 4 st. / Anon. / CG1874.
O WIE UNAUSSPRECHLICH SELIG WERDEN WIR IM HIMMEL SEIN   1038
    Mel.: Alle Menschen müssen sterben / 3 st. / Diterich, after
    Schmolck (Koch; Julian; SAG1851) / Tr.: Julian / KPS1858.
OB ICH SCHON WAR IN SÜNDEN TOT, ENTFREMDET VON DEM LEBEN   1039
    Mel.: Nun freut euch, lieben Christen / 5 st. / Neander (GLU);
    DP1718) / KDP1744.

PFLANZEN DER GERECHTIGKEIT MÜSSEN REICHLICH TRAGEN   1040
    Mel.: Mache dich, mein Geist / 2 st. / P. F. Hiller (GLK) / DB1874.
PFLICHTMÄSSIG GELEBT, ZU GOTT FEST GEKLEBT, DASS NICHTS VON IHM TRENNT 1041
    Mel.: Ich sage gut' / 9 st. / Gruber (Farlee; DP1718, ZW) / KDP1744.
PRÄCHTIG KOMMT DER HERR, MEIN KÖNIG, LAUT ERSCHALLT DER JUBELTON   1042
    Mel.: Sieh, hier bin ich, Ehrenkönig / 6 st. / Anon. / KDP1797-G.
PREDIGET VON DEN GERECHTEN, DENN SIE HABEN'S EWIG GUT   1043
    Mel.: O Jerusalem, du Schöne / 5 st. / P. F. Hiller (GLK) / CG 1874.
PREIS, LOB, EHR'R, RUHM, DANK, KRAFT UND MACHT SEI DEM ERWÜRGTEN LAMM   1044
    Mel.: e. M. / 7 st. / Anon. (Koch; Julian; DP1718, F) / GGB1720.
PREISE DEN HERREN, DER WUNDERLICH UNS ALLHIER FÜHRET, IN LIEBESWEGEN   1045
    Mel.: Lobe den Herren, den / 6 st. / Anon. / GGB1720.
PROBIERT MUSS SEIN DER GLAUB', DAMIT ER WERD' RECHTSCHAFFEN   1046
    Mel.: Holdselig's Gotteslamm / 5 st. / Anon. (DP1718, ZW) / KDP1744.

QUILL AUS IN MIR, O SEGENSQUELLE, DIE DU ENTSPRINGST VON OBEN HER   1047
    Mel.: Verliebtes Lustspiel / 4 st. / Anon. (DP1718, ZW) / KDP1744.

REINE FLAMMEN, BRENNT ZUSAMMEN, MACHT MICH LICHT DURCH EUREN SCHEIN   1048
    Mel.: Seelen-Weide / 7 st. / Anon. (DP1718, ZW) / KDP1744.
RINGE RECHT, WEIL GOTTES GNADE DIR DEIN ARMES HERZE REGT   1049
    Mel.: O der alles hätt' verloren / 12 st. / Stoll (GGG) / GGG1806.
RINGE RECHT, WENN GOTTES GNADE DICH NUN ZIEHET UND BEGEHRT   1050
    Mel.: O der alles hätt' verloren / 23 st. / Winkler (Knapp, Koch;
    Julian, Yoder; DP1718, F) / GGB1720.
"RINGET NACH DEM SELIGWERDEN° UNSER SELIGMACHER SPRICHT'S   1051
    [Mel.: 116] / 4 st. / P. F. Hiller (GLK; Knapp; EGS1850) / NS1870.
ROSEN WELKEN UND VERSCHWINDEN, MANCHER FÄLLT ALS KNOSPE AB   1052
    Mel.: Gott des Himmels und der / 2 st. / Anon. (SEL1842) / CG1874.
RUFT LAUTE, IHR WÄCHTER, BEI TAG UND BEI NACHT, BIS ALLE GESCHLECHTER   1053
    Mel.: Ach lass dich jetzt finden / 2 st. / Anon. / ES1893.
RUHE IST DAS BESTE GUT, DAS MAN HABEN KANN. STILLE UND EIN GUTER MUT   1054
    Mel.: Seele, was ist Schön'res wohl / 19 st. / Schade (Knapp, Koch;
    Julian; DP1718, F, ZW) / KDP1744.

SALB UNS MIT DEINER LIEBE, O WEISHEIT, DURCH UND DURCH   1055
    Mel.: Herr Christ, der ein'ge Gott's Sohn / 6 st. / Anon. (in
    Arnold, EUL; Julian; DP1718, ZW) / Tr.: Julian / KDP1744.
SANFTE LEBENSQUELLE, LAUTER, KLAR UND HELLE, STROM DER HEILIGKEIT   1056
    Mel.: Jesu, meine Freude / 4 st. / Stoll (GGG) / GGG1806.
SCHAFF IN MIR, GOTT, ZU DEINEM DIENST EIN HERZ VON SÜNDEN FREI   1057
    Mel.: C. M. / 6 st. / Dreisbach, tr. (Yoder; EGS1821) / Or.: C.
    WEsley / NS1870.
SCHAFFET, SCHAFFET, MEINE (MENSCHEN-) KINDER, SCHAFFET EURE SELIGKEIT   1058
    Mel.: Freu dich sehr, o meine Seele / 10 st. / Gotter (Knapp, Koch,
    Westphal; Julian; DP1718) / KDP1744.
SCHATZ ÜBER ALLE SCHÄTZE, O JESU, LIEBSTER SCHATZ   1059
    Mel.: Valet will ich dir geben; Herzlich tut mich verlangen / 7 st.
    / Liscow (Koch, Kulp; Julian, Yoder; DP1718, F) / KDP1744.
SCHAU DORT MEIN' HEILAND UND GOTT, SCHAU DORT MEIN' HEILAND   1060
    Mel.: Saw ye my Saviour / 4 st. / Dreisbach, tr. (Yoder; EGS1821)
    / Or.: Saw ye my saviour (?) / CG18974.
SCHAU, GROSSER GOTT DER HERRLICHKEIT, VOM THRON DER MAJESTÄT   1060
    Mel.: C. M. / 4 st. / Schlegel (SGG; DGM1865) / NS1870.
SCHAU, LIEBER GOTT, WIE MEINE FEIND', DAMIT ICH STETS MUSS KÄMPFEN   1062
    Mel.: Ach Gott, vom Himmel sieh / 10 st. / Gesenius-Denicke
    (Fischer; DP1718, F) / KDP1744.
SCHENKE, HERR, MIR KRAFT UND GNADE, DASS ICH MAG MIT ERNST UND TREU'   1063
    Mel.: Ringe recht / 10 st. / Sasse (Yoder; EGS1821) / KPS1858.
SCHICKET EUCH, IHR LIEBEN GÄSTE, ZU DES LAMMES HOCHZEITSFESTE   1064
    Mel.: Liebe, die du mich zum Bilde / 26 st. / Anon. (DP1718, ZW) /
    KDP1744.
SCHLAF SANFT IN DEINEM STILLEN GRAB, FRÜH BRACHT DES TODES STURM   1065
    Mel.: Kommt her zu mir, spricht / 1 st. / Anon. (SAG1851) /
    KPS1858.
SCHON LANG HÖRT' ICH EINE STIMM' IN MIR SO DAUERND ZU MIR SAGEN   1066
    Mel.: Es ist gewisslich an der Zeit / 3 st. / Gerlach (KPS) /
    KPS1858.
SCHÖNSTER ALLER SCHÖNEN, MEINES HERZENS LUST   1067
    Mel.: Liebster aller Lieben / 8 st. / Bernstein (Julian; DP1718, F,
    ZW) / Tr.: Julian / KDP1744.

SCHÖNSTER IMMANUEL, HERZOG DER FROMMEN, DU MEINER SEELEN TROST   1068
    Mel.: e. M. / 6 st. / Anon. (Julian; DP1718, F) / Tr.: Julian /
    GGB1720.

SCHÖNSTES SEELCHEN, GEHE FORT, ENGEL, GEHE VON DER ERDEN   1069
    Mel.: Binde meine Seele wohl / 2 st. / Bornmeister (Fischer;
    SAG1851) / CG1874.

SCHREIBT ALLES FEST IN MEINEN SINN, DASS ICH NICHT NUR EIN SINGER BIN   1070
    Mel.: Herr Jesu Christ, dich zu uns / 2 st. / Anon. / CG1874.

SCHREIB ALLES, WAS MAN HEUT' GELEHRT, IN UNSER HERZ HINEIN   1071
    Mel.: Mein Gott, das Herz / 2 st. / Anon. / CG1874.

SCHWEIGT VOM GLÜCKE UND GESCHICHTE, DIE IHR GOTTES TUN NICHT WISST   1072
    Mel.: Sieh, hier bin / 4 st. / P. F. Hiller (GLK; Knapp) / CG1874.

SCHWING DICH AUF ZU DEINEM GOTT, DU BETRÜBTE SEELE   1073
    Mel.: Christus, der uns selig macht; Jesu Leiden, Pein und Tod /
    17 st. / Gerhardt (GL; Knapp, Koch, Kulp; DP1718, F) / KDP1744.

SCHWINGT, HEILIGE GEDANKEN, EUCH VON DER ERDE LOS   1074
    Mel.: Aus meines Herzens Grunde / 7 st. / Cramer (Koch) /
    KDP1797-G.

SEELE, DU MUSST MUNTER WERDEN, DENN DER ERDEN BLICKT HERVOR   1075
    Mel.: Wo ist die Sonne / 14 st. / Canitz (Knapp, Koch; Julian; F) /
    Tr.: Julian / KH1792.

SEELE, GEH AUF GOLGATHA, SETZ DICH UNTER JESU KREUZE   1076
    Mel.: Jesus ist der schönste Nam' / 4 st. / Schmolck (Knapp,
    Westphal; NVG1806) / CG1874.

SEELE, JESUS RUFT (RED'T) DIR ZU: KENNST DU IHN, SO FOLGE DU   1077
    [Mel.: 33] / 5 st. / P. F. Hiller (GLK; Knapp) / NS1870.

SEELE, WAS ERMÜD'ST DU DICH IN DEN DINGEN DIESER ERDEN   1078
    Mel.: Guter Hirte, willst du nicht / 12 st. / Wolff (Knapp, Koch,
    Westphal; Julian; DP1718, F, ZW) / Tr.: Julian / KDP1744.

SEELE, WAS IST SCHÖN'RES WOHL ALS DER HÖCHSTE GOTT   1079
    Mel.: Ruhe ist das beste Gut / 6 st. / L. Stark (Koch; DP1718, F) /
    KDP1744.

SEELEN, SUCHT EUCH SCHÖN ZU SCHMÜCKEN, NICHT MIT GOLD UND   1080
    Mel.: Treuer Vater, deine / 5 st. / P. F. Hiller (GLK) / CG1874.

SEELENBRÄUTIGAM, JESU, GOTTES LAMM   1081
    Mel.: e. M. / 15 st. / Drese (Koch, Nelle, Westphal; Julian;
    DP1718, F) / Tr.: Julian / GGB1720.

SEELEN-WEIDE, MEINE FREUDE, JESU, LASS MICH FEST AN DIR   1082
    Mel.: e. M. / 12 st. / Drese (Koch; DP1718, F) / GGB1720.

SEGNE DEINER KNECHTE LEHREN, ÖFFNE SELBER IHREN MUND   1083
    Mel.: Gott des Himmels und der Erden / 2 st. / Anon. / ES1893.

SEHET, SEHET AUF, MERKET AUF DEN LAUF DERER ZEICHEN DIESER ZEITEN   1084
    Mel.: Seelen-Bräutigam / 20 st. / Anon. (DP1718) / GGB1720.

SEHT, WELCH EIN MENSCH, ACH SEHT, MIT SCHMACH   1085
    Mel.: O Gott, du frommer / 9 st. / Schlegel (SGG) / KDP1797-G.

SEHT, WIE MIT ERHITZTEM GRIMME NUN DER DRACHE MIT DEM LAMME   1086
    Mel.: Auf, Triumph / 12 st. / Anon. (DP1718, F, ZW) / KDP1744.

SEI GEGRÜSST, DU KÖNIGS-KAMMER, GASTHAUS DER BARMHERZIGKEIT   1087
    Mel.: Unser Herrscher / 13 st. / Anon. (DP1718) / KDP1744.

SEI GETREU BIS AN DAS ENDE, DASS NICHT MARTER, ANGST UND NOT   1088
    [Mel.: 35] / 5 st. / B. Prätorius (Knapp; Julian; A1718) / Tr.:
    Julian / NS1870.

SEI GETREU BIS IN DEN TOD, SEELE, LASS DICH KEINE PLAGEN   1089
    Mel.: e. M. / 8 st. / Schmolck (Koch; Julian) / Tr.: Julian /
    ELEL1812, KLS1826.

SEI GETREU IN DEINEM LEIDEN, LASS KEIN KREUZ NOCH UNGEMACH   1090
    Mel.: Psalm 42 Lobwasser / 4 st. / J. Preiss (GAL) / GAL 1753.

SEI GETREU IN DEINEM LEIDEN, LASSE DICH KEIN UNGEMACH   1091
    Mel.: Freu dich sehr, o meine / 7 st. / B. Prätorius (Koch; DP 1718,
    F) / GGB 1720.

SEI GETREU, SEELE, SEI GETREU DER HAND, DIE DICH WILL DURCH DORNEN   1092
    Mel.: Fahre fort, Zion / 8 st. / Rambach (PF) / KPS 1858.

SEI GOTT GETREU, HALT SEINEN BUND, O MENSCH, IN DEINEM LEBEN   1093
    Mel.: Was mein Gott / 8 st. / M. Franck (Koch; DP 1718, F) /
    GGB 1720.

SEI HOCHGELOBT, BARMHERZ'GER GOTT, DER DU DICH UNSER ANGENOMMEN   1094
    Mel.: Preis, Lob, Ehr', Ruhm / 16 st. / Gotter (Knapp, Koch;
    Julian; DP 1718, F, ZW) / Tr.: Julian / KDP 1744.

SEI LOB UND EHR' DEM HÖCHSTEN GUT, DEM VATER ALLER GÜTE   1095
    Mel.: Mein Herzens-Jesu; Es ist das Heil uns / 9 st. / Schütz
    (Knapp, Koch, Kulp, Nelle; Julian; DP 1718, F) / Tr.: Julian /
    GGB 1720.

SEI UNVERZAGT, O FROMMER CHRIST, DER DU IM KREUZ UND UNGLÜCK BIST   1096
    Mel.: In dich hab ich gehoffet / 9 st. / Ziegler (Koch; DP 1718, F)
    / KDP 1744.

SELIG, DIE GEISTLICH ARM SIND, DIE IHR ELEND RECHT ERKENNEN   1097
    Mel.: Guter Hirte, willst du / 11 st. / J. Preiss (GAL) / GAL 1753.

SELIG IST, DER SICH ENTFERNET VON DES WELTGETÜMMELS GEIST   1098
    Mel.: Ach was mach ich in / 28 st. / Anon. (DP 1718, ZW) / KDP 1744.

SELIG SIND DIE GEISTLICH ARMEN, DENN DAS HIMMELREICH IST IHR   1099
    8 st. / Anon. / NS 1870.

SETZE DICH, MEIN GEIST, EIN WENIG UND BESCHAU DIES WUNDER GROSS   1100
    Mel.: Sieh, hier bin ich / 13 st. / Tersteegen (GBG; Knapp, Koch;
    ZW) / KDP 1764.

SIE IST NICHT MEHR, DIE TREUE SEELE, ACH, UNSRE MUTTER IST NICHT MEHR   1101
    Mel.: Wer weiss, wie nahe mir / 3 st. / Anon. (GGLR 1828) / CG 1874.

SIE STARB, ACH STARB MIR VIEL ZU FRÜH, ZU FRÜH AUCH FÜR DIE MEINEN   1102
    Mel.: Aus tiefer Not / 2 st. / Anon. (SAG 1851) / CG 1874.

SIEH DOCH, HOLDER EHREN KÖNIG, MIT ERBARMEN JA AUF MICH   1103
    Mel.: Sieh, hier bin ich / 9 st. / Stoll (GGG) / Tr.: BLT 19:4,
    p. 233 / GGG 1806.

SIEH, EIN WEITES TOTENFELD, VOLLER DÜRRER TOTENBEINE   1104
    Mel.: Guter Hirte / 5 st. / C. H. Zeller (Knapp, Koch) / ES 1893.

SIEH, HIER BIN ICH, EHRENKÖNIG   1105
    Mel.: e. M. / 6 st. / Neander (GLU; Knapp, Koch; Julian; DP 1718, F)
    / Tr.: Julian / GGB 1720.

SIEH, WIE LIEBLICH UND WIE FEIN IST'S, WENN BRÜDER EINIG (FRIEDLICH)
SEIN   1106
    Mel.: Gott sei Dank / 14 st. / M. Müller (Knapp, Koch; DP 1718, F) /
    GGB 1720.

SIEHE, ICH GEFALL'NER KNECHT VOLLER BLUT UND SCHLÄGE   1107
    Mel.: Straf mich nicht / 12 st. / Gotter (Julian; DP 1718, F) / Tr.:
    Julian / KDP 1744.

SIEHE, MEIN GETREUER KNECHT, DER WIRD WEISLICH HANDELN   1108
    Mel.: Bleibe bei mir / 18 st. / Gerhard (GL; Knapp, Koch; DP 1718,
    F) / KDP 1764.

SINGET DEM HERREN EIN NEUES LIED, SINGE, DENN ER HAT WUNDER   1109
    Mel.: Grosser Prophete / 6 st. / Anon. (DP 1718, F, ZW) / KDP 1744.

SINGET DEM HERRN NAH UND FERN, RÜHMET IHN MIT FROHEM SCHALL   1110
    Mel.: e. M. / 9 st. / Herrnschmidt (Koch; DP 1718, F, ZW) / KDP 1744.

SINGT UNSERM GOTT EIN NEUES LIED, IHM, DER NUR WUNDER SCHAFFT   1111
  Mel.: Mein Gott, das Herz ich bringe dir / 2 st. / Anon. / ES1895.

SO FLIEHEN UNSRE TAGE HIN, AUCH DIESER IST NICHT MEHR   1112
  Mel.: C. M. / 9 st. / Anon. (PUL1785) / NS1870.

SO GEH DENN EIN ZU GOTTES RUH', DURCH TOD UND GRAB DEM HIMMEL ZU   1113
  Mel.: Ach bleib bei uns, Herr / 3 st. / Anon. (SAG1851) / ES1893.

SO GEHE NUN IN DEINE GRUFT, BIS JESUS CHRISTUS AUS DER LUFT   1114
  Mel.: Nun lasst uns den Leib / 4 st. / Anon. / KLS1826.

SO GEHST DU, JESU, WILLIGLICH, DEIN LEIDEN ANZUTRETEN   1115
  Mel.: e. M. / 6 st. / Schlegel (SGG; PUL1785) / KDP1797-G.

SO GRABET MICH NUN IMMERHIN, DA ICH SO LANG VERWAHRET BIN   1116
  Mel.: So gehe nun in deine Gruft / 4 st. / Anon. (F) / KLS1826.

SO IST NUN ABERMAL VON MEINER TAGEN ZAHL EIN TAG VERSTRICHEN   1117
  Mel.: Mein Jesu, der du mich / 10 st. / Freylinghausen (Knapp; F) /
  KDP1744.

SO JEMAND SPRICHT, ICH LIEBE GOTT, UND HASST DOCH SEINEN BRUDER   1118
  Mel.: Nun lobet alle Gottes Sohn / 3 st. / Gellert (GL; Knapp,
  Koch; GKW1841) / CG1874.

SO LASS DEIN BILD AUFGEHEN, WOVON WIR ABGEWANDT, UND UNSERN WILLEN   1119
  [Mel.: 125] / 1 st. / Anon. / NS1870.

SO SOLL ICH DANN NOCH MEHR AUSSTEHN, O JESU   1120
  Mel.: Unser Vater / 6 st. / Neander (GLU; DP1718) / GGB1720.

SO WIRST, DU, LIEBES HOLDES KIND, ZU UNSERM SCHMERZ BEGRABEN   1121
  Mel.: Mir nach, spricht Christus / 2 st. / Anon. (SAG1851) /
  CG1879.

SO ZART IST KEINE LIEBE, ALS CHRISTI LIEBE IST   1122
  Mel.: Zeuch ein zu deinen Toren / 3 st. / P. F. Hiller (GLK; Knapp)
  / CG1874.

SOLL ICH NACH DEINEM WILLEN, O GOTT, GEBÜCKET SEIN UND HIER MEIN MASS   1123
  Mel.: Von Gott will ich nicht / 13 st. / Anon. (DP1718, F) /
  KDP1744.

SOLL SICH MEIN GEIST, O GOTT, ZU DIR ERHEBEN UND DIE ZU KENNEN   1124
  Mel.: Herzliebster Jesu / 11 st. / Anon. / KDP1797-G.

SOLLT' ES GLEICH BISWEILEN SCHEINEN, ALS WENN GOTT VERLÄSST DIE   1125
  Mel.: Liebster Jesu, du wirst kommen / 10 st. / Tietze (Knapp,
  Koch, Kulp, Westphal; DP1718, F) / KDP1744.

SOLLTE MAN WOHL JESUM KENNEN UND SEIN GLIED UND JÜNGER SEIN   1126
  [Mel.: 35] / 4 st. / Anon. (EGS1821) / NS1870.

SO OFT EIN BLICK MICH AUFWÄRTS FÜHRET   1127
  Mel.: e. M. / 17 st. / Arnold (LF; Knapp, Koch; DP1718, F) /
  KDP1744.

SORGEN, FURCHT UND MANCHE PLAGEN SETZEN UNS IM LEBEN ZU   1128
  [Mel.: 35] / 5 st. / Anon. / NS1870.

SORGLOSER SÜNDER DU, ICH BITT DICH, KOMM, DIE WELT VERGEHT IM NU   1129
  Mel.: e. M. / 9 st. / W. Preiss, tr. (KPS) / KPS1858.

SPAR DEINE BUSSE NICHT VON EINEM JAHR ZUM ANDERN   1130
  Mel.: Nun danket alle Gott / 7 st. / J. F. Starck (Koch; NVG1806) /
  ELEL1812, CG1874.

STEH, ARMES KIND, WO EILST (WILLST) DU HIN? ERKENNE DEIN VERDERBEN   1131
  Mel.: Mir nach, spricht / 4 st. / Anon. (ANH1795) / KLS1826.

STIMMT UNSERM GOTT EIN LOBLIED AN MIT FREUDIGEM GEMÜTE   1132
  Mel.: Allein Gott in der Höh' / 7 st. / Anon. / KDP1797-G.

STREITER JESU WERDEN SIEGEN; MAN SIEHT JETZT SCHON IN DER WELT   1133
  [Mel.: 35] / 8 st. / Anon. (EGS1821) / NS1870.

SULAMITH, VERSÜSSTE WONNE, LICHTER GLANZ, ERHÖHTE SONNE   1134
     Mel.: O wie selig / 11 st. / Arnold (GGS; DP1718, ZW) / KDP1744.
SÜNDER, LERNT DAS BLUT ERKENNEN, DAS DAS LAMM VERGOSSEN HAT   1135
     [Mel.: 35] / 5 st. / Anon. / NS1870.
SÜNDER, LERNT DIE ORDNUNG FASSEN, DIE ZUM SELIGWERDEN FÜHRT   1136
     [Mel.: 35] / 5 st. / Anon. / NS1870.
SÜNDER, SÜNDER SELIG MACHEN, DAS IST MEINES JESU AMT   1137
     [Mel.: 35] / 4 st. / Anon. (Yoder; EGS1821) / NS1870.
SÜSSER CHRIST, DU, DU BIST MEINE WONNE   1138
     Mel.: e. M. / 8 st. / Sieber (Fischer, Koch) / ELEL1812.

TOCHTER VON ZION, STEH AUF VON BETRÜBNIS, STEH AUF   1139
     Mel.: e. M. / 3 st. / Ch.: Tochter von Zion, steh auf von
     Betrübnis / W. Preiss, tr. (KPS) / Or.: Daughter of Zion, awake
     from thy sadness, awake / KPS1858.
TOD, WIE BIST DU DURCHGEDRUNGEN DURCH DES ADAMS GLIEDER ALL'   1140
     Mel.: Schaffet, schaffet, meine Kinder / 8 st. / Anon. / KPS1858.
TOLLE MENSCHEN, SCHÄMT DOCH EUCH   1141
     Mel.: Gott sei Dank / 6 st. / P. F. Hiller (GLK) / CG1874.
TRAUERN, JESU, HAT UMGEBEN DEINER JÜNGER TREUES HERZ   1142
     Mel.: Zion klagt mit / 5 st. / Birken (Fischer; DP1718) / KDP1744.
TRAURIG MUSS MAN OFTMALS SEIN, TUT MAN ÜBERLEGEN   1143
     Mel.: Jesu, wahres Gottes-Lamm / 6 st. / Anon.: "Author's name
     withheld" (KPS) / KPS1858.
TRAUTSTER JESU, EHREN-KÖNIG, DU MEIN SCHATZ, MEIN BRÄUTIGAM   1144
     Mel.: Eins ist not, ach Herr, dies eine / 6 st. / T. S. Schröder
     (Kulp; Julian; DP1718, F, ZW) / KDP1744.
TREUER GOTT, ICH MUSS DIR KLAGEN MEINES HERZENS JAMMER-STAND   1145
     Mel.: Zion klagt / 12 st. / Heermann (Koch, Mützell; Julian;
     DP1718) / Tr.: Julian / KDP1744.
TREUER GOTT, WIE BIN ICH DIR JETZT UND EWIGLICH VERPFLICHTET   1146
     Mel.: Liebster Jesu, wir sind hier / 10 st. / Anon. / KDP1760.
TREUER VATER, DEINE LIEBE, SO AUS EINEM HEISSEN TRIEBE   1147
     Mel.: Ach, was soll ich Sünder machen / 23 st. / Gotter (Knapp,
     Koch; Julian; DP1718, F, ZW) / KDP1744.
TREULICH ZEIGET GOTTES SOHN, DASS DIE ZEIT VERBORGEN   1148
     Mel.: Straf mich nicht in deinem / 7 st. / Anon. (GG1700) /
     GGB1720.
TREUSTER MEISTER, DEINE WORTE SIND DIE RECHTE HIMMELS-PFORTE   1149
     Mel.: Liebster Jesu, du wirst kommen / 6 st. / Scheffler (HS;
     Knapp, Koch; DP1718, ZW) / KDP1744.
TRIUMPH, TRIUMPH, ES KOMMT MIT PRACHT DER SIEGES-FÜRST   1150
     Mel.: Wie schön ist unsres Königs Braut / 11 st. / B. Prätorius
     (Knapp, Koch, Kulp; DP1718, F, ZW) / KDP1744.
TRIUMPHIERE, GOTTES STADT, DIE SEIN SOHN ERBAUET HAT   1151
     [Mel.: 33] / 4 st. / Anon. (GGLR1828) / NS1870.
TUT MIR AUF DIE SCHÖNE PFORTE, FÜHRT IN GOTTES HAUS MICH EIN   1152
     [Mel.: 116] / 5 st. / Schmolck (Kulp; EGS1821) / NS1870.

ÜB IMMER TREU UND REDLICHKEIT BIS AN DEIN STILLES GRAB   1153
     Mel.: Mein Gott, das Herz / 6 st. / Hölty (G; Julian) / Tr.: Julian
     / ES1893.

ÜBER ALLE MENSCHENKINDER IST MEIN JESUS KLUG UND WEIS'   1154
    Mel.: O der alles hätt' verloren / 10 st. / Mack, Jr. (Heckman) /
    Tr.: Colonial, p. 585; Heckman.

ÜBERSCHLAG DIE KOST, SPRICHT JESUS CHRIST   1155
    Mel.: Mir nach, spricht Christus / 13 st. / Mack, Sr. (Ephrata
    Chronicle) / Tr.: Origins, p. 408 / GGB1720.

UM CHRISTUS SCHÄTZ ICH ALLES HIN UND HEISSE SONST NICHTS MEIN   1156
    Mel.: Mein Gott, das Herz ich / 9 st. / P. F. Hiller (GLK; Knapp)
    CG1874.

UNERSCHAFF'NE GOTTESLIEB', BRÄUTIGAM DER SEELEN   1157
    (Paraphrase of Arnold's Unerschaff'ne Gotteslieb')
    Mel.: Mache dich, mein Geist / 5 st. / Anon. (ANH1795) / KH1792.

UNSCHÄTZBARES EINFALTS-WESEN, PERLE, DIE ICH MIR ERLESEN   1158
    Mel.: Liebster Jesu, du wirst kommen / 9 st. / Anon. (DP1718, ZW) /
    KDP1744.

UNSER HERRSCHER, UNSER KÖNIG, UNSER ALLERHÖCHSTES GUT   1159
    Mel.: e. M. / 6 st. / Neander (GLU; Knapp, Koch; Julian; DP1718, F)
    / Tr.: Julian / GGB1720.

UNSER JOSEPH LEBET NOCH, DER WIRD UNS ERNÄHREN   1160
    (= st. 3 and 4 of 655)
    Mel.: Jesus, wahres Gottes-Lamm / 2 st. / Mack, Jr.? / ES1895.

UNSER LEBEN BALD VERSCHWINDET, ES VERGEHET WIE EIN TRAUM   1161
    Mel.: Zeuch mich / 5 st. / Anon. (DP1718) / KDP1744.

UNSER WANDEL IST IM HIMMEL, RICHTE DOCH DEIN HERZ DAHIN   1162
    Mel.: e. M. / 9 st. / Schwedler (Knapp, Koch; DP1718) / GGB1720.

UNSRE ZEIT IST KURZ UND BÜNDIG, DIE WIR NOCH AUF ERDEN SIND   1163
    Mel.: Alle Menschen müssen sterben / 5 st. / Anon. / CG1874.

UNTER JESU KREUZE STEH'N UND IN SEINE WUNDEN SEH'N   1164
    [Mel.: 33] / 8 st. / P. F. Hiller (GLK; Knapp, Koch) / NS1870.

UNTER LIEBEN MENSCHENKINDERN LIEBT MEIN JESUS FEST UND REIN   1165
    Mel.: Ringe recht / 10 st. / Mack, Jr. (Heckman) / Tr.: Colonial,
    p. 583; Heckman.

UNTER REICHEN MENSCHENKINDERN IST UND BLEIBT MEIN JESUS REICH   1166
    Mel.: Wo ist Jesus, mein Verlangen / 10 st. / Mack, Jr. (Heckman) /
    Tr.: Colonial, p. 588; Heckman.

UNTER SCHÖNEN MENSCHENKINDERN IST MEIN JESUS TAUSEND-SCHÖN   1167
    Mel.: Wo ist Jesus, mein Verlangen / 10 st. / Mack, Jr. (Heckman) /
    Tr.: Colonial, p. 582; Heckman.

UNVERFÄLSCHTES CHRISTENTUM, ACH WIE BIST DU DOCH SO SELTEN   1168
    Mel.: Liebster Jesu, wir sind / 9 st. / Anon. (DP1753, F) / KH1792.

VATER, DEIN WILL' SOLL GESCHEHEN UND DER MEINE SOLL NICHT SEIN   1169
    Mel.: O Durchbrecher / 4 st. / P. F. Hiller (GLK) / CG1874.

VERBORGENHEIT, WIE IST DEIN MEER SO BREIT   1170
    Mel.: Nur frisch hinein / 10 st. / Arnold (LF; Knapp; DP1718, ZW) /
    KPD1744.

VERBORG'NE GOTTESLIEBE, DU, O FRIEDENS-FÜRST   1171
    Mel.: Gott lob, ein Schritt / 10 st. / Tersteegen (GBG; Julian; ZW)
    / Tr.: Julian / KDP1744.

VERBORG'NER ABGRUND TIEFER LIEB', O LAUT'RE QUELL   1172
    Mel.: Kommt her zu mir, spricht / 3 st. / Anon. (DP1753) / KDP1764.

VEREINIGT ZUM GEBETE WAR EINST DEINER JÜNGER ERSTE SCHAR   1173
    Mel.: L. M. / 6 st. / Lavater (Julian; GGLR1828) / NS1870.

VERGISS MEIN NICHT, DASS ICH DEIN NICHT VERGESSE   1174
    Mel.: Wie wohl ist mir, dass / 6 st. / Arnold (Knapp, Koch; DP1718,
    F) / GGB1720.

VERLIEBTES LUSTSPIEL REINER SEELEN   1175
    Mel.: Die Tugend wird durchs Kreuz geübet / 11 st. / Arnold (EUL;
    Koch; DP1718, F) / GGB1720.

VERMEHRE STETS DES HERREN PREIS, O DU MEIN GEIST, MIT ALLEM FLEISS   1176
    Mel.: L. M. / 7 st. / Anon. (DGM1865) / NS1870.

VERSUCHET EUCH DOCH SELBST, OB IHR IM GLAUBEN STEHET   1177
    Mel.: Nun danket alle Gott mit / 12 st. / Breithaupt (Röbbelen);
    Breithaupt? (Kadelbach, Knapp); anon. (Koch, Nelle); (DP1718, F) /
    KDP1744.

VIELLEICHT IST DIES DAS LETZTE MAL, DASS WIR BEISAMMEN SEIN   1178
    Mel.: Mein Gott, das Herz / 4 st. / Anon. (EGS1821) / CG1874.

VON GOTT WILL ICH NICHT LASSEN, DENN ER LÄSST NICHT VON MIR   1179
    Mel.: e. M. / 9 st. / Helmbold (Knapp, Koch, Kulp; Julian; DP1718,
    F) / Tr.: Julian / GGB1720.

VON GRÖNLANDS EISGESTADEN, VON INDIENS PERLENSTRAND   1180
    Mel.: Befiehl du deine Wege und was dein / 4 st. / Anon. tr.
    (Knapp, Yoder; EGS1821) / Or.: Heber: From Greenland's icy
    mountains (Knapp; Julian, Yoder) / ES1893.

WACH AUF, DU GEIST DER TREUEN ZEUGEN   1181
    Mel.: Entfernet euch, ihr matten Kräfte / 15 st. / Francke (Koch,
    Kulp; DP1718, F) / GGB1720.

WACH AUF, MEIN HERZ, DIE NACHT IST HIN, DIE SONN' IST AUFGEGANGEN   1182
    Mel.: Mein Herzens-Jesu, meine Lust / 10 st. / Laurenti (Knapp,
    Koch, Kulp, Westphal; Julian; DP1718, F) / Tr.: Julian / KDP1744.

WACH AUF, MEIN HERZ UND SINGE DEM SCHÖPFER ALLER DINGE   1183
    Mel.: Nun lasst uns Gott, dem Herren / 10 st. / Gerhardt (GL;
    Knapp, Koch, Kulp; Julian; DP1718, F) / Tr.: Julian / KDP1744.

WACH AUF, MEIN HERZ UND SINGE NUN ZU DEINES JESU PREIS UND RUHM   1184
    Mel.: Ihr jungen Helden, aufgewacht / 7 st. / Anon. / KPS1858.

WACH AUF ZUM DANK, O MEIN GEMÜT UND PREISE GOTTES TUN   1185
    Mel.: C. M. / 3 st. / Anon. / NS1870.

WACHET AUF, RUFT UNS DIE STIMME DER WÄCHTER SEHR HOCH AUF DER ZINNE 1186
    Mel.: e. M. / 3 st. / Nicolai (Knapp, Koch, Kulp, Westphal; Julian;
    DP1718, F) / Tr.: Julian / GGB1720.

WACHT AUF, IHR CHRISTEN ALLE, ES IST NUN HOHE ZEIT, DIE STIMM' RUFT 1187
    Mel.: Herzlich tut mich verlangen / 10 st. / Anon. / GGB1720.

WACHT AUF, RUFT UNS DIE STIMME IN DIESER LETZTEN ZEIT, O BRAUT HÖR 1188
    Mel.: Wacht auf, ihr Christen alle / 12 st. / Anon. / GGB1720.

WALTE, WALTE NAH UND FERN, ALLGEWALT'GES WORT DES HERRN   1189
    [Mel.: 33] / 7 st. / Bahnmeier (Koch; Julian; EGS1850) / Tr.:
    Julian / NS1870.

WANN ERBLICK ICH DICH EINMAL, MEINE LIEBE? EILE BALD VON LIBANON   1190
    Mel.: Jesu, meines Herzens Freud', sei / 12 st. / Petersen (Farlee,
    DP1753; DP1718, F) / GGB1720.

WANN WILLST DU, MEINER SEELEN TROST, EIN WENIG MICH ERQUICKEN   1191
    Mel.: So wünsch ich eine / 12 st. / Anon. / KDP1744.

WANN WIRD DOCH MEIN JESUS KOMMEN IN DAS WILDE TRÄNEN-LAND   1192
    Mel.: Jesu, meines Lebens Leben; Jesu, der du meine Seele / 8 st. /
    Anon. (Fischer; F) / KDP1744.

WANN ... see also: WENN ...

WARUM BIST DU SO BETRÜBT, ARMES HERZ, DA GOTT DICH LIEBT   1193
    Mel.: P. M. / 5 st. / Anon. (DGM1865) / NS1870.
WARUM SOLL ICH MICH DENN GRÄMEN   1194
    Mel.: P. M. / 4 st. / Gerhardt (GL; Kulp, Röbbelen); Christian
    Cassel (Stoudt); / (DP1718, F) / NS1870.
WARUM WILLST DU DOCH FÜR MORGEN, ARMES HERZ, IMMERWÄRTS   1195
    Mel.: Warum sollt ich mich denn grämen; Fröhlich soll mein Herze /
    17 st. / Laurenti (Koch, Westphal; DP1718, F) / GGB1720.
WAS CHRISTI BOTEN LEHREN UND WAS SIE VON IHM HÖREN   1196
    Mel.: Nun ruhen alle Wälder / 15 st. / Anon. (DP1718, F) / KH1792.
WAS ERHEBT SICH DOCH DIE ERDE? WAS RÜHMT SICH DER WÜRMER SPEIS'   1197
    Mel.: Ei, was frag ich / 6 st. / Neander (GLU; DP1718) / KDP1744.
WAS FREUT MICH NOCH, WENN DU'S NICHT BIST   1198
    Mel.: O heil'ger Geist, kehr bei / 1 st. / P. F. Hiller (GLK;
    Knapp; Julian) / Tr.: Julian / CG1874.
WAS GIBST DU DENN, O MEINE SEELE, GOTT, DER DIR TÄGLICH ALLES GIBT   1199
    Mel.: Ach sagt mir nichts von Gold; Wer nur den lieben Gott / 4 st.
    / Lochner (Fischer; DP1718, F) / GGB1720.
WAS GOTT SAGT, DAS BLEIBT WAHR GESAGT   1200
    Mel.: Was Gott tut, das ist / 3 st. / P. F. Hiller (GLK) / CG1874.
WAS GOTT TUT, DAS IST WOHL GETAN   1201
    Mel.: e. M. / 6 st. / Rodigast (Knapp, Koch, Kulp, Westphal;
    Julian; DP1718, F) / Tr.: Julian / KDP1744.
WAS HAT UNS DOCH BEWOGEN, ZU GEHEN AUS VON HEIM   1202
    Mel.: Ermuntert euch, ihr Frommen, zeigt / 8 st. / H. Danner
    (Stoudt) / KLS1827.
WAS HERRLICHKEIT UND FREUDE, WENN ZIONS SCHÖNE SCHAR   1203
    Mel.: Kommt, Kinder, lasst uns gehen / 4 st. / Anon. / KPS1858.
WAS HIER DEM FLEISCH OFT BITTER SCHMECKT UND SEHR ZUWIDER IST   1204
    Mel.: Was mich auf dieser Welt betrübt / 4 st. / Anon. / GGB1720.
WAS ICH EUCH NUN SAGE HIER, NEHMT ES AN AUS LIEB' ZU MIR   1205
    Mel.: Jesu, komm doch selbst / 6 st. / W. Preiss (KPS) / KPS1858.
WAS IN DEM HIMMEL LEBET, WAS AUF DER ERDE SCHWEBET   1206
    Mel.: O Welt, sieh hier dein / 5 st. / P. F. Hiller (GLK) / CG1874.
WAS IST DAS LEBEN DIESER ZEIT? ICH SEHN MICH NACH DER EWIGKEIT   1207
    Mel.: Du unbegreiflich höchstes Gut / 8 st. / Naemi (Viehmeyer) /
    KH1792.
WAS IST DIE GEBÜHR DER CHRISTEN ANDERS ALS EIN ERNSTER STREIT   1208
    Mel.: Wie nach einer Wasserquelle / 5 st. / Anon. / KDP1764.
WAS IST DOCH DIESE ZEIT, WAS SIND DIE LEIDEN   1209
    Mel.: O Jesu, komm zu mir / 18 st. / B. E. Zeller (Koch; DP1718, F)
    / GGB1720.
WAS IST WOHL DAS, DAS REGET SICH IN MIR, IST'S DER TOD?   1210
    Mel.: All is well / 3 st. / Anon. tr. (Yoder; EGS1821) / CG1874.
WAS LOBES SOLLEN WIR DIR, O VATER, SINGEN   1211
    Mel.: Danket dem Herren, denn er ist / 12 st. / Anon. (Koch;
    DP1718, F) / GGB1720.
WAS MACHEN DOCH UND SINNEN WIR? ACH, DASS WIR MUNTER WACHTEN   1212
    Mel.: Was Gott tut, das ist wohlgetan / 6 st. / Anon. / GGB1720.
WAS MAG UNS VON JESU SCHEIDEN? WEDER LEIDEN, FALSCHE FREUDEN   1213
    Mel.: Auf, Triumph, es kommt die Stunde / 13 st. / Anon. / GGB1720.
WAS MICH AUF DIESER WELT BETRÜBT, DAS WÄHRET KURZE ZEIT   1214
    Mel.: e. M. / 4 st. / M. Franck (Koch) Schütz (Julian); (DP1718, F)
    / Tr.: Julian / GGB1720.

WAS SOLL ICH MICH MIT SORGEN PLAGEN, MEIN JESUS SORGET SELBST FÜR MICH 1215
    Mel.: Wer nur den lieben Gott / 8 st. / Schmolck (LS) / KDP1764.

WAS SOLL ICH WEITER SAGEN? O DU MEIN ARMES HERZ   1216
    (= st. 8, part VII of 1320)
    Mel.: e. M. / 1 st. / Mack, Jr. / KLS1829.

WAS VOR VIEL LOB UND LIEB'S-GETÖN' WIRD NOCH GEHÖRET WERDEN   1217
    [Mel.: 19] / 6 st. / J. Preiss (GAL) / GAL1753.

WEG, LUST, DU UNLUSTVOLLE SEUCH', DU PEST DER SEELEN   1218
    Mel.: Nun lasst uns den / 7 st. / Anon. (DP1718, F, ZW) / KDP1744.

WEG MIT ALLEM, WAS DA SCHEINET IRDISCH KLUG IN DIESER WELT   1219
    Mel.: Zeuch mich / 5 st. / Neander (GLU; Knapp, Koch; DP1718, F) /
    GGB1729.

WEIL CHRISTUS UNS ERSCHIENEN IST MIT SEINEM WORT UND LEBEN   1220
    Mel.: Aus tiefer Not / 8 st. / Anon. / GGB1720.

WEIL ICH NUN SEH DIE GÜLD'NEN WANGEN DER HIMMELSMORGENRÖTE   1221
    Mel.: Ach, Jesu, meiner Seelen Freude / 11 st. / Scheffler (HS;
    Koch; DP1718, F) / KDP1744.

WEISHEIT, O ALLER HIMMEL ZIER   1222
    (= 1029)
    Mel.: Mein Gott, das Herz / 3 st. / Tersteegen (GBG) / KDP1764.

WEIT FÜR ALLEN MENSCHENKINDERN IST MEIN JESUS FROMM UND TREU   1223
    Mel.: O der alles hätt' verloren / 10 st. / Mack, Jr. (Heckman) /
    Tr.: Colonial, p. 590; Heckman.

WELCH EINE SORG' UND FURCHT SOLL NICHT BEI CHRISTEN WACHEN   1224
    Mel.: O Gott, du frommer / 15 st. / Hedinger (Knapp, Koch; DP1718,
    F) / GGB1720.

WELCHE AUF DEN HERREN HOFFEN, SIND NOCH NIE UMSONST GELOFFEN   1225
    Mel.: Schmücke dich / 3 st. / P. F. Hiller (GLK) / CG1874.

WELT, HINWEG, ICH BIN DEIN MÜDE, ICH WILL NACH DEM HIMMEL ZU   1226
    Mel.: Alle Menschen müssen / 3 st. / Albinus (Fischer; DP1718) /
    CG1874.

WELT, PACKE DICH, ICH SEHNE MICH NUR NACH DEM HIMMEL   1227
    Mel.: e. M. / 15 st. / Sieber (Koch; DP1718, F) / GGB1720.

WEM DU, O JESU, NAH, DES HERZ MUSS BRENNEN   1228
    Mel.: Wer Jesum bei sich hat / 4 st. / P. F. Hiller (GL1840) /
    CG1874.

WENIG SIND, DIE GÖTTLICH LEBEN UND FÜR GOTTES ANGESICHT   1229
    Mel.: Gott des Himmels und der Erden / 10 st. / Anon. / KDP1760.

WENIG WAREN MEINE TAGE, DA ICH LEBTE IN DER ZEIT   1230
    Mel.: Abermal ein Tag / 2 st. / Anon. / CG1874.

WENN AN JESU ICH GEDENKE UND AUCH LENKE MEINE SINNEN DA HINAN   1231
    Mel.: Wenn an meinen Freund ich denke / 14 st. / Anon. / GGB1720.

WENN AN MEINEN FREUND ICH DENKE UND VERSENKE IN SEIN LEIDEN   1232
    Mel.: Wo ist meine Sonne blieben / 22 st. / Anon. / GGB1720.

WENN DEINE GNADEN OHNE ZAHL MEIN STAUNEND HERZ DURCHDENKT   1233
    Mel.: C. M. / 6 st. / Knapp, tr. (Knapp) / Or.: Addison (Knapp):
    When all Thy mercies, o my God, my rising soul surveys / NS1870.

WENN DIR DAS KREUZ DEIN HERZ DURCHBRICHT UND MANCHER SCHARFE DORN   1234
    Mel.: Da Jesus an dem Kreuze / 11 st. / Anon. (DP1718) / GGB1720.

WENN EIN GLÄUBIGER GEFALLEN, SO GIBT OFT DER SATAN EIN   1235
    Mel.: Gott des Himmels und der / 3 st. / P. F. Hiller (GLK) /
    CG1874.

WENN ENDLICH, EH' ES ZION MEINT, DIE SEHR GELIEBTE STUND' ERSCHEINT   1236
    Mel.: e. M. / 9 st. / Astmann (Koch; DP1718, F) / GGB1720.

WENN HEIL'GE WINDE WEHEN VOM THRON DER HERRLICHKEIT   1237
    [Mel.: 161] / 1 st. / Anon. (DGM1865) / NS1870.

WENN ICH BEI MIR ZU HAUSE BIN, SO ZIEHT MEIN HEILAND MEINEN SINN   1238
    Mel.: Herr Jesu Christ, meins Lebens / 3 st. / P. F. Hiller
    (Ehmann; Knapp) / CG1874.

WENN ICH ES RECHT BETRACHT UND SEHE TAG UND NACHT   1239
    Mel.: Ach treib aus meiner Seel' / 14 st. / Anon. / KDP1744.

WENN ICH IN ANGST UND NOT MEIN AUGEN HEB EMPOR   1240
    Mel.: e. M. / 8 st. / Kelpius (Fischer) / ELEL1788.

WENN ICH MIT GEISTLICHER HABE VERSEHEN, ALS MICH ALLEINIG VERLANGET   1241
    Mel.: Höchster Formierer / 25 st. / Anon. (ZW) / KDP1764.

WENN ICH, O SCHÖPFER, DEINE MACHT, DIE WEISHEIT DEINER WEGE   1242
    Mel.: Es ist gewisslich an / 6 st. / Gellert (GOL; Knapp, Koch) /
    KPS1858.

WENN JESU HIRTENSTAB UNS FÜHRT, EIN TIGER   1243
    Mel.: Brunn' alles Heils, dich / 2 st. / anon. Brethren (ESL1832)

WENN KLEINE HIMMELS-ERBEN IN IHRER UNSCHULD STERBEN   1244
    Mel.: Nun ruhen alle Wälder / 3 st. / Rothe (Knapp, Koch; SAZ1744)
    / KPS1858.

WENN MAN ALLHIER DER WELT IHR TUN BESCHÄMT IN KEUSCHEM LEBEN   1245
    Mel.: Es ist das Heil uns kommen her / 6 st. / Anon. / GGB1720.

WENN MEIN GEMÜT ERFÜLLET IST MIT KUMMER MANCHERLEI   1246
    Mel.: Mein Gott, das Herz ich / 2 st. / W. Preiss (KPS) / KPS1858.

WENN NACH DEM FRIEDENS-LAND WIR GEH'N UND CANAANS HÜGEL FERNE SEH'N   1247
    Mel.: e. M. / 3 st. / W. Preiss, tr. (KPS) / KPS1858.

WENN SICH DIE SONN' ERHEBET, DIE DIESES RUND BELEBET   1248
    Mel.: Nun ruhen alle / 9 st. / Tersteegen (GBG; Kulp) / KDP1764.

WENN UNS GOTT DAS HERZ BESICHTIGT UND DURCH SEINE GNADE ZÜCHTIGT   1249
    Mel.: Alles ist an Gottes / 4 st. / P. F. Hiller (GLK) / CG1874.

WENN UNSRE AUGEN SCHON SICH SCHLIESSEN, DA NOCH GEFAHR WACHT   1250
    Mel.: Wer nur den lieben Gott / 3 st. / Anon. (DP1740) / KDP1744.

WENN WIR DES HERREN WORT ALS HEILSBEGIERIG LIEBEN, SO FINDEN WIR   1251
    Mel.: Der Gnadenbrunn' fleusst / 1 st. / Anon. / CG1874.

WENN ... see also: WANN ...

WENNGLEICH AUS TIEFER MITTERNACHT GEWITTER UM MICH BLITZEN   1252
    Mel.: Nun freut euch, lieben / 4 st. / Anon. / KDP1797-G.

WENN'S DOCH ALLE SEELEN WÜSSTEN, JESU, DASS DU FREUNDLICH BIST   1253
    [Mel.: 35] / 3 st. / Sasse (Yoder; EGS1821) / NS1870.

WER AUSHARRT BIS ANS ENDE, WIRD ENDLICH SELIG SEIN   1254
    Mel.: Valet will ich dir / 4 st. / P. F. Hiller (GLK; Knapp;
    Julian) / Tr.: Julian / CG1874.

WER DA HAT, DEM GIBT MAN NOCH, DASS ER FÜLLE HABE   1255
    Mel.: Mache dich, mein Geist / 5 st. / P. F. Hiller (GLK; Knapp) /
    CG1874.

WER DIE WEISHEIT IHM ERKOREN UND DER TUGEND HAT GESCHWOREN   1256
    Mel.: Immer fröhlich / 7 st. / Dach (Bachmann; GG1700) / GGB1720.

WER EIN OHR HAT, HÖRE DIES: WAS DER GEIST SAGT, IST GEWISS   1257
    Mel.: Gott sei Dank in aller / 3 st. / P. F. Hiller (GLK) / CG1874.

WER HIER WILL FINDEN GOTTES REICH, DER WERDE EINEM KINDE GLEICH   1258
    Mel.: Ich hab mein Sach' Gott / 8 st. / Anon. / GGB1720.

WER IN DEM SCHUTZ DES HÖCHSTEN IST UND SICH GOTT TUT ERGEBEN   1259
    Mel.: Ach Gott, vom Himmel sieh darein; Mein Herzens-Jesu, meine /
    9 st. / Heyd (Koch; F) / GGB1720.

WER IST DER BRAUT DES LAMMES GLEICH? WER IST SO ARM UND WER SO REICH 1260
    [Mel.: 90] / 2 st. / Woltersdorf (Knapp; Julian) / CG1874.

WER IST WOHL WIE DU, JESU, SÜSSE RUH'   1261
    Mel.: Seelenbräutigam / 14 st. / Freylinghausen (Knapp, Koch,
    Nelle, Westphal; Julian; DP1718, F, ZW) / Tr.: Julian / KDP1744.

WER ISTS'S, HERR, DER IN DEINEM ZELT UND DER AUF ZION RUHT   1262
    Mel.: C. M. / 4 st. / Anon. (SEL1842) / NS1870.

WER JESUM BEI SICH HAT, KANN FESTE STEHEN   1263
    Mel.: e. M. / 6 st. / Connow (Fischer, Knapp, Koch) / KPS1858.

WER KANN DOCH DIE WÜRDE ZEIGEN, DIE DORT DENEN WERDEN SOLL   1264
    [Mel.: 35] 4 st. / Anon. (EGS1821) / NS1870.

WER NOCH DIE LÜSTE DIESER WELT FÜR STÄRKUNG DES GEMÜTES HÄLT   1265
    Mel.: L. M. / 7 st. / Anon. (DGM1865) / NS1870.

WER NUR DEN LIEBEN GOTT LÄSST WALTEN   1266
    [Mel.: 96] / 4 st. / Neumark (Knapp, Koch, Kulp, Röbbelen,
    Westphal; Julian; DP1718, F) / Tr.: Julian / NS1870.

WER NUR RECHT BEWEINET HAT SEIN VERDORB'NES WESEN   1266a
    (= st. 4 of 655)
    [Mel.: 64] / 2 st. / Mack, Jr.? / CG1874.

WER OHREN HAT ZU HÖREN, DER MERK, WAS ICH IHM SAG, MEIN CHRIST   1267
    Mel.: e. M. / 4 st. / Anon. / KLS1826.

WER PRÜFEN WILL, DER PRÜFE SICH, WIE IST MEIN WERK   1268
    Mel.: Herr Jesu Christ, mein's Lebens / 4 st. / P. F. Hiller (GLK;
    Knapp) / CG1874.

WER SEINEN JESUM RECHT WILL LIEBEN, DER ACHTET NICHT DER EITELKEIT   1269
    Mel.: Wer nur den lieben Gott / 5 st. / Anon. (Bachmann; GG1700) /
    GGB1720.

WER SICH DÜNKET LÄSST, ER STEHET, SEHE ZU, DASS ER NICHT FALL'   1270
    Mel.: O der alles hätt' verloren / 15 st. / Anon. (Fischer, Koch;
    DP1718, F, ZW) / KDP1744.

WER SICH IM GEIST BESCHNEIDET UND ALS EIN WAHRER CHRIST   1271
    Mel.: Wer Christum recht will / 9 st. / Laurenti (Koch; DP1718, F)
    / KDP1744.

WER SICH IN DIE WELT ZERSTREUET UND SICH NICHT IN JESU FREUET   1272
    Mel.: Sollt' es gleich / 6 st. / P. F. Hiller (GLK) / CG1874.

WER SIND DIE VOR GOTTES THRONE, JENE UNZÄLBARE SCHAR   1273
    Mel.: Gott des Himmels und der Erden / 5 st. / H. T. Schenk (Knapp,
    Koch; Julian; SAG1851) / Tr.: Julian / KSP1858.

WER ÜBERWINDET, SOLL VOM HOLZ GENIESSEN, DAS IN DEM PARADIESE   1274
    Mel.: Schönster Immanuel, Herzog / 14 st. / Sinold (Koch; DP1718,
    F, ZW) / KDP1744.

WER ÜBERWIND'T UND SEINEN LAUF MIT EHREN KANN VOLLENDEN   1275
    (= st. 7 and 9 of 98)
    Mel.: Mir nach, spricht Christus / 2 st. / Scheffler / CG1874.

WER, WAS UNS DIE BIBEL LEHRET, NICHT FÜR EINE FABEL ACHT'   1276
    [Mel.: 35] / 3 st. / Anon. (EGS1821) / NS1870.

WER WEISS, WIE NAHE MIR MEIN ENDE, DIE ZEIT GEHT HIN   1277
    Mel.: Wer nur den lieben Gott / 3 st. / Aemilie Juliane of
    Schwarzburg-Rudolstadt (Knapp, Koch, Westphal; Julian) / Tr.:
    Julian / KLS1826.

WER WILL MIT UNS NACH ZION GEH'N, WO CHRISTUS SELBST UNS WEID'T   1278
    Mel.: Mein Gott, das Herz ich / 8 st. / Ch.: O dort wird sein
    Freude, Freude Freude; alternate Ch.: O Himmel, süsser Himmel /
    Walter (Yoder; EGS1821) / Or. Ch.: O that will be joyful (Lorenz) /
    KPS1858.

WERDE MUNTER, MEIN GENÜTE UND IHR SINNE, GEHT HERFÜR   1279
    [Mel.: 192] / 4 st. / Rist (Fischer, Kulp; DP1718, F) / NS1870.

WIE BIST DU MIR SO INNIG GUT, MEIN HOHERPRIESTER DU   1280
    Mel.: Mein Gott, das Herz / 7 st. / Tersteegen (GBG; Knapp, Koch;
    Julian; ANH1795) / Tr.: Julian / KLS1826.

WIE BIST DU SO WUNDERBAR, GROSSER REGENTE   1281
    Mel.: Es glänzet der Christen / 7 st. / N. L. von Zinzendorf
    (Knapp, Koch; HGB1731) / KH1792.

WIE EIN VOGEL LIEBLICH SINGET IN DEM FELD UND GRÜNEN WALD   1282
    Mel.: Freu dich sehr, o meine Seele / 6 st. / Anon. (Knapp; Julian)
    / Tr.: Julian / KDP1760.

WIE EIN BLUM', O MENSCH, DU BIST, DIE SCHÖNE BLUM' VERGÄNGLICH IST   1283
    Mel.: Warum betrübst du dich / 9 st. / J. Preiss (GAL) / GAL1753.

WIE FLIEGT (FLEUCHT) DAHIN DER MENSCHEN ZEIT   1284
    Mel.: Ich hab mein Sach' / 7 st. / Neander (GLU; Knapp, Koch;
    Julian; DP1718, F, ZW) / Tr.: Julian / KDP1744.

WIE FREUET SICH MEIN GEIST UND HERZ IN DEM VERLIEBTEN   1285
    Mel.: Du unbegreiflich höchstes Gut / 11 st. / Jael (Viehmeyer) /
    KH1792.

WIE GÖTTLICH SIND DOCH JESU LEHREN, WIE ÜBERZEUGET SEINE MACHT   1286
    Mel.: Wer nur den lieben Gott / 7 st. / Spreng (Koch) / KDP1797-G.

WIE GROSS IST DOCH DIE GÜTE, WOVON DIE ERDE VOLL   1287
    Mel.: Von Gott will ich nicht lassen / 3 st. / P. F. Hiller
    (Ehmann) / CG1874.

WIE GROSS IST UNSRE SELIGKEIT, O GOTT, SCHON IN DER PRÜFUNGSZEIT   1288
    Mel.: Wie schön leuchtet / 5 st. / Anon. (PUL1785) / KDP1797-G.

WIE HOCHVERGNÜGT BIN ICH, WENN MICH DIE WELT ENTBLÖSSET   1289
    Mel.: O Gott, du frommer Gott / 3 st. / Anon. / KH1792.

WIE LANGE UND SCHWER WIRD DIE ZEIT, WENN JESUS NICHT LÄNGER IST HIER   1290
    Mel.: How tedious and tasteless the hour / 3 st. / Anon. tr.
    (Yoder; EGS1821) / Or.: Newton: How tedious and tasteless the hour
    (Julian) / CG1879.

WIE LANGE WILLST DU NOCH, DU STARKER GOTT, VERZIEHEN, ZU STEUREN   1291
    Mel.: Psalm 50 Lobwasser / 8 st. / Anon. / GGB1720.

WIE LIEBLICH SIND DORT OBEN DIE WOHNUNGEN, O GOTT   1292
    [Mel. 476] / 5 st. / Gesenius-Denicke (Fischer; F) / NS1870.

WIE MANNIGFALTIG SIND DIE GABEN, WODURCH UNS, HERR, DEIN WOHLTUN NÄHRT   1293
    Mel.: Wer nur den lieben Gott / 3 st. / Anon. (GGLR1828) / NS1870.

WIE PRÄCHTIG IST DER NAM'? BRÜDER, SINGT   1294
    Mel.: e. M. / 3 st. / Dreisbach, tr. (Yoder; EGS1821) / CG1874.

WIE SCHÖN IST UNSRES KÖNIGS BRAUT, WENN MAN SIE NUR VON FERNE SCHAUT   1295
    Mel.: Triumph, Triumph, es kommt / 14 st. / Arnold (LF; Knapp,
    Koch; Julian; DP1718, F) / Tr.: Julian / GGB1720.

WIE SELIG IST DAS VOLK DES HERRN, DAS GOTTES WORT HOCH EHRET   1296
    Mel.: e. M. / 5 st. / Woltersdorf (Knapp; Julian) / KLS1829.

WIE SICHER LEBT DER MENSCH, DER STAUB, SEIN LEBEN IST EIN   1297
    Mel.: Ihr jungen Helden, aufgewacht / 3 st. / Gellert (GOL; Julian;
    PUL1785) / Tr.: Julian / KPS1858.

WIE SOMMERS SCHÖN DIE BLUMEN BLÜH'N UND WIE DIE ROSEN PRACHTVOLL   1298
    Mel.: Herr Jesu Christ, dich zu / 4 st. / Anon. (ALS1871) / CG1879.

WIE SÜSS IST DEIN GEBOT, DU SÜSSER LIEBES-GOTT   1299
    Mel.: Herr Jesu, ewig's / 7 st. / Scheffler (HS; Koch) / KH1792.

WIE WICHTIG IST DOCH DER BERUF, DEN UNS DER HERR GEGEBEN   1300
    [Mel.: 129] / 3 st. / Diterich (Koch; NVG1806) / NS1870.

WIE WOHL IST MIR, O FREUND DER SEELEN, WENN ICH IN DEINER LIEBE RUH   1301
    Mel.: e. M. / 6 st. / Dessler (Knapp, Koch; Julian; DP1718, F) /
    GGB1720.

WIE WOHL IST MIR, WENN ICH AN DICH GEDENKE UND MEINE SEEL' IN DEINE   1302
    Mel.: Der Tag ist hin, mein Jesu / 6 st. / Sinold (Koch; DP1718, F,
    ZW) / KDP1744.

WIE WOHL IST MIR, WIE WOHL IST MIR, WENN UNSER GOTT IM GEISTE HIER   1303
    Mel.: Kommt her zu mir, spricht / 8 st. / Anon. / GGB1720.

WIEDERBRINGER ALLER DINGE, WIEDERBRINGER MEINER SEEL'   1304
    Mel.: O Durchbrecher aller Bande / 13 st. / Anon. / GGB1720.

WIEDERBRINGER DES VERLOR'NEN, HÖRE DOCH, WAS VON DIR HEISCHT   1305
    Mel.: Jauchzet all mit Macht / 4 st. / Anon. / KH1792.

WIEDERUM VON GOTTES GNADEN HABEN WIR DIE NACHT ERREICHT   1306
    Mel.: Gott des Himmels und der Erden / 2 st. / Anon. / NS1870.

WIEWOHL WIR GOTTES KINDER SIND, SO REDEN WIR DOCH WIE EIN KIND   1307
    Mel.: Herr Jesu Christ, meins Lebens / 8 st. / P. F. Hiller (GLK) /
    CG1874.

WILL ICH MICH DENN NICHT BEKEHREN? STERBEN MUSS ICH, STERBEN BALD   1308
    Mel.: Alle Menschen müssen sterben / 2 st. / Anon. / KPS1858.

WILLKOMM', VERKLÄRTER GOTTES-SOHN, DER IM TRIUMPH IST AUFERSTANDEN   1309
    Mel.: Preis, Lob, Ehr' / 10 st. / Tersteegen (GBG) / KDP1764.

WILLST DU DEN PILGRIMS-WEG EINGEHEN UND RUH' DER SEELEN FINDEN   1310
    Mel.: Ich dank dir schon durch / 35 st. / Arnold (LF) / Tr.:
    Origins, p. 411 / GGB1720.

WIR DANKEN DIR, DU GROSSER GOTT, DASS DU VON DEINEM THRONE   1311
    Mel.: Sei Lob und Ehr' dem / 4 st. / Anon. / KLS1826.

WIR DANKEN DIR, HERR JESU CHRIST, DU BRUNN' DER SELIGKEIT   1312
    Mel.: Nun sich der Tag geendet hat / 5 st. / Anon. / KH1792.

WIR DANKEN DIR, O TREUER GOTT, IN DIESER MORGENSTUND'   1313
    Mel.: Nun sich der Tag geendet hat / 3 st. / Anon. / NS1870.

WIR HABEN JESUM NICHT GESEHEN UND DENNOCH LIEBT IHN UNSER HERZ   1314
    Mel.: Wer weiss, wie nahe mir / 5 st. / P. F. Hiller (GLK; Knapp) /
    CG1874.

WIR KÖNNEN NICHT SELBST BETEN, DASS ER DIE PROBE HÄLT   1315
    Mel.: Valet will ich dir geben / 3 st. / P. F. Hiller (GLK) /
    CG1874.

WIR LOBEN DICH, O HERRE GOTT, DU VÄTERLICH GEMÜTE   1316
    Mel.: Allein Gott in der Höh' sei Ehr' / 5 st. / Anon. / GGB1720.

WIR SIND HERZLICH SCHÖN VERMAHNT, WIE UNS IST DER WEG GEBAHNT   1317
    Mel.: Jesu, komm doch selbst / 6 st. / Meyer (KPS) / KPS1858.

WIR SINGEN DIR, ERSTAND'NER HELD, TRIUMPH ZUR SIEGESMACHT   1318
    Mel.: C. M. / 5 st. / Orwig (EGS1821) / NS1870.

WIR SINGEN DIR, IMMANUEL, DU LEBENS-FÜRST UND GNADEN-QELL   1319
    Mel.: Erschienen ist der herrlich' Tag / 20 st. / Gerhardt (GL;
    Knapp, Koch; Julian; F) / Tr.: Julian / KDP1744.

WO BLEIBEN MEINE SINNEN, WIE TRÜB IST MEIN VERSTAND   1320
    Mel.: Ihr Sünder, kommt gegangen / 110 st. / Mack, Jr. (manuscript
    note by A. H. Cassel in KDP1744) / KDP1744.

WO FINDET DIE SEELE DIE HEIMAT DER RUH? WER DECKT SIE MIT SCHÜTZENDEN   1321
    (st. 4 = st. 1 of 127)
    [Mel.: 64] / 4 st. / Jörgens (Nelle) / NS1870.

WO GEHT DIE REISE HIN, O DU MEIN LIEBER WANDERSMANN   1322
    Mel.: e. M. / 18 st. / Anon. (ZSGL) / ELEL1812.

WO IST DER SCHÖNSTE, DEN ICH LIEBE, WO IST MEIN SEELENBRÄUTIGAM   1323
    Mel.: e. M. / 6 st. / Scheffler (HS; Koch; DP1718, F) / GGB1720.

WO IST DIE KIRCHE JESU DOCH? WO TRÄGT MAN FREUDIG CHRISTI JOCH   1324
    Mel.: e. M. / 4 st. / Anon. / KLS1829.

WO IST JESUS, MEIN VERLANGEN, MEIN GELIEBTER UND MEIN FREUND   1325
  Mel.: e. M. / 6 st. / Ludämilie Elisabeth of Schwarzburg-Rudolstadt
  (Knapp; EG1732) / ELEL1812, NS1870.

WO IST MEIN SCHÄFLEIN, DAS ICH LIEBE, DAS SICH SO WEIT VON MIR VERIRRT   1326
  Mel.: Wo ist der Schönste / 9 st. / J. P. Schultt (Koch; DP1718, F)
  / KDP1744.

WO IST MEINE SONNE BLIEBEN, DEREN LIEBEN MIR SO WOHL UND SANFTE TAT   1327
  Mel.: Hüter, wird / 12 st. / Richter (Koch; DP1718, F) / GGB1720.

WO IST WOHL EIN SÜSSER LEBEN AUF DER GANZEN WEITEN WELT   1328
  Mel.: e. M. / 11 st. / Arnold (LF; DP1718, ZW) / KDP1744.

WO KOMMST DU DANN HER, PILGER, SO BESCHWERT   1329
  Mel.: Seelenbräutigam / 13 st. / Stoll (GGG) / Tr.: BLT 19:4,
  p. 234 / GGG1806, CG1874.

WO MEIN SCHATZ LIEGT, IST MEIN HERZE, WAS ICH LIEB, DA LEBE ICH   1330
  Mel.: Jesu, meines Lebens Leben / 9 st. / Arnold (GGS; Koch;
  DP1718, F, ZW) / KDP1744.

WO SOLL ICH FLIEHEN HIN, WEIL ICH BESCHWERET BIN   1331
  Mel.: Auf meinen lieben Gott / 11 st. / Heermann (Knapp, Koch,
  Mützell, Nelle, Westphal; Julian; DP1718, F) / KDP1744.

WO SOLL ICH HIN, WER HILFET MIR, WER FÜHRET MICH ZUM LEBEN   1332
  Mel.: Aus tiefer Not / 5 st. / Neander (GLU; Koch; Julian; DP1718,
  F) / Tr.: Julian / KDP1744.

WO SOLL ICH MICH HINWENDEN IN DIESEM JAMMERTAL   1333
  Mel.: Ach Herr / 11 st. / Frentzel (Fischer; DP1718) / KDP1744.

WOHL DEM, DER SICH MIT FLEISS BEMÜHET, DASS ER EIN STREITER   1334
  Mel.: Wer nur den lieben Gott / 11 st. / Wolff (Knapp, Koch;
  Julian; DP1718, F, ZW) / KH1792.

WOHL DEM MENSCHEN, DER NICHT WANDELT IN GOTTLOSER LEUTE RAT   1335
  Mel.: Werde munter, mein Gemüte / 4 st. / Gerhardt (GL; Knapp,
  Koch; DO1718, F, ZW) / KDP1744.

WOHL, JA EWIG WOHL IST DENEN, DIE IN UNSCHULD LEBEN GERN   1336
  Mel.: Ringe recht / 80 st. / Mack, Jr. (Heckman) / Tr.: Heckman.

WOHLAUF, MEIN' SEEL', WOHLAUF, WIRF ALLE FURCHT BEISEIT'   1337
  Mel.: P. M. / 5 st. / Anon. / NS1870.

WOHLAUF, ZUM RECHTEN WEINSTOCK HER, WOHLAUF, UND BRINGET IHM DIE EHR'   1338
  Mel.: Wie schön ist unsres Königs Braut / 15 st. / Gruber (Farlee;
  DP1718, ZW) / KDP1744.

WOMIT GLEICHT SICH DAS HIMMELREICH? IST ES NICHT DEM HAUSVATER GLEICH   1339
  Mel.: Wie schön leucht' / 2 st. / Anon. / CG1874.

WOMIT SOLL(T) ICH DICH WOHL LOBEN, MÄCHTIGER HERR ZEBAOTH   1340
  Mel.: Jesu, meines Lebens Leben / 14 st. / Gotter (Knapp, Koch,
  Westphal; Julian; DP1718, F) / Tr.: Julian / GGB1720.

WUNDERBARER KÖNIG, HERRSCHER VON UNS ALLEN   1341
  Mel.: e. M. / 4 st. / Neander (GLU; Koch, Kulp; DP1718, F) /
  GGB1720.

ZERFLIESS, MEIN GEIST, IN JESU BLUT UND WUNDEN UND TRINK   1342
  Mel.: O finstre Nacht / 12 st. / Anon. (DP1718, F, ZW) / KDP1744.

ZEUCH DURCH DEINES TODES KRÄFTE MICH IN DEINEN TOD HINEIN   1343
  (= st. 10-13 of 1100)
  [Mel.: 136] / 4 st. / Tersteegen / NS1870.

ZEUCH, JESU, MICH SO INNIGLICH, WIE DU BIST AUFGEFLOGEN   1344
  Mel.: Ach Gott und Herr / 7 st. / Anon. / KH1792.

ZEUCH MEINEN GEIST, TRIFF MEINE SINNEN, DU HIMMELS-LICHT   1345
    Mel.: e. M. / 16 st. / Knorr von Rosenroth (Koch; DP1718, F) /
    GGB1720.

ZEUCH MICH, O JESU, GANZ NACH DIR, SO FOLG ICH GERN, SO LAUFEN WIR   1346
    Mel.: C. M. [i.e., L. M.] / 5 st. / Anon. (Knapp) / NS1870.

ZEUCH MICH, ZEUCH MICH MIT DEN ARMEN DEINER GROSSEN FREUNDLICHKEIT   1347
    Mel.: Komm, o komm, du / 6 st. / Neander (GLU; Koch; DP1718, F) /
    GGB1720.

ZEUCH UNS NACH DIR, SO KOMMEN WIR MIT HERZLICHEM VERLANGEN   1348
    Mel.: Ach Gott und Herr / 5 st. / Funcke (Fischer, Kulp; Julian;
    DP1718, F, ZW) / Tr.: Julian / KDP1744.

ZION, BRICH HERFÜR JETZT DURCH TOR UND TÜR, LASS NICHT DEINEN LAUF   1349
    Mel.: Seelenbräutigam / 25 st. / Anon. / GGB1720.

ZION FEST GEGRÜNDET STEHET WOHL AUF DEM HEILIGEN BERGE   1350
    Mel.: Wachet auf, ruft uns die / 3 st. / Anon. (DP1718) / KDP1744.

ZION KLAGT MIT ANGST UND SCHMERZEN, ZION, GOTTES WERTE STADT   1351
    Mel.: Freu dich sehr, o meine / 6 st. / Heermann (Fischer, Knapp,
    Koch, Kulp, Mützell; Julian; DP1718, F) / Tr.: Julian / KDP1744.

ZION SOLL BILLIG FREUDIG SEIN, WEIL GOTTES WAHRHEIT BRICHT HEREIN   1352
    Mel.: Wie schön leuchtet der Morgenstern / 5 st. / Anon. / GGB1720.

ZION, ZION, DU GELIEBTE UND VON HERZEN OFT BETRÜBTE   1353
    Mel.: Auf, Triumph, es kommt die Stunde / 13 st. / Anon. / GGB1720.

ZIONS HOFFNUNG KOMMET, SIE IST NICHT MEHR FERNE   1354
    Mel.: Wunderbarer König / 5 st. / Anon. (DP1718, F, ZW) / KDP1744.

ZU DEINEM FELS UND GROSSEN RETTER HINAUF, HINAUF   1355
    Mel.: Psalm 140 Lobwasser / 6 st. / Neander (GLU; DP1718, ZW) /
    KDP1744.

ZU DEINEM PREIS UND RUHM ERWACHT, BRING ICH DIR RUHM UND PREIS   1356
    Mel.: C. M. / 4 st. / Anon. (NVG1799) / NS1870.

ZU DIR ICH MEIN HERZ ERHEBE UND, HERR, MEINE HOFFNUNG RICHT'   1357
    Mel.: e. M.; Psalm 25 Lobwasser / 10 st. / Lobwasser (PD1710) /
    KDP1744.

ZU DIR VON HERZENSGRUNDE RUF ICH AUS TIEFER NOT   1358
    Mel.: e. M.; Psalm 130 Lobwasser / 4 st. / Lobwasser (PD1710; Koch)
    / KDP1744.

ZU GOTT IN DEM HIMMEL DROBEN MEINE STIMM' ICH HAB ERHOBEN   1359
    Mel.: e. M. / 11 st. / Lobwasser (PD1710) / KDP1744.

ZU WACHEN LEHRT UNS GOTTES SOHN, GERECHT ZU LEBEN FÜR SEI'M THRON   1360
    Mel.: Wie schön leuchtet der Morgenstern / 4 st. / Anon. / GGB1720.

ZULETZT, WENN WIR EINST ZUM ZIELE GELANGEN, WERDEN WIR JESUM OHN' ENDE 1361
    Mel.: Ehre sei jetzo mit Freuden gesungen / 9 st. / Anon. / GGB1720.

ZUM NACH-DENK' WILL DEN MEINEN HIER DEN RAT NUN GEBEN FÜR UND FÜR   1362
    Mel.: Wie schön leuchtet der Morgenstern / 4 st. / Anon. / GGB1720.

ZUR FRIEDENSSTADT, NACH GOTTES WORT UND RAT, DEN ENGEN PFAD NACH SALEM 1363
    Mel.: Nur frisch hinein / 12 st. / Anon. / GGB1720.

APPENDIX X

Publishing Record of Hymns

This index shows in what hymnals the individual hymns listed in the First-Line Index were published. The hymns are listed by their index numbers. Specific reference is made to the six hymnals, Geistreiches Gesang-Buch, Das Kleine Davidische Psalterspiel, Die Kleine Lieder Sammlung, Neue Sammlung, Christliches Gesang-Buch, and Eine Sammlung and the two supplementary hymnals, Die Kleine Harfe and Die kleine Perlen Sammlung. These hymnals are referred to by the abbreviations used throughout the appendixes. In the last column (XXX) publication in occasional hymn-collections and other publications is indicated.

This table should be read as follows. Publication in hymnals with single editions and other collections is noted by a check-mark (x). In hymnals with more than one edition, "all" indicates publication in all editions listed in the bibliography; "year of publication" indicates publication in that particular edition only; "year of publication +" indicates first publication in that edition and in some or all subsequent editions. Asterisks next to the index numbers indicate core hymns (Kernlieder) published in all the editions of the main hymnals.

Number	GGB	KDP	KH	KLS	KPS	NS	CG	ES	XXX
1		all		all		x	all	all	
2							1874		
3	x	all							
4	x								
5					x				
6							all		x
7					x		1879		
8		all							
9									x
10							all		
11							all		
12		all							
13	x	all							
14					x				
15		all							
16						x	all	all	
17								all	
18		all							
19					x				
20							1879	1893+	
21						x		all	
22				1827+					
23	x	all							
24	x								
25							all	all	

Number	GGB	KDP	KH	KLS	KPS	NS	CG	ES	XXX
26			all	all		x		all	
27		all							
28		all		all					
29		1764+							
30									x
31						x		all	
32	x								
33		all							
34	x	all		1829+			all	all	
35				all					
36	x	all		1829+					
37					x				
38		all				x	all	all	
39	x								
40	x	all							
41		all							
42					x				x
43		all							
44		all							
45		all							
46							all		
47		all							
48		all							
49		all							
50					x				
51		all		all					
52		all							
53		all							
54	x	all							
55		all					1874		
56	x	all							
57							all		
58						x			
59		all							
60	x	all							
61	x	all		all		x			
62							all	all	
63							all		
64				1827+					x
65				1827	x		all		
66							all		x
67									x
68	x	all							
69			all						
70					x				
71						x		all	
72						x			
73		all							
74							all	all	
75				all		x	all	all	
76*	x	all		all		x	all	all	
77		all							
78		all							

Number	GGB	KDP	KH	KLS	KPS	NS	CG	ES	XXX
79	x								
80						x			
81									x
82		all							
83	x	all							
84							all		
85						x			
86		all		all					
87							1874		
88							all		
89		1797-G							
90									x
91							all	all	
92					x	x	1879	all	
93					x				
94		all							
95	x								
96							all	all	
97						x			
98*	x	all		all		x	all	all	
99							1874		
100						x			
101		all							
102				1834+				all	x
103		all							
104	x	all							
105		all							
106							all	all	
107									x
108	x	all							
109							all	all	
110		all		all					
111		all		all		x	all	all	
112		all							
113		all							
114							all	all	
115		all							
116						x		all	
117	x	all		all		x			
118									x
119							1874		
120						x	all	all	
121			all						
122	x	all							
123		1764+							
124		all		1826+					
125						x		all	
126				all		x	all	all	
127						x	all	all	
128				1841-O+		x			
129	x								
130		1760+		all		x			
131									x

Number	GGB	KDP	KH	KLS	KPS	NS	CG	ES	XXX
132						x		all	
133		all							
134		all							
135*	x	all		all		x	all	all	
136		all							
137							all	all	
138								all	
139						x		all	
140		all		1829+		x	all	all	
141		all		all		x		all	
142					x				
143		all							
144				1841-O+					
145		all							
146		all							
147							all	all	
148		1764+		all		x	all	all	
149		all							
150						x		all	
151		all							
152			all						
153			all						
154			all				1879	all	
155							all		
156		all							
157		all							
158	x								
159							all		
160									x
161						x		all	
162		all							
163						x	all	all	
164				1829+					
165		all		all					
166		all							
167							1879		
168						x		all	
169							all		
170						x			
171							all	all	
172								all	
173						x			
174							1874		
175							1879		
176			all						
177					x				
178	x								
179*	x	all		all		x	all	all	
180	x	all							
181									x
182							all	all	
183		1797-G							
184		all							

Number	GGB	KDP	KH	KLS	KPS	NS	CG	ES	XXX
185	x	all							
186							1874		
187						x		all	
188								all	
189		all							
190							all		
191		1797-G		all			all	all	
192	x	all							
193		all							
194								1893+	
195							all		
196	x	all							
197					x		all	all	
198		1797-G	all	1834+		x	all	all	
199		1764+		all					
200	x	1764+							
201	x	all							
202			all						
203		all		all		x		all	
204								all	
205						x		all	
206	x	all		all			all	all	
207						x			
208						x	all	all	
209							all		
210							1874		
211							all	all	
212						x		all	
213						x			
214						x		all	
215					x		all		
216							all		
217		1797-G							
218						x			
219			all						
220		all							
221				1841-O+					
222				1841-O					
223						x			
224							all		
225			all	all		x		all	
226		all					1874		
227		all							
228									x
229							1874		
230							1874		
231		1764+							
232		all							
233						x		all	
234	x								
235									x
236	x	all		all			all	all	
237		all		all		x	all	all	

Number	GGB	KDP	KH	KLS	KPS	NS	CG	ES	XXX
238	x								
239	x								
240					x				
241					x				
242		all							
243							1874		
244							1874		
245						x			
246							all		
247		all							
248									x
249							1874		
250									x
251		1764+		all		x	all	1895+	
252				1844+		x			
253				1844+					
254						x		all	
255		all							
256						x			
257							1874		
258	x	all							
259	x	all							
260		all							
261	x	all							
262							1879	all	
263		all						1895	
264		all		all			all	all	
265				1841-O+					
266			all						
267		all		all		x	all	all	
268		all		all		x			
269	x	all							
270							all	all	
271							1874		
272				1844+					
273							all	all	
274	x								
275				1829+			all		
276	x								
277		all							
278	x	all							
279		all							
280		1797-G				x	all	all	
281				1841-O+					
282						x	1879	all	
283				1829+		x			
284	x								
285		all							
286		all							
287						x	all	all	
288					x				
289					x		all	all	
290							all		

236

Number	GGB	KDP	KH	KLS	KPS	NS	CG	ES	XXX
291			all	1829+		x	all	all	
292		1764+							
293	x								
294			all						
295		all							
296		1797-G							
297	x								
298		all							
299		1764+							
300	x	all							
301		all							
302	x								
303		all							
304		all							
305		all							
306	x	all		all			all	all	
307			all						
308		all							
309						x			
310	x	all							
311							1879	all	
312									x
313					x				
314	x	all					all		
315		all							
316	x	all							
317		all							
318						x			
319						x		all	
320		all							
321		all							
322		1797-G							
323							all		
324							all	all	
325						x		all	
326		all							
327							1874		
328									x
329							all	all	
330							all		
331			all			x	all	all	
332	x	all							
333					x				
334							all		
335		1764+		all		x	all	all	
336		all							
337									x
338	x	all							
339	x	all							
340							all	all	
341						x			
342			all						
343				1829+		x			

237

Number	GGB	KDP	KH	KLS	KPS	NS	CG	ES	XXX
344						x		all	
345	x	all		1829+		x	all	all	
346						x		all	
347	x	all							
348*	x	all		all		x	all	all	
349		all				x		all	
350		all							
351		1760+							
352	x	all							
353						x		all	
354		all							
355	x	all					all		
356		all							
357	x	all							
358						x		all	
359	x								
360	x	all				x	all	all	
361	x								
362		all							
363						x		all	
364								all	
365					x		all		
366	x	all							
367		all							
368						x			
369	x	all		1829+		x	all	all	
370									x
371	x	all							
372		all							
373				1841-O+		x			
374				all		x	all	all	
375	x	all							
376							all	all	
377	x	all							
378		1797-G							
379	x	all							
380									x
381		1744							
382		1760+		all		x			
383		all							
384								all	
385							1874		
386	x	all							
387		all							
388		all							
389							1874		
390		all							
391									x
392							all	all	
393				all		x	all	all	x
394						x			
395						x			
396		all							

238

Number	GGB	KDP	KH	KLS	KPS	NS	CG	ES	XXX
397		all							
398		all							
399		1760+							
400				all		x	all	all	
401						x			
402						x			
403	x	all							
404								1895	
405		1744							
406		all							
407		1764+		all		x		all	
408		1760+							
409		1760+							
410		1760+							
411						x		all	
412	x	all							
413									x
414		all							
415				1841-O+		x			
416						x		all	
417		all		all		x	all	all	
418		all							
419						x	all	all	
420							all		
421					x				
422						x			
423					x		all		
424							all	all	
425							1879		
426							1874		
427							1874		
428		all							
429		1764+							
430		all							
431	x	all							
432		1760+							
433				all			all	all	
434		all					all	all	
435		all							
436								all	
437								all	
438		1797-G	all	all		x	all	all	
439	x	all					all	all	
440							1874		
441				all			all	all	
442							all	all	
443				1834+			all	all	
444	x	all							
445	x	all		all					
446							all		
447							1874		
448		1764+							
449							1874		

239

Number	GGB	KDP	KH	KLS	KPS	NS	CG	ES	XXX
450				all		x	all	all	
451		1764+		1827		x	all	all	
452		all							
453									x
454		1760+							
455		all							
456	x	all							
457						x		all	
458	x	all							
459							all	all	
460		all		all			all	all	
461		all							
462			all	all		x	all	all	
463*	x	all		all		x	all	all	
464	x	all		all					
465	x	all							
466								all	
467	x	all							
468		all		all		x	all	all	
469						x		all	
470			all			x			
471	x	all							
472					x		all	all	
473						x		all	
474	x	all		all					
475							1874		
476		all							
477				1841-0+		x		all	
478								all	
479		all							
480				all		x		all	
481						x			
482							all		
483						x			
484		all		all		x	all	all	
485		all							
486		all		all		x	all	all	
487	x	all							
488		all							
489						x			
490		all							
491	x	all		all		x	all		
492				all					
493				1841-0+		x		all	
494		all							
495		1797-G							
496	x	all							
497									x
498	x	all							
499							1874		
500						x		all	
501		all		all		x			
502	x	all							

Number	GGB	KDP	KH	KLS	KPS	NS	CG	ES	XXX
503		all							
504									x
505							all	all	
506	x	all		all					
507							all	all	
508					x				
509							all	all	
510							all		
511		all							
512		all				x		all	
513					x				
514	x	all							
515	x	all							
516	x	all							
517	x	all		all		x			
518		1760+							
519						x		all	
520			all						
521									x
522	x	all							
523		all							
524							1879		
525					x				
526						x			
527								all	
528									x
529							1879		
530							all		
531						x	all	all	
532						x		all	
533		1764+							
534					x				
535	x	all							
536	x								
537							all	all	
538	x								
539	x	all							
540						x			
541		all							
542						x		all	
543		all							
544	x	all							
545		all							
546						x		all	
547							all	all	
548			all						
549			all						
550							all	all	
551	x								
552	x	all							
553	x								
554		all							
555	x								

Number	GGB	KDP	KH	KLS	KPS	NS	CG	ES	XXX
556							all	all	
557		1797-G					all	all	
558		all							
559	x								
560								all	
561	x								
562	x								
563							all	all	
564		all							
565	x	all							
566							all	all	
567									x
568	x	all					all		
569		all							
570	x	all							
571	x	all							
572	x								
573		all							
574						x		all	
575							all	all	
576					x				
577					x		all	all	
578					x		all	all	x
579							all		
580						x	all	all	
581							all	all	
582	x								
583									x
584							all	all	
585									x
586	x								
587	x	all							
588	x	all							
589	x	all							
590		all							
591		all		all		x	all	all	
592									x
593		all							
594							all	all	
595		all		all		x	all	all	
596							all		
597	x								
598		all							
599				all		x	all	all	
600		all							
601					x				
602*	x	all		all		x	all	all	
603							all		
604	x								
605	x	all							
606	x	all							
607	x	all					all	all	
608	x	all							

242

Number	GGB	KDP	KH	KLS	KPS	NS	CG	ES	XXX
609					x				
610	x								
611	x								
612		all		all	x				
613	x								
614									x
615	x								
616					x				
617						x			
618							all		x
619		all							
620							all		
621		all							
622	x								
623	x								
624							1874		
625							all	all	
626					x				
627							1874		
628						x			
629			all						
630					x		1879		
631									x
632					x	x	all	all	x
633							1874		
634		all						all	
635	x	all							
636									x
637									x
638						x	all	all	
639	x								
640						x		all	
641			all						
642						x	all	all	
643		all							
644			all	all					
645		1764+							
646	x								
647	x	all							
648					x				
649								all	
650	x	all							
651			all	all			all	all	
652						x		1893+	
653					x				
654									x
655						x	all	all	
656		all		all		x	all	1895+	
657									x
658		all							
659	x	all							
660		all							
661	x								

Number	GGB	KDP	KH	KLS	KPS	NS	CG	ES	XXX
662		all		all			all		
663		all		1841-O+		x			
664				1844+		x	all		
665		all							
666									x
667	x								
668	x	all							
669									x
670		1760+		all		x	all	all	
671		all		1841-O+		x	all	all	
672	x	all							
673					x		all	all	
674		all							
675	x	all		1829					
676					x				
677	x	all							
678	x	all		1829		x	all	all	
679		all							
680		all							
681		all		all		x		all	
682			all						
683		1744+		all		x		all	
684						x			
685						x	all	all	
686		all							
687									x
688		all		all		x	all	all	
689		all							
690		all							
691						x	all	all	
692							1879		
693		all							
694							1874		
695			all	1834+					
696	x								
697							1874		
698	x	all		all		x		all	
699		all							
700	x	all							
701									x
702		all							
703									x
704					x				
705		all							
706							all		
707						x			
708			all						
709							1874		
710		1764+		1829+		x	all	all	
711						x		all	
712					x		all	all	
713							all		
714							all		

Number	GGB	KDP	KH	KLS	KPS	NS	CG	ES	XXX
715		all							
716							all	all	
717							1874		
718			all						
719							all		
720						x		all	
721		all							
722		all							
723							1874		
724	x	all		all					
725					x		all		
726					x		all		
727	x	all							
728						x		all	
729						x	all	all	
730		all							
731						x			
732*	x	all		all		x	all	all	
733						x			
734		all		all		x	all	all	
735		all							
736						x			
737				1829+					
738						x			
739						x			
740						x	all	all	
741		all		1829+					
742						x		all	
743									x
744	x	all							
745						x		all	
746							all	all	
747		all							
748							all	all	
749						x			
750						x	all	all	
751		1764+		all		x	all	1893+	
752	x	all							
753	x	all							
754							all		
755						x			
756							1874		
757*	x	all		all		x	all	all	
758		1797-G							
759			all						
760					x		all	all	
761							all	all	
762							1874		
763							all		
764						x			
765		all							
766									x
767		all							

Number	GGB	KDP	KH	KLS	KPS	NS	CG	ES	XXX
768							1874		
769	x	all		all					
770								all	
771							all	all	
772							1874		
773		all							
774							1874		
775		all					all		
776					x		all	all	
777						x			
778	x	all		all		x		all	
779				1841-O+					
780							all		
781					x		all	all	
782					x		all		
783		all							
784			all						
785		all							
786				all					
787		all		all			all	all	
788	x	all							
789		all							
790									x
791	x	all							
792	x	all		all			all		
793		all							
794	x	all							
795	x	all		all			all	all	
796		all							
797	x	all							
798	x	all					all	all	
799									x
800		all							
801		all							
802		all							
803*	x	all		all		x	all	all	
804	x								
805	x	all							
806	x	all					all		
807							all		
808		1744+							
809		all							
810		1797-G							
811	x								
812	x	all							
813			all						
814							all	all	
815		all							
816		all		all		x	all	all	
817								all	
818						x		all	
819								all	
820							all		

Number	GGB	KDP	KH	KLS	KPS	NS	CG	ES	XXX
821							1874		
822		all							
823								all	
824							1874		
825								all	
826				1829+					
827		1777+		all					
828						x			
829	x	all							
830			all						
831			all	1829+		x			
832							1874		
833							1874		
834		all							
835	x								
836	x	all							
837				all					
838	x	all							
839		all							
840		all							
841	x								
842		all					all		
843					x				
844		all							
845		all							
846					x		all	all	
847							all	all	
848					x				
849		all							
850		all							x
851							all	all	
852	x	all							
853		all							
854	x	all		all					
855	x	all		all		x	all		
856						x		all	
857	x	all		all		x			
858	x	all							
859		all							
860									x
861					x				
862	x								
863	x								
864	x	all							
865	x	all					all	all	
866		all							
867	x	all					all	all	
868	x	all		all					
869	x	all							
870	x	all							
871				all		x	all	all	
872		all							
873						x			

Number	GGB	KDP	KH	KLS	KPS	NS	CG	ES	XXX
874				all		x	all	all	
875						x	all	all	
876*	x	all		all		x	all	all	
877						x		all	
878						x	all	all	
879		1797-G							
880						x		all	
881		all		1829+					
882		all							
883								all	
884							all	all	
885		all							
886							1874		
887							1879	all	
888		all							
889						x			
890							1874		
891							all	all	
892						x		all	
893		all							
894		1797-G							
895						x			
896						x			
897	x	all							
898			all	1829+		x	all	all	
899				1827+		x	all	all	
900		all					1879	all	
901		all							
902			all						
903							all		
904				all			all	all	
905	x	all							
906								all	
907	x	all							
908			all						
909		all							
910					x				
911				1829+					
912				all		x	all	all	
913							all	all	
914							all	all	
915	x								
916				all			all		
917				1826+		x		1893+	
918	x	all							
919		1760+		all		x	all	all	
920		1744+							
921								all	
922							all	all	
923		1791+		all			all		
924		all							
925				1826+		x	all	all	
926		all							

Number	GGB	KDP	KH	KLS	KPS	NS	CG	ES	XXX
927	x	all		1826+		x	all	all	
928		all		1826+		x	all	all	
929				1844-O+		x		all	
930	x	all							
931	x	all							
932	x	all							
933			all						
934									x
935		all							
936	x	all							
937		1797-G							
938						x		all	
939									x
940						x			
941						x			
942							1879	all	
943	x	all							
944						x			
945						x		all	
946				1841-O					
947	x	all							
948		1744+							
949		all							
950									x
951	x	all							
952					x				
953								all	
954		all							
955								all	
956							all		
957		all							
958								all	
959							all		
960							1879	all	
961	x								
962				1835+					
963	x	all							
964	x	all							
965		1797-G	all				all		
966					x		1879	all	
967*	x	all		all		x	all	all	
968					x				
969								all	
970		all							
971						x		all	
972		all							
973		1797-G							
974							all	all	
975				1827+			all	all	
976	x	all							
977	x	all							
978		all		1826+		x	all	all	
979							all		

Number	GGB	KDP	KH	KLS	KPS	NS	CG	ES	XXX
980		all							
981		all							
982		all							
983	x	all							
984		all							
985	x								
986		all							
987	x	all							
988					x			all	
989		all		all			all	all	
990			all						
991		all		all			all	all	
992	x	all							
993					x				
994							all		
995	x								
996		all							
997	x	all							
998	x	all							
999					x		all	all	
1000			all						
1001		all							
1002	x	all							
1003							all	all	
1004			all						
1005		all							
1006									x
1007	x	all							
1008				all		x			
1009							all		
1010							all	all	
1011									x
1012				all		x	all	all	x
1013	x								
1014							all	all	
1015		all							
1016	x	all							
1017	x	all							
1018		all							
1019							all	all	
1020		all							
1021						x			
1022		all		all					
1023	x	all							
1024		all							
1025		all							
1026	x	all							
1027	x								
1028		all							
1029		1791+all					all	1893+	
1030	x	all		all		x	all		
1031	x	all							
1032							all	all	x

Number	GGB	KDP	KH	KLS	KPS	NS	CG	ES	XXX
1033									x
1034								1895	
1035							all		
1036	x	all					1879	all	
1037							1874	all	
1038					x				
1039		all							
1040							1874		
1041		all					all	all	
1042		1797-G				x		all	
1043							all		
1044	x	all							
1045	x	all							
1046		all							
1047		all							
1048		all					all	all	
1049									x
1050*	x	all		all		x	all	all	
1051						x			
1052							all	1893+	
1053								all	
1054		all							
1055		all		all		x	all	all	
1056									x
1057						x		all	
1058		all		all		x	all	all	
1059		all							
1060							all		
1061						x		all	
1062		all							
1063					x	x	all	all	
1064		all		all		x	all	all	
1065					x		all	all	
1066					x		all	all	
1067		all							
1068	x	all							
1069							all		
1070							all		
1071							all	all	
1072							1874		
1073		all					all	all	
1074		1797-G							
1075			all						
1076							all		
1077						x		all	
1078		all					all	all	
1079		all							
1080							all		
1081	x	all		all		x			
1082	x	all				x		all	
1083								all	
1084	x	all							
1085		1797-G							

Number	GGB	KDP	KH	KLS	KPS	NS	CG	ES	XXX
1086		1744+							
1087		all							
1088						x	all		
1089				all		x	all	all	x
1090									x
1091	x	all							
1092					x				
1093	x	all		1829+					
1094		all							
1095*	x	all		all		x	all	all	
1096		all							
1097									x
1098		all							
1099						x		all	
1100		all		all		x	all	all	
1101							all	all	
1102							all	all	
1103									x
1104								all	
1105	x	all		1829+		x		1893+	
1106	x	all		1829+		x	all	all	
1107		all							
1108		1764+							
1109		all							
1110		all							
1111								1895	
1112						x		all	
1113								all	
1114				all		x	all	all	
1115		1797-G							
1116				all			all		
1117		all		all					
1118							all	all	
1119						x			
1120	x	all							
1121							1879	all	
1122							1874		
1123		all							
1124		1797-G							
1125		all					1879		
1126						x			
1127		all							
1128						x	1879	all	
1129						x	all	all	
1130							all	all	x
1131				all		x	all	all	
1132		1797-G					all	all	
1133						x			
1134		all							
1135						x			
1136						x		all	
1137						x			
1138									x

Number	GGB	KDP	KH	KLS	KPS	NS	CG	ES	XXX
1139					x				
1140					x				
1141							1874		
1142		all							
1143					x		1879		
1144		all							
1145		all							
1146		1760+							
1147		all							
1148	x								
1149		all							
1150		all							
1151						x			
1152						x		all	
1153								all	
1154									x
1155	x								
1156							1874		
1157			all						
1158		all							
1159	x	all				x			
1160								1895	
1161		all		all			all		
1162	x	all				x	1874		
1163							all	all	
1164						x	all		
1165									x
1166									x
1167									x
1168			all						
1169							1874		
1170		all							
1171		1764+							
1172		1764+							
1173						x			
1174	x	all							
1175	x	all							
1176						x			
1177		all					all		
1178							all	all	
1179	x	all					all	all	
1180								all	
1181	x	all							
1182		all				x	all	all	
1183		all							
1184					x				
1185						x	all	all	
1186	x	all		1829+		x	all	all	
1187	x	all		all			all	all	
1188	x								
1189						x		all	
1190	x	all							
1191		all							

Number	GGB	KDP	KH	KLS	KPS	NS	CG	ES	XXX
1192		1744							
1193						x		all	
1194						x			
1195	x	all							
1196			all						
1197		all							
1198							1874		
1199	x	all							
1200							1874		
1201		all					all	all	
1202				1827+		x			
1203					x		all	all	
1204	x								
1205					x	x	all	all	
1206							1874		
1207			all				all	all	
1208		1764+							
1209	x	all							
1210							all	all	
1211	x	all							
1212	x	all							
1213	x	all							
1214	x	all				x	all	all	
1215		1764+							
1216				1829+					
1217									x
1218		all							
1219	x	all							
1220	x								
1221		all							
1222		1764+							
1223									x
1224	x	all							
1225							all		
1226							all		
1227	x	all							
1228							1874		
1229		1760+							
1230							all	all	
1231	x	all							
1232	x	all							
1233						x			
1234	x	all							
1235							all		
1236	x	all							
1237						x		all	
1238							1874		
1239		all		all			all	all	
1240									x
1241		1764+							
1242					x	x	all	all	
1243									x
1244					x		all	all	

Number	GGB	KDP	KH	KLS	KPS	NS	CG	ES	XXX
1245	x	all							
1246					x				
1247					x		all	all	
1248		1764+		all					
1249							1874		
1250		all							
1251							all		
1252		1797-G							
1253						x	all		
1254							1874		
1255							1874		
1256	x								
1257							all		
1258	x	all							
1259	x								
1260							all		
1261		all							
1262						x		all	
1263					x		all		
1264						x			
1265						x			
1266						x	all	all	
1266a							1874		
1267				all			all	all	
1268							all	all	
1269	x								
1270		all				x	all		
1271		all							
1272							1874		
1273					x	x	all	all	
1274		all							
1275							all		
1276						x			
1277				all		x	all	all	
1278					x		all	all	
1279						x			
1280				all		x	all	all	
1281			all						
1282		1760+							
1283									x
1284		all		all					
1285			all						
1286		1797-G							
1287							all		
1288		1797-G							
1289			all						
1290							all	all	
1291	x								
1292						x			
1293						x			
1294							1874		
1295	x	all							
1296				1829+			all	all	

Number	GGB	KDP	KH	KLS	KPS	NS	CG	ES	XXX
1297					x	x	all	all	
1298							1879	all	
1299			all						
1300						x		all	
1301	x								
1302		all							
1303	x	all							
1304	x	all							
1305			all						
1306						x			
1307							all		
1308						x	all	all	
1309		1764+							
1310	x								
1311				all			all		
1312			all	all		x	all	all	
1313						x		all	
1314							1874		
1315							all		
1316	x	all		all			all	all	
1317						x	all	all	
1318						x	all		
1319		all				x	all	all	
1320		all		1834+		x	all	all	
1321						x		all	
1322									x
1323	x	all							
1324				1829+					
1325						x	all	all	x
1326		all							
1327	x	all							
1328		all							
1329							all		x
1330		all							
1331		all		all					
1332		all		all		x	all	all	
1333		all							
1334			all						
1335		all		all		x	all	all	
1336									x
1337						x			
1338		all							
1339							all		
1340	x	all		1826+		x	all	all	
1341	x	all							
1342		all							
1343						x			
1344			all						
1345	x	all							
1346						x			
1347	x	all		all		x			
1348		all							
1349	x	all							

Number	GGB	KDP	KH	KLS	KPS	NS	CG	ES	XXX
1350		all							
1351		all							
1352	x								
1353	x	all							
1354		all							
1355		all		1829+					
1356						x			
1357		all							
1358		all							
1359		all							
1360	x								
1361	x	all							
1362	x								
1363	x	all							

APPENDIX XI

Index of Melodies

1. FIRST-LINE INDEX

This index lists the melody references for the hymns in the <u>First Line Index</u> (Appendix IX). The entries are arranged alphabetically word by word. Every entry consists of several elements in a certain sequence, which are separated from each other by slashes. In the following, each element is described in detail.

1. <u>The name of the melody</u> in German hymnody is given by reference to the first line of a hymn-text for which a melody was composed or which is associated with a certain melody. In this index, these text incipits are printed in capital letters. As the spelling in the various hymnals and reference sources is not uniform, it has been moderately modernized where appropriate. Variant text is enclosed in parentheses. With some hymn-texts, melody references are made to English tune names; these are given within quotation marks. Elisions are indicated by an apostrophe except in the verb forms of the first person singular, present tense, indicative and subjunctive, and the second person singular, imperative. The exclamations "Oh" and "O" are always spelled "O". Although commas have been supplied where required, they have been omitted after the exclamations "Ach" and "O". Vowels displaying an <u>Umlaut</u> are alphabetized in their pure form. Hyphenated words are considered single words. Melody references for a given text often vary in the hymnals. Cross-references, following the first line and enclosed in parentheses, have been made only for French/ Genevan psalm tunes from Lobwasser and English tunes. The abbreviation "Ch", in parentheses, indicates the first line of a chorus. Brackets enclose information supplied by the author. Cross-references follow the first-line entry and are enclosed in parentheses. Capitalization of such a line of text indicates a melody listed in this index.

2. <u>Scansion of the text</u> is indicated in the following manner: the first numeral refers to the number of lines in the stanza; this is followed by one or more letters indicating the meter; the remaining numerals refer to the number of syllables in each line. (In some instances, this information was not available.)

For example, "8t. 8.7.8.7.8.8.8.8" refers to an eight-line stanza in trochaic meter with syllables per line as indicated. The following abbreviations are used to indicate the meter:

        a: anapestic   ab: amphibrachic
        d: dactylic   i: iambic   t: trochaic

3. <u>Source</u> reference for the melody is given by the name of the author of the reference work where the melody is found, followed by the number under which it is listed in that work. All references are made to the earliest appearance of the melody according to the work cited. For some melodies, no sources could be found, because hymnal publishers often no longer knew the original text incipits, which often resulted in multiple and/or reciprocal cross-referencing. In such a case, a suitable melody for the text can be found by one of two methods. First, look up the same text incipit in the <u>First Line Index</u> (Appendix IX), note the melody reference given there, and look up the new melody reference in this index. If this

results in a dead-end search, consult the metric index of melodies and choose any of the melodies listed under the pattern of the original entry.

4. <u>Year</u> of earliest documentation of the melody as cited in the reference work.

5. <u>First publication in Brethren hymnals</u> is indicated by an alpha-numeric symbol referring to the appropriate Brethren hymnal and the year of publication. A letter following the year refers to the place of publication. Where first publication in a hymnal was preceded by publication in a small hymn-collection, both are listed.

6. <u>Hymn-texts</u> sung to the melody in question are listed by the numbers assigned to them in Appendix IX. Numbers that are underlined indicate texts that are sung to their "own melody" (<u>e</u>. <u>M</u>.).

7. <u>The number</u> of the entry by which the melody is referred to in the metric index is given on the right-hand margin.

List of Abbreviations

For full bibliographical records, consult the Selected Bibliography. Asterisks indicate Brethren hymnals and hymn-collections.

CG*	Das Christliche Gesang-Buch.
ELEL*	Etliche liebliche und erbauliche Lieder.
ENGL*	Etliche Neue Geistliche Lieder.
ES*	Eine Sammlung.
ESL*	Eyn schön Lied.
GAL*	Geistliche u. andächtige Lieder.
GGB*	Geistreiches Gesang-Buch, 1720.
GGG*	Stoll, Geistliches Gewürz-Gärtlein.
Hymnal 1872*	The Brethren's Tune and Hymn Book, 1872.
Hymnal 1879*	The Brethren's Tune and Hymn Book, 1879.
Hymnal 1901*	The Brethren Hymnal, 1901.
Jackson A	Jackson, Another Sheaf of White Spirituals.
Jackson D	Jackson, Down-East Spirituals and Others.
Jackson S	Jackson, Spiritual Folk-Songs of Early America.
KDP*	Das Kleine Davidische Psalterspiel.
KH*	Die Kleine Harfe.
KLS*	Die kleine Lieder Sammlung.
KPS*	Die kleine Perlen-Sammlung.
Lobwasser	Die Psalmen Davids.
Lorenz	Glory, Hallelujah!
NS*	Neue Sammlung.
Yoder	Pennsylvania Spirituals.
Zahn	Die Melodien der deutschen evangelischen Kirchenlieder.

ABERMAL EIN TAG VERFLOSSEN / 8t. 8.7.8.7.7.7.8.8   1
    Zahn 6612 / 1680 / KLS1841 / 25, 415, 527, 529, 1230.
ACH ALLES, WAS HIMMEL UND ERDE UMSCHLIESSET / 4ab. 12.12.12.12   2
    Zahn 1478 / 1698 / KDP1744 / 305, 315, 565, 719, 741.
ACH BLEIB BEI UNS, HERR JESU CHRIST / 4i. 8.8.8.8   3
    Zahn 613 / 1646 / ES1893 / 770, 1113.
ACH GOTT, IN WAS FÜR SCHMERZEN / 8i. 7.6.7.6.6.7.7.6   4
    GGB1720 / 622.
ACH GOTT, MAN KENNET DICH NICHT RECHT / 6i. 8.8.7.8.8.7   5
    KPS1858 / 215.
ACH GOTT UND HERR, WIE GROSS UND SCHWER / 6i. 4.4.7.4.4.7   6
    Zahn 2049 / 1616 / GGB1720 / 276, 976, 1344, 1348.
ACH GOTT, VOM HIMMEL SIEH DAREIN / 7i. 8.7.8.7.8.8.7   7
    Zahn 4431 / 1524 / GGB1720 / 52, 53, 405, 479, 485, 963, 1062, 1259.
ACH HERR, MICH ARMEN SÜNDER / 8i. 7.6.7.6.7.6.7.6   8
    Zahn 5412 / 1628 / KDP1744 / 307, 1333.
ACH JAMMER, ES IST UM DICH, JESU, GESCHEHEN / 4ab. 12.12.12.12   9
    GGB1720 / 32.
ACH JESU, MEIN SCHÖNSTER / 4ab. 12.12.12.12   10
    KDP1744 / 28.
ACH JESU, MEINER SEELEN FREUDE / 6i. 9.9.8.9.9.8   11
    Zahn 3007 / 1684 / KDP1744 / 1221.
ACH LASS DICH JETZT FINDEN / 4ab. 6.5.6.5   12
    Zahn 1452 / 1715 / KDP1744 / 38, 241, 385, 846, 921, 1053.
ACH SAGT MIR NICHTS VON GOLD UND SCHÄTZEN / 6i. 9.8.9.8.9.8   13
    Zahn 2800 / 1657 / GGB1720 / 1199.
ACH SIEHET DOCH, DAS LAMME GOTTES / 8i.t. 9.6.9.6.8.8.8.6   14
    Jackson A303 / 1854 / KPS1858 / 50.
ACH TREIB AUS MEINER SEEL' / 6i. 6.6.5.6.6.5   15
    Zahn 2106 / 1744 / KDP1744 / 1239.
ACH WACHET, WACHET AUF / 6i. 6.7.6.7.7.7   16
    Zahn 2216 / 1680 / GGB1720 / 54.
ACH WAS MACH ICH IN DEN STÄDTEN / 6t. 8.7.8.7.7.7   17
    Zahn 3629 / 1659 / KDP1744 / 528, 1098.
ACH WAS SIND WIR OHNE JESU / 6t. 8.7.8.7.8.8   18
    Zahn 3756 / 1710 / CG1874 / 772.
ACH WAS SOLL ICH SÜNDER MACHEN / 6t. 8.7.7.8.7.7   19
    Zahn 3573b / 1661 / GGB1720 / 43, 705, 868, 1147.
ACH WIE GLÜCKLICH IST EIN HERZE / 6i. 9.8.9.8.8.8   20
    KDP1744 / 690.
ALL IS WELL / 8i.-t. 10.6.10.6.8.8.8.6   21
    Jackson S58 / 1844 / CG1874 / 1210.
ALLE MENSCHEN MÜSSEN STERBEN / 8t. 8.7.8.7.8.8.7.7   22
    Zahn 6776 / 1652 / GGB1720 / 10, 75, 76, 102, 128, 191, 250, 461,
    477, 1032, 1033, 1038, 1163, 1226, 1308.
ALLEIN GOTT IN DER HÖH' SEI EHR' / 7i. 8.7.8.7.8.8.7   23
    Zahn 4457 / 1539 / GGB1720 / 77, 101, 183, 220, 243, 321, 898,
    1023, 1132, 1316.
ALLEIN ZU DIR, HERR JESU CHRIST / 9i. 8.7.8.7.8.8.8.4.8   24
    Zahn 7292a / 1541? / GGB1720 / 293.
ALLES IST AN GOTTES SEGEN / 6t. 8.8.7.8.8.7   25
    Zahn 3839 / 1731 / CG1874 / 99, 440, 1249.
AUF, AUF, MEIN HERZ, MIT FREUDEN / 8i. 7.6.7.6.6.6.6.6   26
    Zahn 5243 / 1648 / GGB1720 / 95.

AUF, CHRISTENMENSCH, AUF, AUF ZUM STREIT / 6i. 8.7.8.7.8.8   27
   KDP1744 / 203, 919.
AUF, HINAUF ZU DEINER FREUDE / 8t.-i. 8.7.8.7.4.8.8.4   28
   Zahn 7098a / 1698 / KDP1744 / 103.
AUF MEINEN LIEBEN GOTT / 6i. 6.6.7.7.7.7   29
   Zahn 2162 / 1609 / GGB1720 / 178, 366, 1331.
AUF, SEELE, AUF UND SÄUME NICHT / 4i. 8.6.8.6   30
   KDP1744 / 801.
AUF, SEELE, SEI GERÜST' / 6i. 6.6.5.6.6.5   31
   GGB1720 / 727.
AUF, TRIUMPH, ES KOMMT DIE STUNDE / 6t. 8.8.7.8.8.7   32
   Zahn 3852a / 1698 / GGB1720 / 113, 515, 1086, 1213, 1353.
AUS LIEB' VERWUND'TER JESU MEIN / 4i. 8.8.8.8   33
   GGB1720 / 117, 837.
AUS MEINES HERZENS GRUNDE / 8i. 7.6.7.6.6.7.7.6   34
   Zahn 5269b / 1598 / GGB1720 / 1027, 1074.
AUS TIEFER NOT / 7i. 8.7.8.7.8.8.7   35
   Zahn 4437 / 1524 / GGB1720 / 536, 538, 1102, 1220, 1332.

BALD KOMMT DAS JUBELJAHR HERBEI (Ch) / 2i. 8.8   36
   CG1874 / 96.
BEDENKE, MENSCH, DAS ENDE / 8i. 7.6.7.6.7.6.7.6   37
   Zahn 5526 / 1738 / KPS1858 / 57, 159, 289, 334, 446, 579.
BEFIEHL DU DEINE WEGE / 8i. 7.6.7.6.7.6.7.6   38
   Zahn 5459 / 1659 / KDP1764 / 29, 448, 1180.
BINDE MEINE SEELE WOHL / 6t. 7.8.7.8.7.7   39
   CG1874 / 706, 1069.
BIST DU DANN, JESU, MIT DEINER HILF / 5d. 14.14.4.7.8   40
   KDP1744 / 151.
BLAST DIE TROMPETE, BLAST / 4i. 6.6.6.6   41
   Jackson A7; Yoder 6 / CG1874 / 96, 137?, 273, 1014
BLEIBE BEI MIR, LIEBSTER FREUND / 8t. 7.6.7.6.7.6.7.6   42
   KDP1797 / 327, 810, 1108.
BRICH AN, MEIN LICHT / 8i. 4.6.6.5.4.6.6.5   43
   Zahn 5039 / 1738 / KDP1744 / 294, 317.
BRICH ENDLICH HERVOR, DU GEHEMMETE FLUT / 6ab. 11.12.11.12.12.12   44
   KDP1744 / 802.
BRUNN' ALLES HEILS, DICH EHREN WIR / 4i. 8.8.8.8   45
   KLS1827 / 899, 1243.

CHRIST(US) LAG IN TODESBANDEN / 8i.-t. 7.7.7.7.7.7.7.4   46
   Zahn 7012 / 1524 / KDP1744 / 15, 162.
CHRISTI TOD IST ADAMS LEBEN / 6t. 8.7.8.7.8.8   47
   GGB1720 / 104, 672.
CHRISTUM WIR SOLLEN LOBEN SCHON / 4i. 8.8.8.8   48
   Zahn 297b / 1524 / KDP1744 / 157.
CHRISTUS, DER UNS SELIG MACHT / 8t. 7.6.7.6.7.6.7.6.   49
   Zahn 6283b / 1598 / GGB1720 / 1031, 1073.

DA JESUS AN DEM KREUZE STAND / 5i. 8.8.7.8.7   50
   Zahn 1706 / 1545 / GGB1720 / 1234.

DA JOSEPH SEIN' BRÜDER ANSAH / 8i. 6.6.6.6.6.6.6.6   51
   Jackson D26; Yoder, p. 363 / KPS 1858 / 577.
DANKBAR LASST UNS CHRISTUM PREISEN / 12i. 8.7.8.7.8.8.7.7.8.8.8.8   52
   KLS 1829 / <u>164</u>.
DANKET DEM HERREN, DENN ER IST / 2i. 11.11   53
   GGB 1720 / 1211.
DANKT DEM HERRN, IHR GOTTESKNECHTE / 6t. 8.7.8.7.7.7   54
   Zahn 3649 / 1692 / KDP 1744 / <u>166</u>.
DANN WÜNSCHT IHR ZU ZU SEIN BEREIT (Ch) / 4t. 7.7.7.7.   55
   CG 1874 / 974.
[DAUGHTER OF ZION, AWAKE FROM THY SADNESS?] / 4d. 11.11.11.11   56
   KPS 1858 / 1139?
DEM HERREN DER ERDKREIS ZUSTEHT / 6i. 8.8.9.8.8.9   57
   (= PSALM 24 LOBWASSER)
   Zahn 2665 / 1542 / KDP 1744 / <u>189</u>, 830, 853.
DER AM KREUZ IST MEINE LIEBE / 8t. 8.7.8.7.7.7.8.8   58
   Zahn 6639 / 1712 / GGB 1720 / 192.
DER GNADENBRUNN' FLIESST NOCH / 8i. 6.7.6.7.6.6.6.6   59
   CG 1874 / 771, 1009, 1251.
DER HERR IST MEIN GETREUER HIRT / 7i. 8.7.8.7.8.8.7   60
   Zahn 4507 / 1598 / KDP 1744 / 295.
DER LIEBEN SONNE LICHT UND PRACHT HAT NUN / 8i. 8.7.8.7.6.6.8.8   61
   Zahn 5658 / 1704 / KDP 1744 / <u>226</u>, 387, 388, 585.
DER SCHMALE WEG IST BREIT GENUG ZUM LEBEN / 5i. 11.10.10.9.11   62
   Zahn 1827 / 1704 / KDP 1744 / 231, <u>232</u>.
DER TAG IST FORT UND HIN / 4i. 6.6.8.6   63
   KPS 1858 / 93, 313, 421, 601, 988.
DER TAG IST HIN, MEIN GEIST / 5i.-t. 4.4.7.7.6   64
   Zahn 1924 / 1704 / KH 1792 / 265, <u>266</u>.
DER TAG IST HIN, MEIN JESU / 4i. 11.11.10.10   65
   Zahn 938 / 1680 / GGB 1720 / 48, 199, <u>236</u>, 433, 445, 905, 990, 1302.
DIE GNADE SEI MIT ALLEN, DIE GNADE UNSRES HERRN / 4i. 6.5.6.5   66
   KLS 1844 / <u>252</u>.
DIE GNADE UNSRES HERRN JESU CHRISTI / irregular   67
   Zahn 8648 / 1763 / KLS 1844 / <u>253</u>.
DIE LIEB' ERKALT' JETZT IN DER WELT / 6i. 8.8.7.8.8.7   68
   GGB 1720 / <u>258</u>.
DIE LIEBE LEIDET NICHT GESELLEN / 6i. 9.8.9.8.8.8   69
   370.
DIE LIEBLICHEN BLICKE / 8ab. 11.6.6.11.5.5.5.5   70
   Zahn 6956 / 1677 / GGB 1720 / 87, <u>261</u>, 836.
DIE MACHT DER WAHRHEIT BRICHT HERFÜR / 8i. 8.8.7.8.8.7.8.8   71
   KDP 1744 / 621.
DIE MORGENSTERNE LOBEN GOTT / 8i. 8.7.8.7.8.7.8.7   72
   CG 1879 / 311.
DIE NACHT IST VOR DER TÜR' / 6i. 6.7.6.7.6.6   73
   Zahn 2189 / 1698 / KDP 1744 / 19, <u>267</u>, 959.
DIE SEELE CHRISTI HEIL'GE MICH / 4i. 8.8.8.8   74
   Zahn 636 / 1657 / KDP 1744 / 550, 978.
DIE TUGEND WIRD DURCHS KREUZ GEÜBET / 8i. 9.8.9.8.9.8.9.8   75
   Zahn 6009 / 1704 / GGB 1720 / <u>269</u>, 1020, 1175.
DIE ZEIT IST NOCH NICHT DA / 8i. 6.7.6.7.6.6.9.9   76
   Zahn 5203 / 1714 / KDP 1744 / <u>277</u>.
DIES SIND DIE HEILIGEN ZEHN GEBOT' / 5i.-t. 8.8.8.7.4   77
   Zahn 1951 / 1524 / GGB 1720 / 83.

DIESEN TÄUFLING BRINGEN WIR / 6t. 7.8.7.8.8.8   78
   KLS1829 / 283.
DIR, DIR, JEHOVA, WILL ICH SINGEN / 6i. 9.10.9.10.10.10   79
   Zahn 3066 / 1698 / KDP1744 / 285.
DORT AUF JENEM TOTENHÜGEL / 7t. 8.7.8.7.7.8.7   80
   KPS1858 / 288.
DU ARMER PILGER WANDELST HIER / 7i. 8.6.8.6.8.8.2   81
   KH1792 / 291.
DU GEIST DES HERRN, DER DU VON GOTT AUSGEHST / 4i. 10.10.11.11   82
   Zahn 842 / 1704 / KDP1744 / 549, 715.
DU, O SCHÖNES WELTGEBÄUDE / 8t. 8.7.8.7.8.8.7.7   83
   Zahn 6773 / 1649 / GGB1720 / 724.
DU UNBEGREIFLICHS HÖCHSTES GUT / 4i. 8.8.8.8   84
   Zahn 659 / 1680 / KDP1744 / 6, 268, 280, 484, 1011, 1012, 1207,
   1285.
DURCH BLOSSES GEDÄCHTNIS DEIN / 4ab. 12.12.12.12   85
   Zahn 1474 / 1684 / KDP1744 / 260.

EHRE SEI JETZO MIT FREUDEN GESUNGEN / 4d. 11.11.11.11   86
   Zahn 1499 / 1680 / GGB1720 / 314, 1361.
EI, WAS FRAG ICH NACH DER ERDEN / 6t. 8.7.8.7.8.8   87
   KDP1744 / 775, 1197.
EIL DOCH HERAN UND MACH DEM GUTEN BAHN / 8i. 4.6.6.5.4.6.6.5   88
   Zahn 5037 / 1736 / KDP1744 / 351, 408, 666, 809, 934.
EILT VORWÄRTS, EILT VORWÄRTS, DAS KLEINOD (Ch) / 5ab. 11.11.5.5.11   89
   CG1874 / 190.
EIN LÄMMLEIN GEHT UND TRÄGT DIE SCHULD / 10i. 8.7.8.7.8.8.7.8.8.7   90
   Zahn 7681 / 1666 / KDP1797-G / 322.
EINS IST NOT, ACH HERR, DIES EINE / 8t.-ab. 8.7.8.7.12.12.11.11   91
   Zahn 7126 / 1698 / GGB1720 / 332, 502, 1144.
ENDLICH, ENDLICH MUSS ES DOCH / 6t. 7.8.7.8.7.7   92
   KPD1858 / 576, 676.
ENDLICH SOLL DAS FROHE JAHR / 10t.-d. 7.8.7.8.7.8.7.8.11.11   93
   Zahn 8074 / 1698 / KDP1744 / 336.
ENDLICH WIRD ES UNS GELINGEN / 6t. 8.8.7.8.8.7   94
   181.
ENTFERNET EUCH, IHR MATTEN KRÄFTE / 8i. 9.8.9.8.4.4.8.8   95
   Zahn 5970 / 1698 / GGB1720 / 124, 275, 339, 822, 1181.
ERHALT UNS, HERR, BEI DEINEM WORT / 4i. 8.8.8.8   96
   Zahn 350 / 1543 / KDP1744 / 349.
ERHEB DEIN HERZ, TU AUF DEIN OHREN / 4i. 9.8.9.8   97
   Zahn 750 / 1547 / GGB1720 / 915.
ERLEUCHT MICH, HERR, MEIN LICHT / 7i. 6.7.6.6.6.6.6   98
   Zahn 4252 / 1698 / GGB1720 / 347.
ERMUNTERT EUCH, IHR FROMMEN / 8i. 7.6.7.6.7.6.7.6   99
   Zahn 5521 / ca. 1710 / KDP1744 / 121, 194, 301, 1202.
ERSCHIENEN IST DER HERRLICH' TAG / 5i. 8.8.8.8.4   100
   Zahn 1744 / 1611 / GGB1720 / 597, 1319.
ES GLÄNZET DER CHRISTEN / 8ab. 12.11.12.11.6.6.12.12   101
   Zahn 6969 / 1704 / GGB1720 / 247, 255, 355, 1282.
ES IST DAS HEIL UNS KOMMEN HER / 7i. 8.7.8.7.8.8.7   102
   Zahn 4430 / 1524 / GGB1720 / 179, 217, 296, 480, 598, 1095, 1245.
ES IST GENUG, MEIN MATTER SINN / 6i. 8.4.7.8.4.7   103
   Zahn 2343 / 1667 / GGB1720 / 359, 562.

ES IST GEWISSLICH AN DER ZEIT / 7i. 8.7.8.7.8.8.7   104
    Zahn 4500 / 1588 / GGB1720 / 2, 7, 17, 74, 118, 204, 230, 251, 300,
    360, 442, 478, 547, 560, 581, 596, 599, 714, 734, 825, 884, 906,
    1010, 1066, 1242.

ES IST NICHT SCHWER, EIN CHRIST ZU SEIN / 6i. 8.11.10.11.10.4   105
    Zahn 2734 / 1747 / KDP1744 / 367.

ES IST WIEDER KOMMEN EIN SCHÖNES NEU-JAHR / 4ab. 6.5.6.5   106
    KPS1858 / 365.

ES KOSTET VIEL, EIN CHRIST ZU SEIN / 6i. 8.11.10.11.10.4   107
    Zahn 2727 / 1704 / KDP1744 / 342, 362.

FAHRE FORT, FAHRE FORT, ZION / 7t. 6.7.8.7.8.9.6   108
    Zahn 4791 / 1704 / GGB1720 / 131, 375, 409, 1092.

FOLGET MIR, RUFT UNS DAS LEBEN / 8t. 8.8.7.7.8.8.7.7   109
    Zahn 6864 / 1642 / GGB1720 / 379.

FORT, FORT, MEIN HERZ, ZUM HIMMEL / t.   110
    ELEL1812 / 380.

FREU DICH SEHR, O MEINE SEELE / 8t. 8.7.8.7.7.7.8.8   111
    Zahn 6545 / 1620 / GGB1720 / 1, 90, 371, 418, 865, 1007, 1058,
    1091, 1282, 1351.

FREUDENVOLL, FREUDENVOLL WALLE ICH / 8d. 10.10.10.10.10.10.10.10   112
    (= JOYFULLY, JOYFULLY ONWARD I MOVE?)
    ES1893 / 384.

FREUET EUCH, IHR CHRISTEN ALLE / 10t. 8.7.7.8.7.7.8.8.8.8   113
    Zahn 7880a / 1646 / GGB1720 / 496, 667.

FRIEDE, ACH FRIEDE, ACH GÖTTLICHER / 6d.-ab. 11.11.11.11.12.12   114
    Zahn 4081 / 1704 / GGB1720 / 386.

FRISCH, FRISCH HINACH, MEIN GEIST / 8i. 8.7.8.7.6.6.8.8   115
    KDP1744 / 227.

FRÖHLICH, FRÖHLICH, IMMER FRÖHLICH / 6t. 8.8.7.8.8.7   116
    GGB1720 / 1036.

FRÖHLICH SOLL MEIN HERZE SPRINGEN / 8t. 8.3.3.6.8.3.3.6   117
    Zahn 6481 / 1653 / GGB1720 / 1195.

FROHLOCKET, IHR VÖLKER / 4ab. 12.11.12.11   118
    Zahn 1464 / 1698 / KDP1744 / 390.

GEH AUS, MEIN HERZ, UND SUCHE FREUD' / 6i. 8.8.7.8.8.7   119
    Zahn 2531 / 1666 / GGB1720 / 108.

GELOBET SEIST DU, JESU CHRIST / 5i.-t. 8.7.8.8.4   120
    Zahn 1947 / 1524 / GGB1720 / 403, 597.

GIB DICH ZUFRIEDEN UND SEI STILLE / 9i.-t. 9.8.9.8.4.5.4.5.5   121
    Zahn 7414 / 1666 / KDP1744 / 406.

GLÜCK ZU, KREUZ, VON GANZEM HERZEN / 4t. 8.7.8.7   122
    Zahn 1289a / 1698 / GGB1720, 312, 412.

GOTT DES HIMMELS UND DER ERDEN / 6t. 8.7.8.7.7.7   123
    Zahn 3614a / 1642 / GGB1720 / 46, 328, 425, 513, 732, 746, 869,
    871, 890, 975, 1052, 1083, 1229, 1235, 1273, 1306.

GOTT HAT DIE WELT GELIEBET / 4i. 7.7.7.7   124
    KPS1858 / 423.

GOTT IST MEIN HEIL, MEIN HILF / 7i. 8.7.8.7.8.6.8   125
    Zahn 4421 / 1605 / KDP1744 / 430.

GOTT LEBET NOCH / 10i.-t. 4.7.8.7.8.7.8.8.7.7   126
    Zahn 7951 / 1714 / GGB1720 / 431.

GOTT SEI DANK IN ALLER (DURCH ALLE) WELT / 4t. 7.7.7.7   127
   Zahn 1230 / 1704 / GGB1720 / 376, 678, 694, 697, 723, 1106, 1141, 1257.

GOTTLOB, EIN SCHRITT ZUR EWIGKEIT / 7i. 8.7.8.7.8.8.7   128
   KDP1764 / 211, 407, 1171.

GROSSER PROPHETE, MEIN HERZE BEGEHRET / 6d. 11.10.11.10.11.11   129
   Zahn 3947a / 1680 / GGB1720 / 456, 458, 498, 668, 1109.

GUTE NACHT, IHR MEINE LIEBEN / 8t. 8.7.8.7.7.7.7.7   130
   CG1874 / 807.

GUTER HIRTE, WILLST DU NICHT / 6t. 7.8.7.8.7.7   131
   Zahn 3443 / 1657 / GGB1720 / 335, 361, 533, 1078, 1097, 1104.

HAB ICH NUR GOTT ZUM SEELEN / 4i. 8.4.4.6   132
   GGB1720 / 369, 607.

HALLELUJAH, HALLELUJAH, WIR SIND AUF DER REISE HEIM (Ch) / 4t. 8.7.8.7   133
   Lorenz 7 / KPS1858 / 472.

HAST DU DANN, JESU, DEIN ANGESICHT / 5d. 14.14.4.7.8   134
   Zahn 1912a / 1665 / GGB1720 / 136, 795.

HEIM, HEIM, WIR GEHEN HEIM / 8ab. 6.5.6.5.6.5.6.5   135
   CG1874 / 340.

HELFT MIR, GOTTES GÜTE PREISEN / 8i. 7.6.7.6.6.7.7.6   136
   Zahn 5264a / 1575 / GGB1720 / 13.

HERR CHRIST, DER EIN'GE GOTT'S SOHN / 7i. 7.6.7.6.7.7.6   137
   Zahn 4297a / 1524 / GGB1720 / 474, 491, 1055.

HERR, DEIN' OHREN ZU MIR NEIGE / 8t. 8.8.7.7.8.8.7.7   138
   (= PSALM 77 and 86 LOBWASSER)
   Zahn 6863 / 1547 / KDP1744 / 476.

HERR JESU CHRIST, DICH ZU UNS WEND / 4i. 8.8.8.8   139
   Zahn 624 / 1648 / KLS1829 / 63, 106, 155, 169, 171, 182, 195, 343, 505, 649, 754, 847, 903, 914, 942, 979, 994, 1003, 1070, 1298.

HERR JESU CHRIST, MEINS LEBENS LICHT / 4i. 8.8.8.8   140
   Zahn 533a / 1625 / KDP1744 / 242, 1238, 1268, 1307.

HERR JESU CHRISTE, MEIN PROPHET / 4i. 8.8.8.8   141
   CG1874 / 820.

HERR JESU, EW'GES LICHT / 6i. 6.6.7.7.6.6   142
   Zahn 2156 / 1704 / KDP1744 / 490, 1299.

HERR JESU, GNADENSONNE / 7i. 7.6.7.6.7.7.6   143
   Zahn 4325 / 1745 / CG1874 / 271.

HERRLICHSTE MAJESTÄT / 6d. 11.10.11.10.11.11   144
   KDP1764 / 645.

HERZLICH TUT MICH ERFREUEN / 8i. 7.6.7.6.7.6.7.6   145
   Zahn 5361a / 1552 / KDP1744 / 301, 326, 965.

HERZLICH TUT MICH VERLANGEN / 8i. 7.6.7.6.7.6.7.6   146
   Zahn 5385a / 1601 / GGB1720 / 79, 122, 238, 357, 835, 1059, 1187.

HERZLIEBSTER JESU, WAS HAST DU VERBROCHEN / 4i. 11.11.11.5   147
   Zahn 982 / 1631 / KDP1797-G / 1124.

HEUT TRIUMPHIERET GOTTES SOHN / 6i. 8.8.8.8.8.8   148
   Zahn 2585 / 1601 / CG1874 / 392.

HILF, JESU, HILF SIEGEN / 6ab. 6.6.6.6.5.5   149
   Zahn 3909 / 1698 / KDP1744 / 511.

HÖCHSTER FORMIERER / 7d. 11.10.11.10.5.5.10   150
   Zahn 4932b / 1693 / KDP1764 / 1241.

HÖCHSTER PRIESTER, DER DU DICH / 4t. 7.7.8.8   151
   Zahn 1253 / 1668 / GGB1720 / 81, 517, 518, 785, 813, 886.

HOLDSELIG'S GOTTESLAMM / 8i. 6.7.7.6.7.7.6.6   152
    Zahn 5229 / 1704 / GGB1720 / 133, 522, 961.

HOME, SWEET HOME / 6ab. 11.11.11.11.5.11   153
    Hymnal 1872, no. 647 / NS1870 / 127.

HOW TEDIOUS AND TASTELESS THE HOURS / 8ab. 8.8.8.8.8.8.8.8   154
    Hymnal 1872, no. 785 / CG1874 / 1290.

HÜTER, WIRD DIE NACHT DER SÜNDEN / 6t. 8.4.7.8.4.7   155
    Zahn 3542 / 1704 / GGB1720 / 59, 535, 769, 854, 1327.

ICH BIN HEILIG, SPRICHT DER HERR / 4i. 8.8.8.8   156
    GGB1720 / 639.

ICH BIN VOLLER TROST UND FREUDEN / 6t. 8.7.8.7.7.7   157
    Zahn 3628 / 1657 / GGB1720 / 544.

ICH DANK DIR, LIEBER HERRE / 8i. 7.6.7.6.7.6.7.6   158
    Zahn 5354b / 1662 / GGB1720 / 234.

ICH DANK DIR SCHON DURCH DEINEN SOHN / 4i. 8.7.8.7   159
    Zahn 247b / 1610 / GGB1720 / 36, 158, 989, 998, 1310.

ICH HAB IHN DENNOCH LIEB / 8i. 6.7.6.7.6.6.6.6   160
    Zahn 5145 / 1676 / KDP1744 / 221, 308, 1000.

ICH HAB MEIN SACH' GOTT HEIMGESTELLT / 5i. 8.8.8.4.8   161
    Zahn 1679 / 1601 / GGB1720 / 130, 180, 514, 553, 909, 1258, 1284.

ICH HABE G'NUG IM HIMMEL UND AUF ERDEN / 4i. 11.11.10.10   162
    Zahn 951 / 1715 / GGB1720 / 555.

ICH KOMME SELBST ZU DIR / 4i. 11.9.11.11   163
    GGB1720 / 561.

ICH LEB MIR NICHT, DENN JESUS / 6i. 8.4.7.8.4.7   164
    GGB1720 / 196.

ICH LIEB DEN HERREN UND IHM DRUM DANK SAG / 4i. 10.11.11.10   165
    (= PSALM 47 LOBWASSER)
    KDP1744 / 569.

ICH LIEBE DICH HERZLICH, O JESU / 4ab. 12.12.12.12   166
    Zahn 1481 / 1704 / GGB1720 / 3, 33, 310, 849.

ICH RUF ZU DIR, HERR JESU CHRIST / 9i.-t. 8.7.8.7.8.7.4.6.7   167
    Zahn 7400 / 1535 / GGB1720 / 977.

ICH SAGE GUT' NACHT DEM IRDISCHEN PRACHT / 5ab. 5.5.5.6.5   168
    Zahn 1440 / 1691 / GGB1720 / 568, 570, 1041.

ICH SUCHE DICH IN DIESER FERNE / 5i. 9.9.8.9.8   169
    Zahn 1817 / 1699 / GGB1720 / 27, 571.

ICH TRAUE MEINEM GOTT / 4i. 6.6.8.6   170
    CG1874 / 324.

ICH WILL DICH LIEBEN, MEINE STÄRKE / 6i. 9.8.9.8.8.6   171
    Zahn 2763 / 1657 / GGB1720 / 587.

ICH WILL DICH NICHT VERLASSEN / 8i. 7.6.7.6.7.6.7.6   172
    Zahn 5520 / 1698 / GGB1720 / 588.

ICH WILL NICHT LASSEN AB / 8i. 6.8.8.6.6.8.8.6   173
    (= PSALM 34 LOBWASSER)
    Zahn 5230 / 1551 / KDP1744 / 593.

ICH WILL STREBEN NACH DEM LEBEN / 11t. 4.4.5.4.4.5.7.7.4.4.5   174
    CG1874 / 594.

IHR JUNGEN HELDEN, AUFGEWACHT / 4i. 8.8.8.8   175
    KPS1858 / 240, 530, 648, 653, 910, 952, 1184, 1297.

IHR KINDER DES HÖCHSTEN / 7ab. 12.12.11.11.12.12.12   176
    Zahn 4927 / 1704 / GGB1720 / 278, 605, 606.

IHR KINDER, HABT MUT /4ab. 5.9.6.5   177
   KPS1858 / 616.
IHR KNECHT' DES HERREN ALLZUGLEICH / 4i. 8.8.8.8   178
   (= PSALM 134 LOBWASSER)
   Zahn 368 / 1551 / KDP1744 / <u>612</u>.
IHR LIEBEN, WEINT NICHT / 4ab. 5.9.6.5   179
   KPS1858 / 609, 626.
IHR SÜNDER, KOMMT GEGANGEN / 8i. 7.6.7.6.6.6.7.6   180
   KDP1744 / 35, 912, 1320.
IHR VÖLKER AUF DER ERDEN ALL' / 4i. 8.8.8.8   181
   (= PSALM 100 LOBWASSER)
   Zahn 367 / 1551 / KDP1744 / 567, <u>619</u>.
IMMER FRÖHLICH, IMMER FRÖHLICH / 6t. 8.8.7.8.8.7   182
   Zahn 3826 / 1673 / GGB1720 / 1256.
IN DICH HAB ICH GEHOFFET, HERR / 6i. 8.8.7.4.4.7   183
   Zahn 2459 / 1560 / GGB1720 / 487, <u>635</u>, 870, 1096.

JAUCHZET ALL MIT MACHT / 12t. 8.7.8.7.8.8.7.7.8.8.8.8   184
   Zahn 8353 / 1698 / KDP1744 / 452, 765, 1305.
JEHOVA IST MEIN LICHT UND GNADENSONNE / 8i. 11.10.11.10.10.10.10.10 185
   Zahn 6194b / 1690 / GGB1720, <u>647</u>.
JESU, DEINE LIEBES-FLAMME / 8t. 8.8.7.7.8.8.7.7   186
   Zahn 6880a / 1698 / GGB1720 / <u>659</u>.
JESU, DEINE TIEFEN WUNDEN / 8t. 8.7.8.7.7.7.8.8   187
   Zahn 6571 / 1663 / KDP1744 / 523.
JESU, DER DU MEINE SEELE / 8t. 8.7.8.7.8.8.7.7   188
   Zahn 6767 / 1641 / GGB1720 / 24, 174, 302, <u>661</u>, 724, 789, 1192.
JESU, DU MEIN LIEBSTES LEBEN / 10t. 8.7.8.7.8.7.7.8.7.7   189
   Zahn 7891 / 1642 / KDP1744 / 708, 767.
JESU, HILF SIEGEN / 6d. 11.10.11.10.11.11   190
   Zahn 3953a / 1698 / KH1792 / 153.
JESU, JESU, BRUNN' DES LEBENS / 4at. 8.7.8.7   191
   CG1874 / 290.
JESU, KOMM DOCH SELBST ZU MIR / 4t. 7.7.7.7   192
   Zahn 1187 / 1657 / GGB1720 / 92, 114, 534, 673, 678, 700, 722, 781,
   814, 974, 1205, 1317.
JESU, KOMM MIT DEINEM VATER / 6t. 8.7.8.7.8.8   193
   GGB1720 / 855.
JESU LEIDEN, PEIN UND TOD / 8t. 7.6.7.6.7.6.7.6   194
   Zahn 6288b / 1682 / KDP1744 / 1073.
JESU, MEIN TREUER / 4d. 5.5.5.5   195
   Zahn 6981 / 1684 / KDP1744 / <u>674</u>, 866.
JESU, MEINE FREUDE / 10t. 6.6.5.6.6.5.3.4.8.6   196
   Zahn 8032 / 1653 / GGB1720 / 82, 149, 657, <u>675</u>, 686, 693, 703,
   1056.
JESU, MEINER SEELEN RUH' / 4t. 7.7.7.7   197
   Zahn 1210 / 1665 / KDP1744 / 372, 688.
JESU, MEINES HERZENS FREUD' / 7t. 7.4.7.4.7.4.6   198
   Zahn 4797 / 1698 / GGB1720 / 55, 1190.
JESU, MEINES LEBENS LEBEN / 8t. 8.7.8.7.8.8.7.7   199
   Zahn 6794 / 1659 / GGB1720 / 24, 663, 1192, 1330, 1340.
JESU, RUFE MICH VON DER WELT / 5t. 5.5.4.4.5   200
   Zahn 1850 / 1698 / KDP1744 / <u>683</u>.

JESU, WAHRES GOTTESLAMM / 8i. 7.6.7.6.7.6.7.6   201
   KPS1858 / 70, 630, 632, 1143, 1160.

JESUS IST DER SCHÖNSTE NAM' / 6t. 7.8.7.8.7.7   202
   Zahn 3440 / 1657 / GGB1720 / 135, 582, 613, 629, 695, 698, 867,
   1076.

JESUS IST MEIN HÖCHSTES GUT / 6t. 7.8.7.8.7.7   203
   GGG1806 / 701.

JESUS, MEIN TROST UND HEIL AUF MEINER PILGERREIS' / 6i. 6.6.6.6.8.8   204
   KPS1858 / 704.

JESUS, MEINE ZUVERSICHT / 6t. 7.8.7.8.7.7   205
   Zahn 3432a / 1653 / GGB1720 / 463.

[JOYFULLY, JOYFULLY ONWARD I MOVE?] / 4d. 10.10.10.10   206
   Hymnal 1879, no. 798 / ES1893 / 384?

"JUBILEE" / 4i. 6.6.6.6   207
   (BLAST DIE TROMPETE?)
   CG1874 / 137.

KEIN CHRIST SOLL IHM DIE RECHNUNG MACHEN / 6i. 9.6.6.9.9.5   208
   Zahn 2739 / 1640 / KDP1744 / 202, 721.

KOMM, LIEBSTER, KOMM IN DEINEN GARTEN / 4i. 9.9.8.8   209
   Zahn 1521 / 1657 / KDP1744 / 730.

KOMM, O KOMM, DU GEIST DES LEBENS / 6t. 8.7.8.7.7.7   210
   Zahn 3665 / 1715 / GGB1720 / 60, 284, 417, 429, 455, 466, 472, 525,
   702, 778, 869, 1347.

KOMM, STERBLICHER, BETRACHTE MICH / 7t. 8.7.8.7.8.8.7   211
   KLS1826 / 450.

KOMMET, IHR LIEBEN GESCHWISTER, ZUM FESTLICHEN / 5d. 14.14.4.6.8   212
   KLS1829 / 737.

KOMMT HER ZU MIR, SPRICHT GOTTES SOHN / 6i. 8.8.7.8.8.7   213
   Zahn 2496a / 1530 / GGB1720 / 8, 14, 68, 108, 352, 356, 398, 539,
   744, 1065, 1172, 1303.

KOMMT, KINDER, LASST UNS GEHEN / 8i. 7.6.7.6.6.7.7.6   214
   KPS1858 / 459, 537, 575, 913, 922, 1203.

LASSET UNS DEN HERREN PREISEN / 10t. 8.7.8.7.8.7.7.8.7.7   215
   Zahn 7886 / 1641 / KDP1744 / 643, 662.

LEBT FRIEDSAM, SPRACH CHRISTUS, DER HERR / 10i. 8.7.8.7.4.4.7.4.4.7   216
   KDP1744 / 773.

LIEBE, DIE DU MICH ZUM BILDE / 6t. 8.7.8.7.7.7   217
   Zahn 3667 / 1738 / KDP1744 / 1064.

LIEBSTE WITWE, WEINE NICHT / 8t. 7.6.7.6.7.6.7.6   218
   CG1874 / 329.

LIEBSTER ALLER LIEBEN / 5t. 11.11.6.6.11   219
   KDP1744 / 1067.

LIEBSTER JESU, DU WIRST KOMMEN / 4t. 8.8.7.7   220
   Zahn 1344 / 1698 / GGB1720 / 435, 454, 665, 671, 677, 788, 1125,
   1149, 1158.

LIEBSTER JESU, LIEBSTES LEBEN / 8t. 8.7.7.8.8.7.7.8   221
   Zahn 6513 / 1747 / GGB1720 / 791, 796.

LIEBSTER JESU, WIR SIND HIER / 6t. 7.8.7.8.8.8   222
   Zahn 3498b / 1687 / GGB1720 / 410, 792, 857, 904, 1146, 1168.

LIEBSTER VATER, ICH, DEIN KIND / 8t. 7.6.7.6.7.6.7.6   223
   Zahn 6341 / 1693 / CG1874 / 91.

LOBE DEN HERREN, DEN MÄCHTIGEN KÖNIG / 5d. 14.14.4.7.8   224
    Zahn 1912c / 1680 / GGB 1720 / 144, 165, 377, 644, 1045.
LOBET GOTT ZU JEDER STUNDE / 6t. 8.8.7.8.8.7   225
    CG 1879 / 175, 424.
LOBT GOTT, IHR CHRISTEN, ALLZUGLEICH / 4i. 8.6.8.6   226
    Zahn 199 / 1631 / KDP 1744 / 111, 503.

MACH ENDLICH DES VIELEN ZERSTREUENS EIN END' / 6ab. 11.12.11.12.12.12   227
    KDP 1744 / 146.
MACHE DICH, MEIN GEIST, BEREIT / 8t. 7.6.7.6.3.3.6.6   228
    Zahn 6277 / 1727 / KH 1792 / 109, 1034, 1040, 1157, 1255.
MACH'S MIT MIR, GOTT, NACH DEINER GÜT' / 6i. 8.7.8.7.8.8   229
    Zahn 2383 / 1628 / GGB 1720 / 876.
MEIN BRÄUTIGAM, DU ZARTES GOTTESLAMM / 8i. 4.6.6.5.4.6.6.5   230
    KDP 1744 / 145.
MEIN GEIST FROHLOCKET UND MEIN SINN / 6i. 8.7.8.7.8.8   231
    Zahn 2405 / 1668 / GGB 1720 / 98.
MEIN GEMÜT ERFREUET SICH / 4t. 7.7.7.7   232
    GGG 1806, CG 1874 / 147, 799.
MEIN G'NUG-BESCHWERTER SINN / 8i. 6.6.7.7.6.7.7.6   233
    KDP 1744 / 176, 980.
MEIN GOTT, DAS HERZ ICH BRINGE DIR / 4i. 8.6.8.6   234
    Zahn 224 / 1723 / KDP 1744 / 246, 400, 437, 503, 508, 584, 603, 713,
    817, 823, 824, 843, 874, 925, 969, 993, 999, 1029, 1037, 1071,
    1111, 1153, 1156, 1178, 1222, 1246, 1278, 1280.
MEIN GOTTES HERZ see MEIN GOTT, DAS HERZ ICH BRINGE DIR
HEIN HEILAND, MEIN ERLÖSER, BLICK / 8i. 7.6.7.6.7.6.7.8   235
    KLS 1829 / 826.
MEIN HEILAND NIMMT DIE SÜNDER AN / 10i. 8.9.8.9.8.8.9.9.8.8   236
    Zahn 7774a / ca. 1733 / KDP 1777 / 827.
MEIN HERZ, SEI ZUFRIEDEN / 8ab. 6.5.6.5.6.6.11.11   237
    Zahn 6943 / 1699 / KDP 1744 / 1025.
MEIN HERZENS-JESU, MEINE LUST / 7i. 8.7.8.7.8.8.7   238
    Zahn 8766 / 1767 / GGB 1720 / 184, 257, 345, 405, 444, 468, 558,
    625, 650, 735, 838, 1023, 1095, 1182, 1259.
MEIN HÜTER UND MEIN HIRT IST GOTT, DER HERRE / 6i. 11.11.11.11.11.11   239
    (= PSALM 23 LOBWASSER)
    Zahn 3199 / 1547 / KDP 1744 / 839.
MEIN JESU, DER DU MICH ZUM LUSTSPIEL / 6i. 6.6.5.6.6.5   240
    Zahn 2103 / 1694 / GGB 1720 / 51, 112, 279, 297, 488, 610, 840, 841,
    970, 985, 1117.
MEIN JESU KAUFTE MICH MIT BLUT / 4i. 8.6.8.6   241
    KPS 1858 / 843.
MEIN KÖNIG, SCHREIB MIR DEIN GESETZ / 6i. 8.8.6.8.8.6   242
    Zahn 2443 / 1698 / KDP 1744 / 845.
MEIN LEBEN AUF ERDEN IST MÜHSAM ALLHIER / 8ab. 6.5.6.5.6.5.6.5   243
    CG 1879 / 167, 262.
MEIN SEELENBRÄUTIGAM / 7i. 13.12.12.12.12.12.13   244
    Zahn 4788 / 1667 / KH 1792 / 718, 759.
MEIN VATER, ZEUGE MICH / 4i. 13.12.13.12   245
    Zahn 1121 / 1704 / KDP 1744 / 935, 1024.
MEIN' WALLFAHRT ICH VOLLENDET HAB / 8i. 8.7.8.7.8.7.8.7   246
    Zahn 5704a / 1641 / GGB 1720 / 583, 829.

MEINE ARMUT MACHT MICH SCHREIEN / 6t. 8.4.7.8.4.7   247
   Zahn 3548a / 1704 / KDP1744 / 709.

MEINE HOFFNUNG STEHET FESTE / 7t. 8.7.8.7.3.3.7   248
   Zahn 4870 / 1680 / GGB1720 / 104, 156, 316, 337, 863.

MEINE SEEL' MIT ALLEM FLEISSE / 6t. 8.7.8.7.7.7   249
   (= PSALM 146 LOBWASSER)
   Zahn 3613 / 1562 / KDP1744 / <u>859</u>.

MEINE SEELE LOBE GOTT, DER EIN MÄCHTIG, HEILIG WESEN / 5t. 7.8.8.7.7   250
   GGG1806 / <u>860</u>.

MEINE SEELE SEHNET SICH NACH DER STILLE / 7t. 7.4.7.4.7.7.4   251
   KPS1858 / <u>861</u>.

MEINE SEELE, WILLST DU RUH'N / 6t. 7.7.8.8.7.7   252
   Zahn 3395a / 1657 / GGB1720 / 689, <u>864</u>.

MEINE SORGEN, ANGST UND PLAGEN / 8t. 8.7.8.7.7.7.8.8   253
   KH1792 / 154, 692.

MEINEN JESUM LASS ICH NICHT / 6t. 7.8.7.8.7.7   254
   Zahn 3449 / 1658 / GGB1720 / 373, 374, 432, 656, 699, 862, 872.

MENSCH, WAS SUCHST DU IN DER NACHT / 6t. 7.8.7.8.7.7   255
   Zahn 3451a / 1674 / GGB1720 / 696.

MIR NACH, SPRICHT CHRISTUS / 6i. 8.7.8.7.8.8   256
   Zahn 2399 / 1668 / GGB1720 / 20, 22, 209, 244, 298, 396, 441, 563,
   651, 1121, 1131, 1155, 1275.

MONARCHE ALLER DING / 6i. 6.7.6.7.8.8   257
   Zahn 2234 / 1738 / KDP1797-G / <u>879</u>.

MORGENGLANZ DER EWIGKEIT / 6t. 7.8.7.8.7.3   258
   Zahn 3426 / 1684 / KDP1744 / <u>881</u>, 1004.

NAME VOLLER GÜTE / 8t. 6.6.6.6.6.6.6.6   259
   Zahn 6261 / 1657 / KDP1744 / 660, <u>888</u>.

NEARER, MY GOD, TO THEE / 7d. 6.4.6.4.6.6.4   260
   Hymnal 1879, no. 434 / CG1879 / 887.

NICHTS HILFT UNS DOCH MIT HOHEN GABEN / 6i. 9.8.9.8.8.8   261
   107.

NIE WILL ICH DEM ZU SCHADEN SUCHEN / 4i. 9.6.9.6   262
   Zahn 737 / 1758 / KDP1797-G / <u>894</u>.

NUN BITTEN WIR DEN HEILIGEN GEIST / 5 mixed. 9.9.11.10.4   263
   Zahn 2029 / 1524 / GGB1720 / <u>897</u>.

NUN DANKET ALLE GOTT / 8i. 6.7.6.7.6.6.6.6   264
   Zahn 5142 / 1649 / GGB1720 / 193, 467, 545, <u>900</u>, 992, 1130, 1177.

NUN DAS ALTE JAHR IST HIN / 6t. 7.6.7.6.7.7   265
   Zahn 3321 / 1704 / KDP1744 / <u>901</u>.

NUN FREUT EUCH, LIEBEN CHRISTEN G'MEIN / 7i. 8.7.8.7.8.8.7   266
   Zahn 4427 / 1524 / GGB1720 / 536, 604, 1039, 1252.

NUN KOMM, DER HEIDEN HEILAND / 4t. 7.7.7.7   267
   Zahn 1174 / 1524 / KDP1744 / 434, 512, 671.

NUN KOMMT DIE ABENDSTUNDE / 8i. 7.6.7.6.6.6.7.6   268
   (= WO BLEIBEN MEINE SINNEN?)
   KLS1829 / <u>911</u>.

NUN LASST UNS DEN LEIB BEGRABEN / 4t.-i. 8.8.8.8   269
   Zahn 340b / 1545 / GGB1720 / 126, 306, 1016, 1114, 1218.

NUN LASST UNS GOTT, DEM HERREN / 4i. 7.7.7.7   270
   Zahn 156 / 1575 / KDP1744 / 1183.

NUN LOB, MEIN' SEEL', DEN HERREN / 12i. 7.8.7.8.7.6.7.6.7.6.7.6   271
   Zahn 8244 / 1540 / GGB1720 / 805, <u>918</u>.

NUN LOBET ALLE GOTTES SOHN / 6i. 8.7.8.7.8.8   272
   CG1874 / 1118.
NUN LOBET ALLE WÄLDER / 6i. 7.7.6.7.7.8   273
   (= NUN RUHEN ALLE WÄLDER?)
   KDP1744 / 920.
NUN RUHEN ALLE WÄLDER / 6i. 7.7.6.7.7.8   274
   Zahn 2308 / 1655 / GGB1720 / 229, 249, 449, 743, 831, 852, 923,
   1030, 1196, 1244, 1248.
NUN RUHT DOCH ALLE WELT / 12 mixed. 11.11.11.11.5.5.8.7.8.7.7.7   275
   Zahn 8423 / 1704 / KDP1744 / 924.
NUN SICH DER TAG GEENDET HAT / 4i. 8.6.8.6   276
   Zahn 212a / 1667 / GGB1720 / 116, 399, 816, 927, 928, 1312, 1313.
NUN SIEH, WIE FEIN UND LIEBLICH IST / 8i. 8.7.8.7.8.8.7.7   277
   Zahn 5736 / 1545 / KDP1744 / 494.
NUN, SO BLEIBT ES FEST DABEI, DASS ICH JESU EIGEN SEI / 4t. 7.7.7.7   278
   KLS1841 / 929.
NUN WILL ICH MICH SCHEIDEN / 6ab.i. 11.9.8.9.9.8   279
   Zahn 4052 / 1704 / GGB1720 / 930.
NUR FRISCH HINEIN / 6i. 4.6.11.11.10.4   280
   Zahn 2090 / 1698 / GGB1720 / 932, 1170, 1363.
NUR GOTT ALLEIN, O GÜLD'NES WORT / 10i. 8.8.4.4.8.4.4.5.5.4   281
   Zahn 7733 / 1778 / KH1792 / 933.

O ALLERHÖCHSTER MENSCHEN HÜTER / 5i. 9.8.8.9.5   282
   Zahn 1799a / 1704 / GGB1720 / 936.
O DAS LAMM, DAS LIEBE LAMM (Ch) / 5 mixed. 7.6.6.5.6   283
   Lorenz 24 / KPS1858 / 843.
O DER ALLES HÄTT' VERLOREN / 4t. 8.7.8.7   284
   Zahn 1290a / 1705 / GGB1720 / 9, 497, 687, 939, 943, 1049, 1050,
   1154, 1223, 1270.
O DU LIEBE MEINER LIEBE / 8t. 8.7.8.7.8.7.8.7   285
   Zahn 6693 / 1684 / GGB1720 / 680, 858, 951.
O DU SÜSSE LUST / 6t. 5.5.8.8.5.5   286
   KH1792 / 902.
O DU TOLL UND TÖRICHT VOLK / 8t.-i. 7.8.7.8.3.3.7.4   287
   Zahn 7096 / 1680 / GGB1720 / 811, 950.
O DURCHBRECHER ALLER BANDE / 8t. 8.7.8.7.8.7.8.7   288
   Zahn 6709 / 1704 / GGB1720 / 186, 391, 756, 774, 780, 858, 947,
   1169, 1304.
O EWIGKEIT, DU DONNERWORT / 8i. 8.8.7.8.8.7.8.8   289
   Zahn 5819 / 1642 / KDP1744 / 263, 953.
O FINSTRE NACHT, WANN / 8i. 11.8.11.8.8.8.8.9   290
   Zahn 6170 / 1723 / KDP1744 / 1342.
O GOTT, DER DU EIN HEERFÜRST BIST / 8i. 8.8.9.8.8.9.8.8   291
   (= PSALM 84 LOBWASSER)
   Zahn 5868 / 1562 / KDP1744 / 957.
O GOTT, DU FROMMER GOTT / 8i. 6.7.6.7.6.6.6.6   292
   Zahn 5144 / 1648 / GGB1720 / 89, 129, 138, 206, 303, 304, 552, 559,
   620, 992, 995, 1085, 1224, 1289.
O GOTTES STADT, O GÜLD'NES LICHT / 8i. 8.7.8.7.9.9.8.8   293
   Zahn 5789 / 1642 / GGB1720 / 964.
O HEILAND, IN DEM MEINE SEELE SICH FREUT / 8ab. 11.8.11.8.11.8.11.8   294
   (= O THOU IN WHOSE PRESENCE MY SOUL TAKES DELIGHT?)
   KPS1858 / 966.

O HEIL'GER GEIST, KEHR BEI UNS / 12i.-t. 8.8.7.8.8.7.2.2.4.4.4.8   295
   Zahn 8371 / 1683 / KPS1858 / 436, 712, 955, 1198.

O HERR DER HERRLICHKEIT / 6i. 6.6.5.6.6.5   296
   Zahn 4155 / 1698 / KDP1744 / 160.

O HERRE GOTT, DEIN GÖTTLICH' WORT / 8i. 8.7.8.7.8.7.8.7   297
   Zahn 5690 / 1527 / KDP1744 / 264.

O HIMMLISCHE LIEBE, DU HAST MICH BESESSEN / 6ab. 12.11.12.11.11.11   298
   KDP1744 / 972.

O HOW HAPPY ARE THEY WHO THEIR SAVIOR OBEY / 6a. 6.6.9.6.6.9   299
   Hymnal 1901, no. 448 / 1824 / CG1874 / 1035.

O IHR AUSERWÄHLTEN KINDER / 8t. 8.7.8.7.4.4.8.8   300
   Zahn 6515c / 1738 / KDP1797 / 973.

O JERUSALEM, DU SCHÖNE / 6t. 8.7.8.7.7.7   301
   Zahn 3655 / 1711 / CG1874 / 1043.

O JESU CHRIST, MEINS LEBENS LICHT / 4i. 8.8.8.8   302
   Zahn 533a / 1625 / KDP1744 / 12, 18, 916, 917, 981.

O JESU, DU BIST MEIN / 8i. 6.6.7.7.6.7.6.7   303
   Zahn 5124 / 1692 / KDP1744 / 815.

O JESU, KOMM ZU MIR / 8i. 6.5.6.3.6.5.6.5   304
   Zahn 5059 / 1698 / GGB1720 / 983, 986, 1209.

O JESU, MEIN BRÄUT'GAM / 5ab. 11.11.6.6.11   305
   Zahn 1908 / 1698 / GGB1720 / 987, 1002, 1026.

O JESU, MEINES LEBENS LICHT / 4i. 8.7.8.7   306
   Zahn 247b / 1610 / CG1874 / 84, 509, 1019.

O JESU, SÜSSES LICHT / 8i. 6.7.6.7.6.6.6.6   307
   Zahn 5181 / 1723 / GGB1720 / 623.

O JESU, WANN SOLL ICH ERLÖSET DOCH WERDEN / 6ab. 12.12.11.11.12.12   308
   Zahn 3915a / 1665 / CG1874 / 210, 389.

O LAMM GOTTES, UNSCHULDIG / 7 mixed. 7.7.7.7.7.7.8   309
   Zahn 4361a / 1545 / GGB1720 / 997.

O STARKER GOTT, O SEELENKRAFT / 4i. 8.8.8.8   310
   GGB1720 / 26, 148, 486, 602, 614, 908.

O STARKER ZEBAOTH / 8i. 6.6.6.6.6.6.6.6   311
   Zahn 5071 / 1680 / GGB1720 / 1017.

O SÜNDER, DENKE WOHL / 8i. 6.6.6.6.6.6.6.6   312
   Zahn 5064 / 1680 / KDP1744 / 1018.

[O THOU IN WHOSE PRESENCE MY SOUL TAKES DELIGHT?] / 4ab. 11.8.11.8   313
   Hymnal 1879, no.667 / KPS1858 / 966?

O TRAURIGKEIT, O HERZELEID / 5i.-t. 4.4.7.7.6   314
   Zahn 1915 / 1641 / GGB1720 / 804, 996.

O URSPRUNG DES LEBENS / 8ab. 6.5.6.5.6.6.11.11   315
   Zahn 6949 / 1735 / KDP1744 / 834.

O WELT, SIEH HIER DEIN LEBEN / 6i. 7.7.6.7.7.8   316
   Zahn 2298 / 1653 / KLS1834 / 443, 762, 1206.

O WIE IST DER WEG SO SCHMAL / 8t. 7.6.7.6.7.6.7.6   317
   GGG1806, CG1874 / 66.

O WIE SELIG SIND DIE SEELEN / 6t. 8.8.7.8.8.7   318
   Zahn 3862a / ca. 1710 / GGB1720 / 338, 541, 766, 1134.

"OLD HUNDRED" / 4i. 8.8.8.8   319
   NS1870 / 132.

ON NE VIT PLUS DANS NO FORETS / 6i. 8.9.8.9.8.8   320
   KH1792 / 548.

PREIS, LOB EHR', RUHM, DANK, KRAFT UND MACHT / 6i. 8.9.8.9.10.10   321
   Zahn 2713 / 1698 / GGB1720 / 134, 185, 320, 464, <u>1044</u>, 1094, 1309.
PSALM 6 LOBWASSER / 6i. 7.7.6.7.7.6   322
   (= In deinem grossen Zorn)
   Zahn 2266 / 1542 / KDP1744 / 882.
PSALM 7 LOBWASSER / 8i. 9.9.8.8.9.9.8.8   323
   (= Mein' Hoffnung auf dir, Herr, tut schweben)
   Lobwasser / KDP1744 / 1001.
PSALM 8 LOBWASSER / 4t.-i. 11.11.10.10   324
   (= O höchster Gott, o unser lieber Herre)
   Zahn 923 / 1542 / KDP1744 / 1022.
PSALM 23 LOBWASSER / 6i. 11.11.11.11.11.11   325
   (= MEIN HÜTER UND MEIN HIRT)
   Zahn 3199 / 1547 / KDP1744 / 839.
PSALM 24 LOBWASSER / 6i. 8.8.9.8.8.9   326
   (= DEM HERREN DER ERDKREIS ZUSTEHT)
   Zahn 2665 / 1542 / KDP1744 / 189, 830, 853.
PSALM 25 LOBWASSER / 8t. 8.7.8.7.7.8.7.8   327
   (= ZU DIR ICH MEIN HERZ ERHEBE)
   Zahn 6678 / 1551 / KDP1744 / 1357.
PSALM 34 LOBWASSER / 8i. 6.8.8.6.6.8.8.6   328
   (= ICH WILL NICHT LASSEN AB)
   Zahn 5230 / 1551 / KDP1744 / 593.
PSALM 38 LOBWASSER / 6t. 8.4.7.8.4.7   329
   (= Herr, zur Zucht in deinem Grimme)
   Zahn 3531 / 1542 / KDP1744 / 59.
PSALM 42 LOBWASSER / 8t. 8.7.8.7.7.7.8.8   330
   (= WIE NACH EINER WASSERQUELLE)
   Zahn 6543 / 1551 / GAL1753, KH1792 / 462, 1090.
PSALM 47 LOBWASSER / 12t. 5.5.5.5.5.5.5.5.5.5.5.5   331
   (= Nun, ihr Völker all')
   Zahn 8337 / 1551 / KDP1744 / 564.
PSALM 50 LOBWASSER / 6i. 10.10.10.10.11.11   332
   (= Gott, der über die Völker all' regiert)
   Zahn 3094 / 1548 / GGB1720 / 590, 1013, 1292.
PSALM 58 LOBWASSER / 6i. 9.8.8.9.8.8   333
   (= Sagt mir, die ihr euch Ratsleut' nennet)
   Zahn 2748 / 1562 / KDP1744 / 690.
PSALM 74 LOBWASSER / 4i. 10.11.11.10   333a
   (= Warum verstösst du uns, o Herr)
   Lobwasser / KDP1744 / 564.
PSALM 77 LOBWASSER / 8t. 8.8.7.7.8.8.7.7   334
   (= ZU GOTT IN DEM HIMMEL DROBEN)
   Zahn 6863 / 1547 / KDP1744 / 476.
PSALM 80 LOBWASSER / 6i. 9.9.8.8.8.8   335
   (= Anhör, du Hirt Israel werte)
   Lobwasser / KDP1744 / 45.
PSALM 84 LOBWASSER / 8i. 8.8.9.8.8.9.8.8   336
   (= O GOTT, DER DU EIN HEERFÜRST BIST)
   Zahn 5868 / 1562 / KDP1744 / 957.
PSALM 100 LOBWASSER / 4i. 8.8.8.8   337
   (= IHR VÖLKER AUF DER ERDEN ALL')
   Zahn 367 / 1551 / KDP1744 / 567, 619.

SETZE DICH, MEIN GEIST, EIN WENIG / 7t. 8.7..7.4.4.7   359
    Zahn 7337 / 1779 / KPS1858 / 748, 776.

SHED NOT A TEAR / 11d. 10.4.4.10.4.4.10.10.10.4.4   360
    CG1874 / 891.

"SICILIAN HYMN" / 6 mixed 5.5.7.5.5.5   361
    KLS1841 / 946.

SIE SCHLÄFET SCHON (NUN SCHLÄFET MAN) / 8i. 4.6.6.5.4.6.6.5   362
    Zahn 5040a / 1766 / KDP1777 / 926.

SIEH, HIER BIN ICH, EHRENKÖNIG / 9t. 4.4.7.4.4.7.4.4.7   363
    Zahn 7322a / 1680 / GGB1720 / 235, 589, 591, 592, 633, 779, 1042,
    1072, 1100, 1103, 1105.

SINGT DEM HERRN NAH UND FERN / 12t.-i. 3.3.7.7.7.7.7.4.4.4.4.7   364
    Zahn 8401 / 1831 / KDP1744 / 1110.

SO GEHE NUN IN DEINE GRUFT / 4i.-t. 8.8.8.8   365
    KLS1826 / 1116.

SO GEHST DU, JESU, WILLIGLICH / 10i. 8.7.8.7.8.8.7.8.8.7   366
    Zahn 7714 / 1785 / KDP1797 / 1115.

SO IST DENN NUN DIE HÜTTE AUFGEBAUET / 6i. 11.10.10.11.10.10   367
    Zahn 3126a / 1714 / KDP1744 / 850.

SO OFT EIN BLICK MICH AUFWÄRTS FÜHRET / 6i.-t. 9.9.7.8.4.7   368
    Zahn 4007a / 1698 / KDP1744 / 1127.

SO WÜNSCH ICH IHR (NUN) EIN' / 7i. 8.7.8.7.4.4.7   369
    Zahn 4405 / 1536 / GGB1720 / 4, 239, 274, 637, 1191.

SOLLT' ES GLEICH BISWEILEN SCHEINEN / 4t. 8.8.7.7   370
    Zahn 1348 / 1687 / CG1874 / 1272.

SORGLOSER SÜNDER, DU, ICH BITT DICH, KOMM / 8d. 6.4.6.4.6.6.6.4   371
    KPS1858 / 1129.

STRAF MICH NICHT IN DEINEM ZORN / 8t. 7.6.7.6.3.3.6.6   372
    Zahn 6274a / 1694 / GGB1720 / 143, 803, 1107, 1148.

SÜSSER CHRIST, DU, DU BIST / 6t. 3.3.4.7.7.8   373
    Zahn 3235 / 1660 / ELEL1812 / 1138.

THE ROCK THAT IS HIGHER THAN I / ab.   374
    CG1874 / 190.

TOCHTER VON ZION, STEH AUF VON BETRÜBNIS / 4d. 11.11.11.11   375
    (= DAUGHTER OF ZION, AWAKE FROM THY SADNESS)
    KPS1858 / 1139.

TOCHTER VON ZION, STEH AUF VON BETRÜBNIS (Ch) / 4 mixed. 11.11.6.4   376
    KPS1858 / 1139.

TREUER VATER, DEINE LIEBE / 6t. 8.8.7.8.8.7   377
    Zahn 3855 / ca. 1708 / GGB1720 / 331, 798, 806, 1080.

TRIUMPH, TRIUMPH, ES KOMMT MIT PRACHT / 6i. 8.8.8.8.2.8   378
    Zahn 2631a / 1698 / GGB1720 / 800, 907, 1295, 1324.

UNERSCHAFF'NE LEBENSSONNE / 6t. 8.7.7.8.7.7   379
    Zahn 3596 / 1705 / KDP1744 / 786, 787, 1005.

UNSER HERRSCHER, UNSER KÖNIG / 6t. 8.7.8.7.8.8   380
    Zahn 3735a / 1680 / GGB1720 / 61, 414, 1087, 1157.

UNSER VATER IM HIMMELREICH / 6i. 8.8.8.8.8.8   381
    GGB1720 / 1120.

UNSER WANDEL IST IM HIMMEL / 9t. 8.7.7.8.8.7.7.7.7   382
    Zahn 7349 / 1738 / GGB1720 / 1162.

VALET WILL ICH DIR GEBEN / 8i. 7.6.7.6.7.6.7.6   383
    Zahn 5403 / 1613 / GGB1720 / 122, 348, 447, 627, 833, 1059, 1254,
    1315.
VERLIEBTES LUSTSPIEL REINER SEELEN / 8i. 9.8.9.8.9.8.9.8   384
    KDP1744 / 1015, 1047.
VOM HIMMEL HOCH, DA KOMM ICH HER / 4i. 8.8.8.8   385
    Zahn 345 / 1537 / KDP1744 / 86, 793, 991.
VON GOTT WILL ICH NICHT LASSEN / 8i. 7.6.7.6.6.7.7.6   386
    Zahn 5264b / 1751 / GGB1720 / 34, 119, 292, 499, 751, 752, 1123,
    <u>1179</u>, 1287.

WACH AUF, DU GEIST DER TREUEN ZEUGEN / 8i. 9.8.9.8.4.4.8.8   387
    KDP1744 / 350.
WACH AUF, MEIN HERZ, UND SINGE / 4i. 7.7.7.7   388
    Zahn 171 / 1655 / GAL1753, CG1874 / 216, 420, 636.
WACH AUF, MEIN HERZE / 4i. 7.7.7.7   389
    GGB1720 / 586, 615.
WACHET AUF, RUFT UNS DIE STIMME / 12i.-t. 8.9.8.8.9.8.6.6.4.4.4.8   390
    Zahn 8405a / 1599 / GGB1720 / 105, 427, 471, 475, 600, <u>1186</u>, 1350.
WACHT AUF, IHR CHRISTEN ALLE / 8i. 7.6.7.6.7.6.7.6   391
    GGB1720 / 348, 1188.
WANN ERBLICK ICH DICH EINMAL / 7t. 7.4.7.4.7.4.6   392
    KDP1744 / 460, 679.
WANN ... see also WENN ...
WARUM BETRÜBST DU DICH, MEIN HERZ / 5i. 8.8.6.8.8   393
    Zahn 1689a / 1565 / GAL1753 / 1283.
WARUM SOLLT ICH MICH DENN GRÄMEN / 8t. 8.3.3.6.8.3.3.6   394
    Zahn 6455a / 1653 / GGB1720 / 1028, 1195.
WARUM WILLST DU DOCH FÜR MORGEN / 8t. 8.3.3.6.8.3.3.6   395
    KDP1764 / 451.
WAS FRAG ICH NACH DER WELT / 8i. 6.7.6.7.6.6.6.6   396
    Zahn 5168a / 1679 / GGB1720 / 552.
WAS GOTT TUT, DAS IST WOHLGETAN / 8i. 8.7.8.7.4.4.7.7   397
    Zahn 5629 / 1690 / GGB1720 / 578, 937, 1200, <u>1201</u>, 1212.
WAS MEIN GOTT WILL, DAS G'SCHEH' ALLZEIT / 10i. 8.7.8.7.4.4.7.4.4.7   398
    Zahn 7568 / 1572 / GGB1720 / 397, 1093.
WAS MICH AUF DIESER WELT BETRÜBT / 10i. 8.6.8.6.4.4.6.4.4.6 399
    Zahn 7525 / 1679 / GGB1720 / 1204, <u>1214</u>.
WAS SOLL ICH WEITER SAGEN / 8i. 7.6.7.6.6.6.7.6   400
    KLS1829 / <u>1216</u>.
WELT, PACKE DICH / 5i.-ab. 4.4.5.12.12   401
    Zahn 1965 / 1679 / GGB1720 / <u>1227</u>.
WENN AN MEINEN FREUND ICH DENKE / 6t. 8.4.7.8.4.7   402
    GGB1720 / 1231.
WENN ENDLICH, EH' ES ZION MEINT / 6i. 8.8.9.8.8.9   403
    Zahn 2674 / 1704 / GGB1720 / <u>1236</u>.
WENN NACH DEM FRIEDENSLAND WIR GEH'N / 8i. 8.8.8.8.8.8.4.4 404
    KPS1858 / 142, <u>1247</u>.
WENN WIR IN HÖCHSTEN NÖTEN SEIN / 4i. 8.8.8.8   405
    GGB1720 / 639.
WENN ... see also WANN ...
WER CHRISTUM RECHT WILL LIEBEN / 8i. 7.6.7.6.6.7.7.6   406
    Zahn 5287 / 1642 / KDP1744 / 1271.

WER JESUM BEI SICH HAT / 8i. 6.5..5.6.5.6.5   407
  KPS 1858 / 832, 1228, 1263.
WER NUR DEN LIEBEN GOTT LÄSST WALTEN / 6i. 9.8.9.8.8.8   408
  Zahn 2778 / 1657 / GGB 1720 / 47, 62, 64, 69, 78, 107, 123, 172,188,
  237, 259, 299, 323, 333, 354, 364, 383, 422, 492, 501, 520, 524,
  543, 556, 557, 572, 573, 595, 760, 768, 819, 842, 883, 885, 893,
  940, 958, 1199, 1215, 1250, 1269, 1277, 1286, 1293, 1334.
WER OHREN HAT, ZU HÖREN, DER MERK' / 8i. 7.6.7.6.7.6.7.6   409
  KLS 1826 / 1267.
WER WEISS, WIE NAHE MIR MEIN ENDE / 6i. 9.8.9.8.8.8   410
  Zahn 2775b / 1747 / KPS 1858 / 88, 177, 507, 566, 821, 960, 1101,
  1314.
WER WIRD IN JENER NEUEN WELT / 8i. 8.7.8.7.8.8.8.8   411
  Broadside / 1796 / 248.
WERDE MUNTER, MEIN GEMÜTE / 8t. 8.7.8.7.7.7.8.8   412
  Zahn 6551 / 1642 / GGB 1720 / 198, 201, 330, 382, 504, 710, 783,
  1335.
WIE FLEUCHT (FLIEGT) DAHIN DER MENSCHEN ZEIT / 5i. 8.8.8.4.8   413
  Zahn 1730 / 1691 / GGB 1720 / 180.
WIE NACH EINER WASSERQUELLE / 8t. 8.7.8.7.7.7.8.8   414
  (= PSALM 42 LOBWASSER)
  Zahn 6543 / 1551 / GGB 1720 / 1208.
WIE PRÄCHTIG IST DER NAM', BRÜDER / 10i.-t. 6.6.6.3.6.6.6.6.6.3   415
  CG 1874 / 1294.
WIE SCHÖN BEWOHNT / 11i.-t. 8.8.7.8.8.7.4.4.4.4.8   416
  CG 1874 / 851.
WIE SCHÖN IST UNSRES KÖNIGS BRAUT / 6i. 8.8.8.8.10.10   417
  Zahn 2658 / 1710 / KDP 1744 / 1150, 1338.
WIE SCHÖN LEUCHT' UNS (LEUCHTET) / 12i.-t. 8.8.7.8.8.7.2.2.4.4.4.8   418
  Zahn 8359 / 1599 / GGB 1720 / 256, 281, 438, 465, 641, 844, 956,
  967, 982, 1288, 1339, 1352, 1360, 1362.
WIE SELIG IST DAS VOLK DES HERRN / 7i. 8.7.8.7.8.8.7   419
  KLS 1829 / 1296.
WIE WOHL IST MIR, DASS ICH / 7i. 11.11.10.11.13.8.4   420
  Zahn 4779 / 1698 / GGB 1720 / 1174.
WIE WOHL IST MIR, O FREUND / 10i. 9.8.9.8.9.9.8.9.9.8   421
  Zahn 7791 / 1692 / GGB 1720 / 1301.
WO BLEIBEN MEINE SINNEN / 8i. 7.6.7.6.6.6.7.6   422
  ELEL 1812, KLS 1826 / 37, 618, 911? 1008, 1216?
WO GEHT DIE REISE HIN, O DU MEIN LIEBER / i.   423
  ELEL 1812 / 1322.
WO GOTT DER HERR NICHT BEI UNS HÄLT / 7i. 8.7.8.7.8.8.7   424
  Zahn 4440 / 1525 / GGB 1720 / 4, 39, 40, 479.
WO GOTT ZUM HAUS NICHT GIBT SEIN' GUNST / 4i. 8.8.8.8   425
  Zahn 304 / 1525 / GGB 1720 / 812.
WO IST DER SCHÖNSTE, DEN ICH LIEBE / 8i. 9.8.8.9.9.8.9.8   426
  Zahn 5956a / 1657 / GGB 1720 / 44, 808, 1323, 1326.
WO IST DIE KIRCHE JESU DOCH / 6i. 8.8.8.8.10.10   427
  KLS 1829 / 1324.
WO IST DIE SONNE / 6t. 8.4.7.8.4.7   428
  KH 1792 / 1075.
WO IST JESU, MEIN VERLANGEN / 4i. 8.7.8.7   429
  ELEL 1812, NS 1870 / 521, 1166, 1167, 1325.
WO IST MEIN SCHÄFLEIN, DAS ICH LIEBE / 8i. 9.8.8.9.9.8.9.8   430
  Zahn 5959 / 1744 / KDP 1744 / 49, 554.

276

WO IST MEINE SONNE BLIEBEN / 6t. 8.4.7.8.4.7   431
   Zahn 3547 / 1704 / GGB1720 / 1232.
WO IST WOHL EIN SÜSSER LEBEN / 8t. 8.7.8.7.6.6.7.7   432
   Zahn 6519 / 1738 / KDP1744 / 381, 747, 1328.
WO SOLL ICH FLIEHEN HIN / 6i. 6.6.7.7.7.7   433
   Zahn 2177 / 1679 / KDP1744 / 73, 110.
WOHLAUF, MEIN HERZ, SEI GUTEN MUTS / 6i. 8.8.8.8.4.4   434
   Zahn 2556 / 1648 / KDP1797-G / 495.
WUNDERBARER KÖNIG / 10t. 6.6.8.6.6.8.3.3.6.6   435
   Zahn 7854 / 1680 / GGB1720 / 428, 646, 1341, 1354.

ZERFLIESS, MEIN GEIST / 8i. 11.8.11.8.8.8.9.9   436
   Zahn 6164 / 1698 / GGB1720 / 94, 200, 954.
ZEUCH EIN ZU DEINEN TOREN / 8i. 7.6.7.6.6.7.7.6   437
   Zahn 5294 / 1653 / CG1874 / 1122.
ZEUCH MEINEN GEIST / 4i. 9.9.8.8   438
   Zahn 788 / 1684 / GGB1720 / 506, 1001, 1345.
ZEUCH MICH, ZEUCH MICH, MIT DEN ARMEN / 6t. 8.7.8.7.8.8   439
   Zahn 3747 / 1680 / GGB1720 / 23, 56, 669, 753, 790, 1006, 1161,
   1219.
ZION KLAGT MIT ANGST UND SCHMERZEN / 8t. 8.7.8.7.7.7.8.8   440
   Zahn 6550 / 1640 / GGB1720 / 378, 658, 757, 1142, 1145.
ZU DEINEM FELS UND GROSSEN RETTER / 4i. 9.8.9.8   441
   GGB1720 / 931, 984.
ZU DIR ICH MEIN HERZ ERHEBE / 8t. 8.7.8.7.7.8.7.8   442
   (= PSALM 25 LOBWASSER)
   Zahn 6678 / 1551 / KDP1744 / 1357.
ZU DIR VON HERZENSGRUNDE / 8i. 7.6.7.6.7.6.7.6   443
   (= PSALM 130 LOBWASSER)
   Zahn 5352 / KDP1744 / 1358.
ZU GOTT IN DEM HIMMEL DROBEN / 8t. 8.8.7.7.8.8.7.7   444
   (= PSALM 77 LOBWASSER)
   Zahn 6863 / 1547 / KDP1744 / 1359.

C. M. / 4i. 8.6.8.6   445
   NS1870 / 85, 139, 173, 212, 213, 223, 254, 319, 325, 353, 368, 519,
   628, 711, 729, 971, 1057, 1061, 1112, 1185, 1233, 1262, 1318, 1356.
L.M. / 4i. 8.8.8.8   446
   NS1870 / 58, 97, 125, 168, 208, 214, 218, 233, 245, 309, 341, 344,
   346, 394, 402, 617, 733, 736, 738, 739, 755, 818, 889, 896, 938,
   941, 944, 1021, 1173, 1176, 1265, 1346.
P. M. / 4t. 7.6.7.6 / NS1870 / 945   447
         7.7.7.7 / NS1870 / 100, 161, 1193.   448
         8.7.8.7 / NS1870 / 750.   449
      6i. 6.6.6.6.8.8 / NS1870 / 1337.   450
         8.8.6.8.8.6 / NS1870 / 187.   451
         8.8.7.4.4.7 / NS1870 / 540.   452
      8i. 7.6.7.6.7.6.7.6 / NS1870 / 120.   453
      8t. 8.3.3.6.8.3.3.6 / NS1870 / 1194.   454
S. M. / 4t. 6.6.8.6 / NS1870 / 72, 531, 728.   455

[NO MELODY REFERENCE]

4d.-i.	11.11.11. 5 / 797.	456
4i.	6. 6. 8. 6 / 318.	457
	8. 6. 8. 6 / 740.	458
	8. 7. 8. 7 / 21, 222, 1217.	459
	8. 8. 8. 8 / 419, 493.	460
4t.	7. 7. 7. 7 / 80, 163, 170, 395, 416, 1077, 1151, 1164, 1189.	461
	8. 7. 8. 7 / 150, 282, 287, 411, 473, 684, 685, 691, 742, 745, 749, 777, 873, 877, 878, 880, 892, 1088, 1126, 1128, 1133, 1135, 1136, 1137, 1253, 1264, 1276.	462
6ab.	11.11.11.11. 8.10 / 1321.	463
6i.	8. 8. 6. 8. 8. 6 / 270.	464
	8. 8. 8. 8.10.10 / 1260.	465
	9. 8. 9. 8. 8. 8 / 207, 542, 828, 875, 895, 1266.	466
6t.	5. 5. 8. 8. 5. 5 / 664.	467
	7. 8. 7. 8. 7. 7 / 707, 856.	468
	8. 7. 8. 7. 7. 7 / 483, 1051, 1152.	469
7i.	7. 6. 7. 6. 7. 7. 6 / 1119.	470
	8. 7. 8. 7. 4. 4. 7 / 31.	471
	8. 7. 8. 7. 8. 8. 7 / 205, 580, 638, 640, 1300.	472
7t. —	8. 7. 8. 7. 4. 4. 7 / 1343.	473
8i.	6. 7. 6. 7. 6. 7. 6. 7 / 67.	474
	7. 6. 7. 6. 7. 6. 7. 6 / 546, 1237	475
	7. 6. 7. 6. 7. 7. 7. 6 / 1292.	476
8t.	7. 6. 7. 6. 7. 6. 7. 6 / 655.	477
	8. 7. 8. 7. 7. 7. 8. 8 / 481, 731, 1279.	478
	8. 7. 8. 7. 8. 7. 8. 7 / 500, 631.	479
	8. 7. 8. 7. 8. 8. 7. 7 / 401.	480
	10. 7.10. 7.10.10. 7. 7 / 272.	481
12i.-t.	8. 8. 7. 8. 8. 7. 2. 2. 4. 4. 4. 8 / 489.	482

2. METRIC INDEX

This index groups the melodies listed in the First-Line Index of
Melodies according to the number of lines per stanza, the meter, and the
number of syllables per line. The numbers following the slash refer to
the numbers under which the melodies are listed in the First-Line Index of
Melodies, which entries in turn refer to the hymn-texts using those
melodies.

2i.	8. 8 / 36.
	11.11 / 53.
4ab.	5. 9. 6. 5 / 177, 179.
	6. 5. 6. 5 / 12, 106.
	11. 8.11. 8 / 313.
	12.11.12.11 / 118.
	12.12.12.12 / 2, 9, 10, 85, 166.
4d.	5. 5. 5. 5 / 195.
	10.10.10.10 / 206.
	11.11.11.11 / 56, 86, 375.
4d.-i.	11.11.11. 5 / 456.
4i.	6. 5. 6. 5 / 66.
	6. 6. 6. 6 / 41, 207.
	6. 6. 8. 6 / 63, 170, 457.
	7. 7. 7. 7 / 124, 270, 388, 389.
	8. 4. 4. 6 / 132.
	8. 6. 8. 6 / 30, 226, 234, 241, 276, 445, 458.
	8. 7. 8. 7 / 159, 306, 429, 459.
	8. 8. 8. 8 / 3, 33, 45, 48, 74, 84, 96, 139, 140, 141, 156, 175, 178, 181, 302, 310, 319, 337, 340, 385, 405, 425, 460.
	9. 6. 9. 6 / 262.
	9. 8. 9. 8 / 97, 342, 441.
	9. 9. 8. 8 / 209, 438.
	10.10.11.11 / 82.
	10.11.11.10 / 165, 333a, 338.
	11. 9.11.11 / 163.
	11.11.10.10 / 65, 162, 324.
	11.11.11. 5 / 147.
	13.12.13.12 / 245.
4i.-t.	8. 8. 8. 8 / 365.
4t.	7. 6. 7. 6 / 447.
	7. 7. 7. 7 / 55, 127, 192, 197, 232, 267, 278, 341, 448, 461.
	7. 7. 8. 8 / 151.
	8. 7. 8. 7 / 122, 133, 191, 284, 344, 356, 449, 462.
	8. 8. 7. 7 / 220, 370.
4t.-i.	8. 8. 8. 8 / 269.
4 mixed	11.11. 6. 4 / 376.

```
5ab.        5. 5. 5. 6. 5 / 168.
           11.11. 5. 5.11 / 89.
           11.11. 6. 6.11 / 305.

5d.        14.14. 4. 6. 8 / 212.
           14.14. 4. 7. 8 / 40, 134, 224.

5i.         8. 8. 6. 8. 8 / 393.
            8. 8. 7. 8. 7 / 50.
            8. 8. 8. 4. 8 / 161, 413.
            8. 8. 8. 8. 4 / 100.
            9. 8. 8. 9. 5 / 282.
            9. 9. 8. 9. 8 / 169.
           11.10.10. 9.11 / 62.

5i.-ab.     4. 4. 5.12.12 / 401.

5i.-t.      4. 4. 7. 7. 6 / 64, 314.
            8. 7. 8. 8. 4 / 120.
            8. 8. 8. 7. 4 / 77.

5t.         5. 5. 4. 4. 5 / 200.
            7. 8. 8. 7. 7 / 250.
           11.11. 6. 6.11 / 219, 350.

5 mixed     7. 6. 6. 5. 6 / 283.
            9. 9.11.10. 4 / 263.

6a.         6. 6. 9. 6. 6. 9 / 299.

6ab.        6. 6. 6. 6. 5. 5 / 149.
           11.11.11.11. 5.11 / 153.
           11.11.11.11. 8.10 / 463.
           11.12.11.12.12.12 / 44, 227.
           12.11.12.11.11.11 / 298.
           12.12.11.11.12.12 / 308.

6ab.-i.    11. 9. 8. 9. 9. 8 / 279.

6d.         9. 9. 7. 8. 4. 7 / 368.
           11.10.11.10.11.11 / 129, 144, 190.

6d.-ab.    11.11.11.11.12.12 / 114.

6i.         4. 4. 7. 4. 4. 7 / 6.
            4. 6.11.11.10. 4 / 280.
            6. 6. 5. 6. 6. 5 / 15, 31, 240, 296.
            6. 6. 6. 6. 8. 8 / 204, 450.
            6. 6. 7. 7. 6. 6 / 142.
            6. 6. 7. 7. 7. 7 / 29, 433.
            6. 7. 6. 7. 6. 6 / 73.
            6. 7. 6. 7. 7. 7 / 16.
            6. 7. 6. 7. 8. 8 / 257.
            7. 7. 6. 7. 7. 6 / 322.
            7. 7. 6. 7. 7. 8 / 316.
```

```
6i.          7. 7. 8. 7. 7. 8 / 273, 274.
             8. 4. 7. 8. 4. 7 / 103, 164.
             8. 7. 8. 7. 8. 8 / 27, 229, 231, 256, 272.
             8. 8. 6. 8. 8. 6 / 242, 451, 464.
             8. 8. 7. 4. 4. 7 / 183, 452.
             8. 8. 7. 8. 8. 7 / 5, 68, 119, 213.
             8. 8. 8. 8. 2. 8 / 378.
             8. 8. 8. 8. 4. 4 / 434.
             8. 8. 8. 8. 8. 8 / 148, 381.
             8. 8. 8. 8.10.10 / 417, 427, 465.
             8. 8. 9. 8. 8. 9 / 57, 326, 403.
             8. 9. 8. 9. 8. 8 / 320.
             8. 9. 8. 9.10.10 / 321.
             8.11.10.11.10. 4 / 105, 107.
             9. 6. 6. 9. 9. 5 / 208.
             9. 8. 8. 9. 8. 8 / 20, 333.
             9. 8. 9. 8. 8. 6 / 171.
             9. 8. 9. 8. 8. 8 / 13, 69, 261, 408, 410, 466.
             9. 9. 8. 8. 8. 8 / 335.
             9. 9. 8. 9. 9. 8 / 11.
             9.10. 9.10.10.10 / 79.
            10.10.10.10.11.11 / 332.
            11.10.10.11.10.10 / 367.
            11.11.11.11.11.11 / 239, 325.

6i.-t.       9. 9. 7. 8. 4. 7 / 368.

6t.          3. 3. 4. 7. 7. 8 / 373.
             5. 5. 8. 8. 5. 5 / 286, 355, 467.
             7. 6. 7. 6. 7. 7 / 265.
             7. 7. 8. 7. 8. 7 / 353.
             7. 7. 8. 8. 7. 7 / 252.
             7. 8. 7. 8. 7. 3 / 258.
             7. 8. 7. 8. 7. 7 / 39, 92, 131, 202, 203, 205, 254, 255, 468.
             7. 8. 7. 8. 8. 8 / 78, 222.
             7. 8. 8. 7. 7. 7 / 357.
             8. 4. 7. 8. 4. 7 / 155, 247, 329, 402, 428, 431.
             8. 7. 7. 8. 7. 7 / 19, 379.
             8. 7. 8. 7. 7. 7 / 17, 54. 123, 157, 210, 217, 249, 301, 343,
                                469.
             8. 7. 8. 7. 8. 8 / 18, 47, 87, 193, 380, 439.
             8. 8. 7. 8. 8. 7 / 25, 32, 94, 116, 182, 225, 317, 377.

6 mixed      5. 5. 7. 5. 5. 5 / 361.
             5. 5. 7. 7. 7. 9 / 346.

7ab.        12.12.11.11.12.12.12 / 176.

7d.          6. 4. 6. 4. 6. 6. 4 / 260.
            11.10.11.10. 5. 5.10 / 150, 351.

7i.          6. 7. 6. 6. 6. 6. 6 / 98.
             7. 6. 7. 6. 7. 7. 6 / 137, 143, 470.
             8. 6. 8. 6. 8. 8. 2 / 81.
             8. 7. 8. 7. 4. 4. 7 / 369, 471.
```

7i.   8. 7. 8. 7. 8. 6. 8 / 125.
         8. 7. 8. 7. 8. 8. 7 / 7, 23, 35, 60, 102, 104, 128, 238, 266,
                                 358, 419, 424, 472.
         11.11.10.11.13. 8. 4 / 420.
         13.12.12.12.12.12.13 / 244.

7t.   6. 7. 8. 7. 8. 9. 6 / 108.
         7. 4. 7. 4. 7. 4. 6 / 198, 392.
         7. 4. 7. 4. 7. 7. 4 / 251.
         8. 7. 8. 7. 3. 3. 7 / 248.
         8. 7. 8. 7. 4. 4. 7 / 359, 473.
         8. 7. 8. 7. 7. 8. 7 / 80.
         8. 7. 8. 7. 8. 8. 7 / 211.

7 mixed 7. 7. 7. 7. 7. 7. 8 / 309.

8ab.   6. 5. 6. 5. 6. 5. 6. 5 / 135, 243.
         6. 5. 6. 5. 6. 6.11.11 / 237, 315.
         8. 8. 8. 8. 8. 8. 8. 8 / 154.
         11. 6. 6.11. 5. 5. 5. 5 / 70.
         11. 8.11. 8.11. 8.11. 8 / 294.
         12.11.12.11. 6. 6.12.12 / 101.

8d.   6. 4. 6. 4. 6. 6. 6. 4 / 371.
         10.10.10.10.10.10.10.10 / 112.

8i.   6. 5. 6. 3. 6. 5. 6. 5 / 304.
         6. 5. 6. 5. 6. 5. 6. 5 / 407.
         6. 6. 6. 6. 6. 6. 6. 6 / 51, 311, 312.
         6. 6. 7. 7. 6. 7. 7. 6 / 233, 303.
         6. 7. 6. 7. 6. 6. 6. 6 / 59, 160, 264, 292, 307, 396.
         6. 7. 6. 7. 6. 6. 9. 9 / 76.
         6. 7. 6. 7. 6. 7. 6. 7 / 474.
         6. 7. 7. 6. 7. 7. 6. 6 / 152.
         6. 8. 8. 6. 6. 8. 8. 6 / 173, 328.
         7. 6. 7. 6. 6. 6. 6. 6 / 26.
         7. 6. 7. 6. 6. 6. 7. 6 / 180, 268, 400, 422.
         7. 6. 7. 6. 6. 7. 7. 6 / 4, 34, 136, 214, 386, 406, 437.
         7. 6. 7. 6. 7. 6. 7. 6 / 8, 37, 38, 99, 145, 146, 158, 172,
                                 201, 317, 339, 348, 383, 391, 409,
                                 443, 454, 475.
         7. 6. 7. 6. 7. 6. 7. 8 / 235.
         7. 6. 7. 6. 7. 7. 7. 6 / 476.
         8. 7. 8. 7. 4. 4. 7. 7 / 397.
         8. 7. 8. 7. 6. 6. 8. 8 / 61, 115.
         8. 7. 8. 7. 8. 7. 8. 7 / 72, 246, 297.
         8. 7. 8. 7. 8. 8. 7. 7 / 277.
         8. 7. 8. 7. 8. 8. 8. 8 / 411.
         8. 7. 8. 7. 9. 9. 8. 8 / 293.
         8. 8. 7. 8. 8. 7. 8. 8 / 71, 289.
         8. 8. 8. 8. 8. 8. 4. 4 / 404.
         8. 8. 9. 8. 8. 9. 8. 8 / 291, 336.
         9. 8. 8. 9. 9. 8. 9. 8 / 426, 430.
         9. 8. 9. 8. 4. 4. 8. 8 / 95, 387.
         9. 8. 9. 8. 9. 8. 9. 8 / 75, 384.

```
8i.          9.  9.  8.  8.  9.  9.  8.  8 / 323.
            11.  8.11.  8.  8.  8.  8.  9 / 290.
            11.  8.11.  8.  8.  8.  9.  9 / 436.
            11.10.11.10.10.10.10.10 / 185.

8i.-t.       7.  7.  7.  7.  7.  7.  7.  4 / 46.
             9.  6.  9.  6.  8.  8.  8.  6 / 14.
            10.  6.10.  6.  8.  8.  8.  6 / 21.

8t.          6.  6.  6.  6.  6.  6.  6.  6 / 259.
             7.  6.  7.  6.  3.  3.  6.  6 / 228, 372.
             7.  6.  7.  6.  7.  6.  7.  6 / 42, 49, 194, 218, 223, 317, 352, 478.
             8.  3.  3.  6.  8.  3.  3.  6 / 117, 394, 395, 454.
             8.  7.  7.  8.  8.  7.  7.  8 / 221.
             8.  7.  8.  7.  4.  4.  8.  8 / 300.
             8.  7.  8.  7.  4.  8.  8.  4 / 28.
             8.  7.  8.  7.  6.  6.  7.  7 / 432.
             8.  7.  8.  7.  7.  7.  7.  7 / 130.
             8.  7.  8.  7.  7.  7.  8.  8 / 1, 58, 111, 187, 253, 330, 347, 412,
                                            414, 440, 478.
             8.  7.  8.  7.  7.  8.  7.  8 / 327, 442.
             8.  7.  8.  7.  8.  7.  8.  7 / 285, 288, 479.
             8.  7.  8.  7.  8.  8.  7.  7 / 22, 83, 188, 199.
             8.  8.  7.  7.  8.  8.  7.  7 / 109, 138, 186, 334, 445, 480.
             8.  8.  8.  8.  8.  8.  8.  8 / 349.
            10.  7.10.  7.10.10.  7.  7 / 481.

8t.-ab.      8.  7.  8.  7.12.12.11.11 / 91.

8t.-i.       7.  5.  7.  5.  4.  7.  7.  4 / 345, 354.
             7.  8.  7.  8.  3.  3.  7.  4 / 287.
             8.  7.  8.  7.  4.  8.  8.  4 / 28.

9i.          8.  7.  8.  7.  8.  8.  8.  4.  8 / 24.

9i.-t.       8.  7.  8.  7.  8.  7.  4.  6.  7 / 167.
             9.  8.  9.  8.  4.  5.  4.  5.  5 / 121.

9t.          4.  4.  7.  4.  4.  7.  4.  4.  7 / 363.
             8.  7.  7.  8.  8.  7.  7.  7.  7 / 382.

10i.         8.  6.  8.  6.  4.  4.  6.  4.  4.  6 / 399.
             8.  7.  8.  7.  4.  4.  7.  4.  4.  7 / 216, 398.
             8.  7.  8.  7.  8.  8.  7.  8.  8.  7 / 90, 366.
             8.  8.  4.  4.  8.  4.  4.  5.  5.  4 / 281.
             8.  9.  8.  9.  8.  8.  9.  9.  8.  8 / 236.
             9.  8.  9.  8.  9.  9.  8.  9.  9.  8 / 421.

10i.-t.      4.  7.  8.  7.  8.  7.  8.  8.  7.  7 / 126.
             6.  6.  6.  3.  6.  6.  6.  6.  6.  3 / 415.
10t.         6.  6.  5.  6.  6.  5.  3.  4.  8.  6 / 196.
             6.  6.  8.  6.  6.  8.  3.  3.  6.  6 / 435.
             8.  7.  7.  8.  7.  7.  8.  8.  8.  8 / 113.
             8.  7.  8.  7.  8.  7.  7.  8.  7.  7 / 189, 215.
```

283

```
10t.-d.      7. 8. 7. 8. 7. 8. 7. 8.11.11 / 93.

11d.        10. 4. 4.10. 4. 4.10.10.10. 4. 4 / 360.

11i.-t.      8. 8. 7. 8. 8. 7. 4. 4. 4. 4. 8 / 416.

11t.         4. 4. 5. 4. 4. 5. 7. 7. 4. 4. 5 / 174.

12i.         7. 8. 7. 8. 7. 6. 7. 6. 7. 6. 7. 6 / 271.
             8. 7. 8. 7. 8. 8. 7. 7. 8. 8. 8. 8 / 52.

12i.-t.      8. 8. 7. 8. 8. 7. 2. 2. 4. 4. 4. 8 / 295, 418, 482.
             8. 9. 8. 8. 9. 8. 6. 6. 4. 4. 4. 8 / 390.

12t.         5. 5. 5. 5. 5. 5. 5. 5. 5. 5. 5. 5 / 331.
             8. 7. 8. 7. 8. 8. 7. 7. 8. 8. 8. 8 / 184.

12t.-i.      3. 3. 7. 7. 7. 7. 7. 4. 4. 4. 4. 7 / 364.

12 mixed   11.11.11.11. 5. 5. 8. 7. 8. 7. 7. 7 / 275.
```

APPENDIX XII

Index of Hymn-Writers

This index is an alphabetically arranged list of all authors and translators cited in the First-Line Index of Hymns. Each entry consists of several elements which are separated from each other by slashes. Not every entry contains all of these elements. For a key to the abbreviations, consult the list below.

1. Author's name: variant spellings are enclosed in parentheses.
2. Years of birth and death.
3. The religious movement with which the author is associated.
4. The chief geographic region(s) of the author's activity.
5. Personal data: religious and literary affiliations, occupation(s).
6. Bibliographic references to biographical information about the author. For the sake of brevity, no page references are provided for works in which authors' names can be located in the index.
7. Publication of the author's hymn-text(s) in Brethren hymnals and hymn-collections is indicated by a symbol or abbreviation referring to the appropriate work.
8. The hymns associated with authors/translators are referred to by the numbers under which they are listed in the First-Line Index of Hymns (Appendix IX). No distinction has been made between texts of undisputable, attributed, or doubtful authorship.

List of Abbreviations

For full bibliographical records, see the Selected Bibliography. Asterisks indicate Brethren hymnals and hymnal-collections.

Brethren Enc.	The Brethren Encyclopedia.
CG*	Das Christliche Gesang-Buch.
Cunz	Geschichte des Kirchenliedes.
Eastern Dist.	History of the Church of the Brethren of the Eastern District of Pennsylvania.
ELEL*	Etliche liebliche und erbauliche Lieder.
ENGL*	Etliche Neue Geistliche Lieder.
ES*	Eine Sammlung.
ESL*	Eyn schön Lied.
GAL*	Geistliche u. andächtige Lieder.
GGB*	Geistreiches Gesang-Buch, 1720.
GGG*	Stoll, Geistliches Gewürz-Gärtlein.
Julian	Dictionary of Hymnology.
KDP*	Das Kleine Davidische Psalterspiel.
KH*	Die Kleine Harfe.
KLS*	Die kleine Lieder Sammlung.
Knapp	Evangelischer Liederschatz.
Koch	Geschichte des Kirchenlieds.
KPS*	Die kleine Perlen-Sammlung.
Kulp	Die Lieder unserer Kirche.
Mennonite Enc.	The Mennonite Encyclopedia.
Mützell	Geistliche Lieder der evangelischen Kirche.

Nelle	Geschichte des deutschen evangelischen Kirchenliedes.
NS*	Neue Sammlung.
Stoudt	Pennsylvania German Poetry.
Willard	Johannes Kelpius.
Wolkan	Die Lieder der Wiedertäufer.
Yoder	Pennsylvania Spirituals.

The Hymn-Writers

ADAMS, Sarah, nee Flower / 1805-1848 / England / Unitarian; author, poet / (Julian) / CG, ES / 887.

ADDISON, Joseph / 1672-1719 / England / dramatist, journalist, poet / (Julian; Knapp) / NS / 1233.

ADOLPH, Gottlob / 1685-1745 / Orthodox / Upper Lusatia / hymnal publisher, preacher / (Knapp, Koch) / NS / 828.

AEMILIE JULIANE, Reichsgräfin von Schwarzburg-Rudolstadt / 1637-1706 / Forerunner / Thuringia / Lutheran; 2nd Silesian circle / (Knapp, Koch, Kulp, Nelle; Julian) / KDP, KLS, NS, CG, ES / 543, 1277.

ALBERT (ALBERTI), Heinrich / 1604-1651 / Königsberg; Prussia / Lutheran; Königsberg circle; composer, organist / (Knapp, Koch, Kulp, Nelle; Julian) / KDP, KLS, NS, CG, ES / 329, 417.

ALBINUS (WEISSE), Johann Georg / Forerunner / 1624-1679 / Saxony / Lutheran; P. Gerhardt's circle; educator, pastor / (Fischer, Knapp, Koch, Kulp; Julian) / GGB, KDP, KLS, NS, CG, ES / 76, 1226.

"ANDREAS" / GGB / 79.

ANNONI (D'ANNONE), Hieronymus / 1697-1770 / Radical Pietist / Switzerland / Reformed; pastor, poet / (Knapp, Koch, Nelle) / KDP, KLS, NS, CG, ES / 670.

ANTON ULRICH, Herzog von Braunschweig-Wolfenbüttel / 1633-1714 / Forerunner / North Germany / Catholic convert from Protestantism; Fruchtbringende Gesellschaft / (Fischer, Knapp; Julian) / GGB / 359.

ARNOLD, Gottfried / 1666-1714 / Early Pietist / Hesse / Separatist; historian, pastor, professor / (Knapp, Koch, Kulp, Nelle; Julian) / GGB, KDP / 49, 145, 146, 184, 185, 242, 260, 305, 336, 339, 372, 383, 471, 498, 502, 522, 735, 808, 809, 845, 935, 943, 949, 951, 1005, 1024, 1127, 1134, 1170, 1174, 1175, 1295, 1310, 1328, 1330.

ARNSCHWANGER, Johann Christoph / 1625-1696 / Forerunner / Nuremberg / Fruchtbringende Gesellschaft; pastor / (Fischer, Knapp; Julian) / KDP / 105.

ASTMANN, Johann Paul / 1660-1699 / Early Pietist / Franconia; Berlin / Lutheran / (Koch) / GGB, KDP / 1236.

BACHMEISTER, Lucas / 1570-1638 / Saxony / Lutheran / (Koch) / GGB, KDP, KLS, NS, CG, ES / 678, 1023.

BAHNMEIER, Jonathan Friedrich / 1774-1841 / German church renewal / Württemberg / pastor, professor / (Knapp, Koch, Nelle; Julian) / NS, ES / 1189.

BAMBERGER (BOMBERGER), C(hristian) / 1801-1880 / German-American / Pennsylvania / Brethren; elder, physician / (Brethren Enc., Eastern Dist.) / KPS / 142, 240.

BAUMGARTEN, Jakob / 1668-1722 / Halle Pietist / Berlin, Halle / educator, pastor / (Knapp, Koch, Kulp) / GGB, KDP, KLS / 724.

BECKER, Peter / 1687-1758 / German-American / Palatinate, Pennsylvania / Brethren; early leader; weaver / (Brethren Enc.) / KH, KLS, NS, CG, ES / 291.

BEHM (BEHEM, BEHEMB, BÖHEIM, BOHEMIUS, BÖHM), Martin / 1557-1622 / Upper Lusatia / Lutheran; educator, pastor / (Knapp, Koch, Kulp, Nelle; Julian) / KDP, KLS, NS, CG, ES / 978.

BEISSEL, Conrad / 1690?-1768 / German-American / Palatinate, Pennsylvania / Brethren, Ephrata Community; author, baker, musician / (Brethren Enc.) / KDP, KH / 202, 645, 908.

BERNSTEIN, Christian Andreas / d. 1699 / Halle Pietist / Saxony / educator, pastor / (Knapp, Koch) / GGB, KDP / 456, 589, 606, 1067.

BERTOLET, Daniel / 1781-1867 / German-American / Pennsylvania / Evangelical; bush-meeting poet / (Yoder) / NS, CG, ES / 147, 208, 270, 509, 878.

BETZ (PETZ), Hans / fl. 1530 / Anabaptist / South Germany / (Mennonite Enc., Wolkan) / GGB / 158.

BIRKEN (BETULIUS), Sigismund von. / 1626-1681 / Forerunner / Nuremberg / Lutheran; Blumenorden; educator, poet laureate / (Fischer, Knapp, Koch, Kulp, Nelle; Julian) / KDP, KLS, NS / 663, 767, 1142.

BOGATZKY, Karl Heinrich von / 1699-1774 / Late Pietist / Saxony, Lower Silesia / author, preacher / (Knapp, Kulp, Nelle; Julian) / NS, ES / 745.

BÖHMER, Justus Hennig / 1674-1749 / Halle Pietist / North Germany / chancellor of University of Halle, jurist / KDP / 937.

BÖHMER, Maria Magdalena / d. 1743 or 1744 / Halle Pietist / North Germany / (Koch; Julian) / KDP / 44.

BONIN, Ulrich Bogislaus von / 1682-1752 / Halle Pietist / Saxony / court official, theologian / (Knapp, Koch) / KDP, KLS / 124.

BORNMEISTER, Simon / 1632-1688 / Forerunner / Nürnberg / Blumenorden; educator, historian / (Fischer, Knapp) / CG / 1069.

BREITHAUPT, Joachim Justus / 1658-1732 / Halle Pietist / North Germany; Saxony / theologian / (Knapp, Koch, Kulp, Nelle; Julian) / KDP, CG / 1177.

BÜCHEL, Hans / 16th century / Anabaptist / South Germany / (Mennonite Enc.) / GGB / 158.

BUCHFELDER, Ernst Wilhelm / 1645-1711 / Pietist / Lower Rhine; North Germany / Reformed; pastor / (Knapp, Koch, Nelle; Julian) / GGB, KDP / 347.

BUCHOLTZ, Andreas Heinrich / 1607-1671 / North Germany / professor / (Fischer, Koch) / GGB, KDP, KPS / 534, 907.

CANITZ, Friedrich Rudolph Ludwig, Freiherr von / 1654-1699 / Early Pietist / Prussia / Lutheran; statesman / (Knapp, Koch; Julian) / KH / 1075.

CLAUDIUS, Mathias / 1746-1815 / North Germany / author, journalist / (Knapp, Koch, Kulp; Julian) / NS / 173.

CLAUSNITZER, Tobias / 1618-1684 / Forerunner / Palatinate / author, pastor / (Fischer, Knapp, Kulp; Julian) / GGB, KDP, KLS, CG / 792.

CLOCK, Lenaert / 16th century / Anabaptist / Lower Rhine; Netherlands / Mennonite; preacher / (Mennonite Enc., Wolkan) / KDP / 773.

CONNOW (CUNOW), Christian Friedrich / 1648-1706 / Forerunner / North Germany / P. Gerhardt's circle; educator, pastor / (Fischer, Knapp, Koch) / KPS, CG / 1263.

CONZ, Karl Philipp / 1762-1827 / German church renewal / Württemberg / preacher, professor, translator / (Knapp, Koch) / NS, ES / 71.

CRAMER, Johann Andreas / 1723-1788 / Denmark; North Germany; Saxony / Lutheran; court preacher, pastor, professor / (Knapp, Koch, Kulp, Nelle; Julian) / KDP, ES / 188, 217, 1074.

CRASSELIUS (CRASSEL, KRASSEL), Bartholomäus / 1667-1724 / Halle Pietist / Hesse; Lower Rhine; Saxony / Lutheran; pastor / (Knapp, Koch, Kulp, Nelle; Julian) / GGB, KDP / 285, 386, 465, 471, 490, 924.

DACH, Simon / 1605-1659 / Königsberg / Lutheran; Königsberg circle; educator, poet, theologian / (Fischer, Knapp, Koch, Kulp, Nelle; Julian) / GGB, KDP / 721, 1256.

DANNER, Heinrich / 1742 - before 1814 / German-American / Pennsylvania / Brethren / (Brethren Enc.) / KPS, NS, CG, ES / 846, 1202.

DANNER, Jakob / fl. 1800 / German-American / Pennsylvania / Brethren; elder / (Brethren Enc.) / KH, KLS, NS, CG, ES / 462.

DECIUS (a CURIA, DEEG, von HOFE, HOVESCH, HÖVISCH, TECK, THECIUS), Nicolaus / 1485 - after 1546 / Orthodox / Lutheran; composer, court preacher, educator / (Knapp, Koch, Kulp, Nelle; Julian) / GGB, KDP / 77, 997.

DENHAM, David / 1791-1848 / England / Baptist; minister / (Julian) / NS, CG, ES / 127.

DENICKE, David / 1603-1680 / North Germany / hymn-text reviser, jurist, professor, theologian / (Fischer, Knapp, Koch, Kulp, Nelle; Julian) / GGB, KDP, KLS, NS, CG, ES / 478, 598, 757, 963, 1023, 1062, 1292.

DESSLER, Wolfgang Christoph / 1660-1722 / Early Pietist / Nuremberg / Nuremberg circle; educator, linguist / (Fischer, Knapp, Koch, Nelle; Julian) / GGB, KDP / 387, 1301.

DITERICH, Johann Samuel / 1721-1797 / Enlightenment / Berlin / Lutheran; hymn-text reviser, theologian / (Koch, Kulp, Nelle; Julian) / KDP, KPS, NS, CG, ES / 89, 106, 810, 825, 884, 1038, 1300.

DOCK, Christoph / d. 1771 / German-American Mennonite / Pennsylvania / author, educator, farmer / (Brethren Enc., Mennonite Enc.) / KLS / 35.

DREISBACH, Johannes / 1789-1871 / German-American / Pennsylvania / Evangelical / (Yoder) / NS, CG, ES / 137, 195, 287, 532, 537, 575, 584, 603, 713, 729, 777, 914, 1057, 1060, 1294.

DRESE, Adam / 1620-1701 / Early Pietist / Saxony, Thuringia / Lutheran; author, composer, conductor / (Knapp, Koch, Kulp, Nelle; Julian) / GGB, KDP, KLS, NS, ES / 683, 947, 1081, 1082.

EDELING, Christian Ludwig / 1678-1742 / Halle Pietist / Saxony, Upper Lusatia / Lutheran; court official / (Knapp, Koch) / KH / 153.

ERHARD, Johann Ulrich / d. 1718 / Württemberg Pietist / Lutheran / (Koch) / KDP / 866.

F., J. / GGB / 79.

FALKNER (FALCKNER), Justus / d. 1724 / Halle Pietist / Saxony, America / Lutheran; pastor / (Knapp, Koch; Julian) / GGB, KDP / 104.

FINX (FRANCISCI), Erasmus / 1627-1694 / Forerunner / Nuremberg / Nuremberg circle; jurist, scholar / (Fischer, Knapp, Koch, Nelle; Julian) / GGB, KDP / 259, 326, 872, 981, 1031.

FLITNER, Johann / 1618-1678 / North Germany / composer, pastor / (Knapp, Koch, Kulp, Nelle; Julian) / KDP / 679.

FRANCK, Johann / 1618-1677 / Forerunner / Lower Lusatia / Lutheran; P. Ger-
     hardt's circle; author, jurist, mayor, poet / (Knapp, Koch, Kulp, Nel-
     le; Julian) / GGB, KDP, KLS / 149, 302, 675, 868.
FRANCK, Michael / 1609-1667 / Forerunner / Thuringia / Lutheran; P. Ger-
     hardt's circle; baker, composer, poet laureate, teacher / (Fischer,
     Knapp, Koch, Kulp, Nelle; Julian) / GGB, KDP, NS, CG, ES / 1093,
     1214.
FRANCK, Salomo / 1659-1725 / Thuringia / Lutheran; Fruchtbringende Gesell-
     schaft/ court official, court poet, jurist, librarian / (Knapp, Koch,
     Kulp, Nelle; Brethren Enc., Julian) / ES / 364.
FRANCKE, August Hermann / 1663-1727 / Halle Pietist / Saxony / educator,
     pastor, theologian / (Knapp, Koch, Kulp, Nelle; Julian) / GGB, KDP,
     KLS, CG / 275, 444, 1181.
FRANKENBERG, Abraham von / 1593-1652 / Silesia / (Fischer, Koch, Kulp) /
     KDP / 156.
FRENTZEL, Johann / 1609-1674 / Saxony / imperial poet laureate, professor
     / (Knapp, Koch) / KDP / 1333.
FREYLINGHAUSEN, Johann Anastasius / 1670-1739 / Halle Pietist / Lutheran;
     hymnal publisher, theologian / (Knapp, Koch, Kulp, Nelle; Julian) /
     KDP, KH, KLS, NS / 266, 320, 831, 879, 1117, 1261.
FREYSTEIN, Johann Burkhardt / 1671-1718 / Early Pietist / Saxony / Luther-
     an; court official, jurist / (Knapp, Koch, Kulp, Nelle) / GGB, KDP,
     KLS, NS, CG, ES / 803.
FRITSCH (FRITZSCH), Ahasverus / 1629-1701 / Forerunner / Saxony, Thuringia
     / 2nd Silesian circle; author, court official / (Fischer, Knapp,
     Koch, Kulp, Nelle) / GGB, KDP, KH, CG / 55, 201, 641, 686, 849, 987.
FUNKE (FUNCKE), Friedrich / 1642-1699 / Early Pietist / North Germany / P.
     Gerhardt's circle; cantor, composer, pastor / (Fischer, Kulp, Nelle;
     Julian) / KDP / 1348.

GARVE, Carl Bernhard / 1763-1841 / Moravian / Lusatia / (Knapp, Koch,
     Nelle; Julian) / ES / 204.
GELLERT, Christian Fürchtegott / 1715-1769 / Enlightenment / Saxony /
     author, philologist, poet, professor / (Knapp, Koch, Kulp, Nelle,
     Julian) / KDP, KPS, NS, CG, ES / 280, 346, 856, 883, 894, 1118, 1242,
     1297.
GERHARDT, Paul / 1607-1676 / Forerunner / North Germany / pastor / (Fi-
     scher, Knapp, Koch, Kulp, Nelle; Julian) / GGB, KDP, KH, KLS, NS, CG,
     ES / 52, 95, 122, 301, 322, 383, 398, 406, 581, 920, 923, 965, 977,
     1030, 1073, 1108, 1183, 1194, 1319, 1335.
GERLACH, David / ca. 1811-1879 / German-American / Pennsylvania /
     Brethren; elder, preacher / (Eastern Dist.) / KPS, CG, ES / 1066.
GESENIUS, Justus / 1601-1673 / North Germany / church official, court
     preacher, hymn-text reviser / (Knapp, Koch, Kulp, Nelle; Julian) /
     GGB, KDP, KLS, NS, CG, ES / 598, 757, 1023, 1062, 1292.
GMELIN, Sigmund Christian / 1679-1707 / Württemberg Pietist / Separatist;
     pastor; found religious refuge at Schwarzenau, Wittgenstein / (Koch,
     Kulp; Julian) / KDP, KLS / 51.
GOTTER, Ludwig Andreas / 1661-1735 / Halle Pietist / Thuringia / court
     official, court preacher / (Knapp, Koch, Kulp, Nelle; Julian) / GGB,
     KDP, KH, KLS, NS, CG, ES / 412, 491, 650, 1058, 1094, 1107, 1147,
     1340.

GRAMANN (GRAUMANN, GROMANN, POLIANDER), Johann / 1487-1541 / Orthodox / Prussia / Lutheran; court official, educator, theologian / (Knapp, Koch, Kulp, Nelle) / GGB, KDP / 918.

GREBIL (GRAYBILL), S[amuel?] / 1809-1881 / German-American / Pennsylvania / Brethren; minister / (Eastern Dist.) / KPS / 19.

GRUBER, Eberhard Ludwig / 1665-1728 / Radical Pietist / Hesse / Inspirationist leader / (Brethren Enc.) / KDP, CG, ES / 689, 699, 1041, 1338.

GRUMBACHER, U. / d. ca. 1745 / German-American / Pennsylvania / Mennonite; teacher / (Stoudt) / ELEL / 391.

GRÜNWALD, Georg / ca. 1490-1530 / Anabaptist / Tyrol / (Kulp; Mennonite Enc.) / GGB, KDP / 744.

GÜNTHER, Cyriakus / 1650-1704 / Thuringia / educator / (Knapp, Kulp, Nelle; Julian) / KDP, KLS, NS, CG, ES / 468.

HAACK, Daniel, / 1629?-1702 / Franconia / Nuremberg circle; pastor / (Fischer) / GGB, KDP / 588.

HALLER, J[akob] / ca. 1777-1865 / German-American / Pennsylvania / Brethren; elder, preacher / (Eastern Dist.) / KPS, CG, ES / 673.

HART, Joseph / 1712-1768 / England / Independent; minister / (Julian) / CG, ES / 748.

HEBER, Reginald / 1783-1826 / England, India / bishop, missionary / (Julian; Knapp) / ES / 1180.

HEDINGER, Johann Reinhard / 1664-1704 / Württemberg Pietist / court preacher, jurist, professor / (Knapp, Koch) / GGB, KDP / 1224.

HEERMANN, Johannes / 1585-1647 / Lower Silesia / Lutheran; 1st Silesian circle; imperial poet laureate, preacher / (Knapp, Koch, Kulp, Nelle; Julian) / GGB, KDP, KLS, NS, CG, ES / 84, 281, 392, 443, 639, 658, 720, 763, 959, 979, 982, 1145, 1331, 1351.

HEINE, Georg / 17th century / Early Pietist / Pommerania / Lutheran; pastor / (Knapp, Koch) / KDP / 112.

HELD, Heinrich / 1620-1659 / North Germany; Silesia / Lutheran; 1st Silesian circle; jurist / (Fischer, Knapp, Koch, Kulp, Nelle; Julian) GGB, KDP, KLS, NS, CG, ES / 434, 732.

HELMBOLD, Ludwig / 1532-1598 / Thuringia / educator, poet laureate, professor / (Knapp, Koch, Kulp, Nelle; Julian) / GGB, KDP, KPS, CG, ES / 910, 1179.

HERBERT (HUBERTUS), Petrus / ca. 1530-1571 / Czech Brethren / early leader / (Knapp, Koch, Kulp, Nelle; Julian) / NS / 245.

HERMAN, Nikolaus / ca. 1480-1561 / Orthodox / German Bohemia / Lutheran; cantor / (Knapp, Koch, Kulp, Nelle; Julian) / KDP / 801.

HERR, Christian / 1780-1835 / German-American / Pennsylvania / Mennonite; bishop / (Mennonite Enc.) / KLS, CG, ES / 22, 63, 906.

HERRNSCHMIDT, Johann Daniel / 1675-1723 / Halle Pietist / Halle / Lutheran; pastor, professor / (Knapp, Koch, Kulp, Nelle; Julian) / GGB, KDP, KH, KLS, CG, ES / 200, 342, 439, 741, 784, 1110.

HERZOG (HERTZOG), Johann Friedrich / 1647-1699 / Forerunner / Saxony / Lutheran; P. Gerhardt's circle; jurist / (Fischer, Knapp, Koch, Kulp, Nelle; Julian) / GGB, KDP, KLS, NS, CG, ES / 927.

HETZER, Ludwig / martyred before 1600 / Anabaptist / GGB, KDP / 258.

HEYD (HEYDEN), Sebald / 1494-1561 / Orthodox / Franconia / Lutheran; educator / (Koch, Kulp, Nelle) / GGB / 1259.

HILLER, Friedrich Konrad / 1662-1726 / Württemberg Pietist / Lutheran; court official, jurist / (Knapp, Koch, Kulp, Nelle; Julian) / KLS, CG, ES / 975.

HILLER, Philipp Friedrich / 1699-1769 / Württemberg Pietist / Lutheran; pastor / (Knapp, Koch, Kulp) / KDP, KLS, KPS, NS, CG, ES / 87, 99, 119, 161, 163, 170, 174, 186, 191, 207, 209, 210, 211, 229, 230, 243, 244, 249, 252, 254, 257, 271, 319, 330, 376, 389, 415, 420, 422, 426, 440, 447, 449, 475, 499, 550, 556, 563, 594, 624, 625, 627, 632, 633, 652, 653, 694, 697, 709, 711, 717, 719, 723, 738, 756, 762, 768, 772, 774, 780, 821, 824, 832, 833, 875, 886, 890, 975, 1040, 1043, 1051, 1072, 1077, 1080, 1122, 1141, 1156, 1164, 1169, 1198, 1200, 1206, 1225, 1228, 1235, 1238, 1249, 1254, 1255, 1257, 1268, 1272, 1287, 1307, 1314, 1315.

HÖFEL, Johann / 1600-1683 / South Germany / jurist / (Fischer, Knapp, Koch; Julian) / NS / 1021.

HOFFER, J. / 19th century / German-American / Pennsylvania / Brethren? / KPS, CG / 365.

HOFFMANN, Gottlieb Wilhelm / 1771-1846 / German church renewal / Saxony / (Kulp; Julian) / KPS, NS, CG, ES / 92.

HOJER (HÖIER), Conrad / fl. 1600 / (Cunz, Mützell) / KDP / 18.

HÖLTY, Ludwig / 1748-1776 / Hesse / pastor, poet / (Julian) / ES / 1153.

HOMBURG, Ernst Christoph / 1605-1681 / Forerunner / Saxony, Thuringia / P. Gerhardt's circle; Fruchtbringende Gesellschaft; jurist / (Fischer, Knapp, Koch, Kulp, Nelle; Julian) / KDP, KLS, NS, ES / 681.

HÜBNER, Johann / 1668-1731 / Orthodox / Saxony / author, educator, theologian / (Knapp, Koch) / KDP, KH, KLS, NS, CG, ES / 121, 198.

HUNTER, William / 1811-1877 / Ireland, America / Methodist / preacher, professor / (Julian) / ES / 384.

J. F. / GGB / 79.

JÄEL, Sister (MEYER, Barbara) / 18th century / German-American / Pennsylvania / Ephrata Community; prioress / KH / 1285.

JÖRGENS, Ludwig / 1791-1837? / Germany, America / (Nelle) / NS, ES / 1321.

KEIMANN (KEYMANN), Christian / 1607-1662 / Forerunner / Saxony / Lutheran; P. Gerhardt's circle; author, educator, poet laureate / (Fischer, Koch, Kulp, Nelle; Julian) / GGB, KDP, CG, ES / 867.

KELLNER von ZINNENDORF, Johann Wilhelm / 1665-1738 / Halle Pietist / Saxony / pastor (Knapp, Koch; Julian) / KDP / 151.

KELLY, Thomas / 1769-1854 / Ireland / Evangelical; preacher / (Julian) / KPS / 525.

KELPIUS, Johann / 1673-1706 / German-American / (Fischer; Willard) / ELEL / 67, 637, 1240.

KLOPSTOCK, Friedrich Gottlieb / 1724-1803 / Enlightenment / author, poet / (Knapp, Koch, Kulp, Nelle; Julian) / KLS, NS, CG, ES / 126, 233.

KNAPP, Albert / 1798-1864 / German church renewal / Württemberg / Lutheran; hymnologist, pastor / (Knapp, Koch, Kulp, Nelle; Julian) / KPS, NS, ES / 436, 733, 944, 968, 1233.

KNEPPER, Wilhelm / 1691-ca. 1743 / German-American / Palatinate, Pennsylvania / Brethren; weaver / (Brethren Enc.) / GGB, KDP, KLS, NS, CG, ES / for hymns attributable to him, see Appendix I/5.

KNORR, Christian Anton Philipp, Freiherr von Rosenroth / 1636-1689 / Fore-
    runner / Palatinate / Lutheran; 2nd Silesian circle; court official,
    scholar / (Fischer, Knapp, Koch, Kulp, Nelle; Julian) / GGB, KDP,
    KLS, CG, ES / 206, 310, 516, 674, 881, 885, 1345.
KOITSCH (KOITSCHE), Christian Jakob / 1671-1735 / Halle Pietist / Saxony /
    Lutheran; educator / (Koch; Julian) / GGB, KDP / 765, 836, 1025.
KONGEHL, Michael / 1646-1710 / Forerunner / Prussia / Lutheran; Blumen-
    orden; jurist, mayor / (Fischer, Knapp, Koch, Nelle) / GGB, KDP /
    932.
KRAUSE, Jonathan / 1701-1762 / Orthodox / Lower Lusatia / Lutheran; pastor
    / (Knapp, Koch, Nelle; Julian) / ES / 466.
KREUZIGER (CREUTZIGER, CREUZIGER, CRUZIGER), Elisabeth, nee Meseritz /
    1504-1535 / Orthodox / Saxony / Lutheran / (Knapp, Koch, Kulp, Nelle;
    Julian) / GGB, KDP, KLS / 474.
KUNTH, Johann Sigismund / 1700-1779 / Late Pietist / Upper Lusatia /
    pastor / (Nelle; Julian) / NS, ES / 363.
KURTZ, Heinrich (Henry) / 1796-1874 / German-American / Germany, America /
    Lutheran; Brethren; pastor, publisher / (Brethren Enc.) / 631.

LACKMANN, Peter / d. 1713 / Halle Pietist / Lutheran; educator, pastor /
    (Knapp, Koch) / GGB, KDP, KLS, NS, CG, ES / 61, 108, 345, 445, 515.
LAMPE, Friedrich Adolph / 1683-1729 / Pietist / North Germany / Reformed;
    pastor, professor / (Knapp, Koch, Kulp, Nelle) / CG, ES / 847.
LANGE, Joachim / 1670-1744 / Halle Pietist / North Germany; Saxony /
    Lutheran; professor / (Knapp, Koch, Kulp, Nelle; Julian) / GGB, KDP /
    496, 992.
LANGE, Johann Christian / 1669-1756 / Halle Pietist / Hesse; Saxony /
    Lutheran; professor / (Knapp, Koch, Kulp; Julian) / GGB, KDP / 113,
    838, 840, 844.
LAURENTI (LORENZEN), Laurentius (Lorenz) / 1660-1722 / Early Pietist /
    North Germany / Lutheran; cantor / (Knapp, Koch, Kulp, Nelle; Julian)
    / GGB, KDP, KLS, NS, CG, ES / 15, 308, 348, 371, 378, 909, 1010,
    1182, 1195, 1271.
LAVATER, Johann Kaspar / 1741-1801 / Switzerland / Reformed; author,
    pastor / (Knapp, Kulp; Julian) / NS / 1173.
LEHR, Leopold Franz Friedrich / 1709-1744 / Halle Pietist / Saxony /
    courtier, educator / (Knapp, Koch, Kulp, Nelle; Julian) / KDP, KLS /
    231, 827.
LEON, Johannes / ca. 1530-1597 / Thuringia / pastor / (Knapp, Kulp, Nelle;
    Julian) / GGB / 553.
LIEBICH, Ehrenfried / 1713-1780 / Enlightenment / Silesia / Lutheran; edu-
    cator, pastor / (Knapp, Koch, Kulp, Nelle; Julian) / KLS, NS, CG, ES
    / 116, 899.
LISKOW (LISKOV), Salomo / 1640-1689 / Forerunner / Saxony / P. Gerhardt's
    circle; pastor, poet laureate / (Fischer, Knapp, Koch, Kulp; Julian)
    / GGB, KDP, NS, CG, ES / 120, 869, 1059.
LOBWASSER, Ambrosius / 1515-1585 / Königsberg / Lutheran; jurist, pro-
    fessor / (Kulp, Nelle; Julian) / KDP, KLS, NS / 189, 476, 564, 593,
    612, 619, 839, 853, 859, 957, 1357, 1358, 1359.
LOCHNER, Karl Friedrich / 1634-1697 / Forerunner / Nuremberg / Blumenorden
    / (Fischer) / GGB, KDP / 1199.
LODENSTEIN, Jodocus von / 1620-1677 / Netherlands / Reformed; pastor /
    (Koch, Kulp; Julian) / GGB, KDP / 471, 589.

LÖSCHER, Valentin Ernst / 1673-1749 / Orthodox / Saxony / Lutheran; pastor, professor / (Knapp, Koch, Kulp, Nelle) / NS, ES / 344, 519.

LOSKIEL, Georg Heinrich / 1740-1813 / German-American / Moravian; preacher / (Knapp, Koch, Kulp) / KLS, NS / 128.

LUDÄMILIE ELISABETH, Gräfin von Schwarzburg-Rudolstadt / 1640-1672 / Fore-runner / Thuringia / 2nd Silesian circle / (Fischer, Knapp, Koch; Julian) / KDP, ELEL, NS, CG, ES / 38, 702, 1325.

LUISE HENRIETTE, Kurfürstin von Brandenburg / 1627-1667 / Forerunner / North Germany / Reformed / (Fischer, Knapp, Kulp; Julian) / CG / 596.

LUTHER, Martin / 1483-1546 / Orthodox / Saxony / (Knapp, Koch, Kulp; Julian) / GGB, KDP, NS / 157, 162, 403, 897.

MACK, Alexander / 1679-1735 / German-American / Germany, Netherlands, Pennsylvania / Brethren; minister / (Brethren Enc.) / GGB / 1155.

MACK, Alexander, Jr. / 1712-1802 / German-American / Germany, Netherlands, Pennsylvania / Brethren; elder, author / (Brethren Enc.) / KDP, KH, KLS, KPS, NS, CG, ES / 107, 181, 294, 312, 328, 337, 370, 413, 453, 497, 504, 521, 540, 578, 654, 695, 898, 911, 934, 1154, 1160, 1165, 1166, 1167, 1216, 1223, 1266a, 1320, 1336.

MENKEN (MENCKE, MENCKEN), Lüder / 1658-1726 / Orthodox / Saxony / jurist, professor / (Knapp, Koch; Julian) / GGB, KDP, KLS / 36.

MENTZER, Johann / 1658-1734 / Early Pietist / Saxony / pastor / (Knapp, Kulp, Nelle; Julian) / NS / 940.

MEUSLIN (MÄUSSLIN, MEUSEL, MOSEL, MÖSEL, MUSCULUS, MÜSSLIN), Wolfgang / 1497-1563 / Orthodox / South Germany; Switzerland / Lutheran; edu-cator, theologian / (Koch, Kulp, Nelle; Julian) / KDP / 220.

MEYER, J[acob W.?] / 1832-1906 / German-American / Pennsylvania / Brethren; elder / (Eastern Dist.) / KPS, CG, ES / 421, 609, 1317.

MILLER, A[braham?] / d. 1843 / German-American / Pennsylvania / Brethren; minister / (Eastern Dist.) / KPS / 313.

MILLER, S. D. / 19th century / German-American / Pennsylvania / Brethren? / KPS, CG, ES / 93, 601, 760, 988, 993.

MÖCKEL (MÖCKHEL), Johann Friedrich / 1661-1729 / Orthodox / South Germany / court preacher, pastor / (Knapp, Koch, Kulp; Julian) / KDP, KLS, NS, CG, ES / 928.

MOLLER (MÖLLER), Martin / 1547-1606 / Saxony / Lutheran; author, cantor, pastor / (Knapp, Koch, Kulp, Nelle; Julian) / KDP, KLS, CG, ES / 18, 991.

MÜLLER, Heinrich / 1631-1675 / Forerunner / North Germany / 2nd Silesian circle / author, pastor, professor / (Fischer, Koch, Nelle) / GGB, KDP / 60, 73.

MÜLLER, Michael / 1673-1704 / Halle Pietist / Württemberg / Lutheran; tutor / (Knapp, Koch, Kulp, Nelle; Julian) / GGB, KDP, KLS, NS, CG, ES / 111, 901, 1106.

NAAS, Johann / 1669-1742 / German-American / Lower Rhine, Pennsylvania / Brethren; minister / (Brethren Enc.) / KH, NS, CG, ES / 331, 470.

NAEMI, Sister (EICHER, Naomi) / 18th century / German-American / Pennsyl-vania / Ephrata Community / KH, CG, ES / 1207.

NEANDER (NEUMANN), Joachim / 1650-1680 / Forerunner / North Germany / Re-formed; educator, pastor / (Knapp, Koch, Kulp, Nelle; Julian) / GGB, KDP, ELEL, KLS, NS, CG, ES / 1, 27, 48, 54, 59, 236, 306, 314, 316, 458, 512, 536, 539, 540, 590, 634, 647, 795, 855, 936, 950, 1016,

1017, 1018, 1039, 1105, 1120, 1159, 1197, 1219, 1284, 1332, 1341, 1347, 1355.

NEHRING, Johann Christian / 1671-1736 / Halle Pietist / Rhineland; Saxony / Lutheran; educator, pastor / (Knapp, Koch, Kulp; Julian) / GGB, KDP / 269.

NEUMANN, Kaspar / 1648-1715 / Orthodox / Silesia / pastor, scholar / (Knapp, Koch) / KLS, NS, CG, ES / 481, 786, 960.

NEUMARK, Georg / 1621-1681 / Forerunner / Thuringia / Lutheran; Fruchtbringende Gesellschaft; court poet, educator / (Fischer, Knapp, Koch, Kulp; Julian) / NS, CG, ES / 1266.

NEUMEISTER, Erdmann / 1671-1756 / Orthodox / Lower Lusatia; North Germany; Saxony / court poet, pastor, theologian / (Knapp, Koch, Kulp, Nelle; Julian) / CG, ES / 138, 706.

NEUSS, Heinrich Georg / 1654-1716 / Early Pietist / Thuringia / Lutheran; educator, pastor / (Knapp, Koch, Kulp, Nelle; Julian) / KDP / 166, 418, 980.

NEWTON, John / 1725-1807 / England / Independent; minister / (Julian; Knapp) / NS, CG, ES / 733, 1290.

NICOLAI (NIKOLAI, RAFFLENBEUL, RAFFLENBÖHL), Philipp / 1556-1608 / North Germany / Lutheran; pastor / (Knapp, Koch, Kulp; Julian) / GGB, KDP, KLS, NS, CG, ES / 1186.

ODERBORN, Paul / 16th century / Baltic countries / pastor / (Knapp) / GGB / 234.

OLEARIUS, Johannes / 1611-1684 / Forerunner / Saxony / Lutheran; P. Gerhardt's circle; court preacher, educator / (Fischer, Knapp, Koch, Kulp, Nelle; Julian) / KDP / 545.

ORWIG, William W. / 1810-1889 / German-American / Pennsylvania / Evangelical; bishop / (Yoder) / NS, CG, ES / 246, 649, 728, 755, 1318.

PAPPUS, Johann / 1549-1610 / Orthodox / Alsace / Lutheran / (Mützell) / GGB / 553.

PAULI, Hermann Reinhold / 1682-1750 / Pietist / North Germany / Reformed; tutor / (Knapp, Koch) / KDP / 796.

PETERSEN, Johann Wilhelm / 1649-1727 / Radical Pietist / North Germany / pastor / (Knapp; Julian) / GGB, KDP / 791, 1190.

PFEFFERKORN, Georg Michael / 1646-1731 / Thuringia / 2nd Silesian circle; educator, pastor / (Fischer, Koch; Julian) / ELEL, KLS / 64.

PFEIL, Christian Karl Ludwig, Reichsfreiherr von / 1712-1784 / Württemberg Pietist / Lutheran; court official, diplomat / (Knapp, Koch, Kulp, Nelle; Julian) / NS, ES / 473.

PLANK (PLANCK), Karl Johann Christoph / 1801-1825 / Bavaria / preacher, student / (Knapp) / KPS, CG, ES / 289.

PRÄTORIUS, Benjamin / 1636-1674 / Forerunner / Saxony / P. Gerhardt's circle; pastor, poet laureate / (Knapp, Koch, Kulp; Julian) / GGB, KDP, NS, CG / 1088, 1091, 1150.

PRÄTORIUS (SCHULZE SCULTETIUS), Christoph / 17th century / North Germany / jurist / (Knapp, Koch) / KH / 152.

PREISS (PRICE), Johannes (John) / 1702-1724 / German-American / Pennsylvania / Brethren; poet / (Brethren Enc., Eastern Dist.) / GAL / 81, 160, 228, 567, 583, 614, 636, 666, 766, 1090, 1097, 1217, 1283.

PREISS (PRICE), Wilhelm (William) Weidner / 1789-1849 / German-American /
Pennsylvania / Brethren; elder, musician, poet, teacher / (Brethren
Enc., Eastern Dist.) / KPS, NS, CG, ES / 37, 333, 472, 525, 577, 616,
626, 704, 712, 843, 1129, 1139, 1205, 1246, 1247.

QUIRSFELD, Johann / 1642-1686 / Forerunner / Saxony / P. Gerhardt's
circle; pastor / (Fischer) / GGB, KDP / 261.

RAMBACH, Johann Jakob / 1693-1735 / Halle Pietist / Halle / hymnologist,
poet, professor / (Knapp, Koch, Kulp, Nelle; Julian) / KPS, NS, CG,
ES / 457, 505, 542, 1092.

REISSNER (REUSNER), Adam / 1496-ca.1575 / Schwenkfelder / Hesse, Saxony /
historiographer / (Knapp, Koch, Kulp, Nelle; Julian) / GGB, KDP /
635.

REISSNER, Johann Conrad / 1795-1877 / German-American Evangelical / Pennsylvania / (Yoder) / CG, ES / 748.

RENAU, E. / d. 1577 / Orthodox / Lutheran / (Koch) / KDP / 430.

RICHTER, Christian Friedrich / 1676-1711 / Halle Pietist / Halle / Lutheran; educator, physician / (Knapp, Koch, Kulp, Nelle; Julian) / GGB,
KDP, GGG, KLS, CG, ES / 232, 355, 362, 367, 506, 535, 850, 854, 1036,
1327.

RINGWALDT, Bartholomäus / 1532-1599 / North Germany / Lutheran; author,
educator, pastor / (Knapp, Koch, Kulp, Nelle; Julian) / GGB, KDP, NS,
CG, ES / 360, 485.

RINKART (RINCKHART), Martin / 1586-1649 / Saxony / Lutheran; cantor, educator, pastor / (Fischer, Knapp, Koch, Kulp, Nelle; Julian) / GGB,
KDP, KLS, CG, ES / 86, 465, 900.

RIST, Johann / 1607-1667 / North Germany / Lutheran; Blumenorden; pastor,
poet / (Fischer, Knapp, Koch, Kulp, Nelle; Julian) / GGB, KDP, ELEL,
KLS, NS, CG, ES / 379, 510, 662, 743, 805, 903, 953, 964, 1279.

RODIGAST, Samuel / 1649-1708 / Forerunner / Thuringia / Lutheran; P. Gerhardt's circle; educator / (Fischer, Knapp, Koch, Kulp, Nelle;
Julian) / KDP, CG, ES / 1201.

ROSENMÜLLER, Johannes / ca. 1620-1684 / North Germany; Saxony / cantor,
educator / (Knapp, Koch) / GGB, KDP, KLS, NS, CG, ES / 76.

ROTHE, Johann Andreas / 1688-1758 / Halle Pietist / Upper Lusatia / Lutheran; pastor, tutor / (Knapp, Koch, Kulp, Nelle; Julian) / KDP, KPS,
CG, ES / 557, 1244.

RUBE (RUBEN), Johann Christoph / 1665-1746 / Hesse / jurist / (Knapp;
Julian) / NS, ES / 212.

RUOPP, Johann Friedrich / 1672-1708 / Halle Pietist / Alsace, Saxony /
Lutheran; professor / (Knapp, Koch, Kulp, Nelle) / KDP, NS, ES / 349.

SACER, Gottfried Wilhelm / 1635-1699 / Forerunner / North Germany / Lutheran; P. Gerhardt's circle; jurist / (Knapp, Koch) / KDP, KLS, NS, CG,
ES / 183, 734.

SACHSE, Christian Friedrich Heinrich / 1785-1860 / Saxony / court
preacher, tutor / (Knapp, Kulp; Julian) / ES / 770.

SASSE, Bernhard Heinrich / fl. 1800 / German-American / Pennsylvania /
Evangelical / (Yoder) / KPS, NS, CG, ES / 62, 109, 1063, 1253.

SATTLER, Michael / martyred 1527 / Anabaptist / South Germany / scholar /
(Mennonite Enc.) / GGB, KDP / 83, 882.

SAUER (SAUR, SOWER), Christoph, II / 1721-1784 / German-American / Pennsylvania / Brethren; elder, printer / (Brethren Enc.) / KH, CG, ES / 154.

SCHADE (SCHAD), Johann Caspar / 1666-1698 / Early Pietist / Berlin / Lutheran; pastor (Knapp, Koch; Julian) / GGB, KDP, KLS, NS, CG, ES / 12, 103, 816, 857, 1054.

SCHARNSCHLAGER, Leupold / 16th century / Anabaptist / Austria, South Germany / (Mennonite Enc.) / GGB, KDP / 258.

SCHECHS (SCHECHSIUS), Jakob Peter / 1607-1659 / South Germany / pastor / (Koch) / CG / 11.

SCHEFFLER, Johann (ANGELUS SILESIUS) / 1624-1677 / Forerunner / Silesia / Roman Catholic convert from Protestantism; 2nd Silesian circle; court councillor, court physician, priest / (Fischer, Knapp, Koch, Kulp, Nelle; Julian) / GGB, KDP, KH, KLS, NS, CG, ES / 47, 94, 98, 203, 268, 298, 304, 395, 396, 397, 463, 517, 518, 544, 587, 671, 690, 698, 722, 730, 778, 785, 864, 876, 888, 930, 976, 1149, 1221, 1299, 1323.

SCHENK (SCHENCK), Hartmann / 1634-1681 / Forerunner / Thuringia / pastor / (Fischer, Knapp, Koch, Kulp) / KLS, CG, ES / 904.

SCHENK, Heinrich Theobald / 1656-1727 / Halle Pietist / Hesse / educator, pastor / (Knapp, Koch; Julian) / KPS, NS, CG, ES / 1273.

SCHIRMER, Michael / 1606-1673 / Forerunner / Berlin / educator / (Fischer, Knapp, Koch, Kulp, Nelle; Julian) / GGB, KDP, KLS, NS, CG, ES / 916, 917, 967.

SCHLATTER, Anna / 1773-1826 / German church renewal / Switzerland / (Knapp) / NS / 628.

SCHLEGEL, Johann Adolf / 1721-1793 / Enlightenment / North Germany; Saxony / educator, pastor / (Knapp, Koch) / KDP, NS, ES / 97, 1061, 1085, 1115.

SCHLICHT, Levin Johann / 1681-1723 / Halle Pietist / North Germany / educator, pastor / (Knapp, Koch) / KDP / 43.

SCHMIDT, Johann Eusebius / 1669-1745 / Halle Pietist / Thuringia / pastor / (Knapp, Koch, Kulp) / GGB, KDP / 375.

SCHMOLCK, Benjamin / 1672-1737 / Orthodox / Silesia / author, pastor, poet laureate / (Knapp, Koch, Kulp; Julian) / KDP, ELEL, KLS, KPS, NS, CG, ES / 25, 78, 335, 374, 399, 432, 533, 546, 707, 819, 1038, 1076, 1089, 1152, 1215.

SCHNEEGASS, Cyriakus / 1546-1597 / Thuringia / educator, pastor / (Fischer, Knapp, Koch, Kulp; Julian) / CG, ES / 182.

SCHRADER, Johann Hermann / 1684-1737 / Orthodox / North Germany / Lutheran / (Koch) / NS, ES / 205.

SCHRÖDER, Johann Heinrich / 1666-1699 / Halle Pietist / North Germany / Lutheran; pastor / (Knapp, Koch, Kulp, Nelle; Julian) / GGB, KDP / 332, 667, 668.

SCHRÖDER, Tranquilla Sophia, nee Wolff / 1667-1697 / Halle Pietist / North Germany / Lutheran / (Koch, Kulp) / KDP / 643, 1144.

SCHULTT, Juliane Patientia von / 1680-1701 / Halle Pietist / Saxony / Lutheran / (Koch, Kulp) / KDP / 1326.

SCHULTT, Rudolph Friedrich, Freiherr von / fl. 1700 / Halle Pietist / Saxony / Lutheran / (Koch) / GGB, KDP / 672.

SCHÜTZ, Johann Jakob / 1640-1690 / Early Pietist / Frankfurt am Main / Lutheran; jurist / (Knapp, Koch, Kulp, Nelle; Julian) / GGB, KDP, KLS, NS, CG, ES / 1095.

SCHWÄMLEIN (SCHWÄMMLEIN), Georg Christoph / 1632-1705 / Forerunner / Nuremberg / Nuremberg circle; educator / (Fischer, Knapp, Koch) / CG, ES / 114.

SCHWEDLER, Johann Christoph / 1672-1730 / Halle Pietist / Upper Lusatia / pastor / (Knapp, Koch, Kulp, Nelle; Julian) / GGB, KDP, NS, CG / 1162.

SCHWERIN, Otto, Reichsfreiherr von / 1616-1679 / North Germany / Reformed; church official, educator / (Knapp, Koch, Kulp) / KDP / 957.

SCRIVER, Christian / 1629-1693 / Forerunner / North Germany / Lutheran; 2nd Silesian circle; author, pastor / (Knapp, Koch, Kulp, Nelle; Julian) / KDP, NS, CG, ES / 139, 226.

SELNECCER (SELNECKER), Nicolaus / 1530-1559 / Saxony / Lutheran / (Knapp, Koch, Kulp, Nelle; Julian) / ELEL, CG / 6.

SENITZ, Elisabeth von / 1629-1679 / Forerunner / Silesia / lady-in-waiting / (Knapp, Nelle) / GGB, KDP / 947.

SIEBER, Justus / 1628-1695 / Forerunner / Saxony / Lutheran; P. Gerhardt's circle; pastor, poet laureate / (Fischer, Knapp, Koch) / GGB, KDP, ELEL, ES / 560, 1138, 1227.

SINOLD, Philipp Balthasar / 1657-1742 / Orthodox / Hesse / court official, scholar / (Knapp, Koch, Nelle) / KDP / 1274, 1302.

SÖMEREN, Theodor von / 17th century / CG / 159.

SONNEMANN, Ernst / 1630-1670 / North Germany / educator / (Kulp) / GGB, KDP, KLS, NS, CG, ES / 678.

SOPHIA, Queen of Denmark / 1498-1568 / Denmark / (Kulp) / KDP / 430.

SPITTA, Karl Johann Philipp / 1801-1859 / German church renewal / North Germany / pastor, tutor / (Knapp, Kulp, Nelle; Julian) / KLS, NS, CG / 128, 323.

SPORLEDER, Christoph August / 18th century / (Koch) / KDP / 973.

SPRENG, Johann Jakob / 1699-1768 / Switzerland / Reformed; pastor, professor / (Knapp, Koch, Kulp) / KDP / 1286.

STARCK (STARK), Johann Friedrich / 1680-1756 / Halle Pietist / Frankfurt am Main / author, pastor / (Knapp, Koch, Kulp, Nelle) / ELEL, CG, ES / 620, 1130.

STARK (STARKE), Ludwig / 1630?-1681 / Forerunner / Thuringia / P. Gerhardt's circle / (Fischer, Koch) / KDP / 1079.

STEINHOFER, Christoph Ludwig / 1747-1821 / Moravian / Württemberg / pastor / (Knapp) / KLS, ESL, CG, ES / 102, 290.

STOLL, Jacob / 1731-1822 / German-American / Pennsylvania / Brethren; author, elder, weaver / (Brethren Enc., Eastern Dist.) / GGG, KPS, CG, ES / 9, 30, 42, 66, 118, 235, 250, 592, 657, 669, 687, 701, 703, 782, 790, 799, 860, 939, 1006, 1011, 1032, 1033, 1049, 1056, 1103.

STRATTNER, Georg Christoph / 17th century / GGB, KDP, CG / 568.

STÜBNER, Conrad Gebhard / fl. 1720 / Orthodox / Nuremberg / (Knapp) / NS, CG, ES / 638.

STURM, Christoph Christian / 1740-1786 / Orthodox / North Germany / author, educator, pastor / (Knapp, Koch; Julian) / NS, CG, ES / 580.

SWAIN, Joseph / 1761-1796 / England / Baptist; engraver, minister / (Julian) / KPS, CG, ES / 966.

TERSTEEGEN (ter STEEGE), Gerhard / 1697-1769 / Pietist / Lower Rhine / Reformed Separatist; author, poet weaver / (Knapp, Koch, Kulp, Nelle; Brethren Enc., Julian) / KDP, KH, KLS, KPS, NS, CG, ES / 14, 82, 130, 148, 165, 176, 199, 368, 407, 428, 433, 451, 454, 486, 548, 644, 660, 710, 751, 787, 830, 919, 926, 933, 984, 989, 990, 1001, 1003, 1029, 1100, 1171, 1222, 1248, 1280, 1309.

TIETZE (TITIUS), Christoph / 1641-1705 / Forerunner / South Germany / Lutheran; Nuremberg circle; pastor, poet / (Fischer, Knapp, Koch, Kulp, Nelle; Julian) / KDP, CG / 1125.

WALTER, Johannes / 1781-1818 / German-American / Pennsylvania / Evangelical / (Yoder) / KPS, NS, CG, ES / 740, 817, 1278.

WATTS, Isaac / 1674-1748 / England / Independent; author, minister (Julian) / NS, CG, ES / 132, 341, 353.

WEBER, Paul / 1625-1696 / Forerunner / Nuremberg / Nuremberg circle; pastor / (Fischer) / KDP, KLS, NS, CG, ES / 267.

WEINGÄRTNER, Sigismund / fl. 1600 / South Germany / Lutheran; pastor / (Fischer, Knapp, Koch, Kulp) / KDP, KLS / 110.

WEISE, Christian / 1642-1708 / Orthodox / Saxony / Lutheran; poet, scholar / (Knapp, Koch) / GGB / 39.

WEISS(E), Michael / ca.1448-1534 / Czech Brethren / early leader / (Knapp, Koch, Kulp, Nelle; Julian) / GGB, KDP / 83, 793.

WEISSEL, Georg / 1590-1635 / East Prussia / educator, pastor / (Knapp, Kulp; Julian) / GGB, KDP / 1023.

WESLEY, Charles / 1707-1788 / England / Methodist; poet, minister / (Julian) / NS, CG, ES / 137, 318, 324, 532, 1035, 1057.

WEYDENHEIM, Johann / 17th century? / (Knapp 1837) / KDP / 479.

WILHELM II, Herzog von Sachsen-Weimar / 1582-1662 / Thuringia / Fruchtbringende Gesellschaft / (Fischer, Knapp, Koch, Kulp; Julian) / KDP, KLS, NS, CG, ES / 484.

WILLIAMS, William / 1717-1791 / Wales / preacher, revivalist / (Julian) / KPS, CG, ES / 776.

WINKLER (WINCKLER), Johann Joseph / 1670-1722 / Halle Pietist / North Germany / pastor / (Knapp, Koch, Nelle; Julian) / GGB, KDP, KLS, NS, CG, ES / 469, 1020, 1050.

WOLFF, Jakob Gabriel / 1684-1754 / Halle Pietist / North Germany / Lutheran; jurist / (Knapp, Koch, Nelle; Julian) / KDP, KH, CG, ES / 1028, 1078, 1334.

WOLTERSDORF, Ernst Gottlieb / 1725-1761 / Halle Pietist / Silesia / pastor / (Knapp, Koch, Nelle) / KLS, KPS, NS, CG, ES / 57, 144, 402, 411, 726, 820, 929, 945, 962, 1260, 1296.

ZELLER, Bernhard Eberhard / d. 1714 / Early Pietist / Hesse / (Koch) / GGB, KDP / 1209.

ZELLER, Christian Heinrich / 1779-1860 / German church renewal / South Germany; Switzerland / Lutheran; court official, educator / (Knapp, Koch, Nelle; Julian) / NS, ES / 971, 1104.

ZIEGLER, Caspar / 1621-1690 / Saxony / Lutheran / (Koch) / KDP, KLS, NS, CG, ES / 267.

ZIEGLER, Johann Conrad / 1692-1731 / Radical Pietist / South Germany; Switzerland / (Koch) / KDP / 1096.

ZIHN, Johann Friedrich / 1650-1719 / Orthodox / Thuringia / Lutheran; educator, pastor / (Koch; Julian) / GGB, KDP / 431.

ZINZENDORF, Christian Renatus von / 1727-1752 / Moravian / Germany / (Koch) / KLS / 272.

ZINZENDORF, Nikolaus Ludwig, Graf von / 1700-1760 / Moravian / Germany / (Knapp, Koch, Kulp; Brethren Enc.; Julian) / KDP, KH, KLS, NS, CG, ES / 80, 155, 307, 477, 500, 664, 682, 758, 779, 874, 1281.

ZWICK, Johann / ca.1496-1542 / South Germany / Reformed; jurist, preacher, professor / (Knapp, Koch, Kulp, Nelle; Julian) / KDP / 101.

298

A SELECTED BIBLIOGRAPHY

I. PRIMARY SOURCES

1. Hymnals.

A. Brethren Hymnals and Hymn Collections.

Das Christliche Gesang-Buch. Eine Zusammenstellung der Besten Lieder der alten und neuen Dichter, zum Gottesdienstlichen Gebrauch aller Gott suchenden und heilsbegierigen Seelen ... . Lancaster, Pa.: Druck und Verlag von Johann Bär's Söhnen, 1874.

--------. [2nd ed.] 1897.

Das Kleine Davidische Psalterspiel Der Kinder Zions; von Alten und Neuen auserlesenen Geistes-Gesängen; Allen wahren Heyls-begierigen Säuglingen der Weisheit, Insonderheit aber Denen Gemeinden des Herrn, Zum Dienst und Gebrauch mit Fleisz zusammengetragen, und in gegenwärtig-beliebiger Form und Ordnung, Nebst einem doppelten darzu nützlichen und der Materien halben nöthigen Register, ans Licht gegeben. Germantown: Gedruckt bey Christoph Sauer, 1744.

--------. Germantown: Christoph Sauer, 1760.

--------. Germantown: Christoph Sauer, 1764.

--------. Germantown: Christoph Sauer, 1777.

--------. Philadelphia: Steiner & Cist, 1781.

--------. Chestnuthill: Samuel Saur, 1791.

--------. Ephrata: Salomon Mayer, 1795.

--------. Baltimore: Samuel Saur, 1797.

--------. Germantown: M. Billmeyer, 1797.

--------. Germantown: M. Billmeyer, 1813.

--------. Baltimore: Schäffer und Maund, 1816.

--------. Philadelphia: M. Billmeyer, 1817.

--------. Harrisburg: Wm. Wheit, 1824.

--------. Germania: 1829.

--------. Philadelphia: Mentz und Rovoudt, 1830.

<u>Die Kleine Harfe</u>, Gestimmet von unterschiedlichen Lieblichen Liedern oder Lob-Gesängen, Welche gehöret werden Von den Enden der Erden, zu Ehren dem Gerechten. Diese Kleine Harfe klinget zwar lieblich, aber doch noch im niedrigen Thon; Bis das grosse Harfen-Spieler Heer den Gesang erhöhen wird. Gott und dem Lamm sey die Ehre und das Lob in Zeit und Ewigkeit! Amen. Zum ersten mal ans Licht gegeben. Chesnuthill: gedruckt bey Samuel Saur, 1792.

--------. Baltimore: Samuel Saur, 1797.

--------. Philadelphia: M. Billmeyer, 1813.

--------. Baltimore: Schäffer und Maundt, 1816.

--------. Philadelphia: M. Billmeyer, 1817.

--------. Germania: 1829.

--------. Philadelphia: Mentz und Rovoudt, 1830.

<u>Die Kleine Lieder Sammlung</u>, oder Auszug aus dem Psalterspiel der Kinder Zions, zum Dienst inniger heilsuchender Seelen, Insonderheit aber der Brüderschaft der Täufer zum Dienst und Gebrauch zusammengetragen in gegenwärtiger Form, und mit einem zweyfachen Register versehen. ... Erste Auflage. Hägerstadt: Gedruckt bey Gruber und May, 1826.

--------. Ephrata: Joseph Baumann, 1827.

--------. Canton: Solomon Sala, 1829.

--------. Neu Berlin: Geo. Miller, 1832.

--------. Osnaburg: H. Kurtz, 1833.

--------. Gettysburg: H. C. Neinstedt, 1834.

--------. Osnaburg: H. Kurtz, 1835.

--------. Gettysburg: H. C. Neinstedt, 1836.

--------. Osnaburg: H. Kurtz, 1837.

--------. Harrisburg: G. S. Peters, 1838.

--------. Gettysburg: H. C. Neinstedt, 1841.

--------. Osnaburg: H. Kurtz, 1841.

--------. Harrisburg: G. S. Peters, 1843.

--------. Poland: H. Kurtz, 1844.

--------. Harrisburg: G. S. Peters, 1847.

--------. Gettysburg: H. C. Neinstedt, 1848.

--------. Poland: H. Kurtz, 1848.

--------. Harrisburg: G. S. Peters, 1849.

--------. Harrisburg: Lutz und Scheffer, 1850.

--------. Poland: H. Kurtz, 1950.

--------. Poland: H. Kurtz, 1853.

Die kleine Perlen-Sammlung, oder Auswahl Geistreicher Lieder, Mehrsten-
        theils von Manuscripten genommen, zum Dienst, Gebrauch und Auferbau-
        ung aller Gottliebenden Brüder und Schwestern in Christo. Zusammen-
        getragen in gegenwärtig kleiner Form, von J. E. Pfautz. ... Erste Auf-
        lage. Ephrata: Gedruckt bey J. E. Pfautz, 1858.

Ein Lied von der Taufe. Broadside. (Lancaster: H. W. Ville, [n.d.])

Ein schön' Lied. [n. p.]: 1832.

Eine Sammlung von Psalmen, Lobgesängen, und Geistlichen Liedern, zum
        Gebrauch für den Privat, Familien- und Öffentlichen Gottesdienst der
        Brüder (German Baptist Brethren) und aller innigen, heilsuchenden
        Seelen, zusammengetragen auf Anordnung der Jährlichen Versammlung,
        von einer Committee. ... Mount Morris, Ill.: The Brethren's Publish-
        ing Company, 1893.

--------. Mount Morris, Ill.: The Brethren's Publishing Company, 1895.

--------. Elgin, Ill.: The Brethren's Publishing Company, 1903.

Etliche liebliche und erbauliche Lieder. Germantown: Peter Leibert, 1788.

--------. Chambersburg: Joh. Herschberger, 1812.

Etliche neue geistliche Lieder. Rorristaun: David Saur, 1807.

Geistliche u. andächtige Lieder. Aufgesetzt von Br. Johann Preisz.
        Germantown: Christoph Sauer, 1753.

Geistreiches Gesang-Buch/ Vor alle Liebhabende Seelen der Warheit/ sonder-
        lich Vor die Gemeine Des Herrn In sich fassend Die Auserlesenste und
        nöthigste Lieder/ Aus andern Gesang-Büchern ausgezogen/ Nebst 100.
        neue Lieder/ so zum ersten mahl aufgesetzt worden/ zum Trost und Er-
        quickung allen wahren Nachfolgern des Herrn Jesu/ und in gegenwärti-
        ger Form ans Licht gegeben/ Zum Lobe Gottes. Berlenburg: Gedruckt
        bey Christoph Konert/ Anno 1720.

Neue Sammlung von Psalmen, Lobgesängen und Geistlichen Liedern, zum
        Gebrauch für den Privat-, Familien- und Öffentlichen Gottesdienst der
        Alten Brüder und aller innigen, heilsuchenden Seelen, zusammengetra-
        gen auf Anordnung der jährlichen Versammlung aus unsern älteren, so-
        wie aus neuern Gesangbüchern von einem Committee. ... Covington,
        Miami Co., O.: Herausgegeben von James Quinter, 1870.

Stoll, Jakob. Geistliches Gewürz-Gärtlein Heilsuchender Seelen; Oder Geistlichen Lieder und Andachten ... . Ephrata: Johann Baumann, 1806.

The Brethren Hymnal. Authorized by Annual Conference, Church of the Brethren. Elgin, Ill.: House of the Church of the Brethren, 1951.

The Brethren Hymnal, a Collection of Psalms, Hymns and Spiritual Songs, Suited for Song Service in Christian Worship, for Church Service, Social Meetings and Sunday Schools. Compiled under Direction of the General Conference of the German Baptist Brethren Church by the Committee. Elgin, Ill.: Brethren Publishing Co., 1901.

The Brethren's Tune and Hymn Book, Being a Compilation of Sacred Music Adapted to All the Psalms, Hymns, and Spiritual Songs in The Brethren's Hymn Book. Singer's Glen, Va.: Benjamin Funk, Dale City, Pa.: H. R. Holsinger, 1872.

The Brethren's Tune and Hymn Book, Being a Compilation of Sacred Music Adapted to All the Psalms, Hymns and Spiritual Songs in The Brethren's Hymn Book. Carefully revised, re-arranged and otherwise improved. Mt. Morris, Ill. and Huntingdon, Pa.: The Brethren's Publishing Co., 1879.

B. Other Hymnals and Hymn Collections.

Ausbund, Das ist Etliche schöne Christliche Lieder, wie sie in dem Gefängnüsz zu Bassau in dem Schlosz von den Schweitzer-Brüdern, und von anderen rechtgläubigen Christen hin und her gedichtet worden. Allen und jeden Christen welcher Religion sie seyen, unpartheyisch fast nützlich. Germantown: Gedruckt bey Christoph Sauer, 1751.

Bickel, P. W. Das Singvögelein, oder Melodien und Lieder für Sonntags-Schulen. Berlin, Ont.: Oberholtzer und Bowman, 1871.

Churländisches vollständiges Gesangbuch, Darinnen D. Martin Luthers, und anderer Geistreichen Männer, wie auch viele aus dem Preussischen, und Rigischen Gesangbuch auszerlesene Gesänge ... zusammengetragen. Mitau: George Radetzki, 1695.

Crüger, Johann, comp. Praxis Pietatis Melica: Das ist Übung der Gottseligkeit in Christlichen und trostreichen Gesängen, Herrn D. Martini Lutheri ... wie auch anderer ... und nunmehr mit Johann Heermanns Evangelien bis in 1220. Gesängen vermehret ... . Edition XXIV. Berlin: David Salfelds Witwe, 1690.

Das Aller Neueste Harfenspiel, oder Zugabe einiger Lieder; auf Begehren von J. Engel, P. Eby, C. Grosch und anderer Mitglieder der Vereinigten Brüderschaft in Pennsylvanien. Zum ersten mal zusammengetragen. [1795?]

    United Brethren. First hymnal to be published by a German camp-meeting group (Yoder).

Das Geistliche Saitenspiel, oder Eine Sammlung auserlesener, erbaulicher, Geistreicher Lieder, zum Gebrauch aller Gottliebenden Seelen. Insonderheit für die Gemeinden der Evangelischen Gemeinschaft. ... Neu-Berlin, Pa.: 1817.

Evangelical Association. Later editions: 1836, 1840.

Das Gemeinschaftliche Gesangbuch zum Gottesdienstlichen Gebrauch lutherischen und reformierten Gemeinden in Nord-Amerika ... . 5. Auflage. Grünsburg: J. S. Steck, 1828.

Das Klug'sche Gesangbuch 1533. nach dem einzigen erhaltenen Exemplar der Lutherhalle zu Wittenberg ergänzt und herausgegeben von Konrad Ameln. Kassel und Basel: Bärenreiter-Verlag, 1954.

Das neue und verbesserte Gesangbuch, worinnen die Psalmen Davids samt einer Sammlung alter und neuer Geistreicher Lieder ... enthalten sind ... vor die Evangelisch-Reformirten Gemeinen in den Vereinigten Staaten von America. 2. Auflage. Germantown: Michael Billmeyer, 1799.

--------. 3. Auflage. Germantown: Michael Billmeyer, 1806.

Davidisches Psalter-Spiel Der Kinder Zions; von Alten und Neuen auserlesenen Geistes-Gesängen; Allen wahren Heyls-begierigen Säuglingen der Weisheit, Insonderheit aber Denen Gemeinden des Herrn, Zum Dienst und Gebrauch mit Fleisz zusammengetragen, und in gegenwärtig-beliebiger Form und Ordnung, Nebst einem doppelten darzu nützlichen und der Materien halben nöthigen Register, ans Licht gegeben. [n. p.]: 1718.

--------. Hamburg: Johann Philip Helwig, 1740.

--------. Frankfurt: Tobias Conrad Landgraf, 1753.

--------. Ebenezer, N.Y.: 1854.

Der Christliche Sänger, Eine Sammlung der vornehmsten und gebräuchlichsten Lieder, zum Gebrauch des öffentlichen und privat Gottesdienstes für alle heilsuchende Seelen Jeder Christlichen Benennung. Skippacksville, Pa.: Samuel K. Cassel, 1855.

Des Neu-verbesserten Gesang-Buchs Anderer Theil, in sich haltend, Den Kern Alter und Neuer Geistreicher Lieder, Zur Erweckung und Erbauung bey dem öffentlichen Gottesdienst Derer Christlichen Gemeinden des Gräflich Wittgensteinischen Landes ... . Berlenburg: Christoph Michael Regelein, 1749.

Deutsches Gesangbuch der Bischöflich Methodisten Kirche. Eine Auswahl geistlicher Lieder für Kirche, Haus und Schule. Cincinnati: Cranston und Stowe, [1865].

Die allgemeine Lieder-Sammlung zum privat- und öffentlichen Gottes-Dienst. Elkhart, Ind.: John F. Funk, 1871.

Die Lieder der Hutterischen Brüder. Gesangbuch Darinnen viel und mancherlei schöne Betrachtungen, Lehren, Vermahnungen, Lobgesänge und Glaubensbekenntnisse ... . Herausgegeben von den Hutterischen Brüdern in America. 2. Aufl. Winnipeg, Canada: The Christian Press, 1953.

[Dreisbach, Johannes and Heinrich Niebel, comp.] Die Geistliche Viole, oder Eine kleine Sammlung alter und neuer Geistreicher Lieder, zum Gebrauch in den Gemeinden der Evangelischen Gemeinschaft und Aller Gott liebenden Seelen. 8. Aufl. Neu Berlin, Pa.: T. Buck, 1842.

Ein Unpartheyisches Gesang-Buch enthaltend Geistreiche Lieder und Psalmen ... . Auf Begehren der Brüderschaft der Menonisten Gemeinen aus vielen Liederbüchern gesammelt. Lancaster: Johann Albrecht, 1804.

Eine auserlesene Sammlung Geistlicher Lieder. Lancaster: Joseph Ehrenfried, [before 1811].

Eine Hell-Posaunende Zionitische Wächter-Stimme/ Zur Offenbahrung der Wider-Christen und ihrer Verwüstung/ und zur Ermunterung der wahren Christen zur heiligen Rüstung auf die Zukunfft des Herrn; Nach dem Hall und Schall derer Heil. Apostel und Propheten ehmals angestimmet und erschollen Durch einen um den Schaden Joseph Bekümmerten Christen. Und nun/ Wegen seiner Würdigkeit/ nebst etlichen dergleichen kräfftigen Zeugnissen vom wahren und falschen Christenthum/ Aufs neue zum Druck befördert. [n. p.]: 1718. Bound with: Davidisches Psalter-Spiel (1718).

Eine Sammlung Evangelischer Lieder, zum Gebrauch der Hoch-Deutschen Reformirten Kirche in den Vereinigten Staaten von Nord Amerika ... . Chambersburg, Pa.: Verlag der Druckerei der Hochdeutsch Reformirten Kirche, 1842.

Eine Sammlung von Geistlichen Liedern angepasst den verschiedenen Arten des Christlichen Gottesdienstes, und besonders bestimmt für den Gebrauch der Brüder in Christo, bekannt als die "River-Brüder." Zusammengestellt nach den Bestimmungen der General-Conferenz. Lancaster, Pa.: 1874.

Eine unparteiische Lieder-Sammlung zum Gebrauch beim Oeffentlichen Gottesdienst und der Häuslichen Erbauung. Lancaster, Pa.: Johann Bär, 1860.

Einige Psalmen Israels oder Geistliche liebliche Lieder und Lobgesänge ... gedichtet und ... gesungen von einigen Erweckten Seelen unserer Zeiten ... . Berlenburg: 1725.

Eisenachisches Neu-vermehrtes und beständiges Gesang-Buch, Darinnen D. Martin Lutheri und anderer reinen alten und neuen Evangelischen Lehrer geistreiche Lieder und Lob-Gesänge enthalten. ... Eisenach: Johann Adolph Boëtius, 1732.

Erb, Jacob. Sammlung von Geistlichen, Lieblichen Liedern, Aus verschiedenen Gesangbüchern gesammelt zum Gebrauch des Oeffentlichen und privat Gottesdienst. Harrisburg, Pa.: 1830.

Evangelisches Gesangbuch. Die kleine Palme mit Anhang. Harrisburg, Pa.: Verlag der Vereinigten Evangelischen Kirche, [1897?].

Evangelisches Gesangbuch, oder, eine Sammlung geistreicher Lieder. Neu Berlin, Pa.: W. W. Orwig, 1821.

————————. 1850.

Evangelisches Gesangbuch und Gebete für den öffentlichen Gottesdienst sowohl, als für die häusliche Andacht. Erfurt: im Evangelischen Waisenhause, 1848.

Eyn Enchiridion oder Handbüchlein, eynem ytzlichen Christen fast nutzlich bey sich zu haben ... . [Erfurt]: 1524; reprint ed.: Kassel: Bärenreiter, 1929. "Erfurter Enchiridion."

Freylinghausen, Johann Anastasius, comp. Geistreiches Gesang-Buch, den Kern alter und neuer Lieder in sich haltend ... . Halle: Waysenhaus, 1741.

Geistliche Lieder D. Martin Lutheri und anderer Geistreichen Männer. Leipzig: Michael Lantzenberger, 1612.

Geistlicher Liederschatz. [n. p.]: 1832.

Geistreiches Gesangbuch, Vormahls in Halle gedruckt ... . Mit einer Vorrede Eberhard Philipps Zuehlen ... . Darmstadt: Sebastian Griebel, 1700.

Gerhart, Isaac, comp. Choral Harmonie. Enthaltend Kirchen-Melodien, Die bey allen Religions-Verfassungen gebräuchlich ... . Harrisburg: John Wyeth, 1822.

Gesangbuch der Vereinigten Brüder in Christo. Dayton, Ohio: 1854.

Geystliche Lieder. Mit einer newen vorrhede D. Mart. Luth. Leipzig: Valentin Babst, 1545; reprint ed.: Kassel: Bärenreiter, 1929. "Babstsches Gesangbuch."

Harmonisches Gesangbuch. Theils Von andern Authoren, Theils neu verfasst ... . Oekonomie, Pa.: 1827.

[Hermann, Charles G.]. Der Sänger am Grabe. Eine Auswahl Lieder zum Gebrauch bei Leichenbegängnissen, wie auch Trost-Lieder für solche, die um geliebte Tote trauern. Philadelphia, P.: J. Rohr, 1851.

Hertz, Daniel. Poetischer Himmelsweg, oder Kleine, geistliche Lieder Sammlung Zum Gebrauch des öffentlichen und häuslichen Gottesdienstes und Erbauung aller gottliebenden Seelen jeder Confession. Lancaster: H. W. Villee, 1828.

Hertz-inniger Andachts-Spiegel, oder Vollständiges und kurtzgefasstes Gebet-Buch ... . Jena: Johann Felix Bielcken, 1713.

Kern Geistlicher Lieblicher Lieder, Dem Herrn mit Hertz und Mund zu sin-
     gen, Oder Neu-auserlesenes Gesang-Buch In welchem Tausend der besten
     alten und neuen Kirchen-Lieder, deren die meisten nach bekannten
     Melodien können gesungen werden, enthalten sind ... . Nürnberg:
     Lorenz Bieling, 1731.

Lobwasser, Ambrosius. Die Psalmen Davids Nach Frantzösischer Melody in
     teutsche Reimen gebracht. Marburg: Joh. Heinr. Stock, 1710.

Lorenz, F. A. Zions Pilgerschatz. Milwaukee: the author, 1902.

Neu-Eingerichtetes Gesang-Buch in sich haltend eine Sammlung (mehrenteils
     alter) schöner lehr-reicher und erbaulicher Lieder ... . Nach den
     Haupt-Stücken der Christlichen Lehr und Glaubens eingetheilet ... .
     Germantown: Christoph Saur, 1762.

Neu-vollständiges Nassau-Dillenburgisches Kirchen Gesangbuch, Worinnen
     befindlich die Psalmen Davids, in Deutsche Reimen gebracht ... . Bene-
     benst Den erbaulichsten und gebräuchlichsten Gesängen und Liedern
     durch D. Luther und viele andere Gotts-gelehrte Männer gestellet;
     Welchen Neanders Bundes-Lieder, Und sonst noch verschiedene noch nie-
     mals gedruckte ... beygefüget ... . Herborn: Johann Nicolaus Andreä,
     1711.

Orwig, Wilhelm W. Evangelisches Liederbüchlein für Sonntagsschulen. 2.
     Aufl. Neu Berlin, Pa.: W. W. Orwig, 1843.

     Other editions: 1853, 1863, 1864, 1866.

Psalmen und Lieder zum Gebrauch der Evangelischreformirten Gemeine in
     Danzig. Danzig: J. E. F. Müller, 1785.

Sammlung Geistlicher und lieblicher Lieder, Eine grosse Anzahl der
     Kern-vollesten alten und erwecklichsten neuen Gesänge enthaltende ...
     . Leipzig: August Martini, [1725]. "Berthelsdorfer Gesangbuch."

Sammlung von Geistlichen Liedern zum gemeinschaftlichen Gesang zusammenge-
     tragen. [n. p.]: 1801.

Schaff, Philipp, comp. Deutsches Gesangbuch. Eine Auswahl geistlicher
     Lieder aus allen Zeiten der christlichen Kirche. Nach den besten
     hymnologischen Quellen bearbeitet ... . Probe-Ausgabe. Philadel-
     phia: Lindsay und Blakistan, Berlin: Wiegand und Grieben, 1859.

Sonntagsschul-Gesangbuch der Reformirten Kirche in den Vereinigten Staa-
     ten. ... Cleveland, O.: Deutsches Verlagshaus der Reformirten Kirche
     in den Vereinigten Staaten, 1876.

Stimmen aus Zion, Oder: Erbauliche Lieder, Zur Verherrlichung Gottes und
     Erbauung vieler Seelen herausgegeben. ... 2. Aufl. Stuttgart: Joh.
     Christian Falck, 1744-1745.

[Weisze, Michael]. Ein New Geseng buchlen. 1531. Reprint ed.: Kassel:
     Bärenreiter.

Zinzendorf, Nikolaus Ludwig von, comp. Sammlung Geist- und lieblicher Lieder, eine grosse Anzahl der Kern-vollesten alten und erwecklich- sten neuen Gesänge enthaltende ... . Nebst einer Vorrede des Edito- ris ... . Herrnhuth: Waysenhaus, [1731].

"Marchesches Gesangbuch," i.e., 3rd enl. ed. of "Berthelsdorfer Gesangbuch."

Zionitischer WeyrauchsHügel Oder: Myrrhen Berg ... . Germantown: Gedruckt bey Christoph Sauer, 1739.

Zwanzig neue geistliche Lieder, Das Erste: Von einem Drucker Gesellen Thomas von Imbroich genannt, welcher zu Cöllen an Reyn um der Wahr- heit willen enthauptet worden ... 1558. [n. p.]: 1758.

Zwey schöne geistliche Lieder ... . [n. p.: 18th century?]

2. Devotional Works.

Arndt, Johann. Paradiesz-Gärtlein Voller Christlichen Tugenden ... . Ne- benst einem Gesang-Büchlein Zu desto mehrerer frommer Seelen Vergnü- gung vermehret ... . Stuttgart: Bernhard Michael Müller, 1718.

--------. Tübingen: Johann Christoph Löffler, 1751.

Arnold, Gottfried. Göttliche Liebes-Funcken ... . Dritte Edition mit neuen Göttlichen Liebes-Funcken aus des sel. Autoris Göttlichen Sophia vermehret. Leipzig: Samuel Benjamin Walther, 1724.

Beissel, Johann Conrad et. al. Göttliche Liebes und Lobesgethöne, Welche in den Hertzen der Kinder der Weiszheit zusammen ein und von da wie- der aussgeflossen Zum Lob Gottes ... . Philadelphia: Benjamin Franklin, 1730.

--------. Jacobs Kampff- und Ritter-Platz. Allwo der nach seinem ur- sprung sich sehnende Geist der in Sophiam verliebten seele mit Gott um den neuen Namen gerungen, und den Sieg davon getragen. Entworffen in Unterschidlichen Glaubens und Leidensliedern ... . Philadelphia: B[enjamin] F[ranklin], 1736.

Bogatzky, Carl Heinrich von. Evangelische Uebung des wahren Christen- thums, oder Erbauliche Betrachtungen von der Freyheit der Gläubigen vom Gesetz ... . Halle: Im Verlag des Waysenhauses, 1730.

--------. Die Uebung der Gottseligkeit in allerley Geistlichen Liedern, zur allgemeinen Erbauung ... . Halle: Im Verlag des Waysenhauses, 1750.

Gellert, Christian Fürchtegott. Geistliche Oden und Lieder. Leipzig: 1757.

Gerhardt, Paul. Paulus Gerhardts geistliche Lieder getreu nach der bei seinen Lebzeiten erschienenen Ausgabe wieder abgedruckt. 6. Aufl. Gütersloh: C. Bertelsmann, 1874.

Gruber, Eberhard Ludwig. J. J. J. Jesus-Lieder Für seine Glieder, sonderlich für seine Kleine und Reine ... gelallet Von einem Der nun suchet wie Er der Ewigen Liebe Gefalle. [n. p.]: 1720.

Helleleuchtender Hertzens- und Andachts-Spiegel ... nach der tiefen Grund- und Kraft-Lehre ... Johannis Thauleri ... . 4. Aufl. Amsterdam und Frankfurth: Johann Felix Bielcken, 1713.

Hiller, Philipp Friedrich. Geistliches Liederkästlein zum Lobe Gottes, bestehend aus 366 kleinen Oden über ebenso viele Bibelsprüche. Kindern Gottes zum Dienst aufgesetzt. Stuttgart: 1762-1767.

--------. Reutlingen: Christoph Jakob Friedrich Kalbfell, 1840.

Hölty, Ludwig. Gedichte ... besorgt durch seine Freunde Friederich Leopold Graven zu Stolberg und Johann Heinrich Vosz. Frankfurt und Leipzig: 1785.

Hübner, Johann. Des frommen Thomas a Kempis goldenes Büchlein von der Nachfolge Jesu Christi ... . Leipzig: 1727.

Klopstock, Friedrich Gottlieb. Geistliche Lieder und Oden. Leipzig: Georg Joachim Göschen, 1823.

Neander, Joachim. Glaub- und Liebes-Übung: Auffgemuntert Durch Einfältige Bundes-Lieder und Danck-Psalmen ... . Bremen: Hermann Brauer, 1698.

--------. Vermehrte Glaub- und Liebes-Übung ... . Nebst einem mercklichen Anhang geistreicher und schrifftmässiger Himmels-Lieder; Durch Georg Christoph Strattner. Frankfurt und Leipzig: Joh. Philipp Andreä, 1691.

Oetinger, Friedrich Christoph. Geistliche Lieder. Metzingen, Württ.: Ernst Franz, 1967.

Rambach, Johann Jacob. Poetische Fest-Gedanken Von den höchsten Wohltaten Gottes ... . Fünfte und vermehrte Auflage. Jena: Joh. Friedr. Ritter, 1740.

Sasse, Bernhard Heinrich. Geistliche Lieder, von ... einem Hausmann in Kirchenlengern. Lancaster: Heinr. und Benj. Grimler, 1811.

Scheffler, Johannes. Heilige Seelenlust oder Geistliche Hirtenlieder ... . München: Allgemeine Verlagsanstalt, 1924.

Schlegel, Johann Adolf. Sammlung Geistlicher Gesänge, zur Beförderung der Erbauung. Leipzig: M. G. Weidmanns Erben und Reich, 1766.

Schmolck, Benjamin. Der Lustige Sabbat, In der Stille zu Zion ... . Mit Heiligen Liedern gefeyert ... . Schweidnitz: Christian Reinmann, 1714.

--------. Eines andächtigen Hertzens Schmuck und Asche, Oder Neue Sammlung allerhand Freud- und Trauer-Lieder, ... Breslau und Liegnitz: Michael Rohrlach, 1717.

Spitta, Carl Johann Philipp. Psalter und Harfe. Eine Sammlung christlicher Lieder zur häuslichen Erbauung. 14. Aufl. Leipzig: August Robert Friese, 1847.

Starck, Johann Friedrich. Tägliches Hand-Buch in guten und bösen Tagen ... . Erste Amerikanische Auflage. Philadelphia: Conrad Zentler und Georg W. Mentz, 1812.

Tersteegen, Gerhard. Geistliche Lieder. Herausgegeben von Wilhelm Nelle. Gütersloh: C. Bertelsmann, 1897.

--------. Geistliches Blumen-Gärtlein Inniger Seelen. Fünfte und vermehrte Edition. Duisburg: Johann Sebastian Straube, 1751.

Tersteegen, Gerhard, ed. Gott-geheiligtes Harfen-Spiel Der Kinder Zion; Bestehend in Joachim Neandri sämmtlichen Bundes-Liedern und Danck-Psalmen, Nebst einer Sammlung vieler anderer auserlesenen alten und neuen Geist- und lieblichen Liedern: Andächtigen Hertzen zum Dienst und Gebrauch mit Fleisz zusammen getragen. Solingen: Johann Schmitz, 1747.

5th enlarged edition: 1768.

Thomas a Kempis. Der kleine Kempis oder kurze Sprüche und Gebätlein, aus dem meistens unbekannten Wercklein des Thomae a Kempis. Zusammengetragen zur Erbauung der Kleinen. Siebente und verbesserte Auflage. Germantown: Peter Leibert, 1795.

Watts, Isaac. The Psalms and Hymns of Dr. Watts, Arranged by Dr. Rippon, with Dr. Rippon's Selection. Philadelphia: David Clark, 1831.

Woltersdorff, Ernst Gottlieb. Einige neue Lieder Oder Evangelische Psalmen ... . Zweyte Sammlung, welche die kürtzeren Lieder in sich fasset. Jauer: Heinrich Christoph Müller, 1752.

3. Other Works.

Arnold, Gottfried. Das Eheliche und Unverehelichte Leben der ersten Christen, nach ihren eigenen Zeugnissen und Exempeln beschrieben ... . Franckfurt: Thomas Fritsch, 1702.

--------. Das Geheimnisz der Göttlichen Sophia oder Weiszheit ... . Leipzig: Thomas Fritsch, 1700.

Christliche Glaubens Bekantnuss Der Waffen-losen und fürnemlich (under dem Namen der Menonisten) wohlbekanten Christen ... . Wobey gefüget Etliche Geistliche Lieder Alles zur Erbauung, Auffmunterung und Lehr unser Jugend zum besten gestellet und geordnet worden. [n. p.]: 1686.

Chronicon Ephratense, a History of the Community of Seventh Day Baptists at Ephrata, Lancaster County, Penn'a, by "Lamech and Agrippa." Translated from the original German by J. Max Hark. Lancaster, Pa.: S. H. Zahm, 1889.

Chronicon Ephratense, Enthaltend den Lebens-Lauf des ehrwürdigen Vaters in Christo Friedsam Gottrecht, Weyland Stiffters und Vorstehers des geistl. Ordens der Einsamen in Ephrata in der Graffschaft Lancaster in Pennsylvania. Zusammengetragen von Br. Lamech u. Agrippa ... . Ephrata: 1786.

Ein Geistliches Magazien, Oder: Aus den Schätzen der Schriftgelehrten zum Himmelreich gelehrt, dargereichtes Altes und Neues. Germantown: Christoph Sauer, 1764, 1770.

Francke, August Hermann. Oeffentliches Zeugnisz Vom Werck, Wort und Dienst Gottes ... . Halle: in Verlegung des Waysen-Hauses, 1702.

Gellert, Christian Fürchtegott. "Vorrede," Sämmtliche Schriften. Zweyter Theil. Neueste verbesserte Auflage. Wien und Prag: Franz Haas, 1808.

Herder, Johann Gottfried. Briefe, das Studium der Theologie betreffend. Nach der zweiten verbesserten Ausgabe, 1785. Herausgegeben durch Johann Georg Müller. Dritter und vierter Theil. Stuttgart und Tübingen: J. G. Cotta, 1829.

Kirchner, Johann Georg. Kurzgefasste Nachricht von ältern und neueren Liederverfassern. Anfangs von Johann Heinrich Grischow im Druck ertheilet, nunmehro aber verbessert und vermehrter herausgegeben. Halle: im Verlag des Waisenhauses, 1771.

Mack, Alexander. Eberhard Ludwig Grubers Grundforschende Fragen, welche denen Neuen Täuffern, im Wittgensteinischen, insonderheit zu beantworten, vorgelegt waren ... . [Berleburg: Christoph Konert?], 1715.

--------. Later editions Germantown: Christoph Saur, 1774 (Zweyte Auflage); Baltimore: Samuel Sauer, 1799 (Dritte Auflage).

--------. Kurtze und einfältige Vorstellung, Der äussern aber doch heiligen Rechten und Ordnungen des Hauses Gottes ... . [Berleburg: Christoph Konert?], 1715.

--------. Later editions Germantown: Christoph Saur, 1774 (Zweyte Auflage); Baltimore: Samuel Sauer, 1799 (Dritte Auflage).

Minutes of the Annual Meetings of the Church of the Brethren. Containing All Available Minutes from 1778 to 1909. Published by The General Mission Board Under Authority of Annual Conference, June 1-3, 1909. Elgin, Ill.: Brethren Publishing House, 1909.

Sangmeister, Ezechiel. Das Leben und Wandel Des in Gott ruhenden und seligen Br. Ezechiel Sangmeisters; Weiland ein Einwohner von Ephrata. ... Von ihm selbst beschrieben. Ephrata, Pa.: Joseph Baumann, 1825; reprint ed.: Ann Arbor, Mich.: University Microfilms.

Spener, Philipp Jacob. Theologische Bedenken, Und andere Briefliche Antworten auf geistliche, sonderlich zur Erbauung gerichtete, Materien ... . Vierter und letzter Theil. ... Halle: in Verlegung des Waysen-Hauses, 1715.

310

Tersteegen, Gerhard. "Vorbericht," Geistliches Blumen-Gärtlein Inniger
        Seelen ... . Fünfte und vermehrte Edition. Duisburg am Rhein: Jo-
        hann Sebastian Straube, 1751.

--------. "Vorrede," Gott-geheiligtes Harfen-Spiel Der Kinder Zion ... .
        Fünfte und vermehrte Edition. Solingen: Johann Schmitz, 1768.

II. SECONDARY SOURCES

1. Hymnological Works.

Bachmann, Johann Friedrich. Zur Geschichte der Berliner Gesangbücher.
        Ein hymnologischer Beitrag. Berlin: Wilhelm Schultze, 1856.

        Covers the older Berlin hymnals from 1640 to 1736. These were pub-
        lished during the orthodox church struggle. Orthodoxy of the texts
        was vouchsafed by supplying authors' names. This work includes a com-
        prehensive index. A reliable and valuable source.

Beery, William. Brethren Hymns, Hymnals, Authors and Composers. A Study
        in Our Literary and Musical Heritage. Elgin, Ill.: Church of the
        Brethren, Board of Christian Education, 1945.

        A ten-page booklet.

Bittinger, Emmert F. "More on Brethren Hymnology." Brethren Life and
        Thought 8 (Summer 1963): 11-16.

Blankenburg, Walter. Geschichte der Melodien des Evangelischen Kirchenge-
        sangbuchs. Ein Abriss. Göttingen: Vandenhoeck und Ruprecht, 1957.
        In: Handbuch zum Evangelischen Kirchengesangbuch, Band II, 2. Teil.

Blume, Friedrich. Protestant Church Music. A History. New York: Norton,
        1974.

Buffington, Albert F. "Dutchified German" Spirituals. Lancaster, Pa.:
        1965.

Cunz, F. A. Geschichte des deutschen Kirchenliedes vom 16. Jahrhundert
        bis auf unsere Zeit. [n. p.]: 1855; reprint ed.: Wiesbaden: Martin
        Sändig, 1969.

Eberlein, Hellmut. Lobgesänge in der Nacht. Die geistlichen Sänger
        Schlesiens von der Reformation bis zur Gegenwart. München: Claudius
        Verlag, 1954.

Eberly, William R. "The Printing and Publishing Activities of Henry
        Kurtz." Brethren Life and Thought 8 (Winter 1963): 19-34.

Ehmann, Carl Chr. Eberhard, ed. Philipp Friedrich Hillers sämmtliche
        Geistliche Lieder, nebst einem Abriss seines Lebens, unverändert
        herausgegeben. Stuttgart: Verlag der Evangelischen Brüderstiftung,
        1858.

Farlee, Loyd Winfield. "A History of the Church Music of the Amana Society, The Community of True Inspiration." Ph.D. thesis, University of
Iowa, 1966.

Valuable for its history of Davidisches Psalter-Spiel. The value of
the first-line index is limited by its omission of numerous hymns
from the 1718 edition and by its documentation which is based on the
"Amana Manuscript" (AMANA MS), a handwritten list of hymns and
authors of the eighth edition (1854) prepared by William Moershel
(1828-1895), which is not entirely reliable.

Fellerer, Karl Gustav. Das deutsche Kirchenlied im Ausland. Münster:
Aschendorff, 1835.

Fischer, Albert, comp. Das deutsche evangelische Kirchenlied des 17.
Jahrhunderts. Vollendet und herausgegeben von W. Tümpel. Hildesheim: Georg Olms Verlag, 1964. 6 vols.

A continuation of Wackernagel's work, this is a valuable and reliable
anthology.

Fischer, Nevin W. The History of Brethren Hymnbooks. Bridgewater, Va.:
Beacon Publishers, 1950.

Sections dealing with German hymnbooks predate later original research and therefore contain several errors.

Foote, Henry Wilder. Three Centuries of American Hymnody. Cambridge,
Mass.: Harvard University Press, 1940.

Gabriel, Paul. Geschichte des Kirchenliedes. Ein Abriss. Göttingen:
Vandenhoeck und Ruprecht, 1957. In: Handbuch zum Evangelischen Kirchengesangbuch, Band II, 2. Teil.

Garber, Ora. "Six Hymns. Jacob Stoll." Brethren Life and Thought 19
(Autumn 1974): 229-236.

Haussmann, William A. German-American Hymnology 1683-1800. [Baltimore]:
Johns Hopkins University, 1895.

Heckman, Samuel B., comp. The Religious Poetry of Alexander Mack, Jr.
Elgin, Ill.: Brethren Publishing House, 1912.

Based on primary sources. Contains prose translations; German and
English on opposite pages.

Heine, Herbert. Die Melodien der Mainzer Gesangbücher in der ersten
Hälfte des 17. Jahrhunderts. Mainz: Selbstverlag der Gesellschaft
für mittelrheinische Kirchengeschichte, 1975.

Hennig, Kurt. Die geistliche Kontrafaktur im Jahrhundert der Reformation.
Ein Beitrag zur Geschichte des deutschen Volks- und Kirchenliedes im
16 . Jahrhundert. Halle: Max Niemeyer, 1909.

Hinks, Donald R. Brethren Hymn-Books and Hymnals, 1720-1884. Gettysburg, Pa.: Brethren Heritage Press, 1986.

Hohmann, Walter H. Outlines in Hymnology with Emphasis on Mennonite Hymnody. Bethel College, Kans.: 1941.

Hollweg, Walter. Geschichte der evangelischen Gesang-Bücher vom Niederrhein im 16. bis 18. Jahrhundert. Hildesheim: Georg Olms Verlag, 1971.

Jackson, George Pullen, comp. Another Sheaf of White Spirituals. Gainesville, Fla.: University of Florida Press, 1952.

--------. Down-East Spirituals and Others. New York: J. J. Augustin, 1942.

--------. Spiritual Folk-Songs of Early America. New York: J. J. Augustin, 1937.

--------. White Spirituals in the Southern Uplands. Chapel Hill: University of North Carolina Press, 1933.

Julian, John, ed. A Dictionary of Hymnology. London: John Murray, 1892.

--------. 2nd ed. 1907.

Kadelbach, Ada. Die Hymnodie der Mennoniten in Nordamerika (1742-1860). Eine Studie zur Verpflanzung, Bewahrung und Umformung europäischer Kirchenliedtradition. Mainz: 1971.

Knapp, Albert, comp. Evangelischer Liederschatz für Kirche und Haus. Eine Sammlung geistlicher Lieder aus allen Jahrhunderten. Stuttgart und Tübingen: J. J. Cotta, 1837.

A pioneer work but lacking the benefit of the documentation of later hymnological research.

--------. 4. Aufl. Stuttgart: J. J. Cotta, 1891.

Newly revised and continued to the time of publication by Joseph Knapp, the author's son, who drew on the findings of the latest research.

--------. Geistliche Gedichte des Grafen Zinzendorf. Stuttgart: 1845.

Koch, Eduard Emil. Geschichte des Kirchenlieds und Kirchengesangs der christlichen, insbesondere der deutschen evangelischen Kirche. Dritte verbesserte und vermehrte Auflage. Stuttgart: Chr. Belser, 1866- 1877.

Kulp, Johannes. Die Lieder unserer Kirche. Eine Handreichung zum Evangelischen Kirchengesangbuch. Bearbeitet und herausgegeben von Arno Büchner und Siegfried Fornacon. Göttingen: Vandenhoeck und Ruprecht, 1958.

Lorenz, Ellen Jane. _Glory, Hallelujah! The Story of the Campmeeting Spiritual_. Nashville: Abingdon, 1978.

Langen, August. _Der Wortschatz des deutschen Pietismus_. Tübingen: Max Niemeyer Verlag, 1968.

Martin, Betty Jean. "The Ephrata Cloister and its Music, 1732-1785: The Cultural, Religious, and Bibliographical Background." Ph. D. thesis, University of Maryland, 1974.

Michaelis, Otto. _Lebensbilder der Liederdichter und Melodisten_. Herausgegeben von Wilhelm Lueken. Göttingen: Vandenhoeck und Ruprecht, 1957.

Moser, Hans Joachim. _Die evangelische Kirchenmusik in Deutschland_. Berlin-Darmstadt: Carl Merseburger, 1954.

Mützell, Julius. _Geistliche Lieder der evangelischen Kirche aus dem siebzehnten und der ersten Hälfte des achtzehnten Jahrhunderts von Dichtern aus Schlesien und den umliegenden Landschaften verfasst_. Braunschweig: C. A. Schwetschke, 1858; reprint ed.: Hildesheim: Georg Olms Verlag, 1975.

Nelle, Wilhelm. _Geschichte des deutschen evangelischen Kirchenliedes_. 4. Aufl. Hildesheim: Georg Olms Verlag, 1962.

Pfeiffer, Johannes. _Dichtkunst und Kirchenlied. Über das geistliche Lied im Zeitalter der Säkularisation_. Hamburg: Wittig, 1961.

Pratt, Waldo Selden. _The Significance of the Old French Psalter Begun by Clement Marot in 1532_. The Papers of the Hymn Society of America, no. 4.

Reed, Luther D. _Luther and Congregational Song_. The Papers of the Hymn Society of America, no. 12.

Ressler, Martin, comp. _A Bibliography of Mennonite Hymnals and Songbooks, 1742-1972_. Quarryville, Pa.: the Author, 1973.

Röbbelen, Ingeborg. _Theologie und Frömmigkeit im deutschen evangelisch-lutherischen Gesangbuch des 17. und frühen 18. Jahrhunderts_. Göttingen: Vandenhoeck und Ruprecht, 1957.

Routley, Eric. _Church Music and Theology_. Philadelphia: Muhlenberg Press, 1959.

Sachse, Julius Friedrich. _The German Sectarians of Pennsylvania. A critical and legendary history of the Ephrata Cloister and the Dunkers_. Philadelphia: the author, 1899.

---------. _The Music of the Ephrata Cloister_. Lancaster, Pa.: the Author, 1903.

Sallee, James. _A History of Evangelical Hymnody_. Grand Rapids: Baker Book House, 1978.

Sauer-Geppert, Waldtraut-Ingeborg. Sprache und Frömmigkeit im deutschen Kirchenlied. Kassel: Johannes Stauda Verlag, 1984.

Seipt, Allen Anders. Schwenkfelder Hymnology and the Sources of the First Schwenkfelder Hymn-Book Printed in America. Philadelphia: Americana Germanica Press, 1909.

Statler, Ruth B. and Nevin W. Fisher. Handbook on Brethren Hymns. Elgin, Ill.: Brethren Press, 1959.

Tucher, G. von., comp. Schatz des evangelischen Kirchengesangs im ersten Jahrhundert der Reformation. Leipzig: Breitkopf und Härtel, 1848.

Ulrich, Winfried. Semantische Untersuchungen zum Wortschatz des Kirchenliedes im 16. Jahrhundert. Lübeck und Hamburg: Matthiesen Verlag, 1969.

Viehmeyer, L. Allen. "An Index to Ephrata Hymnological Materials." (Forthcoming.)

Wackernagel, Philip, comp. Bibliographie zur Geschichte des deutschen Kirchenliedes im 16. Jahrhundert. Leipzig: B. G. Teubner, 1855.

--------. Das deutsche Kirchenlied von der ältesten Zeit bis zu Anfang des 18. Jahrhunderts. Mit Berücksichtigung der deutschen kirchlichen Liederdichtung im weiteren Sinne und der lateinischen von Hilarius bis Georg Fabricius und Wolfgang Ammonius. Leipzig: B. G. Teubner, 1864-1877. 5 vols.

Westphal, Johannes. Das evangelische Kirchenlied nach seiner kirchlichen Entwicklung. Sechste erweiterte und verbesserte Auflage. Berlin: Union deutsche Verlagsanstalt, 1925.

Willard, Martin. "Johannes Kelpius and Johann Gottfried Selig: Mystics and Hymnists on the Wissahickon." Ph. D. thesis, Pennsylvania State University, 1973.

Winkworth, Catherine. Christian Singers of Germany. London: Macmillan, 1869.

Winterfeld, Carl August. Der evangelische Kirchengesang und sein Verhältnis zur Kunst des Tonsatzes. Leipzig: Breitkopf und Härtel, 1843-1847. 3 vols.

Wolkan, Rudolf. Die Lieder der Wiedertäufer. Ein Beitrag zur deutschen und niederländischen Litteratur- und Kirchengeschichte. Berlin: B. Behr, 1903; reprint ed.: Nieuwkoop: B. de Graaf, 1965.

Yoder, Don. Pennsylvania Spirituals. Lancaster, Pa.: Pennsylvania Folklife Society, 1961.

Yoder, Paul M. Four Hundred Years With the Ausbund. Scottdale, Pa.: Herald Press, 1964.

Zahn, Johannes, comp. *Die Melodien der deutschen evangelischen Kirchenlieder, aus den Quellen geschöpft und mitgeteilt.* Gütersloh: C. Bertelsmann, 1889-1893. 6 vols.

2. Other Works.

Blough, Jerome H. *History of the Church of the Brethren of the Western District of Pennsylvania.* Elgin, Illinois: The Brethren Publishing House, 1916.

Brumbaugh, Martin Grove. *A History of the German Baptist Brethren in Europe and America.* Mount Morris, Ill.: Brethren Pub. House, 1899.

Durnbaugh, Donald F., ed. *European Origins of the Brethren.* Elgin, Ill.: The Brethren Press, 1958.

--------. *The Brethren in Colonial America.* Elgin, Ill.: The Brethren Press, 1967.

Erb, Peter. "The Brethren in the Early Eighteenth Century: an Unpublished Contemporary Account." *Brethren Life and Thought* 22 (Spring 1977): 105-112.

Ernst, James E. *Ephrata. A History.* Lancaster, Pa.: Pennsylvania Folklore Society, 1963.

Flory, John S. *Literary Activity of the Brethren in the Eighteenth Century.* Elgin, Ill.: Brethren Publishing House, 1908.

Funk, J. F. *A Biographical Sketch of Bishop Christian Herr, Also a Collection of Hymns Written by Him in the German Language.* Elkhart, Ind.: 1887.

Goedeke, Karl und Julius Tittmann. *Deutsche Dichter des 16. Jahrhunderts.* 2. Aufl. Leipzig: Brockhaus, 1881-1882. 17 vols.

Deutsche Dichter des 17. Jahrhunderts. Leipzig: Brockhaus, 1869- 1885. 15 vols.

History of the Church of the Brethren of the Eastern District of Pennsylvania. Lancaster, Pa.: New Era Printing Co., 1915.

Sappington, Roger E., ed. *The Brethren in the New Nation.* Elgin, Ill.: The Brethren Press, 1976.

The Brethren Encyclopedia, Donald F. Durnbaugh, ed. Philadelphia, Pa. and Oak Brook, Ill.: The Brethren Encyclopedia, Inc., 1983.

The Mennonite Encyclopedia. Hillsboro, Kan.: Mennonite Brethren Publishing House, 1955-1959. 4 vols.

ADDENDUM

At the very time when the manuscript of this study was ready to go to press, a valuable source came to hand. It would have been far too complicated and time-consuming to incorporate its data at this stage; it is therefore provided in this addendum. Only the bibliographical citation was included in the bibliography.

The source in question is a companion to Freylinghausen's hymnal, published in 1771 and entitled <u>Kurzgefasste</u> <u>Nachricht</u> <u>von</u> <u>ältern</u> <u>und</u> <u>neuern</u> <u>Liederverfassern</u>. It contains brief biographies of the hymn-writers and a first-line index to all the texts in the 1771 edition with names of the authors where known. The editor of this work was Johann Georg Kirchner, a pastor (<u>Archidiacon</u>) at Our Lady, the main church of Halle, Germany. The original research, however, had been done by Johann Heinrich Grischow, (church-) inspector and head of the Halle Bible publishing office. In his preface, Kirchner explains that Grischner had undertaken his study upon the publication of the first one-volume edition of Freylinghausen's hymnal in 1741, prompted by personal interest and intended entirely for private use. He was greatly aided in this enterprise by the numerous contacts and wide correspondence connected with his station in life and work.

While Grischow was conducting his research, two other persons were engaged in similar endeavors. The first was an unnamed count who pursued hymnological studies out of avocational interest sparing no cost to locate primary sources in order to carry the research as far as possible. This information he later placed at Grischow's disposal. The second was Kirchner himself who was engaged in revising the official hymnal of the city of Halle and ascertaining the names of the authors in the process.

Grischow and Kirchner corresponded with each other about their work and the former generously shared copies of his notes with the latter. When friends of the count and of Grischow's learned about their valuable hymnological studies, they urged them to publish their index to Freylinghausen's hymnal. The count was disinclined to publish his writings and Grischow seems to have been a perfectionist, who wanted to make his index as complete as possible but at last he did allow himself to be persuaded to publish. Thus in 1753, a very limited number of copies were printed comprising four signatures in large octavo format matching that of the hymnal. As this publication had never been intended to be sold on the book market but only to oblige certain patrons and friends, title-page and preface were omitted.

Kirchner never felt compelled to publish any hymnological work himself, mainly because he felt that there were enough such resources available already and secondly, because his work in the ministry left no time for extensive research. However, as more and more hymnals were provided with names and indexes of the authors and as Freylinghausen's hymnal in the course of its numerous editions had never been supplied with such features, he agreed to edit and revise Grischow's index, which, almost twenty years since its original publication, was no longer to be had, "not even for money." The title-page and foreword, which Grischow had never published, were incorporated by Kirchner into the prefatory matter.

Grischow had based his research as much as possible on primary sources, namely the collected hymn-texts of authors whether published or in manuscript. Where such sources were not available, he consulted other well-known hymnals and writings where information about specific author-ship could be found. It appears that a large portion of the information was supplied by the anonymous count who is given credit by the annotation Gr. v. ... (i.e., Graf von ..., or, "Count of ..."). The biographies, arranged in alphabetical order, were kept as brief as possible by listing only the last office and place of residence along with the year of death where known. The index of hymns is arranged as follows:

[Number of hymn in Freylinghausen, 1771] [First line of text] [Author] [Number of author in biographical list]

The information provided by Kirchner's work is compiled and listed in the following. All numbers refer to the numbers of hymns in the first-line index of The German Hymnody of the Brethren, 1720-1903.

I. Authors.

A. This list records those names found in Kirchner's work that are dif-ferent from or in addition to those in the First-Line Index:

8	Laurenti	452	Herrnschmidt	815	Richter
32	Schade	461	Hippe	822	Herrnschmidt
33	Koitsch	465	anon.	849	anon.
41	Koitsch	471	Crasselius	943	anon.
46	Edeling	479	anon.	947	anon.
53	Nehring	511	Nehring	954	Breithaupt, G.F.
76	Albinus	554	Beckhof	970	Petersen
86	anon.	558	Ruopp	987	anon.
103	Schröder, J.H.	561	Semler	1023	Bachmeister
105	Arnschwanger	565	Semler	1055	Rambach
110	Weingärtner	569	Neander	1062	Heine
115	Müller, M.	589	Bernstein	1068	Fritsch
120	anon.	596	anon.	1079	Fritsch
159	Graff	598	anon.	1086	Herrnschmidt
214	Lange, E.	658	Damius	1106	Müller, M. (st. 1-4)
220	Meuslin	659	Neander		Nehring (st. 5-14)
261	Richter	678	Bachmeister	1109	Müller, M.
267	Ziegler	679	anon.	1116	Neumark
301	Gerhardt	733	Neander	1196	Lange, E.
309	Freylinghausen	741	Herrnschmidt	1212	Gesenius
336	Arnold	757	Denicke	1227	Fritsch
360	Ringwald	800	Koitsch	1292	anon.
390	Gotter	805	anon.	1342	Lackmann
435	Neuss	864	Scheffler/Schade	1348	anon.

B. This list enumerates those items in the <u>First-Line Index</u> in which the author information is identical with that found in Kirchner's work:

3, 6, 15, 18, 27, 36, 39, 43, 44, 47, 48,
52, 54, 55, 59, 60, 61, 73, 77, 95, 98,
101, 104, 108, 111, 113, 122, 124, 149,
151, 152, 153, 156, 157, 166, 182, 184, 185, 193
200, 206, 226, 232, 236,
256, 259, 266, 268, 269, 285, 298,
302, 310, 320, 322, 326, 329, 332, 339, 345, 347, 348, 349,
355, 362, 367, 371, 372, 378, 379, 386, 387, 392, 396, 397, 398,
403, 406, 412, 414, 417, 418, 431, 439, 443, 444, 445, 458,
463, 468, 474, 478, 484, 485, 490, 491, 496, 498,
502, 503, 506, 510, 512, 516, 517, 522, 534, 535, 539, 541, 545,
552, 560, 571, 581, 587,
606, 635, 641, 643, 647,
650, 661, 662, 663, 667, 668, 671, 672, 674, 675, 677, 681, 683, 689, 690,
721, 722, 724, 734,
765, 767, 778, 784, 788, 789, 791, 792, 793, 795, 796, 797,
801, 803, 808, 816, 831, 834, 836, 838, 840, 844, 845
850, 854, 855, 857, 858, 869, 870, 872, 876, 879, 881, 885, 888, 897,
900, 901, 904, 905, 907, 918, 924, 927, 928, 930, 932, 936, 937, 940, 949,
951, 959, 963, 964, 965, 967, 976, 977, 979, 980, 981, 982, 983, 986, 991,
992, 996, 997,
1018, 1023, 1025, 1028, 1030, 1036, 1044,
1050, 1054, 1058, 1059, 1067, 1073, 1075, 1078, 1081, 1082, 1091, 1093,
1094, 1095,
1105, 1107, 1108, 1110, 1117, 1123, 1125, 1127, 1144, 1145, 1147,
1150, 1159, 1168, 1174, 1175, 1177, 1179, 1181, 1182, 1183, 1186, 1190,
1192, 1194, 1195, 1199,
1201, 1209, 1214, 1218, 1219, 1221, 1224, 1226,
1259, 1261, 1266, 1270, 1271, 1274, 1277, 1279, 1284, 1295,
1301, 1302, 1323, 1327, 1331, 1332, 1334, 1335, 1340, 1341, 1345, 1347,
1351, 1354.

II. <u>Biographies</u>.

The following biographical information is condensed from Kirchner's work and pertains to authors listed there but not present in the <u>Index</u> <u>of</u> <u>Hymn-Writers</u>:

BECKHOF / 1665-after 1745 / jurist.

BREITHAUPT, Georg Friedrich.

DAMIUS, Otto Christian / superintendent.

GRAFF, Simon / 1603-1659 / Bohemia / pastor.

HIPPE, Johann Heinrich / fl. 1676 / Hesse / court official.

LANGE, Ernst / d. 18th cent. / Danzig / jurist.

SEMLER, Gerhard Levin / d. 1737 / North Germany / pastor.

INDEX TO CHAPTERS I - IX

A. <u>Authors</u> and <u>Subjects</u>.

Anointing 118, 119
Awakening 69-70, 94-95

Balsbaugh, J. H. 110
Bamberger, C. 84
Baptism 20-22, 74-75, 87, 96, 107-109, 117, 126
Beatitudes 125
Becker, Peter 41, 63

Christian life 83-84, 86, 87, 124
Christmas 65, 86
Church 23-24, 35, 65, 75, 97, 118
Church dedication 117, 119
Clock, Lenaert 48
Consolation 87
Conversion 83, 84, 85, 87, 88
Cross 65

Danner, Heinrich 74, 84
Danner, Jakob 63
Death 53-54, 72, 84, 87, 119, 124, 125, 127
Denham, David 95
Denial of the world 26-27, 35, 125-126
Denicke, David 37
Discipleship 28-29, 35, 36-37
Dock, Christoph 71

Easter 95
End-time 32-34, 54, 72, 124, 125
Eternal life 86
Evening 106

Following Jesus 87, 124
Footwashing 22-23, 73, 96, 107, 118
Francke, August Hermann 14
Freylinghausen, Anastasius 14
Funeral 87, 106

Gerlach, David 85
Gesenius, Justus 37
Government (<u>Obrigkeit</u>) 27
Grebil, Samuel 85
Gruber, Eberhard Ludwig 48
Grumbacher, U. 125
Grünwald, Georg 19

Haller, Jakob 85
Heaven 84, 87, 88, 109, 124
Hiller, Philipp Friedrich 106-107
Hoffer, J. 85

Individual, The 27
Invitation 71

Jesus Christ 27-28, 85
------------: Incarnation and birth 98
------------: Passion 31-32, 49
------------: Resurrection 98-99
Jesus hymns 52-53, 84, 88, 124
Judgment 109-110

Kelly, Thomas 83
Kelpius, Johann 125-126
Knapp, Albert 82-83
Knepper, Wilhelm 12, 37, 69
Kurtz, Henry 73, 92-93, 126

Lobwasser, Ambrosius 45-46
Lord's Supper 73, 96, 119
Love-feast 23, 75, 118

Mack, Jr., Alexander 63-64, 73, 95, 98-99, 126, 128
Mack, Sr., Alexander 15, 20, 37, 41, 76, 98
Meeting 76, 118
Meyer, Sr., Jakob W. 86
Miller, Abraham 86
Miller, S. D. 86-87
Missions 117, 119
Morning 124
Müller, Michael 37
Mutual aid 56
Mystical eros 31
Mysticism 30-31, 53

Naas, Johann 64
New Year 85-86

Office of the keys 76

Parting 51, 72, 87, 88
Petersen, Wilhelm 18
Piety 125
Praise (and thanksgiving) 86, 88, 89, 106, 118, 124
Prayer 51-52, 72-73, 83, 84, 124
Preiss, Johannes 124-125
Preiss, Wilhelm 87-88

Reissner, Adam 19

Sanctification 100
Sauer II, Christoph 64-65, 98
Scharnschlager, Leupold 19
Schütz, Johann Jakob 18
Scriptures, Holy 37
Social concern 35-37, 125
Spitta, Philipp 107
Stoll, Jakob 88-89, 127
Swain, Joseph 83

Table hymns 106
Teaching the faith 51
Trinity 97-98

Universal restoration 29-30, 54-55, 65

Walter, Johannes 83
Weisse, Michael 19
Weltangst 25-26
Wilhelm II of Sachsen Weimar 19
Williams, William 83
World 24

Ziegler, Johann Conrad 48
Zion 34

B. The Hymns.

2 106	154 . . . 64-65, 126	276 32
19 85	158 18	278 . . . . . 24, 32
23 23	160 124	283 74-75
28 . . . 48-49, 51	161 . . . . 97, 118	286 51
31 96	164 76	291 63
32 31-32	169 107	294 63-64
34 22	172 119	313 86
35 71	178 . . . . 23, 34	321 52
37 87	179 . . . . 29, 30	323 107
40 21	187 118	331 64
42 88	190 109	333 87
55 106	194 119	338 . . . . 26, 28-29
56 . . . . . 26, 31	196 23	340 109-110
67 125	202 . . . . . 62, 65	345 36
68 22	216 107	348 70
81 . . . . 124, 125	221 76	356 51
83 19	226 106	357 32
90 125	228 124	365 85-86
93 87	237 52	391 125
127 95	238 27	400 . . . . . 69, 117
129 25	240 84	404 118
133 51	241 84	421 86
134 52	247 52-53	436 117
135 31	258 19	437 119
137 117	279 52	441 72
142 84	274 31	450 72

462 63	712 87	1063 83
469 100	718 65	1006 85
470 64	725 83	1083 118
472 87	727 27	1090 124
478 117	733 48	1093 35-36
482 108	736 96	1095 51
484 19	737 75	1096 48
486 76	744 . . . . 19, 36	1097 125
488 53	752 23	1104 117
489 96	757 37	1106 37
501 52	760 87	1111 118
514 31	766 124	1114 72
525 . . . . 83, 88	776 83	1119 100
527 119	782 98	1129 88
529 . . . 110, 119	788 28	1139 88
530 108-109	791 18	1155 20-21
540 98	795 36	1180 117
542 117	804 22	1184 88
551 30	806 24	1187 32
559 72	813 65	1188 29
562 . . . . . 30, 31	835 27-28	1189 117
566 109	837 72	1190 18
567 124	843 88	1191 53-54
577 87	846 84	1202 74
578 128	848 83-84	1207 62
583 124	863 27	1212 32
588 36	870 36	1217 125
595 54-55	876 45	1229 55
602 . . . 26-27, 69	889 97-98	1231 31
604 24	898 64	1232 31
605 23-24	908 62	1234 36
609 86	912 . . . . . 73, 118	1240 126
610 . . . . 22, 23	915 28	1241 55
613 32	921 118	1245 . . 22, 24, 37
614 124	925 72	1246 88
616 87	931 33	1247 88
621 54	938 118	1250 56
626 87	941 97	1258 27
630 89	961 32-33	1267 72
631 126	966 83	1278 83
635 19	969 . . . . 118, 119	1283 125
636 124	988 87	1285 62
637 125	993 87	1291 25-26
645 55	1002 27	1299 62-63
655 . 95, 98-99, 118	1008 73	1304 29-30
656 118	1013 . . . . 27, 30	1305 65
666 124	1025 88	1311 72
673 85	1026 31	1317 86
687 36	1027 26	1320 . . 49-50, 128
688 51	1033 127	1324 . . 75-76, 97
689 48	1037 106	1338 48
695 . . . . 64, 126	1041 48	1352 27
699 48	1050 100	1353 34
704 87	1053 119	1361 25
708 65		